ENTREPRENEURSHIP DEVELOPMENT

(OBSTACLES AND SOLUTIONS)

DIPESH D. UIKE
B.E., M.B.A.
Professor, Dr. Ambedkar Institute of Management Studies and Research.
Rashtrasant Tukadoji Maharaj Nagpur University,
Nagpur - 440 010, Maharashtra, India.

First Edition : 2012

Himalaya Publishing House

MUMBAI • NEW DELHI • NAGPUR • BENGALURU • HYDERABAD • CHENNAI • PUNE • LUCKNOW • AHMEDABAD • ERNAKULAM • BHUBANESWAR • INDORE • KOLKATA • GUWAHATI

First Edition : 2012 **Edition : 2017**

Published by : Mrs. Meena Pandey for **Himalaya Publishing House Pvt. Ltd.,**
"Ramdoot", Dr. Bhalerao Marg, Girgaon, **Mumbai - 400 004.**
Phone: 022-23860170/23863863, Fax: 022-23877178
E-mail: himpub@vsnl.com; Website: www.himpub.com

Branch Offices :

New Delhi : "Pooja Apartments", 4-B, Murari Lal Street, Ansari Road, Darya Ganj, New Delhi - 110 002. Phone: 011-23270392, 23278631; Fax: 011-23256286

Nagpur : Kundanlal Chandak Industrial Estate, Ghat Road, Nagpur - 440 018. Phone: 0712-2738731, 3296733; Telefax: 0712-2721215

Bengaluru : No. 16/1 (Old 12/1), 1st Floor, Next to Hotel Highlands, Madhava Nagar, Race Course Road, Bengaluru - 560 001. Phone: 080-32919385; Telefax: 080-22286611

Hyderabad : No. 3-4-184, Lingampally, Besides Raghavendra Swamy Matham, Kachiguda, Hyderabad - 500 027. Phone: 040-27560041, 27550139; Mobile: 09390905282

Chennai : No. 8/2, Madley 2nd Street, Ground Floor, T. Nagar, Chennai - 600 017. Mobile: 09345345055

Pune : First Floor, "Laksha" Apartment, No. 527, Mehunpura, Shaniwarpeth (Near Prabhat Theatre), Pune - 411 030. Phone: 020-24496323/24496333; Mobile: 09370579333

Lucknow : House No 731, Shekhupura Colony, Near B.D. Convent School, Aliganj, Lucknow - 226 022. Mobile: 09307501549

Ahmedabad : 114, "SHAIL", 1st Floor, Opp. Madhu Sudan House, C.G. Road, Navrang Pura, Ahmedabad - 380 009. Phone: 079-26560126; Mobile: 09377088847

Ernakulam : 39/176 (New No: 60/251) 1st Floor, Karikkamuri Road, Ernakulam, Kochi - 682011, Phone: 0484-2378012, 2378016; Mobile: 09344199799

Bhubaneswar : 5 Station Square, Bhubaneswar - 751 001 (Odisha). Phone: 0674-2532129, Mobile: 09338746007

Indore : Kesardeep Avenue Extension, 73, Narayan Bagh, Flat No. 302, IIIrd Floor, Near Humpty Dumpty School, Indore - 452 007 (M.P.). Mobile: 09301386468

Kolkata : 108/4, Beliaghata Main Road, Near ID Hospital, Opp. SBI Bank, Kolkata - 700 010, Phone: 033-32449649, Mobile: 09883055590, 07439040301

Guwahati : House No. 15, Behind Pragjyotish College, Near Sharma Printing Press, P.O. Bharalumukh, Guwahati - 781009, (Assam). Mobile: 09883055590, 09883055536

DTP by : Prerana Enterprises, Mumbai.

Printed at : M/s. Aditya Offset Process (I) Pvt. Ltd., On behalf of HPH.

To

My Parents

&

My Wife

PREFACE

The entrepreneurs play an important role in the economic development of a country. They generate wealth and employment for the country. So for economic development, a nation cannot depend on just government activities. America, Japan and European countries are the developed and fast growing economic countries in the world. The entrepreneurs of these countries have a major part in the development of these countries. If a nation wants to develop and progress, the importance of entrepreneurs cannot be neglected. Most of the literature, magazines, articles and research have focused on the importance of entrepreneurs' development for the development of the nation.

Several textbooks have been written on entrepreneurship development. However, none has focused in deep on the obstacles faced by the new entrepreneurs. This book has been written specifically to focus on the obstacles that are faced and are facing by the new entrepreneurs who want to become an entrepreneur but they face so many obstacles in this process and therefore very few become entrepreneurs. Description of all the obstacles are given in this book so that the new entrepreneurs can get an idea about obstacles prior to open the business and ultimately can take benefits from this book. The book combines important issues and challenges, with a strong emphasis on their impact on new entrepreneurs' business.

While preparing this book, I have collected relevant material from direct interaction with new small entrepreneurs who are running their business, books, government publications, journals, articles by eminent scholars. My friends who are running their business, other friends from Management College have offered me valuable suggestions and support in the preparation of the manuscript. My sincere thanks are due to all of them.

The academic encouragement received from my college DAIMSR, my director Mr. Sujit Metre, my parents Mr. D.F. Uike and Mrs. Sheela D. Uike, my wife Mrs. Shweta D. Uike and my friends in preparing this book is acknowledged with great respect.

I request colleagues in the teaching profession, my entrepreneur friends, students and all others who are interested in the study of entrepreneurship development to send their valuable suggestions for the further improvement of the book.

Nagpur

Dipesh D. Uike
dipesh83_star@yahoo.co.in

Contents

ENTREPRENEUR AND ENTREPRENEURSHIP

LEARNING OBJECTIVES

On completion of this chapter, you should be able to:

- ☺ *Explain who is an entrepreneur and what his characteristics are.*
- ☺ *Describe why to become an entrepreneur.*
- ☺ *Describe entrepreneurship.*
- ☺ *Describe need for entrepreneurship.*
- ☺ *Describe benefits of entrepreneurship.*
- ☺ *Describe intrapreneur and Intrapreneurship.*
- ☺ *Describe role of entrepreneur in economic development.*

1.1 Who is an Entrepreneur?

An entrepreneur is considered as a person whose main purpose is to set up his own business or industry. Entrepreneur is a person who always wants his own business instead of working in other business. He takes initiative to open his own business, always looks for an opportunity, tries to come up with the innovative idea and wants to achieve his goals by doing his best. He always comes up with the new idea that is unique to the society and benefits to the society. His focus is on to transform the opportunity into economic gain. Entrepreneurs are very important for the nation as those are the persons who perfectly exploit the resources of the country and generate wealth for the nation that ultimately help the citizens of that country to get the employment. He is the one who knows the perfect combination of human resources and non-human resources that will be required for the production. Entrepreneur turns the environment of the country into the good one.

BOX 1

Small and Medium Enterprises (SMEs) play a vital role for the growth of Indian economy by contributing 45% of industrial output, 40% of exports, employing 60 million people, create 1.3 million jobs every year and produce more than 8000 quality products for the Indian and international markets. SME's Contribution towards GDP in 2009 was 17% which is expected to increase to 22% by 2012. There are 26.1 million MSME Units in India and 12 million persons are expected to join the workforce in the next three years. SMEs are the fountain head of several innovations in manufacturing and service sectors, the major link in the supply chain to corporate and the PSUs. By promoting SMEs, the rural areas of India will be developed.

SMEs are now exposed to greater opportunities than ever for expansion and diversification across the sectors. Indian market is growing rapidly and Indian entrepreneurs are making remarkable progress in various Industries like Manufacturing, Precision Engineering Design, Food Processing, Pharmaceutical, Textile and Garments, Retail, IT and ITES, Agro and Service sector.

Source: Information received from "SME Chamber of India".

However, we tend to think of entrepreneurs as people who have a talent for seeing opportunities and the abilities to develop those opportunities into profit-making businesses.

Are entrepreneurs born or made? The debate still rages, but the current consensus is that successful entrepreneurs share a constellation of personality traits. In other words, some people are naturally more entrepreneurial than others.

A common misperception about entrepreneurs is that entrepreneurs are wild risk-takers. Entrepreneurs do take risks, but only calculated ones. One of the abilities which the successful entrepreneurs share is the ability to evaluate risks. But remember, you don't need to have all the traits associated with entrepreneurship to be a successful entrepreneur. The main quality you need is a determination to make your business venture successful. The rest of the qualities necessary to being a successful entrepreneur, you can learn. Anyone who has ever looked at problems and seen it as an opportunity is a likely prospect. The same goes for anyone who feels as if his ambition is held in check by corporate red tape. But it takes more than just cleverness and frustration with the *status quo* to get an entrepreneurial venture off the ground.

While there's no single entrepreneurial archetype, certain common traits indicate an entrepreneurial personality. For instance, the entrepreneurial adult first often appears as an entrepreneurial child. And although it's far from a necessary ingredient for entrepreneurship, the need to succeed is often greater among those whose backgrounds contain an extra struggle to fit into society.

In addition, contrary to popular belief, entrepreneurs aren't generally high-risk takers when they can't affect the outcome of the situation, they tend to set realistic and achievable goals and when they do take risks, they're usually calculated ones based on facts and experience, rather than instincts. Entrepreneurs are driven not by the need to make money, but by the need to make their dreams a reality. More often than not, money is a by-product of an entrepreneur's motivation rather than the motivation itself.

Entrepreneurs are participants, not observers; players, not fans. And to be an entrepreneur is to be an optimist, to believe that with the right amount of time and money, you can do anything.

The entrepreneur word is derived from the French word Entreprendre which means to undertake, *i.e.,* the person who is ready to accept the challenges, risks, whatever will come to his way while starting a new business. In early sixteenth century, the Frenchmen who organized and led military expeditions were referred to as entrepreneurs. A French economist Richard Cantilon used the word entrepreneur for first time for business activities. According to Cantilon "An entrepreneur is a person who buys factor services at certain prices with a view to selling its product at uncertain prices". Thus to Cantilon an entrepreneur is a person who takes risk to open a business.

According to Jean Baptiste, another French economist, "An entrepreneur is the economic agent who unites all means of production, the labour force of the one and the capital or land of the others and who find in the value of the products which results from their employment, the reconstitution of the entire capital that he utilizes and the value of the wages, the interest and the rent which he pays as well as profit belonging to himself". An Entrepreneur is an economic agent who better knows all the means and their perfect combination that will be useful for the production.

In the words of **J.A. Schumpeter**, "The entrepreneur in an advanced economy is an individual who introduces something new in the economy, a method of production is not yet tested by experience in the branch of manufacture concerned, a product with which consumers are not yet familiar, a new source of raw material or of new markets and the like". According to him an entrepreneur is an innovator, who brings new things into the economy; Innovation may be a new product, new methods of production, creating new markets, new sources of raw materials, new processes adopted into the organization that are not at all adopted by any organization.

The Entrepreneurs: Some Important Definitions

1. **Peter F. Drucker** defines an entrepreneur as one who always searches for changes, responds to it and exploits it as an opportunity. Innovation is the basic tool of entrepreneurs, the means by which they exploit change as an opportunity for a different business or service.
2. **Gillian Murphy,** leader of San Joaquin Delta College Small Business Development Center, says: "An entrepreneur is not static but fluid...continues to seek opportunities and/or different methods of operation."
3. **Author of the book, "*Low-Risk, High-Reward:*** *Starting and Growing Your Small Business with Minimal Risk*", **Bob Reiss**, presented a holistic definition of an entrepreneur. "He was a person who can recognize a good opportunity and will pursue it whether or not resources are available. The entrepreneur is also confident, adaptable and determined to succeed, even when there are setbacks".
4. An entrepreneur, **Daile Tucker,** said that, "Entrepreneurs compete with themselves and believe that success or failure lies within their personal control or influence."

5. **Kilby:** Emphasizes the role of an imitator entrepreneur who does not innovate but imitates technologies innovated by others, are very important in developing economies.
6. **Schumpeter:** According to him entrepreneurs are innovators who use a process of shattering the *status quo* of the existing products and services, to set up new products, new services.
7. **David McClelland:** An entrepreneur is a person with a high need for achievement [n-Ach]. He is energetic and a moderate risk taker.

1.2 Characteristics of an Entrepreneur

Entrepreneur is not a simple man who lives normally like the other people but he is one who continuously thinks something for his progress, challenges, business, new ideas etc. Most of the characteristics of the entrepreneur are his achievement motivation. A successful entrepreneur must be the combination of qualities like innonvation, initiation, leadership, self-confidence, creativeness and so many qualities that ultimately help the entrepreneur to achieve his goals. The following are the characteristic features of a successful entrepreneur:

Do you have what it takes?

If you think you want to be your own boss and run your own business, but are not sure you have the right qualifications to be an entrepreneur, read on. What are the characteristics of an entrepreneur? How does an entrepreneur think? Is your personal profile similar to that of a successful entrepreneur?

Until recently, entrepreneurs were not widely studied. There was a general lack of knowledge and information about what made them tick. Most business universities now offer courses in entrepreneurship. As a result, business professionals have learned a lot about what it takes to become a successful entrepreneur. Although no one has found the perfect entrepreneurial profile, there are many characteristics that show up repeatedly. The following cover several important characteristics of entrepreneurs for you to consider and dispel the entrepreneurial myths.

1.2.1 Entrepreneurial Characteristics

A series of interviews were conducted with distinguished entrepreneurs. They were asked what characteristics they felt were essential to success as an entrepreneur. Good health was a characteristic mentioned by every entrepreneur interviewed. Entrepreneurs are physically resilient and in good health. They can work for extended periods of time and while they are in the process of building their business, they refuse to get sick.

In small businesses, where there is no depth of management, the leader must be there. You may not be able to afford a support staff to cover all business functions and therefore you will need to work long hours. We all know people who use part of their sick leave each year when they are not sick. Entrepreneurs are not found in this group. At the end of the eight-hour day, when everyone else leaves for home, the entrepreneur will often continue to work into the evening, developing new business ideas.

Self-control

Entrepreneurs do not function well in structured organizations and do not like someone having authority over them. Most believe they can do the job better than anyone else and will strive for maximum responsibility and accountability. They enjoy creating business strategies and thrive on the process of achieving their goals. Once they achieve a goal, they quickly replace it with a greater goal. They strive to exert whatever influence they can over future events.

In large, structured organizations, entrepreneurs are easy to recognize by the statements they make: "If they wanted that job done right, they should have given it to me." A dominant characteristic of entrepreneurs is their belief that they are smarter than their peers and superiors. They have a compelling need to do their own things in their own way. They need the freedom to choose and to act according to their own perception of what actions will result in success.

Self-confidence

Entrepreneurs are self-confident when they are in control of what they're doing and working alone. They tackle problems immediately with confidence and are persistent in their pursuit of their objectives. Most are at their best in the face of adversity, since they thrive on their own self-confidence.

Sense of urgency

Entrepreneurs have a never-ending sense of urgency to develop their ideas. Inactivity makes them impatient, tense and uneasy. They thrive on activity and are not likely to be found sitting on bank fishing unless the fish are biting. When they are in the entrepreneurial mode, they are more likely to be found getting things done instead of fishing.

Entrepreneurs prefer individual sports, such as golf, skiing or tennis, over team sports. They prefer games in which their own brawn and brain directly influence the outcome and pace of the game. They have drive and high energy levels, they are achievement-oriented and they are tireless in the pursuit of their goals.

Comprehensive awareness

Successful entrepreneurs can comprehend complex situations that may include planning, making strategic decisions and working on multiple business ideas simultaneously. They are farsighted and aware of important details and they will continuously review all possibilities to achieve their business objectives. At the same time, they devote their energy to completing the tasks immediately before them.

Accounting reports illustrate this characteristic. Accountants spend hours balancing the accounts and closing them out. For them, the achievement is to have balanced books. The entrepreneur only wants to know the magnitude of the numbers and their significance for the operation of the business.

Realism

Entrepreneurs accept things as they are and deal with them accordingly. They may or may not be idealistic, but they are seldom unrealistic. They will change their direction when they see that change will improve their prospects for achieving their goals. They want to know the status of a given situation at all times. News interests them if it is timely and factual and provides them with information they need. They will verify any information they receive before they use it in making a decision. Entrepreneurs say what they mean and assume that everyone else does too. They tend to be too trusting and may not be sufficiently suspicious in their business dealings with other people.

Conceptual ability

Entrepreneurs possess the ability to identify relationships quickly in the midst of complex situations. They identify problems and begin working on their solution faster than other people. They are not troubled by ambiguity and uncertainty because they are used to solving problems. Entrepreneurs are natural leaders and are usually the first to identify a problem to be overcome. If it is pointed out to them that their solution to a problem will not work for some valid reason, they will quickly identify an alternative problem-solving approach.

Status requirements

Entrepreneurs find satisfaction in symbols of success that are external to themselves. They like the business they have built to be praised, but they are often embarrassed by praise directed at them personally. Their egos do not prevent them from seeking facts, data and guidance. When they need help, they will not hesitate to admit it especially in areas that are outside of their expertise. During tough business periods, entrepreneurs will concentrate their resources and energies on essential business operations. They want to be where the action is and will not stay in the office for extended periods of time.

Symbols of achievement such as position have little relevance to them. Successful entrepreneurs find their satisfaction of status needs in the performance of their business, not in the appearance they present to their peers and to the public. They will postpone acquiring status items like a luxury car until they are certain that their business is stable.

Interpersonal relationships

Entrepreneurs are more concerned with people's accomplishments than with their feelings. They generally avoid becoming personally involved and will not hesitate to sever relationships that could hinder the progress of their business. During the business-building period, when resources are scarce, they seldom devote time to dealing with satisfying people's feelings beyond what is essential to achieving their goals.

Their lack of sensitivity to people's feelings can cause turmoil and turnover in their organization. Entrepreneurs are impatient and drive themselves and everyone around them. They don't have the tolerance or empathy necessary for team building unless it's their team and they will delegate very few key decisions.

As the business grows and assumes an organizational structure, entrepreneurs go through a classic management crisis. For many of them, their need for control makes it difficult for them to delegate authority in the way that a structured organization demands. Their strong direct approach induces them to seek information directly from its source, bypassing the structured chains of authority and responsibility. Their moderate interpersonal skills, which were adequate during the start-up phases, will cause them problems as they try to adjust to the structured or corporate organization. Entrepreneurs with good interpersonal skills will be able to adjust and survive as their organization grows and becomes more structured. The rest won't make it.

Emotional stability

Entrepreneurs have a considerable amount of self-control and can handle business pressures. They are comfortable in stress situations and are challenged rather than discouraged by setbacks or failures. Entrepreneurs are uncomfortable when things are going well. They'll frequently find some new activity on which to vent their pent-up energy. They are not content to leave well enough alone. Entrepreneurs tend to handle people's problems with action plans without empathy. Their moderate interpersonal skills are often inadequate to provide for stable relationships. However, the divorce rate among entrepreneurs is above average.

1.2.2 Entrepreneur Profile

For the business that wants to develop the business skills for telltale personality traits that most entrepreneurs exhibit is a great place to start. The personality traits to look out for include:

Determination to succeed

All entrepreneurs are by their nature strong willed. They know what they want and are relentless in their pursuit of goals. In a business, these individuals are usually very easy to identify. They will have drive and enthusiasm and are not easily discouraged by setbacks.

Risk taking

Often, the entrepreneur is typically described as a risk taker. Some of the most successful business people took huge risks in the early days of their businesses. They are open to taking a level of risk that is most likely to possess a level of entrepreneurial attitude. The risk taking capability is one of the most important factors in the life of the entrepreneurs. They take the risk because they are very much confident about the outcome. They apply all the tools to know about the results. They do through R & D to reach near to the success.

Common sense

Coupled with risk taking is a level head that may take risks, but risks that have been carefully calculated. Entrepreneurs do take risks, but these are not haphazard. Common sense still prevails. They take risk with the help of all information, knowledge of market trends, their competitors. They do continuous research and after deep analysis they form conclusion.

Decision makers

One of the strongest entrepreneurial traits to identify in family members is the ability to make clear and concise decisions. Strong entrepreneurial tendencies will always make fast decisions that they always stick to.

Hard working

All entrepreneurs are adept at getting their hands dirty. They work long hours until they have achieved their goals. Those family members in your business that are strong willed and self starters are clearly in possession of personality traits that could translate into the development of leading business people.

1.2.3 Entrepreneur Characteristics: Personal Qualities of An Entrepreneur

What makes an entrepreneur is a complex question. It includes factors from the environment in which an individual was raised, his or her family situation and his or her personality traits. This question has been the subject of a great deal of both study and research. The following discussion is a summary of my own observations plus some of the conclusions of others.

About 20 or 25 years ago if you asked almost any expert to describe a successful entrepreneur, you would probably have been given a list similar to this:

- Male
- Only child
- About 35 to 45 years old
- Bachelor's or Master's degree in Engineering
- Born in the Midwest
- Father owns a hardware store

However, much recent research and many of my own observations seem to indicate that there are qualities commonly found in successful entrepreneurs and there are things that you can do if you are concerned about any you may lack.

1.2.4 Personal Qualities Common in Successful Entrepreneurs

➢ **Motivations to achieve**

In almost every case, successful entrepreneurs are individuals who are highly motivated to achieve. They tend to be doers, people who make things happen. They are often very competitive. Many researchers have concluded that the most consistent trait found in successful entrepreneurs is the sheer will to win, the need to achieve in everything they do. They don't want to come in third, they don't want to come in second, but they want to come in first.

➢ **Nonconformity**

Entrepreneurs tend to be independent souls, unhappy when forced to conform or toe the line. They are people who find it difficult to work for others, who want to set their own goals. It is hard to imagine anyone who is more nonconformist than Steve Jobs and Steve Wozniak, the founders of Apple Computer or Bill Gates, founder of Microsoft.

➢ **Hard work**

The successful entrepreneurs are very handworkers. They are not the lazy people. They believe in smart work. They think logically and then act. They continuousty make planning. They never sit idle. They always try to progress expand the business.

➢ **Strong leadership**

Starting a new company can be a harrowing experience full of uncertainty and risk. Successfully bringing a small organization through these trying periods requires a lot of leadership skills.

➢ **Street smarts**

We all know owners of some very successful businesses who were lucky to finish high school and never even considered college. Yes, they always seem to make the right moves. Call it common sense, instinct, whatever you want. Successful entrepreneurs seem to have intuitive good judgement when making complex business decisions.

1.2.5 The Key Steps to Becoming Successful in Today's Society

Learn how you can start living successfully as an entrepreneur. Before you start your journey, let's first define "entrepreneur," and examine some of the characteristics of an entrepreneur in today's world. The definition of "entrepreneur" is a person who organizes, operates and assumes the risk for a business venture. What are some of the typical characteristics that make up an entrepreneur in today's world?

- Entrepreneurs have **passion** for what they do in life.
- Entrepreneurs express a great amount of **enthusiasm** in their line of work.
- Entrepreneurs are **goal-oriented** in their quest to reach their desired outcomes.
- Entrepreneurs have a **creative imagination** when it comes to their ideas in business.
- Entrepreneurs have a **positive attitude** when it comes to building their business and business relationships.
- Entrepreneurs are very quick **decision-makers** in their business endeavors and ideas.

These are some of the amazing characteristics of an entrepreneur.

After applying the steps below, you will have a good understanding of the entrepreneur personality test. The entrepreneur personality test is a test for you to discover the mindset you have now, compared to the new entrepreneurial mindset that you will be creating. Also, your new entrepreneurial mindset will help you to understand the importance of a network of business opportunities. It is important for you to start networking with other like-minded individuals to help assist you in accomplishing your business goals. Most of the wealthy entrepreneurs today are living successfully due to the many benefits of having a small business as an entrepreneur that's home-based in the state they live in now. So let's go into the key steps of what it takes to become successful.

Prepare yourselves to new entrepreneurial mindset:

Before you can become successful, you have to create a new mindset to achieve the things you want in your life. You have to think thoroughly on that. Examine your current mindset; know your mental and physical level of becoming entrepreneur and how that way of thinking has gotten you to where you're at right now. Be honest with yourself when looking over your current results, because this will give you an accurate measure of the choices that you have made over the years. Only then will you begin to see for yourself that it is time for you to work on your new mindset in order to start living the life you want to experience, regardless of your current circumstances. Find out the successful entrepreneurs, read about them and know what they do and how they have reached to their business height. Once your new entrepreneurial mindset is in motion, you will start making very creative choices to move you faster to your desired goals.

Read success stories of different entrepreneurs. Books will also help you for achieving your goals. Attain business seminars, get information from business news, business journals etc. Maintain and keep your new entrepreneur mindset growing everyday. Your level of awareness will increase greatly with the new mindset that you are creating to go after the things you want in your life. Having an open mind as an entrepreneur will also help you make better decisions quickly and become more creative.

Clearly write down what exactly you want:

Keeping in mind about your ideas and thoughts will not work unless you write it down. You should clearly write down the following:

- What is your business purpose?
- What you want from your business?
- As an entrepreneur what you want to achieve?
- How are you going to achieve those?

This will help you in recalling what you want to do in near future and therefore you will move in the right direction.

Write down all of your new ideas in detail as an entrepreneur:

Now think on your ideas. What exactly you want. Describe it in detail. Take sufficient time to think on your ideas. Write down all information about your ideas. Whether it may be small or big write down all relevant information. The ideas that you are writing down now are the ones that you have been thinking about in your mind that you want to create and achieve in your physical presence now. For example, if you have a burning desire in your heart to start your own fruit center, restaurant, hotel or create a product for people to buy, then write down all of your ideas in every detail. Write down how big the fruit center is going to be, where it is going to be located, what coluru the building is going to be, where will be the parking facility, how many customers can come into your centre, how many people you will staff. This is a perfect example of how you can start writing down all of your ideas as an entrepreneur.

Write your short, middle and long-term goals:

A short-term goal is something you want to achieve in one day, one week or one month. A middle-term goal is something you want to achieve in ninety days to six months. A long-term goal is something you want to achieve in one year or more. Write down what you want to achieve as an entrepreneur. Your goals must be the realistic one. Try to keep such goals which you can achieve. Do not try to jump directly on very hard goals. Keep simple goals first, after achieving those, then set some hard goals. Be creative when writing down your goals because this is your life that you will be experiencing in the near future.

Improve your personality every day:

If you want to become a successful entrepreneur then you must continuously improve your personality. Try to bring all the qualities of the successful entrepreneurs. How they communicate, how confident they are! How they use their logic and intelligence to solve the problems? With the new mindset you have now, you should continue to feed your mind everyday with personal development. There are so many institutes that provide personality development courses. You must join the class of personality development. It will really help you to update your personality. Read a good book on personal growth, listen to meditation music, have a conversation with a positive person and people or obtain a personal development program to help keep your mind on track in accomplishing your goals. So you see this is some great stuff to add as a part of your daily life and it will certainly help move you in the right direction.

Keep your new mindset positive:

Positive thinking is the base of entrepreneurship. If you want be a successful entrepreneur then you must think positively. You must have positive attitude. Eliminate the word impossible from your dictionary. For a successful entrepreneur nothing is impossible. They never become sad from situation, they learn from their failures. Instead of winding the business they come up with more perfect planning to win the situation. To get positive attitude always be with the people who have positive mindset. Make good friends from where you can gain useful learning. Hanging around individuals that have the same entrepreneurial concepts that you will keep your mindset in a positive state and on the right track to achieve your goals. You can hang around like-minded individuals by either listening to a group of individuals on the phone via conference calls, attending seminars, being part of an online forum of positive people like yourself and keeping in contact with the positive like-minded people you have formed a relationship with, on your journey in achieving your goals.

Visualize the end result of your goal in your mind:

Visualize the end result of your goal that you have decided to achieve within a specific time frame. For example, if you have decided to own your own fruit center, then you could spend few minutes in the day visualizing about every aspect of your fruit center as if you currently owned it in the present moment. Then tally all the activities of your business with the goals and ideas that you have written down. By comparison you will have idea about your business progress. You will have a track of your business activities and about your goals and continue to dwell on that end result a few minutes of everyday until it became a part of his experience in life.

Never give up on your new ideas and goals until you see them manifest in your life:

Do yourself a huge favour right now and go ahead make the decision to never give up on your new ideas and goals until you see them manifested in your life as an entrepreneur. Many unsuccessful entrepreneurs in today's society give up their goals and ideas at the first sign of temporary defeat. There is no such thing as failure, only temporary defeat in life, period. When a successful entrepreneur has a temporary defeat, he remains calm, relaxed and confident in his quest to achieve his goal because he understands that every temporary defeat is backed by a great or equal number of successes in his life. That's why many successful entrepreneurs always get what they want in life; they never give up on what they want.

Take action on your new ideas and goals as an entrepreneur:

Take action everyday on your new ideas and goals as an entrepreneur. You deserve the best that life has to offer, so the only gap between knowing what to do and doing it is action. Take action everyday regardless of your current circumstances in life. As an entrepreneur with a new mindset, you are the leader and it's time for you to start living successfully as an entrepreneur in today's world.

1.3 Who can be an Entrepreneur?

Anyone can become an entrepreneur who wants to become. Becoming an entrepreneur requires all those factors that form an entrepreneur. If a person wants to become an entrepreneur then he has to change his mindset first, the mindset of being protective, always plays under security, don't want to take risk, not ready to do much hard work. Such kind of person can never be an entrepreneur he always sticks to his traditional path. But an entrepreneur is always ready to take risk, creative mind, confidence and the most important thing is he is motivated to achievement, he wants to achieve something in his life that lead him to success. Some entrepreneurs have entrepreneurial qualities from the childhood itself but the person who wants to generate those qualities can also generate it by proper training and exposing to the entrepreneurial environment.

The people who do jobs bind themselves to that organization only, they have very narrow place, their boundary is fixed to that organization only, but the entrepreneur never binds himself to a small boundary, his scope is large and because of this, his chances of getting benefits increases and he enjoys reputation, social status though the chances of getting failure is also there but his hunger of achievement motivates him to accept challenges and risks and his entrepreneurial qualities and skills support him to overcome the barriers.

Do you think you're an Entrepreneur?

Follow these secrets of prosperity to guide you on your entrepreneurial quest.

Ability to solve problem – To "think on your feet". You will not accept failure and will continue forward with ACTION. Learn from the best their lessons of failure and how they trudged through the thick mire of adversity until they ultimately broke through. The entrepreneurs are the best problem solver. They are expert in solving the problem. They take the help of creativity, technology and art to solve the problems.

Change the way you think – You are the creator of your life. Learn how to plant different seeds of thoughts in your mind. The entrepreneurs are not the common people. They think differently. They have different perception, different attitude towards the world. They see the opportunity where the common people cannot see any opportunity. They convert the opportunity into reality. They utilize the resources in a better way to accomplish their tasks.

No complacency – To accept life as it is and do nothing more to improve. Transformation through change is necessary to become a successful entrepreneur. The entrepreneurs never get satisfaction. They enjoy the success but then they set their other targets to achieve. They never follow the single goal. Once they achieve the first goal they shift to the other goal. They always try to spread their business and do ail that is necessary for the business. They are always active and think continuously.

No room for failure – Giving up leads to destruction. A majority of very successful self-made entrepreneurs have not had a "soft place to fall" nor a safety net to rely.

1.4 Why to Become an Entrepreneur?

I've always wanted to do this

For some strange reason, ever since I was a kid I have always wanted to build my own business. The question for me always was "when" and not "if". Somehow, other than a brief dalliance with the idea of becoming a fighter pilot, I've never really floundered on what I want to do for a living. It's always been business.

For a higher purpose

It's not just about the money. It's also about listening to a different piper's tune. It's about wanting to do something very different from the mainstream. I have grandiose dreams of being able to inspire a lot of other would-be entrepreneurs out there to take the leap of faith and begin their own ventures. Directly or indirectly I have always wanted to promote entrepreneurship within India, because that's what pumps up the economy - the pursuit of the creation of wealth. It creates opportunities for financial empowerment of all sectors of society and it helps create a shared goal and shared vision of what a country should strive to achieve.

Because it's very creative

The process of starting a business, building and nurturing it is very creative. It requires constant ideation and forces you to keep the creative juices flowing. More so, when things are going good and there is a tendency to rest on one's laurels.

For the sheer challenge of it

Most of the people select it because they like challenges. They want to face the challenges and want to overcome the challenges. They want to become entrepreneur because they think that they can fulfill their desire by becoming an entrepreneur.

For the creation of wealth

Oh yes! There's no denying the fact that the creation of wealth is one of the primary goals of any enterprise and most entrepreneurs dream of material wealth and possessions. But there's more to it than just money. Creation of wealth is not just cash in the bank or assets, but also good will, reputation, camaraderie, experience and most importantly intellectual capital.

Desire for achievement and self-fulfillment

For many, having a business of their own is a childhood dream or a lifelong aspiration. The natural desire to fulfill this ambition will drive some people to pursue their aspirations to become entrepreneurs. Having your own business can bring a lot of satisfaction and a deep sense of achievement. This is especially true for people who have an inborn entrepreneurial spirit: they are excited by the challenge and they enjoy taking risks.

Willingness to invest their current resources

People who are already wealthy may find that setting up a business can be a very good way of creating more wealth and generate a steady flow of income.

For the independence

The independence to do what I wanted to do and to do it in a way where my principles and values would not be compromised. Where my potential would not be capped by the potential of a boss. They want to become the entrepreneur because they cannot work under any boss, they have their own plans what they want to implement. They do not want to go for a job because they do not get the complete freedom for their work and always have to follow the boss's instruction.

Need for money

The current state of the economy has resulted in a dramatic increase in the unemployment rate. Many of the people who lost their jobs are forced by the circumstances to search for new ways of earning a living and supporting their family. For some, setting up a business can be the way to regain their financial stability.

Because I am crazy

That hardly needs much explanation, but a certain amount of eccentricity is almost essential to a successful business.

Need for financial independence and security

Setting up and managing your own business can be a tricky and stressful endeavor; however, it can prove to be very profitable. Having your own business can provide total financial independence and this is an enormous accomplishment for most people, especially when the economy is in a period of decline.

Because it's cool

Yes, running your own business is definitely cooler than slogging it out in the corporate machinery. Which is not to say that it doesn't have its ups and downs and an entirely different set of problems and stressful situations?

Frustration with their current workplace or career

Some people become frustrated with their past achievements and feel like their current career path is not going the way they expected or fulfilling their goals. This is when they make the brave decision to give up on their current job and take on the difficult challenge of setting up their own business.

Because I'm inspired

Whether it is Akio Morita or Warren Buffet or Richard Branson, self-made capitalists have always been a tremendous inspiration. Most of the people want to become an entrepreneur because they are inspired by the successful entrepreneurs. They also want to follow the path of the success what is followed by the successful entrepreneurs. They also want to open their business. They are motivated by the stories of the entrepreneurs, how they have faced the challenges and become the successful businessmen. They think that they can also overcome the problems and can pen a big business.

1.5 Reasons to Start a Business

What drives people to become entrepreneurs-to start companies? It's a question with many answers. Often these individuals are not entirely sure themselves and the answers to the question are apt to change over time as their perceptions change.

People start business for two reasons: first reason is personal reason. They want to open business for their own satisfaction i.e., they want to do something for their own; for example, to earn fame, to bring creative products or services etc. The second reason is general reason. They want to earn profit; huge business scope etc.

Personal Reasons:

Inequity between contribution and reward

People who are by nature high achievers tend not to get along well in large organizations. They want rewards based upon accomplishment, not on seniority, conforming to the culture or political clout. The person who just made a major contribution does not want to be told, "Be patient-your turn will come."

Fame and recognition

It is the opinion of some that, this is an important reason why people start companies. Most of the people open the business because they want to become famous in the world. They want that people should know them. They see in their daily life that how the entrepreneurs have earned the fame. They also want to become like that and they are motivated by the life and business of the big entrepreneurs. People also want recognition from the world. They want to show their talent, intelligence to the world. They try to do something unique for the society and they want that people should remember them for their act.

Participation in all aspects of a business

Nothing is more exciting than to be broadly involved in the operation of a business. The entrepreneur helps conceive the product or service, helps design it, goes out and gets orders, makes sure the factory runs well, helps the customer put it into operation and finally sees the effect that all of this has on the profits of the firm. What a thrill!

Personal financial gain

For some people this is very important, for others less so. Gains can come more quickly and can be much greater than when working for someone else; this is not a negligible consideration. For most people becoming an entrepreneur is the only way available to make a lot of money.

Joy of winning

Entrepreneurs are the ultimate achievers. They like to win. Starting a company is a good way to satisfy the achievement instinct. Starting a new company, working for a new company, being involved in any way with a new company is just plain fun. It is satisfying and exciting. We spend more hours at our job than at anything else we do. Why shouldn't we enjoy it?

Entrepreneurs come from all the paths of life. The diverse motivations of people that become entrepreneurs account for a large number of businesses being opened at any given time. The same diversity of reasons to become an entrepreneur also explains why some businesses are a huge success, while others fail. Nevertheless, the amount of people who get involved in business is growing quite rapidly and having a positive effect on the economy.

1.6 What is Entrepreneurship?

According to Peter Drucker Entrepreneurship is defined as 'a systematic innovation, which consists in the purposeful and organized search for changes and it is the systematic analysis of the opportunities such changes might offer for economic and social innovation.'

Entrepreneurship is a discipline with a knowledge base theory. It is an outcome of complex socio-economic, psychological, technological, legal and other factors. It is a dynamic and risky process. It involves a fusion of capital, technology and human talent. Entrepreneurship is equally applicable to big and small businesses, to economic and non-economic activities. Different entrepreneurs might have some common traits but all of them will have some different and unique features.

If we just concentrate on the entrepreneurs then there will be as many models as there are ventures and we will not be able to predict or plan, how and where and when these entrepreneurs will start their ventures.

Entrepreneurship is a process. It is not a combination of some stray incidents. It is the purposeful and organized search for change, conducted after systematic analysis of opportunities in the environment. Entrepreneurship is a philosophy- it is the way one thinks, one acts and therefore it can exist in any situation be it business or government or in the field of education, science and technology or poverty alleviation or any others.

What is Entrepreneurship? An entrepreneur is an individual who owns a firm, business or venture and is responsible for its development. Entrepreneurship is the practice of starting a new business or reviving an existing business, in order to capitalize on new found opportunities.

Generally, **entrepreneurship is a tough proposition** as a good number of the new businesses fail to take off. Entrepreneurial activities differ based on the type of business they are involved in. It is also true that entrepreneurial ventures create a number of new job opportunities. A large number of entrepreneurial projects look for venture capital or angel funding for their startup firms in order to finance their capital requirements. Besides, government agencies and some NGOs also finance entrepreneurial ventures.

Entrepreneurship, therefore, is about helping other people achieve their goals. It's not about you. Successful entrepreneurs focus on others. Take Derek Sivers, for example. As the leader of a successful touring band, he needed a way to make his CDs available to fans everywhere, all the time — not just at concerts.

But Derek and his group were unattached to a major label and big sellers like CD Now and Amazon required bands to have in-place agreements with large distributors. What was a hard-working, independent musician to do?

Derek decided to set up his own modest online sales channel and soon friends from other bands were asking for help selling their music. Within a couple of years, the store, renamed CD Baby, was distributing the work of more than 90,000 artists. To date, its paid out is more than $70 million to the 200,000 independent artists it now represents. Derek focused on helping others.

Successful entrepreneurs like Derek undertake ventures that benefit many people. Ventures are successful to the degree that they generate social benefits. About Microsoft's products or business practices, who can deny that the company enabled personal computing for a billion citizens? Success as an entrepreneur isn't about you — it's about helping others achieve goals *you* care about.

Entrepreneurship is often associated with uncertainty, particularly when it involves creating something new for which there is no existing market. Even if there is a market, it may not translate into a huge business opportunity for the entrepreneur. A major aspect in entrepreneurship is that entrepreneurs embrace opportunities irrespective of the resources they have access to.

Entrepreneurship involves being resourceful and finding ways to obtain the resources required to achieve the set objectives. Capital is one such resource. Entrepreneurs need to think out-of-the-box to improve their chances of obtaining what they need to succeed. According to management experts, vast majority of entrepreneurs desire to be in control of their own life and they can't find this beyond entrepreneurship. Studies have demonstrated that people derive great satisfaction from their entrepreneurial work.

A number of entrepreneurs are of the opinion that managing their own business offers far greater security than being an employee elsewhere. They feel entrepreneurship enables them to acquire wealth quickly and cushion themselves against financial insecurity. Additionally, an entrepreneur's future is not at peril owing to the faulty decisions of a finicky employer. So, while some people feel that being employed is less risky, entrepreneurs feel that they are better off starting a business of their own.

Today, there is the increasing awareness about entrepreneurship. People aren't confining themselves to one business. They are following one business with another. Such entrepreneurs are referred to as "serial entrepreneurs." Sometimes these entrepreneurs become angel investors and invest their money in startup companies. As a person gains greater insight into business and entrepreneurship, his chances of succeeding in business improve.

Entrepreneurs are a different set of people. They often see things that others fail to notice. They endeavor to bring about change and foster growth. They believe in themselves. Entrepreneurship propels them to strive and move forward, to get to where they want to be.

Enterprise

Entrepreneur is a person who starts an enterprise. The process of creation is called entrepreneurship. The entrepreneur is the actor and entrepreneurship is the act. The outcome of the actor and the act is called the enterprise. An enterprise is the business organization that is formed and which provides goods and services, creates jobs, contributes to national income, exports and overall economic development.

What entrepreneurship is not?

Successful entrepreneurs told the same thing, "It's not about the money."

What, then, is entrepreneurship about? Exploiting a market opportunity? Fame? Fortune? Proving yourself?

First, some tips as to what entrepreneurship's not about:

- Entrepreneurship is not about *you.*
- It's not about *you* getting rich.
- It's not about *you* proving something to the world.
- It's not about *you* struggling to overcome the odds.

Rather, entrepreneurship is about you helping *other people* to achieve their goals. This is obvious when you think about it. Business is all about satisfying customers, right? Well, to satisfy customers, you need to help them save money, solve annoying problems, experience more satisfaction or pleasure or earn a better living. Put simply, in order to succeed as an entrepreneur, you must help other people.

1.7 Need for Entrepreneurship

According to A.H. Cole, "Entrepreneurship is the purposeful activity of an individual or group of associated individuals, undertaken to initiate, maintain or aggrandize profit by production or distribution of economic goods or services".

Entrepreneurship promotes small business in the society. Government has accepted the fact that small firms have a crucial role to play in the economic development of the country. Most economists today agree that entrepreneurship is a necessary ingredient for stimulating economic growth and employment opportunities in all societies. Small businesses are an essential part of our future economic prosperity because of the following reasons;

Employment generation: entrepreneurial development is looked at as a vehicle for employment generation through promotion of small business. India, being far more developed and forward looking country than some of the third world countries, can provide lead to entrepreneurial development activities. However, India can benefit from the well- documented success experiences of developed countries like USA, Japan and UK in the field of employment generation and small business promotion. Steady growth in consumer spending, expanding retail sales, a strong housing market, continued expansion of the service sector, low rates of inflation and of labor cost increases and falling interest rates contributed to a healthy environment for small business. In India, the government policies, political and economic environment greatly encourage the establishment of new and small enterprises. Self- employment and small scale industry schemes have been further liberalized during the last decade.

Small business dynamism: great dynamism is one of the qualities of the small and medium enterprises. This quality of dynamism originates in the inherent nature of the small business. The structure of small and medium enterprises is less complex than that of large enterprises and therefore facilitates quicker and smoother communication and decision- making. This allows for the greater flexibility and mobility of small business management. Also, small enterprises, more often make it possible for owners, who have a stronger entrepreneurial spirit than employed mangers, to undertake risk and challenges.

Balanced economic development: small business promotion needs relatively low investment and therefore can be easily undertaken in rural and semi-urban areas. This in turn creates additional employment in these areas and prevents migration of people from rural to urban areas. Since majority of the people are living in the rural areas, therefore, more of our development efforts should be directed towards this sector. Small enterprises use local resources and are best suited to rural and underdeveloped sector. This in turn will also lead to dispersal of industries, reduction in concentration of economic power and balanced regional development.

Innovations in enterprises: business enterprises need to be innovative for survival and better performance. It is believed that smaller firms have a relatively higher necessity and capability to innovate. The smaller firms do not face the constraints imposed by large investment in existing technology. Thus they are both free and compelled to innovate. Entrepreneurship development is accelerating the pace of small firm's growth in India. An increased number of small firms are expected to result in more innovations and make the Indian industry compete in the international market.

1.8 Benefits of Entrepreneurship

Entrepreneurs enjoy the freedom of making their own business decisions and becoming their own bosses. In addition, they also gain the stability and control that could never be achieved as a regular employee. Compared to being regular employees, entrepreneurs enjoy much excitement beginning from the planning stage of the business up to development and realization. Thrill-seekers obviously love being entrepreneurs as they are exposed to too much risk. You should never forget, that all business risks that you agree on taking, should be calculated. Most people who are employed generally feel that they are not being compensated for the work they do. In addition, they must follow the salary structure set by their employers. Entrepreneurs, on the other hand, earn money that is commensurate to their efforts

1.8.1 Advantages of Being a Successful Entrepreneur

Becoming a successful entrepreneur takes a lot of time, patience and perseverance. Successful entrepreneurs are extremely passionate about their business; they create a vision, focus on their strengths and work hard to accomplish their goals. Often they are strong social networkers and shameless self promoters who strive to become the expert in their trade. Once they have achieved that expert status, they begin reaping the benefits of a successful entrepreneur.

No set timetable

Successful entrepreneurs work flexible schedules and are free to come and go as they please. They do not have to punch a time clock every day nor do they have to sit behind a desk for eight hours. Because of the flexibility they are often able to spend more quality time with their friends and family. They have complete freedom to do anything what they want. They can any time move out of the day, if they feel they have some other important work to do.

Passion for their career

Successful entrepreneurs often build their business around something they love to do. For example, someone who cares about car and mechanics may open their own auto repair shop. Because it is something they are passionate about they are more like to work harder and succeed. They live their dream. They are happy with their business. They can achieve what they want because they are not the employee of any one; they are free to do what they want to do with their business.

Job satisfaction

Successful entrepreneurs have the satisfaction of using their skills, interests and creativity to make money. They do not have a set job description and can work on whatever project interests them the most. They are the satisfied one for at least what they want they do that. They do not work under any influence and therefore they are not restricted by any one. They implement new ideas; they do not have to take the permission of the others for their work.

Increased self confidence

Successful entrepreneurs often build their business from the ground up. Seeing it succeed increases their self confidence and gives them a strong sense of accomplishment. They feel proud of themselves. They overcome the problems; they face the challenges after that too they get success in their business. It gives them the complete satisfaction with increase in the confidence. They now become relaxed; they do not fear about any challenge and have a faith that they will overcome the problems.

Giving back to the community

Successful entrepreneurs are able to give back to their communities by building symbiotic relationships with local business owners as well as increasing local job opportunities. They may also bring a sense of prestige and recognition to their community. They are the job creator. Their business runs many families. They produce the products for the customers. They fulfill the needs of the people in a society. They give satisfaction to the society. They come up with the new ideas to solve the problems of the people.

Job security and friendly work environment

Because successful entrepreneurs are their own boss, they do not have to worry being laid off or losing their job. Also if something in their work environment displeases them, they can easily make adjustments to improve the situation. They are not dependent to anyone. They are independent person. They survive by themselves. They run their own business, create the environment of peace, they give facilities to their employees from medical insurance to education of the employees' children. They create the happy environment in the society.

Financial Freedom

Successful entrepreneurs work hard to achieve financial freedom. Their salary is based on their efforts and not on what an employer offers them. Countless small business owners have been able to build their business into a secure financial empire. Financial freedom can also be obtained when an entrepreneur sells a successful small business. If the work is no longer rewarding and challenging, they can sell the business, reap the benefits and come up with a new business idea.

Excitement

Due to its high capacity for risk, there is a lot of adventure. What they do' they enjoy it very much? They come up with the new and new strategies apply them in the market and remain excited about the outcome. They are very hopeful about the outcome. They always form the strategies like the strategies formed by the military officers. They get enjoyment after defeating the others but they are also ready to get defeated.

Rules and regulations

Work in a current job is difficult to do because of all the "red tape" and consistent administrative approval is needed. In a job someone has to follow all the rules and regulations. Those may be wrong but as an employee the person has to follow the rules. But in a business they form their rules; they have a complete authority to make the rule. They are free to work.

Originality

Some people feel that they can offer a new service/product that no one else has offered before. The entrepreneurs have a complete freedom to implement their ideas. They come with their creative ideas and produce a new product that has not been produced by anyone. They do not follow others, idea. They have their own idea and product.

Competition: Employees feel they can offer their current company's product / service at a lesser expense to the public.

Independence

Some people wish to be their own boss and make all the important decisions themselves. They are not connected by anyone else. They take their own decisions. They feel satisfied in taking their decisions. They do what they want. They run the complete business independently.

Salary potential: Generally, people want to be paid for the amount of work they do in full; they do not want to be "short-charged."

Flexibility

Entrepreneurs can schedule their work hours to spend quality time with family or for any other reason. They can do many tasks at the same time. They are not attached to only one place. They can handle many projects. They can freely move to other places for their other work.

Rational salary: They are not being paid what they're worth and would rather work on their own and earn the money they should be earning for their efforts.

Freedom

Entrepreneurs can work whenever they want, wherever they want and however they want. They can implement their ideas at any time. They are the boss, they have complete authority. They are not required to work at the same place for the long time. They can run simultaneous business. They can handle more than one project at the same time. The employee does not have such freedom.

1.8.2 Disadvantages

Salary

Starting your own business means that you must be willing to give up the security of a regular paycheque. The entrepreneurs do not get regular salary. They are dependent on the business for their payment. They are not secured about the salary. They will earn if the business will do well otherwise they will suffer. Here the employees have an advantage over entrepreneurs.

Benefits

There will undoubtedly be fewer benefits, especially when considering that your business will be just starting off. Definitely in the starting stage of the business, entrepreneurs cannot be the confident ones. If they run it very well then they will achieve success, otherwise there is a fear of business failure. They have to take many efforts to survive the business. They are not the free person, at the initial stage of the business they work for even 12 hours or more.

Work schedule

The work schedule of an entrepreneur is never predictable; an emergency can come up in a matter of a second and late hours will have to be put in. They do not have fix schedule. They can go anywhere whenever it becomes urgent to go for business work. They cannot say that they will come home at sharp 5 evening.

Administration

The entrepreneurs have to take the burden of making decisions. They are the only higher authority in the business and therefore they are responsible for the decisions and their consequences. They are ready to accept the failure if business suffers from their decisions. They have to manage their employees also that is not the easy task. They have to better utilize the resources without any wastages because already they have limited resources. All the decisions of the business must be made on your own; there is noone ranked higher than you on the chain of command in YOUR business. So as an entrepreneur he has the burden of whole business progress.

Incompetent staff: Often times, you will find yourself working with an employee who "doesn't know the ropes" as well as you do due to lack of experience.

Procedures: Many times during your entrepreneurial life, you will find that many policies do not make sense, nor will they ever make sense

1.8.3 Benefits of Entrepreneurship and Entrepreneur Risks

According to Diane Wells an online entrepreneur and author, the following are the benefits of entrepreneurship.

In times when opportunities to earn money from jobs are less, you got to make opportunities for yourself through entrepreneurship. The benefits of entrepreneurship towards the economy and towards the entrepreneur himself or herself are tremendous. Starting out small and working your way up is always a good idea when it comes to entrepreneurship; small entrepreneurial activities are what keeps world economies afloat and not few big businesses. And the benefits of entrepreneurship towards an individual are no less than life changing.

First, entrepreneurship can be your ticket towards financial independence. How much you make really depends on you; you set your own goal and by it you determine how much you compensate your efforts. Of course there are necessary things you need in place before you could realize total financial independence, but working towards your goal is another exciting thing that you could do for yourself as a person. A study by Michael T. Childress and others in 1998 (Entrepreneurs and Small Business - Kentucky's Neglected Natural Resource) found that entrepreneurs make more money and pay more money to their employees, than working in big businesses or corporations.

Second, entrepreneurship allows flexibility in your life. Once the necessary things are set in place and operation is properly delegated, the entrepreneur can start to experience flexibility in work schedule than working for somebody else. After all, one of the top benefits of entrepreneurship is that you are your own boss. When all aspects of your business are fully functional, you can start to do other things that you love. You can finally make time for your sport, hobby and most of all, for your family.

Moreover, entrepreneurship can open endless possibilities for the entrepreneur. Working for somebody else often force people to do jobs they don't like; entrepreneurship can free you from the drudgery of imposed tasks. In fact, your business should be a self-expression, a form of outlet for your creativity and the things that you love to do. It's simply doing the things that you love to do and making money while doing it. No longer will you be in the mercy of seniority and office politics to rise and achieve growth. Entrepreneurship will bring you to new heights that not even your limitations can hold you back if your determination is solid.

Other more noble benefits of entrepreneurship are that you're helping to provide opportunities for other people and contribute to the society through responsible business. In fact, small business owners are respected people in the community because they are responsible for spurring community development starting at creating local jobs. Jobs provided by entrepreneurs are even more fulfilling in terms of pay and recognition compared to jobs in high-rise offices. You're not only providing for yourself and your family, you're also providing for the community in your own little way. No economy in the world can survive without the ingenuity, creativity and labour provided by entrepreneurs.

The best part about entrepreneurship is that it doesn't discriminate: men, women, young, old, educated or not, everyone can become an entrepreneur through hard work and dedication to continuous learning and improvement.

1.9 Intrapreneurship

What is intrapreneurship? Difference, features and examples of Intrapreneurs

Entrepreneurship is the practice of embarking on a new business or reviving an existing business by pooling together a bunch of resources, in order to exploit new found opportunities.

What is Intrapreneurship? Intrapreneurship is the practice of entrepreneurship by employees within an organization.

1.9.1 Difference between an Entrepreneur and an Intrapreneur

Intrapreneurs share the same traits as entrepreneurs such as conviction, zeal and insight. As the intrapreneur continues to expresses his ideas vigorously, it will reveal the gap between the philosophy of the organization and the employee. If the organization supports him in pursuing his ideas, he succeeds. If not, he is likely to leave the organization and set up his own business.

1.9.2 Example of Intrapreneurship

A classic case of intrapreneurs is that of the founders of Adobe, John Warnock and Charles Geschke. They both were employees of Xerox. As employees of Xerox, they were frustrated because their new product ideas were not encouraged. They quit Xerox in the early 1980s to begin their own business. Currently, Adobe has an annual turnover of over $3 billion.

Examples of Intrapreneurs

A lot of companies are known for their efforts towards nurturing their in-house talents to promote innovation. The prominent among them is "Skunk Works" group at Lockheed Martin. This group formed in 1943 to build **P-80 fighter jets**. Kelly Johnson was the director of the project, a person who gave "14 rules of intrapreneurship".

At "**3M**" employees could spend their 15 per cent time working on the projects they like for the betterment of the company. On the initial success of the project, 3M even funds it for further development.

Genesis Grant is another 3M intrapreneurial program which finances projects that might not end up getting funds through normal channels. Genesis Grant offers $85,000 to these innovators to carry forward their projects.

Robbie Bach, J Allard and team's XBOX might not have been feasible without the Microsoft's money and infrastructure. The project required 100s of millions and quality talent to make the product.

1.9.3 Features of Intrapreneurship

Entrepreneurship involves innovation, the ability to take risk and creativity. An entrepreneur will be able to look at things in novel ways. He will have the capacity to take calculated risk and to accept failure as a learning point. An intrapreneur thinks like an entrepreneur looking out for

Table 1.1: Difference between an entrepreneur and an intrapreneur

Entrepreneur	*Intrapreneur*
"An **Entrepreneur** is someone who has the skills, passion and financial backing to create wealth from new business opportunities and is willing to take full responsibility for its success or failure."	"An **Intrapreneur** is someone who manages that business with entrepreneurial flair in line with the expectations of the shareholders."
The Entrepreneur is typically a visionary who spots an opportunity in the marketplace and has the passion, guile and contact base to set the wheels in motion.	The Intrapreneur has passion and drive but also has the operational skills of running the "clockwork" of the business to enable a good idea to be turned into commercial reality. He is the "inside entrepreneur".
Entrepreneur refers to a person who undertakes and operates a new enterprise or venture.	Intrapreneur - The spirit of entrepreneurship within an existing organization.
An entrepreneur takes substantial risk in being the owner and operator of a business with expectations of financial profit and other rewards that the business may generate.	On the contrary, an intrapreneur is an individual employed by an organization for remuneration, which is based on the financial success of the unit he is responsible for.
Entrepreneurs take personal financial risk.	Intrapreneurs have a different mindset. They can perform many similar acts to entrepreneurs, but they tend to do so without taking the personal financial risk.
Entrepreneurs lose houses.	Intrapreneurs lose career development points.
Entrepreneurs are the boss.	Intrapreneurs are the employees.

opportunities, which profit the organization. Intrapreneurship is a novel way of making organizations more profitable where imaginative employees entertain entrepreneurial thoughts. It is in the interest of an organization to encourage intrapreneurs. Intrapreneurship is a significant method for companies to reinvent themselves and improve performance.

In a recent study, researchers compared the elements related to entrepreneurial and intrapreneurial activity. The study found that among the 32,000 subjects who participated in it, five percent were engaged in the initial stages of a business start-up, either on their own or within an organization. The study also found that human capital such as education and experience is connected more with entrepreneurship than with intrapreneurship. Another observation was that intrapreneurial startups were inclined to concentrate more on business-to-business products while entrepreneurial startups were inclined towards consumer sales.

Another important factor that led to the choice between entrepreneurship and intrapreneurship was age. The study found that people who launched their own companies were in their 30s and 40s. People from older and younger age groups were risk averse or felt they have no opportunities, which makes them the ideal candidates if an organization is on the lookout for employees with new ideas that can be pursued.

Entrepreneurship appeals to people who possess natural traits that find start ups arousing their interest. Intrapreneurs appear to be those who generally would not like to get entangled in startups but are tempted to do so for a number of reasons. Managers would do well to take employees who do not appear entrepreneurial but can turn out to be good intrapreneurial choices.

1.10 Role of Entrepreneur in Economic Development

We Need Entrepreneurs — How Vital They are to Our Economy

The Great Recession has made it abundantly clear how important are entrepreneurs. We need their creativity to start businesses and create jobs. We do not do enough to cultivate this special breed of vital change agents on which our economic future depends.

Entrepreneurs are the lifeblood of any economy. Policies have to favour risk-taking and have to reward those with the energy and zeal to start businesses. Without entrepreneurs, there are no jobs. The large enterprises of today were all started by single entrepreneurs willing to take risks to claim the rewards from risk-taking. Americans sometimes take for granted that there is gainful employment, but the Great Recession of 2008 made it abundantly clear that no one can take employment for granted. There are simply not always jobs available. It is imperative to continually increase the supply of jobs for a stable and productive society of working citizens.

Can the government create jobs? Actually no, although the politicians do try to "sell" their legislation by claiming they are creating jobs. In fact, the best the government can do is take money from citizens and pay a government official to do something that the private sector was not willing to pay for. Does this create a job? It does create a government job, but it does not create a 'net' number of new jobs. This is so because when the government takes money from citizens, they have less to spend for their activities. Thus, they will not spend that extra tax money at the hardware store, the movies, a restaurant, fixing a car, etc. Jobs will be lost or not added at the hardware store, a restaurant, the movies, the car repair shop, etc.

An entrepreneur on the other hand creates a new product or service that citizens voluntarily wish to buy. They shift their expenditures to this new product or service and the entrepreneur hires people to satisfy the demand for the new product or service. Everyone is made better off because everyone chooses voluntarily what to buy and sell. Rather than being forced into giving up a meal at a restaurant in order to hire a new government official, a person wants to give up that meal to buy the new product or service from the entrepreneur. A person who loses their job at the restaurant might work for the entrepreneur in the new business. If the business is successful, it will add more and more jobs, creating a demand for employees. With greater demand for employees, their wages will rise. Google was just two employees about 15 years ago, now it has many thousands of employees in a new industry that did not exist 15 years ago. It was created by entrepreneurs.

What do we need to do to stimulate entrepreneurial activity to create more jobs? One, allow entrepreneurs to keep more of what they earn — lower tax rates. Create incentives for starting a business. Two, stimulate employment by making employees less expensive. If every business has to pay huge employer taxes (social security, Medicare, unemployment insurance, workers compensation) and be subject to lawsuit for the smallest of infractions, then those are disincentives to hiring workers in the U.S. Reduce those legal costs to hiring. Third, reduce government mandated paperwork. The government requires a lot of paperwork to run a business. That takes time and detracts from the time for running a business. Starting a business is already more than a full time job; layering on useless paperwork is a big disincentive to the vital economic function of entrepreneur.

We need entrepreneurs to do their magic more now than ever. Let's give them room and stay out of their way so that they can create great businesses and help us through this economic downturn.

1.11 Developing an Entrepreneurial Environment

The nature versus nurture debate with entrepreneurs' development still rages. What is clear; however is that the environment within a family business can have a major impact on the development of entrepreneurial skills of family members? Use checklist below to help you develop an environment within your family business that supports any family members that may want to start their own businesses in the future:

Dynamic business environment

For any entrepreneur to flourish in your family business, the business itself should be as dynamic as possible. Forward thinking businesses that are constantly evolving and adopting new business practices and technologies give any family member that has a start-up business in mind a template they can use for their enterprise.

Can do attitude

Encouragement is often cited as one of the single most important aspects of a young entrepreneur's development. Management and colleagues within a family business should encourage family members that want to start-up on their own to move forward with their plans. Anything is possible attitude, is key to developing the skills of new entrepreneurs.

Training and help

Some entrepreneurial skills are innate, but many can be taught. Sometimes family businesses will shun training as this could mean a valued family member then leaves the business. Training should be offered where possible. Standing in the way of a family member developing their own business start-up plans will only cause resentment and ultimately damage the family business overall.

Mentoring and support

Entrepreneurs tend to identify in others similar personality traits to their own. If several family members have these traits it is only natural that they will be attracted to each other to form new start-up businesses. Look for ways in which these family members can be mentored by either other family members or by people and organizations outside of the family business itself.

Developing Entrepreneurial Skills

Research has indicated that the family business is one of the most effective environments to develop the skills that all entrepreneurs need to succeed. What's more, family businesses have been shown to be the ideal place for female entrepreneurs to thrive. It is not surprising that research has revealed these results. Family businesses tend to be hotbeds of business activity. The skills that new entrepreneurs need are developed within the safe environment of the family business.

1.12. Women Entrepreneurship

Women Entrepreneurs may be defined as the women or a group of women who initiate, organize and operate a business enterprise.

OECD (Organisation for Economic Co-Operation and Development) (1998) has referred women entrepreneur as equally to someone who has started a one-woman business, to someone who is a principal in a family business or partnership or to someone who is a shareholder in a publicly held company which she organizes and runs. Marcellina et al. (2002) has defined women enterprises as ones that were planned, started, owned and managed by women.

Government of India has defined women entrepreneurs as an enterprise owned and controlled by a women having a minimum financial interest of 51 per cent of the capital and giving at least 51 per cent of employment generated in the enterprise to women. Like a male entrepreneur a woman entrepreneur has many functions. They should explore the prospects of starting new enterprise; undertake risks, introduction of new innovations, coordination administration and control of business and providing effective leadership in all aspects of business.

1.12.1. Women's Small Enterprise Development and Its Affecting Factors

There are different factors influencing woman to become an entrepreneur. Such factors can be divided into two: (1) the *push* and (2) the *pull* factors (Robinson, 2001). The *push* factor is allied with negative environment and the *pull* factor is attributed to the push factor may result from low income, low job satisfaction or lack of job opportunities and strict working hours. The *pull* factor, however, may result from the need of fulfilling the desire to help others and self accomplishment. Dhaliwal (1998) found the push factor to be evident in the developing countries. Empirical evidence on the push and pull factors revealed that women entrepreneurs in the developed countries were influenced by the need for achievement, while women entrepreneurs in the developing countries were influenced by a combination of push and pull factors (Orhan and Scott, 2001). Women are influenced by socio-cultural complexities to become an entrepreneur in developing countries (Nilufer, 2001). Because of such complexities in the factors influencing women entrepreneurship development in developing countries, many international organizations adopted strategies to overcome such complexities.

A study conducted by International Labour Organization (ILO) (2006) has found four personal and four external factors that influence women entrepreneurs' success.

Personal factors comprise: (1) motivation and commitment; (2) abilities and skills; (3) ideas and markets; and (4) resources.

While external factors consist of: (1) business development organizations; (2) broader enabling environment; (3) economic/market environment; and (4) socio-cultural context.

The *business development organizations factor* considers the roles of government, NGOs, private sector, membership organizations and donors.

The *broader enabling environment* factor mulls over regulations, policies, institutions and processes.

The *economic/market environment* factor ponders opportunities and threats (e.g., inflation, interest rates, economic trends etc.).

The *socio-cultural context* factor considers attitudes, aspirations, confidence etc.

Ulrich (2006) has examined five factors and found that all of them influence youth entrepreneurship development. The five factors include: (1) entrepreneurship education and training, (2) socio-cultural, legitimacy and acceptance, (3) access to finance, (4) business assistance and support and (5) administrative and regulatory framework.

1.12.2. Problems of Women Entrepreneurs in India

Women in India are faced many problems to get ahead their life in business. A few problems can be detailed as;

1. The greatest deterrent to women entrepreneurs is that they are women. A kind of male dominant social order is the stumbling block to them in their way towards business success. Male members think it a big risk financing the ventures run by women.

2. Changing the perceptions about the likely success of women-owned businesses depends on increasing women's visibility in leadership positions within the greater business community. In an assessment of women's presence as CEOs or Directors of large business enterprises, it has been anticipated that the exodus of women to entrepreneurial growth firms might be because women believe that they have greater representation in strategic leadership positions in privately-held or family-owned firms as they provide better opportunities for leadership than available to women in publicly-traded companies.
3. The financial institutions are skeptical about the entrepreneurial abilities of women. The bankers consider women loanies as higher risk than men loanies. The bankers put unrealistic and unreasonable securities to get loan to women entrepreneurs. The financial institutions discourage women entrepreneurs on the belief that they can at any time leave their business and become housewives again.
4. Another significant need of many women business owners is obtaining the appropriate assistance and information needed to take the business to the next level of growth. Women entrepreneurs required assistance and training in implementing the business idea, identifying initial sources of financing and advertising/promotion. The entrepreneurs, who were already established, had a somewhat different set of needs including financing for expansion and increasing sales.
5. Women hardly interact with other women who are successful entrepreneurs. This results in a negative impact on their networking skills.
6. The women entrepreneurs are suffering from inadequate financial resources and working capital. The women entrepreneurs lack access to external funds due to their inability to provide tangible security. Very few women have the tangible property in hand.
7. Socio-cultural Barriers: Women's family and personal obligations are sometimes a great barrier for succeeding in business career. Women's family obligations also bar them from becoming successful entrepreneurs in both developed and developing nations. The overlapping of the family and the firm is not significant for women business owners. As the boundaries between the firm and the family tend to be indistinct, women operating family businesses face a unique set of issues related to personal identity, role conflict, loyalties, family relationships and attitudes towards authority. "Having primary responsibility for children, home and older dependent family members, few women can devote all their time and energies to their business" Additionally, family businesses owned by women are at a disadvantage financially and are forced to rely on internal resources of funding rather than outside sources.
8. Lack of Confidence: women lack confidence in their strength and competence. The family members and the society are reluctant to stand beside their entrepreneurial growth. Women are very critical when it comes to themselves – can I really do this, am I good enough, maybe I have to learn more, others can do it better. It is quite interesting that many successful women have been educated in only girls colleges and schools, which often deliver a safe environment to try out ones personal strengths, learn to overcome weaknesses and be proud of oneself. The confidence to travel across day and night and even different regions and states are less found in women compared to male entrepreneurs. This shows the low level freedom of expression and freedom of mobility of the women entrepreneurs.
9. Married women have to make a fine balance between business and home. More-over the business success depends on the support the family members extended to women in the business process and management. Very few societies accept fathers taking

over the role of staying home and taking care of the children. Once these children are old enough to take care for themselves, they have to bear an additional responsibility of taking care of elder parents. If they want to become entrepreneurs, the society expects them to be able to do both: take care of family and home and do business.

10. Market-oriented risks – Stiff competition in the market and lack of mobility of women make the dependence of women entrepreneurs on middlemen indispensable. Another argument is that women entrepreneurs have low-level management skills. They have to depend on office staffs and intermediaries, to get things done, especially, the marketing and sales side of business. Here there is more probability for business fallacies like the intermediaries take major part of the surplus or profit. Marketing means mobility and confidence in dealing with the external world, both of which women have been discouraged from developing by social conditioning. Even when they are otherwise in control of an enterprise, they often depend on males of the family in this area.
11. Discrimination – it is hard to believe but women are still treated differently in our society. Women do get lower salaries compared to men doing the same job; women do not have access to men dominated networks who take their decisions about successors in the company during golf plays or meetings.
12. Motivational factors – Self motivation can be realized through a mind set for a successful business, attitude to take up risk and behavior towards the business society by shouldering the social responsibilities. Achievement motivation of the women folk found less compared to male members. The low level of education and confidence leads to low level achievement and advancement motivation among women folk to engage in business operations and running a business concern.
13. Missing networks – through centuries business men have build up their networks but women still have to learn to catch up.
14. The male-female competition is another factor, which develop hurdles to women entrepreneurs in the business management process. Despite the fact that women entrepreneurs are good in keeping their service prompt and delivery in time, due to lack of organizational skills compared to male entrepreneurs women have to face constraints from competition. In spite of constitutional equality, in practice the attitude of men is not only tradition-bound but even of those who are responsible for decision-making, planning and research is not equality. They still suffer from male Reservations. This attitude of reservation creates difficulties and problems at all levels i.e., Family support, training, banking, licensing and marketing.
15. Women are hesitant to find out the access to cater their needs in the financial and marketing areas. In spite of the mushrooming growth of associations, institutions and the schemes from the government side, women are not enterprising and dynamic to optimize the resources in the form of reserves, assets mankind or business volunteers.
16. Knowledge of latest technological changes, know how and education level of the person are significant factors that affect business. The literacy rate of women in India is found at low level compared to male population. Many women in developing nations lack the education needed to spur successful entrepreneurship.
17. Low-level risk taking attitude is another factor affecting women folk decision to get into business. Low-level education provides low-level self-confidence and self-reliance to the women folk to engage in business, which is continuous risk taking and strategic cession making profession.
18. High production cost of some business operations adversely affects the development of women entrepreneurs. High cost of production undermines the efficiency and stands in the way of development and expansion of women's enterprises. Government

assistance in the form of grant and subsidies to some extent enables them to tide over the difficult situations. However, in the long run, it would be necessary to increase efficiency and expand productive capacity and thereby reduce cost to make their ultimate survival possible, other than these, women entrepreneurs also face the problems of labour, human resources, infrastructure, legal formalities, overload of work, lack of family support, mistrust etc.

19. Lack of right public/ private institutions: Most public and private incentives are misused and do not reach the woman unless she is backed by a man. Also many trade associations like ministries, chambers of commerce do not cater to women expecting women's organizations to do the necessary thing. At a government level, the licensing authorities and labour officers and sales tax inspectors ask all sorts of questions like what technical qualifications you have, how will you manage labourers , how will you manage both house and business, does your husband approve, etc.

1.12.3. Progress of Women Entrepreneurship

- **Entrepreneur Dr. Kiran Mazumdar-Shaw, Chairman and Managing Director of Biocon Ltd.**
  The business and managerial skills of Dr. Kiran Mazumdar-Shaw has made her one of the richest business entrepreneurs in India. She ranks among the elite ranks of the Indian business fraternity and is a member of premier business organizations like CII, IIM Bangalore and others.

- **Ekta Kapoor, creative head of Balaji Telefilms**
  The daughter of star actor Jeetendra and sister of Tushar Kappor, Ekta Kapoor is known in almost all Indian households for her K series serials. She is one of the front runners of Indian television industry and has been responsible for the huge profits of her company Balaji Telefilms. Balaji has made crores of profit under her.

- **Sunita Narain, an environmentalist and political activist**
  A renowned social activist fighting for the importance of the Green concept of sustainable development, Sunita Narain has made India proud. She has been currently chosen as the director of the Society for Environmental Communications. She was also awarded the prestigious Padma Shri award in 2005.

- **Neelam Dhawan, Microsoft India managing director**
  A major name in the Indian business scene, Neelam Dhawan is the managing director of the Microsoft's sales and marketing operations. She is well known for implementing business strategies which have earned enormous profits for Microsoft.

- **Naina Lal Kidwai**
  Naina Lal Kidwai was listed by Fortune magazine as the World's Top 50 Corporate Women. She is the first Indian woman to crack the prestigious Harvard Business School. She is one of the top ten business women and the first woman to head the operations of HSBC in India was awarded the Padma Shri award for her work.

- **Sulajja Firodia Motwani**
  Sulajja Firodia Motwani, a known name in Indian business is currently the Joint Managing Director of Kinetic Engineering Ltd and manages the overall operations and business development strategies. She has been nominated as the business 'Face of the Millennium' by magazine *India Today* and also as the 'Global Leader of Tomorrow' by the World Economic Forum."

- **Mallika Srinivasan, Director of TAFE India**
  Named as the one of the top ten business women of the year in 2006, Mallika Srinivasan is the director of TAFE India. Her skills and strategies have helped the company earn profits from a meagre ₹ 85 core to a mammoth ₹ 2,900 cores. She is also a leading figure in social services.

- **Dr. Jatinder Kaur Arora**
  Dr. Jatinder Kaur Arora has made India proud through her scientific research for development of women. Presently serving the prestigious post of a joint director in the Punjab State Council for Science and Technology, she was honoured with the national award for her brilliant works.

- **Zia Mody, Senior Partner**
  Zia Mody was listed as one of the top 25 most powerful business women by *Business Today*. Her strategies have helped AZB and Partners earn great profits. She has also been awarded as the Best Knowledge Manager by *Financial Express*.

- **Ritu Nanda, CEO, Escolife**
  The daughter of ace film personality, Raj Kapoor, Ritu Nanda has made her presence felt as one of the prominent business women of India. Currently serving as the CEO of Escolife, she was awarded the Best Insurance Advisor and entered the Guinness Book of Records for selling 17,000 pension policies in a day.

1.12.4. How to Develop Women Entrepreneurs?

Right efforts in all areas are required in the development of women entrepreneurs and their greater participation in the entrepreneurial activities. Following efforts can be taken into account for effective development of women entrepreneurs.

1. Consider women as specific target group for all developmental programmes.
2. Empower rural women economically, socially, politically and thereby promote sustainable development;
3. Promote popular participation and bottom-up approach in decision making;
4. Develop skills, improve knowledge, promote culture and consultation in decisional process;
5. Strengthening the public administration to make the regulatory and administrative environment more conducive for women entrepreneurs.
6. Setting up labour organizations for all working women and reorganizing the existing organizations to act more effectively and for the better representation of women within them.
7. Give poor rural women a sense of belonging and the opportunity to benefit from and contribute to the development of country;
8. Women's education would be made a policy priority and women's integration in the development process would be enhanced in order to maximize social welfare and women's share within it.
9. Give the youth a sound knowledge of the local technology, tradition and culture that are sustainable for economic development.
10. Re-structuring the existing institutions and programmes, such as credit and guarantee cooperatives, in such a way as to increase their capacity and tendency to provide credit to the growing number of small enterprises; in case of the failure of this strategy in increasing the number of women entrepreneurs, supporting the institutions owned by women.

11. Holding regular consultations with key factors like women entrepreneurs, women entrepreneurs' associations, financial institutions, etc., to review progress and identify new bottlenecks.
12. Examining differential impacts of governmental policies, programmes and actions on their performance. Whether those policies and programmes are affecting women positively or negatively.
13. Another measure that may be considered in line with the target of enhancing women's entrepreneurship is about the development of specific programmes towards job experience acquisition for the unemployed and the measure is specified to target women and youths, whose participation in the labour market is most desired.
14. Better educational facilities and schemes should be extended to women folk from government part.
15. Human resource development for increased competitive entrepreneurship, technology absorbing capacities and women's control over asset management.
16. Adequate training programme on management skills to be provided to women community. Vocational training to be extended to women community that enables them to understand the production process and production management. Skill development to be done in women's polytechnics and industrial training institutes. Skills are put to work in training-cum-production workshops.
17. Policies, laws and overall regulatory environment are frequently seen as barriers and disincentives to expansion and growth. However, they need to be promoted in such a way that women entrepreneurs see the advantages of and benefits that come with compliance.
    - Identifying those instruments that act as barriers to expansion and growth;
    - Modifying or dismantling these instruments;
    - Taking account of the social and cultural contexts affecting policy implementation and redress inequalities and abnormalities;
    - Making use of IT and associations so as to minimize the administrative burdens on women entrepreneurs;
18. Trying to "push" more women entrepreneurs into growth situations as well as ensuring that laws and regulations do not stand in their way. Facilitating and "pulling" the women entrepreneurs into situations where they can actively pursue growth strategies.
    - Providing incentives for expansion and growth after removing barriers and disincentives
    - Promoting strong links and synergies with existing major economic players
    - Promoting and rewarding programmes that serve women entrepreneurs
19. Training on professional competence and leadership skill to be extended to women entrepreneurs. Training in entrepreneurial attitudes should start at the high school level through well-designed courses, which build confidence through behavioral games.
20. Counseling through the aid of committed NGOs, psychologists, managerial experts and technical personnel should be provided to existing and emerging women entrepreneurs. Continuous monitoring and improvement of training programmes.
21. Making provision of micro credit system and enterprise credit system to the women entrepreneurs at local level.
22. Ministry should provide outlets to women in trade shows to display products made by women.
23. District Industries Centres and Single Window Agencies should make use of assisting women in their trade and business guidance.

24. Programmes for encouraging entrepreneurship among women are to be extended at local level.
25. More governmental schemes to motivate women entrepreneurs to engage in small scale and large-scale business ventures.

1.12.5. The Needs of Women Entrepreneurs in India

1. More and better access to finance/credit is mentioned very frequently. Give a woman 1000 rupees and she can start a business. Give her another 1000 rupees and she will be able to feed not only for her family, but for her employees as well.
2. Access to business support and information, including better integration of business services.
3. Access and vigilance on the latest information science and technology to match the basic characteristics of entrepreneurs and the fundamental character of the Indian woman is necessary to show that a lot of potential among Indian women for their entrepreneurial skills. This potential can be considered as suspended and for use in manufacturing and services for the development of the nation.
4. The challenges and opportunities for women in the digital age are growing, as job seekers turn to job creation. They are growing as a designer, interior designers, exporters, publishing, clothing and always looking for new modes of economic participation. They have better access to local and foreign markets.
5. Day care centres and nurseries for children and also for the elderly;
6. Even as women are receiving education, they face the prospect of unemployment. In this background, self employment is regarded as a cure to generate income .The Planning commission as well as the Indian government recognizes the need for women to be part of the mainstream of economic development. Women entrepreneurship is seen as an effective strategy to solve the problems of rural and urban poverty.
7. Positive image-building and change in mentality amongst women, whereby women see themselves as capable achievers and build up confidence.
8. Self-motivation is the keyword: For establishing successful businesses learn to take risk and change their attitude towards business society by taking up social responsibilities. Understand the government business policies and get monetary help from public and private institutions.
9. Breaking through traditional patterns and structures that inhibit women's advancement.
10. Develop confidence: Women in India lack self-assurance in their potency and proficiency. However, over the last few years the outlook of Indian women is changing and they are fast emerging as potential entrepreneurs.
11. Role modeling of women in non-traditional business sectors to break through traditional views on men's and women's sectors.
12. Understanding of Business Administration: Women should be highly educated and trained in their area of knowledge so that they can attain expertise and understanding of all the major operational aspects of business administration. This will assist a woman to take balanced decisions beneficial for expanding her business network. For example, someone may have a tailoring shop but doesn't know how to sell its services to the military. So it is necessary to help them out in filling out the tenders, getting their organization registered, etc. It's a form of marketing support.
13. Women companies are fast-growing economies in almost all countries. The latent entrepreneurial potential of women have changed little by little by the growing awareness of the role and status of economic society. Skills, knowledge and adaptability of the economy led to a major reason for women in business.

14. To give them more involvement and participation in legislation and decision-making processes.
15. Women entrepreneurs in India are handicapped in the matter of organizing and running businesses on account of their generally low levels of skills and for want of support system. The transition from homemaker to sophisticated business woman is not that easy. But the trend is changing. Women across India are showing an interest to be economically independent. Women are coming forth to the business arena with ideas to start small and medium enterprises. They are willing to be inspired by role models- the experience of other women in the business arena.
16. Removing of any legislation which impedes women's free engagement.
17. The role of women entrepreneurs is especially relevant in the situation of large scale unemployment that the country faces. The modern large scale industry cannot absorb much of labour as it is capital intensive. The small scale industry plays an important role, absorbing around 80 per cent of the employment.
18. Awareness-raising at the governmental as well as private level to truly and really create entrepreneurial opportunities and not just programs that stay on paper.
19. While women entrepreneurs have demonstrated their potential, the fact remains that they are capable of contributing much more than what they already are. In order to harness their potential and for their continued growth and development, it is necessary to formulate appropriate strategies for stimulating, supporting and sustaining their efforts in this direction. Such a strategy needs to be in congruence with field realities and should especially take cognizance of the problems women entrepreneurs face within the current system

1.12.6. Reasons of Women Entrepreneurship

In spite of the growing number of female entrepreneurs, the share of female entrepreneurs is still significantly low when compared to their participation rate. However, there are several factors responsible for increasing the level of female entrepreneurship in India:

1. **Nature of Entrepreneurship:** Women enter into entrepreneurial activity because regular employment does not provide them with the flexibility, control or challenge offered by business ownership.
2. **Empowerment:** Indian women are becoming more empowered now-a-days. Legislations are being progressively drafted to offer them more opportunities at various levels.
3. **Social Conditions:** For women, in particular, the relatively high involvement in necessary entrepreneurship indicates that self-employment is used as a way to circumvent institutional and cultural constraints with respect to female employment, as well as a way to provide supplemental family income.
4. **Literacy and Education:** Increased levels of education have played a crucial role in initiating the process of entrepreneurship. It is not only the illiterate that are starting the businesses but those with education and skills are also exploiting profit opportunities.
5. **Multitask oriented:** Women are known for juggling many tasks at the same time and still producing excellent results. A woman can talk on the phone, open and read her email and schedule what else she needs to finish for the rest of the day all at the same time. Men have more trouble with this multitasking thing; therefore sometimes they miss many opportunities.

6. **Being patient with the process:** This is an extremely important attribute for entrepreneurs to have. Too often we hear of visionary entrepreneurs who tried to start their businesses and after a few months gave up. Very often we find these entrepreneurs gave up on their dreams too soon. They became impatient with the process. Women know naturally that you must wait in order to receive positive outcomes.

7. **Branding and marketing themselves:** Women are natural marketers. They are so passionate and enthusiastic about what they choose to do that they just do not stop talking about it. They don't forget to emphasize the benefits of their services to their potential customers. They understand how to emphasize the positive.

8. **Collaborator:** Women entrepreneurs are becoming more and more successful because they are natural collaborators and love doing project together. When they find likeminded women whom they like and think they can accomplish something with by combining their talents they do it. A collaborative spirit and attitude reigns with women a competitive attitude is rarely seen and considered unsavory when witnessed. Women do work they love to do and they feel great when they can do it with other women.

9. **Structural Shift:** One of the primary drivers is a structural shift. Women are now a greater part of the economic make-up of society; there are more women in the workforce. They are resourceful, leaving the workforce to stay home and raise a family, re-entering when the kids are grown or working a flex schedule when their kids go to school.

10. **It's the Blend:** One of the biggest reasons women entrepreneurs are now in the forefront is their desire to blend career and life ambitions. Their personal goals are oftentimes meshed with career goals. They put their passions into practice and it shines through in entrepreneurial endeavors. For them it's not just a job, it's a significant part of who they are.

11. **Relating To Customers' Needs:** One of the biggest reasons women entrepreneurs are so successful is they are more conscious of their customers' needs. Men for the most part are not customers they're consumers. It is the big difference. As a woman they shop for price of course, but what is just as important is the buying experience. If the service is poor or they can't relate to the employees then it doesn't matter what it costs. It's all about word of mouth and customer loyalty.

12. **Integrity of Relationships:** Women's ability to nurture the whole relationship is what makes them great as entrepreneurs. They naturally listen to understand, so they can connect across business boundaries to give solid integrity to relationships. Whether they are talking to a major account, negotiating with a vendor or coaching an employee, it's more than just about that one issue. Their want of making a wide and deep relationship is one thing of many that makes them great entrepreneurs.

13. **Resourcefulness of Women:** There are a growing number of work-at-home moms starting a business from their homes while taking care of their families. Most do it to augment the income of their families, without leaving their homes. Others want to do something economically and financially productive with their time if a corporate career is out of the question at this point. Still others have stumbled upon an opportunity that can be done while staying at home to be with their children.

14. **Women Are Social:** Entrepreneurs now have to be engaged in social media to be successful. By nature, women are social. They can leverage social media in ways that can help jumpstart new businesses quickly and cheaply. Whether it is engaging customers via Twitter, blog, forum or Facebook, they are good at gathering people and starting conversations.

1.13. Six Stages of Entrepreneurship

There are six stages of an entrepreneurial venture that founders of companies will encounter. The six steps are as follows:

1. **Idea Certainty**
2. **Business Idea**
3. **Business Concept**
4. **Venture**
5. **Business**
6. **Sustainable Business**

Stage 1: Idea Certainty

Every entrepreneur must address certainty to be an entrepreneur. He must be confident enough to become an entrepreneur. This is important if you want to become an entrepreneur and want to open your business. It should be the first step; however, many entrepreneurs wait until the Venture stage to address it. This can lead to serious problems. In the Idea Certainty stage, an entrepreneur needs to figure out whether he is able to face the issues of the entrepreneurship. He should not fear or demotivate by facing so many problems. Lots of problems will come on the way but your certainty will decide your progress to the next stage.

➢ **Entrepreneurs must ask few questions to themselves:**

– Am I ready to open a business?
– Am I ready to become an entrepreneur?
– Am I willing to lose the money of investors who may be my friends and family?
– Am I ready to face failure?
– Am I ready to spend my 24 hours?

Stage 2: Business Idea

The Business Idea stage is the stage where you think what exactly you want to do. Everyone has an idea for a business what they want to make real. Everyone see dream about their ideas. It is the foundation stage of business. It ultimately decides the failure and success of the business. The Idea stage is the basis for every other stage so it should be taken seriously.

➢ **Entrepreneurs must trust in their business:**

You must be truly committed to your idea. Entrepreneur must believe in their idea because their belief will decide the success of the idea. You must take all your efforts to make your idea the productive one. Remember, the Idea stage is the point in the venture where the entrepreneur is typically most enthusiastic. They are yet to be confronted with the real situation. Thinking idea and making it real is very difficult task but you can make it real by your efforts, knowledge and creative work.

➢ **Evaluate your idea from every corner:**

You must be careful enough to evaluate your idea before implementing it. You should evaluate the idea with respect to finance and your capability to execute the idea. You must also consider customers for evaluating your ideas, ultimately they are going to make your idea a successful one. You must have a thorough knowledge of what are the requirements of your idea execution in terms of resources, expertise required and technology and how much you are committed to your idea. You can imagine any idea but the important thing is that are you able to execute it.

Stage 3: Business Concept

It is the structure that you are going to develop for business. In the Business Concept stage, you take your idea and employ a certain intellectual firmness which includes:

— Doing market research and survey
— Applying successful business model
— The team of expertise, technician required for execution
— Appointment of the advisors, scholars for their valuable suggestions

↳ **Entrepreneurs must do market research**

As an entrepreneur you want to be optimistic and believe in your product idea, but entrepreneurs often overlook one important aspect of their business: *market research.* The fundamental questions to consider before you start a business include: Is there a buyer for your product? If there is, then how many buyers are there? What is the ultimate maximum number of buyers in the market today? In five years? ten years? And most importantly, how much revenue you could generate from these buyers?

Investigating these questions is called market research and is something every entrepreneur must do to substantiate their product idea before starting the venture. Use a common-sense approach. Part of the process is a description of the marketplace or *market model*, which includes actual customer spending rupees, today and projected for the future. Certainly buying market research from a market research firm is an option, but often their research does not relate you a new product idea and could even be useless if the market for new product does not exist yet. Besides, it costs money!

↳ **Consider a good business model**

Your business model will explain who your customers are, what they value and how you'll profit from providing them that value in your product or service. In other words, how are you going to make money? Business models depend on developing qualities that help the business succeed: finding high-value customers, sustaining customers, offering satisfactory services to customers and delivering significant margins. Great business models also avoid unsatisfactory services to the customers, lagging in the market competition and problems generating funding for growth.

↳ **Bring together the required teams to execute the business**

Entrepreneurs must find out the required skilled teams that will need to execute on this business concept. As the business will progress accordingly, the need of the skilled team will be required because as the business expands new tasks, new methods of doing business also get into the business.

↳ **Start involving advisors**

Taking advice from the advisors and experts are very essential in business. They are the perfect person who will tell you about the way your business must follow. They are the experienced one in their field and better know about the problems and their consequences.

↳ **Don't wait to get fund**

Most entrepreneurs get frustrated and give up in this stage because they wrongly believe that the Business Concept stage is the period during which they will receive their first investment. Getting investment for your business is not very easy as the investors also want to earn the profit and they are very strict in evaluating your business ideas. Investors are interested in the overall growth of your business not in short term but also in long term too.

Stage 4: Venture

Unless you personally have deep pockets, such as inherited wealth, figuring out where you're going to get the money to start your own business and getting the financing in place beforehand is going to be one of the most important components of planning your business. This is the most challenging stage of the business and for many entrepreneurs the most fun...well at least in the beginning. The Venture stage is characterized by significant investment. A business that has performed studies and research into their chosen market and is ready to take their product into the public is prepared to receive start-up capital from venture capitalists. Start-up money can help with the initial marketing push, helping to distribute your product in the market. This investment typically comes in two forms: money and time. In most cases, as the entrepreneur, it is "your" money and "your" time; and those can often be significant.

Finding adequate business start up money is especially critical because there's no guarantee that your business is going to make money right away and certainly no guarantee that your new business will bring in enough money for you and your family to live on. You can't start a business without start-up capital, the total amount of money you need to open your doors for business and to keep them open until sufficient revenue can be depended on. No matter what the economic situation, someone somewhere, eyes bright with potential, is looking to start a new business. Funds are often the biggest hurdle to what could otherwise be a lucrative opportunity.

You can get fund from your family and friends, they will always be willing to help those with who they have personal relationship. Family and friends will always give you money blindly if you are trustworthy.

- **Personal savings:** There's nothing like having your own money saved, to put into your startup. You have the satisfaction of having saved it on your own and the knowledge that you don't owe anyone.

Approaching private investors otherwise known as angels is an option you might want to consider when raising fund to finance your business. Angels are rich individuals that use their wealth to encourage young entrepreneurs with viable business ideas in their community. If you have an angel in your community, you can consider taking your business idea to them.

- **Get a bank loan:** If you have a solid business plan and the lender agrees, this can often be the cheapest (interest rate-wise) loan sources available.

In some states and countries of the world, the government of that region maps out a certain amount of money to encourage the development of small and medium scale enterprises. This money is given out as grants to those it may concern. Governments grants can be a source of fund for you if you are a citizen of that region and you are able to fulfill the stipulated requirements.

Determine the legal structure

The first step in setting up a business is figuring out what type of legal structure you want. There are several options which include:

- Sole Proprietorship
- General Partnership
- Limited Partnership (LP) and Limited Liability Partnership (LLP)
- Corporation
- Company (Private or Public)
- Limited Liability Corporation (LLC)

Determine the short-term business objective and goals

Objectives should be clear and concise. Goals do not have to be specific enough for you to act on, but should give you a future target or list of things you want to work on. Objectives, however, need to be *SMART* — specific, measurable, action-oriented, realistic and timely — to accomplish the goals set for your business.

Specific objectives should be as detailed as possible. In order for the objectives to be measurable, you should state them in terms of rupees or quantities. Objectives are clear targets of performance you can use to evaluate the operation. Action oriented objectives state which actions need to be taken and who will take them. Objectives should be realistic but challenging, with set deadlines in order to be timely.

- **Determine team decision making process**

You must form a team according to the business need and skills required. This will enable you in proper management and as the teams are specialized in their field and can take better decisions in complex situation. You must have a criterion in decision making process and you must also appoint a person who will be the ultimate decision maker.

- **Make Initial Investment**

The VENTURE stage is typically where the entrepreneur makes a meaningful investment. This investment may come in the form of money and/or time. In this stage the entrepreneur has to invest money from their pocket. At the initial stage you have to invest money and do not expect that someone will come to invest money in your business.

- **Identify Customers, Employees and Investors**

In the VENTURE stage your first customers, employees and investors are likely to be those people who trust on your business and ready to engage themselves with your business. Find out the customers who believe in your products or services. Their trust will win the trust of other customers. Find out the employees who are intelligent and knowledgeable who by their hard work will grow your business. Win the trust of the investors by explaining them how your business is going to be a successful business and how you are going to give a big ROI.

- **Entrepreneurs should protect Intellectual Property**

The venture stage is when you should make the investment in protecting your intellectual property. This includes: patents, copyrights and trademarks. The patent process is fairly long and expensive. You also have a discreet period of time after the process or product is publicly released to patent it.

Stage 5: Business

This stage of the entrepreneurial process is the actual establishment and opening of the business. During this stage, the entrepreneur goes from being just a visionary to a visionary with a business to run. One way to examine the changing managerial activities of the entrepreneur is to look at the different roles filled by the entrepreneur as the business develops. As the founder of the organization, the entrepreneur sets the philosophy of the organization, establishes the strategic focus and educates new employees. In this role, the entrepreneur lays the groundwork for the emerging corporate culture. In addition, most entrepreneurs serve as the primary promoters for their new start-ups. They must act as the new venture's chief spokesperson in contacts with financial backers, prospective clients, employees, suppliers and others. In addition, as founders (or founding team members) of organizations, entrepreneurs are often called upon to provide counsel or advice to community members or employees. The roles that an entrepreneur must fill are demand flexibility and creativity. In order to successfully manage a new venture, an entrepreneur must be comfortable in all the roles.

- **Take decision on Buy vs. Build**

At this stage you start evaluating growth in a different way. You don't need to build everything yourself. Sometimes buying is the best option and sometimes building is the best option. Select the one requires less cost. You start to consider acquisition as a viable growth options. Once again, this requires different competencies within the organization.

Evaluate Financing Options

The best thing about the Business stage is that the financing options are much more plentiful. There are a number of potential sources of finance to meet the needs of small and growing businesses:

- Existing shareholders' and directors' funds ("owner financing")
- Overdraft financing
- Trade credit
- Equity finance
- Business angel financing
- Venture capital
- Factoring and invoice discounting
- Hire purchase and leasing
- Merchant banks (medium to longer term loans)

Consistency in Business

Consistency is a necessary ingredient in success. It's strange, because most people do not seem to know its true power. When it wears off things can get rough that is when you truly want to know you're doing something you love. For consistency in business you have to continuously evaluate your resources, way of doing business, competitors and your customers.

Succession Planning

In order to reach the Sustainable Business stage, the business must be able to survive the founder. This requires succession planning at the CEO / founder level as well as in other key managerial roles. The business needs to be building its "bench" in order to get to the next level.

Stage 6: Sustainable Business

Although most entrepreneurs are satisfied to build a Business, they should strive to become a Sustainable Business. There are unique challenges to creating a sustainable business and it can be defined in different ways. It is typically characterized by time. Ventures those last 10+ years may be thought of as sustainable; however, the real challenge is for a business to outlast the involvement of its founders. That is a more relevant definition of a sustainable business.

The concept of sustainable development has received growing recognition, but it is a new idea for many business executives. For most, the concept remains abstract and theoretical. Protecting an organization's capital base is a well-accepted business principle. Yet organizations do not generally recognize the possibility of extending this notion to the world's natural and human resources. If sustainable development is to achieve its potential, it must be integrated into the planning and measurement systems of business enterprises. And for that to happen, the concept must be articulated in terms that are familiar to business leaders.

1.14. McClelland's Achievement Motivation

In attempting to understand employee motivation, Abraham Maslow proposed a hierarchy of needs. David McClelland furthered this idea in his learned needs theory. McClelland's experimental work identified sets of motivators present to varying degrees in different people. He proposed that these needs were socially acquired or learned. That is, the extent to which these motivators are present varies from person to person and depends on the individual and his or her background.

McClelland's experiment — the Thematic Apperception Test (TAT) — consisted of showing individuals a series of pictures and asking them to give brief descriptions of what was happening in the pictures. The responses were analyzed in terms of the presence or absence of certain themes. The themes McClelland and his associates were looking for revolved around the following motivators: achievement, affiliation and power.

According to David McClelland, regardless of culture or gender, people are driven by three motives:

- Achievement;
- Affiliation;
- Power.

Since McClelland's first experiment, over 1,000 studies relevant to achievement motivation have been conducted. These studies strongly support the theory.

1. Achievement (nAch)

The need for achievement is characterized by the wish to take responsibility for finding solutions to problems, master complex tasks, set goals, get feedback on level of success.

Specifically, achievement motivation is defined as a non-conscious concern for achieving excellence through individual efforts. Such individuals set challenging goals for themselves, assume personal responsibility for goal accomplishment, are highly persistent in the pursuit of these goals, take calculated risks to achieve the goals and actively collect and use information for purposes of feedback.

High achievement motivated managers are also strongly inclined to be personally involved in performing their organizational tasks. However, they may also be reluctant to delegate authority and responsibility. Thus, high achievement motivation may be expected to result in poor performance of high- level executives in large organizations.

High achievement motivation is predicted to contribute to effective entrepreneurship and effective leadership of small task-oriented groups.

Achievement motivation is positively related to the leadership of small task-oriented groups and small entrepreneurial firms and negatively related to the effectiveness of high- level managers in complex organizations or in political situations.

2. Affiliation (nAff)

The need for affiliation is characterized by a desire to belong, an enjoyment of teamwork, a concern about interpersonal relationships and a need to reduce uncertainty.

Affiliative motivation is defined as a nonconscious concern for establishing, maintaining and restoring close personal relationships with others. Individuals with high affiliative motivation tend to be non-assertive, submissive and dependent on others.

Such managers are expected to manage on the basis of personal relationships with subordinates. This may result in them showing favouritism towards some.

As managers, highly affiliative individuals are predicted to be reluctant to monitor the behavior of subordinates, give negative feedback to others or discipline their subordinates. However, when the power motive is higher than the affiliative motive, individuals are disinclined to engage in dysfunctional management behaviors such as submissiveness, reluctance to monitor and discipline subordinates and favoritism.

3. Power (nP)

The need for power is characterized by a drive to control and influence others, a need to win arguments, a need to persuade and prevail.

According to McClelland, the presence of these motives or drives in an individual indicates a predisposition to behave in certain ways. Therefore, from a manager's perspective, recognizing which need is dominant in any particular individual affects the way in which that person can be motivated.

Power motivation is defined as the concern for acquiring status and having an impact on others. McClelland used power motivation as a measure of social influence behaviours. Clearly, since most management activities require the use of social influence behaviors and since power motivation measures an individual's desire to influence, the power motive is important for leadership effectiveness.

David McClelland proposed the Leader Motive Profile Theory (LMP theory) in which he argued that a high power motivation, greater than the affiliation motive, is predictive of leader effectiveness.

Highly power-motivated individuals obtain great satisfaction from the exercise of influence. Consequently, their interest in the exercise of leadership is sustained.

High power motivation is predicted to result in effective managerial performance in middle and high-level positions. However, unless constrained in some manner, some power-motivated managers may also be predicted to exercise power in an aggressive manner for self-aggrandizing purposes, to the detriment of their organizations.

1.15. Maslow's Theory of Motivation

Motivational theories dealing with the needs of employees fall under the general rubric of **Content Theories of Motivation**.

Content theories Posit that workers' **behaviors** are **a function of** the workers' abilities to satisfy their **felt needs** at the workplace. A basic assumption of all need theories is that, when need deficiencies exist; individuals are motivated into action in order to satisfy them. The best known of the **Content Theories** of Motivation is **Maslow's Hierarchy of Needs**. (Abraham Maslow)

Maslow's Hierarchy of Needs is based on the assumption that people are motivated by a series of five universal needs. These needs are ranked, according to the order in which they influence human behavior, in hierarchical fashion.

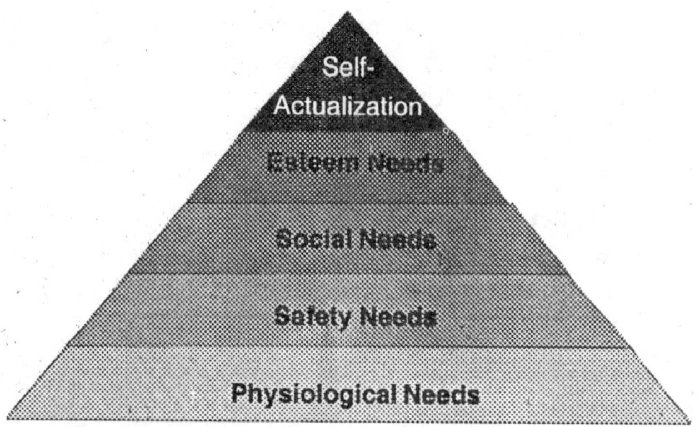

Fig. 1.1: Maslow's hierarchy of needs

Table: 1.2: Maslow's hierarchy of needs

Level	Type of Need	Examples
1	Physiological	Thirst, sex, hunger
2	Safety	Security, stability, protection
3	Love and Belongingness	To escape loneliness, love and be loved and gain a sense of belonging
4	Esteem	Self-respect, the respect to others
5	Self-actualization	To fulfill one's potentialities

1. **Physiological needs** are deemed to be the lowest- level needs. These needs include the need for food, oxygen, sex and drink.
   - **So long as** physiological **needs are unsatisfied, they exist as a driving or motivating force** in a person's life. A hungry person has a felt need. This felt need sets up both psychological and physical tensions that manifest themselves in overt behaviours directed at reducing those tensions (getting something to eat). Once the hunger is sated, the tension is reduced and the need for food ceases to motivate. At this point (assuming the needs for sex, drink and other physiological requirements are also satisfied) the next higher order need becomes the motivating need.

2. Thus, **safety needs** — the needs for shelter and security — become the motivators of human behavior.
   - Safety needs include a desire for security, stability, dependency, protection, freedom from fear and anxiety and a need for structure, order and law. In everyday life, we may see this as a need to be able to fall asleep at night, secure in the knowledge that we will awake alive and unharmed. In the workplace these needs translates into a need for at least a minimal degree of employment security; the knowledge That we cannot be fired on a whim and that appropriate levels of effort and productivity will ensure continued employment.

3. **Social needs** include the need for belongingness and love.
   - Generally, as gregarious creatures, human have a need to belong. In the workplace, this need may be satisfied by an ability to interact with one's coworkers and perhaps to be able to work collaboratively with these colleagues.

4. After social needs have been satisfied, **ego and esteem needs** become the motivating needs.
   - Esteem needs include the desire for self-respect, self-esteem and the esteem of others. When focused externally, these needs also include the desire for reputation, prestige, status, fame, glory, dominance, recognition, attention, importance and appreciation.

5. The highest need in Maslow's hierarchy is that of **self-actualization**; the need for self-realization, continuous self-development and the process of becoming all that a person is capable of becoming.

1.16. Expectancy Theory of Motivation

In recent years, probably the most popular motivational theory has been the Expectancy Theory (also known as the Valence-Instrumentality- Expectancy Theory). Although there are a number of theories found with this general title, they all have their roots in **Victor Vroom**'s 1964 work on motivation.

Alternatives and Choices

Vroom's theory assumes that behavior results from conscious choices among alternatives whose purpose it is to maximize pleasure and minimize pain. The key elements to this theory are referred to as **Expectancy (E), Instrumentality (I)** and **Valence (V).** Critical to the understanding of the theory is the understanding that each of these factors represents a belief.

Vroom's theory suggests that the individual will consider the outcomes associated with various levels of performance (from an entire spectrum of performance possibilities) and elect to pursue the level that generates the greatest reward for him or her.

1. **Expectancy:** *"What's the probability that, if I work very hard, I'll be able to do a good job?"*

Expectancy refers to the strength of a person's belief about whether or not a particular job performance is attainable. Assuming all other things are equal, an employee will be motivated to try a task, if he or she believes that it can be done. This expectancy of performance may be thought of in terms of probabilities ranging from zero (a case of "I can't do it!") to 1.0 ("I have no doubt whatsoever that I can do this job!")

A number of factors can contribute to an employee's expectancy perceptions:

- the level of confidence in the skills required for the task
- the amount of support that may be expected from superiors and subordinates
- the quality of the materials and equipment
- the availability of pertinent information

Previous success at the task has also been shown to strengthen expectancy beliefs.

2. **Instrumentality:** *"What's the probability that, if I do a good job, that there will be some kind of outcome in it for me?"*

If an employee believes that a high level of performance will be instrumental for the acquisition of outcomes which may be gratifying, then the employee will place a high value on performing well. Vroom defines **Instrumentality as a probability belief linking one outcome (a high level of performance, for example) to another outcome (a reward)**.

Instrumentality may range from a probability of 1.0 (meaning that the attainment of the second outcome — the reward — is certain if the first outcome — excellent job performance — is attained) through zero (meaning there is no likely relationship between the first outcome and the second). An example of zero instrumentality would be exam grades that were distributed randomly (as opposed to be awarded on the basis of excellent exam performance). Commission pay schemes are designed to make employees perceive that performance is positively instrumental for the acquisition of money.

For management to ensure high levels of performance, it must tie desired outcomes (positive valence) to high performance and ensure that the connection is communicated to employees.

The VIE theory holds that people have preferences among various outcomes. These preferences tend to reflect a person's underlying need state.

3. **Valence:** *"Is the outcome I get of any value to me?"*

The term **Valence refers to the emotional orientations people hold with respect to outcomes (rewards).** An outcome is positively valent if an employee would prefer having it to not having it. An outcome that the employee would rather avoid (fatigue, stress, noise, layoffs) is negatively valent. Outcomes towards which the employee appears indifferent are said to have zero valence.

Valences refer to the level of satisfaction people expect to get from the outcome (as opposed to the actual satisfaction they get once they have attained the reward).

Vroom suggests that an employee's beliefs about Expectancy, Instrumentality and Valence interact psychologically to create a motivational force such that the employee acts in ways that bring pleasure and avoid pain.

People elect to pursue levels of job performance that they believe will maximize their overall best interests (their subjective expected utility).

There will be no motivational forces acting on an employee if any of these three conditions hold:

(a) The person does not believe that he/she can successfully perform the required task.

(b) The person believes that successful task performance will not be associated with positively valent outcomes.

(c) The person believes that outcomes associated with successful task completion will be negatively valent (have no value for that person).

SUMMARY

In the words of **J.A. Schumpeter**, "The entrepreneur in an advanced economy is an individual who introduces something new in the economy, a method of production is not yet tested by experience in the branch of manufacture concerned, a product with which consumers are not yet familiar, a new source of raw material or of new markets and the like".

The characteristics that help an entrepreneur to become successful are Self-centre, Self-confidence, Sense of urgency, Comprehensive awareness, Realism, Conceptual ability, Status requirements, Interpersonal relationships and Emotional stability.

Personal qualities common in successful entrepreneurs are Motivations to achieve, Nonconformity, Hard work, Street smarts and Strong leadership.

The key steps to becoming successful in today's society are you must prepare yourselves to new entrepreneurial mindset, Clearly write down what exactly you want, Write down all of your new ideas in detail as an entrepreneur, Write your short-, middle- and long-term goals, Improve your personality every day, Keep your new mindset positive, Visualize the end result of your goal in your mind, Never give up on your new ideas and goals until you see them manifest in your life and Take action on your new ideas and goals as an entrepreneur.

You can become an entrepreneur if you have the Ability to solve problem, Change the way you think, No complacency and No room for failure.

Why one wants to become an entrepreneur? The reasons given by entrepreneurs are as I've always wanted to do this, For a higher purpose, Because it's very creative, For the sheer challenge of it, For the creation of wealth, Desire for achievement and self-fulfillment, Willingness to invest their current resources, For the independence, Need for money, Because I am crazy, Need for financial independence and security, Because it's cool, Frustration with their current workplace or career, Because I'm inspired.

Entrepreneurs want to start a business, there are two reasons for that one is personal and the second one is general. The personal reasons are Inequity between contribution and reward, Fame and recognition, Participation in all aspects of a business, Joy of winning and Personal financial gain. The general reasons are they want to earn profit; huge business scope etc.

What is Entrepreneurship? An entrepreneur is an individual who owns a firm, business or venture and is responsible for its development. Entrepreneurship is the practice of starting a new business or reviving an existing business, in order to capitalize on new found opportunities.

There is a need for entrepreneurship because of Employment generation, Small business dynamism, Balanced economic development, and Innovations in enterprises.

The advantages of being a successful entrepreneur are *No set timetable, Passion for their career, Job satisfaction, Increased self confidence, Giving back to the community, Job security and friendly work environment, Financial Freedom,* Excitement, Rules and regulations, Originality, Competition, Independence, Salary potential, Flexibility, Rational salary, and Freedom.

What is Intrapreneurship? Intrapreneurship is the practice of entrepreneurship by employees within an organization.

The Difference between an entrepreneur and an intrapreneur is "An **Entrepreneur** is someone who has the skills, passion and financial backing to create wealth from new business opportunities and is willing to take full responsibility for its success or failure." But "An **Intrapreneur** is someone who manages that business with entrepreneurial flair in line with the expectations of the shareholders."

The Entrepreneurs have a very great role in Economic Development. Entrepreneurs are the lifeblood of any economy. Policies have to favour risk-taking and have to reward those with the energy and zeal to start businesses. Without entrepreneurs, there are no jobs. The large enterprises of today were all started by single entrepreneurs willing to take risks to claim the rewards from risk-taking.

Entrepreneurial Environment can be developed by Dynamic business environment, can do attitude, Training and help, Mentoring and support, and Developing Entrepreneurial Skills.

OECD (Organisation for Economic Co-Operation and Development) (1998) has referred women entrepreneur as equally to someone who has started a one-woman business, to someone who is a principal in a family business or partnership or to someone who is a shareholder in a publicly held company which she organizes and runs.

A study conducted by International Labour Organization (ILO) (2006) has found four personal and four external factors that influence women entrepreneurs' success. **Personal factors comprise**: (1) motivation and commitment; (2) abilities and skills; (3) ideas and markets; and (4) resources. **While external factors consist of**: (1) business development organizations; (2) broader enabling environment; (3) economic/market environment; and (4) socio-cultural context.

The Problems faced by Women Entrepreneurs in India are skepticism about the entrepreneurial abilities of women, lack of proper assistance, inadequate financial resources, Socio-Cultural Barriers, Lack of Confidence, balance between business and home, Market-oriented risks, Discrimination, Motivational factors, Missing networks, Lack of Knowledge of latest technological changes, Low-level risk taking attitude, and Lack of right public/private institutions.

In spite of the growing number of female entrepreneurs, the share of female entrepreneurs is still significantly low when compared to their participation rate. However, there are several factors responsible for increasing the level of female entrepreneurship in India. Those factors are empowerment, social conditions, literacy and education, multitask oriented, being patient with, the process, branding and marketing themselves, collaborator, **structural shift, it's the blend, relating to customers' needs, integrity of relationships, resourcefulness of women, and nature of entrepreneurship**.

There are six stages of an entrepreneurial venture that founders of companies will encounter. The six steps are Idea Certainty, Business Idea, Business Concept, Venture, Business, and Sustainable Business.

According to David McClelland, regardless of culture or gender, people are driven by three motives:

- Achievement;
- Affiliation;
- Power

Achievement – The need for achievement is characterized by the wish to take responsibility for finding solutions to problems, master complex tasks, set goals and get feedback on level of success.

Affiliation – The need for affiliation is characterized by a desire to belong, an enjoyment of teamwork, a concern about interpersonal relationships and a need to reduce uncertainty.

Power – The need for power is characterized by a drive to control and influence others, a need to win arguments, a need to persuade and prevail.

Maslow's Hierarchy of Needs is based on the assumption that people are motivated by a series of five universal needs. These needs are ranked, according to the order in which they influence human behavior, in hierarchical fashion. These needs are Self-actualization, Self-Esteem, Love and Belongingness, Safety and Physiological.

***Expectancy Theory of Motivation* -** Vroom's theory assumes that behavior results from conscious choices among alternatives whose purpose it is to maximize pleasure and minimize pain. The key elements to this theory are referred to as **Expectancy (E), Instrumentality (I)** and **Valence (V)**. Critical to the understanding of the theory is the understanding that each of these factors represents a belief.

Keywords

Entrepreneur: Peter F. Drucker defines an entrepreneur as one who always searches for changes, responds to it and exploits it as an opportunity.

Entrepreneurship: It is the practice of starting a new business or reviving an existing business, in order to capitalize on new found opportunities.

Enterprise: An enterprise is the business organization that is formed and which provides goods and services, creates jobs, contributes to national income, exports and overall economic development.

Intrapreneur: An **Intrapreneur** is someone who manages that business with entrepreneurial flair in line with the expectations of the shareholders.

Intrapreneurship: It is the practice of entrepreneurship by employees within an organization.

Women Entrepreneurs: Women or a group of women who initiate, organize and operate a business enterprise.

QUESTIONS

1. How will you define entrepreneur? What are the characteristics of an entrepreneur?
2. Why entrepreneurs start a business? What are the advantages and disadvantages of being a successful entrepreneur?
3. What is entrepreneurship? What is the need for entrepreneurship? What are the benefits of entrepreneurship?
4. What is intrapreneurship? What is the difference between intrapreneurship and entrepreneurship?
5. What are the six stages of entrepreneurship?
6. What is motivation? What is the role of motivation in entrepreneurship?

CHAPTER – 2

FIRST GENERATION ENTREPRENEURS

LEARNING OBJECTIVES

On completion of this chapter, you should be able to:

☺ *Explain first generation entrepreneurs.*

☺ *Describe qualities of first generation entrepreneurs.*

☺ *Describe issues and challenges.*

2.1 Six E's for the New Entrepreneurs

The first time entrepreneurs must have at least the following qualities if they want to start the business. These are the qualities that will help the new entrepreneurs to move their business.

- Energetic
- Enthusiastic
- Ethics
- Efforts
- Excitement
- Enjoyment

BOX 2

Credit Guarantee Scheme (CGS) Objectives

Availability of bank credit without the hassles of collaterals / third party guarantees would be a major source of support to the first generation entrepreneurs to realize their dream of setting up a unit of their own Micro and Small Enterprise (MSE). Keeping this objective in view, Ministry of Micro, Small and Medium Enterprises (MSME), Government of India launched Credit Guarantee Scheme (CGS) so as to strengthen credit delivery system and facilitate flow of credit to the MSE sector. To operationalize the scheme, Government of India and SIDBI set up the Credit Guarantee Fund Trust for Micro and Small Enterprises (CGFTMSE).

The main objective is that the lender should give importance to project viability and secure the credit facility purely on the primary security of the assets financed. The other objective is that the lender availing guarantee facility should endeavor to give composite credit to the borrowers so that the borrowers obtain both term loan and working capital facilities from a single agency. The Credit Guarantee scheme (CGS) seeks to reassure the lender that, in the event of a MSE unit, which availed collateral free credit facilities, fails to discharge its liabilities to the lender, the Guarantee Trust would make good the loss incurred by the lender up to 75 / 80/ 85 per cent of the credit facility.

Source: *Information received from Credit Guarantee Fund Trust for Micro and Small Enterprises (CGFTMSE).*

2.2 First Generation Entrepreneurs

Many may want to start their own business organization and to make more money ultimately. Many will see great pride in establishing a business organization and running it successfully. Establishing an organization and running it successfully is not a simple thing and in course one has to sail through some difficulties and one must be prepared to be patient, adjustable and courageous. He should prepare himself that the journey of becoming entrepreneur is not easy and many hurdles will come across the way. Than before, with the globalization, the overall economic development and communication technology, many are venturing to start their own business rather investing all their talent for someone. Many look to the entrepreneurs like Bill Gates, Dhirubhai Ambani, Lee Iacocca, Infosys Narayan Murthy etc., in the course, but, you may not focus on the hurdles they have faced to become what they are now. These big names have faced the difficult challenges in their life and business, they have overcome those difficulties and now they are the successful businessmen. But, in an era, where knowledge is believed to be power and with the excellent communication technology connecting the entire world, the scope for establishing an organization without much background has become more.

But, establishing and successfully running an organization requires great ability and qualities. It requires determination, hard work and your passion about your business. This passion will help you and your business throughout your journey. There are three kinds of young people who want to start their own business. In first category, the young people with good financial and business background and in the second category, the young people with enormous zeal and ability, but, without much financial and business background. And in third category, the young people with good financial background but no business background. We need to see many young entrepreneurs when come to business there should be fair environment for them to grow. The young entrepreneurs want to come in the business; they are very excited in opening their business. It is believed that the environment for the young to grow in business is more in developed countries like USA and UK and it is true in part. But, under any circumstances, one can rise and come-up in life if he puts his heart.

The young and first generation entrepreneurs should first realize that nothing will come so easily in business. To realize this fact, they should look at the success stories of young and successful entrepreneurs like Bill Gates, Dhirubhai Ambani, Sir Sorabji and Infosys Narayana Murhty etc.

The issues connected to the young and first generation entrepreneur, are as follows:

1. He must have a clear plan and discipline to pursue the plan.
2. He must concentrate on contacts which can be useful for raising needed funds.
3. He must be broad minded to work in joint ventures and to strike deals.
4. He must understand that managing people is one of the toughest jobs and he must master at that with special concentration on human behavior.
5. He should acquire theoretical knowledge as much as he can.
6. He must have basic understanding about the laws, corporate laws, the auditing issues etc., without which an organization can't function.
7. He must be patient, planned, vigilant, determined and courageous to pursue his goal.

Thus, for young one without business background, it can be a thrilling challenge to establish an organization, to start a business and to make it big and global ultimately.

2.3 First Generation Entrepreneurs (FGEs) – Constructing Businesses in India

How should First Generation Entrepreneurs (FGEs) go about building businesses in India?

First things first, only during the last ten years India has started seeing bootstrapped or garage startups by talented, educated, experienced and passionate folks who don't have access to a lot of capital but have the skills, will to solve problems and the staying power. They have the ability to build the business and run it successfully. The number of successes out of these has been limited and has not been really. The first time entrepreneurs really take all efforts to get success in the business.

BOX 2A

Credit Guarantee

Any collateral / third party guarantee free credit facility (both fund as well as non fund based) extended by eligible institutions, to new as well as existing Micro and Small Enterprise, including Service Enterprises, with a maximum credit cap of ₹ 100 lakh (Rupees Hundred lakh only) are eligible to be covered.

The guarantee cover available under the scheme is to the extent of 75 per cent / 80 per cent of the sanctioned amount of the credit facility, with a maximum guarantee cap of ₹62.50 lakh / ₹65 lakh. The extent of guarantee cover is 85% for micro enterprises for credit up to ₹5 lakh.

The extent of guarantee cover is 80 per cent (i) Micro and Small Enterprises operated and/or owned by women; and (ii) all credits/loans in the North East Region (NER). In case of default, Trust settles the claim up to 75% (or 80%) of the amount in default of the credit facility extended by the lending institution.

The lender should cover the eligible credit facilities as soon as they are sanctioned. In any case, the lender should apply for guarantee cover in respect of eligible credits sanctioned in one calendar quarter latest by end subsequent calendar quarter. Guarantee will commence from the date of payment of guarantee fee and shall run through the agreed tenure of the term credit in case of term loans / composite loans and for a period of five years where working capital facilities alone are extended to borrowers or for such period as may be specified by the Guarantee Trust in this behalf.

Source: *Information received from Credit Guarantee Fund Trust for Micro and Small Enterprises (CGFTMSE).*

FGEs in India: What to focus on?

First thing to ensure is to build a cash flow positive business within the initial capital that you have managed to raise (self, friends, family and tools). Keep lowest possible costs and create early revenues. Expenses should ideally be low. For the first time entrepreneurs the cash flow management is very essential. They should know where exactly they should invest their money so that they can earn the profit. They should get revenue to run the business. The proper financial requirement analysis will help to do proper estimation about cash flow.

Internet as a tool

Internet only business models targeting Indian market is not going to be viable for at least coming years (or more). View internet as a cheap way to build products and get the initial users with zero marketing budgets. From day one build alternate channels: mobile, call center, SMS, kiosks, shops, sales team into your model. For the new entrepreneurs using all the existing technology will help the business to spread more vastly. Use technology as an enabler to drive costs down and to drive quality upwards, but do not depend on customers using it directly via internet. The entrepreneurs should use all possible means to lower down the cost and at the same time to use the technology to make their business more effective and efficient. India still has lower costs and we are very bullish on build here – sell to the developed world model.

One has to keep an eye on the scalability aspect

Most of the successful Indian entrepreneurs have followed the path of building stuff in their own capital reaching profitability and building it further. Examples: Dhirubhai, Subhash Chandra, Mittals, Narayan Murthy, Sanjiv Bhikchandani etc.

There is potential to build a scalable business without incurring too much cost. It has a two-pronged problem:

- Indian entrepreneurs do not have experience of bringing products to market and
- Indian angel investors do not have an intuitive understanding of how products are built or marketed.

Hence, on both sides we have inexperienced people. Thus, we have a blind leading the blind situation and, predictably, deals don't happen. Angels don't trade. Unless angel investors who do have the experience start playing in India, the vitally important "mentor capital" component will continue to be absent. And without that mentorship, the entrepreneurs will not be successful in bringing product or innovation to market." The mentor places an important place in the life of the new entrepreneurs. Mentor explains about the business concepts. Give knowledge about the business; teach how to proceed in the business.

There is a huge need for a public innovation and entrepreneurship platform that will help teaming amongst Idea stage Entrepreneurs with Contributors and create huge visibility of Ideas and Entrepreneurs.

First time entrepreneurs need a lot of good mentoring than huge investment

1. First and the biggest obstacle. You need lot of energy and time to raise funds. Indian financial institutes have a tendency to take a lot of time in evaluating a company before funding them. They want to know everything about the business. They look into every minute side of the business. This could lead to your losing a lot of crucial time at an early stage of your startup. The time when you should be searching for new customers, features instead of working on your Business Plan PPT, financial models, exit strategy. Distractions are your worst enemy and going after financial institutes at an early stage can be a big distraction.
2. Try to ensure that you require money to grow, not to survive. The entrepreneurs do not perfectly use the money. You should think of moving forward your business instead of just running the business. You should have an aim of building revenues from the fund. Your venture should be making enough money to at least fund your current operations. Your aim should be to become independent business and earning the profit in the future.
3. Work on a milestone not on a date when you should start looking for funds. The milestone could be to become number one company in the region. Set revenue targets. But get that milestone first, before even working on your business plan PPT. This will help you to focus all your energy on your venture. The milestones recall you what you have to do in your business. Without milestones you will not get the excitement of the business. You cannot measure your achievement. You should try to achieve triumph in your business.
4. Look for mentors, advisers and friends rather than investors. They will give you a right direction. At the early stage of the business, the entrepreneurs do not have enough knowledge. They lack the market information; they do not know the market game rules. Mentor is the right person to update you with all the relevant information.
5. Keep your costs as low as you can, take the advice of the experienced one on better utilization of the finance. Try to take help of economics concepts to overcome the problems.

There is no shortage of enterprising individuals in India. Still, there is this gaping lack of commercial development. The reasons for this are manifold. Among them, however are two important reasons, viz., the lack of adequate capital and the difficulty in setting-up an enterprise. The bureaucratic hurdles involved in the various stages of set-up is a major dissuading factor even to the most enthusiastic of entrepreneurs, making them literally "run out" of the country in desperation, looking for alternate places to get their footing! They almost always expand into India later, but then, they are not in any sense *Indian* companies.

Researches, time and again by various experts have found that family-run enterprises are usually the most stable to economic perturbations. We entrepreneurs have unlimited potential.

2.4 First Generation Entrepreneurs' Lessons They Have Learnt

1. Information Technology Engineer turned Java Programmer turned Software Salesman shares the lessons he has learnt as a first generation entrepreneur

Dream big, but make sure that there is some arrangement for running your day to day life. If your father has left you a fortune then it is good for you. Another option is to have one spouse working full time while the other is chasing his/her dreams. My entire risk taking is possible only because of the solid support of my wife, who takes more than her share of the family burden.

2. Techie turned restaurateur Madman offers similar advice to wannabe entrepreneurs

It is good to dream, but not to day-dream. You need hope, but not delusion. That said, you should realize that to boldly go where no one has gone before does indeed require a leap of faith and a hope for a market that may not even exist yet (certainly true in my case.) Just be sure that your decision is an informed one and based on solid research, not solely on an impulsive moment. We have to deal with the constraints of the world we live in and one of those is earning a livelihood.

It's weird that I came across these two posts today, because, since yesterday, I have been thinking of doing a series of interviews with people who have made similar career shifts. The thought itself was triggered off by a conversation I had with one of my (much older) dealers who left his corporate career to start off his own business a few years back.

3. Samruddhi ventures forge ahead

Samruddhi Vyapari Kalyankari Sanstha (SVKS) is an organization of traders or businessmen. Members of this group are all first generation businessmen. They don't hail from families owning traditional businesses; in fact their forefathers didn't have a clue about enterprise.

Like typical Marathi middle class families, they were taught to study to get a good job. But, these people dared to change the trend they had witnessed from generations and literally jumped into the business sector.

Today they are successful businessmen who have created job opportunities for many youngsters but initially even their families were skeptical about their venture. With such a background and without proper guidance about business, function of markets and happenings around them they remained firm on their path. They had to struggle to make their own business stable.

However, the things did not stop there. Nine likeminded full-time businessmen came together and decided to gather others like them. It was the beginning of Samruddhi Vyapari Kalyankari Sanstha (SVKS).

SVKS, popularly known as 'Samruddhi Club' was formed on the occasion of Vijayadashmi in 2004 and within just five years it has only gathered 60 members from Thane. It has also opened branches in Borivli, Pune, Alibag and Chiplun. Today it has more than 250 members who are masters in their business and have created opportunities for many others. Every month these people come together not for parties but to share their experiences with each other. Surprisingly after every meeting everybody gets additional knowledge and new techniques of expansion of their business.

According to founders, the objective is to act as a catalyst for growth of existing businesses and offering opportunities to those wanting to enter the business community. The institution acts as a link between Marathi-speaking businessmen and corporate groups. Members of Samruddhi Club are marching ahead and are known as the drivers of Thane's economy.

2.5 Notes From A First Generation Entrepreneur

I entered the trucking business along with my brother in law, tentatively by buying a single truck with almost all our savings put together. I had taken time to prepare the business plan and had calculated my break even conservatively; still the fear was always there. In the initial days, I used to check up on how much we made each trip. Each rupee of profit gave a new high. There are people for whom the process of making money is an end in itself rather than spending the money. I am one of them, who enjoys the thrills of pitting wits with the market and trying to come out on top. The first year was good, so the next year I added one more truck to the fleet. Things were going smooth and steady until a dollop of good fortune came our way, with one of the major players falling out of the market. Someone had to fill the vacuum and due to a combination of timing, service levels and plain good luck we were able to step into that gap.

Till this point of time, we didn't have much to do other than deal with the drivers and a couple of clients, so part time entrepreneurship worked fine. But once this opportunity rose, I had to spend more time traveling. This started eating into my current job of potato selling. Hence I was faced with a choice, whether to quit the day job and plunge into business or not. Around the same time things started to get a little sour at the current work place too. I half heartedly tried for other jobs, but didn't get anywhere, probably because of my unconventional resume. So that sort of made the decision for me. I am now a fully fledged transport fleet operator.

Lessons the first time entrepreneurs have learnt:

1. Think why you want to do it. If you want to start a business just because you can't get along with your boss, don't do that. You must have some purpose of the business. You should have your own objective of opening the business. You must open the business to get something may be achievement, social help anything.
2. Prepare a business plan. Keep your expenses low and your revenues high in your plan. You should have a complete picture of what you want to do in the business. You should have an idea from where you will get all the resources to run your business. What will be the exact cost? Your plan should reflect all that information. If you still think it is feasible, do check with others to see what you have missed.
3. If nobody is doing a business, then there must be a good reason. Find out why others aren't thinking like you. From there itself you can get an idea. What is the difference between your thinking and their thinking? Try to find out who is thinking more positively.
4. Tap your email lists of college friends and ex colleagues for funds. It works. Don't feel shy about it. You should use all possible sources of the finance. You aren't asking for a personal loan, you are offering them a business proposition. Make it clear upfront what the returns that you are promising are. Make them excited about your business so that they suddenly get ready to invest in your business plan.

5. Keep a close watch on the way the business is doing in the initial days. You will be your own accountant, auditor, clerk and peon. Focus on the cash flow; check whether you are making operating profit. Many entrepreneurs are not able to keep the record of the expenses and therefore they are not able to calculate exact profit and loss.
6. Read a lot. Not the self help books, but those about businessmen who succeeded. Read business journals you will find much information out of that. Many magazines about entrepreneurs are there in the market. It has all the information of building the business, starting, running and many more. Go through that. Read about their business strategies. How they have faced the problems? What they have done to overcome the problems?
7. Dream big, but make sure that there is some arrangement for running your day to day life. If your father has left you a wealth then it is good for you. Another option is to have one spouse working full time while the other is chasing his/her dreams. All risk taking is possible only because of the solid support of wife; family members who take more than her share of the family burden.
8. Have a mentor, preferably an older person who has been in the business. Check notes with him; don't feel shy to ask for help. You need lots of them.
9. Pay your staff well. In transportation, the success or failure is in the hands of the driver. Make sure that you pay them more than the market rate and they pay it back by working doubly harder. All businesses boil down to people, so treat them well.

2.6 Young And First Generation Entrepreneur – The Issues

Two great personalities

Steve Jobs:

1. Steve Jobs is a drop-out from Stanford University and he had to struggle a lot to get admitted at Stanford.
2. Steve Jobs could venture discontinuing his education and there was something else in his mind at that time.
3. Steve Jobs has shown an enormous courage to pursue what his inner heart says.
4. Established Apple at a very young age and it was successful.
5. Steve Jobs has brought one management guy into Apple and because of that guy; Steve Jobs had to quit Apple at the age of 30.
6. Steve Jobs wanted to leave the valley with the big setback at 30, but, finally decided to stand.
7. Steve jobs had started two companies after leaving Apple and one is Next and the second one is Pixar Communications.
8. Both companies have become successful and in a dramatic turn of events. Steve has returned to Apple again and he leads a very happy and successful life now.

Sir Sorabji:

1. Many may not know about Sir Sorabji, but, he is the founder of first Indian Bank being Central Bank of India.
2. Sir Sorabji had to discontinue his education and shoulder the family responsibilities at 19.
3. Despite having enormous energy and will, he had to wait for six months to join a Bank as a clerk.

4. Despite working as a clerk in Bank, Sorabji had bigger dream to become big.
5. Despite all the success wherever he works, he had to face all the discrimination from Europeans at that time.
6. Among Indians who works for European Banks, Sorabji had a great recognition.
7. Sorabji had pursued his quest for knowledge along with working experience.
8. Sorabji had pursued his education simultaneous to his work and in the course Sorabji had rejected good offers from other corporate.
9. Sorabji had patiently waited for ten years before taking a decision to start an Indian Bank run by Indians only.
10. There were no endorsements for Sorabji's idea at that time and even family has not supported him.
11. Sorabji has done his level best to raise finances and to get endorsements.
12. A Small Bank started by a young entrepreneur has become very big soon and now it is one of the successful banking networks in India.

By looking at the struggles of Steve Jobs and Sir Sorabji, it is clear that there tend to be struggles in the process and one has to tolerate and come-up.

2.7 Traits of First Generation Entrepreneurs

So much success in business comes down to a great concept and even better execution. Inevitably there are hurdles in the road, so keeping a positive outlook can really inspire others to stay with them through the ups and downs of the journey. An entrepreneur never lets their dreams or vision die. They are bold, take a stance and stick to it, whether the position is popular or not. Oftentimes they see opportunities where others don't, so a little brashness may be required. The best entrepreneurs are courteous, charming and candid, a great combination indeed. They're also determined to turn their ideas into reality.

Energetic

Everyone talks about the importance of time-management skills, but managing your energy is critical as well. Most entrepreneurs are energetic to a fault, which is a great quality because it'll take every bit you have some days just to get through. Staying focused on the important things, not the small stuff is critical so that you don't get derailed or distracted along the way. Being gregarious and generous will help you make friends before you need them, which can never hurt and will certainly pay dividends down the road. Never underestimate the power of good deeds and small gestures; others will love you for them and remember them when you least expect it.

Humour

Having a great sense of humour and being able to laugh at yourself as needed will get you through many a late night. A funny joke or happy comment can go a long way in the trenches.

Innovative

Innovation is the key to creativity and growth today and it will inspire thinking big and broad so others want to join your cause. The ability to juggle many tasks simultaneously without dropping any balls along the way is a great quality and comes in handy often. Every entrepreneur has had a few kooky ideas that just might work, so give them a shot, you never know. Sometimes it's those crazy ones along the way that make all the difference.

Leading capability

The best entrepreneurs lead others to a place where they had no idea they even wanted to go. They mentor others along the way, sharing their experience and stories. Creating a new path can be daunting, so it's important to encourage promising ideas; that's where the magic happens and they can learn as much as they give. When entrepreneurship comes naturally as part of your DNA, you've chosen the right career. Entrepreneurs are born more and can be made and the best ones can't imagine doing anything else. Authenticity always rules. Not everyone is cut out to start a company, so play to your strengths for the best results.

Optimistic

The ability to be optimistic yet realistic is an important trait. It helps you think of creative ways to solve problems that pop up along the way so that you keep trying to find possible answers and exploring ideas. Striking the right balance of being pleasantly persistent as needed is tough to master. Success is about the follow-up and follow-through, not just the great idea. Successful entrepreneurs always question the *status quo* and they never get complacent. They also ask a lot of questions to uncover opportunities and issues that exist.

Remarkable

In today's world you have to be remarkable in some way so you stand out from the pack. Blending into the wallpaper will get you nowhere. Be known for doing something better than anyone else out there. Successful entrepreneurs are strategic yet opportunistic so they can take advantage of the right offers along the way. By having a roadmap, you're able to take detours and sometimes you end up getting to a better place than you ever imagined. But you need a plan so that you can recognize which paths are worth pursuing as you go. There are no shortcuts to paying your dues, so entrepreneurs must be technically competent and have their homework done along the way.

Unflappable

Great entrepreneurs are unflappable with thick skin and don't take it personally when things don't go their way. They know that's part of the experience and what makes it exciting. Entrepreneurs create value and are incredibly valuable to their most important customers. They wow them at every opportunity they get so they're remembered. The best entrepreneurs create extraordinary experiences every time. It's really the experience more than the actual product or service that's important and it's what brings customers back for more of what you're selling. They're young at heart and never lose their sense of curiosity and wonder. Their eyes still sparkle when they get excited by a great idea. And finally, entrepreneurs are zealous about life; after all, if you're not having fun, why bother?

2.8 An Entrepreneur's Challenge

The challenge was literally in formatting the dream and scheduling the conceptual steps and the processes by which the dream would be realized.

Creating the dream

A good business fills a need. You must realize a need. Through a need of your own, you may realize that other people have the same need and the cure for your needs could also be a cure for the needs of others with similar needs. Fulfilling the needs of the others is the base of the business. Try to follow your dream. You may face many challenges but have a confidence in you and continue with your dream.

Realizing the Viability

A good business can fill the need at a profit. Take your dream one step further; determine if the product/service that could be a solution to your problem is worth paying for. The business should have feasibility. The business you see is good for you and very attractive one also but it is not necessary that those businesses will be easy also. Try to evaluate the business idea whether you are perfect with the business or not before starting the business.

Conformation

A good business must have a substantially saleable product. Specifically describe the product/ service and how you could build/design/create it. Determine if the value of the product/service is worth the cost of producing it. Some business cannot be done unless you have a huge amount of money. The business should have a capability to sale. It should attract the customers. The customers should like your products or services.

Marketability

A good business must be marketable at a profit. Developing a market feasibility plan was the next step. By determining the marketability of the product/service and orchestrating the process within the sphere of location, pricing/value, accessibility and dispensation, it is possible to realize the maximum profit from the product/service within a specific market during the initial phase of distribution. By establishing a marketing plan based on the feasibility of marketing your product/ service during this phase of the business development process, your business can become profitable from the earliest stage possible.

Targeting Profit

A good business must operate regularly IN THE BLACK. Often, developing a profitable business is an accidental event that can't be explained. More often, businesses fail within first five years because owners plan to FAIL by failing to PLAN. The new one does not follow the rule of business plan. The business plan is must for opening the business. However, profitability in business can be explained, planned and projected, if the business owner establishes a plan of business and manages his business according to that plan. You can show with the help of business plan from where profit will come, who will be the valuable customers?

Determine the requirements of making a profit in your business and incorporate that process into your plan. That is what targeting profit is all about; making sure that your business plan has 'profit' directly in sight.

Care about your people

A good business must serve its people. Occasionally a company will forget its purpose for being in business. The only REAL reason for being in business is to help other people. No matter what your product/service might be, your purpose is helping others. When this concept becomes genuine within the people who work in your business, they will acquire the ability to serve with objectivity the clients who purchase your products/services. Recognize your business priorities and keep them at the top of the list. Customer Service is not where you want to cut costs.

Plan your business

A good business follows a solid business plan. A solid business plan based on marketing strategies, prioritized business practices and a sound proposal of profitability will project your company to triumph. A complete business plan will include concepts and procedures for day-to-day operations that will lead regularly to the level of success planned for and projected. If you are following your business plan in an organized manner, with periodic reevaluations for business development changes, your company will have its very own success story and history of success.

All-inclusive development

A good business is based on a solidly proven business history. Even if you are new to the business industry, there are proven examples of businesses for you to follow. You should read about the stories of successful business, how they have achieved the success? You can also go through the failure story of the business, why they have failed in the business? Find a successful 'mentor' within your chosen industry and follow their guidance. Do not try to do everything by your own. Trying to reinvent the helm doesn't work. It's been invented and it works, so why mess with perfection by trying to reinvent it. This means that there is a proven method of doing business and it does work, so when you find a person who is successful in your chosen field, use their proven strategies and update for current technical abilities, but do not try to reinvent the processes. You will be in advantage because no need to put your time for inventing the new process for your business.

Maintain business record

A good business uses a consistent record keeping method. Prepare an office for your business that is capable of tracking daily activities within your business, marketing practices and financial records. The new one becomes so busy that they do not get the time to record the daily activities in the business. Sometime they record sometimes they forgot. This record keeping will help you to analyze your business properly. You will know your mistakes and good things also. You must consistently record financial records in a clearly defined manner that will properly project your financial situation at any given time. Weekly, monthly and annual reports are necessary for managing the profitability of your business. Be certain that these reports are available for weekly, monthly and annual evaluation and religiously do those evaluations based on your business plan. Be prepared to revamp and revitalize your business plan based on the evaluations you do.

Use the four E's

A good business promotes enthusiasm, effort, energetic and ethics. Enthusiastically promote what you do. If you believe in what you are doing and put your best attitude towards accomplishing the job at hand, you will be promoting your business in the best possible way, with personal enthusiasm. Following legal practices in business actually helps you in attracting the customers and expanding the business. No customer wants to use the products where they see unethics and fraud. Be sure that majority of effort you put into your business every day is intended for profit. You should use your energy for earning profit. You can give small tasks to other employees in the business and you can focus more on the influential tasks of your business so that you will be more focused. If you are working all day and accomplish nothing towards making a profit, your business will not be profitable in the long run. Personal ethics are a choice. If you value your business you will maintain a high standard of ethics. Honesty and Integrity cannot be regained once they are lost. Don't allow anyone to take those from you for any reason, hold your personal values dearly and promote your business based on solid values.

Enjoy the life

A good business allows for the enjoyment of life along with the requirements of work. As with any job, burnout is a threat if you don't take time out to enjoy life while you work. It often amazes the number of people who indicate that they have no time for family, fun and hobbies, as they are working to own their own business. What ARE they working for? If you don't take time to enjoy life, you will burnout and be no good to anyone and definitely not capable of succeeding in your business. Take time out for you, for family, for LIFE. Your job will still be there when you get back and you will be more capable when you go back to it.

Without specific details that make a business work successfully towards a profit, you don't actually have a business; you have a great idea. An idea won't actually get you very far in the land of profit margins, it actually will cost you more than it will make. An idea is something that is incomplete and surrealistic, until it has been scripted and formatted into the reality of a series of goals that work together to make a profitable business.

SUMMARY

The first time entrepreneurs must have at least the following qualities i.e., Energetic, Enthusiastic, Ethics, Efforts, Excitement, and Enjoyment. If they want to start the business, these are the qualities that will help the new entrepreneurs to move their business.

First Generation Entrepreneurs (FGEs) – Constructing Businesses in India

FGEs in India: What to focus on?

First thing to ensure is to build a cash flow positive business within the initial capital that you have managed to raise (self, friends, family and tools). Keep lowest possible costs and create early revenues.

Internet as a tool

Internet only business models targeting Indian market is not going to be viable for at least coming years (or more). View internet as a cheap way to build products and get the initial users with zero marketing budgets.

One has to keep an eye on the scalability aspect

Most of the successful Indian entrepreneurs have followed the path of building stuff in their own capital reaching profitability and building it further. Examples: Dhirubhai, Subhash Chandra, Mittals, Narayan Murthy, Sanjiv Bhikchandani etc.

There is potential to build a scalable business without incurring too much cost. It has a two-pronged problem:

- Indian entrepreneurs do not have experience of bringing products to market and
- Indian angel investors do not have an intuitive understanding of how products are built or marketed.

First time entrepreneurs need a lot of good mentoring than huge investment

- First and the biggest obstacle. You need lot of energy and time to raise funds.
- Try to ensure that you require money to grow, not to survive.
- Work on a milestone not on a date when you should start looking for funds.
- Look for mentors, advisers and friends rather than investors.
- Keep your costs as low as you can, take the advice of the experienced one on better utilization of the finance.

Lessons the first time entrepreneurs have learnt:

- Think why you want to do it
- Prepare a business plan
- If nobody is doing a business, then there must be a good reason
- Tap your email lists of college friends and ex colleagues for funds

- Keep a close watch on the way the business is doing in the initial days
- Read a lot
- Dream big, but make sure that there is some arrangement for running your day to day life
- Have a mentor, preferably an older person who has been in the business
- Pay your staff well. In transportation, the success or failure is in the hands of the driver

Traits of first generation entrepreneurs are as follows:

- Energetic
- Humour
- Innovative
- Leading capability
- Optimistic
- Remarkable
- Unflappable

An Entrepreneur's Challenges are:

- Creating the dream
- Realizing the Viability
- Conformation
- Marketability
- Targeting Profit
- Profit
- Care about your people
- Plan your business
- All-inclusive development
- Maintain business record
- Use the four E's.
- Enjoy the life

KEYWORDS

First Generation Entrepreneurs: Who first time starts their own business and do not have any business background.

Entrepreneur: Peter F. Drucker defines an entrepreneur as one who always searches for changes, responds to it and exploits it as an opportunity.

Self recognition: Entrepreneurs want to open the business because they want to show their expertise to the world.

Internet: Technology used for online business.

Mentoring: Entrepreneurial mentoring can be viewed as a business development process for owner-managers.

***Angel investor*:** A wealthy individual who invests in a start-up company with his or her own money.

Cash flow: Cash which comes into a company from sales (cash inflow) or the money which goes out in purchases or overhead expenditure (cash outflow).

QUESTIONS

1. What do you mean by First Generation Entrepreneurs?
2. What are the issues with young and first generation Entrepreneurs?
3. What are the traits of first generation Entrepreneurs?

Chapter – 3

Entrepreneurs' Personality and Motivation

LEARNING OBJECTIVES

On completion of this chapter, you should be able to:

- ☺ *Explain different types of personality and their impact on new business.*
- ☺ *Describe a lifestyle entrepreneur.*
- ☺ *Describe the importance of entrepreneur's advisor.*

Entrepreneurs' personality plays an important role in opening the business. It is their personality which decides the success and failure of business. Different people have different personalities and accordingly they live their life and get achievement in their life. For becoming entrepreneur you must have a great personality. You must have intelligence, positive attitude, energy, capability and many more. If your personality will have all positive factors, then definitely you will progress but if you are narrow minded, ego, do not give importance to others, then from there itself you start declining and as a result of that your business suffers.

BOX 3

Indian and Chinese Entrepreneurs

In 2007, a group of Georgia State students travelled to India to answer one central question – "Was the Indian government assisting or halting entrepreneurship?"

The findings were that there were plenty of opportunities to start a business in India, that the bureaucratic process often hindered the speed of a start up and that the Indian Government's best policy would be to get out of the way.

A recent study on Entrepreneurial levels in India and China confirm these findings and added some very interesting information:

- *Major motivation for Indian entrepreneurs is to be their own boss.*
- *Major motivation for Chinese entrepreneurs is to make more money.*
- *American entrepreneurs generally follow the Indian motivational factor of being their own boss.*
- *23% of Chinese entrepreneurs say they are using training obtained in school to start their business.*
- *Only 9 per cent of Indian entrepreneurs say the same about school.*
- *Family expectations were stronger in India compared to China (21 per cent to 9 per cent, respectively) as a motivation to start a business.*
- *Inspiration from entrepreneurial friends and family were cited as the reason. 27 per cent of Indians started their business and just 18 per cent of Chinese.*
- *For Financing, 49 per cent of Indians rely on start-up funding from Friends, Family and Fools (the 3 F's).*
- *Only 25 per cent of Chinese entrepreneurs sought family funding.*
- *49 per cent of Chinese entrepreneurs obtained funds from banks.*
- *Only 27 per cent of Indian entrepreneurs obtained funds from banks.*
- *As for the reasons for success for a new start-up, 93% of Chinese say "Guanxi" is the main reason. A Guanxi is the personal relationships necessary to navigate China's political, legal and regulatory climate.*
- *81 per cent of Indians say "jugaad" is the reason for entrepreneurial success. A Jugaad is the ability to be creative and innovative in getting around governmental regulations.*

As Students saw in their 2007 trip to India, entrepreneurs in India say getting around the government's hefty bureaucracy is the main key to success. For the Chinese, it appears that the ability to navigate within this bureaucracy is the key to success.

Source: *Information received from "The Entrepreneur School Blog", 2010.*

3.1 Important Types of Personality

I. Highly Motivated Entrepreneur

Highly motivated entrepreneur is an entrepreneur who is in the business because he wants to do something in the business or wants to use the business for fulfilling his personal satisfaction. The motivation behind becoming an entrepreneur may not be necessary to get economic reward instead there could also be some psychological reasons that motivate the person for entrepreneurship. The psychological satisfaction may be in terms of getting economic rewards, self achievement or to use his intelligence for achieving the tasks. Highly motivated entrepreneurs are motivated by their inner feelings, desires or need and these are the forces that control the action of individual. These forces decide the direction of the person where he wants to go. The reasons for motivation behind entrepreneurship are as follows:

(i) Self achievement fulfillment
(ii) To prove his excellence in business
(iii) To influence others by his brainpower
(iv) To gain economic rewards
(v) To reap opportunities in market
(vi) Influence of highly successful entrepreneurs

(a) Self achievement fulfillment

Self achievement fulfillment entrepreneur is one who is motivated for achievement, refers to the need for personal accomplishment by the person through excellence. This category of person is very responsible to his tasks always wants to achieve the tasks by his all possible means. High achiever believes in personal achievement rather than reward of success. He is ready to take risks in getting things done. He is not motivated to money but takes money as a source of his achievement.

David C McClelland's motivational needs theory

In the late 1940 American David Clarence McClelland (1917-98) and his associates developed the theory of achievement motivation. McClelland is chiefly known for his work on achievement motivation, but his research interests extended to personality and consciousness. David McClelland pioneered workplace motivational thinking, developing achievement-based motivational theory and models and promoted improvements in employee assessment methods, advocating competency-based assessments and tests, arguing them to be better than traditional IQ and personality-based tests. His ideas have since been widely adopted in many organizations and relate closely to the theory of Frederick Herzberg.

David McClelland is most noted for describing three types of motivational need, which he identified in his 1961 book, *The Achieving Society*:

- achievement motivation (n-ach)
- authority/power motivation (n-pow)
- affiliation motivation (n-affil)

David McClelland's needs-based motivational model

These needs are found to varying degrees in all workers and managers and this mix of motivational needs characterizes a person's or manager's style and behaviour, both in terms of being motivated and in the management and motivation of others.

The need for achievement (n-ach)

The n-ach person is 'achievement motivated' and therefore seeks achievement, attainment of realistic but challenging goals and advancement in the job. There is a strong need for feedback as to achievement and progress and a need for a sense of accomplishment.

The need for authority and power (n-pow)

The n-pow person is 'authority motivated'. This driver produces a need to be influential, effective and to make an impact. There is a strong need to lead and for their ideas to prevail. There is also motivation and need towards increasing personal status and prestige.

The need for affiliation (n-affil)

The n-affil person is 'affiliation motivated' and has a need for friendly relationships and is motivated towards interaction with other people. The affiliation driver produces motivation and need to be liked and held in popular regard. These people are team players.

McClelland said that most people possess and exhibit a combination of these characteristics. Some people exhibit a strong bias to a particular motivational need and this motivational or needs 'mix' consequently affects their behaviour and working/managing style. McClelland suggested that a strong n-affil 'affiliation-motivation' undermines a manager's objectivity, because of his need to be liked and that this affects a manager's decision-making capability. A strong n-pow 'authority-motivation' will produce a determined work ethic and commitment to the organization and while n-pow people are attracted to the leadership role; they may not possess the required flexibility and people-centered skills. McClelland argues that n-ach people with strong 'achievement motivation' make the best leaders, although there can be a tendency to demand too much from their staff in the belief that they are all similarly and *highly* achievement-focused and results driven, which of course most people are not.

McClelland's particular fascination was for achievement motivation and this laboratory experiment illustrates one aspect of his theory about the effect of achievement on people's motivation. McClelland asserted via this experiment that while most people do not possess a strong achievement-based motivation, those who do, display a consistent behaviour in setting goals:

Volunteers were asked to throw rings over pegs rather like the fairground game; no distance was stipulated and most people seemed to throw from arbitrary, random distances, sometimes close, sometimes farther away. However a small group of volunteers, whom McClelland suggested were strongly achievement-motivated, took some care to measure and test distances to produce an ideal challenge - not too easy and not impossible. Interestingly a parallel exists in biology, known as the 'overload principle', which is commonly applied to fitness and exercising, i.e., in order to develop fitness and/or strength the exercise must be sufficiently demanding to increase existing levels, but not so demanding as to cause damage or strain. McClelland identified the same need for a 'balanced challenge' in the approach of achievement-motivated people.

McClelland contrasted achievement-motivated people with gamblers and dispelled a common pre-conception that n-ach 'achievement-motivated' people are big risk takers. On the contrary - typically, achievement-motivated individuals set goals which they can influence with their effort and ability and as such the goal is considered to be achievable. This determined results-driven approach is almost invariably present in the character make-up of all successful business people and entrepreneurs.

McClelland suggested other characteristics and attitudes of achievement-motivated people:

- Achievement is more important than material or financial reward.
- Achieving the aim or task gives greater personal satisfaction than receiving praise or recognition.

- Financial reward is regarded as a measurement of success, not an end in itself.
- Security is not prime motivator, nor is status.
- Feedback is essential, because it enables measurement of success, not for reasons of praise or recognition (the implication here is that feedback must be reliable, quantifiable and factual).
- Achievement-motivated people constantly seek improvements and ways of doing things better.
- Achievement-motivated people will logically favour jobs and responsibilities that naturally satisfy their needs, i.e., offer flexibility and opportunity to set and achieve goals, e.g., sales and business management and entrepreneurial roles.

McClelland firmly believed that achievement-motivated people are generally the ones who make things happen and get results and that this extends to getting results through the organization of other people and resources, although as stated earlier, they often demand too much from their staff because they priorities achieving the goal above the many varied interests and needs of their people.

***(b)* To gain economic rewards**

Some new entrepreneurs are in the business because they want to get the economic reward with the help of their business. They are purely in the business because they think that by doing business, they can earn money. They do not have any other intention to be in the business. It is seen that most of the new small entrepreneurs are in the business because they are motivated to earn money from the business. They may have their other purposes but the main purpose is to earn money.

II. Protective Entrepreneur

These are the entrepreneurs who do not take risk in their business. They are happy with their current situation. They do not take risk until and unless it becomes mandatory to take the risk. They are satisfied with their earnings. They want to expand their business but not by taking risk. They do not change the things easily. They are the ones who do not like change in the business.

- They set goals mainly to impress others, to avoid confronting fears – including the fear of personal freedom and success – and to conform to a comfort zone rather than pushing to learn more and gain new experiences.
- Because of self-imposed limitations, they prefer to follow someone else's game plan and they lack the desire to become a self-motivated and self-reliant entrepreneur.
- They focus primarily on personal security and their emotional motivation derives from a fear of insecurity and a desire to be within the comfort zone of a secure situation.

Those who want a greater sense of responsibility and control over their lives and have the confidence to experiment with that possibility often rise up from the ground level of entrepreneur status to the upper level of entrepreneurship.

III. Enthusiastic Entrepreneur

Enthusiastic entrepreneurs are very excited to open their business. They have a dream to open the business. They have some plans to implement after opening the business. They just wait to implement the plans. Their main motive is not to earn profit but to make the dream true through business. They are very energetic and fulfill all the requirements of the business. They take all responsibilities of the business by their heart and put their all efforts to move forward their business. They are very hopeful about the positive outcomes of business.

IV. Visionary Entrepreneur

Visionary entrepreneurs open business because they have a vision which they want to achieve. They want to reach their business up to the level where they want to see their business and in that direction they proceed. They have a perfect direction to their business. They know their destination and keeping in mind their destination they form strategies and make plans. They continuously analyze all those factors that can get into their way. For example if an entrepreneur opens a business of beauty parlor and has a vision of becoming number one in city or state then they continuously analyze all the competitors, market trends and customers. As a result of that they have perfect information of the market situation and which help them to grow their business.

V. Innovative and Creative Entrepreneur

The main reason to open the business is to present their ideas and creativity to the world. They want to give something new to the society that can help them. They believe in innovation and therefore they open their business. They want to solve the problems of customers by their innovative products. Innovative and creative entrepreneurs have made the life of society comfortable. For example, refrigerator, i-pod, mobiles, shaving machines, ATM, paper napkin, these are all examples of innovative products that are available in the market. They think very differently their products really help others. They continuously analyze the environment and if they see any scope, then suddenly come up with their products in the market. They may come up with innovative process, innovative methods or innovative services. Once their products are accepted by the customers they feel satisfied and successful.

VI. Lazy Entrepreneur

These are the entrepreneurs who open the business and try to run their business but they are very lazy. They do not have activeness in their work; they are not enthusiastic about their work. They take the work as a formality. They never work under deadline just extend the work. They keep their work pending and always throw today's work on the next day. They do not entrap themselves into the competition. They lack the craze about their business. They just want to run the business without thinking about the progress about the business.

VII. The Wealth Creation Entrepreneur

The particular individual creates a business with the ultimate goal of reaching the largest available market whilst making the highest profit. These are the guys who build businesses like Google, Microsoft, Sony, Apple, Facebook and so on. These entrepreneurs generally make the Forbes list of wealthiest people in the world over and over again. They don't think small, it's not in their vocabulary. They deal with vast sums of money and are responsible for thousands and tens of thousands of people's livelihoods. These guys are good for any country. Their bank accounts will usually start from one million dollars a year to billions. They can be extremely innovative businesses that change the way we see the world like Facebook, Twitter or they can be pretty run of the mill like Wal-Mart or Toyota.

VIII. The Social Entrepreneur

A social entrepreneur is someone *who recognizes a social problem and uses entrepreneurial principles to organize, create and manage a venture to make social change.* Whereas a wealth creation entrepreneur typically measures performance in terms of profit and return, a social entrepreneur assesses success in terms of the impact on society as well as in profit and return.

They often operate through non-profits or charities but increasingly, they are doing so from a private standpoint.

Just as entrepreneurs change the face of business, social entrepreneurs act as the change agents for society, seizing opportunities others miss and improving systems, inventing new approaches and creating solutions to change society for the better.

One of the best examples of Social entrepreneurs is Muhammad Yunus, founder and manager of Grameen Bank in India, who was awarded a Nobel Peace Prize in 2006. He essentially invented the concept of Micro finance banks by giving ridiculously small loans to poor people, even beggars and yet still managing a 95 per cent repayment from borrowers. He definitely changed the world of banking.

3.2 Entrepreneurs' Personality

Starting and growing your own business requires many skills to be successful. Take a look at the business personality types and find out what you need to succeed. Are you Bill Gates, a Visionary, or an Improver like Body Shop founder, Anita Roddick?

Your business personality types are the traits and characteristics of your personality that blend with the needs of the business. If you better understand your business personality, then you can give your company the best part of you. Begin identifying your dominant personality theme and understand how you operate in your business.

The business developer

If you operate your business predominately in the developer mode, you are focused on using your company as a means to develop the world. You want to do something for the welfare of people, society as a whole. Your overarching motto is: morally correct companies will be rewarded working on a noble cause. You believe on noble work. Improvers have an unwavering ability to run their business with high integrity and ethics. They never follow any unethical practices even though they have advantages in that. They try to do the business with legal practices. They never take the help of any illegal practices. They try to do something for the society for the welfare of the people. They see the business to improve the status of the society or the nation as a whole.

The people advisor

This business personality type provides an extremely high level of assistance and advice to customers. The advisor's motto is: the customer is right and we must do everything to please them. Companies built by advisors become customer focused. They think that their business must provide a complete satisfaction to the customers. They try to provide all the possible facilities to their customers. They take care of their customers and try to solve the problems faced by their customers.

Personality warning: Advisors can become totally focused on the needs of their business and customers that they may ignore their own needs and ultimately burn out. But very much focused on customers may harm the business also because they should focus on the customers keeping in mind the situation of the business. If the entrepreneurs cannot provide many facilities to their customers because they do not have many resources but still they continue with providing services i.e., they are compromising with the other parts of the business.

The organizer

An entrepreneur is one who is expert in organizing the resources for building the business and running it successfully. He combines labour, land, machines, finance and material for the business and has a great knowledge of utilizing all the resources in an optimum way. He sells products in the market earns profit, pays loan, distributes salaries of employees, purchases required stuff for business and keep remaining for his own. He is an organizer because he organizes every task in the business. He tries to manage a balance between every activity that has been taken to run the business and to earn the profit.

Risk Takers

Entrepreneurial success is usually experienced by people who are not afraid to take a chance with a new idea or concept. These folks are more daring than most and tend more of a 'what if' approach by following through on innovative ideas that others may shy away from. These people are not only thinking outside the box but they are also living there as well and in most cases quite comfortably! They watch the crowd and go in the opposite direction because they know there will be less competition!

The creative or artist

This business personality is the reserved but highly creative type. Their creativity moves forward their business. Often found in businesses demanding creativity such as web design and ad agencies. As an artist type you tend to build your business around the unique talents and creativities you have. They are very artistic person and also they show their artistic work in the business. They mold the things in a different way. They have expertise in providing the things in a different way. They have the unique ideas.

Being a successful entrepreneur also means being innovative and creative. Successful entrepreneurs are able to take an existing product or service and make it better. They also need creativity for all aspects of their business, such as advertising, special promotions and rewarding deserving employees. Without this entrepreneurial personality trait, entrepreneurs will fall short.

The visionary

An entrepreneur builds a business because it is exciting and challenging. It requires every part of them to make it successful. They have a picture, a clear vision of how that business is going to work in every detail and the result it is going to produce. They never work in their business; rather they work on their business. An entrepreneur rarely starts a business in his or her own field of knowledge. They put the right system in place to make their vision become a reality. An entrepreneur looks at systems. They don't get tied up in the day-to-day activities of their business. This frees them up to start new businesses and either sells their existing businesses or takes them public.

The systematic business analyst

If you run a business as an Analyst, your company focuses on fixing problems in a systematic way. Often the basis for science, engineering or computer firms, Analyst companies excel at problem solving. They have logic for every task. They try to take help of science and art to solve the problems. They think in a scientific way. They have a proper approach to their business. They are well aware about the different situation and accordingly they act. They have a proper reason for their act.

Ambitious and driven

Without motivation, it will take a lot to justify the hard work and time required to get a business off the ground. No one should care more about your success than you and if you're not driven to achieve your goals, every obstacle will provide the perfect opportunity to quit.

The energizer

A business owned and operated by an energizer is full of life, energy and optimism. Your company is life-energizing and makes customers feel the company has a get it done attitude in a fun playful manner. The customers suddenly get trust on the company.

The leader

They have an incredible will and ability to lead the world and their business through any challenge. They do not fear; they are ready to face any difficulties. They are the essence of entrepreneurship and can assemble great companies. They are in the business to do something. They want to touch the heights in the business. They overcome any problem. They never give up.

Each business personality type can succeed in the business environment if you stay true to your character. Knowing firmly what your strong traits are can act as a compass for your small business. If you are building a team, this insight is invaluable. For the solo business owners, understand that you may need outside help to balance your business personality.

3.3 What is a 'Lifestyle Entrepreneur?

Running Your Business

Most lifestyle entrepreneurs start businesses that they are passionate about. Any business, even if it is in pursuit of a passion or interest, still requires all the essential elements of a successful set-up, like a plan, a service or product, funding and a market to sell the service or product. To start a successful business, lifestyle entrepreneurs have to pay attention to following factors:

- Choosing suitable people to work with
- Selecting and managing technology to keep up with competition
- Attaining the perfect blend of control and growth
- Proper administration
- Intelligence
- Gaining profits

Whether it is closed, passed on to a family member or sold, every business has an end. Lifestyle entrepreneurs need to make sure their business is profitable. By maintaining good financial records and using good business tactics, the business can generate a good income and profits.

Entrepreneurs' Lifestyle

The entrepreneurial lifestyle is one of the major factors that drive many entrepreneurs to the decision to start their own business. It usually involves long hours, especially when starting out, but a great deal of flexibility as well. Juggling work and personal life can be a daunting challenge. A lifestyle entrepreneur is someone who goes into business for a reason other than the financial rewards of owning a business, but because of their lifestyle. What they are looking for is to work around their lifestyle. They often use their passion to build their career and simply use their passion to build a business.

A lifestyle entrepreneur doesn't expect to make six figures a year doing what they love to do. They just want to be able to live their life doing what they love and being able to support themselves and their family as well. They find much happiness doing what they love to do. All work and no play are making too many entrepreneurs a rather dull bunch in this day and age. With their careers taking up a major part of their time, they have very little time and energy left for their friends and family and even their personal well being.

The term "lifestyle entrepreneur" is given to anyone who starts a business not for financial gains, but for lifestyle rewards. The biggest motivation for all lifestyle entrepreneurs is an overwhelming desire for independence. They want to live their life by their own way. They have their own attitude and perception what they want to follow. They dream of working for themselves and running a business that is in tune with their lifestyle. They select the business which suits to their lifestyle. Therefore, practically anyone with an independent bent of mind can take up lifestyle entrepreneurship.

Even within the free enterprise system there are some factors more highly prized than money, especially for lifestyle entrepreneurs who don't measure the true worth of their small business strictly by the bottom line. For them, the fact that they are pursuing their dream and making a living doing what they love is what matters most.

These aspiring entrepreneurs made their former companies lots of money but they know that now it's time to start their own business. With the acceptance of the home office and the advent of information technologies spurring that movement, things started to evolve and many start-ups began springing up with home bases. These are people who truly love what they do and they don't need to make a million dollars. It could be an IT person, a graphic designer or an artist. Key factors for a growing percentage of entrepreneurs starting their own ventures are a desire for freedom, independence and control over their lives.

Controlling your own destiny

One of the things that a true entrepreneur looks at is governing themselves and being able to do what they think is right without having to go through red tape. It comes from sitting in board rooms and having everybody sign off for each decision that's made.

Controlling one's business destiny is perhaps the biggest draw for lifestyle entrepreneurs who take sole credit for the success or failure of their operation.

Ways to Create Success as a Lifestyle Entrepreneur

The success of a rewarding lifestyle is by far one of the greatest achievements you can attain. Lifestyle entrepreneurs strive to achieve such a success. Here are some ways to become a successful entrepreneur:

- **Define your values:** To become a successful lifestyle entrepreneur, you must define certain values and principles and honour them in both your personal as well as business life. Successful lifestyle entrepreneurs are required to know exactly what is important for their business.
- **Define solid purpose:** The entrepreneurs must have a strong purpose for their business. This purpose will give direction to your business. If you will just open the business without any purpose then it will become direction-less. You must have concrete reasons for running your business.
- **Create a vision:** Visualize what you will be doing three years down the line. Realistic conceptualization is one of the key factors of becoming a successful lifestyle entrepreneur. Not only will this provide a goal, but can also be useful in formulating methods of achieving it.
- **Make a plan of action:** Knowledge is not enough, application is more important. Top performers will tell you that lasting success can only come through hard work. The more you work the better results you reap. Create a plan of action that is result oriented. Your plan must work within a specific period of time. Once you form the plan you know exactly what next you have to do. You have a direction and you do not waste time. You get specific system to move forward your business.

- **Hire support:** It is advisable to hire support in areas that do not fall under your expertise. Hiring people to do your work will provide you with more freedom and time to focus on gaining profits for your business. If you will try to do everything then you may fail also. You should involve yourselves only on those areas where you think you are very good reaming should be left to the other experts. This way, your business will be your main concern and not other lesser tasks that form an intrinsic part of any business.
- **Attend business conference:** They always attend every business conference. They participate in meeting, business exhibitions or seminars. They are ready to get information from every possible source. They give importance to every business information and try to use that for their business progress.
- **Highly interactive:** They are very interactive. They meet with so many persons in their life. They share their experience and gain others experience. They do not hesitate to communicate with others. They try to attach themselves with every person who can give benefits to their business.
- **Generate passive income:** Generating a stream of passive income will build your brand name. Passive income involves referral programs, affiliate programs and pay-for-inclusion committees.

Whether you are a lifestyle entrepreneur or dream of becoming one, following these guidelines will prove useful. Lifestyle entrepreneurship eliminates the usual drawbacks that apply to traditional entrepreneurship, which will provide the motivation and scope for growth, to achieve success. Therefore, if you are ready to live a more meaningful and interesting life, becoming a lifestyle entrepreneur could be the right choice for you.

Lifestyle entrepreneurs' balanced and controlled life

Lifestyle entrepreneurs are people who go into business primarily for lifestyle reasons, as opposed to a desire for financial wealth. They become business owners so they can do the kind of work they want, work the hours they want, live where they want and spend time with people they like and admire.

Lifestyle entrepreneurs judge their success by how much they enjoy their work and their lives as a whole, rather than by their status or their net worth. They want to live their own life. They do not want any interference in that. They do hard work for their business simultaneously enjoy the success also. Lifestyle entrepreneurs love it and delight in helping others find their own path to an entrepreneurial life that works for them.

There are so many people that work their jobs in a career that they chose for all the wrong reasons and the main reason is to have money to pay for their house and the bills. But it's unhealthy for so many reasons. You hardly have any time to play all you do is work and the little time that you do have you just don't have the energy to do anything.

By becoming a lifestyle entrepreneur you can have the best of both worlds and live your life as you have always wanted to. So how do you begin? First thing you should do is that anyone can become a lifestyle entrepreneur, all it takes is some hard work and dedication, so if you have that then you have all that you need. They are the ones who not only enjoy their life but also run their business with full focused mind.

First you need to figure out what your ability is. If you also want to be the lifestyle entrepreneurs then you ask to yourselves basically what you are good at. What do you love doing, your passion is most likely going to make you money and offer you a great business. Try to find out your passion. Try to know in which topic or business you have interest. Now collect information about that. Know everything about that and start your business and you will see that now you are enjoying your life according to you. You are living your dream you are doing your interest business. You enjoy the life.

You will have the ability to spend more time at home with your family and there will be no more waking up so early in the morning. It is ridiculous to assume that you can't make money online, because there are so many people doing it and they are successful at it. There is one important thing that you will need to do before you jump right into this headfirst. You will need to make sure that you research any market that you are entering in and be sure that there is actually money in it. This is the downfall of many people. They think that they will make tons of money and be a huge success but there is just not anybody there to buy what they are selling. So research and more research is the key to making a wonderful life as a lifestyle entrepreneur.

3.4 Entrepreneur's Advisor

The advisor plays an important role in the life of entrepreneurs. If entrepreneurs will have such a good advisor then entrepreneurs can save themselves from many mistakes.

The power of peers

The advisor plays an important role in the success of the business. They give the direction to the business. The new entrepreneurs though have all the knowledge but somewhere they require advice of the experienced one for running their business. It is seen that the business owners achieve greater success and ease in solving problems when they have peers and advisors with whom they can brainstorm. The entrepreneurs who do not have any advisor they mostly face many problems. They do not know the minute things of the business where they require help but when they do not have any one who can help them then they become hopeless. In the absence of the experienced one they take decision whatever they think is good for the business. Absence of the advisor is also one of the factors responsible for the failure of the business.

Role of small business advisor

You know your business? That is why you ventured into your field in the first place, but do you "know business"? Many small business owners know their respective fields but lack specialized knowledge about good business practices. This is the point where they require the help of advisor. The advisor protects them from hidden risks that the new one does not know. If you find that your business could use some help establishing good business practices consider hiring a small business advisor. Small business advisors can help the budding entrepreneur in a variety of ways.

Business coaching

First and foremost, small business advisors can help by actually coaching you and your business to becoming better. They direct you in each and every aspects of the business. Whereas a business consultant outlines problems and develops a course of action, a small business coach outlines current and potential issues but also assumes the role of teacher and trainer, providing instruction on how to invest in your business, how to avoid mistakes and how to implement change. Taking coaching is the best option for the new entrepreneurs. They can learn a lot from the experience of the coach. The coach helps the entrepreneurs' business for surviving. The small business advisors have, by virtue of the work they do, seen first-hand the mistakes made by various businesses and have played party to their recovery.

Marketing training

Small business advisors also provide marketing training to help you navigate your chosen market successfully and avoid marketing mistakes. They help you identify market opportunities and find ways to make the most of those opportunities. They tell you how to compete with others; they provide you all the market information that helps in taking the decision. Small business advisors can really make an impact here because they are involved in the market through their own business and the businesses of the other people they coach. They know the exact sources of the information. They know the perfect timing of the market when to sell, to give discount or to launch the product. As a result, they have a better understanding of the current market situation and can provide advice as to how to enter other markets, some of which you may not have thought of, such as a different geographic area or moving all or part of your business online. They also help you with issues such as effective branding, advertising, lead generation and the creation of an actual marketing plan.

Financial advice

Using a small business advisor can also benefit your bottom line. Small business advisors can help you make sure that you are investing your money in your business and yourself, in the right places and can assist you to increase your income and lower your overhead costs at the same time. They tell you the perfect combination of the finance. They have knowledge about when to purchase, when to lease, when to give credit and when to take debt. They help in better utilization of the finance. By offering advice, training and direction, a small business advisor can help make sure that you reach all your financial goals, including eventually transitioning into passive income from your business.

3.5 How can New Entrepreneurs Learn from The Experiences of Others?

Mentoring - it is a term historically used to describe a teacher-student relationship.

In the business world, a student/teacher relationship occurs when a more experienced professional (the advisor) gives significant career assistance to a less-experienced professional (the protégé). A counselor's knowledge, experience, tenacity and skills offer the growing entrepreneur guidance, advice and training. However, while an advisor can steer a protégé in the right direction to reach her potential, protégés must still rely upon themselves to succeed.

Roles and Responsibilities of advisor

- Provide guidance based on past business experiences.
- Create a positive counseling relationship and climate of open communication.
- Protect the business from the hidden risks of the market.
- Help dependent identify problems and solutions.
- Give direction to the business.
- Lead dependent through problem solving processes.
- Offer constructive criticism in a supportive way.
- Share stories, including mistakes.
- Assign "homework" if applicable.
- Develop business logic.
- Refer dependent to other business associates.
- Be honest about business expertise.
- Solicit feedback from dependent.
- Come prepared for each meeting to discuss issues

Finding an advisor that's right for you

- Look for someone who has knowledge and business experience in areas you don't.
- The mentor is friendly in nature.
- Ready to share information.
- Make sure the mentor you choose desires to be your advisor. A quality relationship requires consent by both parties.
- Look for what you can offer the person willing to invest time in you - make the relationship mutually beneficial.

Many organizations have advisor programs. Look for one in your community. Contact your local business center for more information.

Checklist: be careful about following points?

If you want an advisor for the business then go through the following points that will decide whether you are ready to take mentor or not?

- I know the kind of mentoring I want.
- I'm willing to accept help, if it is appropriate.
- I'm a good listener. I hear what the other person is saying.
- I'm a good follower.
- I do not have ego.
- I am friendly in nature.
- I love to get new information.
- I share my thoughts.
- I can be counted on to carry out commitments.
- I learn most new things quickly.
- I'd be willing to speak up (diplomatically) if I disagreed with an advisor. I'm not a "yes" person.
- I appreciate people who help me.
- I feel that my "entrepreneurship potential" is high.

Myths about the mentor/new entrepreneur (dependent) relationship

- Mentoring is going out of style.
- Advisor is the guarantee of the success.
- Getting advisor is very costly.
- It is best if the advisor is older than the entrepreneur.
- Student/teacher relationships need to be close and last a long time.
- The relationship benefits one party more than the other.
- A person cannot have more than one advisor or dependent at a time.
- Healthy mentor/dependent relationships won't run into difficulties.
- Getting an experienced advisor is the easy way of getting ahead.

SUMMARY

Important Types of Entrepreneur's Personality – the entrepreneurs have different personalities, those are Highly Motivated Entrepreneur, Protective Entrepreneur, Enthusiastic Entrepreneur,

Visionary Entrepreneur, Innovative and Creative Entrepreneur, Lazy Entrepreneur, The Social Entrepreneur, and The Wealth Creation Entrepreneur.

Highly motivated entrepreneur is an entrepreneur who is in the business because he wants to do something in the business or wants to use the business for fulfilling his personal satisfaction. The reasons for motivation behind entrepreneurship are Self achievement fulfillment, To prove his excellence in business, To influence others by his brainpower, To gain economic rewards, To reap opportunities in market, and Influence of highly successful entrepreneurs.

David McClelland is most noted for describing three types of motivational need, which he identified in his 1961 book, *The Achieving Society*:

The need for achievement (n-ach)

The n-ach person is 'achievement motivated' and therefore seeks achievement, attainment of realistic but challenging goals and advancement in the job.

The need for authority and power (n-pow)

The n-pow person is 'authority motivated'. This driver produces a need to be influential, effective and to make an impact.

The need for affiliation (n-affil)

The n-affil person is 'affiliation motivated' and has a need for friendly relationships and is motivated towards interaction with other people.

Protective Entrepreneurs do not take risk in their business. They are happy with their current situation. They do not take risk until and unless it becomes mandatory to take the risk. They are satisfied with their earnings. They want to expand their business but not by taking risk. They do not change the things easily. They are the ones who do not like change in the business.

Enthusiastic entrepreneurs are very excited to open their business. They have a dream to open the business. They have some plans to implement after opening the business. They just wait to implement the plans. Their main motive is not to earn profit but to make the dream true through business.

Visionary entrepreneurs open business because they have a vision which they want to achieve. They want to reach their business up to the level where they want to see their business and in that direction they proceed. They have a perfect direction to their business. They know their destination and keeping in mind their destination they form strategies and make plans.

For innovative entrepreneurs the main reason to open the business is to present their ideas and creativity to the world. They want to give something new to the society that can help them. They believe in innovation and therefore they open their business. They want to solve the problems of customers by their innovative products.

Lazy entrepreneurs open the business and try to run their business but they are very lazy. They do not have activeness in their work; they are not enthusiastic about their work. They take the work as a formality.

The Wealth Creation Entrepreneur - The particular individual creates a business with the ultimate goal of reaching the largest available market whilst making the highest profit. These are the guys who build businesses like Google, Microsoft, Sony, Apple, Facebook and so on.

A social entrepreneur is someone *who recognizes a social problem and uses entrepreneurial principles to organize, create and manage a venture to make social change.*

Starting and growing own business requires many skills to be successful. There are different entrepreneurs with different personalities those are The business developer, The people advisor, The organizer, Risk Takers, The creative or artist, The visionary, The systematic business analyst, Ambitious and driven, The energizer, and The leader.

Entrepreneur's Lifestyle - The entrepreneurial lifestyle is one of the major factors that drive many entrepreneurs to the decision to start their own business. It usually involves long hours, especially when starting out, but a great deal of flexibility as well. Juggling work and personal life can be a daunting challenge. A lifestyle entrepreneur is someone who goes into business for a reason other than the financial rewards of owning a business, but because of their lifestyle.

Ways to Create Success as a Lifestyle Entrepreneur - The success of a rewarding lifestyle is by far one of the greatest achievements one can attain. Lifestyle entrepreneurs strive to achieve such a success. Some ways to become a successful entrepreneur are Define your values, Define solid purpose, Create a vision, Make a plan of action, Hire support, Attain business conference, Highly interactive, and Generate passive income.

The advisor plays an important role in the life of entrepreneurs. If entrepreneurs will have such a good advisor then entrepreneurs can save themselves from many mistakes. The entrepreneurs can learn and get knowledge from the power of peers, Role of small business advisor, **Business coaching, marketing training, and financial advice.**

Mentoring - it is a term historically used to describe a teacher-student relationship. In the business world, a student/teacher relationship occurs when a more experienced professional (the advisor) gives significant career assistance to a less-experienced professional (the protégé).

Keywords

N-ach: The n-ach person is 'achievement motivated' and therefore seeks achievement, attainment of realistic but challenging goals and advancement in the job.

N-pow: The n-pow person is 'authority motivated'.

N-affil: The n-affil person is 'affiliation motivated' and has a need for friendly relationships and is motivated towards interaction with other people.

Protective entrepreneurs: They do not take risk in their business.

Enthusiastic entrepreneurs: They are very excited to open their business.

Visionary entrepreneurs: Visionary entrepreneurs open business because they have a vision which they want to achieve.

Innovative entrepreneurs: The main reason to open the business is to present their ideas and creativity to the world.

Lazy entrepreneurs: They do not have activeness in their work.

The wealth creation entrepreneurs: The particular individual creates a business with the ultimate goal of reaching the largest available market whilst making the highest profit.

Social entrepreneurs: A social entrepreneur is someone *who recognizes a social problem and uses entrepreneurial principles to organize, create and manage a venture to make social change*

Lifestyle entrepreneurs: Lifestyle entrepreneurs start businesses that they are passionate about.

Business Coach: He outlines current and potential issues but also assumes the role of teacher and trainer and provides useful information on business.

Marketing training: Marketing training to help you navigate your chosen market successfully and avoid marketing mistakes.

Mentoring: In the business world, a student/teacher relationship occurs when a more experienced professional (the advisor) gives significant career assistance to a less-experienced professional.

QUESTIONS

1. What is the importance of good entrepreneurs' personality?
2. Describe different types of entrepreneurs' personality?
3. What do you mean by 'Lifestyle entrepreneurs'?
4. What is the role of advisor in the life of entrepreneurs?

❑ ❑ ❑

Chapter – 4

Entrepreneurs' Achievement and Business Failure

LEARNING OBJECTIVES

On completion of this chapter, you should be able to:

☺ *Explain how the level of desire of achievement affects small new entrepreneurs' business.*

☺ *Describe the role of achievement in business failure.*

☺ *Describe how fear of failure affects the business of entrepreneurs.*

☺ *Describe how unhealthy self esteem creates obstacles for the entrepreneurs.*

4.1 Desire of Achievement

Entrepreneurship is a dynamic process of creating wealth whether in small organizations or large organizations. Entrepreneurship is a continuous search for change, responding to it and exploiting it as an opportunity. Most successful organizations are successful because of the entrepreneurial behaviour of their leaders and the entrepreneurial culture prevalent in the organization. The key entrepreneurial behaviours include the following:

BOX 4

Educating Students Worldwide

Junior Achievement is the world's largest organization dedicated to inspiring and preparing young people to succeed in a global economy. Through a dedicated volunteer network, Junior Achievement provides in-school and after-school programs for students which focus on three key content areas: work readiness, entrepreneurship and financial literacy. Today, 127 individual area operations reach four million students in the United States, with an additional 5.8 million students served by operations in 123 other countries worldwide.

382,637 Junior Achievement volunteers teach 403,849 classes to 9,866,143students a year. That's 27,030 students a day and nearly 1,126 students every hour who become empowered to own their economic success!

Junior Achievement is a partnership between the business community, educators and volunteers — all working together to inspire young people to dream big and reach their potential. JA's hands-on, experiential programs teach the key concepts of work readiness, entrepreneurship and financial literacy to young people all over the world.

Source: *Information received from "Junior Achievement Website".*

The desire to win and succeed coupled with vision

Entrepreneurs want to succeed. They are goal-oriented and focus their attention and energy on the achievement of specific goals. Many business people go to business without clear goals and therefore they fail to succeed as entrepreneurs. In her book, *Change Masters*, Rosabeth Moss Kanter (1993) cites visionaries who led companies out of problems. She cites cases of General Electrics, IBM, as institutions where the entrepreneurial spirit either made or unmade these giant companies. Steve Jobs, the founder of Apple Computer, founded the computer at the age of 21 (Michael Hammer, 1994). Prahalad and Gamel, (1994) talk of successful companies that rest on the creativity of visionaries whose entrepreneurial spirit led to the success of various companies. Kinyanjui (1993) in her study found that market opportunity. Desire for independence and income generation constituted over 60 percent of reasons why small enterprises were formed in Kenya. These are typical entrepreneurial characteristics.

Entrepreneurship therefore has been a leading factor in the success of many businesses both large and small

The small scale enterprises are much more numerous than the large ones and the tendency has been to believe that they are automatically entrepreneurial. However this is not the case as the growth of these businesses would have been taken for granted. Small businesses are established for various reasons. Some are income (Elkan, 1988), others to grow big (McCory, 1956) and others are forced (Kinyanjui, 1993). Not all these are entrepreneurial characteristics. This is a limitation for small business success.

BOX 4a

New National Poll: Risk and Failure Top Deterrents for Aspiring Teen Entrepreneurs

A new Junior Achievement survey in USA found that more than half of teen respondents (51 percent) would like to own their own business someday. However, in the face of a prolonged economic recovery, many teens fear the risk of starting a business venture. Of those polled, 74 percent identified risk (39 percent) and failure (35 percent) as the biggest discouragements from starting their own business, compared to 56 percent who cited lack of money to fund their ideas. The Junior Achievement 2010 Teens and Entrepreneurship Survey was sponsored by Sam's Club.

***Source:** Information received from "Sam's Club Website", Sam's Club is a division of Wal-Mart Stores, Inc.*

A need for achievement

Related to the need to win is the need to achieve. McClelland (1961) argues that successful entrepreneurs are characterized by a strong need for achievement and that drives them to achieve. This drive makes them creative and enables them to take risks. What else does a business require? Goals to achieve, the desire to achieve them, the intensity of purpose and the drive to do what it takes to achieve the goal.

They love change

Entrepreneurship is a continuous search for change and a continuous exploitation of the change as an opportunity (Drucker, 1993). Entrepreneurs are thrilled by anything knew and frustrated by a slackness of things. In today's changing environment, with ups and downs that characterize the business environment, the only organisation sure to survive is the one that is entrepreneurial (Kanter, 1993). The one that loves change. There is evidence that the success of Microsoft, Toyota, British Airways, is a result of their ability to cause change themselves. And the failure of many companies is a result of their inability to keep up with the change (Kanter, 1993).

They are the creative type

Creativity is the generation of ideas and precedes innovation. Innovation is a specific function of an entrepreneur (Drucker, 1993). Innovation is something new or different. To be able to adjust to change or manage change, business must continuously come up with new ideas, new products and new processes. These can only come from creative people. The Entrepreneurs, come with ideas as a result of changing needs and changing environmental factors and translate these ideas to create wealth.

Risk taking

While entrepreneurs are not high risk takers, (Hisrich, 1992) they do take risks. And risk is the source of reward. Business reward. Entrepreneurs take risks and succeed. Risk involves looking into the future and believing that there is a probability of the occurrence of certain events. And on this basis a decision is taken to do or not to do something.

In several studies that have been undertaken (Sewannyana, 1997; Mutazindwa, 1997), there has been evidence that there is a relationship between entrepreneurship behaviour and business growth. Mutazindwa (1997) surveyed over 100 small scale enterprises in different areas of business, metal, textile, trade, carpentry and motor repair and established that there was a relationship between entrepreneurship and business growth. Amongst the key entrepreneurship behaviour patters, she noted a positive relationship between successful enterprises and vision, risk taking and the need for achievement. She came to the conclusion that entrepreneurship behaviour existed amongst successful companies but also further that it was not a panacea for business success. Sewannyana (1997) in his study finds that amongst the small proprietors, who were the subject of his study, the entrepreneurship behaviour is exhibited in the majority of proprietors. Unlike earlier thinking, he comes to the conclusion that the poor performance of small business is attributed to factors other than entrepreneurship mainly bad financial management.

These findings tend to conclude that entrepreneurial behaviour exists in many small firms but despite that they are not successful. Further research in this area is necessary.

4.2 Role of Achievement in Business Failure

No involvement

Most of the entrepreneurs do business but they do not run the business from their heart. They run the business and earn normal profit. The entrepreneurs should involve themselves into the business. Many entrepreneurs never involve to them completely in the business. The success will come whenever they will take business seriously and give their full efforts to the business. The entrepreneurs who do not involve themselves to the business, they lack setting the targets. They do not see the business as an achievement. They do not have any goals in the business. So such entrepreneurs have very less chances of success in the business because they do not want to achieve anything in their business.

No excitement

Some entrepreneurs are never excited by their business. They are the dull people. They have no enthusiasm about the business. They never think more about the business. How business will progress? How money will come? What can we do for the business? They take effort to run the business but that is not enough for the business. The excitement of the entrepreneurs will take them high in their business. The excited entrepreneurs always think to do for the business. They want to bring new innovative things in the business that will provide benefits to business. If the entrepreneurs do not have the excitement about their business then they will never be able to do something unique about the business, they will never think of new strategy or techniques for the business and ultimately they remain static about their business or fail in the business.

Take it as a formality

When the entrepreneurs start taking their business as a formality then they have more probability to fail in the business. The main problem of the small new entrepreneurs is that they never think of any scope of the business. They just earn money and run the business. They never think of increasing the customers, selling more products, decreasing the cost etc. Business runs until and unless customers by themselves come but once competition will increase then they may fail into their business.

No goal setting

The entrepreneurs who lack need of achievement and do business. They lack in setting the business goals. They never set proper goals for the business. Even if they set the goals they never take efforts to achieve the targets. They run their business in a normal way. They do not have any excitement and zeal to run the business. They do not have any mission in the business.

Thinking inside the Box

Entrepreneurs are famous for having great ideas. That's what they do—think up brilliant business ideas. The problem for many entrepreneurs is that they never think of any new idea for their business which will benefit the business and help in growing the business. They can only think of ordinary ways to carry it out. If you want to build a business beyond the idea state, "a vision of extraordinary possibility" is needed.

Can't let go of control

Because many entrepreneurs are so attached to the ideas they come up with, many of them insist on controlling every single aspect of the business building process. While the ideal scenario for an entrepreneur is to do the least amount of work possible while still achieving the highest level of results, they often have problems letting go and letting other people make some of the decisions.

Delegate the responsibility

The entrepreneurs never delegate the responsibilities rather they delegate the tasks. But some entrepreneurs never do their work by their own. They just try to protect them from the work. They are not ready to take the efforts. They give burden to employees. They just want to supervise the business but they forget that it is their business if they will not work for their own business then who will work. Such kind of entrepreneurs have all the set ups but they lack in taking the efforts because they do not have any idea about the achievements. They put their task, responsibilities and burden to the employees and make them free from any kind of burden. When the entrepreneurs behave like this then the chances of failure increase.

Inappropriate relationships

It has been proven that people who grew up in dysfunctional families often replicate those dysfunctional relationships in the workplace. These dysfunctional relationships are one of the major reasons that many entrepreneurs fail to take their brilliant ideas any further than the idea stage. Unhealthy relationships with the people in their business support network (employees, clients, business partners) keep them from moving forward.

If you find that you are having trouble in building a successful business venture from your brilliant idea, it is quite possible that you have fallen into dilemmas that cause your business to stagnate.

4.3 The Achievement Motive

Harvard psychologist David McClelland's studies point out the achievement motive as possibly the single largest factor in the success of an entrepreneur. People with a high need for achievement are characterized by the desire to do something better, faster, more efficiently and with less effort. More importantly, they are moderate risk takers with a need for constant feedback on performance. These individuals prefer working on moderately difficult tasks in which the probability of success is between 30 per cent and 50 per cent (McClelland). They show great persistence when failing at moderately difficult tasks and low persistence with high difficulty tasks. This combination of characteristics uniquely suits the high achievement-oriented individual, to entrepreneurial activity.

The High achievement-oriented individual is usually successful at entrepreneurial start-up and generally makes quite a lot of money (money for him is a means of keeping score - a performance feedback). However, this individual is often unable to expand further because he finds it difficult to delegate and to motivate people under him. Start-up firms need a high achievement-oriented founder. But as the business grows, ironically, the same qualities that made him a successful entrepreneur now contribute to his downfall. He finds it difficult to expand the business. He may start subsidiaries or new ventures; but because of his difficulties in delegation, these usually lose money and have to be shut down, creating a drain on the resources of the parent company - perhaps leading to the closure of that company. The achievement-oriented individual has to learn to delegate and to let go of controls.

4.4 Fear of Failure

People with a high fear of failure tend to have low achievement motivation. These people have very often had negative reinforcement in childhood. Parents typically punished (verbally or physically) for failure and were neutral for success, thus leading to high test or competition anxiety in the child. In contrast the parents of those with high achievement drives (and low test anxiety), rewarded success and were neutral for failure.

Parents of those with fear of failure typically set higher standards of achievement for their children and at the same time took a less than favourable view of their ability to achieve those standards than other parents. In effect saying "you must do better but I don't think you can". Typically these people then adopt internalized, unrealistic standards or they compete internally with unreachable goals all the time. They then expect failure and therefore avoid beginning anything so as to avoid the negative feelings accompanying the expected failure.

The characteristics of the person with high fear of failure are, in most cases, the opposite of the person with high achievement motivation. They tend to attempt either very difficult task - so that if they fail, it is no reflection on themselves or very easy tasks where failure is virtually impossible. They avoid the tasks of moderate difficulty that the achievement oriented people focus on.

4.5 The Fear of Success

Also called the Macbeth complex, individuals with this complex experience guilt whenever they achieve success or come close to it. As a result of this feeling of guilt, they have an urge to undo or to reverse the behaviour that led to the success.

Collins, Moore and Unwalla in their book *'The Enterprising Man'* suggest that most entrepreneurs characteristically have unresolved conflicts with their fathers. According to them, most entrepreneurs have a combination of an emotionally close and rewarding mother and an absent or distant and passive father. The child feels that he has 'won' his mother's love through his own achievement and has therefore displaced his father. This sometimes brings on strong guilt feelings in the boy, causing him to fear revenge from the father.

Success on the job may then bring about anxiety produced by the subconscious fear of the father's revenge. To avoid this anxiety and to assuage guilt when successful, the person seeks punishment and often brings about his own failure. Financial losses lead to relief from this anxiety and produce magnificent behaviour in the face of reversals. Such an individual's career is often marked by a series of ups and downs. A frequent pattern is his striving hard to achieve a goal, but just as the goal is within reach, the person sabotages himself. His inability to tolerate success brings on deficient behaviour.

One entrepreneur – the one discussed earlier who left his father's company to start his own business, has clear unresolved issues with his father. Although a person of considerable ability, he has twice failed when success was within reach. Both times, just when it seemed that nothing could stop him, he made blunders that produced great losses. In the face of these financial losses he behaves magnificently, covering all his creditors who continue to have faith in him. However, to capitalize on his own ability and to justify his creditors' faith in him, he has to first acknowledge and then resolve these subconscious, self-defeating impulses. He chooses to sabotage himself because of his inability to deal with success - for that might mean displacing his father.

Both fear of success and fear of failure are causes of self-inflicted failure. Coping with these, as with most inner conflicts, requires primarily, a self-awareness or insight. Insights - real, genuine glimpses of who we really are and why we behave in the ways we do, are reached only with difficulty and sometimes with real psychic pain.

As Carl Rogers, the famed psychologist says in *'Encounter Groups'*, "...we expect the (awareness) process to be painful if it leads towards growth – in fact, believe all growth is turbulent and disturbing as well as satisfying". Insights, although painful, are the building blocks of growth. Only when we are aware of what holds us back can we do something about overcoming those restrictions.

In general, the fear of failure manifests in starting difficulties - beginning something. People with fear of failure tend to postpone, put off or otherwise avoid doing something until it reaches crisis proportions and then do too little, too late. Fear of success manifests in ending difficulties. These people start strong and pick up strength as they go along and then near the end, just when success is around the corner, make unpressurised, impulsive decisions that negate all the earlier hard work. Your pattern of behaviour can tell you whether you have both of these 'fears' and to what extent.

4.6 Conquering the Internal Factors

Enhancement of the achievement motive seems to reduce the fear of failure as well as internalize the locus of control (attribution of success and failure). Most workshops on entrepreneurial development are generally aimed at enhancing the achievement motive.

If it is not possible to attend one of these workshops, one can often enhance the achievement motive by reducing the fear of failure. This can be done by first understanding that the root of the problem lies in the negative feelings associated with failure. This fear may be diminished by reacting to small, daily failures either neutrally or as if it was normal under the circumstances; and more importantly, persisting in the face of these failures - especially when failing at tasks that 'anybody' can do.

Secondly, most people with fear of failure seem unable to break down a task. They see only the whole task and get intimidated by it. For instance, if one plans a target or is required to do something - say make 50 sales calls, the fear of failure individual typically sees the figure 50, gets intimidated and procrastinates, waiting for a 'suitable' time when he can complete this figure. The achievement oriented individual on the other hand, breaks this down into; say five sets of ten calls each - a much more realistic and reasonable target - and goes about achieving those ten calls.

The fear of failure individual seems unable to break down the task into bite-sized chunks. The difficulty is really one of perception. The fear of failure individual perceives in terms of all or nothing and very often ends up doing nothing. He needs to learn to break down a large task into smaller do-able tasks and succeed at those tasks. The feelings of success, associated with these small do-able wins, go a long way towards enabling completion of the larger task. The greater the number of tasks he completes successfully, the lower his fear of failure becomes.

Thirdly, failure may not be something to fear if we are doing something we like - something we know we are good at - as when we make our hobby/interest our career.

Internal factors contributing to failure have to be tackled on the interest plane. With self awareness and insight, one can overcome these limiting factors.

4.7 Characteristics of A Detrimental Self Esteem People

Living unconsciously

The living style of the entrepreneurs has a great impact on the business. If the entrepreneurs live unconsciously that means they do not have any purpose of their life. They just live, eat and sleep. If such people become entrepreneur and run their business then they also behave same with their business. They forgot that their business needs objectives, goals and targets. They treat the business same as they treat to themselves and because of that they never run their business successfully. To run the business requires some goals but if the business will run in random, then the problem starts.

Not learning from mistakes

Most of the entrepreneurs do not take any learning from the mistakes. The achievement motivated entrepreneurs always try to learn from the mistakes so that whatever they want to achieve can achieve that without repeating the mistakes. But when the entrepreneurs do not have need of achievement then they neglect the mistakes because they do not have any achievement, the mistakes only impact on the earning but as soon as they get small success in the business they forgot about the mistakes they have done in the business. So, for success of the business it is very necessary for the entrepreneurs that they should think about the achievements in the business, that give direction, the zeal to get the goal and motivate the persons to achieve their goals. Otherwise they cannot take their business to the heights where everyone wants to take their business and therefore your business will struggle to survive.

No influence of peers

Some entrepreneurs are not influenced by the achievements of the others. They even do not listen to others. They do what they think. They are reluctant to take advice. They do not believe in following others. They are comfortable with the current situation. They do not bother whether they are selling the same amounts / volumes for many years. They do not want to take any steps. They are very rigid about their behaviour. So such behavior does not allow them to do any new in the business or to follow the foot prints of success of the others.

No sense of purpose, a direction in life

Most of the entrepreneurs are not aware about the purpose of the business. They think that their business is all about just to earn the money. They open business and that's all. Just opening the business is their achievement. They never think beyond. They never think about the purpose or giving direction to the business. Such kind of attitude does not move them forward and that is dangerous for the business.

Do not care about other's point of view

The entrepreneurs who lack achievement never listen to others. The purpose is easy to understand they do not want to do anything special in their life. They take things causally. They do not have any dream to follow. They are happy with their current position. They do not want to move forward. They are not ready to take the others important ideas, clues or points. Therefore the chances of failure of business increase.

Don't value other people differences

The low achievement people think about others in the same way they think about them. They do not think about others qualities, values or importance. They see equally to others. These things restrict them to gain knowledge from others, to interact with others because they are not the hopeful persons. They do not think that they can get something from others what they can implement in their business and can get benefits. We are all different. Respecting other people's differences doesn't mean to agree with them, is to understand that they have the right to be different and deserve respect as human beings. We should learn from others.

Do not understand the importance of the work

Such kind of people do not have any concrete reason. Their participation is just the formality. They do not set any target to achieve. They have very less importance for competition, business success or growing the business. They are the dull one and when any person does not have desire then it becomes difficult for them to grow, to improve or to become success. They lack motivation and achievement. If you want to do business then with this nature you are just wasting the time and money. Business wants creative, innovative, mentally strong, and energetic persons.

4.8 Typical Traits

Typical positive and negative personal character traits with respect to a challenge in achieving a goal or performing a task are:

Table 4.1: Entrepreneurs, Traits

	Attitude	
Challenge	*Positive trait*	*Negative trait*
Danger	Courage	Cowardice
Importance	Careful	Careless
Difficulty	Determined	Depressed
Abilities	Confident	Unsure
Effort	Hard working	Lazy

Measuring entrepreneurship achievements

There should be measurement of the entrepreneurship to know about the achievement of the entrepreneurs. These measurement attempts can range from simple checklists through to complex and detailed computer programmes. This need for a definition and measure of entrepreneurship because, however defined, the entrepreneur is the key to the successful launch of any business. By doing this, the level of the entrepreneurs will be identified. Their achievements will be discovered. For example if the entrepreneur is doing the business for last few years then with the help of measurement the progress of the business will be identified. The achievement of the business may be anything. It is not necessary that the achievement of the entrepreneurs should be the big one it may be the smallest one also depending upon the personality of the different entrepreneurs.

He or she is the person who perceives market opportunity and then has the motivation, drive and ability to mobilize resources to meet it. The major characteristics of entrepreneurs that have been listed by many commentators include the following:

- Self confident and multi-skilled. The person who can 'make the product, market it and count the money, but above all they have the confidence that lets them move comfortably through unchartered waters'.
- Confident in the face of difficulties and discouraging circumstances.
- Innovative skills. Not an 'inventor' in the traditional sense but one who is able to carve out a new niche in the market place, often invisible to others.
- Results-orientated. To make the business successful requires the drive that only comes from setting goals and targets and getting pleasure from achieving them.
- A risk-taker. To succeed means taking measured risks. Often the successful entrepreneur exhibits an incremental approach to risk taking, at each stage exposing him/herself to only a limited, measured amount of personal risk and moving from one stage to another as each decision is proved.
- Total commitment. Hard work, energy and single-mindedness are essential elements in the entrepreneurial profile.

4.9 Personality of Low Self Esteem

- These are the tendency to have thoughts and feelings that are negative.
- To be afraid to make mistakes.
- Constant dissatisfaction and frustration.
- The tendency to be suspicious and defensive.
- Lack of boundaries and assertiveness, because of fear of abandonment.
- Fear of change, evasive and lack of communication.
- Feel and act like a powerless.
- Do not try to change the life.
- Do not follow deadline.
- Break agreements, violate own standards. They don't believe in themselves.
- Exaggerate, pretend and lie because of their insecurity.
- Lack of seriousness.
- Fear of rejection is an irrational fear of not being accepted for who you are. It is cause by lacking confidence and esteem.
- Tendency towards negative attitude and pessimism.
- Rationalize to justify fear of change.
- Perfectionist, fear of failure and afraid to make mistakes.
- Dependencies to others.
- Not liking the work one does.
- Leave tasks and relationships unfinished, lack of intimacy in relationships.
- Judge worth by comparing, feel inferior.
- Doesn't accept or give compliments.
- Excessive worry and anxiety. Those who suffer from low self esteem experience fear and anxiety. They are extremely anxious and lack confidence. The difference between fear and anxiety is that with fear, you can identify the source of your emotion whereas with anxiety the source is unidentifiable.
- Irrational responses, ruled by emotions.

- Lack of purpose in life, no direction, confusion.
- Break promises.
- Feeling inadequate to handle new situations because of insecurity and perfectionism.
- Vulnerable to others' opinion, comment and attitudes. People pleasing and looking for constant approval.

4.10 Right Traits for Achievement

- Self Command To turn on a day when it begins.
- Self Discipline To turn it off when it ends.
- Courage to accept a challenge.
- True Grit to preserve.
- Determination to what others think is impossible.
- Admiration of the good wherever it is found.
- Will to change what should not be accepted.
- Adjustment to accept that which cannot be changed.
- Knowledge of self and honest to face it.
- Friendliness.
- Gentleness that beckons a child to turn after you.
- The Joy that comes from glass of cold water, a delicious meal and a Good bed.

4.11 The Reasons for Failure

A few recurring reasons for failure are:

- Poor interpersonal skills
- Wrong person in the wrong job / business
- Fear of failure
- Plain bad luck
- Fear of success
- Poor focus/ concentration
- Poor management efficiency,
- Poor product /services
- Lack of planning and foresight
- Unrealistic assessment of the market
- Inadequate capitalization
- Leadership/ managerial inexperience
- Poor delegation - either over delegation or under delegation

Summary

Entrepreneurship is a continuous search for change, responding to it and exploiting it as an opportunity. Most successful organizations are successful because of the entrepreneurial behaviour of their leaders and the entrepreneurial culture prevalent in the organization. The key entrepreneurial behaviours include the desire to win and succeed coupled with vision, a need for achievement, they love change, they are the creative type, and Risk taking.

Role of Achievement in Business Failure – if there is no desire of achievement then entrepreneurs suffer from No involvement in business, No excitement, Take it as a formality, No goal setting, Thinking inside the Box, Can't let go of control, Delegate the responsibility and Inappropriate relationships.

Harvard psychologist David McClelland's studies point out the achievement motive as possibly the single largest factor in the success of an entrepreneur. People with a high need for achievement are characterized by the desire to do something better, faster, more efficiently and with less effort.

People with a high fear of failure tend to have low achievement motivation. These people have very often had negative reinforcement in childhood. Parents typically punished (verbally or physically) for failure and were neutral for success, thus leading to high test or competition anxiety in the child. In contrast the parents of those with high achievement drives (and low test anxiety), rewarded success and were neutral for failure.

Enhancement of the achievement motive seems to reduce the fear of failure as well as internalize the locus of control (attribution of success and failure). Most workshops on entrepreneurial development are generally aimed at enhancing the achievement motive. If it is not possible to attend one of these workshops, one can often enhance the achievement motive by reducing the fear of failure. This can be done by first understanding that the root of the problem lies in the negative feelings associated with failure.

Characteristics of a Detrimental Self Esteem People are living unconsciously, not learning from mistakes, No influence of peers, No sense of purpose, a direction in life, do not care about other's point of view, don't value other people differences, and do not understand the importance of the work.

Keywords

Creativity: It is the generation of ideas and precedes innovation.

Innovation: It is something new or different.

A need for achievement: It means, the need to win is the need to achieve.

Measurement of the entrepreneurship: It means to know about the achievement of the entrepreneurs.

Low Self Esteem: These are the tendency to have thoughts and feelings that are negative.

Questions

1. Describe the role of achievement in business failure and success?
2. What do you mean by fear of failure and fear of success?
3. What are the characteristics of a detrimental self esteem people?
4. What are the characteristics of low self esteem personality?
5. What are the right traits for achievement?

❑ ❑ ❑

CHAPTER – 5

ENTREPRENEURS' MOTIVATION

LEARNING OBJECTIVES

On completion of this chapter, you should be able to:

☺ *Explain how low motivation hampers the new small entrepreneurs in overcoming obstacles.*

☺ *Describe the factors responsible for motivation*

☺ *Describe support system for the entrepreneurs.*

☺ *Describe entrepreneurs association.*

5.1 Motivation for Overcoming Obstacles

Most of the entrepreneurs fail in the early stage of their business. There are many reasons for their failure. Some of them try again and run their business. They try to find out the problems and then try to eliminate those problems. Many entrepreneurs who fail in their business but do not stand on their feet but instead of that they give up. There are two reasons for that the first is those entrepreneurs who after failure in the business do not try the business again. They do not want to go ahead with their business rather they do some other work. But there are some entrepreneurs who fail in the business and want to run the business again but they do not get another chance to run the business after failure.

BOX 5

Inspiring TYEcoons: TiE Young Entrepreneurs Program

TiE Young Entrepreneurs (TYE) Global Program coaches and trains young high school students to become the next generation of entrepreneurs. The unique program helps high school children learn about the challenges and rewards of becoming an entrepreneur. Seasoned entrepreneurs and mentors teach high school children (grades 9-12) based on a business-focused curriculum. The TYE program nurtures the creativity, self-confidence, leadership and overall development of the students. The program culminates with global Business Plan Competition for the youth. From this year, the final global competition will involve 3 continents and engage 9 TiE Chapters on April 30th at Raleigh, North Carolina. The program is held in 9 cities around the world – Atlanta, Boston, Carolinas, Seattle, San Diego and Austin, London, Delhi and Jaipur.

Source: *Information received from "TiE Global", 2011.*

There are many reasons for that, those are as follows:

Do not get money again

For the new entrepreneurs who start their business by all efforts and fail in their business they do not get second chance to get money. For the new small entrepreneurs, it is very difficult to gain money again and start the business again. Even if they try to correct their business they cannot because it will require money which they cannot collect. So instead of trying again they leave the business.

The other entrepreneurs run their business but at that time they do not have sufficient money and resources. They run their business not to run the business but to get money invested in the previous business.

In such situation the entrepreneurs give up. Though they have the qualities for becoming entrepreneurs but they do not get second chance.

Family discouragement

After failure in the business the family does not motivate them to continue with the business. Family lost their trust on business; they pressurize the entrepreneurs not to follow the business. The entrepreneurs do not have option other than to leave the business because the small entrepreneurs have great responsibility of their family too. They cannot continue experiment with their business where they gain huge losses. So for the family interest they are not motivated again for the business unless they have sufficient money to come back.

BOX 5A

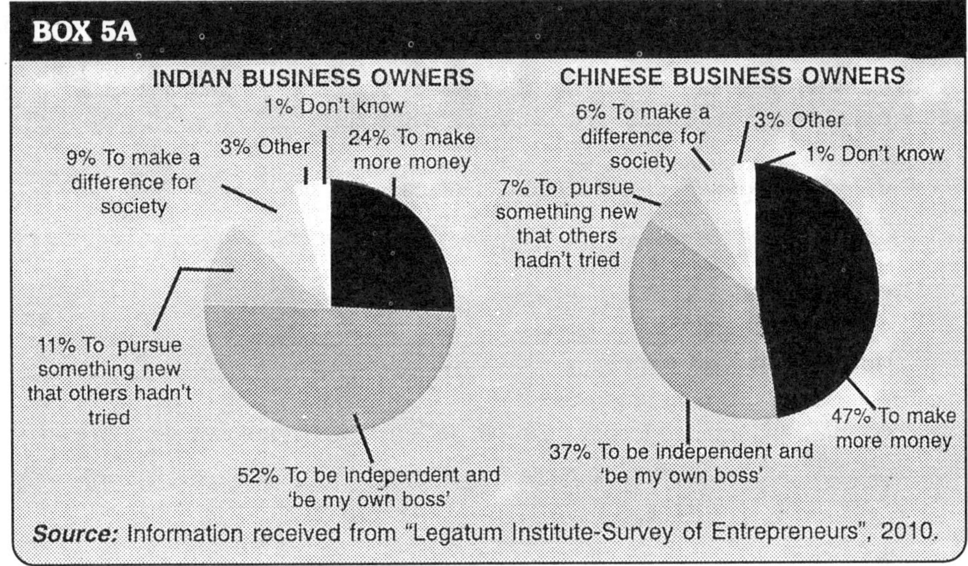

Source: Information received from "Legatum Institute-Survey of Entrepreneurs", 2010.

Pressure for the return/repayment of the bank's loan

The entrepreneurs who fail in their business face two problems as far as loan is concerned. The first is that they have a pressure of returning the loan taken from the bank. After failing they have only one thing in mind that is to return the loan to the bank as soon as possible. This thing diverts the focus of the entrepreneurs from the business. The second is they are not at all trusted by any other financial institutes, even if they want to come back into the business but the others are not ready to show trust on them. They already face many difficulties to get loan but after failing in the business, the chances become rare.

5.2 Factors of Motivation

The driving force: what motivates Indian entrepreneurs?

Motivator

- **Rewards of entrepreneurship**
  - Autonomy
  - Making money/financial independence
  - Saw business opportunity/impact on industry
  - Recognition of self and/or organization
  - Desire to create something new/innovate
  - Build something important/make a difference
  - Grow a business from scratch
  - Desire to be entrepreneur/excitement of entrepreneurship

- **Personal qualities**
  - Intellectual challenge/achieve potential
  - Character
  - Others
- **Career**
  - Career growth/diversification/satisfaction
  - Others
- **Experience**
  - Utilize previous experience
  - Had technology/industry vision
- **Non-monetary factors**
  - Help India in various ways
  - Non-monetary success/personal satisfaction, Create value/jobs/wealth in society

5.3 Entrepreneurship and Self Motivation

Motivation is set of processes that determine individual choices. These processes are influenced from families and friends and the role model that they receive throughout their life. They try to become the same what they see in their role model. This thing motivates them a lot. When speaking with business owners it is clear that they are self-motivated and determined to succeed. How did they reach this point and maybe you have not? It is the result of the interaction of your internalized needs and the external influences you receive.

Past experience influences our thinking. Most people who plan to be entrepreneurs have developed a physiological or psychological need. The person then develops a set of behaviors to satisfy this need. The behavior then results in action towards the goal. At some point in their life, they have been exposed to positive self esteem types of people. They appreciate and can accomplish hard work through employment.

Maslow's Hierarchy of Needs determines that people seek safety and security. This carries over to employment issues. Many people seek positions as employees that will provide long term opportunity with minimal change. What happens when you want to step out of this plan? Anxiety in Excess! Why? You realize that you need to re-train your own thinking process. You are clearly out of your personal comfort zone. You find that you will need a different type of effort to execute successful performance. You realize that there is no one to fall back upon. It comes down to how you operate dealing with all aspects of your own business.

Entrepreneurial motivation, how do you really find it?

Entrepreneurial Motivation can be more difficult to find than your good old fashioned 'motivation' on its own, because most of the time it's a kind of motivation that needs to really be thought about and planned. Which motivational factors influence people's decisions when quitting their jobs; and how these reasons can be used as entrepreneurial motivation for the long haul?

Want to make a name for yourself

A lot of people who ultimately decide to leave the workplace and go off to begin their entrepreneurial endeavors, are fueled by a passion for some kind of celebrity status or authority figure, in a particular field or niche. They want to earn the fame. They want the people should know them for their work. And because of that they quit the job. They want to show the people who they are? How much talent they have? They want to show their expertise to the people. This is especially true when it comes to all the social media sites and applications which are being released daily; you can constantly be marketing yourself.

Want to start a business of your own

People quit their job because they want to be their own boss and start their own business. They dislike to work under any boss. They have their own ideas, their planning and they want to do all by their own way. They are very hopeful about their work. This is their motivation and it can be quite powerful. Owning a business can be a double edged sword; there are so many examples of people try and fail and in business it happens a lot. They want to start the business because they are very much confident about their business. Successful business can be summed up in a couple of words, including that of planning, implementing, analyzing and optimizing; in addition to this: your service or product should be top mark and high quality. A business will only be great if you have a distinct passion for what you're doing. Passion breeds creativity and creativity breeds ideas; most of the time – ideas breed better business.

Want to escape from the workspace

Most of the people do not like the nature of their boss. They become sad; they do not want to be with your boss anymore. They are tired of their boss screaming at them. Frustrated with the workspace in which they spend most of their day, they feel that they can do something more rewarding more excited? All of these questions above are examples of great, long term motivational goals which they use to motivate themselves to continue developing a business model and implementing it. If you have a sound business strategy with a solid foundation, your business is likely to succeed, every time you feel discouraged; just remember you could be chasing trains and catching buses.

Bring professional attitude in you

One thing you need to understand is that there will always be highs and lows...it's only natural. Stress, pressure, money and time constraints may eventually affect you. It is the part of business. Every entrepreneur faces these challenges. The most important message to remember is not to give up into these short term demoralizers; you can and you will get over them. You should continuously learn from your business failures. Those failures teach you a lot. You should take those failures positively. You just think of your goal in life. What you want to do in the business. Think long term, think about the bigger picture and motivate yourself by recalling what you were and envisioning what you will eventually become.

This is where the professional attitude comes in. In everything you do, you should aim for maximized efficiency and productivity; you should have a perfect way of doing the things. You should try the standard processes or methods to accomplish the tasks. If you have a construction crew carrying out work, ensure they know the deadline and that work being executed daily meets quality and standards as well as maintaining and sticking to a rigorous work schedule.

What are the challenges facing entrepreneurs?

- An entrepreneur should lead the business by showing leadership.
- Constantly changing environments demand quick response.
- During times of crisis, an entrepreneur must commit themselves to see their decisions through to the end.
- There is no time limit for an entrepreneur. They have to work for 24 hours.
- Development of the new methods, processes and products to be competitive in the market.

How can you become a better entrepreneur?

- Know yourself before attempting to lead others.
- Your personal philosophy will influence your behaviors.
- Prepare to think situational.
- You must lead by example.
- Allow for team building. A great team can accomplish much more than any individual.
- You must be comfortable using different styles according to the variables at hand.
- Adopt a constant self improvement philosophy.
- Do whatever it takes, whatever is necessary.
- Retain strong customer focus.
- Invest for the long-term.
- Invest in quality.
- Be hands-on.
- Multi-tasking is important.
- The need for the ability to tolerate ambiguity.
- Share profits with employees.
- Government's relative no involvement in the high tech industry is a blessing.

5.4 Why an Entrepreneur Gets Motivated?

Entrepreneur motivation

The entrepreneurs are motivated primarily by the desire to create something new, the desire for autonomy, wealth and financial independence, the achievement of personal objectives and the propensity for action ('doing'). The excitement of entrepreneurship was another major motivator — this was nicely captured by one comment: "We are not sure what's coming down the curve but it is a thrill." Importantly, most entrepreneurs stressed that the objective was never money for its own sake.

They wanted to leave a legacy in the form of a profitable long-lasting business.

Complete autonomy

This is one of the factors that motivate the entrepreneurs for doing entrepreneurship. The people do not want to work under any influence. They want to design their own strategy, their plans and want to work on that. They have their wonderful ideas; they have their own way of doing work. They like autonomy because they are complete by themselves, they rarely need any help to accomplish their task. These things motivate them to become entrepreneurs. They want to implement their own intelligence. They have knowledge and they want to use it in the business. They are very much sure about the positive outcome of the business.

Making money/financial independence

Most of the people want to become entrepreneurs because they want to earn more money. They see the entrepreneurship as a way to earn the money. They are aware about the opportunities in the business. They want to reap those opportunities in the form of money. Most of the entrepreneurs have same objective of doing the business. They want to become financially independent. They cannot earn such huge money from their job so they decide to come into the business so that they can enjoy money by doing business.

Saw business opportunity/impact on industry

People are attracted towards business because they have seen the opportunities in the business. They want to take the advantages of those opportunities. Their prime motto is to take the advantages of the opportunity and the second motto is to earn the money. For example most of the people get attracted towards opening net café as they have seen that it is the need of the people and second thing most of the café remain crowded. They take this as an opportunity to open their own net café to reap the opportunity and they also become successful because they have the complete information about those opportunities.

Self recognition

These type of people are very talented and intelligent. They try to open the business because they want to prove themselves. They want to open the business because they want to show their expertise to the world. They work for their own only. They do all that because they want to satisfy themselves and they choose a way of business to show their talent. They have a confidence and cleverness; they mold the things according to their way. Their primary motto is self satisfaction and self recognition.

Desire to create something new/innovate

The main objective of the entrepreneurs is to bring something new in the market that may be new processes, methods or technology. The entrepreneurs are known for their uniqueness. Most of the people want to open the business because they want to give new product or service for the welfare of the society. They think differently from others, they generate need by their innovation. For example, Sony an electronic products manufacturing company is known for their innovation. They always bring new products in the market. For example walkman, i-pod etc., are the products of the company that have created the market. The people who have a desire to do something new or who have an excellence to think the situation differently or in some innovative way, these things motivate them to open their business.

Build something important/make a difference

Some want to create the difference in the market by their own way. The difference may be in the form of price, quality, volume, services etc. They are capable of differentiating themselves from others. They have the idea about how they can be different from others. For example during 'Power cut', for everyone it is not possible to have the charge tube, so they take the help of either candle or kerosene lamp to get light. These are important stuff for common people to get light in dark. Now in such case the entrepreneurs come up with the small lamps that work with batteries. This has helped a lot to the common people who cannot purchase the costly lamp. It has created the demand and people suddenly take those lamps. So by doing this, they create their value as well as bring the important product or service in the market that is needed by the customers.

Desire to be entrepreneur/excitement of entrepreneurship

Most of the people become entrepreneurs because they want to become entrepreneur. They like to become an entrepreneur. They like the excitement of the entrepreneurship. They like challenges and want to overcome those challenges. They want to live the life of entrepreneur.

5.5 Support Systems for an Entrepreneur

It has been seen that the new entrepreneurs who have got support of someone in their business have become more successful than others. The entrepreneur does not need to worry much as the new entrepreneur without any support worry. An entrepreneur with support of others solves the problems more quickly and easily, though both types of entrepreneurs put their efforts for the success of business. But some entrepreneurs who get support, the chances of their business success increases. It is not necessary that the new entrepreneur who will get support will definitely get success in the business and it is also not necessary that the entrepreneur who will not get the support will fail in the business. But an entrepreneur who gets support the probability of success increases. Now it is up to the new entrepreneurs how they convert the support system into success. For example, in the real life two entrepreneurs have started their career with the same level but one gets the support of shop from their supporter and other did not get. The one who has got the support of free shop from their supporter has gained success easily than the other entrepreneur because the other entrepreneur was facing the problem of getting shop for their business but the first one has solved the problem because of their supporter. Having a supporter and not having the supporter impact on the performance of the entrepreneurs. Indian entrepreneurs rely on friends and family for help in starting the business, with the quality of help from friends, former co-workers and university mates in the startup and management stages being rated the best.

Assistance in terms of manpower was mainly from former co-workers. Help in marketing and access to markets was mainly from friends, former co-workers and university mates. Finance was obtained from relatives and friends but not from former co-workers.

5.6 Success Attributions

Entrepreneurs judge their success not only on the basis of business parameters like revenues, profits, growth and business reputation and monetary rewards, but also on personal factors like satisfaction and goal-achievement.

Most entrepreneurs feel their success was tied to creating something new and durable ('create a world-class company based on intellectual property') and to leaving a legacy ('leaving an indelible mark on the sands of time'). They believe in innovation. They think innovation will grow the business. A few view successes as being able to prove themselves and several emphasized the importance of the contribution of their business to the nation.

The entrepreneurs have attributed their success mainly to hard work and focus or drive. They think that because of hard work only they have successfully grown their business. Other factors were technical knowledge/experience and access to resources. The entrepreneurs who have more technical knowledge easily use that knowledge for their business purpose. They increase the chances of their business success.

Some entrepreneurs feel that success that has come in the business because of emotional or mental strength; resilience ('I can't be kept too down for too long'), perfectionism and patience were other frequently mentioned qualities. They think it is the factor that is required for taking the more successful decision. They do not fear under stress and remain calm. They are mentally fit and ready to face any critical situation.

Leadership skills, particularly communication skills and good employee management, were highlighted as contributors to success.

What hampers the entrepreneurial process?

- Financial struggle — lack of money in the business as well as personally was the most cited negative factor
- No government support — however, a few entrepreneurs disagreed, saying that the government has been supportive and has given lots of concessions to the high tech industry

- Dearth of sophisticated local investors and angel investors
- Lack of a forum for discussing entrepreneurial issues
- Difficulty in finding top-notch resources (for instance, recruiting from good schools)
- Poor infrastructure
- Corruption and bureaucracy

5.7 Recharge Yourselves for New Entrepreneurial Guts

The new entrepreneurs have a lack of motivation. They open their business but immediately they want progress in their business. They want huge customers, maximum sales and reputation of the company. When they do not get them, their motivation level decreases, their faith or interest dangle. But in such situation you should stay connected to your drive and let your passion infuse your business with big-picture thinking by scheduling time for your own private "meeting of one." Setting aside time for this meeting keeps you focused on your current goals and inspires new ideas for taking your business to the next level.

Recharge yourself to the power of new ideas

Most of the entrepreneurs have tired by their average performance of the business. They start thinking that they are not well for the business. Great ideas often come from unexpected sources. You cannot judge that only educated or scholar person can give the idea. One good idea can give a greater boost to your business. Once you will know that your idea has gained the success your confidence will increase; you will think more positively about your business. Create a list of your past accomplishments and define where each achievement originated. Did it develop from a customer suggestion, a visit to a new store or something you read in a magazine? Keep your mind open to new possibilities by adding these specific development channels to your strategic plan.

Create unique ability to improve your customers' lives

Build on your success by focusing on your customers' needs and desires. Customers are the cornerstone of the business. If you will make them happy then definitely you will gain success. Try to explore every activity of your customers. What customers want? When they feel happy or satisfied with respect to your products or services? Integrate these items into your product improvement process. If you don't currently have a mechanism for obtaining customer feedback, devise a plan to glean this information from your most loyal clients. This input is the most valuable data your business can receive, bar none.

Come up with new tastes and flavours

Entrepreneurs become susceptible to competitive forces when they forget to tailor their offerings to specific customer requirements. The entrepreneurs should not serve only those products to the customers that are in the market. They should give something new to their customers. They should provide something unique to their customers. Customers want uniqueness, they want some change and if you are providing their like products or services, then definitely you have won their hearts. Based on the information you collect, ask yourself, "How can a customer request be transformed into a product variation or a completely new product?" Linking customer suggestions to your endeavors keeps your business personal and helps you sustain your competitive edge. Keep your entrepreneurial energy and motivation high by ensuring the new project is something you will enjoy implementing.

Experiment with business execution strategy

Executing your decisions is imperative to your success. Use your new offering as an opportunity to test fresh implementation methods. For instance, if you always launch products through retail stores, investigate how to sell them online. Developing innovative distribution channels can be as profitable for your company as offering additions to your product line. Instead of customers coming to your shop, you move to the customers' door. Provide their needy products or services to their door only. Doing experiment with your business can give you new idea of doing business. Any idea may become very popular and can give benefit to you. Commit to regularly investigating new product developments and distribution possibilities. Conducting an annual meeting of one provides an excellent opportunity to stay energized about growing your business.

5.8 Entrepreneurs' Association

Motivation has a direct impact on productivity and performance. It decides the way of entrepreneurs in the business. In which direction the entrepreneurs will move is decided by the motivation of those entrepreneurs. Although most entrepreneurs are passionate about what they are doing, they can sometimes succumb to the evil clutches of laziness and boredom just like any other human beings. They do not want to move forward with the business.

Entrepreneurs' association helps to generate motivation?

There are a lot of reasons why entrepreneurs should associate among each other to help in self motivation. The following are reasons why association will help to motivate entrepreneurs:

Motivation by others' performance

The entrepreneurs should do the analysis of others' performance. It will help the entrepreneurs to motivate for the business. They should take the example of others how they have progressed in their business? How they have achieved the targets? You do not compete with the others instead you should take all the positive points of the other entrepreneurs. Likewise you should also take the example of the others how they have failed in their business? What they have done to overcome the failure? How they faced the challenges? This will motivate you and give you the direction.

Be in contact with each other

There are many entrepreneurs who are in the same business. You should always be in contact with those entrepreneurs. Try to discuss the issues of your business with the others share your knowledge and gain others' knowledge for your business purpose. The Entrepreneurs are rare and if you are one, it has been really hard to find like-minded people unless you are studying an entrepreneurship course or working with entrepreneurs frequently.

Doing something alone is boring. Make a relationship with other entrepreneurs. Get insight about what they are doing, compare your performance with their performance. Without the right support, you tend to give up easily. Thus, if you want to get to your entrepreneurship goals, start association.

Sharing resources

Just like anyone, we don't have every resources or skills necessary to run a successful venture. Often times, it is lack of resources, be it funds, knowledge, experience or advice that are pulling back entrepreneurs from starting out.

Again, association with fellow entrepreneurs helps to patch these holes. For example, you can share your knowledge with the help of internet also where there is community who share their knowledge about business and give feedback to you also. It is the best source of getting important tips for your business.

How to network with other entrepreneurs?

With the reasons above, the next thing that should come into your mind is how you are going to connect with people who share the same entrepreneurial thoughts as you. What are some of the ways that you prefer to connect with other small business owners and entrepreneurs? Do you think networking with like-minded people can motivate you in getting things done as well as achieving your business goals?

Social networking platforms

Social networking sites like LinkedIn, Facebook and Twitter connect people all around the world together. Apart from using these platforms to find new people to connect with, keeping the relationship going can also be done easily with the incorporated functionalities. Twitter is best for this because the 140 characters limitation makes it much easier for you to approach people that you have not spoken with. Keep this in mind though, you are trying to build an association and develop relationships, not to pitch your product or services to someone else.

Attending events and conferences

Attending trade events and conferences is a must. Here you will find different entrepreneurs, you can interact with them. You can share your knowledge and likewise you can gain others, knowledge also. You can connect with more local small business owners and entrepreneurs. When it comes to networking, nothing beats a face-to-face interaction. Direct talk with the other entrepreneurs gives birth to new thoughts and new solutions.

You will be much comfortable dealing with a person that you had met with him face-to-face. You should shortlist and start attending events and conferences that are relevant to you and your business. Apart from trade events and conferences, local Chamber of Commerce meetings are also popular in some places for small business owners to meet up.

5.9 Consequences of Doing Unpleasant Work

If you are working in a job you hate:

You will spoil relationships around you

Working in a job that you dislike will make you a frustrated and angry person. You will begin to neglect your relationships with people around you because you will take your anger out on them. You will not take any interest in any person who is with you in your project. You will find yourselves alone. You will not take care of any relation.

You will miss opportunities

When you are working in a job that you hate you are so focused on hating your job and so focused on how you wish you didn't work there that you will miss opportunities. You will not concentrate on the work. You will be distracted. Money making opportunities will pass you by everyday because you are so focused on your frustration. That is no way to live and grow.

You will limit your income

Because you are focusing on job, job, job you will limit your income. You will not be thinking of other ways money can come to you. You will be getting the same irrespective of your efforts. Your progress will become slow. You cannot do anything apart from your job and therefore you will miss out on the other multiple streams of income that could be coming your way.

You will box your creativity

Being forced to do something you do not like to do will limit your creativity and shrink your life. You need to be doing something you love to do if you want to become rich. When you are doing something you love to do your creative juices are flowing and that is where million dollar ideas occur. You live in a time where getting rich has never been easier. We live in the information age and the ability for anyone to join the ranks of the rich and mega rich has gotten easier and easier. You just need to know how you can become rich

SUMMARY

Most of the entrepreneurs fail in the early stage of their business. There are many reasons for their failure. Some of them try again and run their business. They try to find out the problems and then try to eliminate those problems. Many entrepreneurs who fail in their business but do not stand on their feet but instead of that they give up. Most of the reasons for their failure are they do not get money again, pressure for the return/repayment of the bank's loan and Family discouragement.

The driving forces for Indian entrepreneurs are Rewards of entrepreneurship, Personal qualities, Career, Experience and Non-monetary factors such as non-monetary success/personal satisfaction Create value/jobs/wealth in society

Entrepreneurial Motivation can be more difficult to find than your good old fashioned 'motivation' on its own, because most of the time it's a kind of motivation that needs to really be thought about and planned. The motivational factors that influence people's decisions when quitting their jobs are they want to make a name for them selves, want to start a business of their own, Want to escape from the workspace, and want to bring professional attitude in them.

Why an Entrepreneur gets Motivated?

The entrepreneurs are motivated primarily because of the following reasons:

Complete autonomy, Making money/financial independence, Saw business opportunity/impact on industry, Self recognition, Desire to create something new/innovate, Build something important/ make a difference, and Desire to be entrepreneur/excitement of entrepreneurship.

Success attribution in entrepreneurs; Entrepreneurs judge their success not only on the basis of business parameters like revenues, profits, growth and business reputation and monetary rewards, but also on personal factors like satisfaction and goal-achievement. Most entrepreneurs feel their success was tied to creating something new and durable ('create a world-class company based on intellectual property') and to leaving a legacy ('leaving an indelible mark on the sands of time'). They believe in innovation. They think innovation will grow the business. A few view successes as being able to prove themselves and several emphasized the importance of the contribution of their business to the nation.

Recharge Yourselves for New Entrepreneurial Guts

The new entrepreneurs have a lack of motivation. They open their business but immediately they want progress in their business. They want huge customers, maximum sales and reputation of the company. When they do not get them, their motivation level decreases, their faith or interest dangle. But in such situation you should stay connected to your drive and let your passion infuse your business and do the following:

Recharge yourself to the power of new ideas

Create unique ability to improve your customers' likes

Come up with new tastes and flavours

Experiment with business execution strategy

Entrepreneurs' Association

Motivation has a direct impact on productivity and performance. It decides the way of entrepreneurs in the business. In which direction the entrepreneurs will move is decided by the motivation of those entrepreneurs. The different way of getting motivated are by making Entrepreneurs' association, Motivation by others' performance, Be always in contact with each other, Share resources, connect with social networking platforms and Attend events and conferences.

The consequences of doing unpleasant work are, you will spoil relationships around you, you will miss opportunities, you will limit your income, and you will box your creativity.

KEYWORDS

Motivation: It is set of processes that determine individual choices.

Self-recognition: Entrepreneurs want to open the business because they want to show their expertise to the world.

Social networking: Social networking sites like LinkedIn, Facebook and Twitter connect people all around the world together.

Entrepreneurs' association: Where entrepreneurs interact with each other and share their thoughts and experience.

Success attribution: Entrepreneurs judge their success not only on the basis of business parameters like revenues, profits, growth and business reputation and monetary rewards, but also on personal factors like satisfaction and goal-achievement.

Support system: It is the system that helps the new entrepreneurs in their business.

Internal factors: Internal factors are those factors for which entrepreneurs themselves are responsible.

External factors: External factors are those factors for which entrepreneurs themselves are not responsible.

Success-Fail Matrix: It gives the different combination of internal factors and external factors with their consequences.

QUESTIONS

1. What is the relationship between motivation and entrepreneurship?
2. What motivates entrepreneurs?
3. What hampers the entrepreneurial process?
4. What do you mean by entrepreneurs association? How does it help an entrepreneur to grow?

My Research Opinion: Entrepreneurs And Qualities – Is It Enough?

I. Influencing Factors

If someone wants to become an entrepreneur, then definitely he must have the required qualities of an entrepreneur. Those qualities make him capable of building the business, facing the challenges and running the business successfully. These are the qualities that every entrepreneur must possess. So many different qualities have been defined by so many authors and entrepreneurs for becoming successful entrepreneur. It is also not necessary that every entrepreneur can have all the qualities. Some entrepreneurs have more qualities, so some entrepreneurs have few qualities but both run business successfully. It is rarely possible that any entrepreneur will have all the qualities of entrepreneurs. Some entrepreneurs are expert in some fields so they reduce the effect of less knowledge by taking help of any other expert. Even most of the entrepreneurs share same qualities. They are confident, well organized, risk taking, leader and many more qualities but even after sharing the common qualities some entrepreneurs fail, some succeed and some remain stable in their business. By law it should be happened that everyone should have been the successful entrepreneurs because they all have the qualities of entrepreneur which is responsible for the success of business but it does not happen.

So there are also other factors too those are responsible for the success of entrepreneurs. It means having all the qualities of the entrepreneurs are not sufficient. The other factors also have an influence over the success of entrepreneurs' business.

All the factors, those have influence over the success of entrepreneurs and their business can be broadly divided into two categories. The first category belongs to the internal factors and the second category belongs to external factors.

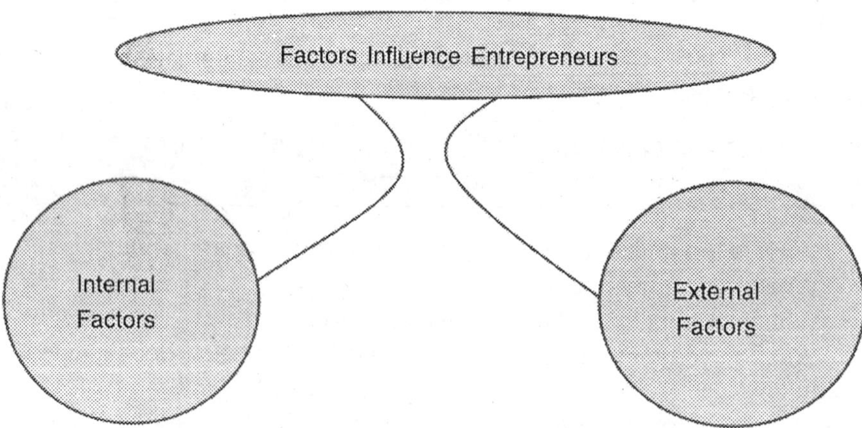

Fig. 5.1: *Factors Influence Entrepreneurs*

II. Internal factors

Internal factors are those factors for which entrepreneurs themselves are responsible. For example: as an entrepreneur you must be very hard worker. If you are hard worker, then only you can think about opening the business. Business requires hard work, efforts and your mind work and sometimes you go out of station to complete business work. As an entrepreneur if you know that hard work is required for business but you are not putting your efforts and not doing hard work for the business, also not visiting other places for your business work then definitely you and your business will suffer. In such situation you will be failing.

Another example if you want to open the business, for that business research is required. As an entrepreneur you must do business research but if you are neglecting that part of business, you are not ready to learn about research and not giving importance to research because you are not at all interested in doing research for your business then definitely again your business will suffer because you are not following the required guidelines.

So internal factors are those factors for which you as an entrepreneur are responsible for the results of your business. Nobody is responsible for that. Your acts decide your way in the business and in turn the direction of the business. You are the alone who has control over those factors. If hard work is required for the business then you will decide that whether you want to do hard work or not? Another can just give suggestions not more than that but you should have a feeling by heart for your business.

Internal factors under will of entrepreneurs

Examples: "I want to appear in horse racing and want to win first prize but it requires efforts and I do not want to take so many efforts".

The following are the internal factors where entrepreneurs have full information about the importance of those factors but they either neglect or completely ignore those factors. Here entrepreneurs are responsible for their behaviour.

- Do not care about research
- Do not work hard
- Lazy
- Unwilling to take responsibilities
- Less energetic
- Do not take efforts
- Very casual approach
- Fear of failure
- Neglect team work
- Ignorance to employees motivation
- Do not focus/ concentrate properly
- Poor delegation - either over delegation or under delegation

III. External Factors

External factors are those factors for which entrepreneurs themselves are not responsible. You do not have control over those factors. Even if you have all internal factors i.e., all the necessary qualities of the entrepreneurs and you are good in those factors also but even after that you and your business will suffer. You will find yourselves helpless. For example: if you have intelligence for opening the business, you are confident, energetic, perfect leader, visionary, risk taker, knowledgeable etc. You have a best plan to open the business. You have done all the planning but you do not have finance, banks are not ready to give you loan because of less trust on you, you cannot purchase land or shop, you cannot hire skilled employees because they demand high salary and facilities, you cannot manipulate humans, you cannot speed up your business documents process in government offices by manipulation, you are the only one in family and therefore cannot take risk otherwise your family will suffer, your family does not support you, you suffer from discrimination, higher caste people, big companies dominate you and many more. The answer is "you cannot become an entrepreneur". These are the factors where you cannot behave according to you. You depend on others. You are on the mercy of others. For example: if any bank is ready to give you loan then only you can think to move forward. Otherwise everything will be stopped.

External factors not under will of entrepreneurs

Examples: "If I want to win the horse race then I must have horse". The first condition is to have a horse if you want to win the race and the second condition is to have knowledge about horsing.

- Unable to manipulate
- Unable to handle bureaucracy
- Government offices delay
- Lack of trust by banks / Financial Institutes
- Do not have Supporting hand
- Do not handle Bribe
- Do not get opportunities to show talent
- Do not get second chance
- Degree of familiarity with others, for example: they do not have many friends and therefore they cannot take advantages of others for their business. If you are familiar with every person in the government office, entrepreneurs, managers of the financial institutes then definitely you can take advantages of them for your business. But if you are not familiar with those people then it has bad impact on your business.
- Lack of facilities
    - R & D
    - Primary research
    - Advanced technology
    - Business infrastructure
- Non availability of sufficient money
    - Improper resources
    - Lack of start up money
    - Higher salary expectations by employees
    - Employees switching
    - Lack skilled labours
    - Do not get suppliers cooperation
- Non availability of land/Shop
- Cultural restriction
- Family compulsion

- Suffer from discrimination
  - Caste system
  - Groupism

So as a new small entrepreneur you will become successful entrepreneur only when you will be able to reduce the influence of external factors. Once you will reduce the influence of external factors and you have all the qualities i.e., internal factors then you will definitely become a successful entrepreneur. High influence of the external factors is the main reason for the failure of the new small entrepreneur.

IV. Success-Fail Matrix

Table 5.1: Success-Fail Matrix

Internal Factors	*External Factors*	*Consequences*
High	High	Success
High	Low	Fail / Poor
Low	High	Medium / Poor
Low	Low	Fail

Note:

- Considering in maximum cases it happens not completely.
- It is only for new small entrepreneurs.

V. Right Traits for Achievement

- Self command to turn on a day when it begins.
- Self discipline to turn it off when it ends.
- Courage to accept a challenge.
- True grit to preserve.
- Determination to what others think is impossible.
- Admiration of the good wherever it is found.
- Will to change what should not be accepted.
- Adjustment to accept that which cannot be changed.
- Knowledge of self and honest to face it.
- Friendliness.
- Gentleness that beckons a child to turn after you.
- The joy that comes from glass of cold water, a delicious meal and a good bed.

VI. The Reasons for Failure

A few recurring reasons for failure are:

- Poor interpersonal skills
- Wrong person in the wrong job / business
- Fear of failure
- Plain bad luck
- Fear of success

- Poor focus/ concentration
- Poor management efficiency,
- Poor product /services
- Lack of planning and foresight
- Unrealistic assessment of the market
- Inadequate capitalization
- Leadership/managerial inexperience
- Poor delegation – either over delegation or under delegation

❑ ❑ ❑

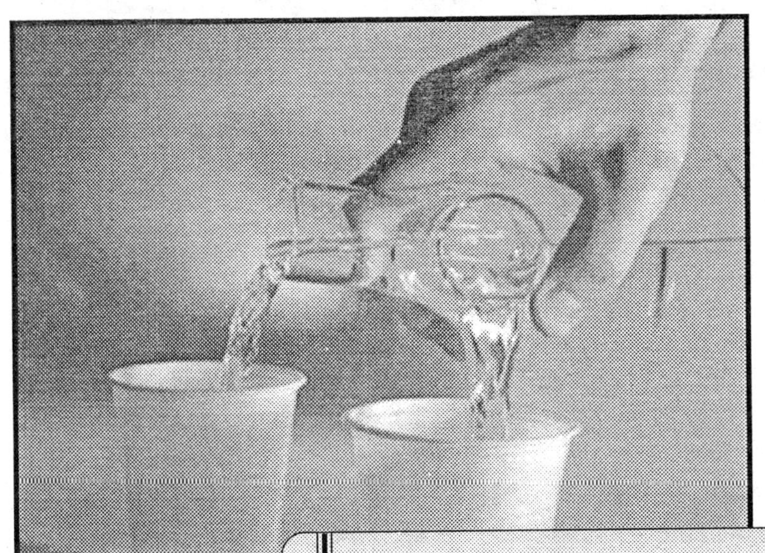

CHAPTER – 6

CREATIVITY AND INNOVATION

LEARNING OBJECTIVES

On completion of this chapter, you should be able to:

- ☺ *Explain creativity and its importance.*
- ☺ *Describe barriers to creativity.*
- ☺ *Describe myths of creativity.*
- ☺ *Describe characteristics of creative personality.*
- ☺ *Describe innovation.*
- ☺ *Describe ways to find innovation.*

6.1 What is Creativity?

Creativity is the act of turning new and imaginative ideas into reality. Creativity is the bringing into being of something which did not exist before, either as a product, a process or a thought.

Creativity involves two processes: thinking, then producing.

You would be demonstrating creativity if you:

- Invent something which has never existed before
- Invent something which exists elsewhere but you are not aware of
- Invent a new process for doing something
- Reapply an existing process or product into a new or different market
- Develop a new way of looking at something (bringing a new idea into existence)
- Change the way someone else looks at something

BOX 6

Society for Innovation and Entrepreneurship

*SINE, **Society for Innovation and Entrepreneurship**, hosted by Indian Institute of Technology Bombay- IIT Bombay is an umbrella for promotion of entrepreneurship at IIT Bombay. SINE administers a business incubator which provides support for technology based entrepreneurship. Thus, SINE extends the role of IIT Bombay by facilitating the conversion of research activity into entrepreneurial ventures.*

IIT Bombay, known as one of the best sources of technology innovation and research excellence in India, was an early adopter of the concept of business incubation in India. IT business incubator was set up at Kanwal Rekhi School of Information and Technology, IIT Bombay in 1999.

The experiment has had manifold effects on the IIT Bombay campus. Apart from successfully incubating a number of companies, the presence of the Information Technology (IT) incubator also created an environment conducive to entrepreneurship. Students and faculty members started thinking of setting up ventures based on their own technologies and ideas, Encouraged by the success of the initial experiment IIT Bombay set up a fully fledged technology business incubator to cover other areas of science and technology.

Thus, SINE came into existence in 2004 to administer the business incubator and accelerate the growth of entrepreneurship in IIT Bombay. Since then it has served as a role model for other business incubators in academia across the country. The Department of Science and Technology of the Government of India has also provided financial assistance to the business incubator. The incubator, with infrastructure spread over 10,000 sq. ft., can accommodate about 15-17 companies.

In fact, we are all creative every day because we are constantly changing the ideas which we hold about the world about us. Creativity does not have to be about developing something new to the world, it is more to do with developing something new to ourselves. When we change ourselves, the world changes with us, both in the way that the world is affected by our changed actions and in the changed way that we experience the world.

Creativity can be used to make products, processes and services better and it can be used to create them in the first place. It is expected that increasing your creativity will help you, your organization and your customers become happier through improvements in your quality and quantity of output.

Creativity (or creativeness) is a mental process involving the generation of new ideas or concepts, or new associations between existing ideas or concepts. From a scientific point of view, the products of creative thought (sometimes referred to as divergent thought) are usually considered to have both originality and appropriateness. An alternative, more everyday conception of creativity is that it is simply the act of making something new. Although intuitively a simple phenomenon, it is in fact quite complex. It has been studied from the perspectives of behavioural psychology, social psychology, psychometrics, cognitive science, artificial intelligence, philosophy, history, economics, design research, business and management, among others. The studies have covered everyday creativity, exceptional creativity and even artificial creativity. Unlike many phenomena in science, there is no single, authoritative perspective or definition of creativity. Unlike many phenomena in psychology, there is no standardized measurement technique.

Creativity has been attributed variously to divine intervention, cognitive processes, the social personality traits and chance ("accident," "serendipity"). It has been associated with genius, mental illness and humour. Some say it is a trait we are born with; others say it can be taught with the application of simple techniques. Although popularly associated with art and literature, it is also an essential part of innovation and invention and is important in professions such as business, economics, architecture, industrial design, science and engineering.

Despite, or perhaps because of the ambiguity and multi-dimensional nature of creativity, entire industries have been spawned from the pursuit of creative ideas and the development of creativity techniques. This mysterious phenomenon, though undeniably important and constantly visible, seems to lie tantalizingly beyond the grasp of scientific investigation.

"Creativity, it has been said, consists largely of re-arranging what we know in order to find out what we do not know." George Kneller

Reasons why people are motivated to be creative:

1. need for new, different and composite stimulation
2. need to communicate ideas and values
3. need to solve problems

6.2 What Is Creative Thinking?

Creative thinking is the process which we use when we come up with a new idea. Creative thinking explores the environment, gets relevant ideas from surroundings and gives them a unique shape that has not been given by anyone earlier. It is the merging of ideas which have not been merged before. Brainstorming is one form of creative thinking: it works by merging someone else's ideas with your own to create a new one. You are using the ideas of others as a stimulus for your own.

This creative thinking process can be **unintentional** or **purposeful**.

Usually in the unintentional way; like a change happening making you think about something in a different way and you then discovering a beneficial change. Other changes happen slowly through pure use of intelligence and logical progression. Using this accidental or logical progression process, it often takes a long time for products to develop and improve. In an accelerating and competitive world, this is obviously disadvantageous.

Using special techniques, purposeful creative thinking can be used to develop new ideas. These techniques force the emergence of a wide range of ideas to spark off new thoughts and processes. Brainstorming is one of these special techniques, but traditionally it starts with unoriginal ideas.

6.3 Characteristics of the Creative Personality

- Creative individuals have a great deal of energy, but they are also often quiet and at rest.
- Creative individuals tend to be smart, yet also naive at the same time.
- Creative individuals have a combination of playfulness and discipline or responsibility and irresponsibility.
- Creative individuals alternate between imagination and fantasy at one end and rooted sense of reality at the other.
- Creative people seem to harbour opposite tendencies on the continuum between extroversion and introversion.
- Creative individuals are also remarkably humble and proud at the same time.
- Creative individuals to a certain extent escape rigid gender role stereotyping and have a tendency towards androgyny.
- Generally, creative people are thought to be rebellious and independent.
- Most creative persons are very passionate about their work, yet they can be extremely objective about it as well.
- The openness and sensitivity of creative individuals often exposes them to suffering pain yet also a great deal of enjoyment.

6.4 What is not Creative?

Problem solving

In general, problem solving is not a creative activity. Problem solving involves applying a known rule or "algorithm" in order to solve problems of an overall type that varies in a minor or predictable way. Successfully understanding and applying a rule is just not the same as discovering it. However, as our discussion of analogy show, sparks of creativity may be involved even in recognizing that a class of new problems can unexpectedly be solved by an old rule. And even in the context of instruction, gifted students may independently rediscover new applications of algorithms they have been taught for more limited purposes.

Learning

Although, as with all skills, some people will do it better and more impressively than others, learning is, in general, likewise not a creative activity: It is the acquisition of knowledge and skills by instruction and example. By its nature it is not something that can give rise to something new and unexpected, although sometimes there are surprises, with creative students discovering (or, just as important relative to what they already know and don't know: rediscovering) things that go significantly beyond the immediate content of what is being taught them.

Imitation

By definition, imitation gives rise to something that is not new; but creativity demands new work. Imitation does not require many physical and mental efforts. Imitation will be creative only when you are doing major changes with that product/service and that's why people can differentiate between old and new product/service. But if there is no change at all then that work is not a creative work. It will be simply a copy of the existing one.

Trial and error

Trial and error work is not a creative work because the type of creativity you are getting is by chance and not by your inspired choice. You are not responsible for that work because you are more dependent on chance instead of your desired choice. It is same with the incident where you win the race by luck but not by your actual efforts.

6.5 The Myths of Creativity

Creativity comes from creative types

There is a common myth that creativity can come from creative type only. For example people believe that R & D department, advertising, marketing people are more creative and these are the areas where there exists creativity. In other areas, people do not have creativity. For example the accounting people cannot have creativity. They are not the creative ones. But the fact is that creativity is not dependent on the work but it depends on the thinking power of the people involved in the work. Over the past couple of decades, there have been innovations in financial accounting that are extremely profound and entirely ethical, such as activity-based costing. The fact is, almost all of the research in this field shows that anyone with normal intelligence is capable of doing some degree of creative work. Past few years, organizations have paid more attention to creativity and innovation.

Time pressure generates creativity

But the fact is that when you are working under pressure then definitely you cannot show your talent easily. Under stress your work will deteriorate. As a result of that you will spoil your current work and that will have impact on your future work also. Creativity is not a food which takes a specific time to cook rather it is uncertain how much time it will require to come up with creative thoughts. Creativity requires an incubation period; people need time to soak in a problem and let the ideas bubble up.

Fear forces step forward

There's this widespread notion that fear and sadness somehow encourage creativity. But creativity is positively associated with joy and love and negatively associated with anger, fear and anxiety. The entries show that people are happiest when they come up with a creative idea, but they're more likely to have a breakthrough if they were happy the day before. When people are excited about their work, then there are more chances of creative work. Their enthusiasm will fuel their creativity. Their happy mind will create as many as thoughts and that ultimately help them to grow.

Competition beats collaboration

There's a widespread belief, particularly in the finance and high-tech industries, that internal competition fosters innovation. Creativity takes a hit when people in a work group compete instead of collaborate. The most creative teams are those that have the confidence to share and debate ideas. But when people compete for recognition, they stop sharing information. And that's destructive because nobody in an organization has all of the information required to put all the pieces of the puzzle together.

Creativity comes from the unconscious

But it is not always the case. Sometimes it may happen that you have got creativity from that way but it is not a law. The unconscious is a notoriously vague term. You cannot define your unconsciousness. Even if we believe in that then what is the application of that in real business. We do not know the time of unconsciousness and when will we get creative ideas by becoming unconscious?

Creativity is a talent

It is not true. Talent is not fixed or we can say talent is not dependent on the mercy of God. God has provided equal opportunity to every human brain. If you can get talent from the time of your birth then you should not worry at all but it is not the case. People say such kind of things just to protect themselves from their weaknesses.

Stanford psychologist Carol Dweck writes, "People who believe in the power of talent tend not to fulfill their potential because they're so concerned with looking smart and not making mistakes. But people who believe that talent can be developed are the ones who really push, stretch, confront their own mistakes and learn from them." Dweck's conclusions are not based on rah, rah self-improvement boosterism; they are based on three decades of pains-taking research. When putting together the iPhone team, Scott Forstall of Apple chose people who were ready to "to make mistakes and struggle." These are the kinds of people that will be great members of an innovative team.

Children are more creative than adults

Children are creative but the fact is that they are not the creator. They cannot sustain their creativity. They do not have any explanation for that. They unknowingly do that. And for having a creative work one cannot depend on children. Adults are also more creative but there are differences and that are; adults create creative work intentionally but the children do not. Adults create creative work because they want to create it but children unknowingly create it. So ultimately we can say adults are more creative but the difficulty is that their business compels them to think in a particular direction and that makes their job more difficult and they have to put all their efforts for generating creative ideas.

Everyone is creative

Though everyone is creative but everyone is not equal in creativity. Some are more creative, some are less creative. All those qualities depend on the personality of the person and the environment under which those people are surviving. So in a company you cannot give the task of creativity to any employee with a belief of everyone is creative. You must be careful while selecting the person for giving them a creative work.

Creativity is the same as originality

This is perhaps the myth of modernism. In most cases, we should rate creativity and innovation by quality, not by originality. Creativity occurs in a domain, whether it is competitive iceboat construction, open source social network software and Hip Hop or Hollywood thrillers. Each of these has an intensely involved group of professional and deeply committed amateurs. In none of these is it a case of anything goes. Each sub-culture is committed to quality and high standards in its domain. Original ideas can create lots of excitement, but quality trumps originality any day. Just think about going out for dinner. It's really cool to have a dinner cooked by a highly originally chef, but only if the meal is good. Originality in cooking is not enough.

Creativity only applies to science and the fine art

If there is a domain that a critical mass of people cares about well then, let them be creative. The history of art, for example, shows us countless examples of genres that were not initially accepted by elites, but have gradually come into the mainstream. Movies, jazz and photography were all on the sidelines initially. As fans and critics began to articulate just what is unique, visionary, or excellent in these art forms they gradually moved into the mainstream of acceptance. Domains, genres and fields go through periods of innovation and stagnation. Possibilities open up and then are exploited. Computer programmers become interested in genetics. Sting sings music from the time of Shakespeare. Let the market place of ideas define what creativity is.

6.6 Creativity and Business Development

The Nomura Institute of Japan classifies four eras of economic activity:

1. Agricultural
2. Industrial
3. Informational... and now through the evolution of technology
4. Creative: constant innovation

Daniel Pink expanding on this idea in *A Whole New Mind* (2005) defines Economic Development as:

1. Agriculture Age (farmers)
2. Industrial Age (factory workers)
3. Information Age (knowledge workers)
4. Conceptual Age (creators and empathizers)

Pink argues that left-brain linear, analytical computer-like thinking are being replaced by right-brain empathy, inventiveness and understanding as skills most needed by business. Pink points to Asia, automation and abundance as the reasons behind the shift.

Pink says "Logical and precise, left-brain thinking gave us the Information Age. Now comes the Conceptual Age — ruled by artistry, empathy and emotion." What does this mean for future jobs? Winners are designers, inventors, counselors, ethnographers, social psychologists and other right-brain folks, while lawyers, engineers, accountants and other left-brainers will see their jobs migrate to Asia.

Creativity at work

Creativity is a core competency for leaders and managers and one of the best ways to set your company apart from the competition. Corporate Creativity is characterized by the ability to perceive the world in new ways, to find hidden patterns, to make connections between seemingly unrelated phenomena and to generate solutions. Generating fresh solutions to problems and the ability to create new products, processes or services for a changing market, are part of the intellectual capital that give a company its competitive edge. Creativity is a crucial part of the innovation equation.

Creativity requires whole-brain thinking:

right-brain imagination, artistry and intuition,

plus left-brain logic and planning.

Creativity is fostered in organizational cultures that value independent thinking, risk taking and learning. They are tolerant of failure and they value diversity. Open communication, a high degree of trust and respect between individuals are crucial.

Can creativity be learned?

A study by George Land reveals that we are naturally creative and as we grow up we learn to be uncreative. Creativity is a skill that can be developed and a process that can be managed. Learning to be creative is akin to learning a sport. It requires practice to develop the right muscles and a supportive environment in which to flourish. Business leaders are increasingly adopting the principles and practices of art and design to help build creative muscle in their organizations.

Design thinking can help organizations manage the innovation process and overcome some of the barriers that prevent leaders from being effective innovators. Art and design processes help people develop fresh thinking through aesthetic ways of knowing, imagination, intuition, re-framing and exploring different perspectives. Art-based processes also help people learn to be comfortable with uncertainty, ambiguity and paradox.

Strategies for developing creativity....

- Skills Training for leaders, managers and staff
- Coaching innovation champions and teams
- Culture Change initiatives

... are based on these findings from global studies on innovation:

- Traditional business models no longer hold.
- Innovation has a higher success rate when it is applied to the business model
- Creative leadership is required for innovation to succeed
- The ability to collaborate at all levels of the organization

Generative research on creativity

Generative research shows that everyone has creative abilities. The more training you have and the more diverse the training, the greater potential for creative output. The average adult thinks of 3-6 alternatives for any given situation. The average child thinks of 60.

Research has shown that in creativity quantity equals quality. The longer the list of ideas, higher the quality of the final solution. The highest quality ideas appear at the end of the list.

"Behavior is generative; like the surface of a fast flowing river, it is inherently and continuously novel... behavior flows and it never stops changing. Novel behavior is generated continuously, but it is labeled creative only when it has some special value to the community... Generativity is the basic process that drives all the behavior we come to label creative." — Robert Epstein PhD, *Psychology Today* July/Aug 1996

6.7 Defining Innovation

Innovation is the production or implementation of ideas.

The **National Innovation Initiative** (NII) defines innovation as "The intersection of invention and insight, leading to the creation of social and economic value."

3M describes innovation as an action or implementation which results in an improvement, a gain or a profit.

Innovation is the production or implementation of an idea. If you have ideas, but don't act on them, you are imaginative but not creative.

"Creativity is the process of bringing something new into being...creativity requires passion and commitment. Out of the creative act is born symbols and myths. It brings to our awareness what was previously hidden and points to new life. The experience is one of heightened consciousness–ecstasy." — **Rollo May, The Courage to Create.**

"A product is creative when it is (a) novel and (b) appropriate. A novel product is original not predictable. The bigger the concept and the more the product stimulate further work and ideas, the more the product is creative." — **Sternberg and Lubart, Defying the Crowd.**

Key Definitions from the IBM Global Innovation Study 2006:

Innovation is defined as using new ideas or applying current thinking in fundamentally different ways that result in significant change. There are three types of innovation that contribute to wealth creation in organizations:

1. Business Model Innovation: Significantly changing the structure and / or financial model of the business.
2. Operations Innovation: Improving the effectiveness and efficiency of core business processes and functions.
3. Product/Services/Markets Innovation: Creating new or significantly differentiated products, services or go-to-market activities.

The nature of innovation—the inherent definition of innovation—has changed today from what it was in the past. It's no longer individuals toiling in a laboratory, coming up with some great invention. It's not an individual. It's individuals. It's multidisciplinary. It's global. It's collaborative. **—Sam Palmisano, Chairman, President and CEO, IBM**

Innovation at Hewlett-Packard

HP's philosophy for fostering an environment for creativity and innovation:

Rules of the garage:

Believe you can change the world.

Work quickly, keep the tools unlocked and work whenever.

Know when to work alone and when to work together.

Share - tools, ideas. Trust your colleagues.

No politics. No bureaucracy. (These are ridiculous in a garage.)

The customer defines a job well done.

Radical ideas are not bad ideas.

Invent different ways of working.

Make a contribution every day. If it doesn't contribute, it doesn't leave the garage.

Believe that together we can do anything.

Invent.

—1999 HP Annual Report

For innovation to flourish, organizations must create an environment that fosters creativity; bringing together multi-talented groups of people who work in close collaboration together - exchanging knowledge, ideas and shaping the direction of the future.

6.8 How to Find Innovation

Take different roles

If you have your own business and you are working as an entrepreneur then you must be ready to take all roles of your business. Switch roles. By this only you will learn what is there in that role. You will learn new things that will help you for your innovation. You will get more knowledge and as a result of that you can think more uniquely about your business. This is the only way to learn and understand what is out there or in there. If you are the manager, become an employee. If you are in Sales, become a customer. If you are the product manager, become the product or the user. Try to adapt the mindset of who you want to do business with. Find new innovative ways to look at the same problem and find a solution that you never thought existed before.

Use knowledge of other domains

Though you are in a particular business but if you take knowledge of other business too that is not at all related to your business then at that condition too you can get idea of conducting the business. You can get idea from the innovation of other business. Try to apply this knowledge to your problem. Say you are trying to market the chocolates to the youths and are not able to determine the appropriate message, the punch line. What if a Kid were to buy your product? How would you explain to the Kid? The key is to use knowledge outside your domain and arrive at a solution.

Ask influential questions

Questions are also a good method to find innovative way because as many as questions you will ask you will find answer for those questions and ultimately you will reach to the point where you know everything. There is no such thing as a silly question. Question everything about what you are trying to accomplish. All those questions that satisfy your needs are important questions for you. Do not hesitate to ask questions. Start with why, what, how, when, what if, so what, where and so on. Ask broader or narrower Questions. Question the merits and even ask how you can make the innovation worse or fail. The more questions you ask and the more answers you try to find, the more innovative ways you would come across in trying to find a way to create a new product or solve a problem.

Foster new knowledge

There are many ways of fostering your knowledge. As an entrepreneur if you want to be more creative then you must have more knowledge of your business and outside world. New knowledge not only comes from your own domain, but when you are out there doing something else. Go attend a trade show of an unrelated business. This will open up your mind to how businesses are creating products for other markets. You may find an application of this in your market. Always analyze your customers. Observe them how they react to a particular product. What they want? How will you make them happy? After analysis and observation you will have enough understanding of your business and customers and therefore you would be able to do an innovation and creativity. Check out what your key competitor is doing outside their place of business, what they are doing to promote and market their products. Do off sites with your creative teams and focus on learning something that is totally unrelated to what you are doing. The creative team should spend time in new places to gain new viewpoints and which in turn will generate new ideas.

Reflect your ideas with pictures

Reflecting your creativity with pictures will improve your creativity. Once you will reflect your creativity with the help of picture you can see the limitations in that and accordingly can remove that limitations and can add more creative thoughts in that. For example if you want to produce a product in an innovative way then if you will draw the picture of that product you can easily make it more creative because you have a complete visual picture which you can see and make changes in that. A picture says a thousand words. To put down your thoughts visually will allow you to think about your ideas from various angles and create clarity of thought. Do drawings of processes, tasks, relationships. Create a habit to write down key ideas, however unrelated and try to associate these with real world scenarios. Create more pictures (don't worry about whether they are pieces of art).And at times, the visuals may create even further complexity. Perhaps it is best to let go of that visual and start a new one. Wherever possible, try to associate visuals with concise thoughts or ideas.

Change the pace of attention

How do you lead groups to find and create innovation? The key is to slow them down and try to get the group to focus on a few key ideas initially. Try to brainstorm on these ideas using creativity techniques such as free association or Question Breakdown. Ask the group to bring their own ideas, however silly they may appear on the surface and evaluate each idea and brainstorm. Give rankings to each idea by having everyone vote. If the group is pressed for time and is moving fast through the thought process, make it a practice of slowing them down. Ask more questions. Try to change the topic to have the group momentarily think of something else. Bring them back. Try to rephrase what you are trying to do.

6.9 How Creative Entrepreneurs Succeed

Collaboration

Connecting and working with partners, clients and other significant players in your network, which will probably be scattered across the globe and contain more 'virtual' relationships than face-to-face ones.

Creative entrepreneurs are not freelancers

Creative entrepreneurs are not freelancers. Freelancers earn a living by doing paid work for clients, usually charging by the hour, day or project. Freelancers think in terms of 'getting more work'. Creative entrepreneurs think in terms of creating opportunities, producing results and making profits. This leads them to create systems and businesses that generate wealth and free up their time for their next big idea.

Stay in contact

Unlike other business that is in touch with their clients only at the time of purchasing of products, you must be in touch with your clients always. For example to make your relationship with the clients more strong you can use many innovative ways such as sending mail/email on their birthday, reminding them about their purchase, home delivery, providing better services etc., innovative entrepreneurs always try to search for such a unique method of servicing that is not at all available in the market and that helps them to become successful in their business. It's easier to maintain a relationship than establish a new one.

Community

This means networks of people. That could be local communities, students, artists entrepreneurs or researchers. The collective has a power beyond the individual. You need to support the exploitation of opportunity. It will provide the anything that is possibly ideal.

What really has to happen is that someone with an idea is able to find someone who can help to make it real. Places like the Digital Hub have shown that if you get a group of like-minded people together they can help each other to succeed. The social media network revolution, already in evidence on the internet today, is the start of things to come.

Communicate with your vendors

Vendors are the best way to know about current happening in the market. Call the vendors you've used most; they know who's buying and succeeding even in a slow economy. Make friends at all levels of your industry. Friends are an important source of information. Take all possible information from them. Utilize that information for your creativity and innovation. You never know where your next job referral will come from.

Maintain industry presence

Maintaining industry presence will help you to collect all relevant information about business. Interact with other entrepreneurs. Know what are they doing? How innovative they are! How are they serving to their customers? Maintain industry presence; even though things are slow, stay active in professional affairs. Attend the monthly meetings, trade shows, exhibitions and work for charity to show off your creative skills.

New clients

Cold call new clients whether you need them or not. Successful entrepreneurs always have a few new clients ready to step in to replace those who step out. What's the real key to success? Get up and get busy — there's no time for sulking.

6.10 Obstacles to Creativity

Not willing to risk

Being creative involves risk-taking, doing something different from the norm. That requires a high degree of confidence and a willingness to face an unpredictable outcome. It is understandable why there may be a preference for the comfort zone of the familiar. Routine has its own attractions: we can switch to autopilot and not have to think too much.

Lack of Experience

Newer organizations, companies or employees might experience a barrier to creative thinking because they are inexperienced. The concern about forgetting information or being thought rude or impertinent can stop creativity in its tracks. Older employees might unconsciously make younger employees less creative due to their lack of experience and the supposed impertinent ideas.

Fears

Fears are a common barrier to creativity. Fear of what others will think, fear of failure and fear that something won't work or even fears of change can prevent creativity. Fears are one of the most common barriers because many of the problems that organizations or companies have relating to creativity is also related to fears. Eliminating the fears is difficult, but there are ways to minimize fears and move past them to get creative thoughts and actions started again.

Judgement

It's not strange at all that judgement is the third barrier. Considering how much of our daily life is made up out of judging in one form or another, it's quite a familiar subject and we eagerly jump at the chance of judge our own as well as other people's ideas.

Judgment is especially damaging when we are trying to come up with new ideas. If every idea you come up with gets shot down, it won't take long till you're bleeding so much you surrender. It's generally damaging because no one knows if an idea is bad until it is has been attempted. There is no way of knowing if an idea is the one that will change everything – just because it happens to look ludicrous at first.

Too much time between creation and implementation

As an entrepreneur you must give value to your employees and your ideas. Taking much time in the implementation of the new ideas will put you in loss. In today's competitive world every second a new idea takes birth. If you will delay in implementation then others may implement it and encash it very quickly. Delay in implementation works against the trust that the system is serious about ideas. The new small entrepreneurs are not active about their creative work. They definitely think on that but they take much time to implement it.

Neglect

Most of the new small entrepreneurs want to open and run traditional business. They try to protect themselves from the fear of risk involved in doing new business. They are ready to sacrifice more money which they could have earned by opening new creative business. They are happy with their current business only. That is the reason why most of the new small entrepreneurs even do not listen to new ideas or try to avoid those ideas. They have less belief in creativity.

Inadequate funding

Getting the start-up funds for creativity often means taking money away from an established program. Getting the money at just the right time is also problematic since organizations often work on annual funding cycles that don't match up well with real-world opportunities. And many an excellent creativity needs more than seed money to survive and is starved out of existence. But broader thinking on needs and resources can help innovators move their ideas along.

Acknowledgement

The entrepreneurs should recognize the creativity of their employees. They should appreciate them for their work. Moreover if they can give them incentives then it encourages the employees to create new ideas for the business. If entrepreneurs will neglect the creativity of their employees and will not give importance to their work then it will discourage employees and therefore they will not try to do anything new for the business because they know nobody gives importance to them. The best acknowledgement for a worker is to see their boss fighting for the idea or it is implemented and making a difference in the workplace.

Valuing only big ideas

There is a myth about idea that is if you have a big creative idea then only it will work or you can earn profit out of that. But it is not the case every creative idea is important for the business. There should not be any concept like small or big. Even small ideas can solve business problems more easily. Anyone can come up with a small idea and every idea is a step closer to a more productive work environment. For example if you want to keep your store room cool then you can even use exhaust fan. It is not necessary that every where you should use A.C.

6.11 Overcoming Barriers to Creative Thinking

We all know how essential creativity and creative thinking is to organization success. Yet seemingly it is an elusive and scarce resource in the workplace. Indeed you frequently find that the work environment acts as a constraint rather than a releasing energy. It focuses on what you, as an entrepreneur and can inform and support coaching and mentoring activities in the workplace and beyond.

- **Educate noncreative**

Educate noncreative people in the time challenges of producing product. Clarify how and why design takes time and costs so much. Use real data and real numbers to enhance understanding. Encourage improved communication to create realistic time lines for new projects and to protect creative people from overwork and burnout.

- **Discourage Group Thinking**

In group thinking, one individual presents an idea and everyone follows it. Discourage this kind of attitude by showing that you don't necessarily implement the first idea that comes up. Create a fun environment in brainstorming sessions. A serious atmosphere can be intimidating to timid individuals. Give everyone a fair chance to express their views. Be open-minded and never discriminate between individuals. Some individuals can be too reserved to speak in public. So be approachable and encourage them to come to you any time.

- **Reverse Creative Thinking**

Creative thinkers often try an opposite idea to what most people would do. They do reverse thinking which loosens the fixed patterns stored in the brain. Try these:

- List three reasons why a person might be drawing UPSIDE DOWN
- List three ways of drinking water WITHOUT holding the glass with your hands
- List three things that you WOULD NOT find in a Tesco or WalMart Supermarket
- List three ways in which a bicycle and a dog are the SAME

Be patient

Realize idea development does not always go smoothly. Sometimes many false starts and blind alleys mark the process. Sometimes nothing short of dogged persistence will succeed in clearing away obstacles to success. Recognize that the creative process generally goes through four cycles: Preparation - the conscious attempt to understand and deal with some personal need ; incubation - sleep on it, leave it for some other task; enlightenment or insight - break through to a new understanding; and discovery - energy to realize the creative idea - the validation or implementation stage.

- **Self imposed barriers**

These can be imposed on ourselves consciously or unconsciously. For example while thinking you become traditional, you do not want to think outside your religion, you do not want to involve modern views etc. So if someone is the traditional thinker and he does not give scope to modern views in his thinking then definitely at that time he has very narrow scope for creativity. They are particularly difficult to recognize but relatively easy to correct.

Try asking yourself – what would be an 'out of the box' solution. Increase your area of thinking. Do not put yourselves into boundary. Try brainstorming different ideas – follow the brainstorming rules – nothing is too outrageous to go on the list. Talk to others, particularly people who you think are creative and get insights into how they think through problems.

- **Patterns or belief in one unique answer**

Most of the time you stick yourselves with the belief of one right answer for a question. You do not give chance to alternate answers. Much of our training is how to establish a pattern or find one right answer. This is difficult to break as we are trained to seek an answer to a problem.

Try to think more than one answer to everything. You must always have alternate answers for the same question. Once you will have list of alternate answers for your question then you can easily select the best fit answer to your question. When you select your preferred solution check this against personal norms – was it predictable that you would choose this solution?

- **Evaluating too quickly**

A powerful idea needs time and research. If you have an idea then try to evaluate that idea from every perspective. For example if you want to come up with a new creative idea of teaching to kids that you think is powerful way of teaching then you must evaluate it with as many as number of kids. You must also consider teachers who will teach them. Take their feedbacks. Take feedbacks from their parents. What do they say? Ultimately you will have an idea about success of your creative idea. Evaluation of an idea is instinctive when ideas are put forward; however doing it too quickly can eliminate possible solutions or areas of thought at an early stage.

- **Believe in your ability to be creative**

Research shows that creativity doesn't belong only to so-called creative types. Most normally intelligent people are capable of doing some degree of creative work. Through perception and understanding creativity can be deliberate. Creativity comes from many different elements: experience (which certainly you have a lot of), knowledge (that too you've accumulated over the years), technical skills, talent and persistence in achieving goals. Creativity is a quality that can be learned, trained and practiced if you put your mind to it.

- **Try new ways of thinking and acting**

Dr. Sylvie Labelle suggests new ways of thinking and acting differently without necessarily changing who you are. Here are some simple steps she recommends for breaking free of constraints:

- Do the opposite of what you are used to.
- Open up uncertain things for discussion.
- Do not focus on what other people think.
- Get out of your comfort zone.
- Do not rely on old solutions from the past.
- Take the time to look deeply into the problem or challenge
- Talk to others, both experts and non-experts in the area.
- Turn the problem upside down by asking what the problem is not or what's missing.
- Sleep on it by taking frequent breaks, distancing yourself entirely for a while or putting it aside while you actually sleep.
- Ask more questions.
- Visualize how different aspects of a problem fit together and storyboard or depict its components.
- Use a graphic organizer to chart what works and what doesn't.

6.12. Why is Idea Generation Important?

The output of the new product development process is only as good as the concepts and ideas being put into it, "garbage in equal's garbage out." Drucker noted that "innovative ideas are like frogs' eggs; of a thousand hatched; only one or two survive to maturity" (Stasch, Lonsdale and LaVenka, 1992, p. 14). Stevens and Burley (1997) have shown it roughly takes from 1,500 to 3,000 raw ideas to equal one business success. With such a poor conversion rate one can understand why a company needs a stream of ideas. Of course, one can argue over the exact conversion rates of raw ideas into business successes, but it would not negate the matter that a large number of raw ideas are needed to develop even one winner. Again, idea generation processes, activities or phase is of great importance, where Stasch, Lonsdale and LaVenka (1992) state, "the objective of all idea-generating activities is to guarantee that the company does not leave the exploration stage of new-product development to chance" (p. 21). Aside from leaving idea generation to chance, changes in the idea generation process may increase the quality of the produced ideas. Several researchers state that idea developed from a deep understanding of the customer usually have higher value and better chances of succeeding (Flint, 2002). So, logically, a business should try to increase the quality of the ideas they are generating in addition to guaranteeing a steady stream of ideas. In addition to generating ideas for new offerings, processes, solutions and so on, development projects periodically require ideas to solve problems. For example, a new product may require new ideas for packaging to help it sell in the stores. So, not only are ideas needed to form the bases of the new product, they are also required to solve problems or create value as the project moves through the development processes. This is backed by Verworn and Herstatt's (2001) statement that "idea generation should take part throughout the whole project".

Good Idea Generation? A Process

It seems incongruous that good idea generation can be a process or that a process may lead to insight. However, if you examine the behaviour of people who regularly generate good ideas? Such as creatives in advertising - you will find that common patterns of behaviour do emerge and it is possible to make insight more likely.

Below are just some elements of the good idea generation process:

1. Read and study as many things about your industry or product and services. You need to investigate specific information of what you are going to sell. Keep up with current events and be ready to take advantage of business opportunities. If you read or watch the news regularly with the conscious intent of finding business ideas, you'll be amazed at how many business opportunities your brain generates. Keeping up with current events will help you identify market trends, news, fads, industry news- and sometimes just new ideas that have business possibilities. You need to have all information about your idea. For example, if you want to be involved in restaurant, you study everything about the subject matter in detail. If you want to start a business, you have to know what's going on in your industry, what sells and at what price, etc.
2. Improve general knowledge. Don't limit yourself to only learn about things in your own industry. Learn as many topics as possible from other industries. It can be any topic. This enables you to think out of your own industry. Once you investigate and research enough, your mind is the storehouse of all the ideas you have studied. You have full knowledge of what to do next with your idea. And this is the main source to your creative ideas. All the knowledge you have learned so far is the raw materials to produce new ideas. Mix all the knowledge and generate the best one.
3. Brainstorming is one group method for generating both business solutions and ideas. It is most effective if performed within a criticism-free zone where group members are encouraged to freely contribute ideas during the brainstorming session. Brainstorming is a way in which you get out of your conscious self and become an idea machine. You take off your "judgment hat" and let any idea come to your mind. Many of the ideas you come up with won't work for you, but you're not looking for many ideas you're looking for one or two ways to solve a problem or create an opportunity.

4. Think on does it make customers' life easier or solve a problem?

   Every product serves a purpose - successful businesses are rarely built on novelty value. Think on whether your idea is really going to solve the problem. How many products are there in the market for the same purpose? It's crucial to be clear about how your product helps people or solves a specific problem. Again, market research will help loads.

   - Know what purpose your product serves?
   - Make sure this responds to a market gap.
   - Market research.

5. Think on; is there a market for your idea?

   Very thorough market research is an absolute must for new business ideas. Market research can prove invaluable in determining your idea's potential. You can gather information from industry associations, Web searches, periodicals, federal and state agencies and so forth. A trip to the library or a few hours online can set you on your way to really understanding your market. Your aim is to gain a general sense of the type of customer your product or service will serve-or at least to being willing to find out through the research process.

   Growing markets are going to appeal more to investors and provide better business opportunities.

   - Do thorough market research.
   - Smaller profit margin requires greater demand.
   - Growing markets are preferable.

6. Checking out the competition. Your aim is to understand what your competition is doing so you can do it better. Maybe their service is poor. Maybe their product has some flaws-something you'll only know if you try it out yourself. Or maybe you've figured out a way to do things better, smarter, more cost-effectively. Market yourself or your product in a way that is completely unique from your competition. Look around at what they're doing and do something different. It's actually easier to do this than it sounds. It just takes a little thought, preparation, trial and error. But no matter what, dare to be different.

   That can be disheartening if you've already spent X amount of hours in the idea stage, plus X amount of hours on market research-only to find that you're not quite ready to get started after all. But taking the time to refocus your energies and determine why your idea needs some tightening is the best predictor of future success

7. Analysis

   Analyze the business idea from three perspectives: company, customer, and competitors. Here's what he looks at for each of the four issues:

   ***(a)* Company.** Think of your idea in terms of its product/service features, the benefits to customers, the personality of your company, what are your promises and commitments to the customers?

   ***(b)* Customers.** There are three different customers you'll need to think about in relation to your idea: purchasers (those who make the decision or write the cheque), influencers (the individual, organization or group of people who influence the purchasing decision) and the end users (the person or group of people who will directly interact with your product or service).

   ***(c)* Competitors.** Think about the competitors, some competitors are good in innovation; some are in setting pricing etc., You must be able to beat the competitors by thoroughly analyzing their core competencies. Their placement within each level is based on how often your business would compete with them and how you would tailor your messages when competing with each of these groups.

8. Think on the viability of the idea?

Unless you have lots of your own money to pour in, you need a business that can operate cheaply to begin with and one that doesn't require dozens of staff. At the initial stage to make the idea practical it should be the economic one. It should not involve number of resources that is difficult to arrange. Your business will only work if your product is technologically possible and manufacturing costs are feasible. Otherwise even if your idea is the best one but if it is not under the reach of maximum people then it is of no use. Work out who would make it and for how much.

- Be realistic.
- Low starting costs and fewer staff are more likely to work.

9. Refine and Narrow

Refine your raw idea until it's up to your satisfaction. You can always do your own research on the raw idea by asking questions to target market to test the feasibility of the idea and how to improve the idea further. Your idea ought to be able to satisfy a very precise need and be readily acceptable once it comes into fruition. Refining will take care of any general indicators and concentrate on the core of the business idea.

10. Can it generate profit?

Work out how you'd make your product and how much you'd sell it for. You need enough profit left over to sustain a business. Factor in employees' salaries, expenses, administration costs, labour, transport and material costs. The smaller your profit margin, the more demand you need to make up for it. Talk to manufacturers to find out about costs.

- Work out all costs.
- Compare with estimated sale price.
- Smaller profit margin needs higher demand.

11. Is there room for growth?

You could gradually offer a bigger range of products, set up business in new locations, make ongoing improvements to your service and reach more customers. Look to web technology for ways to evolve. It's best if plans for growth correspond with how the market working in looks set to develop over the next few years.

Basically new idea is a combination of old ideas. You need to have enough old ideas to come up with new ideas. That's why constant reading and observation are important.

6.13. New Product Development (NPD)

Improving and updating product lines is crucial for the success for any organisation. Failure for an organisation to change could result in a decline in sales and with competitors racing ahead. The process of NPD is crucial within an organisation. Products go through the stages of their lifecycle and will eventually have to be replaced. There are two parallel paths involved in the NPD process: one involves the idea generation, product design and detail engineering; the other involves market research and marketing analysis. Companies typically see new product development as the first stage in generating and commercializing new products within the overall strategic process of product life cycle management used to maintain or grow their market share.

Stage 1: Idea generation

New product ideas have to come from somewhere. But where do organizations get their ideas for NPD? Ideas for new products can be obtained from:

- Within the company i.e., employees
- Competitors
- Company's R&D department
- Focus groups
- Salespeople
- Corporate spies
- Customers
- Trade shows
- Distributors, Suppliers and others

Use creative idea starters like brainstorming to help you find the ideas you're looking for. Try to combine two products you have into a single package or perhaps a product and a service, something to set your offering apart from others.

Stage 2: Idea Screening

This process involves shifting through the ideas generated above and selecting ones which are feasible and workable to develop. The object is to eliminate unsound concepts prior to devoting resources to them. Pursing non feasible ideas can clearly be costly for the company. The screeners must ask at least three questions:

- Will the customer in the target market benefit from the product?
- Is it technically feasible to manufacture the product?
- Will the product be profitable when manufactured and delivered to the customer at the target price?

Stage 3: Concept Development and Testing

The organisation may have come across what they believe to be a feasible idea; however, the idea needs to be taken to the target audience. What do they think about the idea? Will it satisfy the needs of the customers? Will it be feasible? Will it offer the desired benefits? Develop the marketing and engineering details and test the concept by asking a sample of prospective customers what they think of the idea.

Stage 4: Marketing Strategy and Development

How will the product/service idea be launched within the market? A proposed marketing strategy will be written laying out the marketing mix strategy of the product, the segmentation, targeting and positioning strategy sales and profits that are expected. After the testing stage has helped you refine your product a little more, you can move on to actively marketing your new product on a full scale, hopefully with noticeable improvements in sales.

Stage 5: Business Analysis

The company has a great idea, the marketing strategy seems feasible, but will the product be financially worthwhile in the long run? Analyze the potential success by asking some of your customers what they think. The business analysis stage looks more deeply into the profit the product could generate, what the cost will be, what are the expected customers, how much market shares the product may achieve and the expected life of the product. Estimate likely selling price based upon competition and customer feedback, estimate sales volume based upon size of market and estimate profitability and breakeven point.

Stage 6: Product Development

Finally it is at this stage that a prototype is finally produced. The entire desired test will be applied on the prototype and will be presented to the target customers to see if changes need to be made. Accommodate all the required changes as per the audience. Technical Implementation: Involves managerial planning and focusing on feedback. Make necessary adjustments to ensure product is ready for launch.

Stage 7: Test Marketing

Test marketing means testing the product within a specific area. Produce a physical prototype or mock-up. Test the product (and its packaging) in typical usage situations. Conduct focus group customer interviews or introduce at trade show. Make adjustments where necessary. Produce an initial run of the product and sell it in a test market area to determine customer acceptance. Be ready to make instant changes, if necessary, including raising or lowering the price or offering other incentives to move the product.

Stage 8: Commercialization

If the test marketing stage has been successful then the product will go for national launch. Launch the product. Produce and place advertisements and other promotions. Fill the distribution pipeline with product. Critical path analysis is most useful at this stage. There are certain factors that need to be taken into consideration before a product is launched nationally. These are timing, how the product will be launched, where the product will be launched, will there be a national roll out or will it be region by region?

6.14. How to Evaluate Your Business Idea

Whether you want to start an online or offline business, the first thing you need to do is find out whether your product or service will sell. The first step to finding that out is to research the supply and demand of the market. Ideally you want a product or service with high demand and low competition. There are many resources with which you can accomplish that. But, before we get to that, always remember that a business idea is not a business opportunity until you go through the evaluation procedure and judge it to be feasible.

1. Define your product or service. Be specific in your definition. What exactly will be your prospective customers? How will it be produced and/or provided? How will it be delivered to the customer? How much will it cost? What are the options? What is the warranty?
2. Ask Around

   First, bounce your ideas off your family and friends. Here is a list of good questions to ask:

   - Have you ever heard of this product/service before?
   - Would you buy this product/service?

- If yes, what is the maximum that you would pay for it and how often would you buy it?
- If no, why not?
- If you can design this product/service, how could you make it better?

Be prepared to receive many different kinds of answers. Don't get discouraged if some of them are negative; you can't please everyone.

Ask some experts

There are many free resources available to you. Here are just a few:

- Micro Small and Medium Enterprises (MSME): This is a government sponsored organization that helps small businesses with loans, paperwork, education and others services.
- Chamber of Commerce: Most towns and cities have a local Chamber of Commerce to help you with your small business.

When you speak with experts, prepare for and expect hard questions. Make sure your thought process is streamlined. Don't forget survey your potential customers. Develop a list of questionnaires and get as many people to answer them as possible.

3. Analyze the impact of idea (product) on the environment. Today government, customers and investors have become very serious about environment. They are very sensitive about the product that is having bad impact on the environment. Customers try to purchase environment friendly products. Even government may ban the product that is not good for customers' health or for the environment.
4. Describe your customers. Who will buy your product or service? Why will they buy from you rather than your competitor(s)? It is not only customers, but competitors as well, that will determine the success or failure of your new business idea.

   Securing customers in today's cluttered marketplace is difficult and requires creativity and plenty of hard work. Identifying your customer base and attracting them to be potential customers is first and foremost. Keep in mind the old axiom "People don't plan to fail. They fail to plan."
5. Identify your competitors. Learn about their products, services and company. Learn how they do business. You can get plenty of information from the company through annual reports, financial statements, industry publications/reports and marketing materials. Get information from their customers what unique they get from the company. Analyze the competitor's marketing strategies, their methods of promotions. Those information will tell you what they think are the advantages of their products to the customers. Is your product or service better than that of the competitors?
6. Define your competitive advantage. Competitive advantages exist when the company is able to deliver the same benefits as competitors but at a lower cost (cost advantage), or deliver benefits that exceed those of competing products (differentiation advantage). Thus competitive advantage enables the company to create superior value for its customers and superior profits for itself. What makes your product or service better than your competitors' offering? You can gain a competitive advantage in a multitude of ways. You could offer cheaper prices, better quality, faster service or a longer warranty. Perhaps you have a proprietary technology or method of doing business that provides your business with a competitive advantage.
7. To be successful, you must be able to sell your product or service at a price that covers the costs directly associated with producing and delivering that product or service

to your customers plus contribute towards paying other operational costs not to mention providing a profit to the business.

8. How will you communicate the availability of your product or service to your prospective customers? Internet advertising, direct mail, outbound telephone calls, radio, television, print advertising, trade shows and outdoor bill boards are all tools a business can use to educate and inform prospective customers about the availability of your product or service. Selecting a particular tool depends upon the type of product, market and customers to whom you want to communicate. So select a particular or combinations of tools for your product or services.

9. Describe the things that could go wrong to negatively impact your business. Loss of suppliers, insufficient profit, product defects, customer dissatisfaction and better competitors are examples of things that could go wrong. What might go wrong with your business? How will you handle those problems should they arise?

10. **SWOT Analysis**

SWOT stands for strengths, weaknesses, opportunities and threats. Many companies use SWOT analysis to make business decisions. Putting your business ideas through the SWOT test will help you clarify and develop your idea.

Strengths and weaknesses are considered controllable/internal factors while opportunities and threats are considered uncontrollable/external factors.

Examples of strengths:

- Superior expertise in an industry
- Patent protected product

Examples of Weaknesses:

- Weak supply chain
- High learning curve

Examples of Opportunities:

- Product/service is in high demand
- Changes in regulation

Examples of Threats:

- Many established competitors
- Changing technology threaten to make product/service obsolete.

11. **Checklists for idea evaluation**

In normal business life there are always a lot of business ideas but only few of them turn out to be business opportunity and even less turn into a profitable venture. This approach is most appropriate when deciding on starting a business. When there are more than one possible business idea and one needs to decide which one to follow we score business ideas (e.g., idea1,idea2, idea3) by assigning a rating from 1 to 4 for each question, with 4 being highest. After we score the ideas we sum the total and select the idea with the highest score. Following are the checklists for evaluating an idea.

New idea evaluation checklist:

1. Is your idea legal?
2. Please describe in detail the nature of the idea.
3. On what technologies is this idea based?
4. Who will be the customers for this product?
5. Does it need packaging?

6. What benefits will it bring the customers?
7. What is the approximate price range of the product/service?
8. What companies are currently competing in this market?
9. How will the product rank against competing products in terms of price/performance?
10. Is there just one product or a line of products?
11. What is the customer's perception of the current products?
12. Which distribution channel do customers prefer?
13. What is the market size for this new product?
14. What is the lifecycle of the product or service?
15. What is the market growth rate?
16. Does your idea fit into a trend?
17. How much will it cost to get your idea to market?
18. What regulatory threats/trends will influence this market?
19. How many customers are there in the market by segment? (Geography, type of company, industry, application, etc.)
20. What is its environmental impact?

SUMMARY

Creativity (or creativeness) is a mental process involving the generation of new ideas or concepts or new associations between existing ideas or concepts. From a scientific point of view, the products of creative thought (sometimes referred to as divergent thought) are usually considered to have both originality and appropriateness. An alternative, more everyday conception of creativity is that it is simply the act of making something new.

Creative thinking is the process which we use when we come up with a new idea. Creative thinking explores the environment, gets relevant ideas from surroundings and gives them a unique shape that has not been given by anyone earlier. This creative thinking process can be **unintentional** or **purposeful**.

In unintentional way; like a change happening making you think about something in a different way and you then discovering a beneficial change.

Using special techniques, purposeful creative thinking can be used to develop new ideas. Brainstorming is one of these special techniques, but traditionally it starts with unoriginal ideas.

Creative individuals have a great deal of energy, tend to be smart, have a combination of playfulness and discipline, alternate between imagination and fantasy at one end, seem to harbour opposite tendencies on the continuum between extroversion and introversion, remarkably humble and proud at the same time, very passionate about their work, thought to be rebellious and independent, and escape rigid gender role stereotyping.

Problem solving, Learning, Imitation and Trial and error are not considered as creativity.

The Myths of Creativity are: Creativity comes from creative types, Time pressure generates creativity, Fear forces step forward, Competition beats collaboration, Creativity comes from the unconscious, Creativity is a talent, Children are more creative than adults, and Everyone is creative

Creativity is the same as originality and Creativity only applies to science and the fine art.

A study by George Land reveals that we are naturally creative and as we grow up we learn to be uncreative. Creativity is a skill that can be developed and a process that can be managed. Learning to be creative is akin to learning a sport. It requires practice to develop the right muscles and a supportive environment in which to flourish. Business leaders are increasingly adopting the principles and practices of art and design to help build creative muscle in their organizations.

The **National Innovation Initiative** (NII) defines innovation as "The intersection of invention and insight, leading to the creation of social and economic value."

3M describes innovation as an action or implementation which results in an improvement, a gain, or a profit.

Entrepreneurs can find Innovation by taking different roles, using knowledge of other domains, asking influential questions, Fostering new knowledge, reflecting ideas with pictures, and Changing the pace of attention.

Creative Entrepreneurs get success by collaboration with partners, other entrepreneurs, stay in contact with their clients, stay in contact with community, communicate with their vendors, new clients, and maintain industry presence.

Obstacles to creativity are created by not willing to risk, Lack of Experience, Fears of failure, lack of Judgement, Too much time between creation and implementation, Negligence to new ideas, Inadequate funding, non-recognition of creativity of their employees, and Valuing only big ideas.

Barriers to Creative Thinking can be overcome by Educating noncreative, Discouraging Group Thinking, Reverse Creative Thinking, by remaining patient, by overcoming self imposed barriers, patterns or belief in alternate unique answers eveluating with patient. Trying new ways of thinking and acting, and Believing in own ability to be creative.

Some elements of the good idea generation process are:

Read and study as many things about your industry or product and services. Improve general knowledge; Brainstorming is one group method for generating both business solutions and ideas. Think on does it make customers' life easier or solve a problem? Think on is there a market for your idea? Checking out the competition; Analysis of company, customers and competitors; Think on the viability of the idea? Refine and Narrow, Can it generate profit? Is there room for growth?

Improving and updating product lines is crucial for the success for any organization. Failure for an organization to change could result in a decline in sales and with competitors racing ahead. The process of New Product Development is crucial within an organization. Products go through the stages of their lifecycle and will eventually have to be replaced. There are two parallel paths involved in the NPD process: one involves the idea generation, product design and detail engineering; the other involves market research and marketing analysis. The stages for New Product Development are Idea generation, Idea Screening, Concept Development and Testing, Marketing Strategy and Development, Business Analysis, Product Development, Test Marketing and Commercialization.

For evaluating the business idea the entrepreneurs should define product or service, Ask Around the people, Analyze the impact of idea (product) on the environment, Describe customers, Identify competitors, Define competitive advantage of ideas, do SWOT Analysis and Prepare checklists for idea evaluation.

Keywords

Creativity: Creativity is the act of turning new and imaginative ideas into reality.

Creative thinking: Creative thinking explores the environment, gets relevant ideas from surroundings and gives them a unique shape that has not been given by anyone earlier.

Innovation: Innovation is the production or implementation of ideas.

Business Model Innovation: Significantly changing the structure and / or financial model of the business.

Operations Innovation: Improving the effectiveness and efficiency of core business processes and functions.

Product/Services/Markets Innovation: Creating new or significantly differentiated products, services or go-to-market activities.

Collaboration: Connecting and working with partners, clients and other significant players in your network.

Community: This means networks of people. That could be local communities, students, artists, entrepreneurs or researchers.

Idea generation: It is the process of generating new idea either by observation or by R&D.

Idca Screening: This process involves shifting through the ideas generated and selecting ones which are feasible and workable to develop.

Concept Development and testing: The idea needs to be taken to the target audience and test the concept by asking a sample of prospective customers what they think of the idea.

Marketing strategy: A proposed marketing strategy involves the marketing mix strategy of the product, the segmentation, targeting and positioning strategy sales and profits that are expected.

Business analysis: The business analysis stage looks more deeply into the profit the product, the cost, expected customers, market shares and the expected life of the product.

Test marketing: Test marketing means testing the product within a specific area.

SWOT analysis: SWOT stands for strengths, weaknesses, opportunities and threats. Many companies use SWOT analysis to make business decisions.

Questions

1. What do you mean by creativity? Explain with examples.
2. What are the characteristics of creative personality?
3. What are the myths of creativity?
4. What is the role of creativity in business development?
5. What do you mean by innovation? How to find innovation?
6. What are the obstacles to creativity? How to overcome that?

❑ ❑ ❑

Chapter – 7

Entrepreneurs' Thoughts on Business Start Up

LEARNING OBJECTIVES

On completion of this chapter, you should be able to:

☺ *Explain what entrepreneurs think on opening the new business.*

☺ *Describe the bad and good reasons for opening the business.*

☺ *Discuss the advantages and disadvantages of becoming an entrepreneur.*

7.1 Reasons Not To Become An Entrepreneur

You do not want to compromise with your relaxation

If you want to start your own business then you should be ready to work at any time of the day and night. But if you are not at all ready to compromise with your relaxation then definitely you are in the wrong train. You cannot expect job like situation when you are in your business. You cannot work within limited time. So if you want to spend your time with limits then it is not a good idea to open the business.

You're not disciplined

Being an entrepreneur requires discipline since there is no one but you to set your work schedule or deadlines. This is one of the benefits of being an entrepreneur; you can do things when you feel like it, but is also one of the downsides. Think how many times you don't feel like going to work but do anyway or you would lose your job. Because you are your own boss so from here itself your responsibilities increase. If you will shape the situation according to you but not according to business need then you will be in loss.

You give up easily

Most difficult about being an entrepreneur and one of the things that came up repeatedly is to not give up and just keep going. Giving up too early likely contributed to the high failure rates, that entrepreneurs gave up before something great happened because it can be incredibly frustrating sometimes. If you are the type to give up easily, it is almost guaranteed that your business will fail since you will give up when it gets tough and it definitely will get tough, so be honest with yourself as this is a critical key to being an entrepreneur.

Not interested in research and details

Even if you have great idea but if you dislike research to get information then definitely your business is not good for you. If you will think that my idea is good and I have to just start with my business and you will try to avoid business research then it will not work. You have to do a business research to know:

- Is there a market for your products and/or services?
- Who will be your target market?
- What are their demographics?
- How will you reach them?
- Have you set up manufacturing, inventory, delivery and tracking platforms?
- Who's verifying and validating your bookkeeping?
- What type of business structure will/have you set up? Sole proprietorship? Partnership? LLC? Corporation?
- Do you have a lawyer, a patent or a mentor?
- Do you have a budget?
- Do you have a business plan?

The issues above are just a minor sampling of the details that must be addressed. Is it doable? Yes, definitely and it will encourage you to, but only after you throw away your rose-colored glasses, look reality in the face, dive into the research and become acquainted with the possible ramifications.

BOX 7

New Age Entrepreneurs Quit Corporate Jobs to Start Up

The ET-Synovate Entrepreneurship Survey-II among established entrepreneurs across sectors in India found out what is it that pushed them to start up on their own.

Interestingly, 95% of the entrepreneurs have worked in a corporate establishment before starting up. Of the respondents, 67% had 0-5 years of experience before they decided to turn entrepreneurs. It is here that they gained valuable work experience and probably expertise in their domain of choice. And if we go by the ET-Synovate Entrepreneurship Survey a good number of corporate executives usually have business ideas up their sleeve and some even work on their business plans alongside their work in a corporate setting.

While they do get their experience working in a corporate set up, it is here that situations push them towards becoming their own boss. A huge 83% of the entrepreneurs surveyed said they quit because there was an urge to break out and make my own idea come true.

About 56% felt they were making money or doing well for someone else, not for themselves. A similar percentage was not comfortable working as a part of strict hierarchy which exists in some corporate houses. 50% felt they had to cope with seniors whose views were different from their own. 39% recalled that they quit because they were forced to work on ideas that they did not agree with.

When you turn entrepreneur, the basic premise is that you believe in your idea and will work hard to realize the dream of creating a sustainable business model. Over half (56%) of the entrepreneurs decided on quitting and setting up a business because they had a business idea they could no longer hold back. It could be because the idea was linked to some developments in the industry they are operating in. As more time passed by, the idea could lose its effectiveness.

When they were contemplating setting up their business, funding was the biggest barrier in front of them, as indicated by 53% of the respondents. A few said they had problems because the market for their idea was not very well defined, they could not convince partners and could not source quality products consistently. About 11% of the respondents felt one of the barriers was lack of family support.

On the question of mentoring, 58% acknowledged that they did get some kind of support, either in terms incubation or mentoring. About 16% of the respondents said they got incubation support from one of the premier institutions in the country and support from alma mater, alumni network and acquaintances who were successful entrepreneurs. Some said they prefer going without a mentor so that they can make their own mistakes. For some, support from mentors was invaluable when it came to new idea validation and helping them with the fundamentals of running a business. Interestingly, 5% were helped by ex-bosses and academic deans.

Source: Information received from "Economic Times", 2010.

You have a "good" idea

Having a "good" idea does not stir up the fires of passion. Your idea must be great. Your idea must be demanding. It must create within you a passion to defend it against the onslaught of detractors who will be standing in line to tell you why your idea won't work.

- "Someone else is already doing it",
- "It's been tried before and didn't work",
- "What if you fail?"

- "What makes you think you can make a living doing that?"
- "If your idea is so good then why isn't someone else doing it?"

You'll hear all the protests and derogatory remarks. Are you passionate enough to defend your "great" idea? If you're not, then don't waste your time and money. Keep your day job.

You like the idea of being your own boss

When you start out, you get to be the boss and:

- the secretary
- the assistant
- the delivery man
- the promotion guy/gal
- the salesman
- the office manager
- the doorkeeper

So if you have any idea for your business and want to implement it then you should be ready to do all tasks for example, you may be the water boy, the salesman, office boy. If you will hesitate or dislike these tasks then definitely you are not suitable for opening the business. You are the man. You are the go-to guy. The buck stops with you. You make the decisions – all the decisions. There will be no rest for the weary because it all rests on your shoulders. If you can't stand the pressure, then don't put yourself in that position.

7.2 Bad Reasons to Become An Entrepreneur

Risk of Failure

The problem in investing capital into a new business is that if the business fails, you will lose all that money. If you had to take out a bank loan or a second mortgage, in order to come by the money that you required, then you will have to find a way to pay that money back without having a job or a business to assist you. But what can be even more damaging is the sense that you failed, you weren't good enough, your idea was poorly received by peers. Before you set off on your journey as an entrepreneur you should seriously consider whether you are mentally flexible enough to cope with the possibility of failure.

When you actually need a job

Don't do business, if at present you do not have anything to do and therefore you want to do business because that will be the bad option for doing business. You cannot consider opening the business so lightly. You need desire and motivation for your business. Opening the business requires investment, efforts, resources etc., all assets will be of no use if without any mindset you are trying to open the business. The best time to consider entrepreneurship is when you are employed and drawn to doing something else. Then you can truly answer the question of whether you are committed enough to provide steep outlays of time and money to give your business the care it needs.

When you want to work less

It is wrong perception that if you are a boss or business owner then you have to work less, rather you have to work more for your business. Opening a business because you want to work less is a bad option. Running a business is not an easy job. If you want to run a business because you want to work less then there will be more chances that your business will fail. At least initially you need to work hard for growing your business and surviving in the tough competitive market.

You can think about the leisure time when first you will establish your business, you will have your customers and you will settle the problems of your business. If you want to work less then do not start business, otherwise your business will suffer.

Because you hate your boss

When you are frustrating with your boss and you dislike him and therefore want to open a new business, where you can work without any stress. But before taking this decision you need to think on whether are you ready to open the business? Are you able to handle the burden of your business? Are you ready to take such a big responsibility? So many challenges are there for opening a business. You must have all the information of opening the business. You will face the challenges and you must have a gut to face it and overcome it. Now you no longer have someone else to blame for your own shortcomings. You can't thrive in your business unless you've mastered people and processes. If you are so oppressed by your boss or your workplace, consider another job before you consider building a business.

When you want to become wealthy

Just for becoming a rich person is not a good reason of opening a business. So many successful entrepreneurs in the world did not have their prime motive to become wealthy rather they wanted to do something new and unique. They wanted to achieve something in their life and wanted to do something for the welfare of society. The important thing is that if you have a reason for your business then you will definitely succeed in your business. But if you have only one desire to open the business that is to become rich then, your desire is not completely good. You must keep the desire of becoming rich to secondary level but not on the prime level.

Think about the *why*. Why you want to be in business. A lot of people who made a lot of money building businesses have felt this way. A lot of businesses bombed in the Web that was built on less than passion. The need to make money doing what you love leads to innovation. The need to get rich leads to stupid decisions.

When you want to become renowned

People want to do business because they want to be famous. They want that people should know them. The others should respect them, should give value to them. They are impressed by the success stories of the entrepreneurs and what they think by becoming entrepreneur they can also become famous. But the reality is different the entrepreneurs have become rich because of their work, they did not get into the business because they wanted to do the business but they opened the business because they wanted to do something for the society, for people or they had seen the opportunities and after that they have to work hard to turn the opportunities into the reality and because of that they have earned the fame. People have recognized them for their work for their talent and uniqueness. If you want to earn the fame then it is not easy. You must be ready to accept any challenge. You must know about business. You must have purpose to do a business. Becoming famous should not be your goal but it should act as the secondary goal. Your primary goal must be to do some unique thing for the society.

If getting attention is your reason for starting a business, take note: There are much easier ways of becoming famous.

7.3 How to be a Better Entrepreneur

- Don't let emotions cloud your decisions.
- Accept criticism, no matter who gives it to you.

- Never stop networking.
- Learn from your own mistakes.
- Learn from other people's mistakes.
- Around every corner lies an opportunity for you to sell something.
- Try not to mix your family life with your business life.
- No matter how successful you are, you shouldn't stop learning.
- Hiring employees won't solve most of your problems.
- Having a good business partner will be a key factor in your success.
- Don't be afraid of the unknown.
- It is easier to save money than it is to make it.
- You don't always have to innovate; there is nothing wrong with copying.
- Have a marketing plan.
- Don't underestimate your competition; you can't always know what they are doing.
- If you don't have a business mentor, you better get one.
- It doesn't matter what you want, it only matters what your customers want.
- When others are fearful, you should be greedy. And when they are greedy you should be fearful.
- The best chances you have of becoming rich are through your willingness of working hard.
- Even the most idiotic business idea can make money.
- An easy way to make more money is to Upsell to your current customer base.
- Base your business decisions around metrics.
- Raising venture capital is harder than being struck by lightning.
- Learn to be a team player.
- Learn to manage both your personal and business money.
- Live in a location filled with entrepreneurs.
- If you don't take any risks, there will not be any rewards.
- Don't let anything stand in your way.
- Sometimes you have to wait for good deals to come to you.
- The smartest route isn't always the easiest route.
- With networking, it isn't about whom you know, it is about whom your network knows.
- You'll learn more from starting your own business, than going to business school.
- Having a personal blog doesn't only help build your personal brand, but it helps your business as well.
- Your competitors don't have to be your enemies, you can learn a lot from them.
- You can grow your business by working for free.

7.4 Reasons for Becoming an Entrepreneur

Being your own boss

You make all the key decisions. You choose who you sell to, who you buy from, who you work with. Including how much you work and how much you spend on promotion, production and overhead. Desiring to be your own boss is a great motivation to start an enterprise. This is particularly if you are a self-reliant and independent person. To you, life is a risk and a business is no different. Thus 'calling your own shots' is very important and being an entrepreneur allows this. Of course, if your business is successful, you would earn uncommonly more money than most.

Decide what to delegate

A common pitfall for new entrepreneurs is the tendency to try to do everything themselves. In some cases this is necessary due to budget constraints or other reasons. But in time as business grows the owner will increasingly see the need to delegate some of the work to others. At this stage you will get to decide which tasks are not the best use of your time and would be better handed over to someone else. A small retailer might contract with a bookkeeper to take over the day-to-day financial duties, while a writer might hire someone to handle the keyword research portion of writing for online sites.

Because it's very creative

Most of the people want to be in business because they love creativity and they want to show this with their business. The process of starting a business, building and nurturing it is very creative. You can do any experiment with your business. You can present the products or services in your own way. It requires constant ideation and forces you to keep the creative juices flowing. People with such a creativity and efforts always try to do business where they can show their talent. More so, when things are going good and there is a tendency to rest on one's glory.

Income potential

One of the top reasons to be an entrepreneur is that you are not saddles into a yearly salary. You are free to work hard and earn more money. In many cases there is no limit to the amount of money you can earn. You can earn according to your performance and the efforts that you put into the business. The drawback of the job is you can earn only fixed salary irrespective of your performance.

Diversification

You don't have to put all of your marbles in one jar. You can start multiple streams of income, eliminate ideas that do not work and create residual income that makes your money while you sleep. You can play with many ideas. You have a complete freedom to work on more than one idea that you think is feasible for your business.

Excitement and fun

Doing something that you love makes work feel like play. If you can work at something that you enjoy you'll never dread working hard and waking up every day. Your excitement will move you and your business forward. Excitement is one of the important factors to start the business. There's excitement in thinking of new ways to make money.

Confidence

If you are confident then only you should start the business. With fear business cannot be run. It is all about decision making. You should be very much confident while taking decisions about your business. These decisions will decide the future of your business. Showing yourself and others that you can make a living on your own merit can build great self esteem. Being an entrepreneur will help you become better leader.

Satisfaction

There's something to be said for helping out other people. Your product or service will benefit or improve the life of another person which will be very satisfying. Accomplishing your goals and actually having a successful business brings its own satisfaction.

Security

There won't be much security in the beginning but in the long run you will control your own fate. There are no layoffs, no downsizing and no wondering if your job is on the line. A successful entrepreneur will not only bring security to himself but can also bring security to the family and children that might one day take over the business.

Want of freedom

For some, true freedom is defined as being "able to do what you want, when, with whomsoever, wherever and however you want". Others described it as 'being able to wake up when you finished sleeping!". The most common road taken to such freedoms as described above is by becoming an entrepreneur. There are generally major benefits of being an entrepreneur. They mostly explain why anyone would want to face the risk and frustration of owning a business. Starting a new business involves investing in substantial resources, chief of which is money. The initial learning curve is steep, many things can go wrong and a new business owner has to learn things fast to avoid failure. So what are the benefits of becoming an entrepreneur, to make all the frustrations and risks worth taking? Often, the best reason is being able to explore your true passion. (As opposed to dragging yourself everyday to a dead-end job) It may seem silly but sometimes this motivation alone would motivate a person to persist against great odds, when others give up, in the pursuit of his goals.

Opportunity for greater financial success

Entrepreneurs have been shown to amass even personal fortunes through the development of their companies. Certainly this is not all as many entrepreneurs stay small and remain just independent business people. When you work for someone else, you are contributing to their financial future all of the time and to your own financial future to the extent that they decide. People want to open their business so that they can put all their efforts for their business and can have greater success to access finance.

For the creation of wealth

Oh yes! There's no denying the fact that the creation of wealth is one of the primary goals of any enterprise and most entrepreneurs dream of material wealth and possessions. But there's more to it than just money. Creation of wealth is not just cash in the bank or assets, but also goodwill, reputation, camaraderie, experience and most importantly intellectual capital.

Sense of accomplishment

Another great reason for becoming an entrepreneur is the sense of accomplishment you will feel. This will also give you the power to take decisions that will propel you towards greater wealth. Owning a business can make you begin to feel good about what you do and will give you something to look forward to on a daily basis. Though your days may be longer because you are the boss, you can end each one knowing you have taken the necessary steps to insure wealth. You can also grow your business at a pace that can be much faster than waiting for raises and promotions in other job situations.

For a higher purpose

It's not just about the money. The business should have a purpose other than making money out of it. The number of successful entrepreneurs dream was not to make money but they had some other purpose for it.

Various purposes of the successful entrepreneurs:

- Want to help society.
- Want to create wealth for nation.
- Want to generate employment.
- Want innovation and creativity etc.

Likewise you must also have some solid purpose for your business. It's about wanting to do something very different from the mainstream. They have grandiose dreams of being able to inspire a lot of other would-be entrepreneurs out there to take the leap of faith and begin their own ventures. Directly or indirectly they have always wanted to promote entrepreneurship within India, because that's what pumps up the economy – the pursuit of the creation of wealth. It creates opportunities for financial empowerment of all sectors of society and it helps create a shared goal and shared vision of what a country should strive to achieve.

Opportunity to build equity

When you own your own business, you also own the means of production, which can develop into substantial value. This equity represents assets that can be sold to someone else or passed on to your heirs. Entrepreneurship creates the opportunity for philanthropy. Other contributions that entrepreneurs make result from their creating value. New, innovative ideas have been known to change society. Take for example the personal computer or telephone. To have the opportunity to change peoples' lives through your work is personally rewarding and motivation for some entrepreneurs.

For the independence

The independence to do what I wanted to do; and to do it in a way where my principles and values would not be compromised; where my potential would not be capped by the potential of a boss. Entrepreneurs want complete authority; they have their own plan to do. They cannot work under any superior authority and therefore they want to open their own business.

I've always wanted to do this

Most of the people for some strange reason, ever since have always wanted to build their own business. The question for them always was "when" and not "if". Somehow, other than a brief dalliance with the idea of becoming a fighter pilot, they've never really floundered on what they want to do for a living. It's always been business.

Because I am crazy

That hardly needs much explanation, but a certain amount of eccentricity is almost essential to a successful business. Some want to open the business because they anyhow want to open the business. They want their own business, responsibility and authority.

The opportunity to have control over your life and job

It is not just the ability to say what hours you will work but it also involves every step in the operation of a business. This might include environmental sensitivity, social responsibility and benefiting your own community in certain ways. When you are the boss, all decisions from design concept to job creation, sales, business operations and customer relationship management ultimately circle back to the boss and his or her philosophy and motivations.

Many people have made decision to become an entrepreneur so they could take control of every aspect of their lives. This is very important in the stressful world of today. Stress is a great motivator because it prompts people to break away from those factors that are so greatly affecting them and make important decisions that will benefit them in the future. Though owning a business does come with its own set of stresses, it does take you out of the everyday situations that can become the source of anxiety.

Ego satisfaction! Business entrepreneurs have great opportunities to be visible in their community. Membership in chambers of commerce, business awards, community boards and other corporate boards of directors serve the personal esteem and satisfaction motivations of some entrepreneurs.

For a good lifestyle

This would allow you to live a lifestyle associated with material wealth and success. Successful people are admired for their lifestyles; this reason, by itself, gives enough incentives for anyone to become an entrepreneur. The successful entrepreneurs have a very great lifestyle. They enjoy their life. Should you make a lot of money and know how to turn them into solid assets, then your life of never having to worry about money i.e., financial freedom is achieved. Once you achieve your financial freedom then you automatically change your life style. Now, your assets would work for you; making you all the money you need. This reason alone would drive most men to take the risk of starting a new business.

For the sheer challenge of it

Most of the people want to open the business because they love challenges. They love to face the challenges and to overcome the challenges. They want to see themselves in such a critical situation. They have an ability and knowledge to solve the problems. They are the confident people.

Because I'm inspired

Whether it is Akio Morita or Warren Buffet or Richard Branson, self-made capitalists have always been a tremendous inspiration. The success of big entrepreneurs has attracted many new ones to become entrepreneur. They want to be like that. They also want to do business and want to get success in their business. They have a dream to become a successful entrepreneur.

7.5 What to Think When Starting A Business

Thinking about starting your own company? Do you have what it takes? Is it worth all the pain and suffering?

There is no way to eliminate all the risks associated with starting a small business.

However, you can improve your chances of success with good planning and preparation. A good starting place is to evaluate your strengths and weaknesses. Carefully consider each of the following questions.

Who are your target customers?

Before launching your business, you should have already identified for whom you are providing your product. The design and price of your product are also dependent on the needs and wants (potential or present) of your target customers. Your target market or customers determine whether your product will sell or not.

Are you a self-starter?

It will be up to you - not someone else telling you - to develop projects, organize your time and follow through on details. You should know exactly you will be alone or are you starting your business with someone's support? If you are alone then no need to worry but if you are trying to open the business with the help of others then definitely it is better to assure that you will get support for your business.

How much will it cost?

You have to be able to make reasonable estimates on what it's going to cost you to get started and then, after you've started, what it's going to cost you to stay in business.

The maths isn't hard by itself. Your starting costs are essentially two simple lists: a list of expenses and a list of required assets. Expenses are cheques you write before starting for tax-deductible items like fixing the place up, establishing the legal entity, designing a website and so on. Assets are cheques you write for things you have to own to do business: chairs, tables, cars and trucks. And yes, there is a trick question hidden there among the assets — how much money do you have to have stashed away to cover your spending during the early lean period of the business, before sales catches up.

Have You Assessed The Risks Involved?

You need to assess the risks involved in the business. What if it doesn't work? What have you risked to start? How much money are you out? How will you pay that money back? Risk is a huge factor that banks look at when lending you money. They loan out thousands of rupees and they know the risk factors. If your banker doesn't give you the money for your business then you should look closely at the reasons why.

How well do you get along with different personalities?

Business owners need to develop working relationships with a variety of people including customers, vendors, staff, bankers and professionals such as lawyers, accountants or consultants. It is also an art and as an entrepreneur you must have this art. You should feel comfortable while dealing with others. A business requires lot of traveling, you go to others' office; you meet them; you spend your lot of time, sometimes you are not able to solve your problems immediately and easily. Think about it? Can you deal with a demanding client, an unreliable vendor or cranky staff person in the best interest of your business?

How good are you at making decisions?

Small business owners are required to make decisions constantly, often quickly, under pressure and independently. They are the single authority in the business. When new ones start their businesses then they become the single top level person who can take decision. You must think whether you have a capability to take decisions? Can you handle critical situation? Have you taken such kind of decisions before? Do you know the consequences of bad decisions?

Do you have the physical and emotional stamina to run a business?

Business ownership can be challenging, fun and exciting. But it's also a lot of work. Can you face 12-hour work days six or seven days a week? You must be physically and mentally very perfect. When you start your new business then it requires more efforts than established business. You must be ready to give all your 24 hours time to business. You may not have any relaxation in the initial months. If you are physically and mentally weak then think about it.

How well do you plan and organize?

Research indicates that many business failures could have been avoided through better planning. Business is the game of planning and organizing. You must think whether you can do proper planning? Do you have any knowledge about planning? Do you think you can plan different processes of your business? Without proper planning running business is very difficult sometimes it becomes impossible also. Good organization - of financials, inventory, schedules and production - can help avoid many pitfalls.

Is your drive strong enough to maintain your motivation?

Running a business can wear you down. Some business owners feel burnt out by having to carry all the responsibility on their shoulders. Strong motivation can make business succeed and will help you survive slowdowns as well as periods of burnout. Business should not be the passion. You must have strong determination for your business. You must open the business to get success in the business. You should be ready to face failures. It is very necessary in the business. The new entrepreneurs mostly gain failure when they start the business. So they should not give up.

How will the business affect your family?

The first few years of business start-up can be hard on family life. The strain of an unsupportive spouse may be hard to balance against the demands of starting a business. There also may be financial difficulties until the business becomes profitable, which could take months or years. You may have to adjust to a lower standard of living or put family assets at risk.

It's true; there are a lot of reasons not to start your own business. But for the right person, the advantages of business ownership far outweigh the risks.

- You get to be your own boss.
- Hard work and long hours directly benefit you, rather than increasing profits for someone.
- Earning and growth potential are far less limited.
- A new venture is exciting.
- Running a business will provide endless variety, challenge and opportunities to learn.

7.6. Business Success Factors

Each business has its own unique combination of critical success factors, but some are important for all businesses.

1. You should construct a plan to include goal, milestones, deliverables such as contracts, business plans, etc. and accomplishments. This will provide you with a visual as to what you are working for, what milestones you have successfully met and where you need to do better. Being successful also means keeping to a schedule. In addition, you need to learn how much is too much. Good time and resource management will help you ensure that you use your time wisely and that you are not adding third portions onto a plate still overflowing with seconds.
2. Identify and implement the technology needed to support your business and its growth. You can't afford to ignore technology. It can reduce manpower needs, increase efficiency, reduce overall costs and create the means to reach new markets, add new products and significantly improve your bottom line. The key is to know the technology that makes a difference for your business and not to take on technology for its own sake.
3. Communication is the key to unlocking the potential within businesses as well as individuals. When the goals are in alignment with the vision and consistently communicated from top down, then performance excellence is much more likely to happen. Inconsistent communication contributes to missed targets and lowers the performance for the entire organization.

4. Transparency fosters beneficial contagion and excitement among the ecosystem members and interested parties. An examination of any successful business platform reveals alternative futures. Alternative future means options. Options can be valued and hence the investment community can estimate the expected value of such potential futures and model a resulting perpetuity calculation. Transparency attracts new partners and helps existing ecosystem partners to co-create the future of business platform. As momentum builds, transparency also strikes fear in the competitors.
5. Use the skills and resources of others to open growth opportunities and provide support outside the core mission of your business. The virtual nature of today's business means that you can tap into resources that previously would have to be purchased through capital expenditure, employee commitments or long-term arrangements. What you can't provide through core capabilities can probably be better and more efficiently provided through strategic alliances where each alliance partner realizes a benefit from working together.
6. Always make sure you have a positive, pleasing attitude. Watch what you say and do because your employees will be watching. Train and discipline your employees in every aspect of your business, especially a positive attitude towards other employees and customers. Always hire people with a positive attitude, initiative and who are fast learners. These three qualities in people are more important than their education, skill, knowledge and experience. Test their strengths in all these areas.
7. Timing is everything: You have probably heard it before timing is everything. Especially when it comes to opening a business, there is a right and a wrong time to start a business. This would be extremely important if your business has cycles or is seasonal. For example, if you are starting a business to do landscaping, the winter months when snow is on the ground is not the right time. You can be working towards your Business Plan, marketing ideas, finding investors, if required, etc., during those cold months, but you certainly would not want to open your doors for the first time in the heart of winter.
8. Operate from a plan based on your business vision. Even though the speed of business will likely continue to grow, having a basic business operating plan and budget as the framework to keep things in focus and on target is more important than ever. At least quarterly, review the results of actions and update your plan. Staying on top of the financial picture, especially cash flow means problems will be identified early enough that you have time to take corrective action before a crisis occurs.

   Develop your marketing plan. The purpose of the marketing plan is to describe how you will attempt to create and maintain customers for a profit. It needs to state whom you are going to sell to, how you are going to penetrate the market, why you will be successful with your sales campaigns and finally, how much you will sell annually over the next five years. The marketing plan will ultimately become an integral part of your overall business plan, but it must be completed first.

   Finalize your financing needs and create your formal business plan. Starting with the rough business plan put together a full-fledged formal business plan. A business plan should convincingly demonstrate that your business can sell enough of its product or service to make a satisfactory profit and be attractive to potential backers. This is the document you will use to secure the financing you need to get your business off the ground. It will also serve as an operating manual for your business once it's been funded.

9. Find the balance between online and offline activities that's right for your business. This includes marketing, public relations, customer service, business development and, of course, e-commerce. You've probably noticed the onslaught this past year of offline marketing to Web sites. Certainly you'll reach a broader market by waging a multimedia campaign, but if your budget is limited, try weighing your efforts in areas that are less expensive (online, public relations, press coverage). Make sure your online and offline messages are consistent.
10. Persistence is also a key factor for success. In spite of setbacks, hardships, failures and discouragements, persistence propels you to keep trying to develop those skills you initially lacked or continue practicing to achieve your 10,000 hours for expertise and finally reach your goal.
11. Customer Relationship: Keep your line of communication open with your customers. If your customers have a problem, show them the deserved respect and resolve the issue quickly. Make occasional phone calls to see if they have any needs. This will let your customers know that you are there for them and care about their business. This relationship is what is going to keep you on the road to success. After all, the customer is your link between failure and success.
12. Think global, even if your business is strictly local. Today, businesses of all sizes across the globe can interact and share information, technology and products. Consider what global trends are affecting availability of resources, increasing or decreasing demand for your product or service and where there's an unfilled need you might be able to meet. Look at the global marketplace for new ways to compete. Seek global alliances that will allow each partner to enter a new market or augment an existing capability.
13. Profits are essential for your business to succeed - they are what pays you. You don't have to look far to find examples of businesses imploding due to lack of profits. (The current banking and financial crisis immediately comes to mind). Ultimately, profits are the essential key ingredient for business survival - and your focus on them is key. The very existence of your business depends on a steady-stream of profits... to pay your bills... your salary... your employees... your vendors and suppliers... and to secure your financial future.
14. Create an environment where you replicate your passion, caring and sense of ownership in every employee. Clearly communicating your vision, mission and goals to your staff is your job as leader. But by giving the incentives of ownership and decision-making freedom at every level you can attract and keep the most talented and qualified individuals for each job. By fulfilling a mentor role and instilling this attitude in all staff, the strengths of each individual can be directed towards the benefit of the organization.

7.7. Types of Business Ownerships

With job losses everywhere and small business loans being made available easily, people are exploring that hidden entrepreneur inside them. Today, starting a business isn't hard, however remaining dedicated to it is. Before actually registering a business, one needs to know the type of ownership the business would follow. Currently there are three different types of business ownerships: Sole Proprietorships, Partnership Corporation and Limited Liability Company. Each type of ownership has its advantages and disadvantages.

Every business has certain plans and goals for the future. Thus accordingly they should select the type of ownership that would best suit their company. Even though it is possible to change the structure later, selecting the best form in the beginning can be a wise decision since the initial decision can have long term implications on the extent to which a business can progress. All the types of ownership have its advantages and disadvantages, so while selecting the type one should consider them and its consequence on the business.

7.7.1. Sole Proprietorship

Sole Proprietorship is the most common form of business. Sole proprietorships, the easiest and least expensive form of ownership to organize, are usually what the vast majority of the small business starts out as. These types of firms are owned by one single person and he has a complete authority over the company's day-to-day business. Usually all you need to do is register with your state government by purchasing a business license. The most significant downside of operating a sole proprietorship is that you are responsible for all the debts your small business may face. Unlike a corporation, in a sole-proprietorship structure the law views you and your business as one. This means the financial debts of your small business is considered your financial debts. For example if someone decides to sue your business and there's not enough money in your business to cover the costs, your own money and assets (such as your house) are in jeopardy. A good small business insurance policy can reduce lawsuit worries but make sure you have a thorough understanding of what your insurance policy covers. Most of the internet based dot com firms started out as a Sole Proprietorships due to its limited size and many of them have been proved to be a good success.

Advantages

- You have full control over your business- You are your own boss!
- Easiest and least expensive to set up
- Less paperwork to get started than corporations
- You can receive tax breaks for some of your business expenses such as a home office and travel (If the purpose of travel was for business of course)

Disadvantages

- You are fully responsible for your business debts. If something goes wrong with your business, you will have to pay.
- It is often more difficult to raise money for a sole proprietorship
- Selling a small business can be more complicated than selling a corporation since the business assets are involved.
- After you pass away your small business will probably soon follow.

7.7.2. Partnership

1. What Is Partnership?

Partnership is a form of business organization, where two or more persons join together for jointly carrying on some business. It is an improvement over the 'Sole –trade business ', where one single individual with his own resources, skill and effort carries on his own business. Due to the limitation of resources of only a single person being involved in the sole-trade business, a larger business requiring more investments and resources than available to a sole-trader, cannot be thought of in such a form of business organisation. In partnership, on the other hand, a number of persons could pool their resources and efforts and could start a much larger business, than could be afforded by any of these partners individually. In case of loss the burden gets divided amongst various partners in a Partnership.

Essentials of Partnership

According to Section 4 of Partnership Act, the following essentials are necessary to constitute a 'Partnership'.

(i) There should be an agreement between the persons who want to be partners.

(ii) The purpose of creating partnership should be carrying on of business.

(iii) The motive for the creation of partnership should be earning and sharing profits.

(iv) The business of the firm should be carried on by all of them or any of them acting for all, i.e., in mutual agency.

When all the above elements are present in certain relationship then it is known as 'partnership'. Persons who have entered into partnership with one another are called individually 'partners' and collectively 'a firm' and the name under which their business is carried on is called the ' firm name'.

Advantages of Partnership over a Company:

(i) For the creation of partnership just an agreement between various persons is all what you require. In case of a company a lot of procedural formalities which have to be gone through before a company is created.

(ii) The partners are their own masters for regulating their affairs. A company is subject to a lot of statutory control.

(iii) For dissolution of partnership, a mere agreement between the partners is enough but that is not the case of a company which can be wound up by only after certain set of procedure is followed.

(iv) Since all the profits are to be pocketed by the partners in a partnership firm, there is a great incentive for the partners to make business successful but that is not in case of a company.

(v) In a Partnership the persons who have entered into are individually called partners and collectively a firm. A partnership firm does not have a separate legal personality. A company is a legal entity different from its members.

(vi) A partnership firm means all the partners put together, if all the partners cease to be partners, e.g., all of them die or become insolvent, the partnership firm gets dissolved. A company being a person different from the members, the members may come and go but the company's life is not affected thereby.

(vii) The shareholder of a company can transfer his share to anybody he likes but a partner cannot substitute another person in his place unless all the other partners agree to the same. Similarly, on the death of a member of a company his legal representatives will step into his shoes for the purpose of the rights in the company, but on the death of a partner his legal representatives do not get substituted in his place of partnership.

(viii) The minimum number of members in partnership is two and maximum in case of partnership carrying on banking business is 10 and in case of any other business is 20.In the case of a private company the minimum number is 2 and the maximum is 50 whereas in the case of a public company the minimum number should be 7 but there is no limit to the maximum number and therefore, any number of persons can hold shares in a public company.

(ix) The liability of the members of a company is limited but the liability of the partners is unlimited.

Advantages

- Share expenses and losses.
- Easy to set up.
- Two or more heads are better than one.

Disadvantages of Partnership

One of the basic defect of the partnership is that the partners are personally and jointly responsible for all the debts of the firm. The duration of the partnership is always uncertain. If any partner dies, injured, withdraws, sells his interest or a new partner is admitted into the business, the partnership comes to an end. In partnership the misuse of the resources is raised by the partners. In case of any dispute among the partners, a delay may take place in decision-making process. This can cause loss to the firm.

2. Limited Liability Partnership- A Convenient Business Vehicle

A Limited Liability Partnership (LLP) has the best of both partnership and company. It has the features of a partnership, vis-à-vis, agreement, to carry lawful business and motive to make profit, as well as features of a company, vis-à-vis, perpetual succession (coming and going out of members do not affect the continued existence of the company) and legal personality separate from its partners. Thus, LLP is a hybrid of a company and a partnership. But the main attraction of LLP which makes it a popular mode for conducting business is the limited liability of its partners. The liability of the partners is limited to their agreed contribution in the LLP i.e., the partners will be liable only to the extent of their contribution. No partner would be liable on account of the independent or unauthorized acts of other partners. On the other hand, in a partnership originating from the Partnership Act 1932, every partner is liable individually as well as jointly for all acts of the firm. As the firm cannot, literally, act on its own, act of the firm means those acts done through its human agents. Section 2(a) of the Partnership Act 1932 defines "act of the firm" means any act or omission by all the partners or by any partner or agent of the firm which gives rise to a right enforceable by or against the firm.

A LLP has a distinct personality. It is a legal entity separate from its partners having perpetual succession. By being a legal entity, it can sue and be sued in its name. It has perpetual succession just like a company meaning it will continue to exist so long as it is not wound up or dissolved. The death or insolvency of the partners does not affect the continued existence of the LLP. Any change in the partners does not affect the existence, rights or liabilities of the LLP. To form a LLP, there has to be a minimum of two partners and the upper limit in membership is not fixed. This Act permits foreign nationals to be partners in LLP formed in India. Also, LLP's can be formed without even an Indian citizen. All that the Act requires is that at least one must be a resident in India meaning a person who has stayed in India for a minimum period of 182 days during the immediately preceding one year. As the name suggests LLP comes with limited liability and this limited liability is conferred on its partners. According to Section 28, a partner is not personally liable, directly or indirectly for an obligation of the LLP. It is the LLP as a whole that carries the burden of liability. Section 27 states that the LLP is liable if its partner is liable to any person as a result of a wrongful act or omission on his part in the course of the business of the LLP or with its authority. Also, the obligation of the LLP is solely its liability and nobody else's and these liabilities are met out of the property of the LLP. However, the LLP is not bound by anything done by a partner in dealing with a person if the partner is not authorized to do that particular act and the person knows that he has no authority or does not know or believes him to be a partner of the LLP. Yet another distinguishing feature of LLP is the protection for whistleblowers. By virtue of Section 31, the Act has incorporated the concept of whistle blowing which finds no mention in the Partnership Act 1932 or the Companies Act 1956.

This Act protects those individuals who are bold enough to disclose the corruption or irregularities in the administration of the organization.

3. Limited Partnership

A limited partnership is made up of two types of partners; general partner and limited partner. The general partner controls the business and makes all the decisions while a limited partner just invests money in the business. The profits will be shared between partners but losses and debts acquired by the business will be the responsibility of the general partner. The limited partner only risks losing the amount he/she has already put into the business. This form of business ownership can be useful if you want to keep control of your small business but need extra funds. However it also comes with a lot of complicated paperwork. Many entrepreneurs prefer other small business structures when starting a small business because this form of ownership can be quite complicated to set up.

Advantages

- Limited Liability for the limited partner.
- General Partner has all the control.
- Can have unlimited number of owners (however if you have many limited partners it may be better to form a corporation since it offers more flexibility).

Disadvantages

- General partner will be responsible for debts and obligations.
- Need to be in compliance with security laws.
- A lot of paperwork to set up.

7.7.3. Corporation

Is forming a corporation right for your business? What is a corporation?

A corporation is a separate entity that operates independently from the person/ people who formed it. It even has the same legal rights as a person; it has its own social security number, it can own assets and it can sue people as well as be sued, it can even keep operating after you are long gone. Many entrepreneurs are attracted to forming a Corporation because of the benefit of limited liability. Having limited liability means that you only risk the money you put into the business, not your personal money or assets. This means if someone decides to sue your business, you personally will not be liable for any debts encountered assuming you didn't conduct any criminal or negligent acts. The money or assets will be taken from your corporation instead. If there's not enough money and assets in the corporation to cover the costs then that's too bad for the collector.

There are two types of corporations; **C Corporation** and **S Corporation.** The main difference between the two is the way they are taxed. C corporations are subject to double taxation which can mean huge cuts in your profits. C corporations are taxed in the corporate level and after being distributed to the shareholders they are taxed again. S corporations are only taxed at the shareholder level.

Advantages

- You can sell shares to raise money for your business.
- You can easily transfer ownership (by selling shares).
- Limited Liability.
- Better fringe benefits.

Disadvantages

- Selling stocks means selling a percentage of ownership. For example if you sell 20 per cent of the shares of stocks in your corporation, that stock holder will have 20 per cent ownership of the corporation.
- C Corporations are subject to double taxation.
- Increased paperwork.
- Forming a corporation is more complicated and expensive.

7.7.4. Company

I. Private and Public Companies in India

Company is a voluntary association of persons formed for the purpose of doing business having a distinct name and limited liability. It is a juristic person having a separate legal entity distinct from the members who constitute it, capable of rights and duties of its own and endowed with the potential of perpetual succession. The Companies Act, 1956, states that 'company' includes company formed and registered under the Act or an existing company i.e., a company formed or registered under any of the previous company laws.

However, company is not a citizen so as to claim fundamental rights granted to citizens.

1. **Company is a 'juristic person' and it can file a suit as an 'indigent person':** An Expression 'person' includes not merely a natural person but also other juridical persons. A company being a juristic person would be represented before a Court of law or any other place by a person competent to represent it. It is enough that the person competent to represent a company presents the application on behalf of the company. Minors, lunatics or person under any disability are also entitled to file a suit either through guardian or the next friend. In such a case it is the guardian or next friend who is competent to represent the petitioner.
2. **Company is a separate legal entity:** Company is separate legal entity distinct from its shareholders. The major constituents of a company are its members, who are the ultimate owners and its directors. It is an important feature of the company form of business, that there is a gap between the ownership and control over the affairs of the company. In real sense the members are the owners of a company, but it is being managed by the directors who are elected representatives of its members, because it is absolutely necessary for it to have a human agency called as the Company's board of directors. The Board of Directors comprises the directors.
3. **Limited Liability :** The liability of the members of the company is limited to contribution to the assets of the company upto the face value of shares held by him. A member is liable to pay only the uncalled money due on shares held by him when called upon to pay and nothing more, even if liabilities of the company far exceeds its assets. On the other hand, partners of a partnership firm have unlimited liability i.e., if the assets of the firm are not adequate to pay the liabilities of the firm, the creditors can force the partners to make good the deficit from their personal assets. This cannot be done in case of a company once the members have paid all their dues towards the shares held by them in the company.
4. **Perpetual Succession:** A company does not die or cease to exist unless it is specifically wound up or the task for which it was formed has been completed. Membership of a company may keep on changing from time to time but that does not affect life of the company. Death or insolvency of member does not affect the existence of the company.

5. **Separate Property:** A company is a distinct legal entity. The company's property is its own. A member cannot claim to be owner of the company's property during the existence of the company.
6. **Transferability of Shares:** Shares in a company are freely transferable, subject to certain conditions, such that no share-holder is permanently or necessarily wedded to a company. When a member transfers his shares to another person, the transferee steps into the shoes of the transferor and acquires all the rights of the transferor in respect of those shares.
7. **Common Seal:** A company is an artificial person and does not have a physical presence. Therefore, it acts through its Board of Directors for carrying out its activities and entering into various agreements. Such contracts must be under the seal of the company. The common seal is the official signature of the company. The name of the company must be engraved on the common seal. Any document not bearing the seal of the company may not be accepted as authentic and may not have any legal force.
8. **Capacity to sue and being sued:** A company can sue or be sued in its own name as distinct from its members.
9. **Separate Management:** A company is administered and managed by its managerial personnel i.e., the Board of Directors. The shareholders are simply the holders of the shares in the company and need not be necessarily the managers of the company.
10. **One Share-One Vote:** The principle of voting in a company is one share-one vote i.e., if a person has 10 shares; he has 10 votes in the company. This is in direct contrast to the voting principle of a co-operative society where the "One Member - One Vote" principle applies i.e., irrespective of the number of shares held, one member has only one vote.

II. Types of Companies

1. **Public Company** means which is formed with minimum of seven members and three Directors. There is no restriction on maximum number of members. The name of the company shall end with the word 'Limited' which is not a private company.

Public Limited Company

Public Limited Company means a Company which is not a private limited Company and has a minimum Authorized Capital of ₹ 5 Lakhs. It does not carry the word 'private' in its name and also do not have the restrictions as carried out in the private limited companies. A Private Company which is subsidiary of Public Company also functions as Public Companies.

Basic Features are as follows:

- Minimum Authorized Capital of ₹ 5 Lakhs.
- No restriction on number of members.
- Shares are easily transferable.
- Can access Public in case of need of funds.

Advantages

- Better Governed due to large number of compliances.
- No limit to Memberships.
- More financing options in form of Public Issue or Deposits.
- Better Creditworthiness.

Disadvantages

- Number of legal Compliances are too large.
- Approvals of Government for large number of purposes.
- Restrictions on payment of salaries and loans to Directors.
- Not suitable for closely held business..

2. Private Company means a company which by its articles of association:

(a) Restricts the right of members to transfer its shares.

(b) Limits the number of its members to fifty. In determining this number of 50, employee-members and ex-employee members are not to be considered.

(c) Prohibits an invitation to the public to subscribe to any shares in or the debentures of the company.

(d) prohibits any invitation or acceptance of deposits from persons other than its member, directors or their relatives; Provided that where two or more persons hold one or more shares in a company jointly, they shall, for the purposes of this definitions, be treated as a single member.

If a private company contravenes any of the aforesaid three provisions, it ceases to be private company and loses all the exemptions and privileges which a private company is entitled.

Following are some of the privileges and exemptions of a private limited company:

(i) Minimum number of members are two (seven in case of public companies)

(ii) Prohibition of allotment of the shares or debentures in certain cases unless statement in lieu of prospectus has been delivered to the Registrar of Companies does not apply.

(iii) Restriction contained in Section 81 related to the rights issues of share capital does not apply. A special resolution to issue shares to non-members is not required in case of a private company.

(iv) Restriction contained in Section 149 on commencement of business by a company does not apply. A private company does not need a separate certificate of commencement of business.

(v) Provision of Section 165 relating to statutory meeting and submission of statutory report does not apply.

(vi) One (if seven or less members are present) or two members (if more than 7 members are present) present in person at a meeting of the company can demand a poll.

(vii) In case of a private company which is not a subsidiary of a public limited company or in the case of a private company of which the entire paid up share capital is held by the one or more body corporates incorporated outside India, no person other than the member of the company concerned shall be entitled to inspect or obtain the copies of profit and loss account of that company.

(viii) Minimum number of directors is only two. (three in case of a public company)

The Company Law Board on being satisfied that the infringement of the aforesaid three conditions was accidental or due to inadvertence or that on other grounds, it just an equitable to grant relief, may grant relief to the company from the consequences of such infringement. The infringement of the last three conditions does not automatically convert a private company into a public company. It continues to remain a private company; it merely ceases to be entitled to the privileges and exemptions available to a private company.

Advantages

- Suitable for closely held groups.
- Less Legal Formalities.
- Less Government Intervention.
- Better Creditworthiness.

Disadvantages

- Limited financing avenues i.e., no public offer or acceptance of deposits.
- Limited Membership.

3. Companies deemed to be public limited company

A private company will be treated as a deemed public limited company in any of the following circumstances:

(i) Where at least 25 per cent of the paid up share capital of a private company is held by one or more bodies corporate, the private company shall automatically become the public company on and from the date on which the aforesaid percentage is so held.

(ii) Where the annual average turnover of the private company during the period of three consecutive financial years is not less than ₹ 25 crores, the private company shall be, irrespective of its paid up share capital, become a deemed public company.

(iii) Where not less than 25 per cent of the paid up capital of a public company limited is held by the private company, then the private company shall become a public company on and from the date on which the aforesaid percentage is so held.

(iv) Where a private company accepts deposits after the invitation is made by advertisement or renews deposits from the public (other than from its members or directors or their relatives), such companies shall become public company on and from date such acceptance or renewal is first made.

4. Limited and Unlimited companies

Companies may be limited or unlimited companies. Company may be limited by shares or limited by guarantee.

(a) Company limited by shares: In this case, the liability of members is limited to the amount of uncalled share capital. No member of company limited by the shares can be called upon to pay more than the face value of shares or so much of it as is remaining unpaid. Members have no liability in case of fully paid up shares.

(b) Company limited by the guarantee: A company limited by guarantee is a registered company having the liability of its members limited by its memorandum of association to such amount as the members may respectively thereby undertake to pay if necessary on liquidation of the company. The liability of the members to pay the guaranteed amount arises only when the company has gone into liquidation and not when it is a going concern. A guarantee company may be a company with share capital or without share capital.

Unlimited Company: The liability of members of an unlimited company is unlimited. Therefore their liability is similar to that of the liability of the partners of a partnership firm.

5. Section 25 Companies: Under the Companies Act, 1956, the name of a public limited company must end with the word 'Limited' and the name of a private limited company must end with the word 'Private Limited'. However, under Section 25, the Central Government may allow companies to remove the word "Limited/Private Limited" from the name if the following conditions are satisfied:

(i) The company is formed for promoting commerce, science, art, religion, charity or other socially useful objects

(ii) The company does not intend to pay dividend to its members but apply its profits and other income in promotion of its objects.

6. Holding and Subsidiary companies

A company shall be deemed to be subsidiary of another company if:-

1. That other company controls the composition of its board of directors; or
2. That other company holds more than half in face value of its equity share capital.
3. Where the first mentioned company is subsidiary company of any company which that other's subsidiary, e.g., Company B is subsidiary of the Company A and Company C is subsidiary of Company B, therefore Company C is subsidiary of Company A.

The control of the composition of the Board of Directors of the company means that the holding company has the power at its discretion to appoint or remove all or majority of directors of the subsidiary company without consent or concurrence of any other person.

7. Government Companies

Means any company in which not less than 51 per cent of the paid up share capital is held by the Central Government or any State Government or partly by the Central Government and partly by the one or more State Governments and includes a company which is a subsidiary of a government company. Government Companies are also governed by the provisions of the Companies Act. However, the Central Government may direct that certain provisions of the Companies Act shall not apply or shall apply only with such exceptions, modifications and adaptations as may be specified to such government companies.

8. Foreign Companies

Means a company incorporated in a country outside India under the law of that other country and has established the place of business in India.

III. Public and Private Company: Differences.

The main differences between Public and Private Companies relate to the provisions of the Companies Act that are not applicable to private companies. These include:

- Provisions as to the type of share capital, further issue of share capital, voting rights, issue of shares with disproportionate rights, etc.
- Provisions restricting the company from giving financial assistance to subscribe to its own shares.
- Provisions restricting the amount of managerial remuneration paid and certain other provisions relating to managerial personnel.
- Provisions restricting the powers of the Board of Directors.
- Provisions restricting loans to directors.
- Private companies are deemed to be converted into public companies in the following circumstances:
    - When not less than 25 per cent of the paid up capital of the company is held by one or more corporate bodies.

- When the company holds 25 per cent of the paid up share capital of a public company.
- When the average annual turnover of the company exceeds ₹ 100 million.
- When the company accepts deposits from the public.

↳ On becoming a deemed public company, many provisions of the Companies Act, 1956 in respect of which the company had exemption as a private company would become applicable.

Private companies are formed between 2 to 50 members and it prohibits invitation to public for capital issues. Many provisions of the Companies Act are not applicable. Also, there is a restriction on transfer of shares and the taxation rates are higher. Shares of the Public Limited Companies on the other hand, are normally freely transferable. Minimum seven members are required to form the company. The taxation rates are normally lower and there is a wider coverage of Companies Act.

IV. Valuation of Private vs. Public Firms

There are a number of factors that are considered differently in the valuation of privately held vs. public companies-even those that are in the same industry-making a direct comparison for valuation purposes difficult. Following is a list of some of the issues that may result in differences between the valuations of public and private firms:

1. Market liquidity: A lack of market liquidity is usually the biggest factor contributing to a discount in the value of companies. With public companies, we can, if we choose, switch our investment to the stock of a different public company on a daily (if not more frequent) basis. The stock of privately held firms, however, is more difficult to sell quickly, making the value drop accordingly.

2. Profit measurement: While private companies seek mostly to minimize taxes, public companies seek to maximize earnings for shareholder reporting purposes. Therefore, the profitability of a private firm may require restatement in order for it to be directly comparable to that of a public firm. In addition, public-company multiples are generally calculated from net income (after taxes), while private-company multiples are often based on pre-tax (and many times, pre-debt) income. This discrepancy can result in an inaccurate formula for the valuation of a private company.

3. Capitalization/capital structure: Public companies within a specific industry generally maintain capital structures (debt/equity mixes) that are fairly similar. That means the relative price/earnings ratios (where earnings include the servicing of debt) are usually comparable. Private companies within the same industry, however, can vary widely in capital structure. The valuation of a privately held business is therefore frequently based on "enterprise value," or the pre-debt value of a business rather than the value of the stock of the business, like public companies. This is another reason why private-company multiples are generally based on pre-tax profits and may not be directly comparable to the price/earnings ratio of public firms.

4. Risk profile: Public companies usually provide an assurance of continuing operations above that of smaller, privately held firms. Downturns in the economy or a change in the environment (such as an increase in competition or regulatory changes) often have a greater impact on private firms than public firms in terms of performance and market positioning. That higher risk may result in a discount in value for private firms.

5. Differences in operations: It is often difficult to find a public company operating in the same niches as private firms. Public companies typically have operations spanning a broader range of products and services than do private companies. In addition, even if the products and services are the same, the revenue mix is often different.

6. Operational control: Although private companies are more likely to receive valuation discounts than public companies, there is at least one area where they may receive a value premium. While the sale of a private company usually results in the purchase of the controlling interest in the business, ownership of public-company stock generally consists of a minority-share ownership-which may be construed to be less valuable than a controlling-interest position.

7.8. Corporate Social Responsibility

Social responsibility is becoming popular and acquiring an increasing amount of importance day by day. As the world is progressing technically, economically, socially and in so many fields so the needs of the people are also increasing. They look to government for the assistance but it is becoming hard for the government to provide each and every facilities and services to their people because of limited amount of money available to them. Apart from government assistance, the best option to look for assistance is the business sector. Now a days corporates are almost equivalent to a country. They have huge amount of money, resources, intelligence and creative employees to assist communities. Communities' expectations from such a successful entrepreneur are very obvious as such entrepreneurs earn huge profit; they have their presence throughout the world and they are capable and strong enough to assist the people.

Few entrepreneurs are already helping the local community by running a successful business as the economy is being stimulated by its actions. Although this may already seem as a good reason, stimulating the economy is not sufficient. Entrepreneurs want to be the ones controlling the business thus; they also want to be the one making a difference in their local community. It is in this kind of perspective that an entrepreneur can work within a philosophy and put passion on their jobs. An example includes a mediocre entrepreneur walking away from a high ROI business opportunity in order to keep the integrity of the business intact.

Is it the entrepreneur's role to help the community? Is it the social responsibility of the entrepreneur to "give back" to the community? This is a difficult question, but one that will need to be asked by every single entrepreneur. There is no perfect answer; however the most important role for the entrepreneur should always be to keep the business running smoothly and successfully.

What exactly does it mean to be a socially responsible entrepreneur? The Schwab Foundation for_Social Entrepreneurship defines social entrepreneurs as "Those who drive social innovation and transformation in various fields including education, health, environment and enterprise development." In other words, a social entrepreneur is someone who takes actions to make the world a better place while building their business. Does that mean your business has to be about green energy or saving endangered species? No, socially responsible entrepreneurs don't necessarily devote their business to causes. Being a socially responsible entrepreneur is about doing what your business does best and considering other factors, such as the environment, poverty or social equality when making business decisions.

Corporate Social Responsibility means:

- Conducting business in an ethical way and in the interests of the wider community;
- Responding positively to emerging societal priorities and expectations;
- A willingness to act ahead of regulatory confrontation;
- Balancing shareholder interests against the interests of the wider community;
- Being a good citizen in the community.

Social Responsibility is voluntary; it is about going above and beyond what is called for by the legal responsibility; it cannot be imposed by law, thus, it needs willing acceptance and self discipline. As the golden rule says, "Act in a way you would want others to act towards you."

According to Renowned Indian Jurist Nani Palkivala, "What is the point in having laws and laws upon laws if your inner consciousness is not there, which enables you to do right things for a right conclusion. In other words; if you are to looking for fairness and justice all around it has to be found within the heart of the businessmen. If the ethical sense dies in the heart of the businessmen, no constitutions, no law, no court can save it. It is only within yourself that you have to find the ideals you are struggling to establish."

As the world business environment is changing, the requirement for staying and succeeding in business is also changing. As a result large corporations are emphasizing the maintenance of strategic relationship with different section of the society. Hence the social responsibility of entrepreneur embraces multiple stakeholders. In today's world corporations can't isolate themselves from society in which they are operating, rather they are linked to the social, ecological and human fabric and therefore they are responsible in varying degree to all stakeholders. Companies with good social and environmental records perform better in the long run than those that don't behave responsibility.

The community gives the business the right to build or rent facilities, benefit from the tax revenues raised in the form of local services; infrastructure etc. In return for these services, the firm should act in a responsible way. The firm can't expose the community to unreasonable hazards in the form of pollution and toxic waste. A firm's responsibility towards the society includes: Respecting human rights, Supporting public policies and practices that promote human development through harmonious relation between businesses, Collaborating with such activities that aim at improving the standard of health, education, workplace safety and economic well being. Promoting and stimulating sustainable development and playing a leading role in preserving and enhancing the physical environment and conserving the earth's resources, Encouraging charitable donations, educational, cultural contribution and employee participation in community and civic affairs.

This is a social responsibility that will benefit the community in ways that can be more significant than the bottom line in a monetary sense. Beyond that, each and every entrepreneur should look inside of his or herself and ask if there is a higher sense of duty to do more.

7.8.1. Implementation of CSR Framework

International Institute for Sustainable Development (*IISD*) has given the following framework:

When? What? How?

Plan 1.Conduct a CSR assessment

- Assemble a CSR leadership team;
- Develop a working definition of CSR;
- Identify legal requirements;
- Review corporate documents, processes and activities and internal capacity; and
- Identify and engage key stakeholders.

Plan 2. Develop a CSR strategy

- Build support with CEO, senior management and employees;
- Research what others are doing and assess the value of recognised CSR instruments;
- Prepare a matrix of proposed CSR actions;

- Develop ideas for proceeding and the business case for them; and
- Decide on direction, approach, boundaries and focus areas.

Plan 3. Develop CSR commitments

- Do a scan of CSR commitments;
- Hold discussions with major stakeholders;
- Create a working group to develop the commitments;
- Prepare a preliminary draft; and
- Consult with affected stakeholders.

Plan 4. Implement CSR commitments

- Develop an integrated CSR decision-making structure;
- Prepare and implement a CSR business plan;
- Set measurable targets and identify performance measures;
- Engage employees and others to whom CSR commitments apply;
- Design and conduct CSR training;
- Establish mechanisms for addressing problematic behaviour;
- Create internal and external communications plans;
- Make commitments public.

Plan 5. Assure and report on progress

- Measure and assure performance;
- Engage stakeholders; and
- Report on performance, internally and externally.

Plan 6. Evaluate and improve

- Evaluate performance;
- Identify opportunities for improvement; and
- Engage stakeholders.

7.8.2. Contemporary Social Issues

Corporations deal with a wide variety of social issues and problems, some directly related to their operations, some not. This section will briefly discuss three contemporary issues that are of major concern: the environment, global issues and technology issues. There are many others.

(a) Environmental Issues

Corporations have long been criticized for their negative effect on the natural environment in terms of wasting natural resources and contributing to environmental problems such as pollution and global warming. The use of fossil fueis is thought to contribute to global warming and there is both governmental and societal pressure on corporations to adhere to stricter environmental standards and to voluntarily change production processes in order to do less harm to the environment. Other issues related to the natural environment include waste disposal, deforestation, acid rain and land degradation. It is likely that corporate responsibilities in this area will increase in the coming years.

(b) Global Issues

Corporations increasingly operate in a global environment. Critics suggest that globalization leads to the exploitation of developing nations and workers, destruction of the environment and increased human rights abuses. They also argue that globalization primarily benefits the wealthy and widens the gap between the rich and the poor. Proponents of globalization argue that open markets lead to increased standards of living for everyone, higher wages for workers worldwide and economic development in impoverished nations. Many large corporations are multinational in scope and will continue to face legal, social and ethical issues brought on by the increasing globalization of business.

Whether one is an opponent or proponent of globalization, however, does not change the fact that corporations operating globally face daunting social issues. Perhaps the most pressing issue is that of labor standards in different countries around the world. Many corporations have been stung by revelations that their plants around the world were "sweatshops" and/or employed very young children. This problem is complex because societal standards and expectations regarding working conditions and the employment of children vary significantly around the world. Corporations must decide which the responsible option is: adopting the standards of the countries in which they are operating or imposing a common standard world-wide. A related issue is that of safety conditions in plants around the world.

Another issue in global business is the issue of marketing goods and services in the international marketplace. Some U.S. companies, for example, have marketed products in other countries after the products were banned in the United States.

(c) Technology Issues

Another contemporary social issue relates to technology and its effect on society. For example, the Internet has opened up many new avenues for marketing goods and services, but has also opened up the possibility of abuse by corporations. Issues of privacy and the security of confidential information must be addressed. Biotechnology companies face questions related to the use of embryonic stem cells, genetic engineering and cloning. All of these issues have far-reaching societal and ethical implications. As our technological capabilities continue to advance, it is likely that the responsibilities of corporations in this area will increase dramatically.

7.8.3. CSR and Business Advantages

1. **Brand and reputation advantage:** In competitive markets, companies strive for a unique selling proposition that can separate them from their competitors in the minds of customers. Ultimately the value of a company depends largely on how much faith customers have in the business. Successful CSR strategy and its communication will improve a company's overall corporate reputation, thereby strengthening its customers' loyalty and contributing to a sustainable future. For many of the brand name companies, their brand is the core and backbone of their business.
2. **Finance:** Consumers and investors are showing increasing interest in supporting responsible business practices and are demanding more information on how companies are addressing risks and opportunities related to social and environmental issues. A sound CSR approach can help build share value, lower the cost of capital and ensure better responsiveness to markets.
3. **Human resources advantage:** Qualified and talented employees are one of the most valuable assets of a company and companies must provide an attractive working environment to retain them. The results will be committed employees and less staff turnover as well as increases in innovative power and productivity. Many companies

have come to realize the importance of attracting and retaining "the best and the brightest", highly skilled, quality employees as a necessary condition to accomplish challenges. furthermore, the key to firm success is now associated with a firm's ability to create, manage and transfer "knowledge assets", which also stresses the importance of quality employees as a key to a firm's competitive advantage. As there is growing evidence that a company's CSR practices play an increasingly important role in improving recruitment and retention of quality employees, particularly within the competitive market of technical specialists.

4. **Consistency and Community:** Citizens in many countries are making it clear that corporations should meet the same high standards of social and environmental care, no matter where they operate. In the CSR context, firms can help build a sense of community and shared approach to common problems.

5. **Cost advantage:** There are hundreds of examples which show that cost reductions can be achieved through good CSR practices. Many of these reductions are related to the environmental management of operations. Most companies that reduce pollution and hazardous waste, reuse or recycle materials and operate with greater energy efficiency and more efficient use of water can reap significant cost savings. DuPont, for example, has saved over US$2 billion from reductions in energy use from 1990 to 2005. McDonald's changed the materials used to wrap its food and reduced its solid waste by 30 per cent.

6. **Business Tool:** Businesses are recognizing that adopting an effective approach to CSR can reduce the risk of business disruptions, open up new opportunities, drive innovation, enhance brand and company reputation and even improve efficiency.

7. **Risk management:** Reputations that take decades to build up can be ruined in hours through incidents such as corruption scandals or labour rights transgression. Misconduct by Nike's suppliers in using child labour is a good example. Appropriate risk management enhances compliance to ethical business principles and ensures a sustainable future. In addition, it helps to protect a company's license to operate by ensuring the confidence of relevant stakeholders, such as the government.

8. **Sustainable development:** United Nations' (UN) studies and many others have underlined the fact that humankind is using natural resources at a faster rate than they are being replaced. CSR is an entry point for understanding sustainable development issues and responding to them in a firm's business strategy.

9. **Innovation:** For example, a firm may become certified in environmental and social standards to become a supplier to particular retailers. Toyota's response to concerns over automobile emissions is another example. The Toyota's Prius, a hybrid electric/ gasoline vehicle, is the first in a series of innovative car models that have produced a competitive advantage with environment benefits. The Prius was awarded the 2004 Car of the Year Award36 by *Motor Trend magazine*, the world's number one automotive authority, which gave Toyota a unique position in customer's minds.

10. **Globalization:** CSR can play a vital role in detecting how business impacts labour conditions, local communities and economies and what steps can be taken to ensure business helps to maintain and build the public good. This can be especially important for export-oriented firms in emerging economies.

11. **Access to Capital:** Socially Responsible Investing: Increasingly, investors are becoming more and more interested in the CSR policies of the companies they invest in, particularly in issues relating to the environment and human rights. A good CSR

policy will attract investors who will on principle no longer invest in companies who do not have a good reputation for CSR. This means that socially responsible companies will have access to a larger capital base.

12. **Improved relations with regulators:** In some countries, governments use (or are considering using) CSR indicators in deciding on procurement or export assistance contracts. This is being done because governments recognize that without an increase in business sector engagement, government sustainability goals cannot be reached.
13. **Enhanced ability to address change:** A company with its "ear to the ground" through regular stakeholder dialogue is in a better position to anticipate and respond to regulatory, economic, social and environmental changes that may occur. Increasingly, firms use CSR as "radar" to detect evolving trends in the market.
14. **Operational Efficiency:** CSR as part of a corporate business strategy can increase efficiency in operations by, for example, reducing costs through waste reduction, energy efficiency and pollution prevention. Additionally, improved and integrated processes save resources and further increase performance.
15. **Product Differentiation:** Particularly, for organizations that implement socially responsible policies, product differentiation can satisfy the unmet needs of consumers offering both financial and business benefits to the firm. Firms that offer environmentally friendly products experience higher sales growth than firms that sell conventional products and usually such products sell at a higher price.

7.8.4. CSR as A Strategy for Corporate Sustainability

"Strong economic performance and good social and environmental performance are not mutually exclusive. In fact good corporate citizenship improves our bottom line. Firms with social citizenship records and a real commitment to corporate responsibility are arguably more sustainable, better managed and, therefore, better long-term investments."

Ed Zander, Chairman and Chief Executive Officer of Motorola, 2004,

Examples of these effective core ideologies include:

- Procter and Gamble: product excellence, continuous self-improvement, honesty and respect and concern for the individual;
- Wal-Mart: provide value to customers, buck conventional wisdom, work with passion and commitment, run lean and pursue ever-higher goals;
- 3M: dedication to innovation;
- Hewlett Packard: respect for the individual staff;
- Disney: make people happy;
- Sony: elevation of the Japanese national culture and status. Being a pioneer – not following others, but doing the impossible. Respect and encourage individual ability and creativity;
- Merck and Co.: medicine is for patients not for profits. The profits follow; and,
- Marriott: to make people who are away from home feel like they are among friends and really wanted.

7.8.5. An ACTION Plan for Social Responsibility

By Guy Ryder, General Secretary of the International Confederation of Free Trade Unions, United Nations Global Compact Summit, Shanghi, China, 2006.

A simple approach to introducing CSR in a structured way:

1. **Assess:** Whatever you do should be relevant for your business as well as society. Think about the issues that affect you, your staff and your business and what you can do to help support these. Assess where you currently are so you have a benchmark to measure future progress against. This may be formal or informal.
2. **Commit:** To a statement of what being a responsible business means to your business and to clear ethical values from the top down. Appoint a champion/s to ensure the commitment is followed through. You need a champion who walks the talk. The champion, like any boss, has to model the behaviour they want to see in their co-workers if they are going to be credible. They also need to be given the authority to make any necessary changes.
3. **Tell:** Set out your ethical and business cases, communicate them and promote them at every opportunity. Make responsible business an agenda item on all team meetings. Communicate to staff, clients, customers, suppliers and others what you are doing. It is not boasting to tell people what you are doing. Establish effective, two-way dialogue with your key stakeholders (those who can affect or are affected by your business). There are real business benefits to informing people through local/trade press, notice boards, newsletters, websites and achieving awards.
4. **Integrate:** Responsible business behaviour across different functions and activities within the business. Identify issues that are affecting your bottom line and how responsible business practices can help address these.

   Priorities things which you can do as:

   (a) Early wins; (b) things that will need to take some time to prepare; and

   (c) long-term goals.

   List the risks that your company faces or might face and the actions you need to take to address these.
5. **Organize:** The project management, the details, relevant business resources and set targets. Look at one off, individual and team building activities. Look at building a long term relationship with community organization/s. Communicate the aims and boundaries to all staff and stakeholders. Collate the results and thank any staff for their involvement. Make sure all staff know about and are able to get involved in your responsible business practices/opportunities.
6. **Nurture:** Involve your clients and supply chain. Once your programmes are established you can have greater impact and raise your profile by widening your resources. Clients and suppliers will be surprisingly asked and usually very willing to get involved.

Measure and report what you are doing and feedback the learning into your business planning. Measuring the benefits you have made to the business and the wider community helps motivate staff, customers and investors. Reporting can be done informally through word of mouth, staff team briefings, presentations to business networks or more formally through management systems, and achieving relevant standards.

Summary

There are many reasons which motivate the people to become an entrepreneur. But the reasons for what one should not become entrepreneurs are: you do not want to compromise with your relaxation, you're not disciplined, you give up easily, Not interested in research and details, You have a "good" idea, and You like the idea of being your own boss.

The bad reasons for becoming an entrepreneur are Risk of Failure, When you actually need a job, When you want to work less, Because you hate your boss, When you want to become wealthy, and When you want to become renowned.

The reasons given by people for becoming an entrepreneur are: Being their own boss, Decide what to delegate, Because it's very creative, Income potential, Diversification, Excitement and fun, Confidence, Satisfaction, Security, Want of freedom, Opportunity for greater financial success, For the creation of wealth, Sense of accomplishment, For a higher purpose, Opportunity to build equity, For the independence, I've always wanted to do this, Because I am crazy, The opportunity to have control over their life and job, For a good lifestyle, For the sheer challenge of it, and Because I'm inspired.

Before starting a business the entrepreneurs should think, who are your target customers? Are you a self-starter? How much will it cost? Have You Assessed The Risks Involved? How well do you get along with different personalities? How good are you at making decisions? Do you have the physical and emotional stamina to run a business? How well do you plan and organize? Is your drive strong enough to maintain your motivation? How will the business affect your family?

Business success factors are: You should construct a plan to include goal, milestones, deliverables such as contracts, business plans, etc. and accomplishments. Identify and implement the technology needed to support your business and its growth. Communication is the key to unlocking the potential within businesses as well as individuals. Transparency fosters beneficial contagion and excitement among the ecosystem members and interested parties. Use the skills and resources of others to open growth opportunities and provide support outside the core mission of your business. Always make sure you have a positive, pleasing attitude. Timing is everything. Operate from a plan based on your business vision. Develop your marketing plan. Finalise your finascing needs, and create your formal business plan. Find the balance between online and offline activities that's right for your business. Persistence is also a key factor for success. Maintain Customer Relationship. Think global, even if your business is strictly local. Profits are essential for your business to succeed. Create an environment where you replicate your passion, caring and sense of ownership in every employee.

Currently there are three different types of business ownerships: Sole Proprietorships, Partnership Corporation and Limited Liability Company. Each type of ownership has its advantages and disadvantages.

Sole Proprietorship is the most common form of business. Sole proprietorships, the easiest and least expensive form of ownership to organize, are usually what the vast majority of the small business starts out as. These types of firms are owned by one single person and he has a complete authority over the company's day-to-day business.

Partnership is a form of business organization, where two or more persons join together for jointly carrying on some business. It is an improvement over the 'Sole –trade business ', where one single individual with his own resources, skill and effort carries on his own business.

A Limited Liability Partnership (LLP) has the best of both partnership and company. It has the features of a partnership, vis-à-vis, agreement, to carry lawful business and motive to make profit, as well as features of a company, vis-à-vis, perpetual succession (coming and going out of members do not affect the continued existence of the company) and legal personality separate from its partners. Thus, LLP is a hybrid of a company and a partnership.

A limited partnership is made up of two types of partners; general partner and limited partner. The general partner controls the business and makes all the decisions while a limited partner just invests money in the business. The profits will be shared between partners but losses and debts acquired by the business will be the responsibility of the general partner. The limited partner only risks losing the amount he/she already put into the business.

A corporation is a separate entity that operates independently from the person/ people who formed it. It even has the same legal rights as a person; it has its own social security number, it can own assets and it can sue people as well as be sued, it can even keep operating after you are long gone. There are two types of corporations; **C Corporation** and **S Corporation**.

Company is a voluntary association of persons formed for the purpose of doing business having a distinct name and limited liability. It is a juristic person having a separate legal entity distinct from the members who constitute it, capable of rights and duties of its own and endowed with the potential of perpetual succession.

Public Company means which is formed with minimum of seven members and three Directors. There is no restriction on maximum number of members. The name of the company shall end with the word 'limited' which is not a private company.

Private Company means a company which by its articles of association:-

(a) Restricts the right of members to transfer its shares.

(b) Limits the number of its members to fifty.

(c) Prohibits an invitation to the public to subscribe to any shares in or the debentures of the company.

(d) prohibits any invitation or acceptance of deposits from persons other than its member, directors or their relatives;

Companies may be limited or unlimited companies. Company may be limited by shares or limited by guarantee.

Company limited by shares: In this case, the liability of members is limited to the amount of uncalled share capital.

Company limited by the guarantee: A company limited by guarantee is a registered company having the liability of its members limited by its memorandum of association to such amount as the members may respectively thereby undertake to pay if necessary on liquidation of the company.

Unlimited Company: The liability of members of an unlimited company is unlimited. Therefore their liability is similar to that of the liability of the partners of a partnership firm.

Section 25 Companies: Under the Companies Act, 1956, the name of a public limited company must end with the word 'Limited' and the name of a private limited company must end with the word 'Private Limited'. However, under Section 25, the Central Government may allow companies to remove the word "Limited / Private Limited" from the name if the following conditions are satisfied:

(i) The company is formed for promoting commerce, science, art, religion, charity or other socially useful objects.

(ii) The company does not intend to pay dividend to its members but apply its profits and other income in promotion of its objects.

A company shall be deemed to be **subsidiary** of another company if:-

1. That other company controls the composition of its board of directors; or
2. That other company holds more than half in face value of its equity share capital.
3. Where the first mentioned company is subsidiary company of any company which that other's subsidiary.

Government Companies means any company in which not less than 51 per cent of the paid up share capital is held by the Central Government or any State Government or partly by the Central Government and partly by the one or more State Governments and includes a company which is a subsidiary of a government company.

Foreign Companies means a company incorporated in a country outside India under the law of that other country and has established the place of business in India.

Valuation of private and public firms are done on the basis of Differences in operations, Profit measurement, Capitalization/capital structure, Risk profile, Operational control, and Market liquidity.

Corporate Social Responsibility means:

- Conducting business in an ethical way and in the interests of the wider community;
- Responding positively to emerging societal priorities and expectations;
- A willingness to act ahead of regulatory confrontation;
- Balancing shareholder interests against the interests of the wider community;
- Being a good citizen in the community.

Implementation of CSR Framework can be done by Conducting a CSR assessment, Developing a CSR strategy, Developing CSR commitments, Implementing CSR commitments, Assuring and reporting on progress, and Evaluating and improving performance.

Corporations deal with a wide variety of social issues and problems, some directly related to their operations, some not. There are three **contemporary issues** that are of major concern: the environment, global issues and technology issues.

Business Advantages of CSR are: Brand and reputation advantage, Finance, Human resources advantage, Consistency and Community, Cost advantage, Business Tool, Risk management, Sustainable development, Innovation, Globalization, Access to Capital, Improved relations with regulators, Enhanced ability to address change, Operational Efficiency, and Product Differentiation.

A simple approach to introducing CSR in a structured way is Assess, Commit, Tell, Integrate, Nurture and Organize.

Keywords

Good idea: Good idea must be great and demanding.

Equity: This equity represents assets that can be sold to someone else or passed on to one's heirs.

Target customers: You must identify your customers to whom you are providing your product.

Self-starter: When the entrepreneurs start their business alone i.e. without anyone's support.

Emotional stamina: It represents the limit of your mental stress.

Business success factors: Each business has its own unique combination of critical success factors that contribute to the success of the business.

Sole proprietorships: These types of firms are owned by one single person and he has a complete authority over the company's day to day business.

Partnership: Partnership is a form of business organization, where two or more persons join together for jointly carrying on some business.

A Limited Liability Partnership (LLP): A Limited Liability Partnership (LLP) has the best of both partnership and company.

Corporation: A corporation is a separate entity that operates independently from the person/ people who formed it.

Company: Company is a voluntary association of persons formed for the purpose of doing business having a distinct name and limited liability.

Public Company: It means which is formed with minimum of seven members and three Directors.

Private Company: Limits the number of its members to fifty. In determining this number of 50, employee-members and ex-employee members are not to be considered.

Company limited by shares: In this case, the liability of members is limited to the amount of uncalled share capital.

Company limited by the guarantee: A company limited by guarantee is a registered company having the liability of its members limited by its memorandum of association.

Unlimited Company: The liability of members of an unlimited company is unlimited.

Section 25 Companies: Under the Companies Act, 1956, the name of a public limited company must end with the word 'Limited' and the name of a private limited company must end with the word 'Private Limited'.

Government Companies: Means any company in which not less than 51 per cent of the paid up share capital is held by the Central Government or any State Government or partly by the Central Government and partly by the one or more State Governments and includes a company which is a subsidiary of a government company.

Foreign Companies: Means a company incorporated in a country outside India under the law of that other country and has established the place of business in India.

Corporate Social Responsibility means: Conducting business in an ethical way and in the interests of the wider community.

Questions

1. What are the wrong reasons to become an entrepreneur?
2. What are the different reasons for becoming an entrepreneur?
3. What are the different important factors that entrepreneurs must consider before opening a business?
4. What are the different types of business ownerships?
5. What do you mean by Corporate Social Responsibility (CSR)? Explain with examples.

CHAPTER – 8

BUSINESS OPPORTUNITIES TRANSFORMATION OBSTACLES

LEARNING OBJECTIVES

On completion of this chapter, you should be able to:

☺ *Explain the obstacles that are faced by new entrepreneurs while converting opportunities into the business.*

☺ *Describe qualities of business partner.*

☺ *Describe business transformation failure reasons.*

☺ *Describe support and education for business opportunities.*

8.1 Business Opportunity Success and Failure

The biggest challenges faced by the entrepreneurs while choosing a business opportunity are as follows:

- Choosing business that suits an entrepreneur's needs and skills as well as he must have interests.
- Choosing business that pays enough in commissions on goods or services that makes it lucrative enough to turn a healthy profit.
- Choosing the business that is wanted and needed by customers/clients. Where he can flourish his business.
- Choosing business that does not exist in an already glutted market. This would lead to too many choices of other providers and a rather limited market for the business owner. If the entrepreneur will jump into the crowdie market where number of sellers are there

BOX 8

TEN-The Entrepreneurs Network

TEN-The Entrepreneurs Network, a business networking organization, headquartered in Thane (near Mumbai) India is dedicated to helping entrepreneurs succeed. Their activities and programs are focused on building the entrepreneurial and venture community and enabling entrepreneurs to access resources and networks to accelerate their business growth.

The Entrepreneurs Network is a platform for entrepreneurs from different non competing business fields to come together. Members contribute connections, ideas, time and financial resources to help The Entrepreneurs Network grow. Members are rewarded with insights, networks and camaraderie offered by other like-minded entrepreneurs.

The mission of The Entrepreneurs Network is to support, promote and develop entrepreneurs globally.

Their motto is: Share and multiply

All entrepreneurs new or established are welcome to join the business networking group to support this mission. They learn about each other's businesses and the community by having members present themselves before all every week. This allows the entrepreneur to talk about their business and also to ask questions of others or get feedback about their business from others in the group through friendly and interactive discussion. It is also an excellent opportunity to learn about other businesses and sometimes brainstorm solutions to various issues of operating a small business.

The groups meet once a week, from 07.30 a.m. to 09.45 a.m. on specific weekdays at predetermined venues. Details of the venue and meeting day are available on the meet us page. The meeting is attended by the members of the networking group as well as by guests invited by these members. On an average, members get an opportunity to interact in person with about 5-6 business heads each week or about 300 new businessmen in a year.

TEN also helps its members connect with members in other TEN chapters spread across the country over the internet. This helps members tap opportunities beyond local boundaries.

Source: Information received from "TEN-The Entrepreneurs Network".

then in such situation the entrepreneur will not get much, he will just get the small portion of the profit because the customers will have number of options and in such case he has to put his extra efforts to attract the customers and sustain the customers even after that it is not necessary that customers will stick to that entrepreneur business only.

The sad facts are that because of the easy start up and the rather quick "fix" that business opportunities present to potential entrepreneurs, business opportunity members can quickly enter a business to cash the profit in the market and just as quickly leave it when they face reality of the market. Turnover can be quite a problem. Since little initial investment is required, many members "jump into" a business opportunity at whim and quickly find that running a business is a whole heck of a lot of work!

8.2 Fail to Estimate Certain Outlooks and Requirements

The entrepreneurs just run behind the shining of the business without going to in deep knowledge of that business. The reason for the failure rate is also attributable to certain outlooks and requirements that many business opportunity "joiners" fail to consider when joining:

- When entrepreneurs fail to see scope of the opportunity then it becomes problematic to them. Entrepreneurs should ask themselves whether really there exists business opportunity. Is the business opportunity nothing more than empty promises, the old "too good to be true" adage? Unfortunately, these types of offerings run rampant both online and offline.
- When entrepreneurs start their business without considering the market situation i.e., whether it is growing, declining or a mature market. Whether there will be any saturation in the market. Is the business opportunity catering to a dying market? Markets can fluctuate, so due diligence is needed. Research into markets, just as with any other business is paramount. Without any proper research if entrepreneurs will go to that business then it leads to failure of the business.
- When entrepreneurs start a business and they run the business they face many problems some problems are not solved by the entrepreneurs because they did not do a perfect research regarding the problems faced by them in their business. Before going the entrepreneurs should ask, is the business opportunity solvent? Talk to other members and do research. Become aware of any problems in payments/revenues before you join.
- Sometimes opportunities exist in the market but the entrepreneurs face a costly situation when they just go for the opportunities without knowing the cost structure of the opportunities and run the business then slowly they come to know that it is not feasible to them. So the question asked should be, is the business opportunity flexible? Does the Business opportunity restrict members in their advertising methods or are they inflexible and "distant" in their approach to members' concerns/problems. In other words, does the Business opportunity have a great financial track record and does it meet the needs of "you" personally, as far as personal satisfaction and approaches to sales and marketing?

8.3 Failed Business Categories

Because most of the entrepreneurs do the same mistakes then we can broadly categories the entrepreneurs' problems they face:

- Bankruptcies
- Failures
- Terminations

Only one in seven can be considered a true "failure", leaving unpaid obligations in their wakes. Others simply sell or shut their doors for a variety of other reasons because shutting down the business could be the best option rather than continue with the losses.

Since most business opportunities, at least initially, open with less than 20 employees (many are simply the owner, as sole owner and executor of all business "chores"), then most Business opportunity are indeed "small businesses" and as such all the pertinent failure statistics can be applied to them. What is really surprising and rather "staggering" is the fact that most business failures are not due to outside forces, but those that the business owner has complete control over! The entrepreneurs themselves do mistakes. Nobody is responsible for that.

These issues include:

- Lack of marketing know-how,
- Lack of record keeping,
- Lack of intelligence,
- Lack of management competence,
- Lack of financial management and
- Other business basics such as controlling employees and the inability to seek outside assistance and advice!

The wise business owner, whether or not involved in a business opportunity, will seek to learn and implement proper procedures and investigate proper methods of operation throughout the life of a business. The new entrepreneurs face problems of proper management of the business, they don't know the procedure even if known then they do not properly implement it. Business is not all about just dealing with the customers or suppliers there are other important factors too that really want entrepreneurs' attention. If this is done, an entrepreneur, or any small business owner, has less of a chance of becoming the "latest failure statistic"! Full preparation is very important as far as opening and running business is concerned. You should prepare yourself internally and externally. Internally you must have all the qualities to handle the business. You must be knowledgeable, intelligent, confident and business manager etc., externally you must be good in dealing, making communication and interacting with other people.

8.4 Entrepreneurs' Failure to Manage Business

The big entrepreneurs have impressed the small entrepreneurs. The big reputed, rich and famous entrepreneurs have affected the small entrepreneurs positively. It has discovered that small entrepreneurs have learned to think like entrepreneurs. This is what has allowed them to rise to the top of their profession. Each would tell that along the way they have learned how to think differently.

True entrepreneurs struggle with their business opportunities for a variety of reasons. Among the most obvious is a lack of capital, lack of business information, lack of understanding about marketing, competence and personnel issues. **However, there are few major reasons individuals fail in entrepreneurial ventures.**

1. They tie the success of their business with their own self worth
2. They neglect to set realistic goals and plans for themselves and their business.

3. They are not prepared to pay the price of success.
4. They become very much confident with just little success

True entrepreneurs with the right thinking prevail over a period of time. They must understand what should be their tasks in a business? What Goals they should set for their business? And what could be the tax of their business?

Entrepreneurs' tasks in the business

New entrepreneurs are not properly aware of their tasks in the business. When the entrepreneurs fail in the early startups they think that it is obvious many entrepreneurs fail we have also failed without going to the roots of the problems or failure. Entrepreneurs understand that early failure in ventures is a natural part of successful startups. They are able to embrace those experiences, learn from them quickly and move on. They must be willing to face and deal with early failures in order to prevail over time.

Successful entrepreneurs, in contrast to those who struggle, have learned to separate their tasks in life from their self worth or self-identity. People who tend to equate their self-worth to their composite role identity are inherently risk-adverse and look to maintain the *status quo*. Being able to differentiate these two identities allows them to be risk prone vs. risk adverse, a key ingredient to success as an entrepreneur. Individuals who have risked failure, experienced it and learned from it, have not only learned how to differentiate their role identity from their self-identity, they have learned the lessons of risking and failing.

Entrepreneurs' goals and plans in the business

New entrepreneurs are unclear about the goals; they do not have proper understanding of their goals. What they want to do what are their planning about coming years. Goals and plans are necessary for success as an entrepreneur, few people learn the mechanics of successful goal setting and planning. It is not the plan but the planning that is important and the goal setting process allows them to develop the confidence to take risks and fail. New entrepreneurs are not well aware about these things. They just want to earn the profit but want to give less attention to the important factors of the business. Successful entrepreneurs are not only goal driven and goal oriented; they have learned to execute the process of strategic and tactical goal setting and planning. Visualizing goals, writing them down and putting together a detailed plan for achievement provides the confidence and motivation to prevail. More than just business or operational plans, they have goals and plans for all the important roles in their life. They have got it very early that if they will not work for their own ideas and business plans then they are taking efforts for others goals and plans. They make their own way, their identity; position themselves a leader, make adjustments as required and prevail over a course of time.

Consider tax in the business

It will be good for the new entrepreneurs to consider the full tax structure of the business that they want to do. New entrepreneurs face the problems of tax when they do not know the tax structure and their problem increases when they are not earning anything and have to pay the tax. Entrepreneurs must understand that there is a tax to pay. To be successful in any role in life you must be prepared to pay full price one time. Truly one cannot become a successful entrepreneur in one or two days. An entrepreneur needs to learn many more in order to be successful, including the day-to-day mechanics of running a business, producing products, delivering services, making money and dealing with people. The biggest challenge of all is developing an understanding of themselves. Successful entrepreneurs have learned to convert their innovative and successful ideas into a good business and that allows them to prevail where others fail along the way.

8.5 The Core Cause of Transforming Opportunities Failure in Entrepreneurship

Most businesses are guaranteed to fail within the first five years for a number of different reasons.

New entrepreneurs' fear of failure: Less confidence

Without a doubt, an entrepreneur's biggest fear is failing–understandably, because 95 percent of all businesses fail within the first five years.

Reasons for fear

Whenever new entrepreneurs start their business they continuously remain under fear of business failure. The new entrepreneur has much fear in the mind before starting a business. He is very fearful about the things that he will face to open and sustain the business. He has a fear of if I will not be perfect for the entrepreneurship? What if I can't get this last deal? What if I go bankrupt? But the consequences of failure are mostly inside the entrepreneur. The risks may be subjective risk and objective risk: Subjective risk feels scary but is actually safe, whereas objective risk can feel safe but is actually quite dangerous. "Starting a business has a lot of subjective risk, it feels scary, but it's not. At the end of the day, the risk is small." Before begging the business making false assumptions restrict most of the people to become entrepreneur.

"Because entrepreneurs typically work in a random, self-defeating thoughts can become very common. These unconscious thoughts build upon each other, making you feel increasingly negative and scared." These fears lower the confidence of risk taking because business is all about risk we have to trust over selves and should move forward. An entrepreneur must keep tabs on himself by regularly writing a list of accomplishments. Whether he gained three new clients, received positive feedback or sealed a partnership, write it down. "Whenever those fears crop up, he gets a point of reference [that shows] he is actually achieving something. The sad reality, however, is that most of these businesses fail because that have been founded by inexperienced overly-enthused entrepreneurs. This is usually the single most important reason for business failure early in a business.

Erroneous Inspiration

Most of the new entrepreneurs are motivated to money only. As a business owner you are hopefully starting for the right reasons. The entrepreneurs may have any reason for starting the business but entrepreneurs want something else that may not be the money. True entrepreneurs never go for money the primary reason to open a business for them is other than money. They open their business because they either want to help society, want to invent something for the welfare of society or they are passionate about something else that is dear to them which is why they are successful at what they do which is also why they make a lot of money. Having interest in your business is very essential. Without interest running a business will not make you profitable.

Here's the big takeaway: if you start something for the wrong reasons, you will stop for the wrong reasons. The business should be done in the sense of business only. New entrepreneurs must have patient regarding the business. They must also consider the other factors that are generating the employment, solving the customers' problems the entrepreneurs must be passionate about these things also. They should also have a dream of wealth creation for the society, fulfilling the needs of the customers. If your only intention for getting into business is to make lot of money then your resolve and mental toughness will be test greatly if after five years you haven't even turned a profit. Making profit is not at all a bad thing but it should not be the primary motive. You as an entrepreneur should do something for the welfare of the society and such kind of people are the true entrepreneurs. Entrepreneurship does not mean making money but making money in entrepreneurship is the small part of it. Attach the monetary value that you are shooting for to something bigger. Maybe you want to build a school or donate money to charity or retire your mother, something that will keep you going when life hits you upside the head.

The transformation usually fails when it is based on "not-so-credible" strategic planning resources.

The new entrepreneurs try to copy the situation of the big entrepreneurs but they forget one thing that the big entrepreneur situation and the new entrepreneur situation are not same. Your new methods and approaches are not well for your business. You can't trust a research that is based on points or factors that don't have relevance with your respective business environment. For example, you are using as a reference a business that experienced large success in America, but you are investing in Africa. Although there can have similarities, but success depends upon location, culture, customers' perception, government support, opportunities and many more. You can copy but cannot copy A to Z. Copy logically. Your plan should be accurate and appropriate. Go over the real thing before you find some sort of inspiration.

Poor management

Many reports on business failures cite poor management as one of the biggest reasons for failure. The new entrepreneurs focus their whole energy into earning profit only and therefore they do not consider the different aspects of business. New business owners normally have a very poor business and management knowledge. They do not have experience of different business functions and do not have enough capital to hire the needed people who can guide them. Unless they recognize what they don't do well and more importantly seek help, business owners may soon face disaster.

If you can't effectively manage people, learn how to and/ or hire someone who can. Some entrepreneurs are great at this vital skill and others don't have the patience for it. However, the bottom line is you can have a great idea, product and market, but poor management will cause business failure 9 times out of 10. Poor management often evolves into poor employee morale and high employee turn-over, which significantly hampers a company's ability to compete in the market. Management doesn't just entail employee management but also the ability to manage the Company. Having a Good Business Plan, Excellent Profit Management Strategies and Effective Cash Flow Management are just some of the important management tools necessary to run a successful business. Businesses often fail because they haven't owned up to and analyzed their weaknesses, which often stems from poor management practices.

No mentorship and lack of experience

The new entrepreneurs just start their business as soon as have an idea or money. Starting a business requires proper guidance. Without proper guidance running a business is very risky. A lot of setbacks and hiccups, failures and hurdles that are encountered along the way can either be avoided or alleviated with the help of a business mentor. A mentor can help you to identify the hidden risks as well as confirm certain setbacks you will face if you continue what you are doing. He will show you the right path. He will protect you from the wrong direction. They are assets for your business. By taking the valuable suggestions and required information from them you can run your business successfully. Starting a business without proper experience and that too without any advisor will not turn your opportunity into the reality.

When you rush success

Most of the time, investors easily got tempted by success. They indulge themselves into methods or offers they thought will bring them fast to victory. They loosen themselves on things that are too good to be true. This is the time that the strategic plan you established and worked hard lose its purpose. Success is enjoyable if you have got it by your mental and physical hard work. Do not go for instant success that does not persist for long time. It can fade right away because you don't know how to maintain or get it. If you have achieved your success by your own talent then you can repeat it because you know exactly what you have to do to get success. Success is not a onetime process. You need it throughout the lifetime of business. So you need to know the methods that you have adopted to get success. But when you will take short cut that means you are not learning the business but you are copying the business. You may get success by copying but it will be a temporary one but the business is endless process you cannot survive for long time. So as an entrepreneur you must follow every step of the business. Do not try to jump directly to the last step.

Inflexible with changing times

The only constant in business is change. The ability to change with the changing market conditions and to grab the opportunities is the most important quality of any surviving business. Many entrepreneurs do not like change. They like to continue their traditional business even in the new modern age. They are not aware about the changing market climate or they do not want to change. But the business runs according to market trend and customers' desires. If you will not change then your business will be in loss. The challenge is that many new entrepreneurs when like any idea they suddenly go for it without asking others. They ignore the competition in the market. Remember that by not changing and ignoring the changing marketing situations you are actually destroying your established business.

Poor Execution of the business

New entrepreneurs lag behind because they are not well versed of the proper execution of the business. Hard execution — rather than a clever idea — is vital to the success of new businesses. It stands to reason, therefore, that poor execution is the downfall of most startups that go bust. New entrepreneurs require more attention, there are several ways you can avoid execution failure. First, you should try to know about yourselves, your skills and strengths. According to your strengths you should try to grab the opportunities in the market. If you will do something else out of your control and intelligence then definitely you will take very long time or you may not grab the opportunities. Second, it's also wise to surround yourself with talented people who can help you, guide you and can contribute to the growth of business.

Companies with poor direction and leadership usually fail in the first year or two, but even established companies if are not prepared with the good planning, skilled team and required business knowledge can suffer badly. Bill Gates led Microsoft from inception to its current position as one of the largest and most successful companies in history, but this is seldom the case. As a founder, you must have a clear understanding of your expert people to hand over the control of your business to a professional manager who can take your business to the next level.

Improper communication with outside world

Problems arise due to lack of communication between the entrepreneur and the outsider; the partner speaks in business language that an entrepreneur often does not even understand (unless he has the necessary knowledge). The new entrepreneurs must gain insight of the business language. They are not aware of the business language that becomes problematic to them when they interact with the other people. Research shows that for the entrepreneur there is no substitute for a basic understanding of business models, customer wants and cash flow management and so on; these things are not hard to learn, but it must be done. It will be good for an entrepreneur to get the experience of the business before starting it.

Picking a Niche that is too small

Most small businesses compete successfully against larger rivals by specializing in a niche market. That is good strategy because for small company it is not easy to give competition to big companies. However you should be able to find customers in your niche. If you want to serve a niche market then you must first confirm which type of niche you want to serve and know whether it is profitable or not? Make your selection depending on the customers you will get. Serving the niche with the few customers will not fulfill your dream. The small niche is not beneficial as far as profit is concerned. The business should earn profit but not the small profit. Profit means not only saving money but also expanding the business. So you must have money on hand to expand business. Accordingly you must think to earn the profit. You need to know the future growth of your niche and be ready to grab the opportunities. Putting all efforts for few customers does not justify. If the niche will remain stagnant then there will be chances of decline in the profit. If your financial projections require you to hold more than a few percent of market share to remain profitable, be careful.

No Mission and No Vision

The only mission that provides the wrong motivation is money. If the entire dream revolves around profit, failure is likely. A mission is the core of the idea, the heartbeat that keeps the streams of profit flowing. An entrepreneur without a mission is like a tourist without a map. All they are doing is walking around and enjoying the vista before reality sends you back home. No mission, no grandeur. The mission is the soul of business. Without it, success is meaningless and often unachievable.

A dream is not a dream, if it is not dreamt. Everybody dreams. The difference between everybody and entrepreneurs is that the latter takes action. Nevertheless, an entrepreneur who does not dream will not be one for very long. The fuel for the motivation that carries them further and further is the dream itself. It is the vision that provides the enlightenment that makes the difference and such difference provides competitive edge. It all goes around in the cycle of success.

Not doing market research

How do you know if people are going to want your product or service and how much do they think it is worth? Before committing yourself in a new business, do some market research. The Internet is your best source of published information. You can use chat rooms to get instant feedback and input without spending a cent. Or you can test the market using surveys or focus groups among members of your target audience. Testing can keep you from making costly mistakes based on false assumptions about your product, service or customers.

Breakup of the partners

Breaking up is hard on you — and your business

A startup is very complex, busy and lengthy process. When two persons want to open their business in partnership then the chances of conflict is very high among them as they try to implement their own ideas. Two persons may pursue the same idea differently and therefore they may disagree that will lead to a rift within the business. The disagreement between the partners leads to a business destruction.

Solutions

It definitely requires more than maintaining a profit to achieve and maintain overall business success. Avoiding business failure requires constant focus and evaluation of assorted key components.

Business planning is crucial. In order to avoid business failure, any entrepreneur must set out to generate a business plan that is realistic and accounts for all facets of their business. The most important element in planning for business is the financial component. To avoid the potential of failure, it is a good idea to have enough capital on hand to cover for about two years worth of planned or anticipated expense. It is also a must that a business owner keeps about fifty percent of that two year sum as a back-up financial source for unforeseen circumstances that may surprisingly spring up and catch a business owner financially off guard. Business planning doesn't stop with the financial aspect of the enterprise. A business owner must implement and generate a plan that shapes the overall mission and goals of the prospective company. The plan must produce a mission statement, management structure, turn-around options for downward sloping trends and company policies regarding employees.

Research is essential. In order to avoid failure a business owner, or delegated employees, must understand the product or service that is being offered. Product knowledge accounts for an overwhelming majority of the sales process. Customers need to be able to interact with knowledgeable company representatives who can, not only present the product or service effectively, but also who can anticipate and answer customer generated questions.

Marketing is imperative in order to avoid business failure. For a business to survive and thrive, its creators must have an extensive knowledge of the specific market that they will be part of. Market saturation and hot new trends may lead to business failure. As a business owner, it is important to study the trends of the market, become familiar with upward and downward trends for the specific company, as well as the market as a whole. Business owners must be in it for the long haul and comprehend that business success is a fixture of the overall picture and have an understanding that what's hot today, may fizzle out and fail tomorrow. With this understanding of trending, business owners must adapt to change and have effective and creative problem solving techniques.

When you are beginning a new home business, be sure that you have a good handle on managing your time. Most new home business owners fall into the trap that you can work when you want and still make a ton of money. Well, this isn't always true. If you don't spend the time doing the leg work, your new business will fall flat on its face, so you need to know how to manage your time properly. Get a day timer, calendar, or other form of keeping track of your day to day activities so you are able to jot down what you need to accomplish each day and check it off when you have finished. Knowing that you have set tasks to accomplish will help you to keep on track and keep your new business making money.

While it is easy to embark on the new adventure of starting your own business and becoming your own boss, a clear understanding of how to avoid business failure is a prerequisite to establishing and maintaining success.

Go mentally prepared

One of the most important elements to starting a successful business is being mentally prepared. Of course, skills, actions and good old-fashioned luck are also important factors, but it all begins with the right frame of mind. To that end, stay away from people who are negative and may try to bring you down.

8.6 Adding Value to Your Home Business

As with any home business opportunity it's about adding value. A couple of tips worth mentioning:

- Own your own marketing system.
- Understand Internet marketing before you spend money.
- Start a blog.
- Learn from others who have results.
- Have a healthy skepticism but don't be cynical.
- Know what you're trying to accomplish.
- Don't quit until you're done.

It really makes no difference what business opportunity you choose, you have to add value and you have to persist. You will have obstacles, challenges or difficulties, whatever you choose to call them, get over it and enjoy the journey. Help others along the way. Another is "there is so much crap on the Internet". If all you find is crap on the Internet, try looking in a different place. There are dozens of successful people who are very transparent and willing to share the things that have worked for them, it's great. You can buy information online that will save you time or you can spend time and get it all for free. It's up to you. It is a safe bet that you stick with the things that you were genuinely interested in, so find a business idea that really captivates your interest.

There are thousands of good small business ideas, choosing the right one for you requires a little self reflection, don't cut corners, really get into you and what you want to create. You should start a business too; it doesn't have to be a fortune 500, keep it simple, talk to an accountant and learn about the tax benefits to starting a home business or online business. The tax advantages of starting a home business are worth it, check it out.

8.7 Qualities of Business Partner

These are excellent qualities to point out and look for. In addition to being a responsible person, it is important that your business partner possesses and displays a sense of integrity. Is this someone who can be trusted to not only work hard, but to deal with you as well as others in an honest and ethical manner consistently?

Does this person's word match their deeds? This is something that needs to be carefully considered and watched, especially when it affects your own livelihood and reputation. A dishonest business partner can cause a great deal of damage to you personally and professionally. Unfortunately, many family-run businesses learn this lesson in very painful ways.

Here are some simple things that help to look for in your business partner:

- Should have common goal and vision
- Has good creativity level
- Level of commitment in business
- Understand your strength and weakness
- Respect the views/ideas and focus on building trust by talking honestly
- Seek responsibility and take responsibility for decision making
- Financial Position – Have a good experience in related business with strong financial standing

8.8 Supporting for Business Opportunities

The business culture in the USA and in Israel is very forgiving towards failure. USA promotes the entrepreneurship and for that they provide every kind of facilities to the entrepreneurs. It loves serial entrepreneurs and is prepared to provide finance for an entrepreneur who failed in the past but is still highly motivated. But the scenario of the Indian small entrepreneurs are different, the entrepreneurs have to take risk on their own and should solve it.

The new entrepreneurs need a proper training and support for running their business. When the entrepreneur has acquired knowledge and received guidance on setting up and running a venture, his chances of success are considerably increased. There are those who try to solve the problem by having an economics and management person work closely with the entrepreneur. Of course this helps, but research shows that the benefit is not significant. If an outsider (even a partner), rather than the entrepreneur himself, has the business knowledge, the business will never reach its maximum potential.

8.9 Business Transformation Failure

When an entrepreneur made the right and needed **Business Transformation**, but still, he doesn't feel like his business is improving. This maybe because of several reasons that he overlooked.

More probable than not, the problem is in the management and not with the environment. Business transformation is not as plain as what it is. The work he has started should continue with a greater effort this time. The entrepreneurs should not leave the task in between when faced with the difficulties. There are many ways that the step he took can fail, most of the time; entrepreneurs are unconscious of the reasons.

Numerous studies of entrepreneurship have shown that ninety percent of start-up ventures live for only a few months, although there are a range of reasons for these failures. In most cases, failure is not due to bad technology, but rather to the entrepreneur himself, that is, his lack of knowledge and understanding of the business world and in particular on the subject of establishing a business.

If you can point to causes of failure such as lack of cash, mistakes in identifying target customers or even a business model that fails to provide sufficient profit, all these are an indication of a deficiency in the entrepreneur's education and suitability for the world of start-ups.

8.10 Interact Carefully with Partners

One entrepreneur has started a business a year ago. However, he started researching and planning two years before he did any operating. He even moved locations in that two years because he thought the market would be better where he is located now. He also knew he needed help and someone to balance out his very Type A personality and who could be a good finance person. He met a girl whom he thought would be perfect. After a couple of meetings, she was very excited. They met a few more times after that and then he didn't hear from her again for weeks. He was working between 80 and 100 hours a week doing everything and this girl he promised a significant percentage of his business to just hand out her business card and made sure to tell everyone she was the owner. However, he was so busy working and before he knew it, five months had passed.

They sat down and he gave her an ultimatum. She made a bigger effort, but it was still nothing compared to what a part owner should be contributing.

The lesson is this: Be Very Careful of Partners. He should have ended this relationship months ago, but as it turns out, she is a great sales person (fooled him) but definitely not management material. This has been the biggest burden and somehow with divine intervention and lots of support from his family, he has managed to keep this thing moving in a very successful direction. If he had been less prepared, this would have destroyed his business. Not everyone is willing to make the sacrifice, has the life experience and handing out business cards doesn't make you a successful business owner.

So What Could Be the Solution?

8.11 Factors to Consider for New Small Businesses

Save up as much money as possible before starting

You cannot rely on your investors or creditors completely for getting money. You should have enough money to start the business. Government or banks will help you only when you will also invest some amount of money from your side in your business. Without investing any amount you cannot expect any support from these financial institutes. The next thing is that if you take loan then you also have to return it to the bank. In business you cannot give guarantee that your business will do well and you will earn a huge profit. If your business is a failure then you should prepare yourselves for that situation. At that time you must have money to return to bank because earning a profit in business can take months or years. And once a lender discovers a business isn't as profitable as expected, the lender is likely to call in the loan or refuse to renew it for another year. A better plan is to save up as much of the needed investment money as possible, including your living expenses for the first year or even two.

The Time Factor

One issue you hear from new business owners is that they didn't think the business would take as much time as it has in their lives. Time is needed to handle customers and "public" business operations; but time is also needed "privately" to handle paperwork, maintenance, taxes and other items that come with running a business. Each hour you spend in the public eye, expect two hours handling the back office work, travel and daily operations.

Enhance your skills

Continue to brush up on your business skills by attending continuing education classes. These classes are offered at many community colleges and state colleges. They can be very useful in keeping you up-to-date on business activities, new computer software classes and more. These classes do not typically require any prerequisites or prior degrees.

Evaluate the Market

To evaluate the market is to do market research. Lots of entrepreneurs do not have the skills to conduct this research themselves. Some of them don't have enough money to hire professional market researchers. Many Small businesses fail because there is no market for their new products.

Financial Plan

Obtaining startup funding for a new business often reflects an overall estimation of costs. Investors tend to look for such realistic financial projections in the entrepreneur's business plan since it contains, among other things, an outline of exactly how their invested money will be spent. The financial plan section of the business plan should also be supported by market research, illustrating a solid return on investment. While developing the financial forecast, an entrepreneur needs to ask him/herself the following questions: Is the sales forecast reasonable? Are the projected margins achievable? Are the working-capital needs being taken into account? How much are the capital expenditures?

Understand how the things are going on

You should be able to state in just a few sentences how your business plans to make a substantial profit. For starters, you need to know your costs: how much you'll spend purchasing inventory, paying the rent, compensating any employees and covering what is likely to be a surprisingly long list of other costs. Then you can figure out exactly how much you need to sell each month, for how many rupees, to cover those expenses and have an adequate profit besides. These numbers are all you need to create a "break-even analysis."

Make a good business plan, no matter how much perfect

The importance of a comprehensive, thoughtful business plan cannot be overemphasized. Many factors critical to business success depend upon your plan: outside funding, credit from suppliers, management of your operation and finances, promotion and marketing of your business and achievement of your goals and objectives.

Some people assume that if they are not going to seek financial support from lenders or investors to open their business then they don't need to prepare a business plan, but *every* business should have one. Writing a business plan serves as a **roadmap** for your venture when you're starting out.

Try to get and continue a competitive edge

One way to hold on to your competitive edge is to protect your trade secrets, confidential information that gives you a competitive advantage in the marketplace. Examples of trade secrets include customer lists, survey methods, marketing strategies and manufacturing techniques. To protect your trade secrets under the law, you need to take steps to keep the information confidential. This includes marking documents "Confidential," using passwords to protect computer information, using nondisclosure and/or noncompete agreements and limiting access to employees with a reasonable need to know the trade secrets.

Another way to keep your competitive edge is to react quickly to bad news. Once you see that your business faces some kind of adversity, you need to come up with a plan to deal with it immediately. This may involve moving your offices, introducing a new product or service or developing a better way to reach customers.

Always have agreements in writing

The laws require you to put some contracts and agreements in writing:

- Contracts that will last longer than a year.
- Contracts that involve the sale of goods worth of huge amount.
- Contracts that transfer the ownership of copyrights or real estate.

Even if not legally required, it's wise to put almost everything in writing, because oral agreements can be difficult or impossible to prove. This includes leases or rental agreements, storage agreements, contracts for services (such as consulting or electrical work), purchase orders or contracts for goods worth more than a couple of hundred rupees, offer letters of employment and employment policies. Get in the habit of getting and giving receipts for all goods, services and deposits, regardless of how much.

A Solid Hiring Plan

Entrepreneurs need to develop a hiring plan at the same time they develop the business plan. This will help them budget the new business as well as enable them to line up a management team with impressive bios. A solid hiring plan is also very important to an entrepreneur who does not have experience in the business area. By hiring an impressive management team with a proven track record of success, the entrepreneur can convince a business investor that he or she is committed to the project and has the necessary skills to sustain a business and produce or increase profitability.

Concentrate on the legal status of your workers

Most employees you hire will be "at-will" employees — subject to being fired at any time and for any reason (except for illegal motives such as discrimination). It's important to preserve your at-will rights because they protect you from having to prove that you have a valid business-related reason to terminate an employee. Don't make any promises to prospective or current employees that you are offering a permanent job or that they will lose their job only if they perform poorly, because this will limit your ability to terminate the employee for other reasons, such as personality conflicts or finances.

Pay your bills early and your taxes on time

To survive in the market you need to be very honest in the business. You need to be very careful about your business reputation. Your business will earn reputation only when you will be very clear with your suppliers, creditors and your government. If you will pay bill on time and government tax on time then ultimately you will increase your reputation in the market. By giving taxes on time government will appreciate you and in future if you need any assistance from government then government will assist you without any doubt because your track record is very good. You cannot do business alone you have to be honest to your stakeholders.

8.12 Practical Approach for New Entrepreneurs

It's no secret; entrepreneurs are coming up and out from everywhere. With so many people having the gifts, talents and the guts, of which I call an entrepreneur spirit. More people are stepping up and out to take advantage of the opportunity to become an entrepreneur. Fulfilling their dreams and desires to work hard to build and establish something that they can call their own and to be able to leave an inheritance to their children, instead of continuing to work hard, long hours for someone else. It is such an exciting and surely a great time to be an entrepreneur; however it takes work and effort on the entrepreneur's part.

In the last decade technology has leveled the playing field and propelled an entrepreneurial revolution. If you are an entrepreneur, you can most definitely attest to the fact that entrepreneurs now have much more access to free information. Having such access through technology and the internet helps the entrepreneur to access more information that enables him or her to make more intelligent choices quickly. Entrepreneurs have an advantage over big businesses in that they are lighter, more flexible and faster on their feet. Entrepreneurs have the ability to target new markets more quickly and move on them quickly.

However, being a successful entrepreneur requires work, due diligence and that you stay focused and look at the big picture and follow a plan through from beginning to end. Most times the greatest obstacle for a new entrepreneur is staying focused enough to follow their plan through without jumping to something new.

Some practical guidelines that can help you when beginning your own enterprise:

Be Professional

Everything about you and the way you do business needs to let people know that you are a professional running a serious business. That means getting all the accoutrements such as professional business cards, a business phone and a business email address and treating people in a professional, courteous manner.

Find Your Niche

Find a niche and fill it. Find out what's in demand and what is selling well. If you are not already an expert in your chosen trade or profession, you must become one. Either go to work for a competitor for a short while and learn all you can while being paid or study those businesses which are obviously successful to determine exactly why they are successful. Then try to think of how you might be able to compete by offering a cheaper service, a better service or by offering some connected additional service your competitors do not provide.

Have an Online Presence

Your online presence is must to reach to the far customers. Internet can play an important role in promoting your business. Even if you do not have braches of your company to other locations but still you can be in contact to your customers. It's also a great tool for promoting yourself and letting people, even in your own area, know that you're there and what you're doing.

Refuse to Quit

Successful entrepreneurship requires creativity, energy and a drive to keep going when you fail. Few people realize that before Bill Gates created the extremely successful Microsoft 3.0, he created a Microsoft 1.0 and 2.0, both of which flopped — but he kept at it. And that determination and refusal to give up is what will separate successful entrepreneurs from unsuccessful ones. Arm yourself with optimism to get beyond the 'No' or the trouble. There's nothing wrong in failure—just don't repeat the same mistake!

Build Relationships

One of the essentials to business success is the relationships you build up along the way. Try to build relationships with your clients and customers as well as with your other business contacts in order to thrive and grow. Such relationships would provide your business with a lot of opportunities to grow and become successful.

Know Your Personal Goals

Decide what you want out of life and then build a business that supports those plans. Take time to think about the entrepreneurial lifestyle and how it fits in with your personal and family lifestyle. One definition of an entrepreneur is someone who is willing to assume the responsibility, risk and rewards of starting and operating a business. Does that describe you and does it fit with the kind of life you want to live?

Evaluate Market

Market evaluations are a crucial part of each business opportunity. Understanding the demographics of potential customers, the local need for the product or services being offered and the cost of the services or products are all factors that must be considered. For an existing business opportunity, looking at current market share may help with this information.

Get an insurance agent

Find an insurance agent who is honest and willing to give you sound business advice and that is not in business just sell policies. Make sure that she/he is in touch with what your business does and knows what types of coverage you need.

Master the Time

Time will become your most valuable commodity. Treasure it, protect it and use it wisely.

Use time-savers like these:

Organize your work area, so you can find information quickly Rely on a contact management program, such as ACT, to keep track of prospects/clients Start each day with a to-do list, arranged in priority order, Limit the length of phone calls and meal breaks. Outsource work that others will perform well at a reasonable price.

Assemble Your Support Team

Start with the people who will help you do the things you aren't good at. Some examples: bookkeeper, marketing writer, web designer. Then add the people who give you professional business advice: a lawyer, an accountant, a business coach. Finally, include the people who support you personally: your family, friends and colleagues.

You need money

No one will invest in you. If you need large sums of capital to launch your venture, go back to the drawing board. Find a starting point instead of an end point. Scale down pricey plans and high-flying expenditures. Simplify the idea until it's manageable as an early stage venture. Find ways to prove your business model on a shoestring budget. Demonstrate your worth before seeking investment. If your concept is successful, your chances of raising capital from investors will dramatically improve.

Be healthy

Working hard and making a lot of money is important, but being healthy is more important. The best part is being healthy makes you a lot more productive and effective at work! Work out often, spend time with your family and friends, sleep enough and eat healthy foods. When you're burnt out, don't keep working. Get out for a while, play a sport or do something fun.

Support

Believing that you can do everything yourself can be a costly mistake. Enlist the services of a business mentor. A mentor acts as a coach, offering guidance, motivation and practical advice.

Know when to call it quits

Contrary to popular belief, a smart captain does not go down with the ship. Don't go on a fool's errand for the sake of ego. Know when it's time to walk away. If your idea doesn't pan out, reflect on what went wrong and the mistakes that were made. Assess what you would have done differently. Determine how you will utilize these hard-learned lessons to better yourself and your future entrepreneurial endeavors. Failure is inevitable, but a true entrepreneur will prevail over adversity.

SUMMARY

The biggest challenges faced by the entrepreneurs while choosing a business opportunity are: choosing business that suits an entrepreneur's needs and skills as well as he must have interests; that is wanted and needed by customers/clients; that does not exist in an already glutted market; that pays enough in commissions on goods or services that makes it lucrative enough to turn a healthy profit.

The reasons for the entrepreneurs' failure rates are when they just go for the opportunities without knowing the cost structure of the opportunities and run the business; When entrepreneurs start their business without considering the market situation; when they do not do a perfect research regarding the problems faced by them in their business; When entrepreneurs fail to see scope of the opportunity.

There are few major reasons individuals fail in entrepreneurial ventures.

1. They tie the success of their business with their own self worth
2. They neglect to set realistic goals and plans for themselves and their business.
3. They are not prepared to pay the price of success.
4. They become very much confident with just little success

The core causes of transforming opportunities failure in entrepreneurship are Erroneous Inspiration, when it is based on "not-so-credible" strategic planning resources, Poor management, No mentorship and lack of experience, When you rush success, Inflexible with changing times, Poor Execution of the business, Improper communication with outside world, Picking a Niche that is too small, Inadequate goal-setting, No viable market, Breakup of the partners, Solutions and Go without mentally prepared.

Adding value to the home business: As with any home business opportunity it's about adding value. A couple of tips worth mentioning:

- Own your own marketing system.
- Understand Internet marketing before you spend money.
- Start a blog.
- Learn from others who have results.
- Have a healthy skepticism but don't be cynical.
- Know what you're trying to accomplish.
- Don't quit until you're done.

Factors to consider for new small businesses are Save up as much money as possible before starting, The Time Factor, Start on ground level, Evaluate the Market, Protect your personal assets, Understand how the things are going on; Make a good business plan, no matter how much perfect; Try to get and continue a competitive edge, Always have agreements in writing, Hire and keep good people, Concentrate on the legal status of your workers and Pay your bills early and your taxes on time.

Some **practical guidelines** that can help entrepreneur when beginning own enterprise are be professional, find your niche, have an online presence, refuse to quite, build relationships, know your personal goals, Evaluate market, get an insurance agent, master the time, Assemble your suppart team, Arrange required money, be healthy, ask for support and know exactly when to quit.

KEYWORDS

Business Planning: It encompasses all the goals, strategies and actions that you envision taking to ensure your business's survival and growth.

Business goals: It is just something you aim for. Goals give you a framework within which to work. But goals are powerful contributors to successful business growth in several ways.

Bankruptcy: Bankruptcy is a process which permits an individual to announce economic failure.

Business Failure: Closure or cessation of business activity that results in a loss to its creditors.

Business mentor: A business mentor is someone that can provide you with advice, **coaching and** support as you tread the path to the success you plan to achieve.

Niche marketing: It is where you are marketing to a certain sector of people.

Mission: A written declaration of an organization's core purpose and focus that normally remains unchanged over time.

Vision: An aspirational description of what an organization would like to achieve or accomplish in the mid-term or long-term future.

Market research: It is a systematic, objective collection and analysis of data about a particular target market, competition and/or environment.

Financial plan: Financial plan section is the section that determines whether or not your business idea is viable and is a key component in determining whether or not your business plan is going to be able to attract any investment in your business idea.

Competitive edge: A factor that gives a special advantage to nation, company, group or individual when it is competing with others.

QUESTIONS

1. What are the challenges faced by the new small entrepreneurs while selecting the business opportunities?
2. Why new entrepreneur fails to manage the business? What are the reasons?
3. When should you go for partnership? What should be the qualities of a good business partner?
4. What are the different practical approaches for new entrepreneurs?

❑ ❑ ❑

CHAPTER – 9

SELECTING BUSINESS RELATED OBSTACLES

LEARNING OBJECTIVES

On completion of this chapter, you should be able to:

☺ *Explain what are the different obstacles faced by new small entrepreneurs in selecting the business.*

☺ *Describe entrepreneurial opportunity.*

☺ *Describe the role of business coach in new entrepreneurs' business success.*

9.1 Choosing to Run Your Own Business

Choosing to run your own business is a big step that few people take lightly. While the rewards seem self-evident, the challenges are substantial also. Learn more about what making the choice is about from assessing whether taking the step is right for you to looking at business models to help you find the right business.

Undecided about taking the step

Making the choice to start a business can be a difficult decision. Some of the obstacles that keep people from making the choice to run your own business are:

BOX 9

Bharatiya Yuva Shakti Trust

About

BYST, a non-profit organization was set up in 1992 primarily to help disadvantaged Indian youth to develop business ideas into viable enterprises with the guidance and support of a mentor. In the span of over 15 years, BYST has helped young people in Delhi, Rural Haryana, Chennai, Pune, Hyderabad and Rural Maharashtra. BYST extend support through a combination of money and mentor, thereby giving total assistance to disadvantaged youths who wish to set up, or develop their own business. This assistance includes finance, professional advice, training, education and guidance till the venture takes off.

Program description

BYST supports ventures both in the manufacturing and servicing sector, turning job seekers into job creators. On approval of proposal, applicants are provided a whole range of Business Development Services along with a Mentor, who gives guidance until the venture takes off. Presently BYST is operational in six regions of India - Delhi, Chennai, Rural Haryana, Pune, Hyderabad and Rural Maharashtra. Out of these six regions four regions run the urban programme, while two regions run the rural programme.

Participants

BYST is keen on working with young people in the age group of 18 - 35, who are either unemployed or underemployed. BYST invites individuals with sound imaginative business ideas, along with the will and determination to succeed.

Applications

Business proposals from potential entrepreneurs are welcome directly or through vocational schools, entrepreneurial training institutions and well established grass root and NGOs. Bharatiya Yuva Shakti Trust gives assistance to help formulate these proposals. The screening process, done by an Entrepreneur Selection Panel comprises of experts from the industry in marketing, finance, management, etc.

Who's backing BYST?

Founding chairman	*Late JRD Tata*
Vice-chairman	*Late H P Nanda*
Chairman and Managing Director	*Mr. Rahul Bajaj*

Source: Information received from "Bharatiya Yuva Shakti Trust".

- Do you really have what it takes to be an entrepreneur?
- Will I be able to support myself financially?
- How much money will I need to start a business?
- What is the "right" business for me?
- What are all the steps I need to take to start a business?

Decided, but don't know what business you want to start

Perhaps you need to look at different ways to stimulate your creativity. Creativity is important in running any business. So, even if you don't find the right idea for you, know more about creativity will help you be a better business owner.

The actual business you pursue is not the only decision you will need to make. There are a variety of business models that you also should consider in identifying the best way to run your business.

Fear of business failure

Most of the entrepreneurs before selecting the business fear about the failure of the business. It is also natural that they will have a fear; definitely you must take care before starting the business. But fear should not be dominant on you. Business is the game of risk. Not blind risk but calculated risk. Without taking risk doing business is impossible. The new entrepreneurs try to do such a business where they have minimum risk. They do not want to go for something new because they have fear of failure of business because of that they never try new profitable business where they can earn more profit. They never explore new areas or untouched areas of business. For example: most of the new entrepreneurs open their business in city only but they never try to explore rural business. The new entrepreneurs never try to open business in agriculture sector where there is a huge scope.

9.2 Assessment of Entrepreneurial Opportunity

The entrepreneur's common sense and related traits are essential for selecting the business. In the assessment of entrepreneurial opportunity it is necessary for the entrepreneur to have an analytical capacity to be able to determine whether he or she owns the necessary abilities and resources that will enable him or her to undertake the new business. The entrepreneurs do many mistakes if they go for a business without knowing much about it or unable to judge the market situation. It is also important to analyze, as a whole, the potential market of the goods or services produced by the new business. In general terms, the criteria to assess an opportunity is: (1) the need that the goods or services will cover, (2) the possibility to identify the potential clients, (3) the market size, (4) the growth rate of the market, (5) the participation level in the market, (6) the structure of competition, (7) the response to competition, (8) the degree of price control, the distribution chains, (9) the expenditures of production, marketing and distribution, and (10) the profits.

The business plan

New entrepreneurs find obstacles while it comes to prepare the business plan. Though the idea is clear but they cannot convert it into the business plan. Once it is clear that the idea of business is really a business opportunity it is necessary to work out a plan where the purpose of the business, its activities and the required resources are explicitly stated. The business plan is the most important document of the new business. It contains business concept and the activities required to carry out the idea of the business. For making the business plan the entrepreneurs should work with the experienced person who knows detail description of the business plan.

Legal creation of the business

This is the best moment of the creation phase. At this point, the necessary aspects are completed in order to award the business with a legal existence. The legal creation differs from country to country and in some cases, even from region to region within the same country.

Launching and opening

This is the phase that marks the beginning of the actual business. It is the departure on an 'uncertain journey', where the expertise and the capacity of the entrepreneur are important in order to overcome the obstacles that will undoubtedly arise.

Team creation

For the small new entrepreneurs the selection of the team is very essential. The entrepreneurs cannot hire maximum number of employees. They always try to select the multi skilled employees but most of the times they do not get the desired employees for their business. It is an increasingly common fact that the creation of a new business is not the work of a single individual but rather of a group of people interested in the business world. One criterion followed for making a team consists on looking for complementary partners, regarding both –attitudes and capacities.

The team creation is an aspect that requires great attention by the entrepreneur because in a great measure, the future of the new business depends on it. The team should be such that there should not be any confliction but should be a feeling of great cooperation. Entrepreneurs' difficulties in finding perfect team directly affect the business of the entrepreneurs.

Acquisition and organization of resources

Entrepreneurs must know the organization of the resources. Most of the new entrepreneurs start business with partial resources by keeping in mind that rest of the resources will be included when business will start. They do mistake here, they should not be in hurry to open the business. Opening business with partial resources is dangerous for the business because while giving services if customers will not get the required services then definitely image of the business will reduce. On this phase the new business' technical needs have to be determined. They must know the technical requirement of the business. The problems with the entrepreneurs are that they do not exactly know the technical requirement and that's why they do not do proper estimation. Among the technical needs the first decision concerns to the necessary machinery and equipment to start new business activities. If it is an original project the product identification factor and the search for adequate suppliers are typical cases of decisions that have to be taken in unstructured situations, where equally the capacity of the entrepreneur is put to test.

Development of goods or services

Nevertheless, the decision of how to manufacture or produce the goods or service is a fundamental aspect of the new business. They should know the process or the methods. The supplying conditions of the raw material, stockage and certainly the product's design and its presentation must all be taken into account. The new entrepreneurs lag in designing the process for delivery of services and products. They do not have proper process to reach to customers. What they do they simply copy others' business process and try to implement it. But here two factors are important. The first is even if they copy they do not copy completely and as result of that they lag. The second is they do not give importance to develop their own process to get to the customers. They should develop their own unique way of process to give better service and products to customers. For example, if other company is providing Sunday home delivery facility to their customers, then you can develop your own process of delivering throughout the week.

- **Financing**

The capital investment of a business comes in great measure from the founders' or their families' personal resources (47 to 73 per cent of the times). Looking for financing means constitutes a crucial aspect in the new venture. It is usually a long and difficult process because, unless there are good entrepreneurial tracking records, banks are reluctant to provide this kind of financing. It is therefore the entrepreneur's task to use all of his or her capacity to obtain the proper financing. His newness creates many problems. Entrepreneur does not find finance so easily. He has to create his worth; he has to assure the financer that his venture is going to be a profitable venture.

9.3 Choosing A Business to Start

Most of the reasons are there when a person wants to start a business. Whatever reason may be if a person is going to start the business his first motive is to earn the profit. Maybe you have a brilliant idea and you're trying to figure out if it's viable or not. Or maybe you're out of work or just fed up with your current job and looking for an alternative.

Whatever the circumstances that have brought you to this point, the most important thing will be:

- Are you a right person to start a business?
- Do you have knowledge about the business?
- Are you ready to become entrepreneur?
- Are you cut out for entrepreneurship?

Not everybody is. The rewards can be great, but so are the risks. And it will change your lifestyle in ways that you may not be prepared for. If you haven't explored this question yet, take a few minutes to review some of the resources in becoming an entrepreneur. Before going to the business the entrepreneurs should prepare for these questions. Entrepreneurship brings responsibility where your acts will decide the direction of the business. Where you will be responsible for giving the instructions and if you are not ready for this then take a time to prepare yourselves and then try to open a business.

Once you've decided to walk the entrepreneurial path, the next question to ask yourself is, "What type of business do I want to start?" There are, of course, thousands of choices. Number of businesses are there that you can open. Some businesses look great but you may not be able to handle those businesses. So before opening the business it is very important for the entrepreneurs to do analysis of all the business. Many times you go for the business that looks great but then in between you think that you cannot handle the business. As a result of that your business fails. Short of something like pharmaceuticals that requires enormous research and development budgets, there are virtually no limits: automobile manufacturing, food products, import/export and many others are open to even the individual entrepreneur. With infinity of choices, how are you going to decide?

The conventional approach

The conventional approach to entrepreneurship is a methodical, scientific process. Generally speaking, the approach consists of researching the market, identifying a need, looking customers, looking suppliers and creating a business to fill it. More specifically, the steps of the process are:

- Select the industry you're interested in working for.
- Research the kinds of businesses and various business models within that industry.
- Perform market research to see where there is an unmet need — geographically, price wise, complementary products and services, etc.
- Analyze the market situation
- Analyze the competition.
- Analyze the suppliers
- Develop a preliminary business plan for a business to meet that need.
- Do some more market research to assess the realistic market potential for your business. *Will people buy it?*
- Revise the business plan and determine your funding requirements.
- If needed, seek out lenders or investors.
- Start the business.

Needless to say, this is not something you just knock out in a weekend. The most obvious problem to this approach is that it's extremely labour-intensive and potentially expensive to even decide whether or not to go into business. Of course, that time spent on the front end reduces the risk of failure down the road.

The other problem is that you may very well end up realizing far too late that you're doing something you really don't want to be doing, just because you figured you could make some decent money at it. Even when you're the boss, you can still end up feeling stuck and unfulfilled.

9.4 Already Existing Business

When choosing a what business you want to pursue, there are not only many different kinds of businesses you can run, but there are also a wide variety of business models that you should consider when deciding what is the right business for you.

There is more to deciding on the right business other than settling on the actual product or service you will be producing. Here are a number of other factors that may be a consideration in identifying the right model for your business.

Buy a Franchise or Join a Direct Marketing Business or Start from Scratch

This is a question of how ready you are to plan and implement every aspect of your business. Direct marketing businesses and franchises train and support you, but your flexibility of what you offer is limited. It also can be costly to buy into an established business. For new small entrepreneurs it is not possible to suddenly purchase a new business. Franchises do usually have a track record and marketing that can be a bonus to get your business going. Look carefully into any direct marketing businesses you might consider. They can require tremendous investments that often cannot be recovered if you decide it is not the right path for you.

Home-based vs. Office-based

Many people try to open such a business which then can operate out of their home. Entrepreneurs want to operate home based business because by doing this first their investment will decrease because there is no need to purchase any land or infrastructure. Second they will be with their family. Family members can also help them in their business. Doing this entrepreneurs can save money. Some have different attitude, they want to separate their business life from their home life. You also may have space limitations that limit your choices. Home-based businesses can be lonely. Office-based businesses may bring hassles with other tenants if you are renting or cash flow if you purchase.

Invent something new

Invention usually requires lot of knowledge; research work and intelligence. Invention may be new product or new services. Invention should be such that people should have a need of that. Sometimes the new entrepreneurs come up with the new products or services but people do not need that. So be careful while inventing new things. Products require manufacturing facilities, supplies and distribution; services are customer oriented and you should be very perfect regarding time. Independent contracting can be the best of all worlds, although continually finding new contracts can cause cash flow problems.

Long Term Commitment vs. Build a Business to Sell

Some people have every intention of staying in this business forever. They want to move forward their business. They want to become a successful entrepreneur and want to earn profit out of that. Others dream of making their money through starting new businesses, then selling them. Few entrepreneurs are very well in opening the business but they do not want to be in that business forever. They open the business successfully and then sell the business. They enjoy opening the new business. They earn profit by selling a running business. Such folks are sometimes called "serial entrepreneurs." So you must think what kind of entrepreneur you want to become. Are you interested in opening and selling the business? This requires knowledge, efforts and confidence to build a business. But if you want to be in your business forever and want to achieve something with the help of your business, it may be money, recognition, wealth generation etc., then remaining in the existing business is good option. Each way of operating requires a very different financial model. Be honest with yourself about what is right for you so that you can structure your business plan accordingly.

Online vs. Physical Business (or Both)

Online businesses are often the choice of people who want a home-based business, but they are not synonymous. Online business could be the best option if you do not have big space. The advantages of online business are that within small space also you can run your business. No need to decorate your shop because you will be dealing with your customers online only. By doing this you can save your money and can earn more profit. Online businesses can be of any size and in any location. They can be worldwide or local. Physical businesses are almost always local unless there is a mail-order or ecommerce component. Each of these types of businesses is different to manage and run. Most of the entrepreneurs try to run physical business where they can interact with the customers face to face. They do not want to go for the online business. Don't let other factors like wanting to be home-based influence your decision on this. If you have a fear of online business or you think that you will not be able to handle the problems of online business then it is better to switch on physical business.

Size of business

Entrepreneurs when go with big size business then it harms them only because the biggest problems are the first they do not have much experience about the business and second thing, they are not able to handle so many situations at single time. Some entrepreneurs simply want to make enough to live simply. Others are looking to build another TATA. There are two components to consider in size. What is a comfortable size to start for you and how big do you eventually want to get? Some folks who are new to business want to be on their own to learn the ropes before adding employees, others who have managed before may be more comfortable having at least a few employees to share the workload. Your strengths and weaknesses will help you assess your short-term objective. Your own personal goals will help you determine your long-term objective.

Skills needed

You may have a dream of what business you want to have eventually, but not have the skills yet. Education may need to be part of your business plan. Even for those of you who have a basic idea of what the business entails, the more you can learn about it, the better a business you will have. Make certain you know what skills are required for a business and how your strengths and weaknesses fit with those skills.

Urban vs. Rural

Entrepreneurs are reluctant to the rural business. They just want to open their business in city only. They should not think narrowly. That's why they lose profit market. The first constraint is that they do not want to take extra efforts, risk by operating the business in the rural areas. Urban businesses and rural businesses frequently have different constraints and different models. Marketing can be very different. It can make a difference in what business you choose. You may have always wanted to move to a rural location or vice versa and are taking the opportunity of starting a business to explore such a change. Do be aware of the differences in population density, consumer behavior. Learn as much as you can before taking this jump.

Look for the possibilities of Business

There are so many businesses that you can choose to start. You may not be able to select any particular business because of lack of business knowledge. You would like to open such a business which you like and can handle easily. Before starting the business the entrepreneurs must look to the possibilities of the business. Possibilities means you must know customers base, demand of products, competitors etc. One way to start is to look at lists information about different types of businesses to help explore possibilities; however, all lists have limitations. They are nice to scan, through — and great if they describe precisely the business you want to start, but even lists with hundreds of possibilities barely scratch the surface.

Open that business which you love, like and have knowledge about that. If you have a sufficient knowledge about the business which you like then here you can utilize your skills and creativity to operate the business. You can better understand your business and therefore you will see that you are enjoying your business. In a business you must have a desire to achieve something. Unless you have that feeling you cannot get a big success. Knowledge plus interest will lead you towards success. For instance, someone who loves software development can be a software developer, run an IT company. Part of knowing yourself is finding the right fit for what you find fun to do.

For entrepreneurs who do not know their interest and are not sufficient in any knowledge, it is very hard for them to select a particular business. Most of entrepreneurs are not focused to their goals and achievements. In some ways we are blessed because a wide variety of things can make us happy, but it can also provide confusion when there are so many different directions one could go. How do you make the choice?

You cannot become rich within one or two days. You have to think on many aspects. You cannot be in hurry while operating a business. Your decision can put your business in loss. If you are doing a business then you must have patience. Do not look at your business as a money making machine. Business is not just a way of earning money. It is more than that. A successful business is built slowly based on a well-designed business plan, knowledge.

So, how do you know what kind of business to start? You must think on why do you want to open a business? What is the purpose? What do you want to achieve? What are your goals? Are you seeking certain income level? Is this a means of making money so you can do other things or are you seeking a business that is fun in-and-of itself? Describe the ideal business as thoroughly as you can.

Your next step involves using a technique common in strategic planning — SWOT analysis. What you should have at the end of this assessment is a clear set of attributes a business must have to be "right" for you. The next step is to consider how to choose the right one.

This is where you need to get creative. Hopefully, by this point you have some sense of the general area you would like to work in, be it sports, computers, telecommunication or any of the other hundreds of possible industries. Take the SWOT analysis developed earlier and apply it to the industry of interest. What businesses in this industry are best considering your strengths and weaknesses? What businesses are best for the opportunities and threats that are confronting you?

Asking suggestions and discussion with your friends, relatives and the experts who already have a business experience will help you in getting valuable information. At the primary stage of your business you must try to get actual information related to threats, possibilities and scope. The cost of making improvement in mistakes is very high once you start a business with partial facts. So do not take decisions without proper inquiry. You are the one who has to live with this business day-after-day for years to come. It is a major life decision.

SWOT analysis is the best way to take decision. Once you know your weakness, strengths, opportunities and threat you can take better decision. You need to think on as a small business how can you grow your business? How can you make it competent? What is your business long term as well as short term plans? What is the specialty of your business? Will it survive in near future also? How your business is different from others? All this information you have compiled should give you a relatively detailed overview of the qualities you need for a business to have for it to be satisfying.

All these decisions can be overwhelming. Do not show your laziness in taking decisions. Your decisions are very crucial for your business. Entrepreneurs must take right decisions depending upon the situation. Entrepreneurs decisions decide the direction of the business whether it is upward or downward. Entrepreneurs should not fear while taking decisions. If that is one of your weaknesses, perhaps you need to team up with someone else for this venture — or reconsider entrepreneurship.

If you know what you want to do, but are concerned about the financial aspects, write a simple business plan. What your financial obligations will be. If you feel that you are ready to go, move on starting a business. And, remember to have fun!

9.5 Choosing a Business to Start

A number of factors are important in order to start a successful business. Here an effort is made to describe some of the key factors. The process of selecting the right business can go beyond choosing one that fits your personality. Know the other approaches you can use in choosing a business.

Choosing the right business is the first step to entrepreneurial success. Your goal, therefore, as an entrepreneur is to find a business that stands a greater chance of success. Where you as an entrepreneur can explore the opportunity, you will need to determine what you can and cannot do, are you ready to take efforts, research on the potential market and how other similar businesses are doing and what works well in your area or selected business medium.

Total Project Costs

Entrepreneurs just by doing rough calculation of the cost entrap themselves in between the business where there business does not reach to completion and from there they cannot revert back also. It happens because they have partial information of the cost of the business. It is important to correctly assess the total project cost required to set up and run the business successfully.

In a capital intensive business such as starting a manufacturing plant, the start up costs can be very high. You need to identify the total amount which will be spent on the land and building, plant and machinery, furniture and office equipment, vehicles etc.

If a business is of the nature of retail you will need to identify the cost of the store and furniture. Amount required for the decoration of the store needs to be assessed. Similarly in case of an office the major cost will be for the furniture and office equipment. An office or firm can be started at a relatively lower cost initially with only the basic requirements.

One also needs to take care of the working capital requirement. This will mainly consist of the inventory which needs to be maintained and the credit which is extended to the customers. From this the supplier's credit is deducted to arrive at the Working Capital Requirement. The Working Capital Requirement can be quite high for certain industries. For example, inventory will need to be maintained in a garment store. Similarly in case of a grocery shop there is need for huge inventory for which credit may not be given initially by the suppliers.

Financing/Capital

After identifying the initial costs required for starting the business, the financing pattern will need to be decided. The financing pattern will be mainly by way of capital introduction by the owner and borrowed funds.

Depending on how much capital the owner can introduce the balance amount will need to be borrowed. Funds borrowed will be either short term loans or long term loans. The terms and conditions for borrowing funds will need to be studied such as the cost of borrowing, security required, rate of interest and the repayment terms. The owner will need to approach a number of banks to get information about their terms of lending and draw a comparative analysis to identify which funding is the most beneficial for him.

Competition

Before entering new business, information about market competition needs to be found out. In case a product has a monopoly then the competition will not matter. Otherwise the success of the business will depend upon the demand and supply gap. Thus if there is a huge demand then you can enter the business in spite of the market competition. But where there is a tough competition for the customers then you must think on that whether you have sufficient competency or not to open the business in such a tough competitive market. Otherwise you will need to be stronger than the competitors to gain an entry. Normally existing firms will always have an advantage due to the experience they have and because they may be well equipped. They have strong contacts with suppliers, distributors etc., they take advantage of their relationship.

The question which needs to be answered is "What is unique about the product / service which will be offered to survive the market competition"? Information such as who are the competitors, what is their market strategy and what factors are required to compete with them are important.

Less money out

Entrepreneurs mostly deal with the problems of less money or to earn money. Budget decides their business but they do not decide business. The kind of business that you start depends on the amount of capital you can raise. According to budget only you can go for particular type of business. If you have deep pockets, you can go all out with your business - getting first-rate equipment and furnishings, hiring employees, launching the business in grand style and buying loads of inventory. However, if you have little capital, all you can do is to start the business on a much smaller scale.

If you cannot finance your vision, you may need to downscale your business and instead find ways to start on this route but without expense. Entrepreneurs just follow the dream without knowing the fact that whether their money is sufficient for the business or not. One way is to start an e-commerce site where you will not have to pay for furnishings, expensive rent and other overheads that a retail store will need.

Location

Deciding an optimum location for the business is a strategic and an important one. A good location goes a long way in making the business successful. The location needs to be carefully chosen. If your business is in populated area then definitely no need to do much advertising and promotion. You can take an advantage of attracting customers easily, the manpower would be easily available and you can save out on transportation costs because you are located in market area. If you are in backward area, where government gives relief on tax and provides number of facilities to you, you have a great opportunity there. Setting up a business in certain location could lead to subsidy and rebates from the Government. In the case of a retail business one needs to be located in a well populated area and one which is easily accessible.

Laws, rules and regulation

Setting up a new business would require compliance with various laws and regulations. Each country is governed by separate laws and regulations which require that any new business be registered with certain authorities and meets certain compliance. Thus registration of the name of the company may be required with Ministry of Commerce for instance. Further details need to be provided regarding the workforce and certain deductions may be required from the staff (such as tax) which would need to be deposited with the respecting Government bodies. Awareness is required of such rules and regulations. It is always better to consult a lawyer before setting up a new business in an unknown environment.

Return on investment

Return on Investment (ROI) is calculated as Net Profit divided by the Investment made. The ROI is low in the initial years and is expected to grow on a year to year basis. The ROI needs to be compared with the return that would be earned from alternative business options available.

Staff/Manpower

Any business requires efficient manpower to succeed. The staff needs to be carefully chosen since they are the ones who could make or break the business. The cost of manpower varies depending on the location of the business and thus this needs to be factored well. The business needs to be set up in a location where there is sufficient availability of manpower both skilled as well as unskilled.

Technology

Technology would include plant and machinery as well as latest office equipment. One should not exclude the software required to monitor the business. Choosing optimum software is a challenging task. A technologically advanced business is expected to perform much better in the longer run.

Fewer competitors, the better the situation

On the other side of the spectrum from those who believe in safety in numbers are those who think that they are better off in a business with fewer competitors. This is the idea behind the strategy of focusing on a market niche, which has proven to be apt, even a lifesaver, for many small and home-based businesses. Niche entails offering unique products or services to a few concentrated markets.

Self-discovery

Entrepreneurs instead of finding their own interest they just run behind the others suggestions. They try to do particular business because others are also doing the same. Find out what you're truly passionate about and figure out how to make a business out of it. Your interest is must as far as your business is concerned. You will have a business then only you will involve in that business. You will try to find out the new things that will lead you to the success.

Safety in less numbers

As a new entrepreneur, you may also consider a business that has already proven popular, dependable with consistent demand and can be found everywhere. Common businesses include eating places, groceries, used merchandise stores, gift and novelty stores. If these businesses have staying power and are frequently found, then they must be profitable, what you think? But keep in mind that when number of entrepreneurs increase in a particular business then they just only thin the profit of every entrepreneur in the business. As a new entrepreneur you must keep in mind that though a business is looking good but if many players are already there in the market then it is better to avoid that business. Few businesses are very good in nature, less cost is required and profit is good. But the problem with the new entrepreneurs is that they cannot open those businesses easily because so many players have already started their business on that idea. Now if they want to open a business they have to think differently and here they lack knowledge, if they have knowledge then the budget of that business is very high plus they will require more promotion and more advertising for their new kind of business to attract the customers.

Inspiration

That idea that just popped into your head one day may not be so crazy after all. You open the business because you are inspired from someone else who is running the business successfully. Inspiration is good but unless you know about that business and you have proper knowledge about that business you should not try to open that business. If you do not have any advisor then unless you get complete information about the business do not open the business.

Observation

Be constantly looking for unmet needs. Is there a product or service that you would buy if it were accessible and affordable? New entrepreneurs find a problem when they have an idea but they do not convert it into the business. Many entrepreneurs mostly do not care about to know the need of the customers and then to move in that direction. They are lazy to do something by their own. They want to have a set up market instead of creating that market by their own.

Novelty and excitement

For new entrepreneurs the good strategy is to start a business that is on boom. Many entrepreneurs have started the business of computers when it was new and hot and now those entrepreneurs have established their businesses. When you try such a business that is new in the market and hot then you can definitely get success by your efforts, strategies and intelligence. In India people are more attracted towards foreign foods. They eat it with full desire. They like it. You as a new entrepreneur should open the business that is growing. Where there is full scope. Where there are large number of customers and less number of competitors. The new entrepreneurs when open business they do not give proper importance to the analysis of different stages of the business. Whether it is declining, growing or will remain stagnant. You can join in the fray and start a business that has already proven itself to be a moneymaker for others.

Market/Demand

It Entrepreneurs start the business without demand analysis it will become a failure. If already numbers of shops are in the market for the same product then it is not a wise decision to open another shop. By doing this entrepreneurs put them in loss. Once a decision is taken on the business you intend to start, the next step is to explore the demand / market for the product / service. Certain products will only have a domestic market for them whereas others can be successful on an international level. The key question is "Who are the customers?" A market survey can be conducted to identify the market for the business to be started. If the product / service are expected to be sold locally, the demand for it needs to be assessed. In case an international market is expected then rules and regulations for dealing internationally need to be found out.

Limitation

Entrepreneurs must do experiment with different success models. They should read or observe thoroughly different successful entrepreneurs. Imitate their successful business model. But the fact is that they rarely listen to these things. It does not matter what is the source of idea. What is important how you handle it? If you lack money and cannot give sufficient time for market research then you need to do at least informal research to know about the business opportunities for your idea. You can ask your friends and family, what they think? What is their opinion? Take their suggestions on your idea.

Whenever entrepreneurs want to select a business always look for most successful entrepreneurs in that business. (If you don't know that many, you'd better meet some – try to make contact with the successful entrepreneurs. Take their suggestions that will help you a lot. Know how they work? What has made them successful in the business? With this approach, you can pursue your passion, tempered by proven practices and improve your possibilities of prosperity.

Knowledge/Expertise

Entrepreneurs start the business without knowledge and expertise. The reasons are because others are doing well in that business or others are earning profits in that business. Even if any business has a boom in the market it is not necessary that anybody can do that unless they have proper knowledge of that business. Any business requires some amount of basic knowledge and experience. The owner needs to be aware about the business he intends to start. Knowledge and expertise about the product or service are keys to a successful business. In case of limited knowledge the owner may not be able to sustain the business and can be fooled by the vendors, suppliers and competitors.

When you ask yourself a question "What business shall I start?" you need to get a convincing reply about what you intend to do and how you are going to go about it. You must have a plan to start your business. That plan should be in a written format not in mind. Expert knowledge is especially required if the field of business is a niche field. For instance the construction or software industry would require more knowledge as against a retail business selling a particular brand of clothes or shoes.

All the above factors are important to start a successful business. Compromising any of these factors could hamper the growth. Starting a business these days is very challenging and an all round knowledge of various factors is required to run a successful one. It is important to make a Project Report on the basis of the above factors before starting a new business.

9.6 Business Coach Selection

Leaders in any field can benefit from a good coach. As the driving force behind your business venture, you should consider a coach who can help you streamline your production processes, streamline your different business processes, improve your marketing initiatives and contribute to the overall survival and success of your business. Business coaches, like other types of coaches, often specialize in a specific area. If you feel uncomfortable with any of the area of business then you can take help of a business coach. You should not avoid the importance of business coach. If you require them then call them, do not try to do by yourselves. However, use caution when making your decision; business coaching is a self-regulated industry.

Guidelines for finding a business coach who will guide your business down the road to success:

Ask trusted sources for recommendations. Solicit recommendations from trusted service providers, including your accountant, financial planner and banker or from other business providers. It should not happen that after hiring them you are not getting the expected knowledge from them.

Select your uncomfortable area in business. Business coaches specialize in a wide range of topics: marketing, finance or assuring business profitability, building infrastructure for example. Carefully consider in which areas you most need guidance and find a coach who best suits your needs. Make a checklist of each area of your business. Define areas with the help of different existing factors in those areas. Now checklist in which area you have less knowledge and accordingly select your business coach.

Have more numbers of candidates. Judiciously interview several business coaches; this will increase your odds of finding the right match for you. By doing this you will have more options. You can easily compare different personalities and the probability of selecting a good business coach will increase. This decision is as critical as selecting the right financial advisor. You need to be cautious and patient.

Prepare structured interview questions. To find a fitting coach for your business, you'll want detailed answers to specific questions. Preparing structured interview questions for interview will be the best option. Structured questions give direction to your interview. You are more focused. You ask relevant and required questions and get desired answers from candidate. Questions you want to ask include: What is your background in business? What are your experience as coaching business owners? What credentials do you have in coaching or in other related fields? What is your personal coaching style? With what kind(s) of clients do you work best? What are the businesses issues in which you are most qualified?

Seek references. Ask potential candidates for a list of references and contact them. It is crucial to determine if your prospective business coach has satisfied clients. Taking references will assure you about the performance of the coach.

Build solid relationship. Solid relationships are built on trust, safety, honesty, support and quality feedback; the relationship that you form with your business coach is no different. After your interview, reflect upon how you feel about and what you think of your prospective coach. Do you think you can trust them? Could you let your guard down enough to really open up and be honest with this person? Does your guts tell you that this is the right fit or to keep looking?

Have a clear understanding of your mutual roles. An effective business coach helps you build your own capacities and resources to respond more consciously, skillfully and appropriately to your leadership and management challenges. He or she then guides you to execute your decisions with precision. How will this assistance and support be displayed? How will you react to this help?

So What Could Be the Solution?

9.7 Guidelines for Your Business

1. Take on the World

Want your company to go global? Keep these tips in mind when eyeing foreign shores:

1. Research and map out your export journey.
2. Know where you want to go and go there.
3. Take that decisive step and follow it up with sensible judgment. Jump in with both feet first, but keep them firmly planted on the ground.
4. Keep your ego in check. Don't let the prospect of "going global" inflate your ego and cause misjudgments.
5. If it smells, looks or feels bad, don't try to rationalize otherwise. Trust your instincts.
6. Treat people as you yourself want to be treated.
7. Make personal contact with attentiveness, courtesy, professionalism and consistency.
8. Factor in a three-year lead-time for world market penetration. It takes time and patience.
9. In a global marketplace, welcome the unknown.

2. Where to Find Expansion Financing

You may have used personal savings or money borrowed from friends and family to get started, but where do you go when it's time to grow your business? If you've been in business for less than three years or have nothing to offer as collateral, you might find traditional lending institutions unwilling to finance your business. There are options, though — if you know sheer to look. Try these three funding sources to fund your expansion plans:

- **Go back to those same friends and family.** If your first loan wasn't formalized, do it this time by drawing up documents with a set repayment plan and interest.
- **Go the government route.** Many entrepreneurs get financing, including microloans, from MSME-backed lenders.

- **Talk to your vendors.** Another method of obtaining financing for supplies or materials is to approach vendors of those products about opening a line of credit with them so you can stock your inventory or buy raw materials for your product without having to put the cash up front.

3. Ready for another Location?

This might not be your best choice for business expansion, but it's what often comes to mind first for so many entrepreneurs considering expansion. Take a look at the following tips to see if opening a second location is the right move for your business:

- Make sure you're maintaining a consistent bottom-line profit and that you've shown steady growth over the past few years.
- Look at the trends, both economic and consumer, for indications on your company's staying power.
- Make sure your administrative systems and management team are extraordinary-you'll need them to get a new location up and running.
- Prepare a complete business plan for a new location.
- Determine where and how you'll obtain financing.
- Choose your location based on what's best for your business, not your wallet.

4. Franchising and Licensing

Have you ever considered turning your business into a franchise or business opportunity? The key question to ask yourself is if your business can be converted into a business format that somebody else could operate (a franchise) or if you have a standardized product or service that someone could resell multiple times (a business opportunity). While you may think that expanding your business requires raising capital, hiring employees, buying equipment and leasing office or warehouse space, it's often more profitable-and less risky-to license your product to a big corporation with manufacturing capabilities and an existing sales force to do the work for you.

5. How to Target Other Markets

If you sell to teens, start marketing to college students. If you sell to working moms, maybe your product will work for stay-at-home moms with a few modifications. Another strategy is to take a retail-oriented product or service and sell it wholesale. For example, a catering business that specializes in cakes, pies and other tasty desserts can contact local bakeries to sell its goods on a wholesale basis. While the price you get from the bakeries will be lower (because the bakeries need to mark it up to their customers to make a profit), you'll sell more products and generate consistent cash flow that you can bank on.

9.8 Try Bootstrapping

Bootstrapping means "pursuing success with limited resources and with the help of others." By limited resources mean a shortage of money or knowledge. Here are some tips and ideas to help solve these shortfalls for small and entrepreneurial business owners. These ideas are particularly apropos in today's environment.

Barter

Barter, one of the world's oldest forms of commerce, is thriving today because it allows companies to trade their products or services for other needed products or services with little or no cash involved. You can utilize your excess goods, manufacturing capacity or time to obtain needed things of every imaginable variety. Bartering can also help you reach and acquire new customers through satisfied trading partners that, if pleased, will buy again with cash and provide good word of mouth to others.

Free Counseling

MSME and many agencies of government are with the mission to provide resources and expertise to maximize the success of existing and emerging small businesses. All MSME counselors are volunteers, mostly experienced executives who want to give back. There is no charge and everyone who calls gets an appointment.

Mentors

Mentors are experienced, successful businesspeople who are willing to help entrepreneurs get started and grow at no charge. Getting a good mentor will help your business in getting success. Mentors can be found in numerous places: family, former teachers, suppliers, the local Chamber of Commerce, people you admire, etc. If you find a good one, be sure always to keep him or her in the loop and say thank you.

Special Offers to Key Customers

It is very hard for the small businesses to sell to the customers in a very competitive environment. There is a simple way to attract the customers and that is to offer them something that is unique. Unique offers may include innovative products or unique services. Your offer should be such that it should not be provided by anyone in the market. The uniqueness may be terms of cost, usage, consumption or time. For example you can give on-door services to your customers or more durable products than your competitors.

Suppliers

Suppliers are an important part of the business. Your business reputation depends on their quality materials. So every business always wants good and reliable suppliers who can supply on-time and can consider financial problems i.e., should not be very strict regarding payment. Some suppliers may even be willing to invest in your company. The quality of the best suppliers is that they form a strong relationship with you. They want to see your business grow and thus help your business. To gain supplier cooperation, treat suppliers fairly and pay all of their bills on time.

Publicity

Getting coverage about you, your company or your product in print, on TV, on radio or on the web can be more credible than a paid ad you need not be an expert to get such media coverage. Remember that the writer's job is to write and they all need stories. Why not yours? Start by approaching your local media with interesting facts or anecdotes about yourself, your product or service and how you started the company. Writers usually prefer the passion of the company founder to a pitch from a professional publicist.

Outsourcing

Outsourcing helps you in hiring the employees whenever they are required instead of hiring full time employees. You just pay at the time when you hire them instead of paying them full-time. It saves your money and you also become free to select the employees according to their skills and capability. So you can hire employees according to your suitability. You will have no binding to continue with poor employees. Outsourcing does not mean sending work overseas. It is not true. Anything not done in house is outsourced, whether you get it done down the street, in another state or in another country.

Building Trust

If you are trusted, customers will want to do business with you, employees will be motivated and lenders and investors are more apt to give you money. You build trust by refusing to compromise on doing the right thing and conducting business ethically. Trust relentlessly pursued can pay great dividends.

Selling

It's easy for new people to learn selling skills if they stay focused on the sales process. You must first learn the sales process before you learn sales skills required to execute the sales process. The sales process is how sales are developed. So, don't go out and learn sales skills until you have the sales process foundation firmly in place. Only then you are ready for advanced sales training. You'll never look back once you learn sales skills that the top pros use to close more sales.

9.9 Deciding Your Home Business

Selecting the right kind of business is a difficult process for any starting entrepreneur. Many dream of starting their own businesses, but remain frozen in *status quo* mainly because they do not know what business to engage in.

Here are guidelines on selecting the home business most suited for you.

Instead of choosing the first business that comes to mind, take time to explore various options. Do not be so excited. Let's take a sufficient time. Find out and analyze the other business ideas. Read business magazines, newspaper and trade magazines to get an idea about possible home-based or small business. With the tremendous growth of the internet you can find out any information easily.

Find out what type of business appeals to you most. Determine your goals, achievement, desires and knowledge. Your knowledge and interest will give you success in business. If you have a knowledge and interest in opening a restaurant then convert your idea into a business. The important thing is that you must enjoy your business. The most successful entrepreneurs feel passionate about what they are doing. You cannot feel passionate (and hence more driven) about your business if you do not like it!

Choose a business that will be personally satisfying as well as profitable. When you want to open a business which you like, You must first consider the scope of that business. It is good that you want to open a business of your desire but you cannot open a business that has very poor or no demand. You must see whether your desired business is profitable or not? Whether you will get continuous income? What is the demand of the business? How many competitors are there? Is it hard or easy to open a business? Start a business that you think has a solid potential to be profitable. You should do a perfect financial planning. You should have a rough estimation of how much finance you will require for the business? By using break even analysis or by analyzing the market you can do a perfect estimation. This is one of the important steps in assessing whether the business you've selected can make you money.

The most important things you will need to know to decide on starting a new home business is how much time and money it will cost you to get started. You can do business by two ways. First you can establish a business by building the required infrastructure and furniture. Here you will need huge money to invest on physical equipments. Second you can do your business online. Here you can save huge amount of money because no need to have a big infrastructure or furniture. Even in small size room with your computer system you can run a business. Regarding time you can run your online business from anywhere but in offline business you need to be in your shop. So according to time and money you must decide on which business you want to do.

Draw a layout of your intended work area to see how it will fit into its allotted space into your home. Remember, you are opening your business in your home because you cannot afford to purchase a big shop or land to build your business infrastructure, so you must use home space in an effective manner. If you want to start a cake decorating business, you need to have a large kitchen. Forget about starting a dance instruction class if you live in a studio apartment!

You need to decide on which demographic you wish to target, which product or service you want to cater to satisfy the customers' needs and what is the way of marketing? If your chosen product or service is health related, then under it comes kids, youths and older. So to whom you want to provide health related service or product, you must research about it. Which segment you want to cater? Choose according to the demand and your feasibility to serve those customers. You can find your customers in gym, yoga centre and in jogging park, so you can target them in those places for your offers.

Check with an insurance agent to determine the kind of insurance coverage the business is going to need. It is good planning to determine what insurance is necessary to minimize your risks and protect your business. General categories of insurance include property, licensing, liability, health, disability, workers' compensation and life insurance.

Running a business is hard work. Many people think to work from home with the hope that they will now get freedom from job. They fail to realize that freedom does not come so easily unless they work hard. With most home-based businesses, you need to be very hard working, active and disciplined to get success in the business. You will be the one who is selling, planning, promoting, stock-keeping, marketing, purchasing, billing, fulfilling orders, etc. Most times, you will work extra hours than your regular job to build a successful business and that success will give you a true freedom.

Get your family members involved in the business and have fun together working for its success! In home based business you have advantages of your family members. You can take the help of family members in business. It is not always easy, but one way will be to involve your family in your home business. During the holidays you can ask your kids and wife to handle the customers. Even your wife can help you at least three to four hours per day after completion of her home work. The most important thing is that everyone in your family enjoys working in your business.

9.10 Predicting the Success of a New Business

Estimating the success of a new business is an important venture that entrepreneurs need to undertake before they seek funding. After all, no business investor will want to fund a project that does not have evidence for potential growth. There are several common components that predict the success of a new business. Here are just a few of them:

Strength of the work team

Many successful businesses in the world have started with a dedicated and committed work team. These were the team which members were aware about the clear objectives of the business. The businesses with such work team not only sustain their confidence and performance but they also work attentively to satisfy the needs of the customers. In addition to establishing effective leadership abilities towards employees and customers alike, a successful management team is one that tends to work meticulously in resolving any conflicts through effective communication with others.

Efforts of entrepreneurs

The future success of a new business is also indicative of entrepreneurial effort and involvement in the venture. Entrepreneurs who have demonstrated a laborious commitment in establishing their startup and working towards sustaining its operations were more likely to be successful with their new businesses when compared to those who did not dedicate the time and effort. These optimized efforts also paid off in terms of acquired knowledge and skills; the more involvement in a given venture, the more expertise was gained and more credibility among investors was established.

Competitive advantage

Getting success in the business will be more if new business develops their competitive edge. Successful entrepreneurs always want to be superior to their competitors. They continuously scan the market conditions, customers and their competitors' strategies. New business owners use this information to their advantage and lure customers by providing better sale discounts and offering promotions that entice their return. When the new businesses develop a successful competitive edge, they are able to establish a good reputation and dominance in the market as well as gain a considerable amount of loyal customers.

Marketing surveys

Online marketing survey is the easiest way to get information from the customers. It saves time and efforts to collect information. It is a very effective tool for the company. Here the entrepreneurs can get instant feedback from the customers about their products and services. In online marketing survey the customers have to fill up the questionnaire form when they do online shopping from company's website. Apart from online surveys offline surveys are also done by direct mail or one to one interaction with the customer. Such information is useful in improving the mistakes and to design the products or the services according to the need of the customers. By doing this company will generate the demand of their products and will earn more profits. Even though there are many more innovative ways to obtain consumer opinion, marketing surveys are still an effective means that a company can use in order to fully understand consumers' needs. Through this tool, an entrepreneur can predict the outcome of the new business concept and estimate market reaction to a product.

STM's

Compared to the conventional means by which consumer feedback is collected, Simulated Test Markets (STM) is a tool that many new businesses use to predict the success of products and services globally. STM's use a combination of consumer research and prediction markets in order to evaluate a new product before it is mass produced. The advantage of using STM's before seeking funding from business investors is that it helps an entrepreneur gauge reaction of a large number of potential customers as opposed to a smaller cross-section of people. For example, the traditional focus groups involve a small amount of individuals to provide feedback on a new product. STM's, on the other hand, collect data from thousands of consumers.

The data obtained from simulated test markets can provide information regarding the projected profitability of a product. If the results are not so promising, the entrepreneur can consider ceasing mass production until a more viable model can be produced or can abandon the idea completely. More and more small businesses are resorting to STM's for marketing. The cost of using such online marketing tools to estimate a new business proposal is not very expensive and the results are more immediate compared to more traditional marketing tools.

Web analysis

Web analysis is a good online marketing tool to promote a business. Web analysis is an easy tool to collect the customers' information that helps the businesses to form their strategies accordingly. This can be helpful to the new company by giving an analytic report of the site's performance, breaking down which pages of the site are popular and how long a potential customer remains on the site. If feasible, entrepreneurs can tailor their website according to these results in order to increase a customers' chance of making a transaction.

Area of industry

Many successful businesses tend to be in industries of high growth potential, such as information technology, education, science, etc. By meeting the demand of the advancing technological market, entrepreneurs are able to gain a large consumer base. The field of information technology is very competitive and changing so if the entrepreneurs want to be in this field need to be very competitive and should always think about the future. They analyze the market and do new innovations according to the customers' needs. Their products are under the reach of customers. They keep their eyes on the changing market conditions and make sure that the customers should get latest products. There are many predisposing factors indicative to a new business' success. First, startups with strong management teams and skilled and hard working entrepreneurs are both important factors for the success of a business. In addition, a business with a viable competitive edge that is in an industry of growth is also relative to a company's success.

9.11 Keep Your Business Running Optimally with Business Coaching

Running a business can be a lot more than simply crunching numbers or turning a profit. It is an art that can't be learned from books or articles and rarely will it be learned from experience alone. At least, experience will not teach as quickly as a business coach would and in the sink or swim world of today's business, that difference could mean the survival of your business.

What does business coaching do? It teaches you how to properly manage your business for success. Why use a coach? Because coaches deal with a huge array of businesses and can be an indispensable resource for the new entrepreneur or an excellent source of wisdom for the seasoned veteran. Business coaching is an informal, open affair. You will meet with the coach and he will assess your business's needs and then tailor his services to your precise requirements. Of course, if meeting face-to-face is impossible, there are online business coaches available.

No matter what the field or specialty of your business, there is a coach out there for you. By considering your individual situation and working to meet the long and short term goals of your business, business coaching will help foster your company's growth. When you start looking for the right business coach for your business, you should ask each candidate for his or her work histories. Look for someone who has successfully run a business him or herself and who has successfully aided other business to grow and improve.

Finally, when you sit down for your first meeting with your new business coach, be prepared! Have certain goals set in how you want your company to grow, how you would like to manage your personnel, advertising and communication, marketing and how to improve your investment rating.

A business coach will soon become one of your closest friends as you confide in them the ups and downs of your business. Your business coach will not act as a friend though, instead they will help you get right down to the problem and figure out the best solution. A business coach is definitely more than just a friend that will listen to you; they have experience and can offer you indispensable advice.

When looking for a business coach it is important that you talk to them on several different occasions to make sure your business styles and personalities are going to work well together. There is nothing worse than pouring out all your business secrets just to find out your business coach and you don't run on the same philosophies. Take your time in selecting a business coach it will save you a lot of headaches in the long run.

9.12 What Business Coaches Perform

It helps you to improve and achieve the desired success. It enables a business owner to create a unique business plan that would reflect his identity. A business coach emphasizes on the importance of interpersonal communication skills in accomplishing an assignment or a project. He helps to deal with the practical problems and identify realistic solutions to them.

The basic responsibilities of a business coach are as follows:

A business coach enables you to develop the basic qualities required by a self-employed person and helps you to focus on your goals, make concrete plans and work towards executing them in an effective manner. The basic responsibilities of a business coach are as follows:

(a) A business coach works towards strengthening the morale of the student, so that he can take charge of the responsibilities assigned. It will make the student accountable of his actions, as well as the likely consequences. In a way, it helps him to keep an open mind and analyze every situation critically, with respect to the available information.

(b) It is very important to help a new one to identify the right direction and move forward, to achieve the desired results. However, it requires a considerable amount of planning and development of strategies. A business coach reviews the plans and strategies and makes suggestions, to ensure development consistency.

(c) A business coach helps the new one to realize the significance of openness in communication. It forms the basis of a successful business, as it minimizes confusion and clears doubts. It often leads to self-correction and an understanding that is required to focus on performance base issues and behavior.

(d) A business coach enables students to inculcate leadership qualities and teaches them to be leader in their chosen fields. He leads the team by being a part of it.

(e) An experienced business coach believes in sharing views and not dictating them. In case of a conflict, he tries to find a middle path. This path often helps the person to make a profitable decision.

(f) He challenges the student, to widen his horizon and search for options even when there seems no possibility. This boosts his level of confidence.

(g) The coaches teach you to relate to people in an effective manner. This in turn, builds and strengthens partnerships based on mutual appreciation and respect. Eventually, it helps the executives to understand, analyze and find solutions to their problems, with the timely assistance of the business coach.

(h) Business coaches help people understand their strengths and weaknesses in a better way, so that they become aware of their hidden potential and work on their weaknesses.

(i) A business coach acts as a guiding factor in motivating the students. Motivation forms the key to success, for an individual as well as the organization. A business coach helps executives understand the value of motivation, by recognizing employees, privately and publicly. This offers positive reinforcement to the employees, thereby motivating the executives to work harder.

A business coach brings about an understanding of business principles among the employees and helps them develop, unleash and maximize the potential within.

Summary

Making the choice to start a business can be a difficult decision. Some of the obstacles that keep people from making the choice to run your own business are:

- Do you really have what it takes to be an entrepreneur?
- Will I be able to support myself financially?
- How much money will I need to start a business?
- What is the "right" business for me?
- What are all the steps I need to take to start a business?

In general terms, the **criteria to assess an opportunity** is: (1) the need that the goods or services will cover, (2) the possibility to identify the potential clients, (3) the market size, (4) the growth rate of the market, (5) the participation level in the market, (6) the structure of competition, (7) the response to competition, (8) the degree of price control, the distribution chains, (9) the expenditures of production, marketing and distribution, and (10) the profits.

Legal creation of the business involves Launching and opening, Team creation, Acquisition and organization of resources, Financing, and Development of goods or services

In identifying the right model for business here are a number of factors that may be considered: Buy a Franchise or Join a Direct Marketing Business or Start from Scratch, Home-based vs. Office-based, Invent something new, Long Term Commitment vs. Build a Business to Sell, Online vs. Physical Business (or Both), Size of business, Skills needed, Urban vs. Rural, and Look for the possibilities of Business.

Choosing the right business is the first step to entrepreneurial success. The different factors that should be considered by the entrepreneurs are Total Project Costs, Financing/Capital, Competition, Less money out, Location, Laws, rules and regulation, Return on investment, Staff/

Manpower, Technology, Competitors, Self-discovery, Safety in less numbers, Inspiration, Observation, Novelty and excitement, Market/Demand, Limitation, and Knowledge/Expertise.

Guidelines for finding a business coach: Ask trusted sources for recommendations. Select your uncomfortable area in business. Have more number of candidates. Prepare structured interview questions. Seek references. Build solid relationship. Have a clear understanding of your mutual roles.

Bootstrapping means "pursuing success with limited resources and with the help of others." By limited resources mean a shortage of money or knowledge. Some ideas to help solve these shortfalls are Barter, Free Counseling, Mentors, Special Offers to Key Customers, Suppliers, Publicity, Outsourcing, Building Trust and Selling.

The guidelines on selecting the home business most suited for you are:

Instead of choosing the first business that comes to mind, take time to explore various options. Find out what type of business appeals to you most. Choose a business that will be personally satisfying as well as profitable. The most important things you will need to know to decide on starting a new home business is how much time and money it will cost you to get started. Draw a layout of your intended work area to see how it will fit into its allotted space into your home. You need to decide on which demographic you wish to target. Check with an insurance agent to determine the kind of insurance coverage the business is going to need. Running a business is hard work. Get your family members involved in the business and have fun together working for its success!

Predicting the success of a new business depends on Strength of the work team, Efforts of entrepreneurs, Competitive advantage, Marketing surveys, STM's, Web analysis, and Area of industry.

The basic responsibilities of a business coach are to work towards strengthening the morale of the student, to identify the right direction and move forward, to review the plans and strategies and make suggestions, to ensure development consistency, to help the new one to realize the significance of openness in communication, to enable students to inculcate leadership qualities, to teach student to relate to people in an effective manner, to help people understand their strengths and weaknesses in a better way, and to act as a guiding factor in motivating the students.

Keywords

Business plan: A business plan is a document that summarizes the operational and financial objectives of a business and contains the detailed plans and budgets showing how the objectives are to be realized.

Team Creation: Ability to identify and motivate individual employees to form a team that stays together, works together and achieves together.

Direct marketing: Marketing by means of direct contact with potential clients or customers, as by direct mail, telephone solicitation, door-to-door selling, etc.

Franchising: Franchising is where a successful business format is replicated.

On-Line Business: On-Line Business, or "Electronic Business", or "E-Business", may be defined broadly as any business process that relies on an automated information system. Today, this is mostly done with Web-based technologies.

Project Costs: The sum total of all funds required to complete a business purchase transaction.

Business Coaching: A focused conversation that facilitates learning and raises performance at work.

QUESTIONS

1. What are the different challenges faced by the new small entrepreneurs while selecting a business?
2. What are the criterias for assessing the business opportunities?
3. What are the different factors that should be considered while selecting a right model for your business?
4. What is the importance of business coach in the growth of business?
5. What are the responsibilities of business coach?

❑ ❑ ❑

CHAPTER – 10

BUILDING BUSINESS INFRASTUCTURE RELATED OBSTACLES

LEARNING OBJECTIVES

On completion of this chapter, you should be able to:

- ☺ *Describe different obstacles which are faced by entrepreneurs while building business infrastructure.*
- ☺ *Describe how government can help entrepreneurs to overcome difficulties in building business infrastructure.*

Opening business requires proper infrastructure. The infrastructure that is required to conduct the business and to attract the customers. Both are mandatory, without it running business cannot be expected. For the young entrepreneurs if they want to give practical form to their mind idea, then any how they have to arrange for it. For the new entrepreneurs thinking idea is not enough unless they have proper infrastructure for their business. The following are the obstacles that are faced by the new entrepreneurs while building infrastructure for their business:

10.1 In-House Business Problems

Most of the entrepreneurs who had their home business had failed. Most of those entrepreneurs commented on their home based business "failures". In essence they were not moving forward because of past failures. Another was afraid of future failure. They have a fear that they will not become successful in the future. Therefore they are not moving forward their business because of an anticipated failure.

BOX 10

Building India – Financing and Investing in Infrastructure, according to McKinsey and Company

India's infrastructure build-out envisages investments of close to $500bn, with $430bn of this in the core transport and utility sectors. About one-fourth of this investment is expected to be met through Public-Private Partnerships (PPP). Successful implementation of this ambitious plan depends on four interdependent factors, namely the creation of adequate projects for tender by government agencies, the uptake of available projects by private sector developers and cash contractors, the financial closure and start of construction and finally, the execution of projects on-time and within budget.

India faces multiple challenges along all these dimensions in its quest to reach the targets set by the Eleventh Plan. To date, India's success across sectors has been mixed. Capacity under construction or fully constructed relative to the Eleventh Plan (an integrated measure of the first three dimensions mentioned above) reveals that only the power sector is on track, achieving 100 per cent of planned capacity, while the ports sector is at 85 per cent, the airports sector at 75 per cent and the roads sector at 50 per cent (including the National Highway Development Programme (NHDP) that has achieved only 10 percent of planned capacity).

But even assuming the bottlenecks in project creation, uptake and execution are tackled, India is on course to a deficit of $150bn to $190bn in financing core infrastructure sectors. Structural impediments in the financial system coupled with the global credit crisis will constrain capital flows to the sector, perpetuating the deficit in core public goods and persistent inefficiencies in the economy. These consequences can be forestalled only by expeditiously reforming the financial sector to eliminate impediments to existing sources of capital, allowing new investor groups into infrastructure projects and adapting innovative mechanisms to channel investment into the sector.

Nevertheless, the infrastructure sector provides a large opportunity for financial sector players, with potential revenues of $10bn to $12bn between the financial years 2010 and 2014, and a revenue pool of $25bn to $29bn beyond 2014. Several project models with different risk-return implications are available for capital participation across all core sectors. Success will lie in building a profitable business model that earns a high sustained return on capital.

Source: Information received from "McKinsey and Company".

The cruel reality is that most of the entrepreneurs who wanted to do business had a debilitating fear we call Failure. This word is paralyzing entrepreneurs from taking the next step. They are not ready to take risk. With the fear of failure they are not taking the advantages of the opportunities. They do not want to do anything new experiment with their business; they want to run their business as it is with the fear of failure. Their dream flows gracefully through their mind; it is so pleasant and beautiful–just when they believe they can achieve it they reach for it. As entrepreneurs reach for it though they are suddenly stricken with a piercing pain through their insides–fear of failure–stopping them from taking the chance or chances to follow their dream!

The fear of failure demotivates them to turn their dreams into reality. They have no hope of earning the money. They think "whether I will lose my money and I would not be able to do anything then". They take their step back instead of moving forward. And what is failure? How does it has this effect on entrepreneurs? It is not a person, it is a fear. A word defined by entrepreneurs. They make this word tangible! They believe in it and so it is!

Take entrepreneurs fear of failure–and switch it. The entrepreneurs should face the fear confidently. They should have trust on themselves instead of taking step back. They should take the help of professional or market survey to get the true result of market. Starting a business is all about entrepreneurs' confidence on themselves. If under fear entrepreneurs will try to start a business then they will not get success because most of the time they will suffer with their doubts and fear. They will not be able to show their actual performance and will hesitate to try any new thing. But if they without any try will lose the hope then they cannot do anything about their business progress. They should like it, love it and trust in it.

The entrepreneurs' thinking should be the positive one. It will end their fear of failure. They should always think that they will always succeed in their business. They should take the example of the other successful businessmen. How they have succeeded? How they have got confidence? What they have done to remove their fear? And many more they can know from others stories. They should try to learn from the failures and success of others. FEAR does not have what it takes to hold them back! Stop fearing failure and start living home business dream!

10.2 Getting New Land/Shop for Business

To get new land / shop for a business is very difficult for the new entrepreneurs. If anyone wants to do a business for that he requires a perfect place and he searches for that he finds a good place also but the problem comes when he could not be able to purchase that shop. In today's time where the price of the place is increasing day by day, so it remains not under the will of the normal entrepreneur to purchase that shop. If he wants a good place then he has to purchase the shop/ land somewhere outside the city where he probably will not get the perfect market. The customers may not have notice of that because of less crowdedness and far from the city.

Everyone is talking about small businesses. People also have an enthusiasm to register a new business. People register also they take a loan from the banks and run the business but few of them handle the business, rest of them just pressed by the burden of dues. The new entrepreneurs show their enthusiasm about the new business but very soon after starting the business they lose their happiness. When they face the cruel reality of the business they think it is better not to do business.

Why this U-turn? Why people are so enthusiastic about starting a business and then become worried to operate them? Why they are not able to keep their enthusiasm of running the business? Why do they not open the business so easily? The fact is that they lack the knowledge, intelligence and the finance to run the business.

Small business is more than a fashion or a buzzword. In the USA, only small businesses create new jobs. The big dinosaur firms (the "blue-chips") create negative employment - they fire people. This trend has a glitzy name: downsizing. In Israel many small businesses became world class exporters and big companies in world terms. The same goes, to a lesser extent, in Britain and in Germany. Virtually every Western country has a "Small Business Administration" (SBA).

These agencies provide many valuable services to small businesses:

They help them organize funding for all their needs: infrastructure, capital goods (machinery and equipment), land, working capital, license and patent fees and charges, etc. The SBAs have access to government funds, to local venture capital funds, to international and multilateral investment sources, to the local banking community and to private investors. They act as capital brokers at a fraction of the costs that private brokers and organized markets charge.

They assist the entrepreneur in the preparation of business plans, feasibility studies, application forms, questionnaires - and any other thing which the new start-up venture might need to raise funds to finance its operations. This saves the new business a lot of money. The costs of preparing such documents in the private sector amount to thousands per document.

They reduce bureaucracy. They protect their entrepreneurs from the illegal practices. They mediate between the small business and the various tentacles of the government. They become the ONLY address which the new business should approach, a "One Stop Shop". These are the things if not done then properly then the new entrepreneurs find it difficult and sometimes they fail in their business.

10.3 A New Business Needs A Support?

The new entrepreneurs are not competent enough as the big companies are. They definitely start the business. They fulfill the requirements of the business but they do not sustain the business. They need direction, they need a supporter who can support them who can advise them about their business. But unfortunately they do not find such kind of help from others and they try to do the same by their own. But why do new (usually small) businesses need special treatment and encouragement at all? And if they do need it - what are the best ways to provide them with this help?

A new business goes through phases in the business cycle (very similar to the stages of human life).

The first phase - is the formation of an idea. They bring new idea into the market and think that it will be the profitable one for their business. A person - or a group of people join forces, centered around one exciting invention, process or service.

These crystallizing ideas have a few properties:

They are oriented to satisfy the needs of a market niche (a small group of selected consumers or customers) or to provide a new innovative solution to the problems which are not found or to create a market for a totally new product or service or to provide a modified solution to the existing solution in a better way.

This is the stage where entrepreneurs need their expertise. They should be capable enough to handle the tasks completely. They need the advice of marketing professional about market conditions so that they can know whether they can continue with their business or not? They need a help of financial expert about getting funds in each phase of the business cycle - and wherefrom and also if the product or service can produce enough income to support the business, pay back debts and yield a profit to the investors. They need information on financial plan about spending money in a business in an efficient way. They need assistance of technical persons about evaluation of their business idea and what are the ways of getting technologies? They need the information of how much money it takes to practically implement the technology. How much useful the technology is?

Once the idea has been developed to its final form - the proper legal entity should be formed. A partnership? A corporation - and if so, a stock or a non-stock company? A research and development (R&D) entity? A foreign company or a local entity? And so on.

The decision of what kind of business the entrepreneurs want to open is of fundamental importance. It involves many legal issues. The new entrepreneurs are not well to solve the problems. They are blank in such situation so it will be appropriate for the entrepreneurs to contact a lawyer. Getting a supportive and experienced lawyer is very necessary otherwise there will be wastage of money and business. The lawyer may try to exploit the entrepreneurs because the lawyer knows that the new entrepreneurs do not know much about the legal practices. Because this costs a lot of money, one thing those entrepreneurs are in short supplies of. Free legal advice is likely to be highly appreciated by them because for the new small entrepreneurs every time spending the money is not possible. A free counseling should be given to them. Sometimes with the fear of huge fees most of the entrepreneurs try to arrange the knowledge by themselves and then they commit mistakes or they take longer time to take decisions.

When the business is properly legally established, registered with all the relevant authorities and has appointed an accounting - it can go on to tackle its main business: developing new products and services. At this stage the firm should adopt Western accounting standards and methodology.

10.4 Management Techniques Difficulties

A whole host of problems faces the new firm immediately upon its formation.

Good entrepreneurs do not necessarily make good managers. Management techniques are not a genetic heritage. They may be good in opening the business but when it comes about the management of the business they face problems. They may lack the managerial skills. Most of the entrepreneurs do not have MBA or any business relevant degrees. They are not rich enough so that they can hire high skilled managers, most of the work they do by their own and when they start managing their business they are not capable of handling the business. They find it hard to sustain the business by their poor management skills.

They must be learnt and assimilated. Today's modern management includes many elements: manpower, finances, marketing, investing in the firm's future through the development of new products, services or even whole new business lines. That is quite a lot and very few people are properly trained to do the job successfully.

On top of that, markets do not always react the way entrepreneurs expect them to react. Market can change or be static. Market behaves by their own way. Markets are evolving creatures: they change; they develop, disappear and re-appear. Even sometimes all surveys and research do not give perfect estimation. They are exceedingly hard to predict. The sales projections of the firm could prove to be unfounded. Its contingency funds can evaporate. Sometimes it is better to create a product mix: well-recognized brands which sell well - side by side with innovative products. It is the initial stage that requires a lot of money and effort-first phases of creating a business.

10.5 Take Land/Shop on Lease

New business owners have a lot of decisions to make. One of the decisions they need to make early on is whether to buy or lease business space. They remain confused that what should they do? If they will purchase then they will lock their money in purchasing the land which they might have used for their business. If they take on lease then their business runs on the mercy of the leaser and their property does not belong to them.

Buying space for a business puts the new business owner in another business as well- real estate. If the value of the property does very well then the new business owner could sell the property for a profit later on.

However, on the other hand, new business owners may invest more on their property than they can actually afford to. This will result in a drain on the financial resources of the new company. Many small businesses operating one a small and tight budget prefer to lease their space instead of buying business space.

Another factor that new business owners need to consider when buying office property is the tax that they need to pay on it. A lot of new business owners operating on a tight budget prefer to lease properties for business space. This is because the new business owners can avoid making large upfront investment required with a purchase. They can use the reaming money for other purpose also.

Leasing is also attractive option for new business owners who are not really sure about how much space they will require and do not want the responsibility of owning a commercial property. Owning a commercial property is not so much for new business owners as it is for established businesses who want to be in one location for several years and who have the financial resources to take on a significant real estate investment. Of course, a final decision between leasing and owning a commercial property depends on the plans of the new business owner.

10.6 Take Land/Shop on Rent

When an entrepreneur takes a shop or land on rent and does his business there he finds other problems, the first is owner of the shop and land charges high price for that as the owner knows that he will utilize the shop or land commercially here the profit of the entrepreneur decreases because he has fixed cost of rent. Secondly if he earns good money or we can say his business runs very good then automatically the owner raises the rent, here the entrepreneur does not have any option but to obey the owner because owner knows that entrepreneur will not leave the place as his business is doing well.

10.7 Searching Right Environment

The new entrepreneurs most of the time do not get the right environment for their business. Even if they know what kind of environment they want but only some of the entrepreneurs turn it into reality. They find it very difficult to get the proper environment place where they can start their own business.

Create the right environment for success

Entrepreneurs should find it easy to start a business. To do so, most Indians would start slow with capital borrowed from family and friends, a professional team assembled months or perhaps years after the business was created and few, if any, external partners. If it is compared with a start-up in USA: a Venture Capitalist (VC) or angel investor would be brought in early on; a professional management team would drive the business; a multifunctional team would be assembled quickly; and partnerships would be explored early on to scale up the business.

To a large measure, culture, strict rules and regulations shapes this style. Deals are continually being negotiated, teams are pulled together and partners are identified. There is almost unlimited access to multiple VCs and angel investors. Critical support services abound, including professional managers, legal firms, venture capitalists, angel investors and placement agencies. Combine this with excellent infrastructure – connectivity, communication and office space – and getting started is easy.

- **A first challenge for India is to create areas of excellence**

The big problem, the entrepreneurs in India face is of finance or investors the breeding ground where ideas grow into businesses. Some already exist in a very preliminary way (the businesses are there). For example, Gurgaon and Hyderabad for remote services or Bangalore for IT services. But these areas of excellence need strengthening before they can claim to be India's own "Excellence Areas". Most of the small entrepreneurs are not Undergraduates or even the postgraduates they have started the business without any qualification. To gain the excellence the new entrepreneurs must be the trained one and have at least the knowledge of the business which they want to do. They start their business and try to run their business with partial knowledge in an environment where the intelligent competitors already exist. One way of strengthening these areas is to consider the role of universities and entrepreneurship development institutions - places where excellence typically thrives. Creating such educational institutions for starting new ones is going to be very important.

10.8 Ensure that Entrepreneurs have Access to The Right Skills

A survey McKinsey and Company conducted revealed that most Indian start-up businesses face two skill gaps:

- Entrepreneurial (how to manage business risks, build a team, identify and get funding) and
- Functional (product development know-how, marketing skills, etc.,).

In other countries, entrepreneurs either gain these skills by hiring managers or have access to "support systems" such as universities or other institutions that may nurture many regional businesses. In addition, business schools give young graduates the skills and knowledge required for business today.

But the problem is that the persons who start small business they normally do not go for the B-school education. There may be n number of problems for that the first one is they are not able to pay the fees of management colleges so rather they try to invest money in their business. Second it is rarely seen that the persons who are doing business and also going to the management college because they cannot leave their business in between and can devote the time to college, some persons can join the college but in such a situation they have the support of their family members who handle the business in their absence. But the new entrepreneurs without experience and the new entrepreneurs with education there is not much difference in both because they both want only one thing and that is the skill of how to handle the business.

India can move towards ensuring that the curriculum at universities is modified to address today's changing business landscape, particularly in emerging markets and to build "centres of entrepreneurial excellence" in institutes that will actively assist entrepreneurs. For young entrepreneurs a short term entrepreneurship program will be effective. The entrepreneurs before starting the business must take the training of the entrepreneurship where they will spend time developing their own projects, while utilizing state-of-the-art communications technology to interact with members of industry and experts worldwide.

The Centre will help students become successful entrepreneurs by offering a diverse set of programmes, activities and facilities such as a New Business Development Project, an on-campus incubator, an Entrepreneur-in-Residence programme, field projects and a Young Entrepreneurs Club.

10.9 Ensure that Entrepreneurs have Access to "Smart" Capital

For a long time, Indian entrepreneurs have had little access to capital. It is true that in the last few years, several Venture Funds have entered the Indian market and government has extended their support to small entrepreneurs. VCs are providing capital as well as critical knowledge and access to potential partners, suppliers and clients across the globe. However India has only a few angel investors who support an idea in the early stages before VCs become involved. But there is a critical gap between VC and entrepreneurs. While associations such as TIE are seeking to bridge the gap (by working at creating a TIE India Angel Forum), this is India's third challenge: creating a global support network of 'angels' willing to support young businesses.

10.10 Enable Networking and Exchange

Entrepreneurs learn from their experience and that of others. If there will be the network of the all entrepreneurs then it will benefit the whole new entrepreneurs. The problem of the new entrepreneurs is they do not have any advisor or the experienced person who can tell them or can give the direction to their business. Much of the success of Indians in Silicon Valley is attributed to the experience, sharing and support TIE members have extended to young entrepreneurs. Clearly, India would benefit from creating a strong network of entrepreneurs and managers that entrepreneurs could draw on for advice and support.

The rapid pace of globalization and the fast growth of Asian economies present tremendous opportunities and challenges for India. Through planning and focus, India can aspire to create the pool of entrepreneurs who will be the regions – and the worlds – leaders of tomorrow.

10.11 Arranging Machinery

Most of the new entrepreneurs do not want to go for such a business which requires advanced technology or heavy machinery. The problem with the new entrepreneurs is that they feel it very difficult to arrange all the facilities for opening the business. They are not supported by the banks or the government agencies because they are the new ones. Though they have all the potential to run the business but without proper support they do not do the things alone.

10.12 Arranging Business Vehicles

The requirement of the vehicle is based on the kind of business they do. If business requires vehicles then anyhow entrepreneurs have to arrange the vehicles for the business. They try to arrange the vehicles for the business. They try to run the business; they have all the enthusiasm for their work but when they do not fulfill the requirements of the vehicles they face problems. They can become the good entrepreneurs but they do not have a capacity to purchase the extra vehicle for the business. Though they bring work in the business, they expand their business but their capacity does not allow them to expand. Entrepreneurs in such time feel very embarrassing because they do not have any supporting hand that can help them for growing their business.

10.13 Arranging Generator for Electricity

The new entrepreneurs find it very difficult to arrange electricity by their own. They are totally dependent upon the government for electricity. The electricity increases the problems of the new small entrepreneurs because this increases the cost of the product because if they arrange the generator it puts extra burden of cost on the entrepreneurs. The entrepreneurs then not able to keep the price of their product less, they already gain tough competition from the big players and when they do not get proper electricity then it becomes really difficult for them to remain in the market. Arranging for the generator is a big deal for the new entrepreneurs and that too for long time.

10.14 Absence of Supporting Hand

Most of the entrepreneurs do not have a proper support to open a business. They have a support of those people who also do not know about business. For example if the new entrepreneurs want to open a business and if he has a supporter who can tell him about the land, machinery, business information and will help to get those things then those entrepreneurs solve the problems more easily as compared to others who do not have such kind of help. For the entrepreneurs support is must; they want to do a lot but they do not have any one who can tell them the big and minute things about the business. So the probability of becoming success increases. Making use of the supporter's experience he progresses in the business very fast, he solves the problems and also learns to tackle the problems.

10.15 Difficulty to Find Land/Shop in Market Area

For new entrepreneurs to get the desired place in the market is dream only. Even if they know that some particular place is very important to them as far as doing business is concerned they cannot purchase that place easily. Place is one of the factor of success of business. The big players purchase the required place whenever they feel the importance of the place and they start their business. The new entrepreneurs can just see the dream only.

10.16 Transportation Facilities

Top of Form

Transportation has played an important role in improving quality of lives. Railways, shipping, roads and air transport have effected industrialization, diversified international trade and globalization and allowed free movement of people and goods.

There is a close link between efficient transport system and economic prosperity. For example, a 2 per cent reduction in time for all business travels can save crores of rupees. Good roads will ensure low maintenance cost, lesser fuel consumption and safer means of traveling. As individuals, you must have experienced that delays and unreliability of road network can cost people and businesses dearly and affect productivity and innovation. Roads cannot create wealth by itself; they are just means to improve productivity provided other conditions are right.

Transports are the arteries of domestic and international business. They boost competitiveness in imports and exports. Road networks support productivity and success of the urban world. They get people to work, support labour markets and allow the business within the area to reap the benefits. They equally contribute to the development of rural economy by creating new markets and proving the existing ones faster access to sell agricultural products. Government and individuals alike should take the responsibility for superior quality construction, better connectivity and maintenance of roads. If that happens, the road ahead would be a rather comfortable one.

10.17 How can the Government Help?

The entrepreneurs want the help of the government but the fact is that the government help involves so much complexity that the common new entrepreneurs rather select their own way instead of going for the government help. That really creates problems for the new entrepreneurs because they are not able to put their own money into the business because they do not have enough money. The new entrepreneurs most of the time are not aware about the government schemes and therefore they miss the opportunity.

The government can help the new entrepreneurs by setting up an "Entrepreneur's One Station Stop". A person wishing to establish a new business will go to a government agency.

In one office, he will find the representatives of all the relevant government offices, authorities, agencies and municipalities. He will present his business plan that he wishes to develop. In a matter of few weeks he will receive all the necessary permits and licences without having to go to each office separately. It will save entrepreneurs time and efforts.

Having obtained the requisite licences and permits and having registered with all the appropriate authorities - the entrepreneur will move on to the next room in the same building. Here he will receive a list of all the sources of capital available with him both locally and from foreign sources. The terms and conditions of the financing will be specified for each and every source.

The entrepreneur will select the sources of funds most suitable for his business needs - and proceed to the next room. The next room will contain all the experts necessary to establish the business, get it going - and, most important and raise funds from both local and international institutions. For a symbolic sum they will prepare all the documents required by the financing institutions as per their instructions. They will submit the entire relevant documents demanded by the authority.

But entrepreneurs in many developing countries are still fearful and uninformed. They are intimidated by the complexity of the task facing them. They do not have such a great complexity in opening the business. The solution is simple: a tutor or a mentor will be attached to each and every entrepreneur. This will benefit the entrepreneurs a lot. With the help of advisor they will come to know all the ways to solve the problems. This tutor will escort the entrepreneur from the first phase to the last. He will be employed by the "One Station Stop" and his role will be to ease the life for the novice businessman. He will transform the person to a businessman.

So What Could Be the Solution?

10.18 Finding the Best Location

Too many would-be entrepreneurs become so excited about launching their new business venture that they fail to invest the necessary time in finding the right location. But as your company's image and its location are closely tied, finding the right place to set up shop can be critical to your success. If you're preparing to open a business with a storefront, putting your business in the proper location might be the single most important thing you do at startup. In the brick-and-mortar business world, it's said that the three most important decisions [you'll make] are location, location and location, Careful determination of new sites is critical for most businesses.

Get a Flavor for the Community

Before deciding to set up shop somewhere, investigate the community. Read some of the local newspapers. Visit the library and do some research on the history of the place. Speak with other small business owners in the area. Ask them if their business is succeeding and if they think your business would do well there. Try to find out how receptive the established business community is to new businesses that come to town

Check Your Demographics

Making these determinations can be as simple or as complex as you make it. There are, for instance, sophisticated location analysis tools available that include traffic pattern information, demographic and lifestyle data and competitive analyses. An entrepreneur can ask such questions as, 'If I'm looking to add a store to a particular market, what's the optimum level of traffic as it relates to the specific targeted trade area? What is the overall type of traffic? Once consumers are in the store, is there any way to measure the traffic patterns in the store?

Do your due diligence. "Get a demographic overview of the area you're looking at-age, income, households, etc." In addition, you should look at neighbourhood traffic generators, such as other retailers that draw people to the area, industrial or office parks, schools, colleges and hospital complexes. You'll also want to look at both highway and foot traffic.

Demand of Product

To determine the best location for your business, you'll need to look into your area for your product's demand. Your product is whatever you're selling; service or merchandise. Do research for the supply and demand of your product in the area. Sometimes, there's room for more suppliers. But don't guess; do the research. Sometimes you'll want to be in an area with lots of competition. For instance, with a restaurant, you've heard the expression "restaurant row?" That's where people go when they're heading out to dinner. When people go to restaurant row, they know that if one restaurant is too busy, there will most likely be a seat in a restaurant close by. In the restaurant business, a location right next door to a similar business might be just what you need. But like I said, don't guess, do the research.

Competition

Competition can help or hinder a business depending on the location. A good business location is different for each type; gas stations and grocers can do well when competition is nearby or within sight. Service business can also do well in highly competitive markets. Contractors can compliment or contradict each other; complimentary examples include carpenters and painters or concrete and stone. Contradictory examples include any two contractors that do the exact same work but at different skill levels. Make sure you understand the competition and how they can affect your business at the location you are considering.

Talk to Your Neighbours

Think about all of the factors that drive your business before you choose the location. Talk to local grocery stores and retailers near your potential location and figure out what areas their consumers come from. If the number of consumers at these local stores is not as many as you hope to receive for your business, you may want to consider moving to another location.

Do You Need Professional Help?

It's a good idea to hire the services of a real estate agent if you want to purchase the location. Find a reputable agent who can help you out with your concerns. Try to inquire at concerned local or state offices about the legal requirements of your business, especially the zoning restrictions (this will depend on the business that you want to put up). Regulatory issues can also affect your decision. At this point, you may want to seek help from a lawyer so that you won't violate any regulation or law. Location is one of your keys to success. By choosing a poor location, you will lose out on your investment. Some states and countries offer financial incentives to business owners as well as tax credits; again, this will depend on the type of business that you plan to put up. So far, these are the things that you need to look into before you decide on the location of the property. By establishing a budget, you will find it easier to find an ideal location.

Underestimating the costs and the time involved with launching your business-especially when it comes to your location-is one of the most common startup mistakes and one you can avoid if you plan properly. The best advice? Talk to other people in the business-learn from them what they've experienced, what the pitfalls are what things to look out for. You've got to do your homework. You can protect yourself and come out ahead.

Ease of Access

If your business is a customer destination, consider how people get around in the area where your business will be located.

- If you are scouting a location in a suburban area, most people may get around by car. You'll need to make sure you are close to major streets and have plenty of parking.
- If you are scouting a location in an urban area, consider areas around public transportation hubs or areas of the city where there is a lot of foot traffic.

Balance Cost with Other Factors

Obviously, the cost of the location is important to consider, but be sure to look at the big picture as well. For example, no matter how attractive the price of a site might be, if your customers can't get there easily or if the infrastructure can't support the necessary wiring for your Internet business, your business probably won't last very long. Spending more on a good location will probably pay off in the long run with lots of business.

Factors to Be Considered

In choosing an area or type of location within a city you evaluate factors such as:

- Customer attraction power of the particular store and the shopping district.
- Quantitative and qualitative nature of competitive stores.
- Availability of access routes to the stores.
- Nature of zoning regulations.
- Direction of the area expansion.
- General appearance of the area.
- Is the facility located in a safe neighborhood with a low crime rate?
- Is exterior lighting in the area adequate to attract evening shoppers and make them feel safe?
- Are there any competitors located close to the facility? If so, can you compete with them successfully?
- Is the facility easily accessible to your potential customers?
- possibilities for expansion
- Is parking space available and adequate?
- Is the area served by public transportation?
- Can suppliers make deliveries conveniently at this location?

10.19 Knowing What to Ask

Answering these 22 questions for each of the sites you're considering can help you decide on the best location for your business:

1. Is the facility located in an area zoned for your type of business?
2. Is the facility large enough for your business? Does it offer room for all the retail, office, storage or workroom space you need?
3. Does it meet your layout requirements?
4. Does the building need any repairs?
5. Do the existing utilities-lighting, heating and cooling-meet your needs or will you have to do any rewiring or plumbing work? Is ventilation adequate?
6. Are the lease terms and rent favourable?
7. Is the location convenient to where you live?
8. Can you find a number of qualified employees in the area in which the facility is located?
9. Do people you want for customers live nearby? Is the population density of the area sufficient for your sales needs?
10. Is the trade area heavily dependent on seasonal business?
11. If you choose a location that's relatively remote from your customer base, will you be able to afford the higher advertising expenses?
12. Is the facility consistent with the image you'd like to maintain?
13. Is the facility located in a safe neighbourhood with a low crime rate?
14. Is exterior lighting in the area adequate to attract evening shoppers and make them feel safe?

15. Will crime insurance be prohibitively expensive?
16. Are neighboring businesses likely to attract customers who will also patronize your business?
17. Are there any competitors located close to the facility? If so, can you compete with them successfully?
18. Is the facility easily accessible to your potential customers?
19. Is parking space available and adequate?
20. Is the area served by public transportation?
21. Can suppliers make deliveries conveniently at this location?
22. If your business expands in the future, will the facility be able to accommodate this growth?

10.20 Creating an Office Where You Can Work

- Your office must be in a location where you can work without any disturbance. If your office location will be just beside the main road then it will create disturbance for your work. Locate your office in a space you love.
- If you have to share an office, make space for two desks and two sets of files and supplies.
- Situate the workspaces to allow each person maximum quiet and minimal distractions.
- Your office selection must be according to the future need. Project your office's needs for the next year and acquire equipment and furnishings accordingly.
- You cannot change your office location so many times because your business is growing. Purchase systems and furniture that will allow for growth or add-ons.

10.21 Good Merchant Relationships

- You must know your suppliers. Using technology for the communication will be good, be in touch either face to face or by phone conversation.
- Do not treat your suppliers as a separate person. Consider your suppliers as a part of your business team.
- Be clear of what exactly you want from them and how much they know about your needs and expectations.
- Appreciate your suppliers for their good services and quality products.
- Do not delay on payment. If you can't, let your vendors know right away and work out a payment plan. That's when knowing them personally will be invaluable.

10.22 Insurance for Small Business

- You must be careful about the protection of life, health and property.
- "Key man insurance:" Protect your business if you lose a partner or key employee. Also, insure yourself to safeguard your spouse and family.
- Life insurance for employees: Consider offering a term policy. This is a benefit you can offer and even underwrite as an added value.

- Health insurance: A comprehensive health insurance policy will help you recruit and retain good employees. It will also help employees stay healthy and productive.
- Property insurance: Obtain broad property coverage to protect you from a variety of losses in case of theft or disaster.

10.23 Leasing Equipment

- Keep in mind that leasing equipment instead of buying it can help you manage your business without tying up funds needed for working capital. You can use the equipment to make money while you are paying for the lease.
- Use leasing to help you meet objectives that might otherwise be out of reach. Instead of giving a deserving employee a raise, one cash-strapped entrepreneur instead more cheaply leased a new car for the employee.
- Be aware that monthly payments are often tax deductible and may offer a larger tax break than you would get if the equipment were depreciated.
- Leasing is a form of borrowing and usually the interest rate is higher than that of a commercial bank.

10.24 Preparing for Disaster Recovery

- Prepare yourselves if your business suffers natural disaster. Small businesses the world over have been affected by disasters such as hurricanes, tsunamis, floods, earthquakes, volcanic eruptions and fire.
- Develop your plan B if your business suffers natural disaster. Discuss it with your employees so that in emergency everyone will know what to do?
- Take sufficient insurance that should cover important areas of your business. You'll need coverage for property damage and loss (including inventory).
- You must have mobile and telephone numbers of all employees. Give this list of numbers to every employee in your business. That way, you can learn who is all right and who needs help and you can quickly communicate instructions about your business.
- You need to have a backup system for your computer. Keep backup programs and duplicate records (accounts receivable, client information and the like) at a different, safe site.

10.25 The Role of Government in Supporting Entrepreneurship

Small and Medium-sized Enterprises (SMEs) in market economies are the engine of economic development. Owing to their private ownership, entrepreneurial spirit, their flexibility and adaptability as well as their potential to react to challenges and changing environments, SMEs contribute to sustainable growth and employment generation in a significant manner.

SMEs have strategic importance for each national economy due a wide range of reasons. Logically, the government shows such an interest in supporting entrepreneurship and SMEs. There is no simpler way to create new job positions, increasing GDP and rising standard of population than supporting entrepreneurship and encouraging and supporting people who dare to start their own business. Every surviving and successful business means new jobs and growth of GDP.

Therefore, designing a comprehensive, coherent and consistent approach of Council of Ministers and entity governments to entrepreneurship and SMEs in the form of government support strategy to entrepreneurship and SMEs is an absolute priority. A comprehensive government approach to entrepreneurship and SMEs would provide for a full coordination of activities of numerous governmental institutions (chambers of commerce, employment bureaus, etc.,) and NGOs dealing with entrepreneurship and SMEs. With no pretension of defining the role of government in supporting entrepreneurship and SMEs, we believe that apart from designing a comprehensive entrepreneurship and SMEs strategy, the development of national SME support institutions and networks is one of key condition for success. There are no doubts that governments should create different types of support institutions:

- To provide information on regulations, standards, taxation, customs duties, marketing issues;
- To advise on business planning, marketing and accountancy, quality control and assurance;
- To create incubator units providing the space and infrastructure for business beginners and innovative companies and helping them to solve technological problems and to search for know-how and promote innovation; and
- To help in looking for partners in order to stimulate entrepreneurship and improve the business environment for small enterprises.

Training

Basic training differs from product to product but will necessary involve sharpening of entrepreneurial skills. Need based technical training is provided by the Govt. and State Govt. technical Institutions.

There are a number of Government organisations as well as NGOs who conduct EDPs and MDPs. These EDPs and MDPs are conducted by MSME's, NIESBUD, NSIC, IIE, NISIET, Entrepreneurship Development Institutes and other state government developmental agencies.

Marketing Assistance

There are Governmental and non-governmental specialized agencies which provide marketing assistance. Besides promotion of MSME products through exhibitions, NSIC directly markets the MSME product in the domestic and overseas market. NSIC also manages a single point registration scheme for manufacturers for Govt. purchase. Units registered under this scheme get the benefits of free tender documents and exemption from earnest money deposit and performance guarantee.

Promotional Schemes

Government accords the highest preference to development of MSME by framing and implementing suitable policies and promotional schemes. Besides providing developed land and sheds to the entrepreneurs on actual cost basis with appropriate infrastructure, special schemes have been designed for specific purposes like quality upgradation, common facilities, entrepreneurship development and consultancy services at nominal charges.

Government of India has been executing the incentive scheme for providing reimbursement of charges for acquiring ISO 9000 certification to the extent of 75 per cent of the cost subject to a maximum of ₹ 75,000/- in each case. ISO 9000 is a mechanism to facilitate adoption of consistent management practices and production technique as decided by the entrepreneur himself. This facilitates achievement of desired level of quality while keeping check on production process and management of the enterprise.

Concession on Excise Duty

MSME units with a turnover of Rs. 1 crore or less per year have been exempted from payment of Excise Duty. Moreover there is a general scheme of excise exemption for MSME brought out by the Ministry of Finance which covers most of the items. Under this, units having turnover of less than Rs. 3 crores are eligible for concessional rate of Excise Duty. Moreover, there is an exemption from Excise Duty for MSME units producing branded goods in rural areas.

Credit Facility to MSME

Credit to micro, small and medium scale sector has been covered under priority sector lending by banks. Small Industries Development Bank of India (SIDBI) has been established as the apex institution for financing the MSME. Specific schemes have been designed for implementation through SIDBI, SFCs, Scheduled Banks, SIDCs and NSIC etc. Loans up to Rs. 5 lakhs are made available by the banks without insisting on collaterals. Further Credit Guarantee Fund for micro, small and medium enterprises has been set up to provide guarantee for loans to MSME up to Rs. 25 lakhs extended by Commercial Banks and some Regional Rural Bank.

Policies and Schemes for Promotion of MSME Implemented By State Governments

All the State Governments provide technical and other support services to small units through their Directorates of Industries and District Industries Centres. Although the details of the scheme vary from state to state, the following are the common areas of support.

1. Development and management of industrial estates
2. Suspension/deferment of Sales Tax
3. Power subsidies
4. Capital investment subsidies for new units set up in a particular district
5. Seed Capital/Margin Money Assistance Scheme
6. Priority in allotment of power connection, water connection.
7. Consultancy and technical support

Government of India runs a scheme for giving National Awards to micro, small and medium scale entrepreneurs providing quality products in 11 selected industry groups of consumer interest. The winners are given trophy, certificate and a cash price of Rs. 25000/- each.

10.26 Setting up a IT Network Infrastructure for a Business

A number of small businesses are finding success in installing IT networks. They produce higher production rates, better flexible application mobility, easier to reconfigure your office space as your company grows and changing to a network infrastructure is becoming much more affordable.

Below you will find instructions on setting up a network.

- Before jumping into a costly infrastructure change, it may not be a bad idea to bring in a contracted IT professional specializing in network technology to help you determine if a networking solution is right for your company. This will also be helpful if you need help determining what equipment or other resources will be needed to suit your business needs.

- As system requirements grow, it is essential to anticipate changing tech support needs. Computer problems result in downtime, which translates into lost productivity and revenue. How do you plan to adapt to changing system requirements? This may require upgrading staff professionalism or maybe even outsourcing work to specialists. One size may not fit all circumstances. The overall guideline is to anticipate how the network infrastructure will change. The least efficient and costly way to grow a company is to replace hardware and software. Your goal, from both a cost and productivity standpoint, is to plan for system changes. While predicting the future of technology is difficult, failure to think and plan ahead can be costly. Getting the best advice, either in-house or with an external consultant is essential in navigating your current and future network needs.
- It is often seen that the productivity of companies gets hampered due to improper transmission of communication signals. At times, many accidents take place due to defective electric wiring within the official infrastructure. Computers, television sets and other electronic equipment often get damaged due to short circuit. Such unwanted accidents take place because of the negligence of people while selecting wires. Many people overlook the fact that installing wires of good quality into their official building assures safety and efficient working environment for their employees as well as to them. They compromise with the quality of wiring system and prefer saving money for the time being.
- While setting up an infrastructure for businesses it is critical to ensure that there are minimal technical problems such as hard-drive failures so to prevent data loss. The need for e-mail security and archive-management solutions cannot be ignored as it protects the business from being subpoenaed to provide employee e-mails.

Small businesses need to be as cautious of their IT infrastructure setup and its management as larger ones. This involves a variety of approaches and one may choose from either a number of manual processes or licensed software solutions, third-party service providers and various combinations of these.

The business may also seek the help of various solution providers across the major categories of IT Infrastructure Management. It is a common practice to use a number of IT infrastructure management solutions in businesses and organizations. Anti-malware and virus protection solutions are in extensive use within small businesses and companies.

10.27 Business Incubators and Facilitators in India

Business incubators are projects designed to help new businesses develop and successfully launch. In some instances, the projects are overseen by colleges or universities and are based in facilities located on campus. Just about every business incubator program has well-defined qualifications that applicants must meet in order to be accepted into the incubation project. The main goal of a business incubator is to encourage the development of new business within the local community. By assisting a local entrepreneur to start a company in the area, the community is likely to benefit from an increase in the number of available jobs in the area and the additional revenue that is brought to the city or town as a result of the new business activities. Both elements can help to revitalize a local economy that is somewhat sluggish and thus enhance the quality for everyone who lives and works in the area.

Places for business incubators

They can be stand alone business incubators, or based on a science or business park, within a University campus, a laboratory or a private sector large corporate - basically anywhere where there is a demand for intensive business support. Business incubators can be found in all regions and locations; essentially, they are located where the market needs them. This is based upon the needs of the entrepreneur and the sector focus of the business incubator; close proximity to research, technical support and equipment or a dynamic business cluster. For example, where a University has a strong bioscience offering, it is usual to find a business incubator dedicated to commercializing bio businesses or innovations. Similarly, incubators can be used to drive forward the development of a strong cluster of businesses; such as IT, creative industries and environmental technologies, which then act as a magnet to other innovative start-ups or entrepreneurs who want a slice of the action.

How do incubators help start-ups get funding?

Incubators help resident companies secure capital in a number of ways, including:

- Connecting companies with angel investors (high-net-worth individual investors).
- Working with companies to perfect venture capital presentations and connecting them to venture capitalists.
- Assisting companies in applying for loans.
- Assisting companies in accessing government agency business assistance grant programmes.

List of Business Incubators in India

Table: 10.1: List of Business Incubators in India

Name	Contact Person	Address	Contact Information
Centre for Innovation, Incubation and Entrepreneurship (CIIE)	Mr. Kunal Upadhyay - CEO	Indian Institute of Management, Vastrapur, Ahmedabad- 380015	91-79-26324203 / 079 - 26308357 kunal@iimahd.ernet.in www.iimahd.ernet.in/ciie
Society for Innovation and Entrepreneurship (SINE)	Prof. N.L. Sarda- Professor in Charge	IIT Bombay, Powai, Mumbai – 400076	91- 22- 25767072 Direct: 25767710 nls@csc.iitb.ac.in www.sineiitb.org
TBI ON EMBEDDED SYSTEMS AND VLSI DESIGN	Prof.S, Gurunarayanan Co-ordinator, TBI	Birla Institute of Technology and Science, Pilani - 333031 Rajasthan.	91-1596-245073 Extn: 252 sguru@bits-pilani.ac.in www.bits-pilani.ac.in
TBI for Composites	Dr.R. Gopalan, Executive Director	Composites Technology Park, 205, Bande Mutt, Kengeri Satellite Township, Bangalore-560060	91-80-56997605, 56681005 drgopal@blr.vsnl.net.in

Name	Contact Person	Address	Contact Information
Centre for Biotechnology	Dr. S. Meenakshisundaram-Business Manager	Centre for Biotechnology, Anna University Chennai – 600025	91-44-22350772, 9840348173 eenakshi@annauniv.edu www.annauniv.edu/biotech
MITCON Biotechnology Centre	Mr. Kulkarni - Chief Executive	MITCON Biotechnology Centre, BAIF Campus Mr. Manibhai Desai Nagar Pune – 411052	91-20-66289451 kulkarni@mitconbt.com www.mitconindia.com
National Design Business Incubator	Mr. Mahesh. K Rovvidi - Chief Operating Officer	National Institute of Design (NID), Paldi, Ahmedabad – 380007	91-79-2662 3692 Extn 5001 ndbi@nid.edu www.ndbiindia.org
Vellore Institute of Technology	Mr. A. Balachandran, Manager- TBI	VITTBI, Vellore Institute of Technology, Vellore-632014	91-416-2243097 - Directvittbi@vit.ac.in www.vittbi.com
National Institute of Technology, Calicut	Mr. A.V. Francis, Officer on Special Duty, TBI	National Institute of Technology, Calicut - 673601 Kerala	91-0495-2286162, Direct - 2286604 avf@nitc.ac.in
J.S.S. Mahavidyapeetha	Prof. R. Raghunanadan - Chief Executive	J.S.S. Academy of Technical Education, C-20/1, Sector -62 Noida 201301	91-120-2401442 ce@jssstepnoida.org www.jssstepnoida.org
ICRISAT	Mr. S. Karuppanchetty - Deputy COO, Mr. Abdul Rahman Ilyas - COO	ICRISAT, 303 Bldg, Patancheru - 5023224	91-040-30713222 karuppanchetty@cgiar.org
Kongu Engineering College	Prof. S. Balamurugan-Executive Director - TBI	Kongu Engineering College, Perundurai -638052, Erode, Tamil Nadu.	91- 4294 220562, 220171, Direct 226650 balamurugan@kongu.ac.in
Advance Materials Technology Incubator	Mr. Sanjay Bharadwaj - Co-ordinator	International Advance Research Centre for Powder Metallurgy and New Materials, RCI Road, Opp. Ballapur Village, Hyderabad – 500005	91-40-24457104-7
Center for Entrepreneurship - SPJIMR	Prof. M. Suresh Rao - Program Co-ordinator	S.P. Jain Institute of Management & Research, Munshi Nagar, Dadabhai Road, Andheri (West), Mumbai - 400 058.	+91-22-2623 7454 / 0396 / 2401 Ext: 211 msrao@spjimr.org www.spjimr.org/centreentrepreneurship/home.asp

Source: *Information received from "indianwebstartups".*

SUMMARY

In house business problems: Most of the entrepreneurs who had their home business have failed. Most of those entrepreneurs commented on their home based business "failures". In essence they were not moving forward because of past failures. Another was afraid of future failure. They have a fear that they will not become successful in the future. Therefore they are not moving forward their business because of an anticipated failure.

Getting new land/shop for business: To get new land / shop for a business is very difficult for the new entrepreneurs. If anyone wants to do a business for that he requires a perfect place and he searches for that he finds a good place also but the problem comes when he could not be able to purchase that shop.

A new business needs a support: The new entrepreneurs are not competent enough as the big companies are. They definitely start the business. They fulfill the requirements of the business but they do not sustain the business. They need direction, they need a supporter who can support them who can advise them about their business. But unfortunately they do not find such kind of help from others and they try to do the same by their own.

Management techniques difficulties: Good entrepreneurs do not necessarily make good managers. Management techniques are not a genetic heritage. They may be good in opening the business but when it comes about the management of the business they face problems. They may lack the managerial skills. Most of the entrepreneurs do not have MBA or any business relevant degrees. They are not rich enough so that they can hire high skilled managers, most of work they do by their own and when they start managing their business they are not capable of handling the business. They find it hard to sustain the business by their poor management skills.

Take land/shop on lease: New business owners have a lot of decisions to make. One of the decisions they need to make early on is whether to buy or lease business space. They remain confused that what should they do? If they will purchase then they will lock their money in purchasing the land which they might have been used for their business. If they take on lease then their business runs on the mercy of the leaser and their property does not belong to them.

Create the right environment for success: Entrepreneurs should find it easy to start a business. To do so, most Indians would start slow with capital borrowed from family and friends, a professional team assembled months or perhaps years after the business was created and few, if any, external partners.

Ensure that entrepreneurs have access to the right skills: A survey McKinsey and Company conducted revealed that most Indian start-up businesses face two skill gaps:

- Entrepreneurial (how to manage business risks, build a team, identify and get funding) and
- Functional (product development know-how, marketing skills, etc.,).

Transportation facilities

Top of Form

Transportation has played an important role in improving quality of lives. Railways, shipping, roads and air transport have or affected industrialization, diversified international trade and globalization and allowed free movement of people and goods.

There is a close link between efficient transport system and economic prosperity. For example, a 2 per cent reduction in time for all business travels can save crores of rupees.

How can the Government help? : The entrepreneurs want the help of the government but the fact is that the government help involves so much complexity that the common new entrepreneurs rather select their own way instead of going for the government help. That really creates problems for the new entrepreneurs because they are not able to put their own money into the business because they do not have enough money. Many times it happens that the new entrepreneurs are not aware about the government schemes and therefore they miss the opportunity.

The government can help the new entrepreneurs by setting up an "Entrepreneur's One Station Stop". A person wishing to establish a new business will go to a government agency.

Finding the Best Location includes Get a flavor for the community, Check Your Demographics, Demand of Product, Competition, Professional Help, Consider traffic and accessibility, and Balance cost with other factors.

The role of government in supporting entrepreneurship is as follows:

- To provide information on regulations, standards, taxation, customs duties, marketing issues;
- To advise on business planning, marketing and accountancy, quality control and assurance;
- To create incubator units providing the space and infrastructure for business beginners and innovative companies and helping them to solve technological problems and to search for know-how and promote innovation; and
- To help in looking for partners, in order to stimulate entrepreneurship and improve the business environment for small enterprises.

KEYWORDS

Capital: "Capital" is often overused, allowed to describe any asset regardless of how this economic asset is used.

Entrepreneurs Network: The Entrepreneurs Network is a platform for entrepreneurs from different non competing business fields to come together.

Demographics: Demographics are identifiable, measurable characteristics of your best customers and form the basis of your customer profile.

Lease: A lease is a legal agreement in which a property owner (the lessor) grants another party (the lessee) exclusive use or possession of his property for a defined time period, under specified conditions.

Business incubators: Business incubators are projects designed to help new businesses develop and successfully launch.

Credit facility: A credit facility is a type of loan or debt strategy that is often used in a business or corporate setting.

QUESTIONS

1. What are the problems faced by the entrepreneurs while building business infrastructure?
2. What are the different factors to be considered while selecting a location for the business?
3. What is the role of government in supporting entrepreneurship?
4. What is the importance of IT Network Infrastructure in business?
5. What is business incubator? How it has promoted entrepreneurs' business in India?

❑ ❑ ❑

CHAPTER – 11

TECHNOLOGY ACCESS OBSTACLES

LEARNING OBJECTIVES

On completion of this chapter, you should be able to:

☺ *Explain the impact of changing technology on new small entrepreneurs business.*

☺ *Describe web development importance for new entrepreneurs.*

☺ *Describe impact of e-commerce on entrepreneurs.*

11.1 Changing Technology

In today's world, the technology is changing so fast that it becomes quite difficult to remember the technology or to say that my current technology will run long. Even the established entrepreneurs are facing the problems related to the obsolescence of technology. The technology involves huge money. A new entrepreneur if opens business cannot know exactly for what kind of technology he should go, the rapid technology development confuses the new entrepreneur and puts in dilemma what he should do in such situation and that really slows down his growth of business.

In the context of today's global economy, trade, FDI, strategic alliances and other forms of internationalization which are critical for capturing the benefits of globalization offer many opportunities in this regard. Technology and information systems are bringing about deep-seated changes in the ways small firms conduct business. Effective application of new technologies helps entrepreneur to progress themselves. Electronic and mobile commerce and the internet are increasingly important for new and established firms to innovate, improve their products, production and services, expand their markets and become more dynamic.

BOX 11

Science and Technology Entrepreneurs Park (STEP)

The Science Parks and similar initiatives help in creating an atmosphere for innovation and entrepreneurship; for active interaction between academic institutions and industries for sharing ideas, knowledge, experience and facilities for the development of new technologies and their rapid transfer to the end user.

The Science and Technology Entrepreneurs Park (STEP) programme was initiated to provide a re-orientation in the approach to innovation and entrepreneurship involving education, training, research, finance, management and the government. A STEP creates the necessary climate for innovation, information exchange, sharing of experience and facilities and opening new avenues for students, teachers, researchers and industrial managers to grow in a trans-disciplinary culture, each understanding and depending on the other's inputs for starting a successful economic venture. STEPs are hardware intensive with emphasis on common facilities, services and relevant equipments.

The major objectives of STEP are to forge linkages among academic and R&D institutions on one hand and the industry on the other and also promote innovative enterprise through S&T persons.

Objectives

- *To forge a close linkage between universities, academic and R&D institutions on one hand and industry on the other.*
- *To promote entrepreneurship among Science and Technology persons, many of whom were otherwise seeking jobs soon after their graduation.*
- *To provide R&D support to the small-scale industry mostly through interaction with research institutions.*
- *To promote innovation based enterprises*

Facilities and Services Provided by STEPs

- *It offers facilities such as nursery sheds, testing and calibration facilities, precision tool room/central workshop, prototype development, business facilitation, computing, data bank, library and documentation, communication, seminar hall/conference room, common facilities such as phone, telex, fax, photocopying. It offers services like testing and calibration, consultancy.*

- Training, technical support services, business facilitation services, database and documentation services, quality assurance services and common utility services.

The department has so far catalyzed 15 STEPs in different parts of the country, which have promoted nearly 788 units generating annual turnover of around Rs. 130 crores and employment for 5000 persons. More than 100 new products and technologies have been developed by the STEPs / STEP promoted entrepreneurs. In addition, over 11000 persons have been trained through various skill development programmes conducted by STEPs.

Top 10 Business and Technology Priorities in India in 2011

Top 10 Business Priorities	Ranking	Top 10 Technology Priorities	Ranking
Increasing enterprise growth	1	Cloud computing	1
Improving business continuity, risk and security	2	Mobile technologies	2
Reducing enterprise costs	3	Virtualization	3
Implementing and updating business applications	4	Enterprise resource planning (ERP)	4
Increased use of information/ analytics	5	Enterprise applications	5
Attracting and retaining new customers	6	Business Process Management (BPM)	6
Improving technical infrastructure	7	IT Management	7
Improving business processes	8	Networking, voice and data communications	8
Greater control and management of technology	9	Business intelligence (BI)	9
Expanding into new markets and geographies	10	Analytics	10

Source: Gartner EXP, 2011.

Obsolescence of technology

The technology changes according to many factors. Many factors impact the popularity of the technology. Customers and productivity have greater influence on technology. The new technology comes to fill the gap of demand, quality, productivity etc. If the experienced entrepreneurs will not come up with the new technology then it will ultimately hamper their business and market shares. The new technology is brought to give competition to the competitors and attract the customers. New entrepreneur is not well versed of the market situation, the technology, benefits of the technology. He just wants to open his business and purchases the technology where much finance is not involved and goes for that. The new technology is not the cheap one so it also becomes the other reason that he chooses obsolete technology instead of the new one but that really affects the growth of the business of the new entrepreneurs.

Improper technology information

For opening the business, information about the technology is a must. The entrepreneurs are living in the age of the technology where technology becomes the weapon of the entrepreneurs. The more the advanced technology entrepreneurs' chances of success become more. The new entrepreneur faces problems of getting perfect information about the technology that he will use. Some entrepreneurs try to search about the information but they did not succeed. Some entrepreneurs take the situation as it is and don't try to get information of the technology that will be required by their business. The entrepreneur is always in confusion from where he could get the correct information and after no hope of information he begins his business with the partial information whatever he has.

The stock market always looks to the future. This should also be true for first time entrepreneurs. When defining entrepreneurs Start-up Company's business proposition, they need to look at both the general technology and the general market trends of the future. Why, because it is these general trends that will define the future market place for their technology, product or service offering. General trends are often overlooked by entrepreneurs, but venture capitalists always take a "big picture" view as to what technologies and markets will be pervasive five to ten years out in time. As is often the case, what is true and certain today regarding technologies and markets will not be true and certain five to ten years in the future. Therefore, as an entrepreneur he needs to have a "big picture" view of the future and make sure his technology, product or service offering will have a role to play in the future, when defining a given market "problem" or "need".

Unclear understanding of general technology trends

General technology trends change over an extended period of time. Unlike predictions often set forth by the technology pundits, a new technology does not take hold in the market in a year's time frame. It often takes five to seven years or more for a new technology to take hold. It even takes longer than that for a new technology to become pervasive and accepted by the general public. Why, because there are many issues that come into play when rolling out a new technology. These include the following:

- Initial costs of new technologies are generally high,
- Infrastructure roll-out takes time and is very expensive,
- The new technology may not be ready for prime time and
- End-users do not always readily embrace new technologies.

These issues can substantially delay the rollout of new technologies. But in the whole scheme of things, the entrepreneur must be aware of new, general technology trends, their timing and availability to the market. In this context, having a good understanding of general technology trends, their availability and how they can affect entrepreneurs start-up company's product or service offering, in a positive or negative manner, is a key for positioning entrepreneurs' start-up company and its product offering in the future markets. Knowing and properly presenting entrepreneurs' start-up company's technology product or service offering in the context of these general technology trends will not only gain credibility with potential investors, it will provide the underlying and necessary credence to overall potential value of start-up company and its technology, product or service offering.

This is important, as investors need to know and believe that your start-up company's technology, product or service offering has the ability to create long-term value in the context of the general technology trends of the market.

Setting up a computer system

Most of the new entrepreneurs do not understand the power of computer system for their business. They are just fulfilling the formality of the computer system for their business. They are not using the client server architecture for their business still most of the entrepreneurs are working on the outdated computer systems which are slow and not ready to handle the huge data. The new entrepreneur wants to have such facility but then he will not be able to fulfill the other requirements of the business that are very important and he starts cost cut from the computer systems or the systems that he thinks do not matter much more for their business though such systems must be in his business.

Selecting the best software

Software purchase is not under the will of new small entrepreneurs. The cost of software is very high. For example ERP software is so costly that even middle type of company cannot purchase it. Now a days big companies are making use of software for the benefit of the business. For example Decision Support System (DSS) and Expert System (ES) are used by the big companies for forecasting, knowing business and taking decisions. These systems help a lot for the progress of the business. But situation is not same for new small entrepreneurs, they cannot take such systems for their business, they are dependent on their own business only. And somewhere lack of these systems suffers the business of new entrepreneurs or you can say speed of business becomes slow.

Lack of technical equipment

Most of the new entrepreneurs do not want to do a business where technical equipments are needed. They know the business and also have information about technical equipments but the main problem is that they cannot afford those equipments. If they purchase those costly equipments then what can they do about the other requirements of the business? They will not be able to fulfill the other requirements of the business. Small excess in finance is enough to break the motivation of new entrepreneurs. They are not ready to take any risk because who will support and guide them in that critical situation.

11.2 Why You Need a Website

Even if you're not planning on selling online, a well-crafted site is essential for any business.

Small business and website

The small new entrepreneurs do not give much importance to the web site. They want to directly sell their products to the customers. They think it is wastage of time and money to put the things on website and let the people select product from website. Most of the entrepreneurs have traditional thinking of interacting with customers. They do not want to go for it because of its expensiveness. This may affect their business in the modern age where number of customers are large who want to buy the product online. The important thing is that the initial entrepreneurs do not have sufficient money on hand so that they can open a website. This is not on their priority list.

Without website the reach of such kind of entrepreneurs to customers become limited. They cannot sell their products to far customers.

But the fact is that the future of e-commerce is very bright, but even the most futurists agreed that all the signs indicated that a large portion of future business revenues would be derived from online transactions or from offline transactions that were the result of online marketing efforts. Whether your business is small or big website benefits all business. For a small business it is very beneficial to open a website to reach to the far customers. So as an entrepreneur you must seriously think on whether you must have website or not to sell products or services online.

Do not take decision in hurry about selling product online or offline. Nowadays anything can be sold over the internet even customers prefer to buy the products or services online instead of going to the shops. The number of internet surfers are increasing day by day. Million shoppers are now online, purchasing everything from mobiles to laptops to vehicles to real estate to jet airplanes to natural gas to any thing you just name it. If you can imagine it, someone will figure out how to sell it online. Your presence on the website will help you to promote awareness about your products or services to customers, potential employees, business partners and perhaps even investors.

Having presence on website is not enough. Your website look should be professional and attractive. It should be user friendly so that users can easily operate on your website. Consumers are becoming habitual to online search for the primary information about the products or services before actual purchase. If they find your website then this is the time where your website talks to your customers than you. If your website is not attractive or user-friendly and hard to access your chance at making a good first impression will be lost. One of the great things about internet is that it has leveled the playing field when it comes to competing with the big boys. As mentioned, you have one shot at making a good first impression. With a well-designed site, your little operation can project the image and professionalism of a much larger company.

Not ready for online money transaction

Most of the new entrepreneurs are not ready for the online money transaction. They want money on hand or either in the bank's account. They have a fear about money security; they do not have trust on the system. That's why it is not simple for the entrepreneurs to suddenly shift on new system or technology. Even if the entrepreneurs are ready to do online money transaction the customers should also be ready to do online money transaction. So it becomes problematic for the entrepreneurs to do a business where the customers do not have such kind of facilities. Cash flow can make or break a company, especially in its early stages. That's why many online businesses often encourage credit card payments, although it's also helpful to give buyers alternative opportunities to pay with cheques and money orders. Offering a variety of methods for shoppers to pay online increases the opportunity for these buyers to pay in the method they prefer.

Accepting payments online increases revenue and cash flow because money goes into the account immediately. Even more compelling is that there are more than 1.2 billion consumer credit cards worldwide. Credit card payments aren't returned for non-sufficient funds—and credit card holders tend to do more impulse buying than those who write personal cheques.

Businesses have several options when setting up an e-commerce function and accepting payments online, which include:

Processing payments through a merchant account

To accept credit cards online, a small-business owner must first apply for a bank merchant account and then find a way to process transactions. At a brick-and-mortar store, the processing takes place when a card is swiped through the card reader. At an online store, the processing is done when a shopper types in the credit card information, which is then verified by a merchant account processor.

During most online checkout flows, a shopper is asked which method of payment is preferred. If the shopper selects a form of credit card payment, he or she will be redirected to a secure page within the store to enter the credit card information. After the shopper selects "submit," the credit card information will be sent to the correct merchant account, where it will be verified and either accepted or denied by the merchant account service provider.

Merchant accounts may have drawbacks for some small-business owners, however. Most charge set-up, monthly and per-transaction fees. Additional fees may also be involved if a business owner has a pre-existing account for a physical store and wants to convert that account to accept payments online. Moreover, some banks won't approve small online businesses for merchant accounts, considering them high-risk operations.

It may take 30 days or more for a merchant account to be approved and the integration process can be burdensome for business owners to do it themselves. Fortunately, the growth of online sales has given rise to an entire industry of merchant service bureaus that will grant a merchant account and everything else needed to accept online payments.

Ensuring transaction security

Online entrepreneurs have a responsibility to do all they can do to ensure their websites offer a safe shopping experience. But they need not be information technology security expert to have a secure site—the techies already have developed security measures that any online small business can adopt.

There are services in this space that bring together all the security measures that an online small business needs to have in place. PayPal enables businesses to set up a website that accepts credit cards without seeing or having to store the account numbers of its customers. This makes buyers feel even safer because they don't have to share their personal or financial information online. Gateway services like Authorizenet.com, CyberSource or Chase Paymentech Solutions will also handle credit card and electronic cheque payments securely.

11.3 Developing a Privacy Policy

Consumers' fears of identity, theft and the aggravation over spam make privacy policies essential for online businesses. Customers expect merchants to boldly exhibit their privacy policies on their stores' sites, with links from the catalog pages and the shopping cart.

A privacy policy should clearly state how the customers' personal information and financial details will be used and protected from the unauthorized persons. Consumers should be informed before collecting their information and with their consent only their information should be distributed. An online business is very clear about its private policy and never hides it from their customers. Do not change your private policy frequently otherwise customers will not trust you. Your reputation among customers will grow your business. This type of policy shows that the business takes customer privacy seriously and will use information it obtains in a responsible way.

Starting an online store may seem like a daunting challenge, but the reality is it's never been easier. Today there are standardized processes of moving a business online and most of the processes are now automated. Business owners discover an entirely new meaning in their business lives when — through the process of building an online store — they realize they've optimized their new-found markets and won the trust of internet consumers.

The Internet is very useful for any kind of entrepreneurs. Never have entrepreneurs had such a clear, easy and relatively inexpensive opportunity to reach a global marketplace for so many products and services. It's amazing how a business can thrive when its customers only need to lift a finger.

11.4 Requirements of Online Business

1. **Competitor analysis:** Look at competitors online and decide how you will differentiate yourself from them.
2. **URL:** Register a domain name.
3. **Web development:** Hire a web site developer or buy web development software, then determine site design and navigation.
4. **Internet service provider:** Buy a server or find an outsourced Internet service provider.
5. **Payment system:** Find a secure online order solution, including shopping cart and payment service.
6. **Protection plan:** Fight viruses and protect the site and computers with anti-virus software.
7. **Marketing plan:** Develop a marketing plan, which includes determining and publishing customer service policies.
8. **Contracts:** Establish alliances with crucial partners, such as product suppliers, search engine optimizers, fulfillment services, shippers, web technicians, marketing or public relations firms.
9. **Product:** Create an online catalog or listings of all products that you want to sell to the customers.
10. **Maintenance:** Keep inventory, catalogs and listings up to date for your customers.

11.5 Young Entrepreneurs – Online Business Fears

The entrepreneurs are ready to open the business online but they have a fear of the success of the online business. They have a fear that it is very expensive and not under their reach. They fear about the security and about money transaction. Majority of them like online business ideas, but are scared to do so. Below are the reasons they gave for this.

Lack of skills

Most of the entrepreneurs are scared of that they do not have skills about online business. Entrepreneurs are well in finance but technically they feel less. They can handle the business problems of finance, marketing, handling resources but they do not have much technical knowledge. They feel that it is very hard process and if they will not work properly on it then it may harm the business. They do not know how much it will require taking an online business, where to go for that, how the problems will be solved if any problems come.

Self-confidence

Some entrepreneurs would get discouraged too early in the beginning. It all sounds so scary. You have to have confidence, will power and strong guts to take this on. They do not want to take any trouble with their business. They are happy with the traditional one of doing business. Entrepreneurs' fear of failure restricts them to go for the new technology. They are not at all confident about new technology. There may be two reasons the first one is they do not have proper knowledge about the technology therefore they are not very much sure about the success of the technology. The second is they have wrong myths about the new technology that their business may suffer. When they see that others are not getting benefits or becoming fail then these things break their confidence of moving to the online business. They instead of earning much try to remain happy with the current situation. This is typically fear of the unknown and the lasting mythology of entrepreneurship that is perpetuated, unfortunately, because so a lot of entrepreneurs keep making the same preventable mistakes over and over again.

Lack of online business ideas

Some entrepreneurs are not so much creative enough to come up with something unique and incredible. Entrepreneurs have these great business ideas and even then it's not often sufficient to take a new business off the ground." Perception and not conception is the secret to entrepreneurial success: Paying attention is far more essential than creativity. It is all about finding a need or problem and then coming out with an innovative and feasible solutions and not about coming up with an idea and then finding a customer who might need it. The lack of creativity in the new entrepreneurs does not allow them to come up with the new business ideas that will help them in their business. They want to take the existing set up as it is without trying to do some modification in that by their own.

Lack of startup capital

New entrepreneurs are not so much interested in opening an online business because they already run out of money. They do not have sufficient money for their own business. Even if they will have money they will try to expand their business or try to bring some more required stuff into their business. They always try to return their loan taken from the banks or financial institutes. So at the initial level of their business they do not go for extra technology system because of lack of money.

Don't know how to handle failure

If entrepreneurs tried and failed as an internet business entrepreneur, they think they would be crushed, would bear huge losses. They unnecessarily fear about its implementation. They feel like a total failure in the business, it would most likely affect their business, their friendships as well as their reputation and if they came to dislike their day job they wouldn't even be able to daydream about running their own online business, for the reason that they have already tried that and failed. Inc. Magazine carried out a survey about two years ago and found that only one factor correlated strongly with entrepreneurial success: A preceding entrepreneurial failure. Certainly this is how you learn. If you stay away from over-committing and learn how to "fail quick and early", you can have the resilience to be a 'serial home business entrepreneur' and be confident with the reality that no entrepreneur succeeds in all undertaking.

Don't understand the process

Some young entrepreneurs have different problems. They take MBA certificate. They know about business and its running but they don't get any knowledge about online business ideas. From where do they acquire this knowledge? They do not know the implementation process of the technology. They do not know how to handle it. Knowledge will come by spending time with other entrepreneurs at the forums and drawing on the skills and knowledge of experienced people. Most individuals love to see new enterprises do well and those who can assist are usually very liberal with their time as well as counsel.

Lack of time

The new entrepreneurs are totally busy in their business. They are always busy in collecting all the necessary stuff for their business. They are the only single to handle their business. Here two situations may happen the first is even if the entrepreneurs have time they do not want to implement it. Second, they really do not have time to implement online business. The mentality of the small business person is that they never do that work until it becomes necessary. They delay up to the point from where it becomes necessary to implement online business to earn profit. So here the desire of the entrepreneurs is also very important. If they have a desire then they will do it otherwise they will not do it?"

The biggest time-consumer in launching a successful Plug-In Profit Site is the up-front research. But that study can be performed while you are doing other things you are already devoted to such as social occasions, courses, shopping, sales calls, dinners and even watching your kids' after-hours activities are all opportunities to observe. Explore and find the untapped needs that could be the basis for a successful entrepreneurial business enterprise. Take your time and carry out your research properly and you will then be so sure of success that you'll be able to confidently make the time to bring your online business ideas to fruition.

Stress

The home business entrepreneurs are in hock to the bank or to demanding investors, their personal possessions are at stake, their family depends on them for a stable source of income and a single bad debt could sink them. They even do not get time to fulfill all the requirements of the family. The entrepreneurs who have such huge responsibilities are always under stress and because of that they cannot run their business properly. They can now take extra burden of loan or money. For small entrepreneurs everything is not possible. Even if they like the idea they cannot fix it like big businesses. They have to take care about their families also. They are not free to do anything with their business.

Loneliness

"The entrepreneurs are one of the loneliest people in the world. They work day and night and barely have time for anything. Their complete focus is on their business. They continuously think about their business. They are always in search of knowledge and try to do everything themselves because they can't afford professionals/consultant." They implement the knowledge in the business what they learned? The biggest mistake many individuals make when starting their own online business is trying to execute it all themselves. Reports have it that one-man enterprises have the highest rate of failure, because no one person can know everything you need to know or have all the necessary skills and knowledge to succeed in business. One of the most important business decisions is finding a business partner who is having enough business knowledge so that you both can collectively use your skills to start and run a business. Get that right and you can never be lonely.

11.6 Large-Scale Trends That Impact Business

There are several major trends IT enables in our economy that will have a transformational impact on business and the family entrepreneur:

The globalization of intellectual capital

Increasing influence of English as a universal language and easy availability of high speed communication networks have made it possible to have intellectual work such as research and analysis performed by experts anywhere in the world. In today's global market, Indian doctors analyze x-rays for U.K.-based patients and Filipino analysts write Wall Street investment reports. Work is outsourced to the skilled and knowledgeable workers who are ready to work on the lowest cost. The threat of this trend is that someone with similar skills may "underbid" you in his willingness to work at a lower rate. Outsourcing to the skilled labour at lowest cost gives the opportunities to use global intellectual resources up to a larger extent. This is an opportunity to reach to the global market.

The accessibility of information

The easy and speedy availability of valuable information has a great influence on the people and their work. Whether you are searching a local ice-cream shop or toy shop information access has never been easier. The only threat is traditional information-based business models will be vanished. It provides many opportunities such as getting information in less time, ability to work faster and deliver a higher quality and urgent product, often independent of employer location.

The replacement of labour

Advanced technology has automated most of the repetitive low skill work. It is a good opportunity to the small business to fully utilize such technologies. It will solve their maximum problem of lack of skilled employees. Technology has brought efficiency, speed and quality in work. Whether it is automated robot that works independently or computer software that can analyze huge data within seconds, jobs with lower skill content continue to be replaced by IT. This threatens to the job of lower skilled labours who are candidates for replacement, while the opportunities mean a lower cost, higher-quality product for product-based companies.

The increase in spans of control

IT enables faster and easier communication and better monitoring of worker's activities, allowing supervisors to manage larger numbers of workers in disparate locations. While this threatens the jobs of lower-level supervisors, the opportunities for flatter, less hierarchical organizations and leaner, lower-cost production means companies that are more competitive in the marketplace.

The collaborative work environment

More information-based services are delivered through the collaborative efforts of others, many times unknown to each other. From networking sites such as LinkedIn to collaborative information and product communities such as Wikipedia and Linux, information is increasingly delivered as a joint effort of disparate individuals, creating new venues for work. The threats include a loss of market share by companies without collaborative mediums. On the other hand, companies can tap into a vast knowledge pool that directly applies their services, using contract work that results in faster and richer results.

The massive impact of the new economic realities made possible by IT is literally creating a tectonic shift in business. This means opportunities exist for a creative entrepreneurial family leader to translate his skills and experience into a new lifestyle: he can integrate his work and family life by changing the means through which he produces value. This is easier for knowledge workers in information based industries, but possibilities also exist in service- and product-based industries. It could be as simple as redefining the terms of your current employment to work from home or as complex as launching a new venture that delivers an outsourced service at a better price and/or quality than is currently offered.

11.7 Impact of e-Commerce on Entrepreneurs

There are huge potentials in building a business online. With the right tools and marketing strategies, you can come up with a profitable business. Imagine the number of people who regularly use the internet every day. Some people spend hours hooked on the internet. Moreover, with the busy lifestyle that a lot of people have these days, most of them prefer to do their shopping online. For these reasons, there are indeed business opportunities via e-Commerce.

Electronic Marketing had reached new heights in the recent years and business individuals had seen a lot of potential in it. Competition has become very tough among the players. However, there are many ways to promote an online business. With the various services and features specifically made to increase the exposure of websites – from getting a domain name all the way to generating traffic, success in e-Commerce can be achieved without any doubt.

Small business towards internet

The Internet and the World Wide Web (WWW) are revolutionizing the way organizations are functioning around the world. The Web is used by organizations in a myriad of ways, some of which include collaborating, communicating information, obtaining information, providing information and sharing information. One application of the Web that is grabbing headlines in virtually every media is Internet commerce or Electronic Commerce (e-commerce). e-commerce—the marketing, promotion, buying and selling of goods and services over the Internet is experiencing unprecedented growth (Williams, 1999). In the past two or three years, e-commerce growth has been astonishing and is expected to continue at a similar rate over the next four years.

Small business use of the Internet (e-commerce and other applications) has increased. Although statistics provide evidence that smaller organizations are now conducting e-commerce activities, large companies still account for the majority of e-commerce activity. These statistics also fail to tell us whether or not selling online is a better method for small business. Over the past few years, a decrease in the prices for software and hosting services has reduced the barriers to entry in the online environment. Even the smallest of businesses can now have a presence on the web and conduct commerce. Selling online, however, is not without its perils. Blindly diving headfirst into the Internet without a complete understanding of technical, managerial and competitive challenges may result in stressed operations or bankruptcy.

A question, then, arises: should small businesses and potential entrepreneurs embrace the Internet? The answer to this question lies in how well a business understands e-commerce opportunities in its environment and implements strategies to take advantage of these opportunities.

Opportunities in e-commerce

e-commerce takes a number of forms: business-to-consumer (B2C), business-to-business (B2B), e-procurement and e-marketplace. e-commerce is growing much faster in the B2B sector compared to B2C and is largely dominated by larger companies. e-commerce could yet turn into one of the biggest business start-up schemes ever. In a recent study, eBay found some 430,000 people in America alone who now make a full-time living or earn a substantial secondary income from trading on its site. Every year eBay holds a big get-together for its army of online entrepreneurs. Google, too, knows plenty of people who have profited from ads placed on their website.

Retailing or "e-tailing" is the most typical B2C activity. New ventures or small businesses can use the Internet to either start a new retailing or service business, enhance an ongoing business or provide hardware, software or services that allow other businesses to integrate the Internet into their business model. A traditional small business can utilize the opportunity to increase market share and to reach the far customers by creating a website and selling on the Internet.

While there are many large Internet service providers (ISP), there are also many small businesses that provide this service. The number of small businesses that provide Internet services have experienced tremendous growth because of the increase in demand for Internet access. Many of them are finding opportunities in providing additional hardware, software and service opportunities as they see the opportunity to host and design web sites for Internet businesses. They are also providing consulting services for those new businesses.

The greatest opportunities for the small business entrepreneurs will be in the area of B2B. According to Boston Consulting Group, all B2B e-commerce purchases will be made by six sectors: retail trade, motor vehicles, shipping, industrial, manufactured equipment, and the government. This will provide ample opportunities.

Technology

Majority of the small businesses use old techniques of production and outdated machinery and equipment. Up gradation of the technology and achieving economies of scale is one of the major problems facing the sector?

They cannot afford new machines and equipments and are therefore not in a position to use the latest techniques of production. They do not find it possible to conduct research and development on a continuing basis. Therefore, productivity and quality in small scale firms tends to be low while unit cost of production is generally high.

But with liberalization of the economy, the small businesses are facing stiff competition from imports and need technological up gradation in order to produce better quality products at cheap rates. As far as sourcing technology is concerned, small businesses face the following three essential problems:-

- **Obtaining information about technology** is the first important issue. For most of them, information about available technology options is through word of mouth or from a visit to an advanced unit. Few have access to technical literature, professional journals or information about new product launches. But with the advent of internet, new vistas are opening up through electronic journals, catalogue downloads and advanced search facilities.
- **Actual procurement of the technology** is the next important issue because even if information is obtained, there are barriers to import of technology and other problems relating to technology transfer, vendor capability, after sales support, import procedures, etc., which impede procurement.
- **Acquiring finance for technology** up gradation is also a problem. Small enterprises generally look to external sources of funding for upgrading technology as withdrawing money from business entails its own costs. With a view to foster the growth of MSME sector in the country, government has taken up several initiatives:

ISO 9000/14001 Certification Fee Reimbursement Scheme was introduced in order to provide incentives for technological upgradation, quality improvement and better environment management by the MSEs. The scheme provides incentive to those small scale/ ancillary undertaking who have acquired ISO 9000/ISO 14001/HACCP certifications.

In order to reduce the cost of funds, a scheme called **Credit Linked Capital Subsidy Scheme (CLCSS)** for Technology Up gradation in Small Scale Industries has been put into place. It aims at facilitating technology up gradation by providing upfront capital subsidy to small scale industry units, including tiny, khadi, village and coir industrial units, on institutional finance (credit) availed of by them for modernization of their production equipment (plant and machinery) and techniques.

National Manufacturing Competitiveness Programme (NMCP) has been launched by the government in order to help MSMEs improve their competitiveness. The schemes under this Programme are aimed at addressing the technology/quality up gradation needs of the sector, mainly in the public-private partnership mode.

Small Industries Development Bank of India (SIDBI) in collaboration with United Nations-Asian Pacific Centre for Transfer of Technology (UN-APCTT) had established **Technology Bureau for Small Enterprises (TBSE)** to bring synergy between Technology and Finance for Small and Medium Enterprise (SME) sector. The objectives of the company are to:

- Provide professional services for technology transfer in order to enhance market competitiveness of small and medium enterprises and promote sustainable development.
- Maintain and provide data base on technology options available from different countries.
- Provide micro small and medium enterprises information on sources of technology and means of accessing them.
- Provide background information on technology seeking enterprises to technology suppliers and collaborators.
- Identify business partners willing to collaborate and extend support to tie up financial assistance and other requirements such as drafting agreements, obtaining various approvals and preparation of business plans required for transfer of technology.
- Provides financial syndication through banks and financial institutions.

Besides, **National Small Industries Corporation Ltd. (NSIC)** has taken up an initiative to enhance technology options for small scale industries. An ISO 9001 certified company, it has been working to fulfill its mission of promoting, aiding and fostering the growth of small scale industries and industry related small scale services/business enterprises in the country. Over a period of five decades of transition, growth and development, NSIC has proved its strength within the country and abroad by promoting modernization, up gradation of technology, quality consciousness, strengthening linkages with large medium enterprises and enhancing exports - projects and products from small industries.

Also, **Small Industries Development Organization (SIDO)** has set up ten Tool Rooms and Training Centres in the country in order to assist small scale units in their technical up gradation by providing good quality tooling.

Further, in order to facilitate investments for technological up gradation and higher productivity in the micro and small enterprises, the phased deletion of products from the list of items reserved for the exclusive manufacture by such enterprises is being undertaken.

So What Could Be the Solution?

11.8 Entrepreneurs' Mission for New Technology – New Business

Many entrepreneurs start their new companies with the intention of commercializing creative business models and innovative ideas. In a strong sense, many of these startups are high tech and have become a platform in which new business owners can offer simple prolific solutions to existing market problems. Entrepreneurs who wish to launch such high tech startups should always be aware of any emerging technologies, so they can try to commercialize and market those ideas. One important question may remain: how do entrepreneurs find new technologies to start companies?

Discover new technology

By extensively researching and developing new solutions to solve the industrial or customers' existing problems or coming out with a totally unique solution entrepreneurs can find new technology. Although research in the fields of pharmacology, chemistry, cloning, electronics and biotechnology require the utilization of expensive laboratories, other technological research and experimentation can be done in one's home. For example, to develop a new software, an entrepreneur needs computer system and software (operating system) that are easily available and under the reach of entrepreneur. Similarly with few electronic components any small electronic device can be invented. More promising is the fact that a number of technology enthusiasts, who have worked out of their own home garages, have proposed and prototyped several automobiles that run on solar electricity and hydrogen.

Many successful entrepreneurs, who have typically worked from their garages, have invented new technologies that have changed the world. For example, William Hewlett and David Packard, who founded the Hewlett-Packard Company or HP, started their collaborative efforts from their garage. Today, HP has grown to become the world's largest vendor of personal computers. In addition, both Steven Jobs and Steve Wozniak, co-founders of Apple Inc., also began their partnership in the same manner. They assembled the first prototypes from Wozniak's bedroom and later, in Jobs' garage. Today, Apple, Inc. is the leader of consumer electronics and software.

Partner with a technologist

If an entrepreneurs is not able to invent himself then the best way is to partner with professional for inventing new technologies. The term "technologist" refers to skilled individuals who have immense aptitude for electronics, computers and other technologies. They are also most likely to prefer the role of a CTO (chief technological officer) rather than be involved in business development.

Technologist can either be the person who has an expertise in their own domain area where he has a vast experience or are young graduate students who have developed novel technological innovations. It is surprising that most of the technologists do not have business experience and therefore they do not know exactly the way of commercializing their technology. But the entrepreneurs who have business experience can easily encash the technology. For an inventor it is better to make partnership with already existing entrepreneurs. By doing this the technologist will be able to focus on inventing the technology and the entrepreneurs with their vast experience in business will commercialize the technology. On the other hand, the entrepreneur may end up with a disproportionate amount of equity since he/she does not contribute to the technical know-how and may not be given a major stake in the company.

Licensing technologies

Entrepreneurs can licence technologies for a researcher's new invention. These researchers can comprise of scientists, professors, patent owners or just be individual technology enthusiasts. They highly prefer inventing new technologies rather than taking part in the commercialization process. They also tend to remain as technical advisors to the entrepreneurs when their businesses move forward.

Providing licensing technology is not just limited to individual inventors. It can also be provided to large institutions such as universities, federal laboratories, research organizations and other companies. Since many major universities have a technology licence institute, they strive to licence all the technologies that have been developed in their educational facilities. For example, MIT's Technology Licensing Office has diligently helped a number of entrepreneurs by licensing their innovations. Similarly, central laboratories offer technology licensing to entrepreneurs. A good example is NASA, who executes hundreds of technology licensing agreements annually with new inventors.

In addition, some existing companies not interested in commercializing some of their technologies can also provide licence technologies to entrepreneurs. Licensing technologies from institutions are by far the simplest and most effective ways of acquiring technologies to start companies since entrepreneurs have the choice to select among different technologies before investing his/her time into it.

11.9 NSIC (National Small Industries Corporation Ltd.)

NSIC has now emerged as one of the key players for the promotion and development of Micro and Small Enterprises in the country.

At the national level, NSIC was conferred the "Corporate Excellence Award" by Amity International Business School during the year 2006-07 thus, acknowledging the turnaround in overall performance and quality of service delivery. Institute of Economics Studies- New Delhi conferred the 'Udyog Rattan Award' and 'Excellence Award' to NSIC for outstanding performance in the field of industrial development of the country. For participating in the India International Trade Fair organized by India Trade Promotion Organization (ITPO), NSIC was given the award for 'Best Display in Theme Category'.

Corporate Info

National Small Industries Corporation Ltd. (NSIC), an ISO 9001 certified company, since its establishment in 1955, has been working to fulfill its mission of promoting, aiding and fostering the growth of small scale industries and industry related small scale services/business enterprises in the country. Over a period of five decades of transition, growth and development, NSIC has proved its strength within the country and abroad by promoting modernization, upgradation of technology, quality consciousness, strengthening linkages with large medium enterprises and enhancing exports - projects and products from small industries.

NSIC operates through more than 120 offices, supported by a team of over 500 professionals spread across the country. To manage operations in African countries, NSIC operates from its office in Johannesburg.

NSIC carries forward its mission to assist small enterprises with a set of specially tailored schemes designed to put them in a competitive and advantageous position. The schemes comprise of facilitating marketing support, credit support, technology support and other support services.

Marketing

Marketing, a strategic tool for business development, is critical to the growth and survival of small enterprises in today's intensely competitive market. NSIC acts as a facilitator to promote small industries products and has devised a number of schemes to support small enterprises in their marketing efforts, both in and outside the country. These schemes are briefly described as under:

Consortia and Tender Marketing: Small Enterprises in their individual capacity face problems to procure and execute large orders, which inhibit and restrict their growth. NSIC accordingly adopts Consortia approach and forms consortia of units manufacturing the same products, thereby easing out marketing problems of SSIs. The Corporation explores the market and secures orders for bulk quantities. These orders are then distributed to small units in tune with their production capacity. Testing facilities are also provided to enable units to improve and maintain the quality of their products conforming to the standard specifications.

Single point Registration for Government Purchase: NSIC operates a single Point Registration Scheme under the Government Purchase Programme, wherein the registered SSI units get purchase preference in Government purchase programme, exemption from payment of Earnest Money Deposit etc.,

- Issue of tender sets free of cost.
- Advance intimation of tenders issued by DGS&D.
- Exemption from payment of earnest money.
- Waiver of security deposit up to the monetary limit for which the unit is registered.
- Issue of competency certificate in case the value of an order exceeds the monetary limit, after due verification.

Exhibitions and Technology Fairs: To showcase the competencies of Indian SSIs and to capture market opportunities, NSIC participates in select International and National Exhibitions and Trade Fairs every year. NSIC facilitates the participation of the small enterprises by providing concessions in rental etc. Participation in these events exposes SSI units to international practices and enhances their business prowess.

Buyer-Seller meets: Bulk and departmental buyers such as the Railways, Defence, Communication departments and large companies are invited to participate in buyer-seller meets to enrich SSI unit's knowledge regarding terms and conditions, quality standards, etc., required by the buyer. These programmes are aimed at vendor development from SSI units for the bulk manufacturers.

Export of Products and Projects: NSIC is a recognized Export House and exporting products and projects of small industries of India to other countries. The major areas of operation are:

- Export of products such as handicrafts, leather items, hand tools, pipes/fittings, builders' hardware etc.
- Supply of Small Industry projects on turnkey basis.

Credit Support: NSIC facilitates credit requirements of small enterprises in the following areas:

Financing for procurement of Raw Material (Short term)

NSIC's Raw Material Assistance Scheme aims at helping Small Scale Industries/ Enterprises by way of financing the purchase of Raw Material (both indigenous and imported). The salient features are

1. Financial Assistance for procurement of Raw Materials up to 90 days.
2. Bulk purchase of basic raw materials at competitive rates.
3. NSIC facilitates import of scares raw materials.
4. NSIC takes care of all the procedures, documentation and issue of letter of credit in case of imports.

Financing for Marketing Activities (Short term)

NSIC facilitates financing for marketing actives such as Internal Marketing, Exports and Bill Discounting.

Finance through syndication with Banks

In order to ensure smooth credit flow to small enterprises, NSIC is entering into strategic alliances with commercial banks to facilitate long term / working capital financing of the small enterprises across the country. The arrangement envisages forwarding of loan applications of the interested small enterprises by NSIC to the banks and sharing the processing fee.

Performance and Credit Rating Scheme for small industries

To enable small enterprises to ascertain the strengths and weaknesses of their existing operations and take corrective measures to enhance their organizational strength. NSIC is operating a Performance and Credit Rating Scheme through empanelled agencies like ICRA, ONICRA, Duns and Bradstreet (D&B), CRISIL, FITCH, CARE and SMERA. Small enterprise has the liberty to choose among any of the rating agencies empanelled with NSIC. Rating agencies will charge the credit rating fee according to their policies. The benefits to small enterprises are as follows:

- An independent, trusted third party opinion on capabilities and credit worthiness of SSI units.
- Good rating to enhance the acceptability of the SSI units with Banks. FIs, SSI's customers and buyers.
- Facilitate prompter credit decisions from Banks on proposals of SSI units.
- 75 per cent of the credit rating fee subject to a maximum of ₹ 25,000/- will be reimbursed to the small enterprise having a turnover upto ₹ 50 lakh by way of grants.
- 75 per cent of the credit rating fee subject to a maximum of ₹ 30,000/- will be reimbursed to the small enterprise having a turnover above ₹ 50 lakh to ₹ 200 lakh by way of grants.
- 75 per cent of the credit rating fee subject to a maximum of ₹ 40,000/- will be reimbursed to the small enterprise having a turnover above ₹ 200 lakh by way of grants.

Technology Support

Technology is the key to enhancing a company's competitive advantage in today's dynamic information age. Small enterprises need to develop and implement a technology strategy in addition to financial, marketing and operational strategies and adopt the one that helps integrate their operations with their environment, customers and suppliers.

NSIC offers small units the following support services through its Technical Services Centres and Extension Centres

1. Advising on application of new techniques
2. Material testing facilities through accredited laboratories
3. Product design including CAD
4. Common facility support in machining, EDM, CNC, etc.
5. Energy and environment services at selected centres
6. Classroom and practical training for skill upgadation

NSIC Technical Services Centres are located at the following places

Name of the Centre	Focus area
Chennai	Leather and Footware
Howrah	General Engineering
Hyderabad	Electronics and Computer Application
New Delhi	Machine Tools and related activities
Rajkot	Energy Audit and Energy Conservation activities
Rajpura (Pb)	Domestic Electrical Appliances
Aligarh (UP)	Lock Cluster and Die and Tool making

Infomediary Services

Information today is becoming almost as vital as the air we breathe. We need it every minute of our working lives. With increase in competition and melting away of international boundaries, the demand for information is reaching new heights. NSIC, realizing the needs of MSMEs, is offering Infomediary Services which is a one-stop, one-window bouquet of aids that will provide information on business, technology and finance and also exhibit the core competence of Indian SMEs.

Membership Benefits

- Tender and Trade Information.
- Banner display on NSIC Website
- Access to a wide range of technologies from India and abroad.
- Access to national and international business leads, JV opportunities and trade information.
- Comprehensive information on Government policies, rules and regulations, schemes and incentives.
- Access to industrial databases and member's directory.
- Various value added, specialized services for members of Infomediary Service.

Software Technology Parks

NSIC Software Technology Parks (STPs) facilitate small industries in setting up 100 per cent export-oriented units for software exports. They also act as nodal point to activate software exports directly through NSIC. These STPs extend support in terms of the requisite infrastructure to the SSI units to start business operations with a minimum lead time. The scheme is governed by STPI regulations of the Ministry of Information Technology, Government of India. NSIC established the first STP at Okhla, New Delhi in 1995 and second in Chennai in 2001. Several small scale units have taken advantage of these parks and contributed export earnings to the exchequer.

Technology Business Incubators

Enterprise development is one of the thrust areas for nurturing the development and growth of micro and small enterprises in the country that is being facilitated by providing handholding support to the micro and small enterprises in every field of business. Incubation is one of the appropriate tools to achieve this goal, as it provides necessary facilities for the prospective entrepreneurs and start-up companies to learn product manufacturing processes coupled with technology development, business development under one roof. In these incubators working projects depicting appropriate technology for small enterprises are displayed in working conditions.

Small Enterprise Establishment Programme (SEEP)

This programme facilitates setting up of new enterprises all over the country by creating self-employment opportunities for the unemployed persons. The objective of this scheme is to facilitate establishment of new small enterprises by way of providing integrated services in the areas of training for entrepreneurial skill development, selection of small projects, preparation of project profiles/reports, identification and sourcing of plant, machinery and equipments, facilitating sanction of credit facility and providing other support services in order to boost the development of small enterprises in manufacturing and services sectors.

International Cooperation

NSIC facilitates sustainable international partnerships. The emphasis is on sustainable business relations rather than on one-way transactions. Since its inception, NSIC has contributed to strengthening enterprise-to-enterprise cooperation, south cooperation and sharing best practices and experiences with other developing countries, especially those in the African, Asian and Pacific regions. The features of the scheme are:

- Exchange of Business/Technology missions with various countries.
- Facilitating Enterprise to Enterprise cooperation, JVs, Technology Transfer and other form of sustainable collaboration.
- Explore new markets and areas of cooperation:
- Identification of new export markets by participating in sector- specific exhibitions all over the world.
- Sharing of Indian experience with other developing countries

International Consultancy Services

For the last five decades, NSIC has acquired various skill sets in the development process of small enterprises. The inherent skills are being networked to offer consultancy services for other developing countries. This activity has been started during 2004-05 and is expected to occupy a place in the future service profile of the Corporation. The areas of consultancy are as listed below:

1. Capacity Building
2. Policy and Institutional Framework
3. Entrepreneurship Development
4. Business Development Services

Insurance of Export Credit for Micro and Small Enterprises

NSIC is facilitating micro and small enterprises to insure their export credits by entering into strategic alliance with Export Credit Guarantee Corporation of India Limited (ECGC). MSEs would be helped in insuring their export credits through any office of the Corporation, located all over the country. This arrangement is made to strengthen promotion of exports from small enterprises

11.10 National Research Development Corporation (NRDC)

Corporate Goals

To fulfill its mission, the National Research Development Corporation (NRDC) has set for itself a portfolio of corporate goals. Goals that its team of professionals helps to achieve by giving of their best.

NRDC team has a singular purpose - to identify and satisfy the potential investor in the use of innovative, reliable and competitive technologies co-developed or Licensed by the Corporation.

To this purpose, NRDC harnesses its human resources to:

- Promote, through flexible funding schemes, the development of marketable technologies in close association with industry and National R&D institutions.
- Evaluate the technological merits and commercial potential of incipient or mature technologies by conducting techno-economic surveys; technology and business forecasts and investment appraisals.
- Pre-emptively protect intellectual property rights worldwide.
- Design and engineer manufacturing plants of commercial scale.
- Shape and manage technology contracts that are fair and equitable.
- Test - market products.
- Assist in obtaining certifications for products and their quality, where these are prerequisites for entering commerce.

Transforming Innovative Research into Profitable Technology

The accelerating spread of new technologies in a competitive environment worldwide makes it imperative that new ideas and technologies are identified at their source in the scientific world, carried forward by technological innovation and piloted into commercial production.

NRDC is India's premier service enterprise whose business is to be the identifier, the carrier and the pilot of technology transfer. For over fifty years, NRDC has played a key role in speeding the commercial applications of research and in effecting the transfer of technology from laboratory to enterprise. NRDC guides and assists the entrepreneur in executing his technological business plans.

NRDC's extensive network of national and international contacts in scientific bodies, technology transfer agencies, industrial and engineering concerns and venture-capital providers, has enabled it to act as an effective catalyst translating innovative research into marketable industrial products, processes and services.

NRDC works in close conjunction with over 200 national R & D laboratories and has licensed over 2000 technologies for commercial exploitation, of which nearly 1000 are in production with a current annual turnover of about ₹ 12,000 million (₹ 12 billion).

Technologies licensed by NRDC cover areas such as chemicals, drugs and pharmaceuticals, food, agro-processing, bio-technology, metallurgy, electronics, instrumentation, building materials, manufacturing techniques and utility processes including pollution control.

NRDC is the one-stop provider of comprehensive business services, devoted to satisfying the demanding customer of competitive technology. To this end, NRDC nurtures new ideas and inventions by providing finance and rewards; ensuring intellectual property protection; efficiently effecting transfer of know-how from laboratories to industry; providing access to new technologies from India and abroad; exporting Indian technological expertise and offering an array of technology consultancy services.

Technology packages from NRDC include data for the preparation of project reports that meet the requirements of investment banks and financial institutions.

Technology Promotion development and Utilization Programme (TPDU)

NRDC is an active partner in the TPDU programme of the Department of Scientific and Industrial Research (DSIR), Government of India.

Through this programme, the Government catalyses by financial support and institutional networking, the design, development, prototyping and the commercialization of innovations in and by industrial enterprises. NRDC manages the intellectual property generated from such TPDU projects and also it desired licenses the know-how so generated to other industries in India and abroad.

The details of the programme can be attained from DSIR website.

General Technology Consultancy (GTC)

NRDC's new scheme arranges to provide General Technology Consultancy services to Indian industries that have been suddenly exposed to international competition with the introduction of the new industrial policy of the Government of India.

The main objective of the scheme is to study the existing technology and business base of an industrial unit in some detail and on that basis, to identify, select and source new technological inputs needed by that unit and to upgrade its operations, so as to meet domestic as well as international competition.

11.11 Buy Small Business Computers

Advice When Buying Computers

When it comes to buying computers for your small business, one word dominates the conversation. Advances in technology have created a seemingly endless list of choices in computers and computer-related equipment. The decisions you make will inevitably reflect the needs of your business. But to make the right decisions, you'll need to know what your options are. Here is a sampling of the options at your disposal:

New vs. Used

First of all you must ask yourselves whether to buy new ones or the used ones. It also depends upon the budget you have. Now a days the cost of computer systems have gone down and therefore purchasing the new computer systems will be the best option. Used computers will most likely be outdated and beaten up. They may also contain internal problems that you can't see until you set them up. New computers, on the other hand, are warranted and often come with special software deals that are not available with used products. In the end, you'll spend far less time and money going new. But few technologies are still costly so there you can purchase the used ones.

Desktop vs. Laptop

Next you will need to decide whether you'll need laptops, desktops or both. The big advantage of laptops is portability. Today's laptops can go virtually anywhere and do virtually anything you need them to do. But in general, they have smaller processors and less disk space than desktops and they are more expensive. You'll need to weigh those costs against your need for mobility. Many small businesses opt to purchase desktops for the office and laptops for employees who work outside the office. Assess your needs and decide what's right for you.

Mac vs. PC

Computer users are always in confusion whether to favour Macintosh computers or to favour PCs. Quality wise both are good. Both are capable of meeting your small business requirements. Mostly deciding the best computer for your business greatly depends on the type of business you are doing because each business has its own requirement for example whether your business is online business or offline business if online then you will need a strong 'Server' and mostly Linux based servers are used for such requirement. Most small businesses operate in a PC environment and format their files in a PC format. However, businesses that work in graphic arts and other creative activities tend to favour Mac formats. It will be better if you will talk to other business owners about the computer requirement of small business so that accordingly you can take a good decision. Some companies, especially the ones who regularly rely on computer technology to do business, find it best to keep at least one of each on hand to make sure they have the ability to meet all their computing needs.

Wireless vs. Cables

A recent advance in computing has been the move to wireless connectivity. Many computers now come with built-in wireless capability. This technology enables the user to connect to the internet via a wireless hub instead of through clumsy cables and wires. The wireless revolution has been especially beneficial to laptop users who can now surf the internet from virtually anywhere, provided they are in range of the wireless hub connection. Coffee shops, airports and other public areas even provide wireless connections for their customers free of charge.

11.12 Trusting up with Technology

Small Business Technology Advice

Although you can't do business without it, the cost of upgrading your technology can easily kill your company's budget. Luckily, there are ways to minimize the financial impact of technology updates, keeping your technology - and your budget - on track.

Create a Technology Plan

When you want to run your business then it requires a great planning. Technical plan is also very important as the marketing and financial plans are! A technical plan must include the technology that you want to use, when to use, lease or buy decision, upgradation of the hardware, software and networking that is vital to the successful operation of your business. You must be very clear about what kind of technology you want to use for your business? Wrong selection of technology might spoil your business. There are a lot of advantages to a tech plan, but one of one's is that you'll avoid sticker shock because you'll be able to stage your upgrades over a period of time.

Prioritize Technology Purchases

Prioritization is an important decision while you are upgrading the technology. If you want to use new software in website for feasible and speedy interaction with your online customers then it is your priority because you cannot be lenient towards your customers. But if you want to use new software for maintaining an inventory then there you can delay but not neglect. A tech plan will get the prioritization ball rolling, but maintaining a prioritization mentality - that's up to you.

Assess Needs vs. Wants

Technology is constantly changing, making it a potentially bottomless pit for your hard-earned cash. Professional business owner quickly take decision whether to purchase technology or using the old one. As the technology is changing very fast then purchasing a technology on some time is not a good option. When technology is very important for the success of business where you cannot afford long time then purchasing is the good option. But when the technology is not so much important for your business and you can compromise with your time then using old technology is good. It never hurts to have a wish list, but before purchasing upgrades ask yourself the hard question: Do you really need it or do you really want it?

Buy at a Discount

Once you've decided what you need to buy, the next question is where to buy it. Suppliers for specialized technology will be limited, but for your general technological needs you have a lot of options to choose from. Ironically, one option is to use technology to buy technology. E-bay offers products from a variety of suppliers, making it easy to compare prices. It also lists used merchandise, which may be an option in a financial pinch.

Business liquidations are another solid source for technology upgrades. Unfortunately, many small businesses close their doors every day. When a business closes, it's not uncommon for them to liquidate their capital assets - including their technological assets. Although it's sad to see a business close, you might save a bundle by helping them turn their technology into cash.

11.13 Using Technology to Get Customers

1. Use your Web site to build solid, trusting relationships with customers. Trust helps bring customers back.
2. Enhance communication with customers. Some small business CEOs put their email address on the company Web site so customers can contact them directly.
3. Don't forget the basics: Post your company's address and phone number on your Web site.
4. Remember that the Internet is educating your customers and making them smarter buyers. Keep pace with their knowledge.
5. Respond to emails promptly.

11.14 National Science and Technology Entrepreneurship Development Board (NSTEDB)

The National Science and Technology Entrepreneurship Development Board (NSTEDB), established by Government of India in 1982 is an institutional mechanism, with a broad objective of promoting gainful self-employment amongst the Science and Technology (S&T) manpower in the country and to setup knowledge based and innovation driven enterprises.

NSTEDB functions under the aegis of Department of Science and Technology. It has representation from socio-economic and scientific Departments / Ministries, premier entrepreneurship development institutions and all India Financial Institutions.

The major objectives of NSTEDB are:

- To promote knowledge based and innovation driven enterprises.
- To facilitate generation of entrepreneurship and self-employment opportunities for S & T persons.
- To facilitate the information dissemination.
- To network with various Central and State Government agencies for S&T based entrepreneurship development.
- To act as a policy advisory body to the Government agencies for S&T based entrepreneurship development.
- To generate employment through technical skill development using S & T infrastructure.

The Programmes conducted by NSTEDB have created awareness among S&T persons to take up entrepreneurship as a career. The academicians and researchers have started taking a keen interest in such socially relevant roles and have engaged themselves in several programmes initiated by NSTEDB. About 100 organisations, most of which are academic institutions and voluntary agencies, were drafted in the task of entrepreneurship development and employment generation.

Some of the major programmes/activities undertaken by NSTEDB are elaborated on this portal. More programmes are being evolved to suit the changing economic and market scenario.

1. What is a Technology Business Incubator?

A Technology business incubator nurtures the development of technology based and knowledge driven companies helping them to survive and grow during the start up period (2-3 years) by providing an integrated package of work space, shared office services, access to specialized equipment and value added services like management assistance, business planning, access to finance, technical assistance and networking support. The main objective of the TBI (**Technology Business Incubators**) is to produce successful business ventures that create jobs and wealth in their region.

2. How do tenant company's benefit to a TBI?

A decent infrastructure coupled with an integrated package of business support services with moderate costs offered by a TBI enables the tenant companies to start up their venture with a lower initial investment. The TBI also assist the tenant companies by offering critical support services so as to minimize the chances of failure and improve their survival prospects. Various studies report that the survival rate of the incubatees (tenant enterprises) is nearly 70 per cent to 80 per cent. In addition, the networking support provided by the TBI helps the tenants companies to establish credibility and also reduces their time to develop marketable product and services.

3. What are the agencies, which support the establishment of TBI in India?

National Science and Technology Entrepreneurship Development Board (NSTEDB) of the Department of Science and Technology, Govt. of India is the leading Governmental agency to support the establishment of TBI. It provides financial assistance for creating state of the art facilities in the identified thrust areas. It also offers partial /full support for recurring/operational cost for a period of five years. It is expected that the TBI after five years would be in a position to attain the operational self-sufficiency. In addition, the applying host institution also sponsors the TBI by offering land, building, equipments and facilities, technical expertise, etc., and other support services from the institution to strengthen the activities of TBI. In some cases other like-minded organizations and the State Government also join hands to promote the TBI in a suitable location having potential for entrepreneurship development and creation of new enterprises in the chosen technological areas (single/mixed).

4. Are there any technological areas earmarked for the TBI?

A TBI can be set up in any technological (single /mix) area after thorough study and analysis. The area should essentially offer good market potential and institute should have the needed expertise, good facilities, proven track record of R&D work to demonstrate their strength and justify the potential of the selected thrust area. The areas may range from biotechnology, information and communication technology, design, micro-electronics, embedded systems, manufacturing, agri-business, environment and energy, etc.

5. Who can set up a TBI?

An institution in operation for at least five years and having good resource base of R&D work in identified technological area, technology commercialization, some experience and drive for entrepreneurship development would be the primary target group for setting up a TBI. Some of the institutions having focus on business management systems and practices could also apply with proper systems for innovations and technology sourcing.

6. How many TBIs are there in India?

NSTEDB, DST has promoted nearly 40 TBIs in the country and over 15 Science and Technology Entrepreneurship Parks (STEPs). five more TBIs are planned to be set up. Some of the leading institutes like IITs, IIMs, NITs, NID and ICRISAT have set up incubators. Some of the State Governments other agencies have set up initiative similar to that of TBI to promote the growth of specific industry i.e., food processing, bio-technology, etc. Small Industry Development Bank of India (SIDBI) has also set up innovation and incubation set at IIT, Kanpur and BITs Ranchi. With globalization and liberalization, emergence of knowledge driven product and services in sunrise areas and its ensuing benefits to the nation and society, the incubator programme is becoming popular in India.

7. What is the global scenario of TBI?

Incubator programs have been established in many countries to stimulate creation of technology-oriented small businesses. At present, there are nearly 4000 incubators of various types operational in the World. In USA, there are more than 1000 incubators including about 200 Internet incubators. Europe has nearly 1000 incubators including 300 in Germany. Among the developing countries, China has shown exponential growth in the incubators and over a period of ten years has set up almost 400 incubators. Korea too, is reported to have about 300 Incubators. While Japan, Malaysia and Singapore are catching up. High-technology incubators have been particularly successful in U.S., Israel and China.

8. What are the indicators of a successful TBI?

The success of a TBI can be judged from the efficacy of the TBI operations, number of successful enterprises, social impact created in the region and good financial health of the TBI. The TBI should be a visible and known entity in the region for stimulating new enterprises.

9. What makes a TBI programme successful?

Following are the general guidelines in order to make the TBI programme successful:

- Careful selection of the location and host institution
- Careful Identification of thrust area backed up by a feasibility study.
- Identify a champion to steer the process of setting up an Incubator
- Arrange resource mobilization and good support from its sponsors.
- Ensure proper Implementation through
- Appropriate systems and processes to execute the business plan of TBI
- A good service package for tenants
- Committed, competent and dynamic core team
- Effective management board
- Good linkages and networking
- Well laid out entry and exit policies for tenant companies.
- Good infrastructure
- Involvement, commitment and full cooperation from host institute and other stake holders.

10. How do incubators help start up in getting funding?

Incubators can help tenant companies in securing capital in a number of ways:-

- Managing in-house and revolving incubation funds/ seed support fund.
- Connecting companies with angel investors (high-net-worth individual investors)
- Working with companies to perfect venture capital presentations and connecting them to venture capitalists.
- Assisting companies in applying for bank loan.

11. What are the different models of TBIs?

In the developing economies like India, each TBI evolves its model based on the need, its strength and the thrust area of the technology. The TBI model usually has following features.

- Sector specific
- In and around Univ., Technical Institute/R & D/Management Institute
- Well Equipped
- Incubation process may involve the following.
- Select the Tenant – Incubate – Graduate
- Select the idea – test the idea – market feasibility – business plan – start the venture – arrange for seed fund – mentorship program- incubate the start-up-graduate

Select the technology-upscale the technology-match making with the entrepreneur-mentor - incubate-graduate

SUMMARY

Changing Technology

In today's world, the technology is changing so fast that it becomes quite difficult to remember the technology or to say that my current technology will run long. Even the established entrepreneurs are facing the problems related to the obsolescence of technology. The technology involves huge money. A new entrepreneur if open business cannot know exactly for what kind of technology he should go, the rapid technology development confuses the new entrepreneur and puts in dilemma what he should do in such situation and that really slows down his progress of business.

Obsolescence of technology: If the experienced entrepreneurs will not come up with the new technology then it will ultimately hamper their business and market shares. The new technology is brought to give competition to the competitors and attract the customers.

Improper technology information: For opening the business, information about the technology is a must. The entrepreneurs are living in the age of the technology where technology becomes the weapon of the entrepreneurs. The more the advanced technology entrepreneurs' chances of success become more. Some entrepreneurs try to search about the information but they did not succeed. Some entrepreneurs take the situation as it is and don't try to get information of the technology that will be required by their business. The entrepreneur is always in confusion from where he could get the correct information and after no hope of information he begins his business with the partial information whatever he has.

Unclear understanding of general technology trends: There are many issues that come into play when rolling out a new technology. These include the following:

- Initial costs of new technologies are generally high,
- Infrastructure roll-out takes time and is very expensive,
- The new technology may not be ready for prime time and
- End-users do not always readily embrace new technologies.

The other issues are related to Setting up a computer system, Selecting the best software and Lack of technical equipment.

Entrepreneurs Need a Website

Small business and website: The small new entrepreneurs do not give much importance to the web site. They want to directly sell their product to the customers. They think it is wastages of time and money to put the things on website and let the people select product from website.

But the fact is that the future of e-commerce is very bright, but even the most futurists agreed that all the signs indicated that a large portion of future business revenues would be derived from online transactions or from offline transactions that were the result of online marketing efforts.

Not ready for online money transaction: Most of the new entrepreneurs are not ready for the online money transaction. They want money on hand or either in the bank's account. They have a fear about money security; they do not have trust on the system. Accepting payments online increases revenue and cash flow because money goes into the account immediately. Even more compelling is that there are more than 1.2 billion consumer credit cards worldwide. Credit card payments aren't returned for non-sufficient funds—and credit card holders tend to do more impulse buying than those who write personal cheques.

Processing payments through a merchant account: To accept credit cards online, a small-business owner must first apply for a bank merchant account and then find a way to process transactions. At a brick-and-mortar store, the processing takes place when a card is swiped through the card reader. At an online store, the processing is done when a shopper types in the credit card information, which is then verified by a merchant account processor.

Ensuring transaction security: Online entrepreneurs have a responsibility to do all they can do to ensure their websites offer a safe shopping experience. But they need not be information technology security expert to have a secure site—the techies already have developed security measures that any online small business can adopt.

Developing a Privacy Policy

Consumers' fears of identity, theft and the aggravation over spam make privacy policies essential for online businesses. Customers expect merchants to boldly exhibit their privacy policies on their stores' sites, with links from the catalog pages and the shopping cart.

The reasons for **online business fears** are Lack of skills, Self-confidence, Lack of online business ideas, Lack of startup capital, Don't know how to handle failure, Don't understand the process, Lack of time, Stress, and Loneliness.

There are several major trends IT enables in our economy that will have a transformational impact on business and the family entrepreneur: those are *the globalization of intellectual capital, The accessibility of information, The replacement of labour, The increase in spans of control,* and *The collaborative work environment*

Impacts of e-Commerce on Entrepreneurs are as follows:

Small business towards internet

The Internet and the World Wide Web (WWW) are revolutionizing the way organizations are functioning around the world. The Web is used by organizations in a myriad of ways, some of which include collaborating, communicating information, obtaining information, providing information and sharing information.

Opportunities in e-commerce

e-commerce takes a number of forms: business-to-consumer (B2C), business-to-business (B2B), e-procurement and e-marketplace. e-commerce is growing much faster in the B2B sector compared to B2C and is largely dominated by larger companies.

Technology

As far as sourcing technology is concerned, small businesses face the following three essential problems:-

Acquiring finance for technology

Actual procurement of the technology

Obtaining information about technology

ISO 9000/14001 Certification Fee Reimbursement Scheme was introduced in order to provide incentives for technological up gradation, quality improvement and better environment management by the MSEs. The scheme provides incentive to those small scale/ ancillary undertaking who have acquired ISO 9000/ISO 14001/HACCP certifications.

National Manufacturing Competitiveness Programme (NMCP) has been launched by the government in order to help MSMEs improve their competitiveness. The schemes under this Programme are aimed at addressing the technology/quality up gradation needs of the sector, mainly in the public-private partnership mode.

In order to reduce the cost of funds, a scheme called credit Limited Capital Subsidy Schems (CLCSS) for technological up gradation in small scales Industries has been put into place.

National Small Industries Corporation Ltd. (NSIC) has taken up an initiative to enhance technology options for small scale industries. An ISO 9001 certified company, it has been working to fulfill its mission of promoting, aiding and fostering the growth of small scale industries and industry related small scale services/business enterprises in the country.

With a view to foster the growth of MSME sector in the country, government has taken up several initiatives:

Small Industries Development Bank of India (SIDBI) in collaboration with United Nations-Asian Pacific Centre for Transfer of Technology (UN-APCTT) had established **Technology Bureau for Small Enterprises (TBSE)** to bring synergy between Technology and Finance for Small and Medium Enterprise (SME) sector.

Entrepreneurs' Mission for New Technology - New Business

Discover new technology

Entrepreneurs can acquire new technologies by extensively researching and developing new solutions to solve current technological flaws. Although much of the research in the fields of pharmacology, cloning and biotechnology require the utilization of expensive laboratories, other technological research and experimentation can be done in one's home.

Partner with a technologist

Another way in which entrepreneurs can invent new technologies is by partnering with professional experts to start their companies. The term "technologist" refers to skilled individuals who have immense aptitude for electronics, computers and other technologies.

Licensing technologies

Entrepreneurs can license technologies for a researcher's new invention. These researchers can comprise of scientists, professors, patent owners or just be individual technology enthusiasts. They highly prefer inventing new technologies rather than taking part in the commercialization process. They also tend to remain as technical advisors to the entrepreneurs when their businesses move forward.

National Small Industries Corporation Ltd. (NSIC), an ISO 9001 certified company, since its establishment in 1955, has been working to fulfill its mission of promoting, aiding and fostering the growth of small scale industries and industry related small scale services/business enterprises in the country. NSIC carries forward its mission to assist small enterprises with a set of specially tailored schemes designed to put them in a competitive and advantageous position. The schemes comprise of Marketing, Consortia and Tender Marketing, Single point Registration for Government Purchase, Exhibitions and Technology Fairs, Buyer-Seller meets, Export of Products and Projects, Credit Support, Financing for procurement of Raw Material (Short term), Financing for Marketing Activities (Short term), Finance through syndication with Banks, Performance and Credit Rating Scheme for small industries, Infomediary Services, Technology Support, Software Technology Parks, Technology Business Incubators, Small Enterprise Establishment Programme (SEEP), International Cooperation, International Consultancy Services, and Insurance of Export Credit for Micro and Small Enterprises.

NRDC team has a singular purpose - to identify and satisfy the potential investor in the use of innovative, reliable and competitive technologies co-developed or Licensed by the Corporation.

Transforming Innovative Research into Profitable Technology

NRDC is India's premier service enterprise whose business is to be the identifier, the carrier and the pilot of technology transfer. For over fifty years, NRDC has played a key role in speeding the commercial applications of research and in effecting the transfer of technology from laboratory to enterprise. NRDC guides and assists the entrepreneur in executing his technological business plans.

Technology Promotion development and Utilization Programme (TPDU)

NRDC is an active partner in the TPDU programme of the Department of Scientific and Industrial Research (DSIR), Government of India.

General Technology Consultancy (GTC)

NRDC's new scheme arranges to provide General Technology Consultancy services to Indian industries that have been suddenly exposed to international competition with the introduction of the new industrial policy of the Government of India.

The National Science and Technology Entrepreneurship Development Board (NSTEDB), established by Government of India in 1982 is an institutional mechanism, with a broad objective of promoting gainful self-employment amongst the Science and Technology (S&T) manpower in the country and to setup knowledge based and innovation driven enterprises. The Programmes conducted by NSTEDB have created awareness among S&T persons to take up entrepreneurship as a career.

A **Technology Business Incubator** nurtures the development of technology based and knowledge driven companies helping them to survive and grow during the start up period (2-3 years) by providing an integrated package of work space, shared office services, access to specialized equipment and value added services like management assistance, business planning, access to finance, technical assistance and networking support. The main objective of the TBI (**Technology Business Incubators**) is to produce successful business ventures that create jobs and wealth in their region.

KEYWORDS

Obsolete technology: The technology that becomes outdated.

Web site: A Web site is a related collection of World Wide Web (WWW) files that includes a beginning file called a home page.

Online money transfer: Online Money Transfer refers to the process in which funds can be transferred over Internet with the use of debit cards or credit cards.

Merchant accounts: Merchant accounts act as a contract between the business owner and the bank.

***Transaction* security system:** It is a system for ensuring the *security* of financial transactions on the Internet.

Privacy policy: The *privacy policy* describes what personal information we collect and how we use it.

Internet service provider: *Internet service provider* is a company that provides a subscriber with access to the Internet.

e-commerce: *e-commerce* (electronic commerce or EC) is the buying and selling of goods and services on the Internet, especially the World Wide Web.

Software Technology Parks (STPs): Software Technology Parks (STPs) facilitate small industries in setting up 100 per cent export-oriented units for software exports.

Technology business incubator: A Technology business incubator nurtures the development of technology based and knowledge driven companies helping them to survive and grow during the start period.

QUESTIONS

1. What is the role of technology in promoting entrepreneurship?
2. What are the technology related problems of small entrepreneurs?
3. What is the need of website in business in today's business scenario?
4. What are the requirements of online business?
5. What are the online business fears of new entrepreneurs?
6. What is the impact of e-commerce on entrepreneurs business?
7. Write short note on: NSIC, NRDC and NSTEDB.

❑ ❑ ❑

Chapter – 12

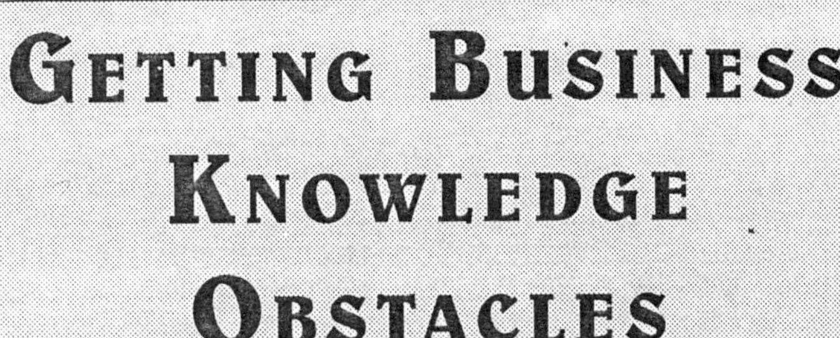

Getting Business Knowledge Obstacles

LEARNING OBJECTIVES

On completion of this chapter, you should be able to:

☺ *Explain why new small entrepreneurs lack in business knowledge.*

☺ *What are the different obstacles faced by entrepreneurs.*

☺ *Describe how entrepreneurs can improve business idea.*

☺ *Describe how entrepreneurs can search a new idea.*

For the new small entrepreneurs it is always the question of confusion, what is this business all about? They always try to get the answer, how can we run this business? What is this business? What are the requirements of this business? When they remain confused, then it makes them weak before opening the business. Having business knowledge is must to open the business. These create basic blocks of the business. If you have all the knowledge of the business then definitely you can minimize most of the risks that otherwise you might encounter after opening the business and running the business. The new entrepreneurs are weak in knowledge about business. They do not have complete idea about business. The following are the obstacles faced by the new entrepreneurs when they are eager to open the business, but their less business knowledge restricts them to open the business correctly.

12.1 Where to Look for Business Issues

An entrepreneur if wants to do something new then in such case he always faces the problems of where to go to get the perfect knowledge of that business even if he wants to be in the known

BOX 12

HP Graduate Entrepreneurship Training through IT (GET-IT)

The HP Graduate Entrepreneurship Training through IT (GET-IT) program is working to provide young people with business and technology skills training they can use to start careers or launch their own businesses. In partnership with the Micro-Enterprise Acceleration Institute (MEA-I) and the United Nations Industrial Development Organization (UNIDO), World ORT and local training centers, HP has made the GET-IT program available in 30 countries in Europe Middle East and Africa (EMEA), particularly in low-income communities with high unemployment rates and limited job opportunities.

GET-IT courses teach 16- to 25-year-olds practical hands-on IT solutions for daily business challenges in areas such as finance, management, marketing and technology management. In 2009, HP opened 30 GET-IT training centers in Africa and the Middle East and Russia and Ukraine, bringing the total number of training centers to 100.

Young entrepreneurs who do not live near a GET-IT center can access training courses through www.get-it-city.net, an online portal that offers hands-on resources and tools to facilitate self-directed learning. For example, Blossom, a role-playing game launched in 2009, offers students the chance to manage their own virtual floral business.

Since the launch of GET-IT in 2007, the program has reached more than 100,000 young people through online and on-site training courses, with the goal of reaching half a million by the end of 2010.

HP Entrepreneurship Learning Program (HELP)

Microenterprises—very small businesses with fewer than five employees—are integral to creating jobs and strengthening local economies, particularly in emerging regions. A total of 9,890 micro-entrepreneurs and youth have participated in the HP Entrepreneurship Learning Program (HELP), since it was launched in 2007 to support the growth of small businesses across the Asia Pacific region. The program now includes 48 centers in ten countries, each targeting microenterprises and unemployed youth in their local communities.

*In 2009, HP made 24 HELP grants with a combined value of approximately $1.55 million and expanded the reach and curriculum of HELP in China, India, Indonesia, Korea and Thailand. In 2011 **HP** is investing more than $4 million for Entrepreneurs (HP LIFE).*

Source: Information received from "hp-Hewlett-Packard".

business, he is not aware of the needs of that business and he does not get proper help for that. He continuously works with the incomplete knowledge of the business and finds many hurdles to run the business. When his issues remain unsolved he tries to solve those issues on his level when he does not get proper help. The new entrepreneurs because of lack of knowledge and source of information, they do not get proper assistance for their business. As a new entrepreneur you can get information from entrepreneurial web sites, books or magazines. If the new entrepreneurs do not have any advisor then they can at least refer to the said sources of information. But it is a fact that without proper advisor, opening and running business is very hard.

12.2 Improper Information of Knowledge Source

Many people may enjoy the notion of starting their own business because of the lure of generating immediate profits for their innovative inventions and ideas. However, it takes more than just having an idea of a establishing a startup that will lead to a company's success. There is a considerable amount of planning that needs to take place prior to the launch of a company in addition to personal and financial dedication. If he has proper or profitable idea he does not know how to turn that idea into the business and earn the profit.

12.3 Improper Business Information

Many entrepreneurs try to do that business which they seem is very lucrative. When they see that other entrepreneurs are earning profits from that business then they suddenly jump into that business. But when they try to do that business then they face many problems because they do not have proper knowledge of that business and after spending so much time and money they cannot also return back from that position. A new entrepreneur always has a shortage of the business knowledge. Whatever he knows is the overview of that business but the details he does not know or if he tries to find out that information he may or may not find that information that leads him to the wrong direction. So if you want to become an entrepreneur then you must first get the knowledge of the business and after that only you should start the business. The best way is to do a job or work under experienced one and then try to open the business.

12.4 Start Business with Partial Knowledge from Relatives or Friends

When the entrepreneurs start business they seek information from the relatives or friends who have their business. Knowing the business and running the business are two different things. The new entrepreneurs think that they know everything about the business and therefore they can run business and they start the business but when they actually put themselves into the real situation of the business they face many hidden challenges of the business. They try to get the information about the business but they do not get the relevant source of the information. When they continue with their understandings they may fail in their business. The important thing is that they do not find any advisor for their business. If you want to open your business then take sufficient time to collect information and once you have sufficient information then you should start your business.

12.5 Improving a New Business Idea

Entrepreneurs are always excited about their new business ideas. However, they should conduct thorough market research and testing to initially examine that their products or services are indeed viable. Research can be completed in numerous ways, including the solicitation of opinions from family, friends, business partners and even potential customers. Research tells them about the market condition. These facts help the entrepreneurs a lot. Feasibility studies can also be conducted to have a stronger sense of the direction of products and to investigate/be aware of any existing competitors. Because new entrepreneurs after opening the business realize that this business are not beneficial for them but from that point they cannot move back because they have already invested so much money in the business. This collective information is vital prior to starting a new business since there is always the risk of a new company failing.

12.6 The Importance of Market Research and Testing

For every successful business idea, there are hundreds that fail. One of the reasons why most business ideas are not successful is because they were introduced to the public without support of sufficient market research. "All are doing the business and that's why we should also do the business" this attitude is wrong. For their business they should have concrete reasons. Therefore, these business ideas did not meet a market demand. Before seeking startup capital for a new business, entrepreneurs should ensure that their business ideas are tested sufficiently before they are formally introduced to the public. Market research and testing during the initial stages of a product's life will determine if a product or service is viable. It will also aid entrepreneurs in identifying the different ways in which they can refine their current business ideas.

12.7 Big Businesses vs. Small Businesses

Unlike giant corporations that invest enormous amounts of money to test potential products, small business owners need to rely on their own knowledge and skills for testing any prospective business ideas. They do not have sufficient money to invest on testing the products. Often times, large corporations are later-stage, high-market capital companies who have already established financial success and can afford to continually test market their products. Small businesses, on the other hand, are an extremely risky venture since most new companies have not established a solid pattern of success. When new business owners introduce a new product into the market without ample preparation (market research and testing), they are risking possible company failure, especially if their product sales remain stagnant. You should at least do a small market research if complete market research is not possible to get new facts about the market. Entrepreneurs are encouraged to be resourceful in market testing, become familiar with the basics of market research and targeted marketing, as well as identify any existing or potential competitors.

12.8 Seek Opinions from Family, Friends and Business Partners

Small business owners can enlist the assistance of their family members and friends in evaluating their new business ideas. Families, friends and business associates can certainly help in detecting any potential problems in the product or service being offered. They can even propose suggestions on improving any current business ideas. In addition, they might be able to convey what they feel will be the most effective marketing strategy for the products.

12.9 Ask Potential Customers

New business owners should also present their current business ideas or prototype to potential buyers and request their opinions. By developing a prototype of their existing concepts, the entrepreneur can easily demonstrate a new product to a prospective buyer. But the entrepreneurs never do that when they have an idea they try to start the business. The new and small entrepreneurs do not have a tendency of asking the customers what they want from the business. They think that they will do the business without checking the viability of the idea but when they start the business they face the results. If the result is positive then they are happy but if the result is negative then they can never do anything but to suffer. The new entrepreneurs do not have a tendency to check the idea before implementing it; they never go to the customers and form a report about their business. Sometimes even they don't have any idea that they have to do this. During this prototype phase, potential customers will be able to provide valuable feedback about the new products and can even offer suggestions about how much they would be willing to pay. As with family and friends, these potential buyers can assist entrepreneurs in fine-tuning their business ideas and concepts more effectively. The entrepreneur can also develop financial projections about their products based on the success of this informal market testing.

12.10 Feasibility Studies

Once the initial results of market testing look positive, entrepreneurs need to employ a feasibility study of their prospective ideas/products. This type of study can help determine how feasible their business ideas are and if there is a need for their products in the marketplace. Most business owners prefer to undertake a feasibility study as part of their own due diligence in researching the industry and determining the capability of their products. For the new entrepreneurs who are opening the business first time for them it becomes necessary to conduct feasibility study. They can find most of the valuable information which will benefit the business. It can also serve as a formal document that will help recruit potential partners, investors or lenders. Feasibility studies essentially address the core of the business idea. It examines the customer's thoughts about the unique features of the new product and how the product should be packaged and delivered. How you are going to handle your business? Whether business is possible for you or not? Feasibility studies also examine the potential target for the business ideas, the size of the market and the costs required to market the products/services.

12.11 Assess the Competitors

In order to improve a current business idea, entrepreneurs should not only be knowledgeable about the market, industry trends and potential consumer base, but should also be aware of their competition. This includes being well-informed about the strengths and weaknesses of any major competitors and, if possible, preventing their previous mistakes. A product should then be introduced to the market once it has been modified to meet consumer needs.

12.12 Not Having a Business Plan

Too many entrepreneurs take the "fly by the seat of my pants" approach to running their business. Nothing could be more dangerous. If you want to be successful, you need to have a plan. Your business plan should include all the details about your business: what you do, who your target audience is, your goals, how you're going to reach your goals, your finances and more. You can find plenty of great books on writing effective business plans or you could enlist the services of an expert.

And remember, a business plan isn't just something you stuff away in a filing cabinet. It's something that should dictate everything you do on behalf of your business.

12.13 Not Knowing when it's Time to Get Help

Sure, there are many tasks you'll be able to handle yourself, but if you want to experience long-term success as an entrepreneur, you need to get help. Do not be in the ego that you do not need help. This is especially true when it comes to all the legal matters surrounding your business. Don't try to go it alone here. Take someone who can better do the work than you. Seek professional help or else the future of your business could be compromised.

As far as the actual tasks of running the business on a day to day basis, if you're constantly swamped, it's probably time to consider hiring an employee. I know it can be hard to give up control of your "baby", but if you get quality help, you can focus on things that will actually help your business grow.

12.14 Hiring the Wrong People

The new entrepreneurs do two mistakes related to the hiring people. First mistake is they do not take hiring of the people seriously. They think opening business is very important and they completely focus on that but at the time of hiring people they take any one who is ready to work in less payment. This hampers the performance of the business. The second mistake is some entrepreneurs intentionally hire any people because they are not ready to pay much to the labours. As a general rule, it's typically best not to mix friends, relatives with business. Too many entrepreneurs hire their friends rather than the person who's most qualified for the position. This often leads to serious complications down the road, jeopardizing the business and the friendship.

Are you an entrepreneur? What are some of the biggest mistakes you've made? Share your experiences and you just might help a fellow reader avoid making the same mistakes.

12.15 Fundamentals of Building a Successful Business

With over 50 per cent of all new businesses failing, there's got to be a better way. Building a successful business is certainly difficult. It's fraught with problems over sales, capitalization and poor management.

The entrepreneurs start the business with no intention of problem solving

The new small entrepreneurs have one problem they start the business but they do not know why they have started the business. What is the purpose of that business? Which section of the customer will be benefited from that? What should be the direction of the business? Unless and until they know about these things they will work at random. Their business will not have any direction and if there is no direction in terms of customers, purpose then they become static or sometimes fail. The one key to all of them was that you should identify a significant problem in each of these markets and then go about to solve that problem using a combination of market research and creativity.

Lack of multi skills

The new entrepreneurs lack multi skills. They may be very much expertise in one part of the business but regarding the other part of the business they lack knowledge. They do not fulfill the requirement of the other parts of the business. So for a new entrepreneurs it is necessary that they should have knowledge about maximum areas of their business otherwise they are not able to mold the situation according to their desire. While there is never a rule about anything, there are certainly people who are better at being entrepreneurs. All the entrepreneurs must have the ability to do a number of things at one time well. Successful entrepreneurs frequently are not experts in any one thing, but they are capable of being the chief, chef and bottle washer all in one. Interestingly, they frequently are not the ones who got the A's in all their classes, but as a rule, they're the most creative ones.

Underestimation of the importance of emotions plays in building a successful business

There are many studies and research on this end, certainly. But entrepreneurs don't always understand how to deal with these things. People simply do not understand that psychology is more important than financial analysis and accounting in building a successful new business. Internally you should be strong. If the entrepreneurs are psychologically confident enough about their business then only they can move to the other areas of the business. Building and running a successful business requires both business acumen and an in depth understanding of what drives customers, employees and themselves. If only entrepreneurs are competent enough they cannot run the business unless they take care about their employees, customers etc., they should have knowledge about these things but the new small entrepreneurs are not aware about these things they think that if they are confident enough then they will run the business. But business requires the bond between employees, management and customers. It's about the right combination of forces working together. With employees, for instance, there's often this "us vs. them" mentality. But your company is only as good as your weakest link and less successful entrepreneurs don't understand the importance emotions play in every part of a successful business.

Small consideration of metrics, search and understanding of the consumer

Most successful entrepreneurs get to a point where they feel comfortable enough with the information they have that they are able to make a decision. That's usually all it takes. Because big companies usually take two to three times as long, at a minimum, to make the same decision a small business can, the small venture can start their business and make their first sales before even the big business competitor has made up its' mind to go into the market or not. You certainly have to do the homework though, especially as it relates to generating sales. Contrary to common belief, the number one reason most new businesses fail isn't because they ran out of money, it's because they were unable to generate the sales numbers they projected. They are not able to take proper decisions because they lack understanding of the business and customers. You have to figure out how to pare down the information to understand what really drives your customers and the market. Your business is for customers only. Give time to understand the customers. After all, it's the doing that makes the money. It amazes how many entrepreneurs lose track of this. Making things happen is the name of the game for new businesses. That's why successful entrepreneurs are doers.

There often ego involved for the businesses that fail

When the entrepreneur falls in love with their own product and their customers simply don't. You have to understand why people buy. First time entrepreneurs who have failed blame their customers for their failure. "They just didn't get it. They think that their product is best but they do not think if they will not consider the problems that exist in the product they will fail. The products or services are not for you but for customers only. The new entrepreneurs should not have any ego problem. They are in the market to sell their products to the customers and they should think in terms of the customers only. The new entrepreneurs do not try to find out the mistakes, they do not find the real reason behind the mistake and this becomes hurdle for their business. Sure, some of its ego, but most of it is due to not knowing better in the first place.

Unaware about small business problems

The new entrepreneurs are not aware about the small problems of the business. They do not take the small problems seriously. They think that if they will not solve the small problems then nothing will be lost. They try to keep their focus on the big problems. But they forget that their business also suffers from the small problems and if they will not solve the problems initially then the problems will become big. They should know that there are ways to do things and there are ways in business to make things work better. It seems so simple, but people start the business and then they simply don't understand why things aren't selling. That's where having an entrepreneur who can move in a number of directions is valuable.

The entrepreneurs should focus on the concepts like priority and value. For example, one of the most important things that is that new businesses are much more likely to be successful with a mediocre product that satisfies a high priority market need than they would be with a top of the line product that only satisfies a mediocre market priority. It's hard enough to sell to customers. A high priority solution is vital to making this as easy as possible. Also, value is the relationship between a product's benefits and its price to customers. Usually when there is a high priority need for a product, there is a lot of competition. The way you beat competition out is through value—if your customer perceives your product delivers more value than your competitors do for them, they will buy it and if not they won't. If they buy, you're on your way and if they don't, it's closing time and lights out.

12.16 To Start a New Business is Easy

Most of the entrepreneurs have a very brilliant business idea to start a new business. The only problem is that most of us, when we have such enlightenment, do not act on this impulse immediately. You should act immediately to implement your idea.

An exceptional business idea can be universal. Often times, many people from around the world and from every walk of life may share similar ideas for starting a new business. They keep the idea and never do anything about that. They just think on it. Among the hundreds and even thousands of people with the same innovative business ideas, only a few will actually be proactive in their approach. They try to implement it. They try to make it real. They do R & D for it. They collect information about it. They take all efforts to encash that idea and most of them even become successful. They are the ones who will take the first step in bringing their thoughts and concepts to the forefront, trying extensively to make their business ideas into a reality.

For those entrepreneurs who have great business ideas but are not sure about how or where to start, there are several resourceful avenues to resort to:

Internet

The internet can be an effective means in which an individual can find information on starting their own business. Many informational sites, blogs and forums regarding startups and marketing one's invention are readily available by just the click of a mouse. By simply typing an inquiry in any browser, the prospective entrepreneur can be given endless facts and opportunities to start their own business.

Entrepreneurs can advertise their business ideas and capital requirements for prospective investors. Likewise, investors can browse through profiles and easily develop potential leads for investments. Entrepreneurs can have access to published articles that can serve as educational tools during the startup process and both parties can correspond with each other for information, support and probable business endeavors.

Books theory and companies' cases

There are plenty of books that can easily explain the basics of startups and how to market one's ideas. Such information can be made available at the local library or bookstore. Specific sections on startups, early-stage investing, advertising and market research are easy to locate since they are organized according to section. Often times, books serve as a valuable resource since many of them have been written by people who are successful entrepreneurs and experienced investors.

College courses

Another way in which one can learn more about the process of launching a new business is through the help of local colleges. Today colleges are more focusing on entrepreneurship. Government and non government institutes are opened to give practical knowledge and training on entrepreneurship. They are also giving all possible support to the new one for opening the business. Government entrepreneurship development institutes are implementing all the government schemes for promoting entrepreneurship in India. Involvement in such instruction and gatherings serve as an excellent means to learn about the startup process and allows the entrepreneur to network with others, gain potential leads and find ways of funding.

Evaluate your ideas

Evaluating new business ideas is an essential skill for any would-be entrepreneur. If you're going to put everything at risk and pour your heart and soul into a new business initiative, the idea had better be a good one. Good entrepreneurs constantly evaluate business ideas. Think about a local store near your home. How much do you think they make? What would you estimate their revenues to be? What are their expenses? Are they filling a market need? Will they make it or will they go out of business?

By constantly making such business evaluations you can hone your skills at differentiating a good business idea from bad business ideas. It's also a great idea to read business publications that walk you through success stories and failure stories. You can learn a lot by reading about other entrepreneurs. When you've got your own idea that you want to evaluate, you'll be in a good position to see if it's viable.

Business plan objectives

If you fail to plan, you are essentially planning to fail. And yet, so many entrepreneurs fail to create a business and marketing plan for their businesses. A business plan can help you see the bigger picture and get organized, as well as. You may have an idea of your company's goals in your head, but if you put them down on paper, it goes a long way towards making them happen. By sharing your business plan with your employees, you make them feel like part of the company's operations. You give them an understanding of what the business' goals and objectives are and they can help achieve them.

Without business goals, entrepreneurs will find difficulty in keeping their business on the right track. In addition, when moving forward with their brilliant business ideas, entrepreneurs must spend some time to devise a series of individual tasks that help achieve the milestones. Such initiatives can be made for themselves, their business partners and employees, which help promote a positive, efficient work environment.

Sources of capital

Finding sources of capital is very important when you want to open a new business. This is extremely important for the launch and development of a startup. You can get finance from your family and friends easily but you need to find out the other sources of capital such as venture capitalists, banks and angel investors are obvious choices to consider. Central government is helping the new entrepreneurs by providing loan on low interest rate, subsidy and taking the loan guarantee of the new entrepreneurs. Once you secure funding for your new business, then you have to focus on hiring employees, purchasing assets, developing infrastructure and many more that are required to start a business. Finding the perfect location for the enterprise may also pose another challenge as well as purchasing any necessary equipment and technologies for the new business.

12.17 Setting-up to Start an Entrepreneur Business

Before applying for small business funding, it is important for an entrepreneur to clarify all the details about the type of business they are starting and what their needs will be. Careful consideration about different scenarios is necessary for an aspiring mogul to start their business the right way. It is always better to be knowledgeable and well-prepared for your new venture rather than be in a situation that is unfamiliar.

The first factor that an entrepreneur must consider is the product or service that they will be offering because the same may be offered by someone else. This may sound obvious to many; however, many people tend to neglect providing others with a clear definition of what their business truly entails. This is the problem because unless others will not have the clear idea about the business then they will avoid your business. As a new business owner, it is important to determine how your product(s) and/or service(s) will be different from what the competitors offer. The differentiation should be such that the others should remember your company or that uniqueness. In addition, since most new businesses will not generate any profit for at least one year, entrepreneurs must be able to envision the amount of money they need for that given period of time in order to get the right type of startup funding. Fund is the blood of the business. The entrepreneurs should plan the finance in such a way so that in slowdown also their business should survive. Starting a new business requires ample planning and research about the specific industry, including how other businesses have been successful in that particular market.

A new entrepreneur with a great business idea should learn how other businesses have fared during different seasons of the year and understand how the economy plays an influential role in a company's success. In addition, some products or services are more successful in certain geographical regions than others, especially in regards to climate differences. The most important thing to remember before starting a small business and applying for the proper funding is being well-prepared. After all, individuals who plan well tend to be the most successful individuals.

12.18 Discovering the New Idea

Is there a market for idea?

There are certain criterias you can use to establish whether there is a market or demand for your product or service:

- Does it satisfy or create a market need?
- Can you identify potential customers?
- Will it outlive passing trends or capitalize on the trend before it dies away?
- Is it unique, distinct or superior to those offered by competitors?
- What competition will it face - direct or indirect, local, national or global?
- Is the product safe for public use and does it comply with relevant regulations and legislation? Seek legal advice before proceeding.
- Will the market want your product or service at a realistic price?

Sharing your ideas with others

At some stage you will probably wish to discuss your idea with a third party. This could be informally, such as seeking advice or encouragement from friends or family or formally, by hiring a professional consultant, talking to your solicitor or accountant or forming a partnership or joint venture with another company. Remember, once you put an idea into the public domain it can no longer be considered confidential or a trade secret. You should therefore take steps to protect your intellectual property. Before talking to third parties, it is a good idea to ask them to sign a non-disclosure agreement to prevent them from sharing the details of your confidential discussion with others

So What Could Be the Solution?

12.19 Various Sources of Business Knowledge

Whatever the size of your business, there are many sources of business knowledge, including the following.

Customer knowledge

You should know your customers' needs and what they think of your business and you. Customers are the best source to share knowledge with you. They can tell you about their present and future requirements. Developing knowledge-sharing relationships with customers will be beneficial for your business that will ultimately give you an idea about how to develop products and services exactly the customers want.

Employee and supplier relationships

As employees are deeply interrelated with the business, they are in better position to explain what are the things going wrong? Ask about their opinions, they'll have their own impressions of how you're performing. You can use formal surveys to gather this knowledge or ask for their views on a more informal basis.

Market knowledge

Analyze market trends. How are your competitors performing? How much are they charging? How creatively they are serving their customers? Are there any new entrants to the market? Have any significant new products been launched?

Knowledge of the business environment

Developments in politics, the economy, technology, society and the environment could all affect your business' development, so you must have all the above information. You could consider setting up a team to monitor and report on changes in the business world.

Professional associations and trade bodies

Get information from publications, academic publications, government publications, reports from research bodies, trade and technical magazines.

Trade exhibitions and conferences

These are the good ways to know about the strategies of your competitors. You can find out what are your competitors doings? What are the new innovations they have done to dominate the other businesses in the market?

Product research and development

R & D, scientist and technical research and development can be a vital source of knowledge that can help you create innovative new products - retaining your competitive edge.

Articles

An entrepreneur can access articles, for example, that discuss legal issues, managing a business office, writing a business plan, online business, buying a business, selling a business, raising capital for your business, marketing, public relations, customer services, sales, leadership, human resource issues and training.

Experience

This is another important resource for the seeker of knowledge. It is said that experience is a great teacher, so learn from your past experiences and the experience of others. Learn from your and others' past and present achievements as well as mistakes.

Your circle of influence

This is where building a network of alliance partners or circle of influence is so critical. It is not just for referrals between yourselves... those closest to you and those you trust, admire and interact with can give you feedback and they can be your ears beyond your own. Once you've established strong relationships with others you know and trust, your business can grow ten-fold.

Collaboration between businesses and associated institutions

Groups of businesses or associated institutions with common interests - known as clusters - sometimes join forces in order to share knowledge at an inter-organizational level.

12.20 Mentorship and Entrepreneurs' Success

What is entrepreneurial mentoring?

Entrepreneurial mentoring involves one entrepreneur acting as 'critical friend' or 'guide' helping to oversee the career and development of a less-experienced entrepreneur (Harrington 1999).The relationship is between entrepreneurs from different businesses and can be characterized as a 'mentor-protégé' relationship. However, within entrepreneurial mentoring, the relationship between mentor and mentee is often one of equals. Each party brings different perspectives and knowledge and in many cases mentees will establish the goals of the relationship. Entrepreneurial mentoring can be viewed as a business development process for owner-managers (Gold et al2003). This is based on the premise that there is a direct link between entrepreneurs' actions and capabilities and the performance of their businesses.

Today's motivation for young entrepreneurs is being fueled through a variety of mentor-based programs that work to assist in the development of great ideas while pointing out potholes to avoid. Organizations like Entrepreneurs Development Institute (EDI) are working to foster growth in young entrepreneurs with a sizeable dream. The organization further encourages philanthropy as part of the goodwill associated with establishing the vision.

Make no mistake, becoming an entrepreneur is as grueling as any class you've ever attended which is why it makes sense to link with an entrepreneurial group or message board that will allow you to ask questions and learn from the collective wisdom of those you are in contact with.

"Mentor: Someone whose hindsight can become your foresight". Experience can come in two flavors. The first is through personal failures and the wisdom gained from those very personal events. The second is by expressing a willingness to learn from the mistakes of others. When developing a business it is in your best interest to seek out someone who's been on the road you are traveling and see what you can learn from him or her.

Some may have had the rare privilege of having a mentor who helped shape them into the human being they are today, but many are still looking for someone to interact with that can assist them in both personal and professional growth. Interestingly, many who could be mentors typically do not see themselves as such. These individuals can pinpoint mistakes they have made in their lives and come away with the decision that they are not qualified to be a mentor.

Whether in business or life one of the most valuable assets you will ever have is a friend who will stand with you in all circumstances. A mentor is in many ways an advocate as well as a voice of reason. They aren't parents and they shouldn't be drill sergeants. In business and in life, a mentor is a goldmine and should be sought enthusiastically and with great care.

12.21 Starting a Successful Home-based Business

Get a head start and save a lot time in building your internet home-based business by learning from the experience of others and understanding the basics that are often overlooked.

Home-Based Business Re-examine

With the increasing popularity of internet, anyone with a computer and internet connection can work from home. It does not require much knowledge of the technology. Many people are doing online home-based business part time so that they can earn some additional money to fulfill their personal needs. Many have devoted all their time to this business as they are getting profit from this business. The people are not having detailed knowledge and they are not professional businessmen. They are all 'new' with only one thing in their minds, to generate passive or residual income. They have not been exposed to the pitfalls that they might encounter during the early period of their home business start-up. How they overcome the challenges that come in many forms and situations during the early period of their business venture will eventually define the path for a successful home-based business.

Home-Based Business Challenges

There are number of challenges in online home-based business. Like any other businesses the first time business owners will also face problems during the initial period. They will be in their learning stage. Learning may happen in few days or it may take years. But one cannot wait for long years to learn. At least in this competitive market if you take long time to learn then it will be your disadvantage. So the idea is to master your own learning curve. If the learning curve will be shorter then you will learn fast and that will help you for fast development of business. Getting knowledge from the experienced one is the best way to learn more in short time. You can take the help of professionals, businessmen, trade magazines or consultancies. Learning curve signifies an important period to get your home-based business up and running. Mistakes, errors, slow progress, impatience and miscommunication can lead to frustrations. One needs to stay focus on the objective(s) of setting up home business to counter all the negatives and look to the future.

Continuing Your Personal Development

Live Life Your Way

Living the life you want to live the way you want to live it is the best part of being a business owner. It is what makes the idea of entrepreneurship so attractive to so many people, especially in the public relations industry. It allows the PR types to express their creativity and make time for the events and people that enticed them to work in the field in the first place. Being self-employed allows you to make your own schedule, operate your company the way you see fit, work with clients you choose to work with and create your own personal working environment. There is no need to request time off for vacations. And speaking of vacations, these are things you can do at your leisure since you can work from virtually anywhere in the world thanks to inexpensive advancements in global technology such as world smart phones and Skype. By living your life at your own pace and by your own schedule, you are essentially the captain of your own ship.

Develop Your Network

Networking brings exposure. It is one of the best methods to expose yourself to the business community and also to spread the world about your brand without being termed as an over-zealous marketer. Lots of businesses strive on relationship. To build fruitful relations, it is important for the entrepreneurs to be good in inter-personal skills. Networking allows to hone these skills and to bring them in effect. Networking allows the entrepreneurs to get better understanding of the market as well as the competition. In fact, entrepreneurs must know their competitors so that they can distinguish themselves to steer ahead in the market shares. While it is possible to meet the competitors, it is also possible that entrepreneurs would meet like-minded people who would like to collaborate or do business together at some point of time. It is of course one of the most intended objective of networking events. As you grow in your network, your expertise in executing your business also gets polished.

Creating a Think Tank for Your Business

As a business professional you will always need updated business knowledge to get business success. You must be aware about the current trends, market conditions, customers' taste, competitors' strategies and technology changes to become competitive. The knowledge you lack is always someone else's specialty, so you can turn to others for help. You must always have people who can help you in your trouble. You should find out professionals and make contact with them so that in emergency you can call them. When you've identified your most important contacts, start connecting with these people to enhance and improve your knowledge network. As you do this, your network and the information you need to build your business will expand and grow.

Undertake a Personal Learning Program

What do you have to do to enjoy the long-term benefits of a personal learning program? Subscribe to business magazines and e-mail newsletters and read them consistently. If you have a Palm or Pocket PC, use e-book software to read business articles and e-books. Commit yourself to reading (or listening to) at least one or two business books each month. Register for seminars and short classes that teach hands-on skills such as marketing, sales, accounting, legal issues, etc., the more you know about each such subject, the better you'll be at supervising people who do those tasks for you.

Never Stop Learning

A common mistake for many entrepreneurs is that they "just don't have time" to work on the things that will make them better at what they do. They get caught up in the daily operations of their business and can't see past that. You must be ready to stay high in the learning mode. Keep reading books about entrepreneurship, attend seminars and listen to broadcast by successful entrepreneurs. Without learning you can never get anywhere. To be a great entrepreneur, you just have to keep on learning. Learning never stops. If you should put a stop to your learning, you've set a limit for your success.

There are great books written by people who have climbed the mountain you are trying to climb. Read about how they manage to make it through and how you can too. Remember that learning is not always the guaranty of success. But by reading books, attending seminars and all that, you will get to know how you can manage possible risk. Every entrepreneur must be ready to take risk so if you are avoiding it, then you will never win in a big way.

12.22 Requirements of Starting a New Business

Many people may enjoy the notion of starting their own business because of the lure of generating immediate profits for their innovative inventions and ideas. However, it takes more than just having an idea of establishing a startup that will lead to a company's success. There is a considerable amount of planning that needs to take place prior to the launch of a company in addition to personal and financial dedication. Despite the fact that the majority of startups will eventually fail in their first year, many of these failures can be prevented if entrepreneurs' simply took the needed time to properly assess if they have what it takes to run their own company.

Ask People

Before starting a small business you should ask people who you know and trust if they think you are qualified to run a small business and why they think the way they do. This will help you get a better handle on things you need to improve on before you jump in with both feet. Starting a small business is a pretty big risk so before you jump in you should ask yourself if you are ready for the risk. Starting a small business will be risking your time, reputation and most likely your hard earned money.

Have a plan

You may think creating a business plan is a waste of time, but this is a big mistake. A business plan maps out, on paper, your goals and how you expect to reach them. It also forces you to think about everything the business will entail and devise solutions ahead of time. Plus, down the road if things feel overwhelming, you can revert back to your business plan to help guide you.

Business experience

The idea of starting a business may seem very attractive but without familiarity and in-depth knowledge of the business entrepreneurs may find themselves helpless. They will start the business with full enthusiasm but when the complexity of the business will increase they may find it difficult to handle the situation. Number of business are flourishing in the market and continuously giving tough competition to each other. In this competitive market running a business without any experience is very dangerous. Lack of experience does not necessarily mean that entrepreneurs should not start a business; however, they should wait until they have developed considerable knowledge in the field. They can accomplish this by talking to other business owners within the same industry who can give practical advice about startup costs, revenue projections, expertise in running a company and other additional company expenses. A prospective entrepreneur should also conduct independent research regarding competitors as well as find out which sort of businesses are needed within their community.

Sincerity and clarity of vision

It is always better for an entrepreneur to start a business with sincerity and clarity of vision. Any new business venture has its underlying uncertainties and speculations. Ever-changing consumer demands make it formidable, if not impossible to adhere to a profitable business strategy.

Determination

You need passion, a fire in your belly, a determination to succeed because you won't get every contract, not every person will want to hire you- and really you don't want them anyway. Not every human being breathing is a good customer for you services. Being an entrepreneur can sometimes be discouraging, so you need to be determined to succeed.

Risky business

Many entrepreneurs will agree that starting a small business is a risky endeavor. If a company is not successful as anticipated, there may be a strong possibility that business owners may have to resort to closing or bankruptcy and lose much of their invested wealth. The first few years of a company is considered to be a very crucial time for entrepreneurs since their startup's fate is unexpected. It is important that an individual evaluate the different risks involved when considering entrepreneurship. If they do not feel comfortable with taking these risks, then perhaps they may need to reconsider whether starting a small enterprise is suitable for them.

Be ready to be the boss

Some business owners may have the misconception that once they launch their businesses, they will be able to finally have more available free time and can live a comfortable, stress-free lifestyle; however, this is not completely true. Becoming your own boss includes an undeniable amount of stress, work and sacrifice. Many business owners may not be ready to face the daily business challenges, difficulties and stress. They may be less motivated or lack willingness to manage their employees, deal with customers, competitors or to make the business more creative. Forthcoming entrepreneurs should encourage themselves to actively participate in entrepreneurship programmes and develop their skills of management to become completely capable of being their own boss and running a company.

Family support

Starting a small enterprise and managing family life are considered to be both demanding, full-time responsibilities. You can and must make time for both family and business. It is important to build a strong family life: It helps to give you a better perspective and balance in business.

Moreover, a key responsibility for each generation is to bring up the next generation — and you need to be present to do this. It is a proven fact that entrepreneurship can be mentally, physically and financially draining. Family members should offer their loved ones understanding, mental and emotional support, especially during the preliminary years of the company launch.

Expect to work

It's common for business owners to work long hours ... much longer than when they were employed. The upside is that all of your hard work is for your own business, not someone else's. However, be prepared to burn the midnight oil if you want your business to get off the ground (especially if you're still working full-time in the meantime).

Once an entrepreneur has evaluated they have what it takes to start a company, they can now follow a few steps to launch a successful business.

1. Visualization and research of product, service and market

The primary step of the successful entrepreneurs is to make the quality products and services and according to the needs of the paid customers. Prospective entrepreneurs must think on which type of business they want to open or which type of business they can run. Entrepreneurs should open such a business where they have vast experience and enough knowledge because that will help them to formulate attractive products or services for customers. Designing such products or services involves extensive research of competitors' strategies and customers' needs in the market. Once the products/services are determined, a product prospectus should be written, documenting how each of the products/services are prepared, used and its competitive edge.

2. Preparation of a marketing strategy and well-written business plan

Once entrepreneurs are over with their target customers and the products and services they are now ready to market their goods and ideas. This involves taking assistance of the paid marketing professionals or market experts for formulating a market strategy for the promotion of products or services. Demo presentation of products / services gives clear idea to the customers. A detailed business plan is also needed for any business, regardless of the size of the company, which documents the company's objectives, their goods/services offered, startup costs and the targeted market and customers. Each business has its own business plan and therefore differs accordingly. MSME, EDI or other entrepreneurial development institutes in India provide assistance in creating a business plan.

3. Seeking professional assistance

There are number of private and government institutes in India that provide assistance in starting a business. For example MSME gives training to the prospective entrepreneurs in their interested area and also helps in starting their own business. The importance of accountants cannot be ignored as finance has a major role to play in business. Lawyers will help regarding legal issues, rules and regulation in business. Many of these professionals can also critique proposed business plans and assist in determining which legal form is most suitable for their company (i.e., partnership, proprietorship, corporation, etc.,).

4. Sources of capital

The final step in starting a business entails obtaining the necessary funding to sustain a company's survival. Some sources include the use of personal savings, angel and venture capitalist financing, borrowed money from business associates, private loans and family and friends. The process of obtaining funding may be time consuming and frustrating; however, it is important to stay motivated until the desired capital is raised.

While many people want to have their own business but some do not get the right path and information to start and sustain the business. Most small enterprise failures can easily be avoided if business owners would simply be aware of the challenges that lie ahead and evaluate within themselves if they are fully prepared to start their own business. Once they are able to determine that they are capable, they can then take the necessary steps needed for startup success.

12.23 e-COMMERCE BUSINESS STRATEGY FOR NEW BUSINESS

e-business strategy characteristics

e-business strategies share much in common with corporate, business and marketing strategies.

These typical quotes summarizing the essence of strategy could equally apply to each, strategy:

- "Is based on current performance in marketplace"
- "Defines how we will meet our objectives"
- "Sets allocation of resources to meet goals"
- "Selects preferred strategic options to compete within a market"
- "Provides a long-term plan for the development of the organisation"

Deciding if e-commerce is right for your business

An entrepreneur must evaluate whether an e-commerce is really beneficial for growing their business and increasing sales of products. e-commerce implementation requires thorough planning, expert people suggestions and assessment of internal as well as external factors of your business. It is not a one day task. For instance, not all products and services can be sold over the internet (i.e., automobile sales) and may require an in-person evaluation for that product's sale. In addition, business owners should take into consideration the different domestic and international shipping costs, especially if they are seeking more than just local recognition. Once an entrepreneur gets the required full information for implementing e-commerce and knows exactly the pros and cons of the implementation then they should plan to design and publicize their company's products and services via a company website.

A professional website for your company

Every business owner who is considering an e-commerce strategy for their company should know the basic principles of electronic buying and selling. They should also be aware of how e-commerce functions before establishing an online business. Help of paid experts can be taken to design the company's website. They know the exact requirements of any website they can design an attractive website with all necessary features i.e., marketing tools to successfully target customers and generate profit. A professional website can yield the necessary traffic flow to the new business while improving the recognition and credibility of the company with its current and potential customers.

The importance of e-commerce

Business executives are getting more and more into the e-commerce website these days. If your website is an e-commerce website, your business store can soon turn into a worldwide web store. There are many advantages of having an e-commerce website such as your customers are just a click away from your product and on top of that your store would remain open for 24×7 for the potential customers. Your prospective clientage extends to different countries worldwide. Anybody can order your product or services just sitting in front of their computer. So it is apparent that an e-commerce website increases your revenue and business considerably.

e-commerce is the cheapest means of doing business, Ready-to-use information about any product or service. e-commerce development has made it possible to reduce the cost of marketing and promotions. It reduces delivery time, labour cost and is surely viable in all its possible ways. On-time alerts for the convenience of the consumers informing about new products. Last but not the least; with the development of e-commerce, it has been possible to save time of both the vendor and the consumer.

e-commerce and customer service

As with every traditional business endeavor, online businesses need to aggressively market the products and services on their website. This often entails offering free gifts or services upon the purchase of products, providing numerous bargains, as well as finding other novel, resourceful ways in generating traffic to their company web page. One way business owners can accomplish this is not only by ensuring their website and services offered surpasses their competitor's, but by making sure their online business has a competent team of customer service support. In fact, customer service is a more vital tool for an e-commerce business rather than the traditional business establishment. Through friendly and skilled customer service support, companies can make the consumer shopping experience hassle-free, address customer inquiries and establish a strong rapport with current and potential customers.

12.24 Searching the Right Business Coach

An entrepreneur can benefit from the wisdom and insights of an experienced business coach. Finding this unique individual is easier than you may think.

Define what do you need help with?

If you need a business coach then you must be very clear what exactly you want from your business coach. You must specify your needs precisely. A business coach can assist with things as specific as making product demo presentations or as broad as developing a long-term business plan for your business. So determining the areas where you need coach help will be helpful for you to find out the expert business coach.

Consider Crossover Expertise

Your coach must have an experience of your trade. Your trade problems should not be new to him. He must have an impressive past wherein he has actually gone through the problems and has given the solutions that have survived the then business. Expert coach does not take much time to solve the business problem. If you want to add franchises to your carpet cleaning business, for example, a coach with a background in the restaurant industry can guide you through the process of evaluating potential markets and structuring contracts.

Ask About Their Success Rate With Clients.

Again anyone who tells you they can generate AMAZING RESULTS with ANY Business may as well tell you they are SUPERMAN! Ask them for an honest account of their success rate with clients similar to yours and how they truly feel about working with you... If they give you some waffle about how they will try but it's all ultimately up to you with no real guarantees of success, then again show them the door. This is probably just a cover the butt sales tactic to help justify taking your money in return for little in the way of results.

Get an Objective Perspective

Entrepreneurs count on friends and family members for many things, but don't expect honest criticism to be among them. Your business coach should be someone who is fair, reasonable and interested in your success, but also willing to tell the truth, even if it's not what you want to hear.

Coaching experience

The first factor that you should look for while searching for a good business coach would be his coaching experience. Experience of a business coach is one of the key factors that could make or destroy the prospects of your success. An experienced coach would guide you to achieve success and help you to understand the intricacies of the corporate world.

Find a Compatible Comfort Factor

Personalities don't always click. You may discover that an otherwise perfect business coach is difficult to work with or doesn't fully understand your perspective. (For example, many female entrepreneurs prefer working with a coach who is also a woman.) Your coach should be someone who earns your trust and confidence, not intimidates you into following his or her advice.

Coaching process

The coaching process includes the duration and frequency of the coaching sessions. It determines the system along which the coach instructs his students. The approach towards the treatment of a subject plays a very important role in understanding the coaching process. Before you select a coach, you should research on the teaching hours and frequency of the coaching sessions.

Make sure you fit with your coach

Trust your instincts when deciding whether or not the coach truly understands who you are and what you need. You may want:

— A coach whose direct and will act as a constant 'swift kick in the behind.'

— A coach who provides advice and talks about his experiences.

— A coach who listens as you pull the answers from inside yourself.

Ultimately, you will want a coach with whom you have great rapport, who you would trust with certain details of your life as well as your observations, who will not judge you.

Where to Find It?

You can find it in www.businesscoachingindia, www.universalconsulting.com, www.drshaileshthaker.co.in.

12.25 Importance of Right Business Coach

A business coach is like a personal trainer—for your business. A good business coach will help you to realize your dreams, goals and achieve success through careful step by step planning and processes. The business coach is there to help you with resources, support, motivation and planning of your business venture. If you already have a business, the business coach is there to help your business succeed and grow in ways that you could only imagine. You can find a business coach in a number of different ways and in many places. The key is to find the right business coach for you and your company.

There are several things to consider when looking for a business coach.

Whether your business is just you or a Fortune 100 Corporation with hundreds of employees, without a Coach to guide you to completing your goals, you may end up wandering aimlessly on the playing field of life. That may seem a bit dramatic, but winners in sports, in business and in life, quickly realize the benefits that coaching has to offer. The coaching industry is growing at a very rapid pace and business professionals of all types are taking advantage of this benefit at full speed. A personal coach will also keep his team motivated and focused on the task at hand while seamlessly guiding them to win the championship. And you may want to win the "Super Bowl" of your business; and you can! But, it's going to take someone to coach you through each individual play in order to win the first quarter, to win the first half, which will lead to winning each game

The most important factor that will determine the success of business coaching is good communication. Building a good rapport with your business coach is crucially important to establish the effectiveness of business coaching. Hence, recruit a business coach who you feel comfortable working with and discuss your problems.

An efficient business coach should be able to understand you and your personality profile. Once he understands your goals, your aspirations, the way you visualize and comprehend, only then can he plan accordingly. Hence, not only should he take into account the problems of your business, but also evaluate your personality so as to determine the most efficient approach that you can adopt comfortably and without any difficulty.

Coaches tend to be charismatic easy to like people very good at selling – selling themselves. Be sure to go deeper than personality and promises. Does the coach bring real-world grounded values to the challenge at hand? Does he possess the expertise that you need? Is she experienced in technical areas critical to combat your problem? Be sure the coach can support sizzle with substance.

While choosing a coach, start by collecting the list of top candidates and then interview them. While interviewing, do not forget to get the names of past clients and contact them as references. It is better to enquire about your business coach in every way to understand him. And find someone who's good at training and teaching. You don't want someone who will do the work for you, but you want someone who can share his experience and help in developing innovative ideas to give your business impetus.

Many business coaches are quite expensive, but there are some that are extremely cost effective. The important thing to remember when considering the cost of a business coach is the cost of not getting the business coach. Starting a business can be difficult and costly, but starting that same business can be more costly if you are not sure what you are doing. When you have a business that seems to be failing or if your business is simply not going anywhere, you are more likely to lose money by doing nothing than by spending the money on a good business coach.

Summary

The issues related to getting business knowledge are as follows:

Where to look for business issues, Improper information of knowledge source, Improper business information, Start business with partial knowledge from relatives or friends, New business idea without proper research, Lack of market research and testing; Seek opinions from family, friends and business partners; Ask potential customers, Not having a business plan, Not knowing when it's time to get help and Hiring the wrong people.

Issues related to building a successful business

- The entrepreneurs start the business with no intention of problem solving
- Lack of multi skills
- Underestimation of the importance of emotions plays in building a successful business
- Small consideration of metrics, search and understanding of the consumer
- There often ego involved for the businesses that fail
- Unaware about small business problems

For those entrepreneurs who have great business ideas but are not sure about how or where to start, there are several resourceful avenues to resort to: Internet, Books theory and Companies' cases, College courses, Evaluation of ideas, Business plan objectives, and Sources of capital.

Various sources of business knowledge are Customer knowledge, Market knowledge, Employee and Supplier relationships, Knowledge of the business environment, Professional associations and trade bodies, Trade exhibitions and conferences, Product research and development, Articles, Experience, Entrepreneurs circle of influence, and Collaboration between businesses and associated institutions.

Entrepreneurial mentoring

Entrepreneurial mentoring can be viewed as a business development process for owner-managers (Gold et al2003). This is based on the premise that there is a direct link between entrepreneurs' actions and capabilities and the performance of their businesses. Entrepreneurial mentoring involves one entrepreneur acting as 'critical friend' or 'guide' helping to oversee the career and development of a less-experienced entrepreneur (Harrington 1999).The relationship is between entrepreneurs from different businesses and can be characterized as a 'mentor-protégé' relationship. However, within entrepreneurial mentoring, the relationship between mentor and mentee is often one of equals.

Home-Based Business Re-examine

With some knowledge about how things operate in the internet realm, anyone with a computer and internet connection can work from home. Many people who have embarked in the online home-based business are basically taken in by the prospect of meeting their personal needs or seeking for a supplemental income or a full-time income.

Home-Based Business Challenges

Working at home to start an online internet home-based business has its fair number of challenges. Just like any other business ventures, first time home business owners will experience a learning curve during the initial period. The idea is to master your own learning curve. A shorter learning curve will expedite your business building process. One of the best ways is to learn from the experience of others who have been successful before in this business.

Live Life Your Way

Not taking a vacation is not a sign of an indispensable business owner; it's proof of an ineffective leader. It's the mark of an irritable boss with high employee turnover.

Develop your network

It's the accumulation of resources developed through personal and professional networks. These resources include ideas, knowledge, information, opportunities, contacts and, of course, referrals.

Creating a Think Tank for Your Business

As a business professional, entrepreneurs need a constant supply of information to achieve success. Entrepreneurs must stay aware of trends and issues and keep up with rapid economic and technological changes to become competitive.

Undertake a Personal Learning Program

What do you have to do to enjoy the long-term benefits of a personal learning program? Subscribe to business magazines and e-mail newsletters and read them consistently.

Never Stop Learning

A common mistake for many entrepreneurs is that they "just don't have time" to work on the things that will make them better at what they do. They get caught up in the daily operations of their business and can't see past that.

Requirements of starting a new business are Ask People, **Have a plan,** Business experience Sincerity and clarity of vision, Determination, Risky business, Be ready to be the boss, Family support, and **Expect to work.**

Once an entrepreneur has evaluated they have what it takes to start a company, they can now follow a few steps to launch a successful business. Those steps are Visualization and research of product, service and market; Preparation of a marketing strategy and well-written business plan; Seeking professional assistance, and Sources of capital.

e-commerce business strategies for new business are e-commerce and customer service, deciding if e-commerce is right for business, a professional website for company, the importance of e-commerce and e-business strategy characteristics.

Searching the right business coach involves Define what do entrepreneurs need help with? Consider crossover expertise, Ask about their success rate with clients, Get an objective perspective, Coaching experience, Find a compatible comfort factor, Coaching process, Make sure entreprenurs fit with their coach, and Where to Find It?

Importance of Right Business Coach

A business coach is like a personal trainer—for your business. A good business coach will help you to realize your dreams, goals and achieve success through careful step by step planning and processes. The business coach is there to help you with resources, support, motivation and planning of your business venture. If you already have a business, the business coach is there to help your business succeed and grow in ways that you could only imagine. You can find a business coach in a number of different ways and in many places. The key is to find the right business coach for you and your company.

KEYWORDS

Market Research: The process of examining the possible sales of a product and the possible customers for it before it is put on the market.

Market testing: An examination to see if a sample of a product will sell in a market.

Feasibility study: The feasibility study usually recommends selection of a cost-effective alternative.

Business plan: A business plan is a document that summarizes the operational and financial objectives of a business and contains the detailed plans and budgets showing how the objectives are to be realized.

Business knowledge: Business knowledge is a thorough understanding of the general business functions and the specific areas under analysis.

Business environment: The elements or factors outside a business organization which directly affect it, such as the supply of raw materials and product demand.

Entrepreneurial mentoring: Entrepreneurial mentoring involves one entrepreneur acting as 'critical friend' or 'guide' helping to oversee the career and development of a less-experienced entrepreneur.

E-commerce: *e-commerce* (electronic commerce or EC) is the buying and selling of goods and services on the Internet, especially the World Wide Web.

Business coach: A business coach can assist with things as specific as making product demo presentations or as broad as developing a long-term business plan for your business.

QUESTIONS

1. Why small new entrepreneurs lack in business knowledge? Explain.
2. What are the fundamentals of building a successful business?
3. What are the different sources of getting business knowledge?
4. What do you mean by entrepreneurial mentoring?
5. What should be the e-commerce strategy for your business?
6. How to get a right business coach?

❑ ❑ ❑

CHAPTER – 13

BUSINESS PLAN

LEARNING OBJECTIVES

On completion of this chapter, you should be able to:

- ☺ *Explain what are the obstacles faced by new small entrepreneurs while creating business plan.*
- ☺ *Describe business plan.*
- ☺ *Discuss the steps required in writing business plan.*
- ☺ *Describe the contents of business plan.*
- ☺ *Discuss do's and don'ts of business plan.*

13.1 What is Business Plan?

The primary value of your business plan will be to create a written outline that evaluates all aspects of the economic viability of your business venture including a description and analysis of your business prospects.

13.1.1 Steps to a Great Business Plan

Start-up entrepreneurs often have difficulty writing out business plans. To make it easier, here are steps that will produce a worthwhile plan:

1. Write out your basic business concept.
2. Gather all the data you can on the feasibility and the specifics of your business concept.
3. Focus and refine your concept based on the data you have compiled.
4. Outline the specifics of your business. Using a "what, where, why, how" approach might be useful.
5. Put your plan into a compelling form so that it will not only give you insights and focus but, at the same time, will become a valuable tool in dealing with business relationships that will be very important to you.

BOX 13

Indian Angel Network (IAN) Incubator

In its continuous endeavour to work for seed and early stage entrepreneurs, Indian Angel Network (IAN), the pioneer of Angel Investing in India, has established the IAN Incubator with the support of National Science and Technology Entrepreneurship Development Board, Department of Science and Technology, Govt. of India. IAN Incubator provides a platform for sound technology/business ideas to become successful and investible businesses at the time when they are most susceptible – the first few months before and after the creation of the venture. The IAN Incubator supports techno-preneurs along their entire journey from an idea to enterprise and beyond.

The IAN Incubator team works very closely with the Incubated companies and supports them through the pre-start-up/start up phase of their business ventures. The Incubator works with entrepreneurs in stabilizing the product/service, business planning, formulating the market strategy and providing full support in operationalizing the business plan. It helps in accessing seed funding, team building, providing strategic and operational guidance, marketing and promotion, advisories on IP and investment and everything else that will help entrepreneurs survive in the competitive market and reach the stage where they can be receiving further funding for growing their venture. Simultaneously, the Incubator also provides a rich training and development program to enhance the skills and knowledge base of the entrepreneurs. The Incubator has a strong and dynamic core team and leverages the Angel network for mentoring and various other services.

The Incubator is also in the process of developing strategic tie-ups with other DST supported incubators, corporate, R&D labs and industry associations to be able to provide comprehensive support to the Incubatees. A robust virtual platform will be used to ensure that any physical distances do not inhibit the effectiveness of the incubation services.

Once selected for Incubation, ventures are incubated over a period of 18-24 months

Source: Information received from "Indian Angel Network Incubator".

6. Review the sample plans we furnish and download the blank format to a MS Word document. Fill in this as you progress though the course.

13.1.2 Why Prepare A Business Plan?

Your business plan is going to be useful in a number of ways

- First and foremost, it will define and focus your objective using appropriate information and analysis.
- You can use it as a selling tool in dealing with important relationships including your lenders, investors and banks.
- It describes all the relevant external and internal elements involved in starting a new business.
- Your business plan can uncover omissions and/or weaknesses in your planning process.
- It addresses both short-term and long term decision making for the first three years of operation.
- It is sometimes referred to as game plan or road plan- answers the questions, where Am I now? Where am I going? How will I get there? Potential investors, suppliers and even customers will request or require a business plan.
- You can use the plan to solicit opinions and advice from people, including those in your intended field of business, who will freely give you invaluable advice. Too often, entrepreneurs forge ahead ("My Way!") without the benefit of input from experts who could save them a great deal of wear and tear. "My Way" is a great song, but in practice can result in unnecessary hardships.

13.2 Contents of Business Plan

- Cover Page
- Table of Contents
- Executive Summary
- General Company Description
- Products and Services
- Marketing Plan
- Operations Plan
- Management and Organization
- Key Personnel
- Financial Plan
- Exit Strategy

- **Cover Page**

Every Business Plan should have a cover page, which includes:

- The Company's name, address, telephone, fax, e-mail, website address, if any. The simpler the access to the entrepreneur's contact details, the more likely the contact will take place.
- The name and designation of the contact person - who should be one of the top executives of the enterprise and one who is familiar with and was part of the team that formulated the business plan and will be able to answer any queries relating to the business plan.
- Names of organizations from where funding is being sought.

The Company's logo - every company being established should have a logo in place, which could be an image, design or picture representing the company's ideology pictographically.

- **Table of Contents**

Once the cover page has been made, a formal table of contents must be written for easy navigation to the rest of the plan, by numbering each section.

- Enables readers to focus on the information they are most interested in.
- It should be easy enough to help navigate the document.
- Could be immediately before the executive summary.
- List of all major sections and sub-sections.

- **Executive Summary**

The executive summary is the most important part of a business plan, especially to the investors. Most investors do not go beyond the executive summary, as they have too many plans to read. So make sure that your executive summary is able of conveying clearly and succinctly exactly what you want your investors to read.

The summary should include:

- Kind of Business - a brief description of the industry your firm is focusing on.
- Profile of the company's management - listing the names of top executives and their qualifications and industry experience.
- Financial requirements - briefly state how much finance is required. Also make sure you indicate the degree of flexibility you are willing to show in case the investor suggests any changes in your plan. This will allow the investor to consider your plan with few changes rather than rejecting your plan outright due to rigidity on your part.

- **General Company Description**

- **Company Purpose:** Define the company/business in a single declarative sentence.
- **Your Business Profile:** Define and describe your intended business and exactly how you plan to go about it. Try to stay focused on the specialized market you intend to serve. What Business are you in? What will you do?
- **A Vision and Mission Statement:** This will be a concise outline of your business purpose and goals. Vision: Defines your long-term dream. It should be slightly out of reach. Mission Statement: A brief but motivating prose description of the organization's purpose for being. It should be short enough to memorize and long enough to inspire and inform any person who wishes to know why the organization exists and whom it serves.
- **Mission:** Defines what you intend to become or accomplish. It should be challenging but achievable
- **Problem:** Describe the pain of the customer (or the customer's customer). Outline how the customer addresses the issue today.
- **Solution:** Demonstrate your company's value proposition to make the customer's life better.
- **Company goals:** plans to be accomplished over coming years (up to five years in advance) and how these are going to relate to the investment you are seeking. Keep the goals realistic and credible.
- **Future plans** for the growth and expansion of the company. Will you keep the business small? Do you plan to expand extensively? Link this to the projected investment. Once again, be moderate and keep things simple and believable.
- The Value of a Situation Analysis

You might also find it useful, after creating your mission statement, to conduct a classic situation analysis. It is a way for you and your readers to understand the current and potential environment in which you will be selling your product or service. You can also refer to a situation analysis as a SWOT analysis: a way to identify your company's internal Strengths and Weaknesses and to examine your external Opportunities and Threats.

It is good to write your SWOT analysis boldly and clearly. For example:

Strengths

- Low personnel turnover.
- Clear and inspirational mission statement.
- Clear need in the marketplace.
- Wide-ranging experience of top executives.
- Complete satisfaction to customers.

Weaknesses

- New CEO with limited industry experience.
- Poorly defined product image.
- Top operations people are nearing retirement.
- Aging machinery.
- Limited finance.

Opportunities

- New CAD/CAM software offers manufacturing efficiencies.
- Customers are increasing so can cater to larger customers.
- Fewer competitors
- Demand is high.

Threats

- Downward trend in core customer incomes.
- New, more efficient technology is in development.
- New competitors from China and Brazil are encroaching on our Markets.

- **Products and Services**

This section of the business plan will describe in a non-technical manner the characteristics of your products/services, stressing upon their competitive qualities. The business plan should be able to convince the investor that the entrepreneur understands the prevailing competitive environment and is able to prove that his/her product/service is a niche product or service with substantial prospects for growth and capable of attaining a competitive position in the market.

- Section that discusses product/service features and the needs or problems they address in the market. A description of the products or services you are offering or plan to offer. A competitive comparison of the products or services your competitors offer in relation to yours. This section describes what your product or service consists of. It should contain detailed descriptions of products and/or services.
- **Make the presentation explicative**, as if addressing a reader who is not familiar with the offered products/services.
- **Product description:** should cover size, shape, color, design, capabilities. Representative pictures might be helpful in retaining the reader's attention. Also add a

brief description of the production technology (needed materials, type of labor) and some things on patent protection.

- **Services:** explain the services — what they are, what needs they address the operations area, needed materials or equipment, operations program (scheduling— days, hours), steps in the service process, benefits for clients.
- A **presentation of the technology** you use in order to produce/maintain/develop your products/services will speak about your ability to put to good use facilities offered by modern science and about your openness to new.
- You may also want to present **future products or services future planning**. It implies describing a product strategy, how you see the relationship between market needs and product development. This topic would mostly appeal to possible investors, who look for the business' perspective than to bankers who would not be interested in ideas of future products but in more concrete things.
- The business plan writer should **treat this subject from the perspective of the customer's needs** and the potential of your product of benefit offers. This chapter is decisive for the holistic impression of the reader — whether the business/company has anything interesting to offer, something that will sell and something that will retain attention and seem attractive.
- The section must be informative enough, offering an easily understandable image without boring details. Emphasis should be placed on the difference your products/services make on the market.
- Products:
  - Pictures
  - Size, shape, colour
  - Cost
  - Design, capabilities, technological life-span
  - Patent protection
  - Components
- Services Overview

Marketing Plan

This section of your business plan presents a market-research survey, locating your business in the market environment. It also determines whether the market is sufficient to support the business. It analyzes the following aspects:

Market characteristics and market segmentation

- Briefly describe here the market you are in or the market you are planning to enter: product coverage area, environment, additional product area if necessary and potential customers.

Analyze the market also from a chronological perspective:

- Provide a historical market survey of the products and producers;
- Analyze the current status of the market — needs and trends;
- Forecast market growth.
- Define the **prospective segments** of your market: fields of interest, reasons for the interest caused by your products or services in particular market segments.

Market analysis and its component parts

- Participants in this industry — seek out the principal representatives in the market of your industry.
- Distribution patterns — analysis of the principal means of distribution of the specific products or services to the customer.
- Competition and buying patterns — **Identify the main competitors** (direct and indirect) and the principal **factors which determine purchasing choices** of the product or service. Here you should analyze your specific target market needs and the means of coverage, identify unexplored or poorly exploited market niches and your opportunities on these territories. Analyze the strengths and weaknesses of the offers of your competitors by comparing their offers to yours.

In this section you must answer these questions:

- Will your sales reach break-even point?
- Is the market large enough?
- Are your products or services competitive enough to break into the market?

• Operations Plan

The operations plan is an essential component to your business plan and it tells the reviewer how you're going to get your product/service out to market. That is, how are you going to get your product out of the production stage to the doorstep of your target customer?

The operational plan may seem ordinary but it will outline some very important answers to such fundamental questions such as:

- Who is doing what?
- What are the day-to-day activities?
- How will the suppliers and vendors be used?
- Who are the suppliers?
- What are the labour requirements?
- What are the sources of raw materials?

Why is this section so important? First, it will outline to the reader how you are going to carry out the delivery of your product or service. What's the use of having a product or service if you don't have a way to get it from the development stage to the consumers' home?

A business plan reviewer gives this section a lot of weight because they want to know what you and your employees are doing to get your product/service out to market. How you keep track of inventory or what type of equipment you need may seem obvious to you, but remember, the reader doesn't know this. These activities may seem like the kind of details that take care of themselves but these are fundamental and critical for your business success.

• Management and Organization

Purpose

Offers a statement of your management philosophy with an in-depth focus on processes and procedures.

Includes

- Management Philosophy
- Structure of Organization
- Reporting System

- Methods of Communication
- Employee Skills and Training
- Employee Needs and Compensation
- Work Environment
- Management Policies and Procedures
- Roles and Responsibilities

- **Key Personnel**

Purpose

Describes the unique backgrounds of principle employees involved in business.

Includes

- Owner(s)/Employee Education and Experience
- Positions and Roles
- Benefits and Salary
- Duties and Responsibilities
- Objectives and Goals

- **Financial Plan**

The financial analysis is the most concrete, practical part of the business plan, the section likely to arouse the greatest interest.

Financially astute readers may well turn to this section of your business plan first of all. This section, the most concrete, deals mainly with numbers. If you can translate your ideas into figures, you will demonstrate both your practical planning skills and the potential profitability of your business.

The financial plan should reflect all the financial aspects of the entire business plan. When you write business plans for existing companies, base your future planning on their past history. For startups, construct the financial plan by taking some premises and assumptions on board. The data you have at hand estimates the costs and investments necessary at starting and the sales, revenue and expenses forecasts made on the basis of the market analysis components and business statistics.

Financial Projections

- Financial projections for three to five years
- Income Statements
  - Year 1 - Monthly Projections
  - Years 2 through 5 - Quarterly or Yearly Projections
  - Existing businesses for last three years
- Balance Sheets
  - Year 1 - Quarterly Projections
  - Years 2 through 5 - Yearly Projections
  - Existing businesses for last three years
- Cash Flows
  - Year 1 - Monthly Projections
  - Years 2 through 5 - Quarterly or Yearly Projections

Behaviour of costs

- Fixed Costs
  - When costs are linked with time. For example: rent.
- Variable Costs
  - When costs are linked with volume of work or production. For example: raw material.

- **Exit Strategy**
  - For an investor, liquidity is very critical, the exit route should be clear. You must have a plan when you will exit. On what conditions and circumstances you would like to exit.
  - This will also depend on the intentions of the founder.
  - Venture Capitalists: Look for a high return and an exit strategy of 3-7 years.

  Exit strategies:
  - Initial Public Offering
  - Merger/Acquisition
  - Buyout by partner

13.3 Documents to be included in Business Financial Analysis Papers

- **The cash flow analysis** — the main aspect of your business, the one that arouses the greatest interest. It deals with the cash revenues and cash outlays over a given period of time (The cash flow does not treat the non-cash expenses). The desirable outcome is to prove that you can maintain a positive cash flow while you pay financing and interest.
- **The pro forma balance sheet** deals with cash and income and also with assets, liabilities and capital. The balance should result in the debit and credit balances ending up equal.
- **The break-even analysis** results from an estimate of income and expenses. It determines whether or not your business will bring in enough money to meet its costs.
- **The sales forecast** which outlines the methodology.
  - The business "inventory" for sale, which is based on value.
  - The business potential of selling based on the market.
  - The business capacity for producing to sell based on resources.
- **The personnel plan** — this subject is also dealt within the Management Team section. The resulting figures should be used further in cost calculations.
- **Profit and loss**. Here you will consider the sales forecast, the sales costs, operating expenses and the profits. Make month-by-month formal estimates of sales and expenses to obtain a profit projection for your first year of operations. It will reveal **gross margin** (obtained from sales, less cost of sales), **gross profit** or profit before interest and taxes (obtained from gross margin, less operating expenses) and **net profit** (obtained from gross profit, less interest and taxes).
- **The business ratio analysis** results from existing figures. The financial sections of business plans require key ratios such as **profitability ratios**, gross margin, return on sales, return on investment and **liquidity ratios** such as current ratio, debt to equity and working capital.

- **The market forecast** is treated in detail in the chapter on Strategy Implementation. A few lines on marketing may be appropriate here. Project the number of potential customers and the impact of market growth on the business.

A hint: Jot down your financial assumptions as you work through each section of the business plan. Always keep in focus the material aspects of the subjects you are dealing with. In this way, when you have finished writing the business plan, you will almost have completed the financial section simultaneously.

- **Appendices**

Purpose

Supporting documents used to enhance your business proposal.

Includes

- Photographs of product, equipment, facilities, etc.,
- Copyright/Trademark Documents
- Legal Agreements
- Marketing Materials
- Research and or Studies
- Operation Schedules
- Organizational Charts
- Job Descriptions
- Resumes
- Additional Financial Documentation

13.3 Imaginary Example: Restaurant Sample Business Plan Outline

Table of Contents

Cover Letter

Executive Summary

Company Description

Industry Analysis

Products and Related Services

The Target Market

The Competition

Marketing Plan and Sales Strategy

Operations

Management and Organization

Long-Term Development and Exit Plan

Financial Data and Projections

Appendices

Company Description

One Destination, a Delhi based company, will operate, a single unit, medium-size restaurant serving healthy, contemporary style food. The Fast Service restaurant will be located at Sadar Street in Mumbai.

Mission Statement

The company's goal is that of a multi-faceted success. Our first responsibility is to the financial well-being of the restaurant. We will meet this goal while trying to consider; 1) the effect of our products on the health and well being of our customers (and our staff), 2) the impact that our business practices and choices will have on the environment and 3) the high quality of attitude, fairness, understanding and generosity between management, staff, customers and vendors. Awareness of all these factors and the responsible actions that result will give our efforts a sense of purpose and meaning beyond our basic financial goals.

Development and Status

The company was incorporated in September of 1995.

The founder is Mr. Bakshi. Mr. Bakshi is the President. A suitable site for the first restaurant was found last month and lease negotiations are in the final stages. The location will be on Sadar Street, just outside Shanti Square and close to a dense population of the target market. When the lease is signed there will be three months of free rent for construction and in that time the balance of the start-up funds must be raised. With that phase completed, Restaurant can then open and the operations phase of the project can begin.

Future Plans

If the business is meeting its projections by month nine, we will start scouting for a second location and develop plans for the next unit. Our five year goal is to have 3 restaurants in Mumbai with a combined annual profit of between Rs. 30,00000 to 40,00000.

Industry Analysis

Although the restaurant industry is very competitive, the lifestyle changes created by modern living continue to fuel its steady growth. More and more people have less time, resources and ability to cook for themselves. Trends are very important and Fast Service is well positioned for the current interest in lighter, healthier foods at moderate to low prices.

The Restaurant Industry Today

The food service business is the third largest industry in the country. It accounts for over $240 billion annually in sales. The independent restaurant accounts for 15 per cent of that total. The average Indian spends 15 per cent of his/her income on meals away from home. This number has been increasing for the past seven years. In the past five years the restaurant industry has out-performed the national GNP by 40 per cent. The reasons given by the Report (November 1994) are (1) lifestyle changes, (2) economic climate and (3) increase of product variety.

There are 600 new restaurants opening every month and over 200 more needed to keep pace with increasing demand.

Future Trends and Strategic Opportunities

The predicated growth trend is very positive both in short and long-term projections. Reports state again that as modern living create more demands, people will be compelled to eat more meals away from home.

Some highlights from the panel's findings:

- "Consumers will spend a greater proportion of their food money away from home.
- Independent operators and entrepreneurs will be the main source of new restaurant concepts.
- Nutritional concerns will be critical at all types of foodservice operations and food flavors will be important.
- Environmental concerns will receive increased attention."

Products and Related Services

Fast Service restaurant will be offering a menu of food and beverages with a distinctive image. There will be three ways to purchase these products; table service at the restaurant, take-out from the restaurant and delivery to home or office.

The Menu

The Fast Service menu (see appendices) is moderate sized and moderate-low priced offering a collection of ethnic and Indian items with a common theme — healthy (low-fat, low cholesterol, natural ingredients), flavorful and familiar. Our goal is to create the image of light satisfying and still nutritious food.

There has been an increased awareness of nutritional and health concerns in recent years and a growing market of people who now eat this style of cooking regularly.

Production

Food production and assembly will take place in the kitchen of the restaurant. Fresh vegetables, meat and dairy products will be used to crate most of the dishes from scratch. The chef will exercise strict standards of sanitation, quality production and presentation or packaging over the kitchen and service staff.

Service

There will be three ways a customer can purchase food. They may sit down at one of the 54 seats in the dining room and get full service from a waitperson. A separate take-out counter will service those who wish to pick up their food. Most take-out food will be prepared to order with orders coming from either the telephone or fax. Delivery (an indirect form of take-out) will be available at certain times and to a limited area.

Future Opportunities

There is a market segment that prefers to eat this type of cooking at home although they do not have the time to cook. There are already caterers and even mail order companies that provide individuals and families with up to a month's supply of pre-prepared meals.

This opportunity will be researched and developed on a trial basis. If successful, it could become a major new source of income without creating the need for additional staff or production space.

The Target Market

The market for Fast Services' products covers a large area of diverse and densely populated groups. Although it will be located in a downtown urban setting, it is an area where people travel to eat out and one that is also frequented by tourists. It is also an area known for and catering to the demographic group we are targeting.

Market Location and Customers

The Shanti Square area is one of the most desirable retail locations in Mumbai. The Mass. Chamber of Commerce rates it as the third best retail market in the state. There are more than 400 businesses in a 1/4 square mile area with average sales of ₹ 3300 per square foot.

The customer base will come from three major segments;

- **Local population** — with a year-round population of 145,000 is centrally located in the Shanti area and is within 15 minutes drive of 8 major suburbs.
- **Colleges and Universities** – Shanti area alone has six different schools within walking distance of Sadar Street and a seasonal population of 22,000. In addition five more colleges near the square have large student bodies.
- **Tourism** — between hotels, motels, bed and breakfast rooms and inns, there are over 8,500 rooms available. Last year they were at 92 per cent occupancy.
- **Local businesses** — The Chamber of Commerce lists over 900 businesses with an average of 12 employees in the Shanti square area.

The food concept and product image of Fast Service will attract three different customer profiles;

- **The student** — more and more young people have developed healthy eating habits. Some also go through a "health food phase" while in college.
- **The health conscious person of any age or sex** — this includes anyone on a restricted or prescribed diet or those who have committed to a healthy diet.
- **Curious and open-minded** — "if you try it, you will like it." Through marketing, publicity and word-of-mouth, people will seek out a new experience and learn that nutritious food can be tasty, fun, convenient and inexpensive.

Market Trends and the Future

The population and demographics of Shanti square have remained steady for the last three years. Tourism has increased 24 per cent over the last three years and is predicted to keep growing. Local businesses are increasing at a rate of 18 per cent yearly.

The idea of a health consciousness through nutritional awareness and dietary change has been slowly building for the last seven years. The extensive government studies and new Food Guide Pyramid have given everyone a new definition of a balanced, healthy diet. This is not a fad but a true dietary trend backed by the scientific and medical community, the media, the government and endorsed by the big food manufacturers.

As people want to stay home more and cook less our strategy of delivering prepared meals on a weekly or monthly arrangement may be a widespread accepted new way of eating.

The Competition

There are over two dozen restaurants in the Shanti Square area that sell food at similar prices. Although this presents an obvious challenge in terms of market share, it also indicates the presence of a large, strong potential. The newest competitors have made their successful entry based on an innovative concept or novelty. Fast Service will offer an innovative product in a familiar style at a competitive price. Our aggressive plans of take-out and delivery will also give us an advantage to create a good market share before the competition can adjust or similar concepts appear.

Competitor's Profile

Competing with Fast Service for the target market are these categories of food providers:

- Independent table service restaurants of similar menu and price structure.
- Chain " " " " "
- Commercial foodservice companies serving students directly.

Independent operators include Grendel's Den, Iako, Bombay Club, Iruna and The Border Cafe. Most are ethnic based and will carry at least two similar menu items. Grendel's and Iruna are long-standing businesses while the others are fairly new. They all are doing very well.

The major chain restaurants are House of Blues, Chili's and Bertucci's. All are relatively new but well established and profitable. They have big resources of marketing and/or a specialty product or attraction (House of Blues is also a live music club). Ogden Foods and Cysco both service 24,000 Management students but their product is not appealing enough to prevent students from eating out 5 to 7 meals a week. In addition there are two local catering companies that deliver prepared meals daily to offices.

Competitive Strategy

There are three major ways in which we will create an advantage over our competitors;

- product identity, quality and novelty
- high employee motivation and good sales attitude
- innovative and aggressive service options.

Fast Service will be the only restaurant among all the competition which focuses the entire menu on healthy, low-fat cooking. Each of the competitors offers at least one "healthy" selection on their menu. Grendel's Den even has an entire section called "On the Lighter Side" but in all cases they are always seen as alternatives to the main style being offered. The target market will perceive Fast Service as the destination location for healthy, low-fat cooking.

Once they have tried the restaurant, their experience will be reinforced by friendly, efficient, knowledgeable service. Return and repeat business will be facilitated by accessible take-out and delivery options. At the time of this writing all of the competitors offered take-out but only two (Bertucci"s and Chili's).

Marketing Plan and Sales Strategy

Market Penetration

Entry into the market should not be a problem. The store has high visibility with heavy foot traffic all day long. The local residents and students always support new restaurants and the tourists do not have fixed preferences. In addition, ₹ 50,000 has been budgeted for a pre-opening advertising and public relations campaign.

Marketing Strategy

Focusing on the unique aspect of the product theme (healthy, tasty foods) a mix of marketing vehicles will be created to convey our presence, our image and our message.

- **Print media** — local newspapers, magazines and student publications
- **Broadcast media** — local programming and special interest shows
- **Hotel guides**, concierge relations, Chamber of Commerce brochures
- **Direct mail** — subscriber lists, offices for delivery
- **Misc.** — yellow pages, charity events

A public relations firm has been retained to create special events and solicit print and broadcast coverage, especially at the start-up.

The marketing effort will be split into three phases;

(1) **Opening** — An advanced notice (press packet) sent out by the PR firm to all media and printed announcement ads in key places. Budget – ₹ 50,000

(2) **Ongoing** — A flexible campaign (using the above media), assessed regularly for effectiveness. Budget – ₹ 50,000

(3) **Point of sale** — A well-trained staff can increase the average check as well as enhancing the customer's overall experience. Word-of-mouth referral is very important in building a customer base.

Future plans and Strategic Opportunities

Catering to offices (even outside of our local area) may become a large part of gross sales. At that point a sales agent would be hired to directly market our products for daily delivery or catered functions.

Operations

Facilities and Offices

The restaurant at Sadar Street is a 2400 Square feet space. It was formerly a restaurant and needs minor structural modifications. The licenses and codes' issues are all in order. New equipment and dining room furnishings will be purchased and installed by the general contractor. Offices of the corporation are presently at Mr. Bakshi's home but will be moved to the restaurant after opening.

Hours of Operation

The restaurant will be open for lunch and dinner 7 days a week. Service will begin at 11:00 AM and end at 11:00 PM. The restaurant will be closed on Independence Day and Republic Day.

Employee Training and Education

Employees will be trained not only in their specific operational duties but in the philosophy and applications of our concept. They will receive extensive information from the chef and be kept informed of the latest information on healthy eating.

Systems and Controls

A big emphasis is being placed on extensive research into the quality and integrity of our products. They will constantly be tested for our own high standards of freshness and purity. Food costs and inventory control will be handled by our computer system and checked daily by management.

Food Production

Most food will be prepared on the premises. The kitchen will be designed for high standards of sanitary efficiency and cleaned daily. Food will be made mostly to order and stored in large coolers in the basement.

Delivery and Catering

Food for delivery may be similar to take-out (prepared to order) or it may be prepared earlier and stocked. Catering will be treated as deliveries.

Management and Organization

Key Employees and Principals

Mr. Bakshi, President, he is also the owner and manager of Grains and Grains, a local natural food wholesaler and retail store. Since 1977 his company has created a high-profile mainstream image for natural foods. In 1992 Grains and Grains opened a small cafe within the retail store that became so popular and profitable, he decided to expand the concept into a full service restaurant.

Mr. Bakshi, brings with him a track record of success in the natural foods industry. His management style is innovative and in keeping with the corporate style outlined in the mission statement.

Compensation and Incentives

Fast Service will offer competitive wages and salaries to all employees with benefit packages available to key personnel only.

Board of Directors

An impressive board of directors has been assembled that represents some top professional from the area. They will be a great asset to the development of the company.

Consultants and Professional Support Resources

At the present, no outside consultants have been retained, excepting the design department at Best Equipment.

Management to be added

We are presently searching for a general manager and executive chef. These key employees will be well chosen and given incentives for performance and growth.

Management Structure and Style

Mr. Bakshi will be the President and Chief Operating Officer. The general manager and chef will report to him. The assistant manager and sous-chef will report to their respective managers and all other employees will be subordinate to them.

Ownership

Mr. Bakshi and the stockholders will retain ownership with the possibility of offering stock to key employees if deemed appropriate.

Long-Term Development and Exit Plan

Goals

Fast Service is an innovative concept that targets a new, growing market. We assume that the market will respond and grow quickly in the next five years. Our goals are to create a reputation of quality, consistency and security (safety of food) that will make us the leader of a new style of dining.

Strategies

Our marketing efforts will be concentrated on take-out and delivery, the areas of most promising growth. As the market changes, new products may be added to maintain sales.

Milestones

After the restaurant opens, we will keep a close eye on sales and profit. If we are on target at the end of year one, we will look to expand to a second unit.

Risk Evaluation

With any new venture, there is risk involved. The success of our project hinges on the strength and acceptance of a fairly new market. After year one, we expect some copycat competition in the form of other independent units. Chain competition will be much later.

Exit Plan

Ideally, Fast Service will expand to five units in the next ten years. At that time, we will entertain the possibility of a buy-out by a larger restaurant concern or actively seek to sell to a new owner.

13.4 Miscalculations in Business Plan

Every business should have a business plan

A perfect business plan shows the success of the business. Unfortunately, despite the fact that many of the underlying businesses are viable, the vast majority of plans are hardly worth the paper they're printed on. The new entrepreneurs are not well experienced in formulating the business plan. They commit most of the mistakes. They do not have any idea about the value of business plan.

Experienced investors constantly examine the business plan of a number of entrepreneurs in order to gain a better understanding of their business ideas and objectives. Often times, investors can notice certain tactical mistakes that many first-time entrepreneurs tend to make. These tactical mistakes often blur the message of the business pitch and, at times, even confuse prospective investors. First-time entrepreneurs, unlike serial entrepreneurs, are often inexperienced in their approach and thus, lack considerable business experience. Entrepreneurs should treat their business pitch similar to a sales process and clearly understand that the goal of the first meeting with an investor is not to get money commitment but to impress them by the business plan. This will make your bond with your investor strong. The investors will themselves take interest in your business. They will provide all possible help for the business.

The following are the mistakes done by the new entrepreneurs:

The plan is poorly written

The problems of the most of the entrepreneurs are that they do not know the way of writing a business plan. They are not able to write a letter in a standard way. They have the thoughts, they are intelligent but they have to reflect those on the paper. Spelling, grammar and style are all important when it comes to getting your business plan down on paper. But they do not take it seriously or they do not know whether they are right or wrong. They are looking for clues about the underlying business and its leaders when they're perusing a plan. When they see one with spelling, punctuation and grammar errors, they immediately wonder what else is wrong with the business. But since there's no shortage of people looking for capital, they don't wonder for long—they just move on to the next plan.

Before you show your plan to a single investor or banker, go through every line of the plan. Check every area of the plan. You should catch spelling and punctuation errors and have someone; you know with strong "English" skills review it for grammar problems. The English should be written in a standard way.

Ethics and professionalism

A major requirement for the survival of an entrepreneur and his/her business is not the ability to successfully raise startup capital but to present his/her ideas in an ethical manner. It is the best way by which they can think that their business can survive. Investors do not want to invest the money on illegal ideas. Any attempts to embellish the facts about their business idea(s) or their own individual backgrounds will be either immediately recognized or discovered later in the due diligence process. Investors are very particular about the entrepreneur's ethical and professional conduct and do not want to fund an entrepreneur who is untruthful in their approach. They never promote unethical environment that will harm the customers, society and as a country whole. An entrepreneur should present his/her business ideas in the best possible way but should never be inclined to grossly exaggerate.

Careless plan presentation

The entrepreneurs lack skills of presenting the business plan. They actually do not know the way of presentation. Sometimes new entrepreneurs miss the contents of their business plan while they deliver. It is the important stage of the business plan. Without proper communication either orally or on paper plan cannot be explained. You should explain what is written in your plan. Nothing disturb investors more than inconsistent margins, missing page numbers, scattered contents, no justification, no highlights, no charts or charts without labels or with incorrect units, tables without headings, no proper explanation about the tables, cannot read it properly, technical terminology without definitions or a missing table of contents. You should check the plan before going to the final investor, banker or venture capitalist. Even if you are working for many months for your plan but if you cannot present it to the final investors then it is of no use.

Follow-up

It becomes very necessary for the entrepreneurs to be in touch with the investors for a few days. After meeting and presenting your proposal you should be in touch with the entrepreneurs either by telephone, mail, email or personal meeting. It also shows your interest for the business and your seriousness. But the new entrepreneurs left all to the investors they never call or ask about their results to the investors. They think investors will call them and they need not to do anything. Entrepreneurs are encouraged to write a letter to each investor, via direct mail or by e-mail, or even make a follow-up telephone call thanking the investor for taking the time out to attend and listen to their business proposal. It usually takes investors (angels and venture capitalists) a few days to research the idea that the entrepreneur presented. By following-up with investors it also shows investors they are truly serious in taking their business ideas forward.

The plan is incomplete

The business plan should be the complete one. The plan should not be taken as the formality. The plan itself can take you to success. The entrepreneurs when prepare the plan forgot to take every aspects of the business. They do not think with a broad mind. They are the new ones so they do not have any experience or knowledge they miss the contents which they should include in the business plan. Every business has customers, products and services, operations, marketing and sales, a management team and competitors. At an absolute minimum, your plan must cover all these features. A complete description of all the features and their interaction with the business should be explained. A complete plan should also include a discussion of the industry, particularly industry trends, such as if the market is growing or shrinking. Finally, your plan should include detailed financial projections—monthly cash flow and income statements, as well as annual balance sheets.

Unclear roadmap

Most of the time the entrepreneurs do not provide the required information in the business plan. When they will start the business? What is the specific date for that? Not mentioning important facts disappoint the investors. The entrepreneurs also do not show the deadline of their tasks. For example how much time they will take to accomplish the tasks? How they have divided the time slots? They do not mention the responsibility. For example who will be responsible for the different functions of the business? What comes under responsibility etc.?

First-time entrepreneurs often make the mistake of not clearly stating WHO their customers are, WHAT problem is being addressed and HOW company can solve the problem. Although experienced entrepreneurs rarely commit this mistake, it is the first-time entrepreneurs who pitch their ideas in such a way that investors have difficulty in understanding the business proposition even 30-minutes into the meeting. Although there is some benefit in explaining the context before putting forth the value proposition, an entrepreneur should take time into consideration and get to the point in a timely manner. This is very important since most investors expect a crisp and precise value proposition.

Entrepreneurs should research the spectators

It is important for the entrepreneurs to be familiar with the audience before they present their pitch. Every entrepreneur should diligently research the particulars of each audience member, especially if they happen to be investors. They should present the idea keeping in mind the nature of the investors. The entrepreneur who is "pitching" their idea to angel investors should know previous and existing investments of the investor and then tailor what he/she presents based on this information. You should have an idea what are the things that will really impress the investors. It is part of the business game. Mostly entrepreneurs are not able to consider these things. They do not try to know the nature and the history of the investors. They do not have any idea about how to impress the investors by using different tactics. When a meeting is confirmed, entrepreneurs should ask the investor about the particulars of the audience who will be attending the meeting.

The plan is too vague

A business plan is not a novel, a story or a song. Most of the entrepreneurs plan does not show consistency that's mean different parts of the plan contradict with each other. They do not have a consistency in their plan. They do not have proper reasons for their act. Therefore investor cannot come on to the conclusion. The contents are not so much clear, investor takes much time to read it. The plan should be such that the investors will become happy at the first moment just by seeing to the business plan. If you want to hide the secrets of the business, confidential material, processes or technologies, then show people your executive summary first (which should never contain any proprietary information). Then, if they're interested in learning more about the business, have an agreement of non disclosure with them.

Demonstrations or presentations that do not work

Most entrepreneurs will present their ideas and demonstrate their prototypes/services during their business presentation. It is quite essential that entrepreneurs use their time as efficiently as possible during the presentation, especially when switching between their verbal presentation and prototype demonstration. They do not use their time properly. They are not able to explain the ideas with calm and patience. They lack presentation skills. Since time is of the essence, entrepreneurs should set up their equipment, connect their laptop to a projector and setup the prototype demonstration, even before the meeting begins. Entrepreneurs are encouraged to resume their business plan presentation should technical difficulties occur, such as equipment and prototype failure. You should look like a confident one. You should give the impression that you are going to solve any problem. Remember: An entrepreneur who appears worried about technical mishaps may present the wrong message to the investors.

The plan is too detailed

The entrepreneurs write the plan in much detail. They provide all the technical or the explanation of the techniques that will be used. They take maximum pages just to explain the technology only. But the fact is that a proper description is enough for the plan instead of giving all the minute details of the technology. The explanation of the technology with respect to business is sufficient for the business plan. The investors just want to know about the technology but not the explanation of the technology, laws or principle of the technology. Keep the technical details to a minimum in the main plan — if you want to include them, do so elsewhere, say, in an appendix. The description of the technology can also be shown in the form of attachment at the last of the business plan. If the investors are interested then they can go through that otherwise the investors can refer it some other time. You can also break your plan into three parts: a two- to three-page executive summary, a 10- to 20-page business plan and an appendix that includes as many pages as needed to make it clear that you know what you're doing.

The time and pace of the pitch is important

The time at which an entrepreneur can clearly communicate his/her idea in order to raise capital for their venture is during their business plan presentation. Therefore, it is vital that the entrepreneur spends a considerable amount of time on each aspect of his business plan. You need not be in hurry to explain the concepts. You can use any examples, case studies or any incident to explain your ideas. The entrepreneurs do the mistake of spending too much time on some topic of their business proposals that they need not to explain much. They take much time to explain their business summary only and sometimes they describe irrelevant business concepts not related to the business idea. It can irritate investor; they may take wrong decision for your proposal because of unclear and boredom presentation. Likewise, mid-stream questions are helpful in allowing an investor develop a better understanding of the business proposal, but the entrepreneur should spend less time on irrelevant topics and communicate only the important ones in his/her full agenda.

The plan makes unfounded or unrealistic assumptions

The entrepreneurs just to attract the investors show their business plan with so many unrealistic assumptions. By their very nature, business plans are full of assumptions. The most important assumption, of course, is that your business will succeed! The best business plans highlight critical assumptions and provide some sort of rationalization for them. The entrepreneurs have some assumption about their business but they do not have any explanation about those assumption. They just want to do all that for achieving the success but they become nil when they are asked about the practical achievement of the assumptions. There should be assumptions but those assumptions should have proper explanation. The entrepreneurs must be in a position to explain the assumptions. They should move on more real world, they should have concrete reasons for their ideas to implement. Market size, acceptable pricing, customer purchasing behavior, sales, future prospects, time to commercialization—these all involve assumptions. Wherever possible, make sure you check your assumptions against benchmarks from the same industry, a similar industry or some other acceptable standard. Tie your assumptions to facts.

The plan includes inadequate research

The business plan should be based on the research. The research helps you to find the exact happening in the market and because of that you will be able to write your business plan more easily. The plan should include all the possible research data. The research data gives strength to your plan. Just as it's important to tie your assumptions to facts, it's equally important to make sure your facts are, well, facts. Learn everything you can about your business and your industry—customer purchasing habits, motivations and fears; competitor positioning, size and market share; and overall market trends. Statistics should be used for explaining the results. That is the best way of representing the data and your assumptions. You can use statistical tools for showing the projections of your business. But the fact is that most of the entrepreneurs do not take many efforts to do all that. They lack knowledge about conducting research and using the statistical tools but they can do this by hiring the people or taking the help of the experienced one.

You claim there's no risk involved in your new venture

Any sensible investor understands there's really no such thing as a "no risk" business. The entrepreneurs may say that there are no risks in the business. There are two reasons for that the first reason is they actually are not able to see the risks in the business, they lack knowledge, they lack information and therefore they say that there are no risks. They definitely take efforts to form the business plan but they are not able to see the risks. The second reason is they intentionally try to hide the risk in the business so that they can win trust of the investors. If here also their innocence is seen, they forget that the investors are the well experienced persons and they cannot be fooled easily. The investors know that there are always risks. You must understand them before presenting your plan to investors or lenders. Since a business plan is more of a strategic tool than anything else. You can show them the proper explanation of how you can reduce the risks. You should have the answers for the questions of the investors about the risks.

You claim you have no competition

It's absolutely amazing how many potential business owners include this statement in their business plans: "We have no competition."

If that's what you think, you couldn't be further from the truth. Every successful business has competitors, both direct and indirect. You should plan for stiff competition from the beginning. If you can't find any direct competitors today, try to imagine how the marketplace might look once you're successful. Identify ways you can compete and accentuate your competitive advantages in the business plan.

13.5 Features to be Considered in Business Plan

What are the different factors that the entrepreneurs should consider while making a business plan bulletproof. The following should be considered.

Think it through

You might have a great idea, but have you carefully mapped out all the steps you'll need to take to make the business a reality? Try to include all the facts in the business plan. Then think about building your management team, hiring salespeople, setting up operations, getting your first customer, protecting yourself from lawsuits, outmaneuvering your competition and so on. Think about cash flow and what measures you can take to minimize your expenses and maximize your revenue.

Do your research

Research is the primary requirement of the business plan. Try to take the help of others research data. Investigate everything you can about your proposed business before you start writing your business plan—and long before you start the business. Know about every possible unit that will interact with your business. For example how will you arrange suppliers, customers and what is the viability of the business area etc.? You'll also need to continue your research while you write the business plan, since inevitably; things will change as you uncover critical information. And while you're researching, be sure to consult multiple sources since many times the experts will disagree. Try to show your data in the form of statistics.

Research your potential customers and competitors

The business plan must include information about the customers and competitors. How the customers will benefit from your business? How the competitors will try to affect your business and as a result of that how will you form the strategy to compete them? Your product or service something people really want or need, or is it just "cool"? Study your market. Is it growing or shrinking? Could some sort of disruptive technology or regulatory change alter the market in fundamental ways? Why do you think people will buy your product or service? What are you providing to them? How are you going to create the value among customers? If you don't have any customers or clients yet, you'll need to convince investors that you have something people really want or need and more important, that they'll buy it at the price you expect.

Get feedback

Obtain as much feedback as you can from trusted friends, colleagues, nonprofit organizations and potential investors or lenders.

Hire professional help

Find a professional you trust to help guide you through the entire process, fill in knowledge gaps (for instance, if you know marketing but not finance, you should hire a finance expert), provide additional, unbiased feedback and package your plan in an attractive, professional format.

13.6 Top Ten Do's and Don'ts

TOP DO'S

1. Prepare a complete business plan for any business you are considering.
2. Use the business plan templates furnished in each session.
3. Complete sections of your business plan as you proceed through the course.
4. Research (use search engines) to find business plans that are available on the Internet.
5. Package your business plan in an attractive kit as a selling tool.
6. Submit your business plan to experts in your intended business for their advice.
7. Spell out your strategies on how you intend to handle adversities.
8. Spell out the strengths and weaknesses of your management team.
9. Include a monthly one-year cash flow projection.
10. Freely and frequently modify your business plans to account for changing conditions.
11. Use simple language in explaining the issues. Make it easy to read and understand.
12. Be flexible early in the process and keep it fluid. Don't commit too early. Expect your first plan to be provisional and subject to revision.
13. Ask yourself if your experience or expertise gives you the right to an opinion on your specific opportunity.
14. Identify your potential deal killers: variables that are likely to prove fatal to the venture.
15. Clearly identify what you see as the key drivers of success. What are you betting on here?

16. Raise money only in sufficient amount to finance the experiment or evaluation you next envision, with a cushion for contingencies.
17. Delay hiring key managers until initial rounds of experimentation has produced a stable business model.
18. At some point, take the plunge and test your product or service on a small scale in the real world through customer research, test marketing or prototypes.
19. Test and refine your business model before expanding your operations.

TOP DON'TS

1. Be optimistic (on the high side) in estimating future sales.
2. Be optimistic (on the low side) in estimating future costs.
3. Disregard or discount weaknesses in your plan. Spell them out.
4. Stress long-term projections. Better to focus on projections for your first year.
5. Depend entirely on the uniqueness of your business or the success of an invention.
6. Project yourself as someone you're not. Be brutally realistic.
7. Be everything to everybody. Highly focused specialists usually do best.
8. Proceed without adequate financial and accounting know-how.
9. Base your business plan on a wonderful concept. Test it first.
10. Skip the step of preparing a business plan before starting.
11. Avoid optimism. In fact, to offset optimism, be extremely conservative in predicting capital requirements, timelines, sales and profits. Few business plans correctly anticipate how much money and time will be required.
12. Do not ignore spelling out what your strategies will be in the event of business adversities.
13. Don't depend entirely on the uniqueness of your business or even a patented invention. Success comes to those who start businesses with great economics and not necessarily great inventions.

SUMMARY

The primary value of your business plan will be to create a written outline that evaluates all aspects of the economic viability of your business venture including a description and analysis of your business prospects.

Why Prepare A Business Plan?

Your business plan is going to be useful in a number of ways: First and foremost, it will define and focus your objective using appropriate information and analysis. You can use it as a selling tool in dealing with important relationships including your lenders, investors and banks. It describes all the relevant external and internal elements involved in starting a new business. Your business plan can uncover omissions and/or weaknesses in your planning process. It addresses both short-term and long term decision making for the first three years of operation.

Contents of Business Plan is Cover page, Table of Contents, Executive Summary, General, Company Description, Products and Services, Marketing Plan, Operations Plan, Management and Organization, Financial Plan And Exit Strategy.

Cover Page

Every Business Plan should have a cover page, which includes: The Company's name, address, telephone, fax, e-mail, website address, if any. The simpler the access to the entrepreneur's contact details, the more likely the contact will take place.

Table of Contents

Once the cover page has been made, a formal table of contents must be written for easy navigation to the rest of the plan, by numbering each section.

Executive summary

The executive summary is the most important part of a business plan, especially to the investors. Most investors do not go beyond the executive summary, as they have too many plans to read. So make sure that your executive summary is able of conveying clearly and succinctly exactly what you want your investors to read.

General company description should include Company Purpose, Your Business Profile, A Vision and Mission Statement, Mission, Problem, Solution, Company goals, Future plans, and SWOT analysis.

Products and Services

This section of the business plan will describe in a non-technical manner the characteristics of your products/services, stressing upon their competitive qualities. It includes product/service features, product/ service description, potential and benefits of the product/services, future products/ services and the technology.

Marketing Plan

This section of your business plan presents a market-research survey, locating your business in the market environment. It also determines whether the market is sufficient to support the business. It analyzes the following aspects:

Market characteristics and market segmentation.

Market analysis and its component parts.

Operations Plan

The operations plan is an essential component to your business plan and it tells the reviewer how you're going to get your product/service out to market. That is, how are you going to get your product out of the production stage to the doorstep of your target customer?

The operations plan may seem ordinary but it will outline some very important answers to such fundamental questions such as: Who is doing what? What are the day-to-day activities? How will the suppliers and vendors be used? Who are the suppliers? What are the labour requirements? What are the sources of raw materials?

Management and Organization

It offers a statement of your management philosophy with an in-depth focus on processes and procedures.

Key Personnel

Describes the unique backgrounds of principle employees involved in business.

Financial Plan

Financially astute readers may well turn to this section of your business plan first of all. This section, the most concrete, deals mainly with numbers. If you can translate your ideas into figures, you will demonstrate both your practical planning skills and the potential profitability of your business.

Financial Plan includes Financial Projections and Behaviour of costs.

Financial Projections describes Financial projections for three to five years, Income Statements, Balance Sheets and Cash Flows.

Behaviour of costs describes Fixed Costs and Variable Costs.

Exit strategies are Initial Public Offering, Merger/Acquisition and Buyout by partner.

Documents to be included in business financial analysis papers are the cash flow analysis, the pro forma balance sheet, the break-even analysis, the sales forecast, the market forecast, Profit and loss, the business ratio analysis, and the personnel plan.

Appendices

Supporting documents used to enhance your business proposal.

Miscalculations in Business Plan

Every business should have a business plan.

A perfect business plan shows the success of the business. Unfortunately, despite the fact that many of the underlying businesses are viable, the vast majority of plans are hardly worth the paper they're printed on. The new entrepreneurs are not well experienced in formulating the business plan. They commit most of the mistakes. They do not have any idea about the value of business plan.

The mistakes made by the new entrepreneurs are the plan is poorly written, Ethics and professionalism are poorly followed. Careless plan presentation, Follow-up, The plan is incomplete, Unclear roadmap, Entrepreneurs should research the spectators, The plan is too vague, Demonstrations or presentations that do not work, The plan is too detailed, The time and pace of the pitch is important, The plan makes unfounded or unrealistic assumptions, The plan includes inadequate research, You claim there's no risk involved in your new venture and You claim you have no competition.

The different features to be considered in business plan are Think it through, Do your research, Research your potential customers and competitors, Get feedback and Hire professional help.

KEYWORDS

Business plan: A business plan is a document that summarizes the operational and financial objectives of a business and contains the detailed plans and budgets showing how the objectives are to be realized.

Cover Page: It is the *first page* of your *business plan.*

Table of contents: Table of contents must be written for easy navigation to the rest of the plan, by numbering each section.

Executive summary: it is a brief description of the industry your firm is focusing on.

Marketing Plan: This section of your business plan presents a market-research survey, locating your business in the market environment.

Operational plan: It tells the reviewer how you're going to get your product/service out to market.

Financial Plan: It includes Financial Projections and Behaviour of costs.

Appendices: **Supporting documents used to enhance your business proposal.**

Exit strategies: Exit strategies are Initial Public Offering, Merger/Acquisition and Buyout by partner.

Questions

1. What do you mean by business plan?
2. Why entrepreneurs should prepare a business plan?
3. What are the contents of business plan? Explain in detail.
4. What are the mistakes done by an entrepreneur while writing a business plan?

❑ ❑ ❑

CHAPTER – 14

BIG COMPANIES RELATED OBSTACLES

LEARNING OBJECTIVES

On completion of this chapter, you should be able to:

- ☺ *Explain how difficult it is for the new small entrepreneurs to overcome the hurdles created by big companies.*
- ☺ *Describe different obstacles created by big companies.*
- ☺ *Describe different obstacles faced by entrepreneurs.*

Opening business in an environment where already number of experienced players are playing with all their skills, knowledge and intelligence is not an easy task for the new entrepreneurs. They open their business with the hope that they will also earn profit like big companies. They try to do all their best to run the business. The new entrepreneurs when open their business faces the following obstacles when they come in competition with the big companies:

14.1 Unable to do Effective Promotion and Advertising

For the new small entrepreneurs the big established businesses give tough competition. The big businesses by means of all promotional and advertising tools become successful to attract the customers. They take all efforts to sell the products and to get new customers in their business. But the new small entrepreneurs do not have much money so even if they want to attract the customers

BOX 14

Is Wal-Mart Killing Your Business?

The best strategies for small business owners struggling to compete with the discount giant

When small retailers see the blue big-box giant Wal-Mart moving into town it can be a scary thing. Wal-Mart has a powerful presence, especially now, as customers are drawn there for their legendary low-prices and wide array of offerings.

According to a study from Dartmouth's Tuck School of Business, the entry of a Wal-Mart does significantly impact sales at other local establishments. After observing the effects of seven Wal-Mart openings, researchers saw a 40 percent sales drop at nearby mass merchandise chains and 17 percent sales drop at supermarkets.

Kusum Ailawadi, the professor of marketing who led the study, was interested in not only the impact of Wal-Mart's entry, but in how different retailers reacted.

"In their reactions, retailers did a mix of everything," she says. "In general, they tend to reduce the number of brands they carried, lowered their price and also cut promotions."

It turns out, Ailawadi found, that these most commonly employed strategies were the least effective. Those stores that reduced prices often could still not match Wal-Mart's offerings. "You can't beat Wal-Mart on price," she says, so those retailers just ended up losing customers and revenue.

Instead of reducing brand offerings, Ailawadi found it was better to diversify and sell products that Wal-Mart won't have—such as higher-tier goods. She says that small businesses will have an easier time competing on this front because they will have less difficulty adjusting inventory in a more nuanced way. "What we found is that big retailers don't have the flexibility to react category by category, but small businesses have much more flexibility to fine tune a reaction."

Finally, she suggests that local retailers that can't match Wal-Mart's "everyday low prices" offer more promotions to draw customers. "If a store is offering weekly specials, it's harder to make exact price comparisons," she says.

The outlook, no matter what tactics retailers use, Ailawadi says, is bleak. While smaller companies may more easily fine-tune a strategic reaction, it's often less about boosting sales and more about survival.

Source: Information received from "Inc monthly magazine", 2009.

by means of all possible tools they can select only selected tools to attract the customers. They cannot use all the type of promotional tools and advertising. They have their limitations in investing money for promotion and the advertising. For example: a big business can distribute sample to as many customers as possible but for the small new business it is not readily possible they run their business under limited budget and if they will do the same as the big businesses do then they will not be able to provide proper money to other parts of the business.

Second reason is that customers are more attracted to the big companies' name. They try to use all big brands. In all that the small businesses' names hide somewhere because they are not popular as much as the big businesses are! So even if the new entrepreneurs' product is good, they are not being able to promote their products to the large customers.

Third reason is that they cannot take reputed celebrities to advertise about their products. The big companies by taking reputed celebrities can make their products easily popular because they can give such a huge amount to the celebrities. The small new entrepreneurs are not able to do such kind of things.

Fourth reason is that the big players have a huge force of the sales executive to promote their products in the market. All the sales executives are intelligent and have all necessary skills. But the new small entrepreneurs do not have such a huge force of the sales executives. They cannot keep such a huge force and their sales executives are also not competent enough. The small businesses do not provide training to their sales executives and therefore they are not competent enough as the big players sales executives are! For small entrepreneurs it takes time to reach to the final customers. The process is slow but the big players grab opportunities as soon as possible. After that nothing or less left for the new small entrepreneurs.

14.2 Tough Competition

New entrepreneurs find it very difficult to give competition to the big players. The big players have all the weapons of success. They can do anything what they want. For example they have technology and quality the most important factors of the products or services. To bring advance technology and make use of it for production is very easy for the big businesses but on the other side it is very difficult for the new entrepreneurs. They cannot purchase advanced technology so they stick to the old technology only and try to serve the market customers. The big players have different effective strategies for their products but the small new entrepreneurs lack this. Even most of the entrepreneurs are not aware about most of the strategies that can be effectively used. The new entrepreneurs are not the experienced one and they formulate the strategies according to their level of experience which may or may not be effective in the market.

14.3 Lack of R & D Facilities

The new entrepreneurs' businesses do not have R & D facilities. They never go for R & D before bringing product in the market. They have one reason for that; they cannot afford R & D facilities in their business because they do not have enough money so that they can invest in the R & D. The new entrepreneurs give little importance to the R & D. They are not completely aware about the importance of the R & D. They try to sell the products without any R & D. The big players on the other hand do every kind of R & D before bringing the product in the market. So they become successful in the market. They know the results of their product launch. The new entrepreneurs do not do any R & D and therefore they do not know the results, what could happen with their products? Therefore their probability of success becomes less as compared to the big players.

14.4 Unable to Maintain the Quality of the Products

Most of the new entrepreneurs definitely sell quality products but they are not able to maintain the quality of the products for long time. They lack consistency in maintaining the quality of the product. Their consistency totally depends upon the money they have on hand. If they do not have much money then they compromise with the quality of the products or sometimes their suppliers do not support them properly. They try to exploit them. The big players are famous for their quality products. They easily curb the small businesses in terms of quality. So for the new entrepreneurs maintaining the quality of the products become hard because they are new in the market, inexperienced, do not have much contact with the quality people and do not have good formula or method to have a quality product.

14.5 Unable to Penetrate Big Companies' Net

The big players already have a tie up with number of suppliers, distributors, retailers and so many people who are valuable for the business. They restrict the new players to enter into the market by all means. For example the big players restrict them by creating hurdles to access good suppliers; the big players make such an agreement with the suppliers so that the suppliers cannot sell raw material to new entrepreneurs. Suppliers become ready for this because they have their own benefits in that. The new entrepreneurs become unable to break these hurdles and as a result of that even if they want to procure good material from the good suppliers they cannot do that. The other example is of retail shop where the big players secure the best places in retail shop for their products. They give huge commission to the retail shop for giving the best places but the new entrepreneurs are not being able to secure the good place for their products in the retail shop. Big players always try to hamper the progress of small business by taking all illegal activities that will restrict the new players to enter into the market.

14.6 Lack of Business Experience

The big players are the experienced one, they know every unit of information of the market. They have database of all the possible activities, trends and affairs that is going on in the market. Nothing is hidden from them in the market. The new players do not have much information about the market. They do not know the sources of the information which are important for the business. Their partial knowledge becomes their problem. They miss the opportunity by not finding the information for their business. They lack in utilizing the information for their business purpose. That's why they lag in the business.

14.7 Protecting the Patent System for Entrepreneurs

Most of the small and new entrepreneurs are not aware about the laws of the patents. Even if they know about patent laws, they do not know how to apply for the patent. They do not have any information about the procedure of the patent. Most of the new small entrepreneurs when have a unique method, process or the products instead of using those methods, procedures or products for their own business sell that to the big companies. The big companies try to attract small one by giving huge amount of money. The small new entrepreneurs get into the attractive money and sell their unique idea. The problem is that the new entrepreneurs can also be the big ones but they should not sell their ideas to the big companies because they could have been achieved the great heights in their business if they have been used their own ideas instead of selling that idea to big companies.

14.8 How to Compete Against Larger Companies

If you are a small business and a bit intimated by competing against larger companies then follow the guideline given below.

Do you think that because you have a small business you can't compete against larger companies? Do you have a fear about your business? If you do then you have to think again. Most small business owners don't feel that they are in the same arena as larger companies so they don't even bother to try. They give up even before the actual race begins. This can be a big mistake and one that can cost your company in the long run.

Growing your company takes some competitive moves. Sure, you can continue to operate as you always have but this routine will not get you ahead. You must think differently. There are some guidelines, however, if you want to expand your business opportunities and compete against the big companies.

14.9 Start Thinking Big

Always have the big picture in mind. Thinking big means picturing what can be more than what already is. Always try to add something to your business. If you will become satisfied with your current situation then from that moment your business will stop progressing or even it may decline. Try to think something new for the business, try to set the big goals and divide those goals into the targets. If you will not think big then you will be doing the same business throughout the life without any additional achievement in your business. The day-to-day routine can get you in a rut and you can get so hung up on it that you fail to look ahead.

14.10 Bring Passion/Excitement into You

Loving what you do can help you get ahead. Passion is the primary condition of being a competent. The passion you have for your business not only helps catapult the company ahead but also helps motivate employees on a daily basis. Without passion the business then becomes only a formality for you. You do not take interest in that. The Passion also translates directly to sales. The passion you feel for your business can be more easily brought to the bottom line when there are fewer employees. You should also generate the same passion into your employees so that they will take the business from their heart. Larger companies have to work twice as hard to get the same feelings across to customers.

14.11 Think Outside the Box

This may sound like an old formula but it is really true. Out of box thinking will help you for formulating unique ideas and that idea will help you to grow in the business. If you can have vision to do things differently you just may get ahead. Business is all about the game of unique things. If you do the same thing in a different and more useful way then definitely you can give a tough competition to the big players. This is particularly true when it comes to competing with larger companies. You must think of ways that your company can provide something better than the large company can. Always try to adopt new processes for the company, try to bring more efficiency and effectiveness with new methods that will help your company.

14.12 Keep Yourselves Ahead

Instead of thinking about this month's numbers you should be looking towards the future. You should always plan for the future. Try to see what will happen to the future and how you will change your business accordingly to take benefits from the future opportunities. Great companies are made by revolutionaries - those who look ahead to the future to see the possibilities. Instead of entrapping yourselves into the current market situation try to think what will happen in the future, what kind of preparation is required for facing the future? A continuous forecasting should be done to reap the future opportunities. Larger companies may use technology to serve the customers but you can use the same technology on a smaller scale to serve the customers. Market is big; numbers of customers are there in the market with their own need so you can serve those customers who need your technical products. By doing this you can provide the same service, features and benefits at a much smaller cost.

14.13 Find Your Niche in the Market

Once you know what your market is you'll be much better able to cater to it. Try to give your business a position in the market for what you should be known in the market. Small new entrepreneurs instead of catering to the whole market customers they should try to cater to specific segment of the market. At initial level this will be the best strategy for you. Larger companies often lose focus and try to market to too broad a group. Instead use your marketing skills to your advantage. Yes, you have a much lower marketing budget than the larger companies do. But you can use your marketing strategies to your advantage if you know your niche. Marketing the specific segment will not create any complexity to you. You will be more focused to your customers and can better serve to the needs of the customers.

14.14 Use Internet to Your Advantage

The web has brought large and small companies to an even playing field. Make sure that you use the Internet to boost your business. Always have a web site presence. Don't skimp when it comes to your website. You don't need lots of pages but you do need a professional look. Be sure to put your website address on all your brochures and business cards. Internet is one of the gifts for the business. The small or big any entrepreneurs can use it. e-commerce has given the new strength to the small companies. Even if they do not have any branches in any area they can do business with the help of their e-commerce.

The products sold in shops and purchased in an organizations are the result of a complex web of relationships between manufacturers, component suppliers, wholesalers, retailers and the logistic infrastructure that links them together.

14.15 Provide What the Big Companies Can't or Don't

Look for weaknesses in your competition and use those to build your business. For example, one place where many larger companies fail is in providing good customer service. Small businesses can give better service because they care about each customer. Be sure to use that to help you win business over the larger competition. Customers are hungry for the good services. It does not matter whether the company is big or small what matters is that whether companies give respect to their customers or not. Whether they take care about their customers or not? Customers want good services and they want complete satisfaction of their needs. You as a small entrepreneur should always think of what extra you can do for the customers. How can you attract the customers? Try to provide those services that are not given by any of the companies. It will help you a lot to grow your business.

14.16 Importance of Best Practices

Today new small business owner are facing new business problems and lacking knowledge in converting the opportunities into a profit. Sustaining a business requires continuous upgradation of the business knowledge and a regular scanning of the market environment for getting new ideas, solutions or best practices. However, borrowing ideas and best practices can be wrought with danger. Learn what big business already knows about benchmarking best practices and how to effectively borrow or steal ideas, tactics and strategies.

What is a Best Practice?

A best practice is the process of searching and getting new ideas, solutions or strategies from outside your business to make effective changes in any area of your business.

Big business has used best practice benchmarking over decades and earned huge profit in all areas of business operations and sales. Small business has an opportunity to get complete benefits from best practices.

Benefits of Best Practices for Small Business

- **Reduce Costs:** Small businesses already do not have enough money for their business and therefore it becomes quite difficult for them to do any new inventions like big companies. By taking the knowledge of what other companies have productively done, a small business can save money and generate revenues without investing enough money in testing new ideas.
- **Avoid Mistakes:** Solving business problems on your own may not be much fruitful because you don't have any exact idea about the outcome of your solution. It can also cost you very badly. Learning what others have done to solve their business problems can keep your business in business.
- **Find New Ideas:** Adopting the "Not-Invented-Here" attitude can spell disaster for small business. Learn to borrow the best from beyond your company.
- **Improve Performance:** When your business looks for best practices outside your business, you learn the new things that you do not know and therefore your performance improves. You do what other businesses do in market and you keep your business according to the current trends in the market. You raise the bar of performance and set new standards of excellence to propel your company forward.

Steps for Best Practices

- First understand thoroughly the existing business processes.
- Look for one metric to measure.
- Analyze others' processes.
- Select one business process or service at a time to develop.
- Compare it with the standard process or with others process.
- Find out the gap and improve processes.
- Execute the process then measure the outcome.

Remember to survey companies of all sizes. And the time to complete a best practice study doesn't have to take months. A few weeks of literature research and telephone interviews are often enough for small business. Borrowing best practices from other businesses and industries can dramatically improve your small business. Take the time to learn the ingredients of success and your business will excel in good times and bad.

SUMMARY

Opening business in an environment where already numbers of experienced players are playing with all their skills, knowledge and intelligence is not an easy task for the new entrepreneurs. They open their business with the hope that they will also earn profit like big companies. They try to do all their best to run the business. The new entrepreneurs when open their business faces the following obstacles when they come in competition with the big companies:

Unable to do effective promotion and advertising: For the new small entrepreneurs the big established businesses give tough competition. The big businesses by means of all promotional and advertising tools become successful to attract the customers. But the new small entrepreneurs do not have much money so even if they want to attract the customers by means of all possible tools they can select only selected tools to attract the customers.

Tough competition

New entrepreneurs find it very difficult to give competition to the big players. The big players have all the weapons of success. They can do anything what they want. For example they have technology and quality the most important factors of the products or services. To bring advance technology and make use of it for production is very easy for the big businesses but on the other side it is very difficult for the new entrepreneurs.

Lack of R & D facilities

The new entrepreneurs businesses do not have R & D facilities. They never go for R & D before bringing product in the market. They have one reason for that; they cannot afford R & D facilities in their business because they do not have enough money so that they can invest in the R & D.

Unable to maintain the quality of the products

Most of the new entrepreneurs definitely sell quality products but they are not able to maintain the quality of the products for long time. They lack consistency in maintaining the quality of the product. Their consistency totally depends upon the money they have on hand.

Unable to penetrate big companies' net

The big players already have a tie up with number of suppliers, distributors, retailers and so many people who are valuable for the business. They restrict the new players to enter into the market by all means. For example the big players restrict them by creating hurdles to access good suppliers; the big players make such an agreement with the suppliers so that the suppliers cannot sell raw material to new entrepreneurs.

Lack of business experience

The big players are the experienced one, they know every unit of information of the market. They have database of all the possible activities, trends and affairs that is going on in the market. Nothing is hidden from them in the market. The new players do not have much information about the market.

Protecting the patent system for entrepreneurs

Most of the small and new entrepreneurs are not aware about the laws of the patents. Even if they know about patent laws, they do not know how to apply for the patent. They do not have any information about the procedure of the patent.

How to compete against larger companies

To compete against the big companies you must start thinking big, Bring passion / excitement into you, Think outside the box, Keep yourselves ahead, Find your niche in the market, Use Internet to your advantage, and Provide what the big companies can't or don't.

What is a Best Practice?

A best practice is the process of searching and getting new ideas, solutions or strategies from outside your business to make effective changes in any area of your business.

The benefits of best practices for small business are Reduce Costs, Avoid Mistakes, Improve Performance, and Find New Ideas.

KEYWORDS

Sales promotion: Sales promotion methods aim to capture the market and increase the sales volume.

Advertising: The act of telling people about products or events in order to make them want to buy them or take part.

R & D: Research and development department in a company that develops new products.

Outside the box: think laterally or unconventionally; look at the broader context of a problem, challenge, etc.

Niche Marketing: Niche marketing means a portion of a market that you've identified as having some special characteristic and that's worth marketing to that market.

Best practice: A best practice is the process of searching and getting new ideas, solutions or strategies.

QUESTIONS

1. What are the problems faced by small companies that are created by big companies?
2. Why small entrepreneurs do not give competition to big entrepreneurs?
3. What are the different threats created by big companies for small companies?
4. What do you mean by best practice? How it is beneficial to the small business?

❑ ❑ ❑

CHAPTER – 15

FINANCIAL OBSTACLES

LEARNING OBJECTIVES

On completion of this chapter, you should be able to:

- ☺ *Explain financial obstacles which are faced by the new small entrepreneurs.*
- ☺ *Describe difficulties which are faced by entrepreneurs in taking loan from financial institutes.*
- ☺ *Describe role of government grants in new business.*
- ☺ *Describe the resources of finance.*
- ☺ *Describe building relationship with lenders.*
- ☺ *Describe business funding myths.*

Most of the new entrepreneurs believe that, initial capital is the main problem to start a business. If proper loan and adequate financial support is easy to receive from Government and Private sector, then number of entrepreneurs would be increased. It also provides enough support for an established business to continue their business properly.

Staring a new business can be a stressful occurrence, especially having to come up with the startup funding that is necessary to better ensure success with your dreams. There are many options available to a prospective new business owner, but it is important that you find a choice that will be beneficial for you and your company. The financial mix is important for getting and maintaining the finance for the business. It pays to do your research and ask around to estimate how other small business owners received their start.

A great place to start when looking for startup funding for your new business is the government. A government entity helps people such as you get their new businesses off the ground. Of great importance is their listing of central and state government grants for individuals looking to start their own business. The most important thing is to know that the grants are highly competitive and skewed for certain industries in certain areas. The grants from the government can be easily got with the conditions that your business idea and plan should have a strong demand.

If you are serious about starting a new business, rest assured there are numerous options available to you. As mentioned before, do your research to find the option that is the most beneficial for your situation.

How to raise capital

When first starting your own business, the issue of how to raise capital will be your first obstacle. The new entrepreneurs are not aware about the way of raising funds for their own business.

BOX 15

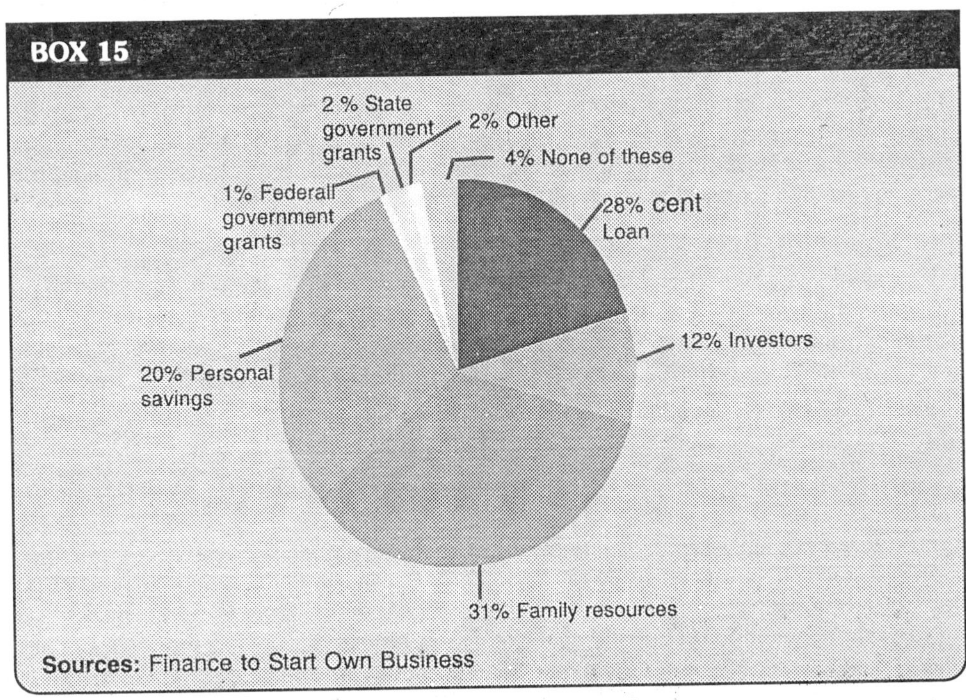

Sources: Finance to Start Own Business

They even do not know about government grants. They have an idea, business plan but they do not have money. It could also be one of the most difficult issues you are confronted with. There are several ways to raise capital that will help you get past these initial business road bumps. It is best to go into your business endeavors with a good idea and present that idea in a good form to investors. In other words, if you elaborate a business plan that sounds promising, you will surely be able to raise capital.

15.1 Financial Resources

It is not easy for the entrepreneur to arrange money for the business. The difficulties one entrepreneur faces are to find out the easiest resources of the finance from where he can get the finance without many hurdles. As a new entrepreneur no one suddenly trusts on the ability of the entrepreneur that he will run the business and as a result of that the entrepreneurs find it difficult to get money even if he has an ability, intelligence, skills etc., to run the business properly. Following are the resources from where entrepreneur can get finance.

- **Family, relatives and friends**

These are the resources from where the entrepreneur can get finance easily mostly on without interest, but these are the resources that do not fully satisfy the need of the business. So an entrepreneur does not have an option other than to go to the commercial banks.

Friends and family members are important sources of startup capital for your new business. If they are able to offer you a loan to get your business going, this could be a very beneficial situation. But at the same time it might not always be a good idea to mix business with friendships since it can cause problems in the future. The most important thing is to treat it like a business agreement with a detailed plan about how much the interest will be and how the loan will be paid back.

- **Commercial banks**

To get a loan from the commercial banks is not easy task for the new entrepreneur while taking loan he has to prove to the bank that he will return money to bank with all interest. His new step towards the entrepreneurship brings obstacles to the entrepreneur. The banks do not readily become ready to give loan to him.

- **Government grants**

The easiest way of getting finance for business is from government. But the real problems of the entrepreneurs are that most of the entrepreneurs don't know whether such kind of grants exist for their support in the business. Even if the entrepreneurs know it, it becomes difficult for them to get money from the government. Most of the new entrepreneurs rarely apply for that because of the complexity involves and delay in the government procedure.

15.2 Raise Capital with the Help of Grants

You have a possibly profitable idea which you strongly believe in for a small business, yet need to raise capital. There is no need to worry. You are not the only one confronted with this issue. You may have tried banks or various other lending institutions, only to find yourself turned down due to not meeting their lending guidelines. For the new entrepreneurs it is hard to meet all guidelines for taking the loan. That does not, however, mean that you need to give up, especially if you believe in the venture you are looking to get involved in. Entrepreneurs have one problem that is they easily do not get the finance for their business. What you and other prospective small business owners do not know is that you may have grants from state agencies and central government at your disposal. But you are unaware about such grants and therefore you miss the chance of getting finance.

The problems of the new entrepreneurs are that they do not get fund easily. They have to put extra efforts to get fund. Government grants involve very complex procedures. Most of the entrepreneurs are not aware about those complex procedures to get fund for the business and it is very time consuming. It takes much time to get fund to clear all the documents.

Who knows why grants are being overlooked, may be they do not want to put themselves into the complex procedure of the government grants but the bottom line is that they could save you some headaches, so that going a bit deeper into this possibility might be more than useful if you want to raise capital for your small business. Do you think that the government is on a tight budget? Think again. Do you want to raise capital? Then you should at least do some additional research if you think that grants may be available to you. Try to impress the investors by your planning. But the problem with the new entrepreneurs is that they do not know the way to get grants for the business. They do not have any idea to deal with the government agency. They do not know where to go, with whom to contact, what are the requirements like so many things. Grants should at least be considered as an alternative way to raise capital.

If you are in certain specialized industries, you might stand a greater chance at being able to raise capital through grants. Government promotes some special kind of businesses. There are many interesting grant opportunities open of sheltered workshops and this is only one example. If you live in an area with a high unemployment rate, then you can be sure that it is in the government's best interest to give you a grant if you want to raise capital for a business which is likely to produce many job opportunities. Opening the business also helps the government to reduce the unemployment rate. If your business has a future and you have all information then your chances are bright. Many people would never be able to raise capital for their business without grants, due to the fact that a lot of assets are required in order to secure the costs of running those businesses.

Depending on your character, academic background and experience, you can be eligible for a grant. If you are from family background, well qualified, experienced and have zeal to open the business then definitely you will get a grant. After you raise capital, you can pay off your debt in a fixed timeframe, but, in general, the schedules with grants are far more flexible that other lending institutions. All types of businesses are eligible for grants. The owners of certain companies know very well how natural disasters or seasonal downturns can negatively affect their business.

The owners may find that they are in a situation where they do not have the necessary cash flow to keep things running smoothly and need to raise capital. As a result, maximum grants may be the solution for them. Many companies would have had to close down after certain downturns due to the lack of working capital without the help of grants. And it would be too bad to let businesses with economical value go waste. That is why the government helps owners of such companies raise capital. These businesses only needed a hand from the government and they have managed to raise capital in order to keep them from getting off-track. If you find yourself needing to raise capital or start a new venture, exploring the various grant possibilities out there is recommended.

15.3 Getting Finance

Entrepreneurs find it very difficult to get fund for their business. They are the young ones and they do not have much experience of their business because of that most of the financial agencies do not show interest as well as trust on them. When finding ways to raise capital, think about how you present your business plan to investors. In some ways, it is like presenting your resume to a potential employer. Every detail is important and critical in persuading investors to contribute to your business. The new entrepreneurs find it difficult to make a business plan. They just try to know how could be the business plan. What are the requirements of the business plan?

Much like you explain your academic background and how it could help in adding value to the company, you are presenting your plan to investors on how to raise capital and to make them confident in your business. Be sure to provide as many details and references as possible. You do not want to leave any question potential investors could ask unanswered.

When thinking of how to raise capital through investors, you need to consider the business not only getting onto its feet, but you should present estimations of the income in the next three to five years. Your plan should seem very profitable. By researching the market you are thinking about entering and putting together a projected cost report, you can easily overcome the issues of how to raise capital on your new business.

Also, you might consider involving forecasts of your potential customers if you are serious about the investment and to have an edge over your competitors. There are many ways to raise capital and to appeal to investors for more than just getting your business off the ground. Many websites and consultants can help in developing your business plan to help find ways to raise capital for your new business.

15.4 Non Availability of Capital

If an entrepreneur wants to set up a business he will need some Startup Business Capital and unless he was born into wealthy family he'll have to look into getting a Business Capital loan. Mostly new entrepreneurs face such type of situation where they become paralyzed because of the lack of capital. They are eager to open the business ready to face challenges but without money they are not able to move forward. They collect money from the relatives, friends but they do not collect the amount that they actually need. Therefore they do not open the business what exactly they want to open.

A business loan is often used by business owners who are just starting to access some much needed cash for their business start up, or for business growth and improvement. On the other hand you may need startup Business Capital in order to provide working capital for a business that can be used to purchase necessary machinery.

Standard Business Capital loans can take on several different forms in specific situations. While there are stringent central guidelines about how banks and other lenders conduct business, there are no definitive standards as to how the various types of Business Capital loans are structured: the terms and conditions may and will probably vary from one lender to the next and minimum and maximum amounts can differ. Private investors are a great source of startup Business Capital that will help your new business reach success.

It would be ideal for small businesses to start planning at least a year even before they put forth their proposal for any venture capital or financial aid. Getting finance is not easy unless they have a solid plan. You need to conduct some market research and business concepts and ideas to be examined and analyzed. Entrepreneurs will also need to find and consult with great financial advisors to guide them towards received approval for grants.

15.5 Improper Estimation of the Cost

A common mistake many first-time business owners make is underestimating the amount needed to start their new business. In fact, this unintentional miscalculation is one of the leading reasons why most businesses tend to fail in the first year of operation. Even though there is never a guaranteed way of knowing a new business will make a substantial amount of profit or that it will "break-even," entrepreneurs still need to properly calculate the different costs before further investing their time and effort into the startup. Entrepreneurship can be a very costly venture and many first-time business owners need to properly assess the many different challenges that lie ahead, especially when it comes to estimating the startup costs.

15.6 Research Estimated Costs

One way entrepreneurs can avoid the underestimation of new business costs is by doing independent research. The entrepreneurs are not interested in doing deep research about their business. By simply taking time out to research the various anticipated expenses for a new business, business owners will be able to educate themselves about the industry, any leading competitors and how much will be needed to launch and sustain their startup. They also need to analyze the performance of similar products in the market and determine different ways in which the product can improve. Research can be conducted through visiting online entrepreneur sites and by reading small business and startup books which include the detailed description of the business startup. In addition, entrepreneurs can also speak to other business owners who have experience and success in the same field. If an entrepreneur does not have the time to conduct independent research, they are able to hire a professional who can do the research for them. For an average cost many business owners can conveniently obtain any needed marketing information for their new business.

15.7 Product Development and Commercialization

One very important component to consider when starting a new business is the process of new product development and the amount of money it takes to effectively create a product. The deep process understanding will clear this doubt. Entrepreneurs do not know what to do for proper calculation of the cost. They themselves do the calculation of the cost that normally fails to consider other cost that the entrepreneurs don't know. They do not think economically. They do not know the different factors that they should consider for the proper cost calculation for example fixed cost or variable costs. Many entrepreneurs will agree this development process not only takes time and effort to execute but it can also be financially draining. During a new product's development, an idea can be generated rather quickly. However, it is the concept development and testing phase that may take a considerable amount of time to complete. In this particular phase, entrepreneurs will be faced with the cost of producing their product. They may also need to invest additional funding into the product's test marketing and technical implementation phase, which may require more specialized revisions before their product can be commercialized.

15.8 Website and Technology Expenses

Entrepreneurs initially do not pay much attention to the website. But when their business slowly grow or when they know that web site is also the requirement then at that time they do not have money to invest because they did not consider website development cost and they face the problem. So even if the entrepreneurs want to advertise their product through websites they remain helpless in such situation. Every new business should have an updated, well-detailed website that proudly introduces their company and its different products and services. Their website should be user-friendly and designed and maintained by skilled technical professionals. A company's website development and maintenance is a necessary cost, especially if the company is interested in making additional revenue outside of the traditional in-store purchases. In addition, business owners need to consider other technological expenses, including computers and accessories with updated specialized software for their company. Website and technological expenses are essential in today's innovative and technologically-adapt society.

15.9 Office Expenses

Another cost to consider when starting a business is office expense. This financial figure can encompass the combined amount of renting (or buying) office space, office furniture, telephone and fax lines, high-speed internet access, office supplies, etc. It can also include licensure costs, down payments and surcharges, office utility bills, inventory, maintenance and company-related miscellaneous expenses. Many entrepreneurs do not realize how important this expense can be in order to properly sustain a business and that is the reason why this cost is most often overlooked. And when they run their business they face the problems of non availability of the money. So in this situation either they have to invest the money or to discard the things. If they discard the things then their business suffers.

15.10 Marketing and Advertising Costs

Every new business should also be aware that in order to gain public recognition and paying customers, they will need to spend money on promoting their company and its products and services. But the fact is that opening business is enough for the new small entrepreneurs. They already dried up by their business opening. They after opening the business live on the mercy of the customers. They do not have any idea about different strategies to propagate the business. Marketing materials can include anything from professional business cards and stationery; local, nationwide and international advertising campaigns; online and in-store promotional offers; public relations, company flyers and brochures; internet and telephone marketing, etc. Depending on the type of industry and the aggressiveness of a company's public relations approach, this process can be very expensive. The new entrepreneurs because of the non availability of the fund do not care about the above requirements but the fact is that they actually create obstacles for their business.

15.11 Basic Living Salary for Business Founders

Business owners need to calculate how much their exclusive salary should be during the initial years of startup development. Even though most entrepreneurs may choose a modest salary, they should take into consideration the cost of living, including rent or mortgage payments, car and gas expenses, food, clothing and other personal costs that are needed to sustain themselves and their families for about one year. A founder's living expense can certainly cost less than their overall startup business costs; however, its significance should be taken into account since most new businesses will not reflect any profit for at least one year.

15.12 Other Employee Payroll and Benefits

When starting a new business, entrepreneurs should take into account the salaries and benefits of their employees. First, they should consider if they will be the sole operator of their business or if employees will work for them. If their business will encompass the assistance of paid staff members, then the business owner needs to determine the hierarchy of workers and the number of full-time and part-time staff so their salaries can be adjusted. In addition, they can also determine who will be qualified for receiving health insurance and other employee-related benefits. Normally the entrepreneurs do not provide most of the facilities given to the employees. They themselves run out of money. Employee payroll and benefits are just two of the many different costs needed for a startup. Entrepreneurs do not have a perfect salary structure for their employees. They even do not bother about the employees' payment. But they forgot the facts that employees are the strength of their business if they will not be happy then they will shift to some other place. Entrepreneurs' salary structure always collapse when they invest the salary of the employees in the business and then employees suffer. In such situation employees leave the business because of improper salary or delay in salary that affects the entrepreneurs' business.

15.13 Monthly Insurance Costs

Another very important expense to keep in mind is the monthly cost of small business insurance. Every new business needs different kinds of insurance in order to protect their company, personal assets and paid employees. For many business owners, the type of insurance they choose is highly dependent on the nature of their business. For example, liability insurance can protect a business' property, while worker's compensation insurance abides by state-specific rules when enforced. In addition, if a new company has a great deal of assets, they may be inclined to purchase property damage or theft insurance.

15.14 Legal and Professional Fees

During the pre-startup phase and throughout a company's progress, an entrepreneur will work with many collaborators (including accountants, investors, advisors, etc.,) in ensuring the successful launch and development of their company. Most of these professionals charge high fees. In fact, they are rather expensive to hire and sustain. For example, many lawyers can charge anywhere from a few thousand to tens of thousands of just for lease negotiations, patent, trademark and logo planning and non-disclosure agreements. Accountants, on the other hand, can also charge just as much, especially since they are needed for financial guidance and company tax purposes. Entrepreneurs should never underestimate the need for these hired professionals since they are the only ones who can provide necessary guidance to an entrepreneur during stressful time of starting a business.

15.15 Travel Expenses

Every company should consider travel expenses in their startup costs. These expenses will usually cover any business-related training outside of the company's center of operations. They can include any educational or technical workshops, seminars or training for employees and founders. Depending on the number of employees, a company's travel expenses may be equally as important as other company expenditures.

So lastly it can be said that....

The predicted costs for starting a company are often underestimated. An entrepreneur needs to properly evaluate all the associated expenses that need to be paid prior to the launch of their new company. Once they are able to consider the different financial costs, these estimated values should be well-documented in their company's business plan. Failure to properly record all financial projections can easily cost a business owner from obtaining the necessary capital from institutional lenders and potential investors.

Once all fundamental costs are carefully measured and well-thought out, the entrepreneur can then find different sources of funding for their new business. If considering different sources other than personal financing, they should then attempt to convince a business investor their product, indeed, shows promise of making a substantial amount of profit.

15.16 Obtaining Short Term and Long Term Loans

Banks are not motivated so much to give loan to the new entrepreneurs. Even if banks become ready the whole loan of the entrepreneur is not passed by banks because of the lack of trust that is shown by the banks towards new entrepreneur unless the new entrepreneur has a good financial background. Here the entrepreneur faces most of the problems.

Banks are of course a common source of Business Capital loans, but they are somewhat conservative in their lending decisions. Entrepreneurs shall have to find a banker that is knowledgeable enough that he understands the world market he can review their summary and can agree in principle to fund project with collateral that is acceptable to the bank. He or she will review the Business Capital loan request and after determining if the project is a viable business situation will state in a letter, that they will fund your acquisition.

15.17 Financial Information Utilization

To many people, starting a business may be a bit overwhelming. Entrepreneurs not only need to define their value proposition but they must also setup operations, offer economically viable solutions, gain credibility, build a customer base and generate revenues. Although entrepreneurs face number of challenges when they commercialize their business ideas, raising startup capital (seed investment) to fund their business efforts is the most challenging of all.

Although the pool of capital available for startup companies is not significantly larger today than a decade ago, the variety of financing options is larger. The large variety of financing sources makes raising funds for different ventures easier. However, every specific source of financing is associated with certain obligations that entrepreneurs must understand before raising capital. The more educated entrepreneurs are, the more likely they are going to succeed in raising startup capital.

The following are the major sources of funding for entrepreneurs:

(i) Personal finances

(ii) Friends and family

(iii) Angel investors

(iv) Debt financing

(v) Equity financing

(vi) Government–sponsored programs

Personal Finances

People start companies at different points in their lives. Some entrepreneurs start companies during the early stages of their career. A majority of entrepreneurs start companies at later stages in their lives and these entrepreneurs often have personal assets that they could use to finance their ideas. They do not find any difficulty to open the business. They have sufficient money to open the business. It is important for entrepreneurs to invest their personal savings in their business ideas as it indicates that the entrepreneur is confident about his or her own idea, thereby encouraging other investors to look at the idea more seriously. After all, who would like to invest in a company wherein the founder does not want to bet on the idea? Additionally, entrepreneurs who do not put their personal savings into the venture can find it hard to raise money from friends and family. They can never implement their idea so easily. Entrepreneurs should think thoroughly before investing their personal finances. If the business idea is not feasible, the entrepreneur loses everything.

Friends and Family

Friends and family are important sources for financing startups since they would like to see the entrepreneur succeed. They help the new entrepreneurs a lot. Entrepreneurs here have one advantage that is they become assure that they will not have a pressure on them like the pressure they have when they take loan from bank. Such loans can be obtained quickly as this type of financing is based more on personal relationships than on financial analysis. However, friends and relatives who provide business loans sometime feel that they have the right to offer suggestions concerning the management of the business. Their suggestions might be orthogonal to the entrepreneur's strategy and might create fissures in the relationships. It is important to minimize the chance of damaging important personal relationships. Therefore, entrepreneurs should plan on repaying such loans as soon as possible even if the business idea fails, thereby ensuring that relationships are maintained.

Angel Investors

A large number of individuals invest in a variety of entrepreneurial ventures. They are affluent people such as successful entrepreneurs, lawyers, physicians, etc., who have moderate to significant business experience. This type of financing is called as informal capital because these individuals do not make such investments in established market places. Such investors are called business angels. Although angel investment is easier to acquire than some of the more formal types of financing, angels can sometimes be very demanding. Entrepreneurs should therefore define their relationships with the angels before finalizing the terms of the agreement. It is imperative to emphasize that any angel investor would be skeptical to fund a company, wherein the founders do want not invest their personal savings.

Debt Financing

Entrepreneurs can also raise capital from banks through the debt financing route. Although some angels provide debt capital, commercial banks are the primary providers of debt capital to small companies. Bankers tend to make business loans through lines of credit, term loans and mortgages.

Equity Financing

As opposed to debt financing, equity financing transfers the risk from the entrepreneur to the investors, but has its own set of drawbacks. Equity financing is when entrepreneurs can raise money only through selling common or preferred stock to investors. This implies that an entrepreneur gives up some of his or her voting rights to investors. Although most angels offer equity financing, institutional venture capitals make the biggest equity financing investments.

Government–sponsored programs

Although there are a number of financing sources, it is important that entrepreneurs plan their strategy to raise capital. The decision to use debt or equity financing depends to a large extent on the type of business, the firm's financial strength and the current economic environment, e.g., whether lenders and investors are optimistic or pessimistic about the immediate future. The entrepreneur should start pitching his or her idea as soon as the business plan is ready to meet the investors' eyes. The entrepreneur should then determine the best suitable capital sources for his or her business idea and focus on those sources only. Entrepreneurs should allow ample time for raising capital, since it generally takes more time than most people think.

15.18 Building Relationship with Lender

The new entrepreneurs are not able to make strong relationship with the lender like the experienced one do. They are not treated well by the lender. They are always suppressed by the lender. Entrepreneurs also do not have any option but to continue with the lender who is providing finance to them for their business.

How to manage the finance function and lender relationships of any business or company goes hand in hand. Poorly managed finance functions of any business or company will lead you to poor lender relationships. You and your business or company will be less likely to get any new credit or other types of funding for any projects that your business or company needs. Here are a few tips on how you can better manage the finance function of your business to improve any lender relationships you have or may have in the future.

The first step in managing the finance function of your business is to keep detailed records of all your accounts. The more detail you have in your books the easier it is to keep track of all your money. You will know where your money comes from and where your money goes. Keeping track of all expenditures will help you in lender relationships because it is easier for you to show or even explain where your business is financially. Detailed records of all your accounts will make it easier for you to obtain credit for your business through lender relationships.

You can manage the finance function and lender relationships by not only keeping good records but also by knowing what your company or business needs and wants financially. Knowing these financial goals will help your lender get you the best loans and rates available to you and your business or company. The lender relationship can be made easier when you both have the same goals in mind. The lender will be better able to work for you when he knows what your business or company's financial goals are.

Another step in how to manage the finance function and lender relationships is to stay in good relations with any lenders your company or business may have. Whenever you and your company have a good relationship with any of your lenders it is easier for you to rely on your lenders through all the normal business cycles no matter if the current cycle is a positive cycle or a negative cycle. As a way to manage your finance function you should go out of your way to let the lenders know that they are important to you and your business so that you keep a good lender relationship.

Managing your finance function and your lender relationships is good for both companies. Both the company and the lender understand that they are strategic partners in any business deal. The company and the lender realize that they need each other and that both can benefit financially from a long-term partnership. In order to manage the finance function and the lender relationships you will need to keep both sides happy to continue complimenting each other.

15.19 Small Business Funding Myths

There exist many misconceptions regarding funding for small businesses. Some prospective business owners may believe that obtaining necessary capital is an easy and straightforward task, when, in fact, the process may be more complicated than initially anticipated. For example, many business owners may feel that it is not needed to implement an effective marketing strategy or prepare a well-devised business plan, which can often greatly contribute to a company's failure. Furthermore, there is an erroneous belief that government can offer financial assistance to those who apply and that entrepreneurs can increase their chances of acquiring angel capital if they actively solicit the help from numerous contacts.

An individual considering the prospect of entrepreneurship should be aware that it takes time to evaluate the different options in order to obtain funding and that they may even experience repeated rejections before the needed capital is raised.

Myth – "I can open my business as soon as possible"

The reality- opening the business is not an easy task. It requires planning, business plan, approvals, marketing plan and financial plan. It takes time. It requires deep study of the business, business environment, competitors etc. You should not be very much excited for opening the business unless you have fully planned about your business otherwise after opening the business you will not be able to give proper time for your business problems or by the time you will know your mistakes you would have invested your valuable resources that cannot be reverted back. Getting all knowledge about business is must. Partial knowledge about business will damage your business because sometimes you may find yourselves in such a problem from where you cannot come out easily. So have patience, do complete planning and then go for the business.

Myth - "I can easily find funding for my new business in a few months."

The reality- Obtaining a start-up funding is not easy rather it is a complex and lengthy process. The new entrepreneurs do not have any idea about time duration for getting finance. The investors have many such business plans, they evaluate different business plans. It takes time to get money. A wise entrepreneur is one who acknowledges this extensive process yet is patient and seeks all means to accomplish this goal. First, these entrepreneurs take time out to meticulously research prospective investors with experience in their field of industry. In the course of this process, they may be rejected multiple times; however, they still find time to optimize their resources by networking extensively with others. They also use their rejections in a positive way. They work on improving the business plan by removing all the mistakes of business plan and devise a well-detailed business plan. Many investors will not help entrepreneurs in investment if entrepreneurs are not ready with their business plan and other preparations. Investors also see how much effort entrepreneurs are taking for their business. The investors thoroughly check the entire business plan; they wait if they can get some more interesting business plan. Investors always search for such a plan that involves less risk and maximum profits. Their invested company's products and services must also prove to be successful in trial marketing, which may also take a considerable amount of time to execute. A good entrepreneur must be able to get all the financial opportunities to launch their business.

Myth - "My business idea is great and unique. I should get funding right away."

The reality- Many times entrepreneurs are very enthusiastic and overconfident about their business ideas and innovations. Just because they feel that their products or services are marketable does not mean that they will convince the investors for their ideas. The investors have their own attitude and perceptions. They think by their own mind and logic. Every year many people come up with their business ideas and think that their ideas are the best but the fact is that most of them only disappoint. Many times it happens that even if the idea is good but inventors are not able to defend it from major competitors in the market. Tough competition destroys their ideas. That is why entrepreneurs need to research market, customers and competitors and then should develop the idea accordingly. An innovative product or service will be successful when customers will be willing to pay for that innovation. This will not only show investors that the company has the potential for producing a large return on investment, but it also gives time to polish any flaws before mass production of a product takes place.

Myth - "I know everything about my business; therefore, I do not need to create a business plan."

The reality- Approximately 90 per cent of all small businesses fail within the first two years of operation. It is very surprising that many do not have business plan. If a business plan exists, it may not be updated or the company may even fail to comply with their existing plan. They do not follow the business plan. They even do not know the actual importance of the business plan. That is why most successful entrepreneurs agree that opening, running and surviving a business requires an effective business plan. Prospective investors start their evaluation from the business plan itself and without business plan they will not be ready for investment. A business plan primarily focuses on purpose of business, daily company operations, customers, competitors, the management team and employees, finances, etc., Business owners and employees are encouraged to follow their business plan and update it accordingly throughout the development of their company.

Myth - "I know how to market my products; therefore, I do not need a marketing plan."

The reality- A marketing plan is a written document that details the advertising objectives of a company. It shows how you will penetrate the market? How will you reach to the customers? What could be the target customers? It documents a business' marketing approach and expenditures in promoting their company, brand or company's product line. Many startups depend on their marketing plan to gain publicity and to promote newly released products or services. But the new entrepreneurs are not able to make a proper marketing plan; they do not have any plan. They want to sell products or run the business without any plan that leaves them at random without direction. Consumers, on the other hand, are highly influenced to buy products from companies with effective marketing plans and strategies. Hired professionals are known to devise successful marketing plans, which are vital components of a company's overall investment. Through an effective marketing strategy, plan and public relations, an enterprise and their product line can gain public recognition, further contributing to their success and profitability.

Myth - "The more investors I contact, the more likely I can find funding."

The reality- In the hope of getting required funds for the business the entrepreneurs contacts many investors through e-mails and direct mail. Investors will admit that this is clearly the wrong approach when trying to find investors since mass mailing is considered a waste of money, time and energy. Entrepreneurs should not be very eager in finding the investors. They should not select any investor. They should select quality investors who have a track record of success. Investors are also an expert. They have knowledge about business and therefore indirectly they help entrepreneurs in their business by evaluating their business plan and suggesting the improvements. If entrepreneurs will see only money then definitely they will get money but what about business success? In the process of searching entrepreneurs may be rejected but the entrepreneurs should not be stopped and should try to find out credible investors. Upon this research, each prospective investor should then be sent a personalized request. By sending these custom-made requirements, the entrepreneur will gain credibility from investors, who will recognize them for conducting their own due diligence.

Myth - "I can easily get funding from the Government"

The reality- This is a very wrong thinking of the entrepreneurs. In real sense government does not give money directly to the businesses owners. Government just gives their guarantee to the lenders on behalf of the new entrepreneurs so that new entrepreneurs should not face any difficulty from the lenders for getting loans for their business. So government provides an opportunity to the prospective entrepreneurs for building their business. Even any one cannot take the benefits of this opportunity; a prospective applicant should have a good credit history, proof of income, a solid business plan, marketing plan, financial plan and collateral in order to be considered. Even though loan is smaller in amount but approval of a government, increases chances of obtaining additional capital from many lending institutions. The fact is that the grant funding is small in size and therefore entrepreneurs cannot use it for financing the business at initial stage. Even after getting grants businesses have to search for the additional sources of capital. It is also a very competitive process to obtain a central grant since there is only limited funding available. Entrepreneurs who strongly believe that their business falls into the category of receiving government grants should target different organizations and propose a grant request.

Myth - "Venture capitalists will give me money for my startup."

The reality- Venture capitalists invest in already established business. They do not invest in a very new business. Venture capitalists collect their money from various sources and select the company with good revenue record. They are very sensitive while selecting the companies for their investment. They want to invest their money in good companies so that they can get return on that. Angel investors, contrary to the venture capitalists invest in startups and early stage businesses, the businesses that are not properly established and not yet seen any success. They use their own money for funding young companies, making their investments more "risky" than that of venture capitalists. However, they are also selective with their applicants, who need to convince them that their company will produce a large return on investment.

So What Could Be the Solution?

15.20 Small Business Finance

Small Business Finance refers to the task of providing funds or capital required for the starting up and daily activities of the Small Business Enterprise. This Small Business Finance should be done in a way that it properly balances risk and profitability. This financing or funding can be long term or short term. The term depends on the nature of the sources from which the funds are coming. These long term and short term finances actually constructs the capital structure of the Small Business Enterprise. Small Business Entities can use several sources for accumulating their required capital. The main sources of funding can be:

- **Self-financing by the owner**

  Owner of the Business can use his own savings for financing his own business. This self-financing can be done through cash or he can take equity loan on his home and can use his other assets.

- **Loans from friends and relatives**

  Generally it has been observed that people who start small business takes loans from their friends and relatives and repay at their convenience.

- **Forming Partnerships**

In a partnership, all partners invests capital in the business. They share profit or loss whatever is generated by the small partnership business as they have contributed capital and sometimes even property.

Partnership can be of three types:

General Partnership-Here all partners have the power to manage the business and they are personally responsible for the debts. Limited Partnerships-In Limited Partnership there are some general partners and some are partners with limited liability. Here only general partners have control over management, the limited partners are only responsible for the debts to the extent of their investment in the business but they have no influence on the management of the business. Limited Liability Partnership-Here all partners have limited liability but all of them have power to manage the business. Here one thing should be mentioned that financing through partnership must be encouraged because in partnership no Dividend Tax (tax imposed on the realized profit) is needed to be paid whereas in private ownership small businesses it has to be paid.

- **Venture Capital**

Venture capital is a kind of private equity capital, which is supplied by the professional investors and given to new growing businesses on submission of sufficiently impressive business venture plans. In this form of funding the financing is actually done by third-party investors who invest from the professionally managed fund, which is generated by managing the pooled money of others.

- **Angel Investors**

By Angel Investor we mean a wealthy person who lends his own personal funds for setting up a business and in return generally acquires ownership equity of the business. Nowadays some Angel Investors are being organized amongst them and are forming Angel Groups or Angel Networks, which will engage them in financing small businesses to a greater extent. Other than the above-mentioned main sources of finance, some small businesses are further funded through Credit Card. But this source of funding should not be encouraged as the interest rates are pretty higher compared to the interest rates associated with bank loan.

Bank Loans also can be a source of funding for a small business but the loan cannot be taken in the name of the business; it has to be taken in the name of the business owner as banks ask for personal guarantee. Donations, Grants and Subsidies can also be sources of finance for small businesses. In Indian Government Small Business Loans are available through Schemes if the small business owners are ready to pledge their personal assets and have a strong business plan and have a good track record of repaying loans. Sometimes these loans have been proved to be better than grants, venture funds or venture investors.

15.21 Government Funding and Schemes

An entrepreneur requires a continuous flow of funds not only for setting up of his/ her business, but also for successful operation as well as regular upgradation/ modernization of the industrial unit. To meet this requirement, the Government (both at the Central and State level) has been undertaking several steps like setting up of banks and financial institutions; formulating various policies and schemes, etc. All such measures are specifically focused towards the promotion and development of small and medium enterprises.

The public sector banks are the major source of financial assistance to the industrial sector. They extend credit support to the firms in the form of loans, advances, discounting bills, project financing, term loans, export finance, etc. Some of the major examples of such banks are:

1. **State Bank of India (SBI)** provides a wide range of financial products and services that can cater to any business or market requirement. It deploys multiple channels to deliver integrated solutions for all financial challenges faced by the corporate universe. Its various funding schemes are:-
   - **Working capital finance**, extended to all segments of industries and services sector.
   - **Corporate term loans** to support capital expenditures for setting up new ventures as also for expansion, renovation, etc.
   - **Deferred payment guarantees** to support purchase of capital equipments.
   - **Project finance**
   - **Structured Finance**

The bank also provides financial assistance to agriculturists through a network of rural and semi-urban branches. These specialized branches have been set up in different parts of the country exclusively for the development of agriculture through credit deployment. Their schemes cover a wide range of agricultural activities like **crop loan**, **finance to horticulture**, **farm mechanization schemes**, **land development schemes**, **minor irrigation projects**, **agricultural term loans**, etc.

1. **Bank of Baroda** offers various products and services that meet the specific requirements of business enterprises, particularly the small scale units. Various schemes relating to the provision of loans and advances by the bank include:
   - Working Capital Finance
   - Term Finance
   - Small and Medium Enterprise (SME) Loan Pack
   - Small Business Borrowers
   - Traders Loan

2. **Andhra Bank** has also devised a host of loan schemes to meet the financial requirements of an enterprise. These particularly cater to the corporate and agricultural sector. Some of its important funding options include:
   - Working Capital Loans
   - Export and Import Finance
   - Advance against Shares
   - Term Finance
   - Corporate Loans
   - Project Finance
   - Infrastructure Project Finance
   - Kisan Vikas Card
   - Kisan Sampathi
   - Self Help Groups-Bank Linkage Programme
   - Kisan Green Card

Small scale industries need **credit support** on a continuous basis for running the enterprise as well as for its diversification and modernization. Recognising the need for a focused financial assistance to such industries, the Government of India, together with the State Governments, has formulated several policy packages including schemes and funds for their growth and development. Most of these programmes of the Central Government are implemented through two principal organisations:

1. **Small Industries Development Organisation (SIDO)** is an apex body for promotion and development of small scale industries in the country. Its major activities include:
   - Advising the Government on formulation of policies and programmes for the small-scale industries.
   - Conducting periodical census/survey of the small scale industry and generating data/reports on various important parameters/indicators of growth and development of the sector.
   - Maintaining close liaison with other Central Ministries, Planning Commission, State Governments, Financial Institutions and other organisations concerned with the development of small-scale industries.
   - Facilitating linkage of small-scale industries as ancillaries to large and medium scale industries.
   - Developing human resource base through training and skill upgradation.

For achieving its objectives, SIDO has devised a comprehensive range of schemes for providing credit facilities, technology support services and marketing assistance, etc. Some of the major **schemes** are:

- Credit Linked Capital Subsidy Scheme for Technology Upgradation
- Credit Guarantee Scheme
- ISO 9000/ISO 14001 Certification Reimbursement Scheme
- Integrated Infrastructure Development (IID Scheme)
- SSI MDA Scheme
- Assistance to Entrepreneurship Development Institutes
- Micro Finance Programme

2. **National Small Industries Corporation Ltd (NSIC)** has been established with the objective of promoting, aiding and fostering the growth of small scale industries in the country. It has been assisting small enterprises through a set of specially tailored schemes which facilitate marketing support, credit support, technology support and other support services.

- **Marketing support schemes:** Sound marketing is critical for the growth and survival of small enterprises. NSIC acts as a facilitator to promote small industries products and has devised a number of schemes to support small enterprises in their marketing.
- **Credit support schemes:** NSIC facilitates credit requirements of small enterprises in several areas. These include:
  - **Equipment financing:** through schemes like 'Hire Purchase' and 'Term Loan' for the procurement of equipments.
  - **Financing for procurement of raw material:** by facilitating bulk purchase of basic raw materials at competitive rates, import of scares raw materials, etc. NSIC also takes care of all the procedures, documentation and issue of letter of credit in case of imports.
  - **Financing for marketing activities:** such as internal marketing, exports and bill discounting, etc.
  - **Financing through syndication with banks:** by entering into strategic alliances with commercial banks so as to facilitate fund requirement of the small enterprises. It involves an arrangement of forwarding the loan applications of the interested small enterprises to the banks.

Performance and credit rating scheme for small industries: so as to enable the small enterprises to ascertain the strengths and weaknesses of their existing operations and take corrective measures accordingly. NSIC is operating the scheme through agencies like ICRA, ONICRA, Duns and Bradstreet (D&B), CRISIL, FITCH, CARE and SMERA.

- **Technology support schemes:** NSIC offers small units various support services through its 'Technical Services Centres' and 'Extension Centres'. The services provided include advice on application of new techniques; material testing facilities through accredited laboratories; energy and environment services at selected centres; classroom and practical training for skill upgradation, etc.

At the State level, various State Financial Corporations (SFCs) have been set up by the respective State Governments for providing financial assistance to the industrial units. For this purpose, these institutions have brought out several funds and schemes, from time to time. There are 18 State Financial Corporation's (SFCs) in the country. For example:

1. **Kerala Financial Corporation (KFC),** incorporated under the State Financial Corporations Act of 1951, is a trend setter in the field of industrial finance. It has been playing a major role in the development and industrialisation of Kerala by extending financial assistance well-suited for the requirements of the entrepreneurs. Its main objective is to extend term loan assistance for establishing new industrial units or to extend credit assistance for meeting expansion/diversification/modernisation costs of the existing units, in small scale or medium sectors. Some of its major **schemes** include:
   - General Scheme For SSI Units
   - General Scheme For SME Units
   - National Equity Fund (NEF) Scheme
   - Working Capital Finance
   - Scheme For Assistance To Information Technology And Software Development Sector
   - Financial Assistance For Infrastructure Projects
2. **Madhya Pradesh Financial Corporation** is the premier institution in the State of Madhya Pradesh engaged in providing financial assistance to small and medium industries. This assistance has been extended in the form of a wide range of fund and non fund based services/ schemes. The fund based schemes are available for setting up of business ventures within the State, whereas, non fund based schemes are available throughout the country.

The **fund based schemes** include:

- Term Loan
- Equipment Finance
- Asset Credit
- Short Term Loan
- Working Capital
- Loan Replenishment
- Finance for Market Activities
- Composite Loan
- Credit Linked Capital Subsidy for SSI

The **non-fund based schemes** include:

- Public Issue Appraisal
- Credit Syndication

Corporate Advisory Services

15.22 Small Business Loan

Small Business Loan refers to the amount of money borrowed by an aspiring small business owner to set up or to run or to expand a small business. So, the small business loans provide necessary economic support to a person who is willing to own a small business or already owns one. There are many advantages of availing a small business loan. Small Business Loan covers all the monetary need of the small business and is available on easy terms and conditions. If a person is able to get small business loan before starting the small business then has not to face any initial financial problem. Moreover, the small business loan boosts the marketing strength of the small business. These small business loans can be availed from different sources like banks, large business organizations and government. The type of small loan actually depends on the personal requirement and the personal repayment capabilities of the small business owners. The various kind of small business loans a person can get are as follows:

Micro loans: Micro loans refer to the small loans which are given to set up new small businesses. Though amount of credit varies, the maximum term of repaying micro loans are generally six years. Micro loans can be availed only if:

1. The aspiring small business owner possesses complete business training.
2. An impressive business plan along with well designed market strategies is submitted.
3. There are strong chances of financial profit.

Government loans: Most Governments offer various kinds of loans to lend a support to the small businesses. There is generally no limit on the loan amount as the governments are really interested in promoting small business ventures. The terms and conditions of repayment are fixed by preparing an agreement signed by the government and borrower. If a person wants to avail this opportunity of taking a loan which has no limit on loan amount, he has to meet the following criteria:

(1) The small business owner has to convince the govt. that his business will be a sincere and authentic venture. He has to serve complete details along with his business plan to the government. Govt. generally believes that if somebody invests his own money in his business then he will be much more determined to earn profits and achieve success.

(2) A strong business plan clearly stating the probable profits should be submitted to the government.

(3) The schedule of repayment must be clearly discussed.

(4) The person applying for small business cannot have any criminal record.

Government offers special loans to worthy businesses or to the people who are unemployable. Some of these loans are:

- Loans for the elderly people to start a small business
- Loans for the minority people to start small business
- Loans for rent, equipment and other office expenditures for the worthy small business

Loans from Banks: Banks provide loans to small businesses if its future growth prospect and prospective profit figures are presented clearly to the bank. Otherwise getting a small business loan from a bank may be proved to be a difficult task. It is very important to mention that there is

Debt and Interest associated with a bank loan and it is essential to make a general agreement between the bank and the borrower. The several ways to ask for a bank loan are:

(1) Request for credit (2) Request for partnership in small business (3) Request for grants with debts (4) Request for free assistance.

Loans by the Large Business Houses Large Business houses also give loans to the small businesses but in order to get the loan the small business has to engage itself in some form of partnership with the investor that is with the large business corporation. For giving this kind of loan the large business organizations consider the locality of the small business, the target market of the business and the growth potential of the small business.

Franchise Loans Some franchise companies provide financial assistance to the small businesses or help them to find a lender.

Export Financing These loans support export financing to small businesses. These loans are provided only on the guarantee of timely repayment of the loan.

The Documents needed to avail any of the above mentioned loans are:

- A Business Plan
- A Statement of Personal Financial Status
- Paper on Cash Flow Projections
- Past Business Tax Returns
- A Credit rating Record.

15.23 Financing The Business

The single biggest obstacle in setting up your business will be convincing your bank to give you a loan. Here are important strategies that could help you:

Buying The Business: Buying an existing business has many advantages over starting a new business. Here you get already made customers, required infrastructure, suppliers and many more. When you buy a business that has good earning record then it is a much easier proposition for a bank to lend you the money. Buying an existing business will require you to add your own ideas and concepts into the already established ideas and concepts of the existing business. The chances of getting success in such business will be higher. Banks appreciate this and fully cooperate. If you are also buying a property-based business, such as a hotel, then the loan can be leveraged against the value of the property. This means that even if your business fails, a bank can get its money back from the property. Again, banks like this.

Banks: For most startups, getting a traditional bank loan is a long shot. That's because banks typically will only consider companies that have been in business for two years. What's more, they need to see a tangible asset that can be used as collateral. The exception is a manufacturing company building or using heavy equipment. The bank is going to loan money based on your ability to pay and they're more likely to finance something that has greater value. One possibility is to apply for a loan guaranteed by the MSME (Micro Small and Medium Enterprises) kind of government institutes. A bank is more likely to take on a company with an MSME guaranty. Even with that seal of approval, however, you may still have to pledge your home as collateral.

Consider buying a franchise: It is a good option when you do not want to waste time in promoting your business. Here customers know your business already you just have to grow it. Your business runs on others concept. Some banks will lend you up to 60 per cent to acquire your franchise. However, the franchise company itself will often be prepared to lend you the money to buy into their concept. It is a well known fact that 90 per cent of franchise concepts that have been established for more than two years are unlikely to fail. Therefore, you are also unlikely to fail, which makes lending you the money more attractive.

Understand the numbers: When asking for money – and it doesn't matter who you ask it from – the lender or the investor will want to make sure you know your numbers inside-out. You must have this information at your fingertips. You need to know exactly how much you want and what it is for – down to the last cent or penny. You need to demonstrate when you will be profitable and how you will become profitable based on a credible forecast of your future costs and sales. This is something that will be backed up by your business plan – which is something you should be able to refer to without actually looking at it.

Get your deposit together: Asking for a business loan without any investment from your side will not be succeeded. If you want to take a loan for your business then you need to invest at least some amount of your own money. If you can put together 30 per cent or 40 per cent of the money you need to start a business or buy a business then a bank is more likely to approve your loan for the rest. This amount of money gives assurance to the banks or investors that you will work seriously because you have invested your own money. This large amount of money shows commitment. It is not at all possible to raise 100 per cent money from loan. So you must start saving from today itself. Your saving will depend on your business. So carefully analyze your business and find out how much initial amount you require.

Get the business plan right: Banks or investors get idea of your business from your business plan only. This means you must have a clear idea about what are you doing? What is your market? What is your product/service? And who are your customers and competitors? What is your cost structure? What would be the price of your product? Know your competitors' turnover, profit, strengths, weaknesses and history. If you know this and it is represented in your plan then your chances of raising the money become better.

Customers and suppliers: Some customers may be willing to help fund your product development if you customize it for them. As for suppliers, you may be able to convince one to hold inventory for you, as long as you guarantee them you'll pay for the material by a certain date. Remember: When you're raising money for your business, it pays to be creative.

Credit Cards: It is very tempting to look at your personal credit cards as a source of money. Don't make this mistake. You need to keep your personal credit and business credit separate no matter how tempting it is to use one for the other. However, you may want to apply for a business credit card. Because they are easier to get than bank loans, this may be helpful.

However, two words of warning:

- Make sure you study the interest rate and penalty clauses before you even think of opening a business credit card account.
- Your business credit card should be only a supplement to your financing.

If the card is the only way you have found to finance your business, walk away from this dream—at least for a while.

Venture Capital: If a bank says no, you might consider contacting a venture capital firm (VC). VCs typically demand a very high percentage of equity for their investment. Ownership at 70 to 80 per cent is not uncommon. Moreover, VCs are a very tough bunch. They are exposed to dozens of business plans and fund only a tiny percentage. They are often frustrating for entrepreneurs because they require a huge return on their investment, often as much as ten times in three to five years. On the other hand, VCs can open doors that you would never be able to open on your own. Their contacts with influential and wealthy individuals and companies can provide you with customers you would never have known. And they can sometimes help you grow faster than you could on your own.

15.24 Business Financial Problems

If you've made it past your first year, congratulations; that's just the first hurdle. Here are the business-related financial problems that you will still face and how to avoid them.

1. **Factoring.** Does your business provide products and services to other businesses or to government agencies? If so, then you know that one of the big problems you face is having to wait 30 to 60 days or longer before your invoices are paid. This can be particularly troubling for your company if your business is growing fast and you are adding new customers and clients on a regular basis, because your supplier's credit terms are much shorter than 30 days as a rule. And you need capital to pay your suppliers and your other overhead and expenses.

   One solution you should consider to this problem is to factor your accounts receivables, which is simply another name for invoices. Many well known and respected businesses today are using this form of financing to provide the working capital they need to more effectively operate and grow. Moreover, an accounts receivable factoring facility is a lot easier and quicker to set up than traditional bank financing. And can be set up in a matter of days, because the factor bases their decision on the credit worthiness of your customers or clients, not upon your personal or business credit.

   This can be particularly important if your business is a relatively new business or your company has had some financial difficulties in the past, because with factoring providing your customers have a good credit position, you can still get the funding you need with factoring.

2. **Lax credit or receivables terms.** Unless you work in a retail environment, there's a good chance that you have some kind of credit terms set up with your customers. For the really nice customers, it's easy to extend a little more credit and a little more credit, perhaps to the point of over-generosity. Are you too lax on your credit terms? Are you giving your customers too much time to pay or not enough incentive (in the form of late-payment interest charges)? Consider these options to help you:
   - Offer prepayment specials, such as 20 per cent off for any purchase paid in full before it's delivered.
   - Increase your interest charges on late payments.
   - Offer a discount (5 per cent to 10 per cent) for invoices paid in less than 30 days.
   - Offer a coupon for invoices paid in less than 15 days.
   - Divide up payments: half up front, one quarter upon delivery and one quarter credit.

3. **Undercapitalization.** This is where many companies fail and not just in their first year. If growth is meteoric but profits are fairly passive, you're setting yourself up for an undercapitalization situation. If your business has experienced fairly aggressive growth in the recent past, you may be in danger. Consider these options to help you:
   - Proactive planning should help solve the problem. Make sure that your current business plan (and all future versions) have a "just in case" contingency for too fast growth.
   - Find an investor (probably a friend or relative) who can act as a pinch hitting investor, if necessary, to bail you out. Avoid using them at all costs, but it's good to have just in case.

- Get a line of credit at the bank.
- Consider emergency options, including selling your car. Not a perfect solution but wouldn't you rather walk than see your business fold?
- Raise your prices to stem the tide of customers.

15.25 Money Shortage Way-out

Basic Strategies

Negotiate everything

Always try to get the best price for the products and services that you require. By merely asking, you can oftentimes purchase at a discount. To sweeten the deal, you can propose to pay early in exchange for a discount particularly if you are paying in cash or if you intend to pay within 5-10 days. In addition to saving money, this arrangement will also allow you to build a strong credit record that your business can surely benefit from. Remember though; always strive for a win-win situation when negotiating with your business partners, suppliers, customers and vendors.

Slowing outflow

Depending upon the nature of the situation prioritize your bills. Decide which bills you must pay first. Remember you must be capable enough to know the nature of your supplier because some suppliers are very strict and some are friendly in nature. So it should not happen that delay in payment will jeopardize your relation. If you intend to pay some of the bills significantly late, advise it of this in advance. If you are fairly certain as to when, specifically, you will be sending payment, consider offering this information as a promise in exchange for continued credit on new purchases.

Crucial creditors

Out of many creditors you must decide which creditor will get first preference for payment. Pay those creditors that are most important to the continuation of your normal business operations first. If it is not possible to pay them on time then request them politely but do not do anything without informing to them. Instead, tell creditors that you have placed them on your payment list. Assure them that you haven't forgotten about them. Let them know they will be paid as soon as possible, but you just can't say when exactly that will be.

Consider working out of a co-working location instead of leasing office space

Co-working is shared office space, generally with a community feel and month-to-month rental agreements. Unlike signing a formal lease for several years, co-working is a lot more flexible. Also, leasing traditional office space requires you to estimate your space requirements and many small business owners overestimate, paying more than they should. Co-working, on the other hand, allows you to simply rent another desk when you need to add someone to your office.

Prioritizing Bills When Money is short

When your cash crunch is looking particularly severe and you can't pay all of your creditors, decide which ones to pay first. While every situation will be different, the following provides a good base strategy for prioritizing payment importance.

Payroll and sales taxes

Unlike income taxes, you collect your employees' shares of payroll taxes and sales taxes as an agent for the appropriate taxing authority. You are merely holding this money in trust until you turn it over to the government. If you can't pay these taxes, it is not the same as not paying an ordinary bill. It is the same as having used the government's money for your own purposes and the government will enforce severe penalties for failure to make payment.

Income and other taxes

While it is usually possible to do some negotiating with the tax authorities regarding income taxes, particularly in arranging installment or delayed payments, the penalties and interest can be stiff. Also, once the tax authority is determined to collect money from you, it will be much quicker than any other creditor to place liens against your bank account or completely freeze your assets.

Utilities

If you are approaching a cutoff date for utility payments, remember that few utility companies will allow business customers to continue service use without paying bills in full. If you need electricity, water, heat or phones, you'd better not fall too far behind in your payments.

Wages

If you miss even one payroll, your best people, if not everyone, will begin looking elsewhere for employment. Suppliers may soon forget or at least forgive a late payment, but your employees never will. Technically, if a company goes bankrupt, you will not be responsible for its debts, including payroll debt. But most companies in this situation find some way to pay their employees in full for work already completed. You should too!

Key suppliers

Pay your key suppliers enough money to continue delivery of those goods, materials and/or services that are absolutely essential to the operation of your business.

Debtors

If you think your business may go under and you have personally borrowed money or personally guaranteed business loans to finance your company, consider paying these types of debtors before paying your key suppliers. No matter what happens to your company, including bankruptcy, funds borrowed from friends or relatives, funds used from home equity loans, any personal loans garnered for business use and/or any business loans with personal guarantees will still be due and payable in full-by you.

15.26 Crisis Financing Alternatives

Bootstrapping

Bootstrapping involves using your own personal income, equity and savings to finance your business. You operate on the lowest possible operating costs and turn inventory as quickly as you can produce it. Many of the world's most successful companies operate according to bootstrapping techniques. Some of these companies include Dell, Coca-Cola and the Clorox Company.

Angel Investors

Angel investors are private parties and sometimes businesses, that invest their own funds into selected businesses. The angel investor becomes, in essence, a stockholder in your company and is as concerned about your business' success as you. Each investor establishes his own guidelines, application methods and standards.

Green Lenders

Green banks are on the rise and if your company meets green standards, you may be able to locate financing with one. Green lenders focus on companies and businesses that strive for energy preservation and use natural resources.

Microloans

Microloans are small loans that are usually issued through micro finance institutions network. The loans can be used for equipment, fixtures, inventory, etc., but cannot be used to pay off existing debts. These loans are short-term and usually quickly approved.

Hard-Money Loans

Hard-money loans should only be used in emergency situations. These loans carry high interest rates and are based on the amount of equity you can show in your business. Hard-money lenders focus on hard-to-finance companies that have little or bad credit.

Asset-backed Financing

While you are unlikely to obtain new or additional unsecured bank lending if you are facing a cash crunch, you may be able to obtain asset-backed financing. Try approaching nonbank sources such as commercial financing companies. Unlike most bank lending, true asset-backed lending focuses primarily on the value of the asset used for security, rather than the ongoing cash from the business.

You do need to keep in mind, however, that such lenders, unlike banks, will seldom hesitate to seize your assets after even a few missed payments. And you may also have to pay a stiff premium over traditional commercial bank loan rates. If you are already borrowing from a bank, you need to be sure that borrowing from another source does not violate your loan agreement. And, even if it doesn't, do keep your bankers apprised of any other borrowing you undertake. If you do look creditworthy to another lending institution, even if it is nonbank, your banker will probably look more favorably upon your account.

Factoring

If you have a good amount of solid receivables, factoring may enable you to raise a lot of cash in a hurry. Factoring firms are private, nonbank lenders that buy, outright, your creditworthy receivables and collect them at their own risk. Even discounting the element of risk that factoring companies assume, they will typically seek a higher premium than bank lenders offer. This is especially true if your business is facing difficulties.

Lease-back

Look around your office. The furniture, computers, fax machines, phones and any other equipment you may own have a cash value. You can realize the value of your assets in instant cash and still retain the equipment for use in your business! You just need to find a leasing firm willing to buy the items from you and lease them back to you.

Leasing is similar to asset-backed lending. First, the financing is based on the value of the asset. Second, you will probably pay a significant premium over that of a bank loan. One major difference, though, is that the leasing firm will actually own everything you lease. Since all the equipment belongs to it, it won't hesitate to take physical possession if you fall behind in your payments. A big advantage to leasing is that, even though it must be disclosed as a footnote in your financial statements, it doesn't actually appear as debt on your balance sheet. It isn't considered to be as onerous as debt by debtors and other lenders or suppliers.

15.27 Influential Way-out to Money Problems

Be on the lookout for used equipment

Visit auction websites or look at the classified ads of newspapers and trade publications for any announcements on used equipment. Many of these machines are sold at 40 per cent of their original price, but of course you should look at the quality before actually forking over your cash. You may not want to buy secondhand computers (especially if they're old and slow) but there's nothing wrong with getting secondhand office furniture or something you need but won't use often, like a scanner or fax machine.

Collecting Payments

Having enough cash flow for your business can become a problem if you're not getting paid on time. Accept credit cards so customers can pay you as soon as a job is finished or if the customer can't pay the whole bill at the time of service, suggest a financing program offered through a bank. Also, make sure you are billing at the time of service or soon afterward. If it's been over two months and the customer hasn't paid, the probability of them paying at all goes down dramatically.

Developing a Debt Payment Plan

If you find yourself with more bills than your monthly income can cover, set up a debt payment plan. Completing this plan will take patience. You will have to stick with it until all your debts are paid. A debt payment plan will work if you really want to get out of debt. You need to start getting out of debt right now. Paying a little back is better than doing nothing or just worrying about the problem. Paying back a small amount will give you a sense of control. It will start you on your way to solving your financial problems.

Cutting costs

The first thing that you must do is stop unnecessary spending. You must determine the total amount that you owe. You should determine the exact amount that you need to settle all your obligations on a monthly basis. For instance, you can say that you need ₹ 30,000 every month. List the assets that you own. Aside from physical assets or possessions, you can also list your skills and knowledge. You can use these assets to earn extra income that you can use to pay your obligations. It will take time before you can repay all your debts but this is better than running away and incurring bad records on your credit report.

Employee participation

Encourage your staff to make savings suggestions. Explain them the reasons and importance of why you are doing all this. Ask suggestions from your employees. If more number of employees will think in this direction then the chances of getting good solution will be more. Even you can reward your employees for their best suggestion. Creating an awareness of the problem and offering each employee the opportunity to be part of the solution boosts morale and breeds loyalty even in the worst of times. If employees participate in suggesting cost-cutting measures, they are more likely to be cost conscious every day as well.

Layoffs

Everyone wants to avoid layoffs. But it is better to lay off a few people at once rather than let everyone go because you are shutting your doors. Employee attitudes can be volatile during a downturn in business. You need to be very careful in your handling of employment issues during this period. Avoid cutting salaries if possible. If you must make cuts, start with your own. Key executives should be next in line for pay cuts. Cut only the salaries of your rank-and-file employees as a last resort. But definitely cut pay before cutting benefits. Employees are generally more attached to their benefits than to the specific amount of their wages.

Summary

A great place to start when looking for startup funding for your new business is the government. A government entity helps people such as you get their new businesses off of the ground. Of great importance is their listing of central and state government grants for individuals looking to start their own business. The most important thing is to know that the grants are highly competitive and skewed for certain industries in certain areas. The grants from the government can be easily got with the conditions that your business idea and plan should have a strong demand.

The financial resources are Family, relatives and friends, Commercial banks, and Government grants.

Raise capital with the help of grants

If you are in certain specialized industries, you might stand a greater chance at being able to raise capital through grants. Government promotes some special kind of businesses. If you live in an area with a high unemployment rate, then you can be sure that it is in the government's best interest to give you a grant if you want to raise capital for a business which is likely to produce many job opportunities. Depending on your character, academic background and experience, you can be eligible for a grant.

Getting Finance

When thinking of how to raise capital through investors, you need to consider the business not only getting onto its feet, but you should present estimations of the income in the next three to five years. Your plan should seem very profitable. By researching the market you are thinking about entering and putting together a projected cost report, you can easily overcome the issues of how to raise capital on your new business.

The other obstacles of entrepreneurs related to finance are Non availability of capital, Improper estimation of the cost, Research estimated costs, problems in Product development and commercialization, Website and technology expenses, Office expenses, Marketing and advertising costs, Basic living salary for business founders, Other employee payroll and benefits, Monthly insurance costs, Legal and professional fees, Travel expenses, and Obtaining short term and long term loans.

The major sources of funding for entrepreneurs are Personal finances, Friends and family, Angel Investors, Debt financing, Equity financing, Customer financing, and Government–sponsored programs.

Building Relationship with Lender

The first step in managing the finance function of your business is to keep detailed records of all your accounts. Another step in how to manage the finance function and lender relationships is to stay in good relations with any lenders your company or business may have. You can manage the finance function and lender relationships by not only keeping good records but also by knowing what your company or business needs and wants financially.

Small business funding myths are "I can open my business as soon as possible", "I can easily find funding for my new business in a few months.", "My business idea is great and unique. I should get funding right away.", "I know everything about my business; therefore, I do not need to create a business plan.", "I know how to market my products; therefore, I do not need a marketing plan.", "The more investors I contact, the more likely I can find funding.", "I can easily get funding from the Government.", And "Venture capitalists will give me money for my startup."

The main sources of funding can be Self-financing by the owner, Loans from friends and relatives, Forming Partnerships, Venture Capital, and Angel Investors.

State Bank of India (SBI) provides a wide range of financial products and services that can cater to any business or market requirement.

Its various funding schemes are Working capital finance, Corporate term loans, Deferred payment guarantees, Project finance and Structured Finance.

Bank of Baroda offers various products and services that meet the specific requirements of business enterprises, particularly the small scale units. Various schemes relating to the provision of loans and advances by the bank include Working Capital Finance, Term Finance, Small and Medium Enterprise (SME) Loan Pack, Small Business Borrowers and Traders Loan.

Small Industries Development Organization (SIDO) is an apex body for promotion and development of small scale industries in the country. SIDO has devised a comprehensive range of schemes for providing credit facilities, technology support services and marketing assistance, etc. **Some of the major schemes are:** Credit Linked Capital Subsidy Scheme for Technology Upgradation, Credit Guarantee Scheme, ISO 9000/ISO 14001 Certification Reimbursement Scheme, Integrated Infrastructure Development (IID Scheme), SSI MDA Scheme, Assistance to Entrepreneurship Development Institutes and Micro Finance Programme.

National Small Industries Corporation Ltd (NSIC) has been established with the objective of promoting, aiding and fostering the growth of small scale industries in the country. It has been assisting small enterprises through a set of specially tailored schemes which facilitate marketing support, credit support, **Performance and credit rating scheme for small industries,** technology support and other support services.

Micro loans: Micro loans refer to the small loans which are given to set up new small businesses. Though amount of credit varies, the maximum term of repaying micro loans are generally six years.

Government loans: Most Governments offer various kinds of loans to lend a support to the small businesses. There is generally no limit on the loan amount as the governments are really interested in promoting small business ventures. The terms and conditions of repayment are fixed by preparing an agreement signed by the government and borrower.

Loans from Banks: Banks provide loans to small businesses if its future growth prospect and prospective profit figures are presented clearly to the bank. Otherwise getting a small business loan from a bank may be proved to be a difficult task. The several ways to ask for a bank loan are:

(1) Request for credit (2) Request for partnership in small business (3) Request for grants with debts (4) Request for free assistance.

Loans by the Large Business Houses: Large Business houses also give loans to the small businesses but in order to get the loan the small business has to engage itself in some form of partnership with the investor that is with the large business corporation.

Franchise Loans: Some franchise companies provide financial assistance to the small businesses or help them to find a lender.

Export Financing: These loans support export financing to small businesses. These loans are provided only on the guarantee of timely repayment of the loan.

Financing the Business

The single biggest obstacle in setting up your business will be convincing your bank to give you a loan. The important strategies that could help you are buying the business, Banks loan, Consider buying a franchise, Understand the numbers (exact ROI), Get your deposit together, Get the business plan right, Find supportive customers and suppliers, Credit Cards, and Venture Capital.

Money shortage way-out: Two strategies are there first are basic strategies and second are strategies related to prioritizing bills when money is short.

Basic strategies include Negotiate everything, Speeding inflow, Slowing outflow, Crucial creditors, and Noncrucial creditors.

Prioritizing bills when money is short strategies includes Payroll and sales taxes, Income and other taxes, Utilities, Wages, Debtors and Key suppliers.

Crisis Financing Alternatives are as follows:

Bootstrapping involves using your own personal income, equity and savings to finance your business.

Angel investors are private parties and sometimes businesses, that invest their own funds into selected businesses.

Green banks are on the rise and if your company meets green standards, you may be able to locate financing with one. Green lenders focus on companies and businesses that strive for energy preservation and use natural resources.

Hard-Money Loans

Hard-money loans should only be used in emergency situations. These loans carry high interest rates and are based on the amount of equity you can show in your business. Hard-money lenders focus on hard-to-finance companies that have little or bad credit.

Asset-backed financing

While you are unlikely to obtain new or additional unsecured bank lending if you are facing a cash crunch, you may be able to obtain asset-backed financing. Try approaching nonbank sources such as commercial financing companies. Unlike most bank lending; true asset-backed lending focuses primarily on the value of the asset used for security, rather than the ongoing cash from the business.

Factoring

If you have a good amount of solid receivables, factoring may enable you to raise a lot of cash in a hurry. Factoring firms are private, nonbank lenders that buy, outright, your creditworthy receivables and collect them at their own risk.

Lease-back

Look around your office. The furniture, computers, fax machines, phones and any other equipment you may own have a cash value. You can realize the value of your assets in instant cash and still retain the equipment for use in your business! You just need to find a leasing firm willing to buy the items from you and lease them back to you.

The influential way-out to money problems are Be on the lookout for used equipment collecting payments, Developing a bet paymentn plan, Cutting costs, Layoffs and Employee participation.

KEYWORDS

***Government* grant:** Central, state, or local *government* organized methods of financial assistance.

Commercial bank: A financial institution that accepts demand deposits and makes loans and provides other services for the public.

Professional fee: *It* is that fee charged for services from university trained professionals; primarily doctors, lawyers and accountants.

Short term loan: Maturity within a relatively brief time, such as a year.

Long-term loan: A *loan* where repayments are made over several years, usually between five and ten years.

Angel investor: A wealthy individual who invests in a start-up company with his or her own money.

Venture capitalist: Private investors who provide venture capital to promising business ventures.

Micro loans: Micro loans refer to the small loans which are given to set up new small businesses.

Factoring: The receivables are sold without recourse.

Bootstrapping: It involves using your own personal income, equity and savings to finance your business.

Green lenders: It focuses on companies and businesses that strive for energy preservation and use natural resources.

Lease-Back: A business arrangement whereby property is simultaneously sold and leased back to the seller for usually long-term continued use.

QUESTIONS

1. What are the different possible financial resources available for an entrepreneur?
2. What are the different financial challenges faced by small entrepreneurs?
3. What do you mean by 'Angel Investors'?
4. Write about different government funding and schemes.
5. What are the different sources of getting small business loan?
6. What are the different strategies of managing money in crises?

CHAPTER – 16

EMPLOYEES RELATED OBSTACLES

LEARNING OBJECTIVES

On completion of this chapter, you should be able to:

☺ *Explain why new small entrepreneurs are not able to keep good skilled employees.*

☺ *Describe the factors responsible for creating obstacles for the new entrepreneurs.*

☺ *Describe the mistakes that are done by entrepreneurs while hiring the employees.*

☺ *Describe the role of employees' motivation in new business.*

Once the entrepreneur obtains the needed finances to start his/her new business, he/she can now begin to hire employees. Hiring employees for a new business can be quite a difficult task since it requires the same amount of time and dedication as developing the business proposal and the process of raising capital. The hiring process of a new business takes ample time and preparation in order to recruit the best-qualified candidates. The entrepreneur first needs to determine how many employees they plan to hire and which job positions need to be filled. After posting employment advertisements and reviewing resumes, the employer should abide by the legal guidelines when hiring new employees. This includes the applicant's consent for prescreening. The entrepreneur of the new business also needs to inform a candidate of their status, including the reasons for rejection. However, before recruiting anyone into the new business, the entrepreneur needs to understand the hiring process whether you've just started a small business or are the head in an entrepreneurial business, any of the following problems of employee hiring mistakes could prove disastrous for your business.

BOX 16

What Employees Want (It's not what you think!)

Just last month, the results of The 2010 Global Workforce Study were released and they revealed some pretty surprising insights about what employees want from their employer today. The study is considered to be the first and most significant read on employees' mindset following the recession and widespread financial woes.

In the decades following the industrial revolution the social contract between employer and employees was predominantly a security-for-loyalty exchange. It was common, even expected, that you would work for a single organization throughout your entire career.

In more recent memory, employers offered increasingly less security and employees responded with little loyalty. Many employees started acting as 'free agents,' trying to gather meaningful development opportunities from a variety of employers. In fact, the workforce of my generation has become very comfortable with the notion that you'll have a dozen or more different jobs throughout your career.

And today, the terms of this contract seem to be shifting again, as the results of the 2010 Global Workforce Study suggests. Feeling the painful after effects of a global recession and financial defaults, employees are now yearning for a longer-term commitment with employers in return for security and meaningful career development. In fact, a surprising 8 out of 10 employees now want long-term relationships with their employer, with 43 per cent saying they want to work for a single company for their entire career.

Employers wanting to retain top talent must respond to the interests and needs of their employees. Sixty percents of respondents in the study were asking for more mentoring and 59 per cent for more clarity on defined career paths. We may want the security of a long-term employer, but we're not willing to perform the same routine function for the next 20 years. Employees who have no sense of future with their employer are vulnerable to external opportunities and those who are unsatisfied in their jobs can become toxic to the work environment. This study suggests that career management has become a key component of the new employment contract. Ergo, the new career management-for-talent loyalty exchange.

The results of this study will inspire a new consciousness among employers. A consciousness that good career fit matters - both to the employee and the employer; that ignoring employees' career development is incredibly costly; and that career management is a key driver of employee attraction, engagement and retention.

Source: Information received from "Global Workforce Study", 2010.

16.1 Partial knowledge of employees

The new entrepreneurs do not have proper information of the employees. If they open business and want employees for their business then they do not know what kind of employees are required for the job? What should be the parameters for selecting the employees? Multi skills or single skill employee who could be better? Where should they go for asking the employees? Many more questions are there that are unanswered. They open business but they require someone who can guide them, tell them from where they can get employees. Most of the time entrepreneurs have to deal with such problems by their own without any support and when they do by their own the results are not good.

BOX 16A

Busy Doing Nothing

Employees at small and midsize businesses spend 50 percent of their day on "necessary, yet unproductive" tasks like filing, communications and dealing with correspondence, according to a survey by Webtorials for business communications company Fonality.

The study of "knowledge workers" — the largest staff component for most SMBs (or the business owners themselves) — found that 36 percent spend their time trying to contact customers, partners or colleagues, find information or schedule a meeting. They spend 14 percent of their time duplicating information (forwarding e-mails or calling to confirm if a communication was received) and managing unwanted communications such as spam e-mails or unsolicited phone calls.

Source: Information received from "Webtorials for Business Communications Company".

16.2 Employees' High Salary Expectation

It is the biggest problem of the new entrepreneurs. When they open business and try to hire best employees they cannot give high salary to them. Some entrepreneurs have a desire to take best employees but again they face the same problem. Employees are assets of the business. Big businesses can easily hire best employees for their business. They are ready to pay any package to their employees for their knowledge and intelligence. Big companies also take advantages of competent employees who create and increase the value of company. But the new small entrepreneurs find themselves very low in doing the same. That is also one of the reasons that why the new entrepreneurs lag behind big companies.

16.3 Ignorance to Job Consultants

The entrepreneurs normally do not take help of job consultants to hire the employees. They lack money for their business. They try to save money for business. In this process they never think about any expenses regarding recruitments. They try to do everything by their own and as a result of that they do not select correct employee for their job. The small entrepreneurs are not always very much interested in giving much time for hiring the employees. They any how apply their brain to select the employees. They just give the small ad or even by informal way they hire the employee. They do not understand that more the applications will come it will help them to select correct employee for the job.

16.4 Employees' Retention Problem

The new entrepreneurs do not know the techniques of retaining the employees. Even they do not have a professional who can tell them how to retain the employees. Most of the times the employees leave their job because of the less salary or the entrepreneurs are not able to give them salary on time. It becomes really hard for the entrepreneurs to retain the employees because they do not have much money so that they can give it to the employees and there is also lack of other facilities that employees want. For the new entrepreneurs the initial stage of the business is very hard. They definitely run the business do investment but at the initial stage their business runs slowly. They find it very difficult to retain the employees because they do not earn much profit and sometimes they pay payment by their own pocket.

16.5 Employment, Health and Safety Regulations

New entrepreneurs do not provide all the facilities that they must provide. Here workers work in the unsafe condition because the entrepreneurs are not capable of supplying the required equipment or dress for the work. Mostly the workers side is neglected by the new entrepreneurs. They should give importance to workers also. Your employees are valuable for you. They help you to build business. But the fact is that even if they want to provide all the facilities they cannot provide to each and every employee the equipment required. They face many problems while running such kind of business which demand many types of equipment. The new entrepreneurs can also run such kind of business that requires equipment and safety but they do not have any supporting hand that could help them financially and logically to build the business.

16.6 Motivating Employees

The new entrepreneurs lack in motivating the employees. They are not aware about the power of motivation. Most of the new small entrepreneurs do not care about their employees. They are very rude with their employees. They think that they have purchased employees like machines or equipments. Though they cannot give their employees incentives or bonus for their good work, should at least motivate the employees on moral level. Sometimes new entrepreneurs even do not know the concept of motivation. If it is not possible for you to give high incentives or bonus to your employees then you can give them low incentives. You should assure them that their performance will definitely get reward. You can either give them monetary incentives or non monetary incentives depending upon your ability.

16.7 A Solid Hiring Plan

Entrepreneurs need to develop a hiring plan at the same time they develop the business plan. This will help them budget the new business as well as enable them to line up a management team with impressive bios. A solid hiring plan is also very important to an entrepreneur who does not have experience in the business area. By hiring an impressive management team with a proven track record of success, the entrepreneur can convince a business investor that he or she is committed to the project and has the necessary skills to sustain a business and produce or increase profitability.

16.8 The Do-No-Wrong Effect

This erroneous employee hiring mistake occurs when the interviewer finds a common element in the candidate and themselves: they went to the same college, have a shared mentor or love a similar hobby. As if by magic the potential employee can do no wrong, an effect quite similar to falling in love. They should think differently as far as selection is concerned. Mostly it has happened that the person who is from the same college, shared same mentor as the entrepreneur is, those persons are selected by the entrepreneur immediately because the entrepreneur and the person share the same value. But when it comes about the selection the entrepreneurs should think from mind not from heart otherwise they can select wrong person for their business.

16.9 Getting Employees for New Business – What Goes Wrong

Improper estimation of the number of employees needed

The entrepreneurs do not have enough budgets to hire the number of employees. They try to select employees who are best and ready to work in less salary but they do not get those kind of employees because in today's business environment salary expectation of the employees are more and that expectation are not fulfilled by the new small entrepreneurs and that create problems for the new entrepreneurs. The new entrepreneurs just to save money hire any employee but that employee is not the competent one. The first step in hiring staff for a new business is determining the number of employees that are needed. This is crucial for new entrepreneurs since each staff member requires a salary, benefits and employer liability. The entrepreneur also needs to decide on the qualification requirements for different positions within the business. The new business owner also needs to make sure that the new hire(s) has/have the necessary educational qualifications and matches the working style required for the new business. Working for a start-up company requires a lot of hard work and can be very challenging; therefore, the entrepreneur needs to find people who share the vision and are committed to the work.

Speedy hiring decisions

Few entrepreneurs and small business owners can focus solely on employee hiring tasks, so it is often tempting to hire quickly so you can get back to your main priorities, whatever they may be. They forgot one thing that these employees are going to impact the business by their performance. Your mistakes will impact the whole business. Unfortunately this employee hiring mistake can leave you open to candidates who interview well but perhaps are unable to do the job or lack the qualifications to fit in. Don't overlook warning signals just to get some stress relief in the short term.

Ignorance to educational qualification

The new entrepreneurs do not take education of the employees much seriously. They just want the employees who can do their tasks. They therefore select the person who is ready to do the work on their conditions. They do not select the employee depending upon the requirements of the job but rather they select the employees according to their suitability. That creates problems because that employee is not the competent one and that's why does not satisfy the requirement of the job. The entrepreneurs face the problem of giving high salary to employees. In today's world expectations of well qualified employees have increased. They are not able to select well qualified employee because they cannot fulfill the need of employee. The demand of employee is more than the ability of the new entrepreneurs. These things compel them to go for lower educated employees. But for the new entrepreneurs it is possible to keep few well educated employees instead of number of low educated employees. Entrepreneurs should give value to the education of the employees. They should not avoid it.

Ignorance or little importance to advertising a job opening

Mostly the entrepreneurs do not advertise much about their job opening. They try to select employees through informal sources. They try to save money for advertisement. If they advertise then also they are not able to select reputed media or costly one that will be effective, instead they try to select media which is cheap because they cannot pay much amount just for selecting the employees. As a result of that most of the applicants are not aware about job openings of the company and because of that entrepreneurs mostly do not get the desired employee for the post. A new business owner who is interested in hiring new employees must use all available resources in recruiting the best possible candidate. By placing job postings in the local paper and on numerous online web-based job sites, the employer can definitely increase the pool of qualified applicants. They can even attend job fairs to recruit potential candidates. In order to assess which candidate qualifies most for a particular job, the new business owner must meticulously compile a list of requirements in an employment ad, including education and work experience. The most qualified candidates should be invited to get interviewed.

Improper selection procedure

Most of the new entrepreneurs even do not follow the whole official procedure that is required to hire the employee. There are number of methods for selecting the employees that gives best results if followed but they do not care about that they follow the procedure but not completely. As a result of that they cannot judge right candidate for the required post. Sometimes employee may be the good one but most of the time the employee does not suit for the job and because of that business suffers. For the proper selection of the procedure you can take help from books, websites or even from professionals.

Poorly prepared interview or no preparation at all

The new entrepreneurs are not aware of the interview techniques. They even do not hire professionals for hiring the employees. When they start their interview they do not follow proper guidelines of the interview they randomly ask whatever they want to ask to the interviewee without any base of the questions. In such situations they commit many mistakes. They even select wrong person for the job but they remain in the illusion that they have done right. They suffer when the employee does not fulfill the requirements of the job. Preparing your questions, keeping formal notes of the process, having a job description in place, knowing how to explain the job requirements and having answers to all of the commonly asked questions are integral to looking professional and polished to your potential employees. Plus, the extra confidence in knowing what you are doing can't hurt.

The legal obligations in hiring

There are no mandatory legal requirements in posting an employment ad; however, the new business owner must abide by several state and central guidelines in order to avoid unfair hiring practices. For example, The Equal Employment Opportunity Act prohibits discrimination in the workforce against race, gender, age, religion, sex and disability. The employer must provide all the necessary equipments for the tasks that are necessary for the tasks. Without necessary equipments, if there is any harm to the employee then new business owners can put themselves in the illegal risk. The employers must provide all legal facilities to their employees for example fresh drinking water, wash room, relaxation room and toilet room. The employers should provide better working conditions to their employees for example in summer fan, proper ventilation etc., most of the entrepreneurs do not take this seriously or they do not know anything about that; they are unaware about their responsibilities towards employees or they do not have much money so that they can provide all the facilities to the employees but the new entrepreneurs should think that if any incident happens with the employees and at that time the employers are not found with the legal facilities then it is risky for the employers. The employer must become familiar with all of these acts when conducting a prospective candidate's background check in order to avoid legal problems and discriminatory practices.

Informal hiring needs

Several recently released studies have shown that most entrepreneurs (around 70 per cent) spend less than five minutes in employee hiring preparation, yet it only seems obvious that less planning increases the risks of not getting the right candidate for the job. If you don't have a clear cut job description - create one. Knowing exactly what needs filling and doing is essential when posting a position, working with recruiters and any human resources departments either internally or externally. Entrepreneurs without giving much time select the employees for their business. They take it as a formality. They never go in deep to explore the employees before selecting them. After some time it is realized that the employees selected are not good for the business. Their performance is not good and therefore such employees affect business of the entrepreneurs.

Appropriate carefulness by checking references

Often times, employers will ask the job applicant to provide at least three sources of references. These legal requirements are not followed by most of the entrepreneurs. The harm is that the employees can any time leave the job without any intimation to the entrepreneur and that time the entrepreneur becomes helpless. The employee may damage the business of the entrepreneurs and can steal the secrets of the business also. These references are a vital tool in determining if the applicant is qualified for the job. By failing to conduct a thorough background and reference check on each candidate, the business will not only be at risk for negligent hiring but it may also create some form of legal liability when violent or serious acts are committed by employee in the workforce.

In addition, negligent hiring can lead to high employee turnover, increased office absenteeism and eventually, poor company reputation. In order to avoid such problems, employers must always check references, as well as verify the educational background and job experience of the applicant. Checking a prospective applicant's references also allows the employer to directly speak to a candidate's past and/or present supervisor in order to validate any information that is presented and to better determine if they are qualified for the job.

If the employer does not have resources to prescreen an applicant, they can utilize many of the available pre-employment screening services when recruiting a new hire. These services conduct a background check and a social security check on the potential applicant. Unlike business practices in the past, an entrepreneur cannot undertake the prescreening process without written permission from the potential candidate.

If you are 100 per cent accountable for your hiring decisions, checking references isn't an option. Realizing there are some limitations to the process, talking to someone who has worked with the applicant will either strengthen your case that they will be a great fit or lead to additional questions that require asking. Either way, you're solidifying your case with concrete information.

Improper spending for hiring a new employee

The new entrepreneurs do not take the procedure of hiring the employees seriously. Even they do not follow the formal procedure. They take employees without any detailed interview. They do not want to spend much money on employees' selection. As a result of that they never get good employees who can work for them for long time. Nowadays, it costs money to recruit, hire and train employees. A recent study revealed that on average, companies spend at least Rs. 30,000 during the hiring process. This amount takes into consideration the time spent on developing a job description, advertising the job opening on and offline, responding to resumes, conducting telephone interviews, performing in-person meetings and the administrative paperwork in hiring the lucky candidate. This hiring process is repeated each time a vacant position needs to be filled and costs associated with this process add up very quickly. The new entrepreneurs can never spend such a huge amount of money on hiring the employees but they can at least follow some steps of the selection procedure to protect themselves from hiring the wrong employees.

Non standard Interview Questions

Every entrepreneur has done it: asked questions plucked from nowhere at the last minute because they didn't take time to do much more than that. They cannot afford to go for consultancy because it needs money and they do not have money. The results, unfortunately, usually speak for themselves. Even they do not have any expert who can formulate the interview questions. Interview is a responsible duty of the entrepreneurs they should properly focus on it. They should do their best to hire the right candidates in the business.

Employee hiring questions should be carefully crafted to determine the candidate's skills, qualifications, on-the-job behaviors, likes and dislikes, work style, motivations and preferred communication methods. It's not enough to know if they can merely do the job. You must know if they will fit.

Gut nature can be both good and bad

Instinct plays a very important role in determining the credibility of an individual. But the new or small entrepreneurs do not take care about those things. They just want the employees who should work for their business. Even they cannot afford high salaried employee. They rarely consider these things. However, it should not be the only factor that should be taken into consideration during hiring process. An employer may feel confident that a certain candidate is well-qualified for a position based on the in-person interview but should not dismiss other candidates quickly. Thorough background and reference checks, as well as follow-up interviews are all needed in deciding if a candidate qualifies for a job.

16.10 Wrong Ways of Employee Hiring

Hiring Your Twin

It only makes sense that many a hiring decision would be based on finding those who share a similar style, view or temperament to one's own. Yet a similar trait in an employee constitutes familiarity, not necessarily the best employee hiring choice. Competence exists in differentiation.

The employees should be selected on the basis of different traits. Selecting twins will not be beneficial as selecting two different persons with different personality traits.

Expecting way too much

A common problem these days is looking for one person to save a sinking ship. An unrealistic, lengthy list of qualifications and background requirements — as frequently seen in employment ads — creates a situation where you settle for someone whom you think can do a little of everything, but does not excel in the key areas. Narrow your focus to the most important aspects of the position.

Rely on the Interview to Evaluate a Candidate

The interview is a lot of talk. And most frequently, because applicants are not prepared in advance, a lot of interview time is spent giving the candidate information about your organization. Even more time is invested in different interviewers asking the candidate the same questions over and over. During an interview, candidates tell you what they think you want to hear because they want to successfully obtain a job offer. Organizations are smart when they develop several methods for evaluating candidates in addition to the interview.

Poorly Chosen Interview Questions

Every entrepreneur has done it: asked questions plucked from nowhere at the last minute because they didn't take the time to do much more than that. The results, unfortunately, usually speak for themselves.

Employee hiring questions should be carefully crafted to determine the candidate's skills, qualifications, on-the-job behaviors, likes and dislikes, work style, motivations and preferred communication methods. It's **not** enough to know if they can merely do the job. You must know if they will *fit.*

16.11 Ways of Hiring the Perfect Employee

Hiring the right employee is a challenging process. Hiring the wrong employee is expensive, costly to your work environment and time consuming. Hiring the right employee will be beneficial for the business productivity and performance. Hiring the right employee enhances your work culture, business value and pays you back a thousand times over in high employee morale, positive forward thinking planning and accomplishing challenging goals. This is not a comprehensive guide to hiring an employee. But, these are key steps to hiring the right employee.

Describe job before hiring an employee

The best way to hire the right person for the job is to clearly define what skills are needed. Once you know what it takes to do the job, you can match the applicant's skills and experience to the job's requirements. This step will probably be easy for you if you're hiring an associate, but how about office help or other support functions?

Once you have a job description on paper, decide what skills the person must have to fill the job. Then, estimate the value of this service to your business. Finally, determine how much other employers in your area are paying for these skills.

When you know the kinds of skills you need in your new employee and his/her market value, you're ready to contact sources that can help you recruit job applicants. Make sure you offer a living wage.

Follow standardized hiring process

In today's modern world traditional way of selection may not count. Many standard selection methods are there you must use that. Your standardized hiring process should include candidates' background check, standardized assessments and structured interviews. Different types of interviews are there to evaluate the candidates. Try those tools all of which will provide much more consistent results than the traditional interview. You can take the help of professionals in selecting the best tools. The more important the position, the more rigorous the hiring process should be.

Employee recruiting strategy

With the job description in hand, set up a recruiting planning meeting that involves the key employees who are hiring the new employee. Prepare plan about how many posts are there? When will you give your ad? Which media you are going to select? Evaluate different media and select the best and effective one. At this meeting, your recruiting strategy is planned and the execution begins. Teams that have worked together frequently in hiring an employee can often complete this step via email.

Select experts, knowledge and experienced person for hiring employees

You should search for such persons who are intelligent, knowledgeable and have much experience about hiring the people. Here you can take help from your friends who are in any business or from any experienced person. If you want help of such persons then you will not find any difficulty to find them. Always keep relationship with such persons. You can develop relationships with potential candidates long before you need them when hiring an employee. Doing this will help you to recruit right person for your job.

Review qualifications and applications carefully

The work of reviewing resumes, cover letters, job applications and job application letters starts with a well-written job description. You must make a list of required characteristics that you want to see in your candidates. The characteristics should be experience, qualification, achievements, skills, personality etc. Screen all applicants against the list of characteristics. Work with an expert who has a good experience of taking interview. This will enhance your knowledge. Get knowledge from those people and write it down so next time when you will need to conduct interview then you will be able to do it by your own.

Prescreen your applicant

Have an informal meeting with your applicants. This meeting will give you idea about the caliber of applicant and you can decide on whether to call him/her for the next round of final interview or not. Sometimes the applicants may look good on paper but when you interact with them face to face then you can somewhat judge about the credibility of your applicant. You can know about applicants' ability and thoughts about your business. You can determine whether their salary expectations are congruent with job. So prescreen helps you to filter the applicants for the final interview.

Ask job interview questions accurately

Prepare your questions in advance so you can use the interview time wisely. One useful technique is to present a hypothetical (or even real) work problem and see what ideas a candidate can contribute towards a solution. Another possibility is to throw out a startlingly difficult question and see how the candidate handles a curve ball. The questions should be designed thoroughly before actual interview. All the factors should be included in the questions list that you want to ask. The questions selection will decide the type of employee you will select. Interview questions that help you separate desirable candidates from average candidates are fundamental when hiring an employee. Job interview questions matter to employers.

Hire for today's need and tomorrow's vision

Your vision must be very clear while hiring the employee. In this competitive world where the market situations are changing continuously you need to hire all rounder, flexible and multi skill employee. Remember that you're hiring for the future. The employee should be such that he can face any challenge without any fear and should accommodate himself to any environment. For example if in near future your business will expand then in such situation the candidate should be ready to go anywhere in the state, country or world. New people should provide the skills you need in the future, not just match the job demands you see today. Be clear about your strategic direction for the future and then hire the talent to help you achieve it.

Check backgrounds and references when hiring an employee

Checking the background of employee is very necessary as you do not know anything about that person. You don't know whatever he is telling is right or wrong. You cannot simply trust on that person for getting information and therefore checking the references and background of the person is very important. The background checks must include work references, especially former supervisors, educational credentials, employment references and actual jobs held and criminal history. Other background checks when hiring an employee, such as credit history, must be specifically related to the job for which you are hiring an employee.

Use effective employment letters

These sample employment letters will assist you to reject job candidates, make job offers, welcome employees and more when hiring an employee. Use these sample employment letters to develop the employment letters you use in your organization when hiring an employee.

The most neglected aspect of hiring

A job analysis is the most neglected aspect of hiring. Each job task should be analyzed according to the knowledge, skills, intelligence, efforts, performance, abilities and attitudes required to perform the job correctly. It will be easy for you if you prepare a checklist of the required characteristics that you want to see in your candidate so that you can remember that easily. Once you are fully aware of the required characteristics then the hiring process becomes faster and the probability of getting right candidate is increased up to large extent. When you know exactly what talents are required — you know what to look for and what to test for.

Focus more on evaluation than talk during interview

Most of the time you forgot that it is an interview and not a normal communication. You do not ask, you talk with your interviewee. You should ask such questions by which you can evaluate a candidate. You should give them a problem and ask them about solutions. By doing this you should try to know the problem solving ability of the candidate. Ask about his or her experience with situations you point out. Try to know the learning ability of the candidate. See how quickly a person learns a particular task. Give them practical situation and observe them what they think about it. Are they confident or cannot handle situation?

So What Could Be the Solution?

16.12 Appointing the Right Person

How you approach hiring the right person for a job depends upon the type of job. It goes without saying that hiring an entry-level person is substantially different than securing the services of a high-level technical person or a number two or three in the chain of command. In every case, however, reference checking is mandatory.

Know exactly what you expect from your new hire: Before you advertise for help, sit down and write a job description. List your goals for the new hire – do you want someone who can fill in on short notice when you need to take a day off or do you want someone who can work a regular schedule? Do you want someone who can meet with clients, set their own schedules and attend meetings and events on your behalf or do you simply need someone who can pick up your overflow? By spending time working through your thoughts on hired help you are setting yourself up for a great working relationship. If you can clearly articulate the job to all applicants, they will have the opportunity to determine if this is a mutually agreeable fit. Be sure to concentrate on specific job-related descriptions and not subjective information.

Define the qualities, characteristics and basic aptitude wanted to find in a potential employee. Those characteristics are:

- Excellent Attendance and Dependability
- Flexibility
- Integrity and Honesty
- Motivated and Dedicated
- Detail-Orientated
- Team-Orientated
- Strong Work Ethic
- Positive, Polite and Approachable
- Continuous Improvement Orientated
- Good Communication Skills

Interviewing Job Applicants: The objective of the job interview is to find out as much information as you can about the job applicant's work background, especially work habits and skills. Your major task is to get the applicants to talk about themselves and about their work habits. The best way to go about this is to ask each applicant specific questions: What did you do on your last job? How did you do it? Why was it done?

As you go along, evaluate the applicants' replies. Do they know what they are talking about? Are they evasive or unskilled in the job tasks? Can they account for discrepancies?

A major contributor: People with a large nose need to make a major contribution in the work place. They will make a significant difference, if given the chance. If micro managed they will bog down and not produce to their potential. When these people are put in positions of manager or supervisor, they will make a solid contribution.

Competencies: Competencies encompass many desired attributes that you want in an employee. They can include:

- Knowledge,
- Skills,
- Attitudes,
- Actions.

For any position you would want to determine the candidate's effectiveness on the job by evaluating their ability to:

- Achieve Results
- Communicate Effectively
- Demonstrate dependability
- Sustain a level of Organizational Knowledge
- Make Effective Decisions
- Plan and organize
- Problem Solve and show good Judgment and decision making skills
- Be Productive
- Take Responsibility

Always check references: when you are recruiting employees-It cannot be overstated that every business manager needs to check references carefully and do background checks. In the litigious society in which we live, business owners need to pursue every avenue to assure that the people they hire can do the job, contribute to the growth of your business and development and have no past transgressions which might endanger your current workforce. Keep in mind that you might be liable if you failed to do a background check, on a person who then attacked another in your workplace.

Do not "buy" their services: Any person who is primarily motivated by an immediate increase in their pay is not looking for the strong, long-term relationships that will contribute to the company's success. Why wouldn't he leave your company six months from now for another immediate increase in basic pay, this is quite different from a candidate's desire to be properly rewarded for an outstanding contribution to the company's objectives? Although you shouldn't "buy" the candidate, you should be willing to "pay for what you get." Good people cost more!

16.13 "Getting Acquainted"

There are several ways to provide the needed training.

1. MSME Training Programs: MSME training programs are quite good in training people in industrial arts, such as machine tool operation, engineering design, computer-assisted design (CAD), computer-assisted manufacturing (CAM) and similar skills. You or the person who is responsible for human resources matters should be well acquainted with any training program in your company's area and the types of skills for which they offer training.

2. Business schools, colleges and universities: These institutions are very good in providing training in the areas of marketing, sales, export-import, accounting, computer operation, clerical skills and others. You can ask to them to design the workshop based on employees work, their responsibilities and knowledge. These institutions can also arrange the classes according to the suitability of the employees so that your employees' working time will remain untouched. Either you can pay the fees of your employees or let the employees pay their own fees or contribute 50 per cent from your side whatever is feasible to you. Most often, these educational opportunities are low cost and, in some cases, free to the participant.

3. Industry schools and seminars: Industry-sponsored seminars or workshops can be an excellent way to provide training to new employees. The experienced and good communication skilled person from any industry can be called as an instructor of the workshop. Such workshops are very effective and time duration is also less. The specialty of such workshop is that it takes the form of get together for the employees of the other companies. It benefits to all employees as employees from the different companies share their thoughts, experience and skills.

4. In-house training: Many small companies are not able to provide the required facilities for training. But small companies can provide on-the-job training. It does not require any additional facilities or extra time and employees get training also. It is an excellent way to give training because employees get knowledge more rapidly. Keep in mind that such training may detract from the efficiency of the trainer but the new hire will learn "our preferred methods," enabling him to contribute more rapidly to the company's performance.

16.14 Motivation and Involvement

Obviously, motivation is not as simple as a pat on the back or a person knowing that they've done well. You must understand the normal desires of people relative to their employment, regardless of the level of their responsibility. Most people desire the following:

- Recognition for their good work
- Meaningful participation in the company's efforts
- A feeling of belonging in a successful organization
- Opportunities for growth and advancement in their competence and responsibility
- Security in their job if they perform to expectation
- Monetary reward for an expected level of performance
- Benefits that protect them and their families from significant monetary loss

Even top-level management personnel, who are typically self-motivated, desire the same things as those in positions of lesser responsibility. A mutual recognition by their peers for a job well done or a project successfully completed may be sufficient. A brief recognition of their success by the top executive goes even further as a motivator!

16.15 Make Employees Happy

How do you make an employee's work something that he or she enjoys? It is called involvement! Keep your people involved. Consider the following:

1. Communicate with them. Make them aware about your business, working culture and environment. Tell them new products and services, about customers and competitors. Make them aware about the company's policies, rules and regulations. Behave friendly with them.

2. Reinforce their contributions to the Business' objective. Informal discussions are needed to bring the employees up-to-date on their role in the business. Check their performance. Tell them about their weaknesses and strengths. Improve their performance by giving them the right direction. Involve them in achieving the objectives.

3. Solicit suggestions for positive changes, whether in customer service, business processes, manufacturing processes or administration. Often, the employees who are closest to a problem will come up with the best solution. If your business is facing problems then ask solutions to employees instead of solving it alone. The employees will feel proud when you will involve them in problem solving. Take their suggestions for improvement. As number of brains will work for the improvement then definitely you will get good ideas. You should reward the employees with recognition and monetary rewards for their good ideas.

4. Encourage a sense of belonging, a sense of being a part of a successful effort. This is much like being a part of a winning sports team, an experience that is never forgotten.

16.16 Searching Good Employees

Finding good employees is crucial to most businesses. The better the employees, the more likely the business will be successful. Similarly, bad employees can cost a business incredible amount of time, resources and money. So it pays to take the time at the beginning to find the best candidates for the position.

What are the best resources for finding great candidates? Here are some ideas:

Industry professionals

Whether you're just starting out or have been a business owner for a while, chances are you have business associates whose opinion you value. Networking with other industry professionals is one resource you can utilize when looking for a good first employee. Don't be afraid to ask around. Oftentimes other business owners know of qualified individuals who have applied for work when there weren't any openings who might be interested in working for you instead.

Referrals

Asking close friends and family members for personal referrals regarding potential employees is another place you could start. Friends and family members generally care about the success of your business and will be more likely to refer quality individuals with whom they have had personal dealings. This is less risky than placing an open advertisement.

Internet

The Internet can be a good source for employees, particularly for entry-level professional positions. The majority of small businesses still use the standard classified advertisement, while a growing number are using employee referral programs. Other possibilities are through business networks, at job fairs and through online job boards.

Temporary personnel agencies

Temporary employment agencies can provide you with virtually any type of employee — accountants, programmers, sales personnel, secretaries, word processing staff and much more. With temporary employees, you get the opportunity to check out their performance, with the possibility of hiring them on a permanent basis. The only downside is that the temporary employment agency will charge you a fee if you do hire one of their temps full-time.

Headhunter

A headhunter is a classic route to take in this situation and is still a good choice. A headhunter will actively search for you, if you do not have the time to do it yourself, within the parameters you request. If your business keeps you tied up, this might be a good option.

Outsourcing

Outsourcing is a great stop-gap solution until you find an employee, but it can also replace positions within your company too. It could be as simple as having a company do your accounting for you, or it could be more complex with the entire process performed by another company. (One excellent example is from General Motors who has entire parts pre-assembled before they even get to the assembly line and are bolted on the car).

Internal candidates

Look at your own employees to fill vacant positions. There may be one who is ready for a promotion. You have the added benefit of already knowing the work habits of this person. Plus, the candidate already knows the organization. Promoting from within is also good for employee morale, as other employees will see opportunities for advancement.

Job Web sites

The Web contains a great number of sites that have job postings, want ads and resumes of prospective employees, such as Monster.com, Naukri.com and Careerbuilder.com. One good way to find these sites is through Internet search engines, such as Google and Yahoo!

Recent graduates

This group is often overlooked because they lack work experience, but they are great to hire because their lack of experience makes them moldable to your processes AND helps to build loyalty towards your company. Their youth, enthusiasm and energy will certainly help your business, too.

Employment Agencies

These organisations will pro-actively search and preselect on your behalf but they are likely to charge at least a flat finder's fee and possibly a commission of first year salary.

Industry/Professional Associations

Many industries have professional associations which are a rich resource for suitable employees, who are members. If you can identify a professional body or association which is linked directly or indirectly to your industry, you're likely to find well qualified people.

Business Networks

Utilize your professional business contacts as a source for information and recommendations over suitable staff. Also, since they are the type of people you associate with, they'll have access to the type of people you want.

16.17 Making a Good Hire

Hiring the right employee comes down to three things: screening, screening and screening. These tips will help you select the right applicant for the job.

Write a realistic job description: Before you begin writing your ad, make a comprehensive list of duties. Prioritize this list in order of importance. Include at least the top three job duties in your ad. If you want the candidate to sit in a dark room, never speak to anyone and count widgets all day, say it! Inaccurate descriptions of job duties only waste your valuable time and limited money.

Clear Qualifications: Be as detailed as you need to be in order to be clear about the qualifications that you require. This is the place to go into detail about the work environment, as well as the skills required to do the job well. This puts everyone on the same page as far as expectations.

Read resumes with a critical eye: To avoid having too many people to interview, it is a good idea to start the short listing from the resumes that applicants have collected because if you schedule for interview everyone who submitted a resume, you will be wasting a lot of your time. When looking at resumes, you should not only look at the credentials of the applicant, you should also call up previous employers to double check the information stated in the resume. Remember, resume falsifications have become so rampant these days that it is already quite difficult to know which applicants are telling the truth.

Checking references: This is your chance to find out the truth behind your potential employee. Checking references will give you valuable insight from the people who know and worked with your potential employee. Be sure to have consent (permission) from your potential employee before calling their references. If they refuse to give you consent, this should be a warning sign.

Don't be surprised that a majority of references will give good recommendations or else your candidate wouldn't give you permission to contact them. References will often give good recommendations just out of fear of being taken to court. They may be the candidates' friends who are told to exaggerate and praise the candidate.

Conduct background checks: If an employee breaks the law while performing his or her duties for your company, you may be held liable. Conducting a background check can help determine if an applicant has a criminal history and can help insulate you against possible lawsuits. You can perform a search on the Web, ask your insurance provider, consult a lawyer or contact your local police authorities for recommendations on companies to conduct this check for you. In each instance, you will need the applicant's signature and understanding that you will have a third party conduct a background check as a condition of employment.

Don't skip drug testing, credit checks and criminal background checks: Some insurance companies give discounts for mandatory new-employee testing and you'll want to know your employees are drug-free and felony-free.

Screen over the phone: During the telephone screening, ask for a brief description of their background, work experience and hobbies. This should give you some idea whether or not the candidate can handle the basics of small talk, telephone etiquette and basic communication.

Employment Testing: Thousands of companies use employment testing of some kind to evaluate candidates prior to employment. Employment testing is an area fraught with legal pitfalls, however, so it is best to seek the advice of a professional employment testing service or an attorney experienced in labour law before implementing such requirements.

The Offer: The hiring manager should personally extend an offer of employment to the selected candidate as soon as possible after the interview. This begins the employee/manager relationship. Define the amount of time the candidate has to consider the offer—a few days to one week is usually enough. The offer can be extended in person or over the phone. It is important to note that an offer, even verbal, may be construed as a contract between the employee and the company. Therefore, construct the offer carefully.

Consider "temp to perm": Using a temporary agency saves you a lot of the legwork of finding the right candidate. But make sure you read the contract carefully and know exactly what you are getting into. If a candidate does not work out, what recourse do you have? Will they refund some or all of your money? Do they only offer replacement candidates? If you do not want replacement candidates from them, are you still entitled to a refund? What are the criteria for unsuccessful placements? Make sure you get the answers to all of your questions in case the placement does not work out.

Look Internally: Now that you are clear about your expectations, the next step is to begin recruiting. The logical place to begin is with current employees. If you are not in the position to hire current employees for an open position, go to them for hiring suggestions. What kind of team members are they looking for? What is missing within the structure that will help them do their jobs better? Do they know people who can get the job done?

16.18 Need of a Recruiter in Small Business

Good employees are important to a business's success. The problem is that most small-business owners don't have the time to do it right. Advertising, culling through resumes and interviewing candidates can be a full-time job. That's why many companies look to third-party recruiters to help them hire better.

Before hiring the recruiter for the company following qualities should be checked:

- **Understanding of business:** He must have a keen understanding of your business. The best recruiters will have years of actual work experience in your field. Barring that, look for recruiters who have studied your field intensively - not just the basics, but the intricacies and the latest trends as well. This knowledge will come in handy and increase the likelihood that your recruiter has an up-to-date network of contacts.
- **Be able to read quickly:** the Statement of Work, the Job Description and the resumes as they are submitted. If the recruiter is a slow reader they will never be able to turn over the bodies in post-to-hire metrics needed for an optimum ROI for the company for which they work.
- **Understand the job inside and out:** by interviewing the supervisor or manager first to get a good feel for the billet before they ever post the first ad. If recruiters don't understand the entirety of the job, they can't recruit effectively for the placement.
- **Well communicator:** he must have a fluency in communication. He must be able to put forward the words before candidates with ease. He should be able to communicate clearly that what are the expectations of company from candidates. His accent should be clear and according to the language he is using. Recruiting is, by its nature, an actively social occupation. Look for recruiters who have extroverted (but not overbearing) personalities and a good eye for detail.
- ***An extroverted personality:*** One of the most important duties of any professional recruiter is approaching and talking to people. You want the recruiter you hire to feel at ease with this prospect - and to have the kind of personality that puts others at ease as well. Remember, executive recruitment agencies will conduct interviews on your behalf, so you need to make sure your recruiter is someone who is up to the task.
- **Interview skills:** Knows and use array of interviewing techniques.
- **Sales skills:** A good recruiter must have strong verbal and written skills, good presentation and negotiation skills. Convince a client for her business-sell your business/company to the client and convince a candidate for the job-sell the job to the candidate.

- **Analytical skills:** Good with numbers and calculations. Resumes sent, shortlisted, interviewed, selected and/or reject - a good recruiter must keep track of these numbers, analyzed and take action wherever necessary to see the increase in number of closures. A good recruiter must always quantify and talk numbers.
- **People skills:** Build and develop internal and external relationships – with client, candidate, colleagues etc.

You might think that hiring a recruiter is too expensive. It can be, but so can all the time and money you've spent in the last year on identifying, recruiting and hiring people. Try to quantify your recruiting efforts. Include the impact that the diversion had on your business. Then compare that to the typical fee of a recruiter, which is anywhere from 20 percent to 35 percent of a candidate's salary. You may be surprised at how close the costs are. In fact, one of the benefits of hiring a recruiter is that you'll have a controlled, fixed cost: You'll know what it's going to cost you to fill that position. Plus, the right recruiter can do the job better and faster than you can.

Finally, a recruiter can help you hire strategically rather than ad hoc. If you retain a recruiter on an ongoing basis, he or she can help you develop a plan for attracting good people, hiring the right people for the right jobs and managing them so that they don't jump ship at the first opportunity.

16.19 Qualities of Home-Based Business Employees

When your home is your office, the thought of hiring an employee may be daunting. It's almost more like finding the right roommate, which makes recruiting and hiring the right match all the more important.

Here are guidelines for finding and hiring:

1. **Know what you're getting yourself into:** Hire is a process that needs preparation. You have to think on many factors before hire such as will you hire full- or part-time employees or independent contractors? Do you need skilled or semi skilled employee? Do you need fresher or an experienced employee? Hiring employees means dealing with payroll and benefits. You must think on whether you will do this process by your own or will outsource that?
2. **Ask for referrals:** Before you place a help wanted ad, ask for word-of-mouth referrals. Call former colleagues and ask friends and family members if they know any trustworthy, hard-working people. Other places to look for and recruit prospective employees include local universities and community colleges, organizations or trade associations and chambers of commerce.
3. **Write down exactly what you want your new employee to do for you:** How will his or her role help you with your job? Your new employee is there to help you, so find tasks you can delegate to your new employee. By listing everything you want your employee to do, you should be able to determine if you need someone who might be full time, part time, or maybe you just need someone to come in on a freelance/independent contractor basis.
4. **Define your compensation package:** Define your compensation package. Determine what you can afford to pay the employee and what benefits you can afford to offer. If you are trying to cut costs, think outside the box. Offering flexible hours or allowing telecommuting can be very attractive advantages for prospective employees.
5. **Perform your due diligence:** You need to decide if you can afford to offer your employees benefits, such as health insurance, vacation time or sick leave. If you only have part-

time or temporary employees, this is not a large concern, but if you plan on having a full-time staff, this is very important. There are some outsourced HR options that can help you afford benefits for employees.

6. **Conduct the interview:** Get as much information from the candidate as possible. In addition to submitting a resume, ask for references and have them fill out an application. If possible, have someone else with you during the interview. This way, you will have another person's impressions of the candidate as well as your own. Ask job-specific questions and try to create scenarios to test how a prospective employee would handle typical situations. Determine how they feel about working in an office where family members and even pets may be around.
7. **Get signed contracts:** Make sure your employees know their job and they will know what they do have access to and what they do not. Those who have access to sensitive materials should be under a contract. Lay out hours they will work, their duties, their salary, if there will be paid sick time, benefits and all the finer details. Have your lawyer check out the contract and have every employee sign one.
8. Preventing the hiring of bad employees can be difficult if you are not looking for warning signs. This can include failure to answer all questions during an interview or on an application, showing up late for the appointment or not meeting all the requirements needed to perform the job. While you can still hire those who lack formal training but who are able to learn quickly or have other skills that will be useful, it is important to set a minimum number of goals so you can find candidates that have the ability to learn how to complete job tasks.
9. **Compile an employee handbook:** This lets your employees know immediately that you take your management duties seriously. Your handbook or operations manual should include policies on sick days, hours, personal use of phones and performance expectations. It should also include job titles and descriptions, office rules and procedures for requesting vacation time or reporting an absence.
10. **Prepare your family members:** You must inform the other employees in the family that you are bringing one new employee into the family. You must give reasons to your employees why you are bringing the new employee so that the new employee can get an acceptance without any confliction. It becomes necessary that you must set the boundaries for the new employee to protect him from exploitation by other employees. Assure them that the employee will not be interfering with their personal space and that they are not obligated to entertain, feed or treat the employee as a guest.

16.20 Ways for Recruiting Online

The Internet can be a powerful tool, but, like all good tools, it can also gobble a lot of your time if you let its features distract you from the job. Here are a few steps to organize your online recruiting and to keep you from veering too far off into the Web's job-related hinterlands.

Step 1: Find out any site that provides free listing. Find out, is your city listed? If yes then select the category in which you want to list. If you find many local companies are listed there then you will get an idea about whether you will be benefited by listing or not? But if you do not find many local companies listed there then you have to think on paid listing sites. You can go to monster.com, naukri.com or any job sites.

Step 2: You can enlist the help of a recruitment agency that will receive the resumes from the candidates on your behalf. The agency will then sift through all the relevant details, such as educational qualifications, skills and experience, which will be submitted in the prescribed format provided in the website. The employer can then scan through the applications received and choose the most eligible candidate.

Step 3: Write your ad. Contact to your hiring manager and get complete information about the position, qualities, qualification and experience required for the post. If you have already posted the ad then you must check it whether it requires any updation or not. Many times it happens that the requirements of the post changes according to the changing marketing conditions. You should investigate the different changing attributes you need and then you should update your ad.

Get Clear Idea About the Post: It is crucial for a recruiter to have a thorough understanding of the post in question. As a recruiter, you need to be well informed about the job description, salary range, job timings, career growth in that field, etc., before contacting the candidate. Since recruiters are the face of the company to fresh candidates, it is important to build your company's impression. Lack of knowledge about the job and its requirements will put off the candidate, which can prove to be a loss to your company.

Remember that your job description will serve a purpose beyond the job-advertisement phase. The job description will be an important document for each of your hires — something you will want to include in the hiring packet and keep on file as a reference. Discussing performance issues will be easier if you can refer to a set of expectations that were laid out at the beginning.

Think of a job title that sells. The title by which you advertise the open position doesn't have to be the company's internal title that goes with the job. While you want to include an accurate job title in the ad, you'll want to come up with a title for the ad itself that will make job seekers want to read more. This is crucial for a small business to compete with the big brand companies on the big job boards! On Monster, Yahoo! Hot Jobs and CareerBuilder your ad is likely to be listed among a huge number of jobs for a given category and the way to get job seekers to notice you among the many calls for salespeople or Web designers is to call out an enticing, distinguishing aspect of your business.

Step 4: Post it! If a small business has yet to set up a home on the web, the ease with which quality candidates can be found on some of the more mainstream online recruitment avenues makes them a very viable option. This also allows the business to reach a broader and many times higher-caliber of potential employee. While a startup business owner might not have access to career fairs at many top schools, the online recruitment channels would provide access to top students, who are more frequently posting their resumes online in addition to other methods of searching for the best positions.

Step 5: Sort, Revise...Repost? If you do not get enough online responses for the post then think on the job description of the post. It might happen that the applicants are confused about the post. So you need to post it again with the simple words and again re-post it. If you do not get the right candidates then contact to any good consultancy. The paid consultancy helps you to find out right candidates for your company. The chances of getting good candidates are high here. Once the consultancy will find out the candidates according to your expectations then they inform you and then you can take interview of those candidates.

SUMMARY

Hiring employees for a new business can be quite a difficult task since it requires the same amount of time and dedication as developing the business proposal and the process of raising capital. The entrepreneur needs to understand the hiring process whether you've just started a small business or are the head in an entrepreneurial business, any of the following problems of employee hiring mistakes could prove disastrous for your business. The problems are Partial knowledge of employees, Employees' high salary expectation, Ignorance to job consultants, Employees' retention problem, Employment, health and safety regulations, lack of employees Motivation, A solid hiring plan, and The Do-No-Wrong effect.

Getting employees for new business – what goes wrong

Improper estimation of the number of employees needed

The entrepreneurs do not have enough budgets to hire the number of employees. They try to select employees who are best and ready to work in less salary but they do not get those kind of employees because in today's business environment salary expectations of the employees are more and that expectations are not fulfilled by the new small entrepreneurs and that create problems for the new entrepreneurs.

Speedy hiring decisions

Few entrepreneurs and small business owners can focus solely on employee hiring tasks, so it is often tempting to hire quickly so you can get back to your main priorities, whatever they may be. They forgot one thing that these employees are going to impact the business by their performance.

Ignorance to educational qualification

The new entrepreneurs do not take education of the employees much seriously. They just want the employees who can do their tasks. They therefore select the person who is ready to do the work on their conditions.

Ignorance or little importance to advertising a job opening

Mostly the entrepreneurs do not advertise much about their job opening. They try to select employees through informal sources. They try to save money for advertisement. If they advertise then also they are not able to select reputed media or costly one that will be effective, instead they try to select media which is cheap because they cannot pay much amount just for selecting the employees.

Improper selection procedure

Most of the new entrepreneurs even do not follow the whole official procedure that is required to hire the employee. There are number of methods for selecting the employees that gives best results if followed but they do not care about that they follow the procedure but not completely.

Poorly prepared interview or no preparation at all

The new entrepreneurs are not aware of the interview techniques. They even do not hire professionals for hiring the employees. When they start their interview they do not follow proper guidelines of the interview they randomly ask whatever they want to ask to the interviewee without any base of the questions.

The legal obligations in hiring

There are no mandatory legal requirements in posting an employment ad; however, the new business owner must abide by several state and central guidelines in order to avoid unfair hiring practices. For example, The Equal Employment Opportunity Act prohibits discrimination in the workforce against race, gender, age, religion, sex and disability.

Informal hiring needs

Several recently released studies have shown that most entrepreneurs (around 70 per cent) spend less than five minutes in employee hiring preparation, yet it only seems obvious that less planning increases the risks of not getting the right candidate for the job. If you don't have a clear cut job description - create one.

Appropriate carefulness by checking references

Often times, employers will ask the job applicant to provide at least three sources of references. These legal requirements are not followed by most of the entrepreneurs. The harm is that the employees can any time leave the job without any intimation to the entrepreneur and that time the entrepreneur becomes helpless.

Improper spending for hiring a new employee

The new entrepreneurs do not take the procedure of hiring the employees seriously. Even they do not follow the formal procedure. They take employees without any detailed interview. They do not want to spend much money on employees' selection. As a result of that they never get good employees who can work for them for long time.

Non standard Interview Questions

Every entrepreneur has done it: asked questions plucked from nowhere at the last minute because they didn't take time to do much more than that. They cannot afford to go for consultancy because it needs money and they do not have money. The results, unfortunately, usually speak for themselves.

Gut nature can be both good and bad

Instinct plays a very important role in determining the credibility of an individual. But the new or small entrepreneurs do not take care about those things. They just want the employees who should work for their business. Even they cannot afford high salaried employee. They rarely consider these things.

Wrong ways of employee hiring are Hiring Your Twin, Unrealistic Job Requirements, expecting way too much, Rely on interview to evaluate a candidate, poorly choosen interview questions.

The different ways of hiring the perfect employee are Describe job before hiring an employee; Follow standardized hiring process; Employee recruiting strategy; Select experts, knowledge and experienced person for hiring employees; Review qualifications and applications carefully; Prescreen your applicant; Ask job interview questions accurately; Hire for today's need and tomorrow's vision; Check backgrounds and references when hiring an employee; Use effective employment letters; Focus more on evaluation than talk during interview; The most neglected aspect of hiring i.e., perform job analysis.

Appointing the right person includes Know exactly what you expect from your new hire, Define the qualities, Interviewing Job Applicants, find a major contributor, Do not "buy" their services. Always check references, and their Competencies.

The several ways to provide the needed training to employees are MSME Training Program; Business schools, colleges and universities; Industry schools and seminars and In-house training.

To make employees happy you must Communicate with them, Reinforce their contributions, Solicit suggestions and Encourage a sense of belonging.

The best resources for finding great candidates are Industry professionals, Referrals, Internet, Temporary personnel agencies, Headhunter, Outsourcing, Internal candidates, Job Web sites, Recent graduates, Employment Agencies, Industry/Professional Associations, and Business Networks.

The guidelines for selecting the right applicant for the job are: Write a realistic job description; Clear Qualifications; Read resumes with a critical eye; Checking references; Conduct background checks; Don't skip drug testing, credit checks and criminal background checks; Screen over the phone; Employment Testing; Giving Offer; Consider "temp to perm." and Look Internally.

Before hiring the recruiter for the company following qualities should be checked: Understanding of business, Be able to read quickly, Understand the job inside and out, Well communicator, *An extroverted personality,* Interview skills, Sales skills, People skills and Analytical skills.

Qualities of home-based business employees

When your home is your office, the thought of hiring an employee may be daunting. It's almost more like finding the right roommate, which makes recruiting and hiring the right match all the more important. Here are guidelines for finding and hiring:

Know what you're getting yourself into, Ask for referrals, Write down exactly what you want your new employee to do for you, Define your compensation package, Perform your due diligence, Conduct the interview, Get signed contracts, Compile an employee handbook and **Prepare your family members.**

The ways for recruiting online are Research by browsing the local sites, enlist the help of a recruitment agency, Write your ad, Get Clear Idea About the Post, Post it and Sort, Revise...Repost.

KEYWORDS

Consultancy: Consultancy is defined as the provision of expert advice, analysis and interpretation, which draws upon and applies the knowledge, skills, techniques and equipment of the consultant to meet a specific external need.

Job Consultancy: Job Consultancy is a recruitment and placement firm that understands the intricacies of human resource management and it creates a platform for jobseekers and employers, to meet and exchange their information.

Hiring plan: A hiring plan can help maximize internal resources by identifying under-utilized talent that already exists within a company.

Recruitment and Selection: It refers to the process of attracting, screening and selecting qualified people for a job.

Prescreen: To examine or interview before further selection processes occur.

Outsourcing: It occurs when a company assigns an outside firm to provide a necessary, but non-core business function which otherwise would have to be done in-house.

Employment agencies: Employment agencies are designed to act as intermediaries between employers and workers.

Business Networking: It is a marketing method by which business opportunities are created through networks of like-minded business people.

Online recruitment: It is the use of technology to attract candidates and aid the recruitment process.

QUESTIONS

1. How skilled employees can contribute to the success of the business? Explain.
2. What are the mistakes done by small entrepreneurs while hiring employees?
3. How to hire a perfect employee? Explain.
4. What are the different ways of providing training to employees?
5. What are the different sources of finding good employees?

CHAPTER – 17

CUSTOMERS RELATED OBSTACLES

LEARNING OBJECTIVES

On completion of this chapter, you should be able to:

- ☺ *Explain what are the obstacles faced by new small entrepreneurs while interacting with customers and attracting them to their business.*
- ☺ *Describe the mistakes which are done by entrepreneurs.*
- ☺ *Discuss the importance of market research and public relation for developing a new business.*
- ☺ *Describe customer service support for the new business.*

Customer service support is extremely important for any new business. It involves hiring competent and knowledgeable staff, finding fast, novel ways to respond to consumer inquiries and abiding by the cardinal rule: the customer is always right. In addition, a strong customer service team can be an effective way in which companies can easily establish a solid rapport with existing and prospective consumers in addition to finding out ways to improve products and services. Providing exceptional customer service will give any company an advantage over their competitors. This practice will also be an immediate means of gaining credibility and public recognition.

BOX 17

24 per cent of US Small Businesses Now Engaged in Social Media Survey Says

American small businesses are pushing the limits on new ways to improve efficiency in the prolonged downturn, including a steady increase in social media adoption according to results of a study from the Small Business Success Index™ (SBSI) sponsored by Network Solutions and the Center for Excellence in Service at the University of Maryland's Smith School of Business . The SBSI reports social media adoption by small businesses has doubled from 12 percent to 24 percent in the last year.

The SBSI found that nearly one out of five small business owners are actively using social media in their business. Small businesses are increasingly investing in social media applications, including blogs, Facebook and LinkedIn profiles. The biggest expectation small business owners have from social media is expanding external marketing and engagement, including identifying and attracting new customers, building brand awareness and staying engaged with customers. Sixty-one percent of the respondents indicated that they use social media to identify and attract new customers.

"Social media levels the playing field for small businesses by helping them deliver customer service," says Janet Wagner, Director of the Center for Excellence in Service at the University of Maryland's Robert H. Smith School of Business. "Time spent on Twitter, Facebook and blogs is an investment in making it easier for small businesses to compete."

Small business owners use social media to attract new customers:

- *75 per cent surveyed have a company page on a social networking site*
- *61 per cent use social media for identifying and attracting new customers*
- *57 per cent have built a network through a site like LinkedIn*
- *45 per cent expect social media to be profitable in the next twelve months*

Small business owners still have concerns with social media:

- *50 per cent of small business social media users say it takes more time than expected*
- *17 per cent express that social media gives people a chance to criticize their business on the Internet*
- *Only 6 per cent feel that social media use has hurt the image of the business more than it helped*

Source: Information received from "Pathwaypr Communications", 2010.

17.1 Attracting Customers to Your Business?

One thing is sure when you are in business; you do not stop hunting for new clients and prospects. Even when business is doing great, you still have to look for and attract new customers so you can ensure that your business keeps on growing. If not, then you might end up losing your customer base, which can lead to your losing your business altogether.

That is why it is very important that you market regularly. Marketing should not stop when you have a solid client base; it should not stop when business is doing very well; and it should never stop even when the economy is down and everybody's curbing their spending activities. You got to attract customers at all times.

But you know for a fact that targeting and attracting customers is a very difficult job. Not only are you introducing your business to your target audience, but more importantly, you are trying to convince them to do business with you. This then means that you have to show them you are different and that you are exactly what they are looking for.

The reasons behind the new entrepreneurs do not get customers are.

Entrepreneurs do not find out what customers are for

Bear in mind that it is all about them; your customers. It is all about what they need and want. If you want to attract as many customers and clients to your business, you have to learn to give them what they are looking for. But the new entrepreneurs are not competent enough to know exactly what their customers want from them. They do not understand market trends; they just try to sell what they want to sell; they do not study what products and services sell the most. They just hear from their known persons about the business and they start with that. They do not find out what problems have yet to be solved by other companies. By doing so, they do not be able to position themselves to show their target clients in their ads.

Give importance to client's money

The new entrepreneurs do not understand the psychology of the customers easily. They sell their products on high rates and low qualities because of that most of the customers are not interested in their products. The problem of new entrepreneurs is that they are not capable of keeping the price of their products less and they are not capable of increasing the quality of the products. They are the initial players and they do not take advantages of their suppliers, transporter.etc. You have to learn that money does not grow on trees. They are earned with hard work and sweat. That is why your target clients would not part with it that easily. Unless you are able to convince them that what you provide are excellent quality products and services, only then will they trust you with their hard-earned cash.

Failure to conduct the primary research

There are many great ideas you can latch on to, but the key in business is to make sure the idea—the central theme or mission of your business venture—can attract customers and generate sales and profits. A great idea in and of itself is not enough to start a business.

Your duty – You must first get the knowledge about business, study companies' case studies, read business magazines and understand what is business? How to run it? What are the drivers of business? How to generate profits? What is the role of customers and competitors? Find hidden information about the business. Find out how you are going to fulfill the requirements of the business?

Failure to follow-up with clients

Many new entrepreneurs are so busy in finding the new customers even they neglect their own current customers. They do not give proper services to customers and as a result their business suffers. Statistics show that it takes seven more interactions to secure a new client than to sell more to a repeated client. So you must develop a useful and organized follow-up system for your customers. Remember that keeping the customers are more important than attracting the customers. Sustain your customers by giving all possible services that they want.

Your duty – Be in touch with your current clients. Number of ways are there through which you can be in touch with your customers. For example wish your customers on their birthday, New Year, festivals; inform them about new offers, discounts and sales. If your customer purchases on monthly bases then remember the products he purchases and be ready with their products. Ask them whether they are comfortable with your services and products. It is essential to build a very, very special relationship with your clients. They are your best audience.

Failure by over-marketing

You may have a thought that your products or services are best in the market. Even after that you cannot sell to every customer. You should select a particular segment where your products best suit to their requirements. Entrepreneurs are always ready to sell anyone in the market but the fact is that they should create themselves a niche in the market about their business. By doing this you will have a more efficient message and will more likely achieve success much sooner.

Your obligation – Carefully identify your segment, your location, your well suited clients, where they go, what they read, what their hobbies are, etc. Once you have a full understanding of your client's profile you will then have a full understanding of how and where to find more of them. Try to have the database of your client. Write down full information about your client that will help you for analysis.

Unable to focus on the business

Many new entrepreneurs are energetic and enthusiastic people (which is essential to success), but they can also be overly optimistic and pursue too many targets and directions at one time. They fail to focus on one thing properly because they want to pursue so many goals at the same time. This typically results in mediocre results. Clearly and in detail write down your business mission. When you will try to achieve everything at once then you will be disturbed and confused. You are likely to fail to execute anything correctly. You won't have the time to sit back and decide on the best way to develop your own marketing plan, create new products or improve your services.

Your task – You must know your mission. Frame it. Your mission must be achievable and realistic. Decide time limit for your mission and accordingly set your targets. Your activities to achieve targets must be measurable. Once you will be clear with your business purpose then running a business is easy.

Do not make marketing a priority

Many new entrepreneurs start their business without determining their target, niche and demography first and as a result have failed to attract any clients. They do not have any marketing plan for the business. How they are going to reach to the customers? Marketing should be one of your top priorities. Devising a marketing plan will help you determine how to promote your products or services and create a system that will generate more clients for your business.

Your duty – you must seriously work on your marketing plan. How will you form it? and how will you implement it? You must be very clear about it. Marketing plan is essential because it gives direction to your business. Think on after opening business what to do? So the marketing plan should be ready to penetrate the market. Work continuously on your marketing plan to make it more powerful.

Do not contact professionals

Many new entrepreneurs ask their friends and family for advice when starting a new business. The problem is that they often ask people who have never started a business; so in reality, these people are not in a position to offer sound advice.

Your duty – Contacting to a professionals or experts will improve your business skill. At least for the initial years of your business you must be continuously in touch with the experts. Team up with professionals who can complement your strengths and cover for your weaknesses.

Do not spend enough time researching the business idea

Number of new entrepreneurs have often failed because they were not truly interested in the business; they were more interested in making money. It is important to start something that you really like, because you will be spending a lot of time on it.

Assignment – You must give sufficient time to your business plan. In business plan you must focus on mission statement, products or services, business strategy and competitors, research on your target market (demographics), industry analysis (size, economics, trends, success factors, challenges, etc.,) your marketing plan, your financial plan and sales and profits.

Improper determination if the business adds value

The most sustainable businesses, those that withstand the test of time, provide value by performing a service that people need. Most of the entrepreneurs are not aware about this. Whether they are providing any additional value to the customers?

Your task – Make sure your products or services provide value and benefit to your clients. Be ready to solve any business problems that your clients may have. The business should satisfy the needs of the customers. After that only customers will come.

Under-budgeting the marketing costs

Market is flooded with the same type of businesses and therefore you need to do a lot of work to differentiate yourselves. That means there is a need to provide unique products or services to your customers so that you will look different. Promotional activities become very essential for your business.

Your assignment – Think on the new strategy that you can bring into the market. Provide adequate publicity, business cards and marketing materials that project a professional image. This is the area where you have to spend money. If you will invest smaller amount of money then your business will suffer because these strategies are reflecting your business. A cheap business card or flyer will not make a professional impact.

Cannot describe the business in one or two sentences

It may happen that because of the complexity of your business you are not able to clearly explain your business in short. Or, you take time to communicate the basic concept of the business. What value or benefits does your business offer?

Your duty – Work on to explain your business in fewer sentences and less time. Explain your business, mission and the benefits that you will provide. Find out the way to define your business in a precise manner.

Do not consider the demographics

When the entrepreneurs become unable to consider the demographics of the customers then they do not able to attract the customers. They do not market to the right people with the right message. They are not capable of determining who would be more interested in their offer, as well as who would have the most capacity to buy their product or service. This creates problem because they do not know how to treat different category customers. You do not go wasting your time and effort trying to advertise to just about everybody. If you target carefully, you can attract the right people who would surely be able to act on your offer right away.

Unable to gain an understanding of the business

Every business runs because there are some reasons behind that. For example fruit business runs because people like to eat fruits. Toys business runs because people like to purchase toys for their kids. Every business has an influence over some segments of the market. Many business leaders, executives and management consultants would say that success largely depends on attention to detail. The entrepreneurs start the business but they do not have complete understanding of the business. They start the business with the hope that they will handle the situation in the business.

Your duty – You must have complete knowledge of your business then only you will be able to think logically. Understand all the important areas of your business and then manipulate that according to your benefits. The important thing in the business is that you should completely understand the business without that you can not apply your brain for the success of the business.

Be different

They are not capable of differentiating themselves from the others. They do not know this valuable concept. They do not know the way how they can differentiate their business from others. Make your own strategy of marketing. But remember that your marketing strategy should be the attractive and influencing one. Without it you will not be able to generate interest in the customers. Give customers a strong reason to come to your shop. The uniqueness of your marketing campaign will help you become distinct to attract the attention of your target audience. It is not always necessary that every time you will need huge finance for your business related activities, even by less expensive method also you can attract your target customers. For example direct mail, on door services and internet marketing are good ways of promotion.

No Means of Differentiation – Just another "Me Too" Business

Many businesses failed because they have simply copied the other existing business. Though two same types of businesses are opened but they must have their own uniqueness. There are number of restaurants but customers prefer only their choice of restaurant. Why because each restaurant has their own uniqueness and therefore customers who like that they go to that restaurant without any second thought. Uniqueness may be in the form of better product / service (better quality, lower prices, broader selection, faster delivery, better location, extended warranty, etc.,). But the restaurants that are unable to create such uniqueness they run on luck. Customers need a reason to come to or to want to do business with your company. If your products or services are the same quality and prices as your competitor(s), why will people buy from you? They already have an existing supplier.

Improper Location

The entrepreneurs are not able to attract the customers because their business is not located in proper place from where they can attract customers. Customers are by nature lazy they do not want to search the location of the business instead they will go to other company. Everywhere you go everyone and anyone will tell you that one of the most important things to making a successful business and to keep customers coming back is the location! Entrepreneurs feel it very hard to attract the customers to their shop. Many times customers abandon the idea of going to a particular area because of the heavy traffic and busy roads. Contrary to this customers want to go to a particular area anytime due to less traffic and crowd.

Some businesses run only on the bases of location; particularly those engaged in retail and hospitality businesses. These businesses need a location that is appropriate, visible and attracts significant traffic. Restaurants and retail stores need a location where there is sufficient parking, a good flow of walk-in and drive-by traffic and little competition.

For home-based entrepreneurs, location depends on the zoning restrictions of the area. You may insist on operating the business from the comforts of your home, but zoning laws (and neighbours) may disagree with you and prevent you from operating the business.

What to do: You must study the area thoroughly before selecting the location for a business. You need to know about population, crowd, traffic, roads, parking, nature of customers, government plan on that area and competitors. You also need to know the business trends in the area for the past year and the number of new businesses that opened as well as those that have closed recently.

If you are operating a home business, be sure to check with your zoning authorities.

Non pleasure appearance

The entrepreneurs find it difficult to have the appearance of their shop at the level of the big companies. When customers come in their shop and try to purchase at that time if the customers expectation is high then the entrepreneurs become helpless but most of the times the entrepreneurs are not aware about the value of services. They neglect this part. It is very true what everyone says in terms of the first impression is a last impression! This is not just true in personal aspects but in business situations as well. If someone walks into a department store that has great prices but garbage on the floor, a bad smell in the air and items thrown all over the shelves and on the floor, what are the chances that they will return just based on the low prices? Very slim to none unless the prices are almost 100 per cent discounted which is highly unlikely.

Product has no sizzle

Your success depends on whether you provide products or services with value to your customers. Many small business entrepreneurs fail to effectively communicate to their customers the benefits of their products or services. This is particularly true of many home-based Internet entrepreneurs, who have been misled to believe the myth that "if you build it, they will come." People will accept your product/service when they will have a positive image of your business in their mind. For example if your hotel provides very delicious food to the customers that too in less price then customers will have an image of "Hotel with tasty food in less price". You will become famous because no other hotel provides such a delicious food and that too in low price. Once you position your product/service by your efforts then after that you will see a huge crowd of customers are coming to your hotel.

Prices

This is obviously one of the most important aspects of the business world. While you want to make a profit to stay afloat in the business world, you also need to make sure you are still fairly competitive with other business of the same kind and maybe a little lower with more products to offer which will offset the lower prices. Nothing is more appealing than knowing if you drive down the road a mile you'll find the same product for fifty rupees cheaper. Now this can be accomplished in many ways with specials, sales, coupons, buy one get one at half off or free and so on. And you can have lower prices but offer more product and more brands which should offset the lower prices and still bring in the amount of revenue you're looking for.

Knowledge of the product you are selling

It is very crucial that all employees have complete knowledge in the product or services being offered in a business. It is very embarrassing that if customers ask you a question and you are not in position to give proper answer. Sometimes you call other or ask them to come on next day or give very poor answer. This is very bad situation for your business. Customers have a tendency to ask many questions and if at that time you will not satisfy them by giving answers to the questions then customers will feel bad about you and customers with such bad experience will never come again. Start a business with at least some basic knowledge of the business so that you can entertain your customers. Your employees need to have sufficient knowledge to satisfy customers' query.

Friendliness

All too often we hear complaints by word of mouth stating that an employee at a certain business was short, rude, callous or uptight while servicing a customer. This creates a huge problem for the business. Word of mouth travels extremely fast and we all know that when we hear something, we take it to heart and usually stay clear of the business without even trying it out for ourselves. Talk to your customers, smile, make suggestions but don't be overbearing at the same time. People like to chat, especially stay at home moms who don't get out often. It gives customers a sense of feeling that he got me, knew what I was about and was truly caring of my needs.

Advertising

It is extremely important to get your business advertised in all the right places. This can be accomplished in so many different ways, newspapers; magazines; internet; coupons; signs out of front; word of mouth and more. Choose something like a coupon or a two day sale, this will get the customers rolling in the door specifically for the sale but then once they see all the products offered and the prices that are available everyday and the excellent customer service that they will receive, it is almost a sure bet that everyone will be coming back over and over whether there is a sale or not.

Underestimating the Competition

Some business owners underestimate the competition because of their overconfidence on their own products or services. They think that if their business is running properly then why they should care about the competitors. But the fact is that if two businesses are of the same kind then you can never sit relaxed just by saying that I have no fear from others. Remember that any business in the world can never attract 100 per cent customers. If you will not take it seriously then your competitors will take your customers away and you will not be able to do anything at that time. You can compete by lowering prices, offering package / bundle pricing, extending terms, introducing new products, improving product quality, extending warranties, increasing marketing activities, etc., therefore do not underestimate the competitive reactions to the start of your business.

Inability to reach desired sales goals

For running your business you will need profit. But if you are not able to make the required sales then your earning will not be sufficient to meet your fixed and variable costs. The problem is that the new entrepreneurs are not able to implement the sales strategies properly. They already have no experience, when they do not sell anything they keep the price of the products as it is. They do not use any promotional strategies. So in such a situation you should use all the promotional activities to increase the sales. This could attract customers, helps cover your costs and buys time until your business rebounds. Reduction in your product price will also increase your sales, especially when your limited budget does not allow you to go for advertising or other expensive promotional activities.

However once you down the price of your product then it is hard to gain the original price. Consumers become habitual to the low price and they will not be ready to pay high price for your product. Consumers may even peg you into the "cheap" category, thus putting your hard-earned image at risk.

Not cost competitive

Before opening a business you must obtain the information of cost structure and product price of your competitors. Even cost structure and product price information of your competitors will give you new ideas for your business. If you find that your cost structure and price are higher than your competitors that mean some where you are lacking. Your business requires improvement.

If your selling prices are the same as your competitors and their operating costs are lower, their margins will be higher. You cannot compete to them because of their lower operating cost. You will have to find ways to reduce the cost disparity if you plan to last in this industry. The lowest cost producer will always win a price war.

Failure to adapt to changing market conditions

Changing market conditions means fluctuation in the market. Changing market conditions may include downturn or upswings in the economy, heightened competition or even common business risks such as Web site business interruption or calamities. It is like a ship in the sea. You as a captain of the business must progress your business by overcoming all the hurdles. You must find out the way of adjusting your business in such a fluctuating market. But the new entrepreneurs are not able to change suddenly to the given market conditions because it requires time and money. Changing market conditions also change the taste of the customers. That means now they want to consume or use different products or services. They want to shift from the traditional to the modern one. But if you are not prepared for the changing conditions and when these changes strike, you may find your business ill-prepared to cope and survive. The new entrepreneurs find it very difficult because they do not have enough money and do not have any preplan about changing market condition.

What to do: You need to know one thing and that is you must be ready for change. You must review your strategy according to the changing business environment. Find out weaknesses and make it more resourceful. By doing this you will be able to change your old strategy and will be able to make it more flexible. It is important that you study your customers thoroughly so you can track customer preferences and buying trends. This will help release your company from the economic ups and downs.

Wallet is not big enough

You have really worked hard to gather all the resources, equipment and materials to start your business. You have taken loans from banks and also convinced your investors to invest in your business. You have started your business with the hope that now you will earn profit. When you open your business for the customers then you realize that it is not so easy to run the business. You do not get enough customers. You wait but you do not get the expected results and on other side you lack money because of less profit. Without money coming in, you decide to cut your losses and close down the business.

Your duty: Any business before start must have a roadmap. In business the roadmap is business plan. In your business you must always have predefined tasks that you want to perform. Business plan gives you right direction of the business. It has all the answers of your business issues. But you need to seriously write down a detailed business plan. If you will run the business without proper business plan then you will never get the success.

17.2 Market Research Importance in a New Business

Market research involves the systematic gathering, recording and analyzing of data about customers, competitors and the market. This links marketers to consumers by supplying essential information to solve marketing challenges and help with marketing decisions.

Market research helps a company create and develop an up-to-date and relevant portfolio of products. Your existing and potential customers fall into particular groups or segments, characterized by their 'needs'. Identifying these groups and their needs through market research and then addressing those needs more successfully than your competitors, should be one of the key elements of your marketing strategy.

Every entrepreneur should ask themselves the following:

The entrepreneur who is planning to introduce their new concept into the market needs to determine the reasons for starting their new business. They should ask themselves the following questions: What technical skills do I have that will contribute to my new business? How Can I Attract More New Customers? What do others believe are my strengths and weaknesses? How Can I Get More Repeat Business? Will I have the finances to fully support my family when I decide to leave my job and start the new business? What's the Most Effective Way to Spend My Promotional Budget? How much available time do I have to invest in my business idea? What services or products will I sell? What new concepts or ideas will I be bringing forth? Could I sell better quality products or services? Could I compete to my competitors?

Benefits of market research

By conducting thorough market research, entrepreneurs will be able to obtain valuable information about starting their new businesses.

First, market research will enable the business owner to learn of industry trends and which products/services will be in demand.

Second, they will be able to see how the general public responds to their business ideas. This step is extremely important because if a business manager cannot show investors (venture capitalists or angel investors) that his/her great business idea(s) has/have potential, they may not be able to secure proper funding for their venture.

Essential Benefits of Market Research

1. Increases overall competency and understanding of critical research concepts and provides an enhanced ability to make well-informed decisions
2. Provides a cost-effective opportunity to supplement a company's internal training (Discounts for group enrollments are available!)
3. Facilitates a common knowledge bridge with all parties involved in the research process.
4. Provides a specific starting point for people entering the profession.
5. Gives company an objective tool to help develop and promote employees.
6. Assists researchers in understanding and differentiating between good research practices and those which undermine objective and impartial research.

Types of market research

There are two distinct types of market research.

A. In secondary research, the business owner gathers already published data, which is easily accessible and nearly free to obtain. Information such as consumer demographics, major competitors and general usage of products is often collected by government agencies and organizations and made available online and in books and publications. One disadvantage of this type of market research is that the data collected may be difficult to validate and may even contain biased information.

B. Primary market research is more specific in nature. It contains information regarding a specific product that is brought forth by a company. Focus groups, field studies and simple observations of customer behavior are some ways in which companies obtain primary market research. Many businesses that are planning to launch new products rely on this form of research since they produce more specific results. However, primary market research can be quite costly. Using both types of research can certainly allow business owners to have accurate information regarding the market and in making wise investment decisions.

Types of customers

There are three main types of customers that every business will encounter. Depending on the product, its cost and position within the sales cycle, they may or may not be influenced to purchase a particular product or service. It is up to the sales person or business owner to understand their customers' thinking in order to successfully win them over and make a sale.

A. The "purchaser" is primarily concerned with the cost of a product, not how effective a particular product may be. These types of customers are aware of all the prices offered by major competitors and will often purchase a product if they believe it is a according to them. To target this type of customer, the business owners should show how their prices are competitive.

B. The "influencer" is not concerned by the cost of a product but rather if the product being offered will be considered a good purchase. They tend to be very knowledgeable about every characteristic of a product, including technical features that the product offers. They have every minute information about the product. To target this type of customer, the business owners should be aware of every aspect of their product and present to potential buyers what the product can do for them.

C. The end-user will not only be glad to purchase the product but he will actually use the product bought. When enticing this type of customer, it is always a good idea to relate to them with their frustrations on their current situation and convey how their new product will alleviate many of the limitations that they may have encountered.

Overall, market research tests the customer response to a product. When developing a great business idea, business owners first need to think how their great business ideas will benefit customers. Shortly after developing great business ideas, entrepreneurs are encouraged to analyze the market in order to determine if their product is similar to what they are considering to develop and if it is already available on the market. If there is already a similar product, business developers then need to determine how they will place their new product to differentiate it from the product already available on the market. The placement of products born out of great new business ideas need to be carefully chosen to attract the maximum attention of customers. In addition, it is product placement that will differentiate this product from other similar products on the market.

17.3 Role of Public Relations Campaign

Public Relation is simply accurate, consistent and timely communications that convey the right message to the right audience. This is true across-the-board for businesses of any size. OR "any activity that creates a positive image, fosters goodwill or increase sales. A poor marketing strategy is one of the leading reasons why most businesses fail. It is no wonder that many new enterprises resort to establishing a strong public relations campaign in order to actively advertise and promote their businesses. Public relations are a vital necessity for a company's success. Without it, entrepreneurs have no outlet to effectively sell their products and services.

Define your audience

New business owners must know who are their target customers? Once it is known then according to the type of customers you can make your strategies of public relations campaign. Your products and services will decide your marketing plan. Make sure which types of customers are going to be benefited most by your products and services. For example, a stationery shop can easily target school children by selling copy, pencils, pen and all, that is required by school students.

Define your competition

Next you have to find out is there any competition in the market in your kind of business? Every type of business has competitors so you must deeply analyze your competitors. Find out what is their reputation? What customers think about their business? Are they stronger or weak? Such information should be obtained by their opponents, customers, websites and their suppliers. For example, a restaurant that is located nearby offers new customers discount. Entrepreneurs can have a competitive edge by offering their existing customers more attractive discount and they can recruit new customers by advertising large posters or by night lightning.

Website development

Now website has reduced the demand for any new land or the desire to open a new branch by new and small entrepreneurs. Website has given tremendous power to the new entrepreneurs. By opening a website small businesses can now attract more customers. If they are unable to interact with their customers face to face then this limitation is overcome by the website. They can run their promotional programmes thorough internet also. Your website should have an attractive look and user friendly. The instructions on your website should be clear and highlighted. Many companies can further raise their profile by employing the help of a professional webmaster for search engine optimization and affiliate posting to increase the flow of online traffic to their company website. For example, if someone is looking to buy print T-shirts they can simply type "print T-shirt" during a web search and will instantly find sites that exclusively sell these products. By linking different sponsors and associates on a company's website, entrepreneurs can easily raise their recognition since they can be listed on many different sites.

Determine your advertising budget

After identifying the target customers and any major competitors, entrepreneurs should now take a decision on how to effectively expose their business. How public will know about business? What are the ways to tell customers about products or services? Advertising about the new business is a difficult task. You should think on the effective way of doing publicity of the business. The entrepreneurs should select the strategy or promotional tools according to their budget by which they can reach to their potential customers. For example, if an entrepreneur runs a business of a toy shop and can afford print media only then he should use his advertising budget towards posters, banners, leaflets, newspapers that can be distributed locally and then use a portion of the budget towards magazine ads. If it is not possible for you to use all print Medias then you can focus on newspapers and magazines because these are more exposed to common people.

Self vs. hired professionals

Once an advertising budget is determined, the entrepreneur can now decide on public relations. Public relations have an important place in promoting the business. Either you can contact to a public relations specialist or you can design your own strategy for the publicity of your business. You can take the ideas from other businesses what they are doing for publicity of business. If you want to do your own business publicity then you can copy others. There are many ways of publicity like use of newspaper advertisements, posters, direct-mail notices, blogs, contests etc., to lure prospective customers. Public relations specialist can effectively convey accurate information to the target audience through more outlets, including local and national television commercials, in-store item positioning and sales and various packaging styles and techniques in order to gain new and repeated customers.

17.4 The Importance of Customer Service Support

Surveys suggest that service driven companies are able to charge up to 9 per cent more for the goods and services they offer and grow twice as fast as the average. These are powerful incentives for becoming the best customer-service company in any industry. Equally, poor service has a cost penalty. It costs up to five times as much to go out and get a new customer as to retain those we have.

According to research the average person who has a bad-service experience tells at least nine others about it and 13 per cent of complaints relate their experience to more than 20 other people. In comparison, people who receive silent service only tell three or four others about it"

The following factors are as follows:

Good customer care matters

Good customer care matters because keeping existing customers is easier than finding new ones and satisfied customers will do a lot of our advertising for us. Most people consider doing business with a certain company because of a recommendation by a friend or acquaintance. Dissatisfied customers spread the bad news and undermine your business, which ultimately threatens everyone's jobs

Competitive edge

You can get a competitive edge over competitors by providing excellent customer service. Customer service is a fast and effective marketing tool and that's why every company is trying to take advantages of it. It has been seen that small enterprises, which heavily focus on their customer service support, were more likely to endure and succeed when compared to their leading competitors who only focused on offering lower prices for their products and services. You can differentiate your business from others by having easily accessible customer service support, maximum facilities, solving customers' problems instantly, reliable and friendly service.

Give the gift of your confidence

Make it easy for employees to up their game and take some ownership. Give them the option to make instant decisions and provide what the customer needs. Tell every employee its okay to go above and beyond to fix a customer issue. Let them know that you will support their judgment in attending to a customer issue. This puts a backbone to the idea that the customer is at the center of the company. Every single customer contact must be friendly, productive and helpful. Every customer interaction is an opportunity to move the relationship to a higher (or deeper) level.

Employee Empowerment and Training

Give your front-line employees some power to solve problems. For instance, let a cashier offer a small discount on damaged merchandise. This provides two advantages: you solve problems quickly; and both customer and cashier feel more valued. Top companies treat their employees well. Motivate employees who deliver top service with rewards.

Media outlets

There are different kinds of media outlets which business owners depend on to promote their enterprises. Print media refers to any image or text that can be produced on paper or on objects. Posters, brochures, catalogs, daily newspapers, business journals, fliers and newsletters are some forms of print media. It can also comprise of billboard advertisements and items which contain company letterhead and promotions (i.e., pens, key chains, etc.,). For example, a fruit store can rent billboard space and place their billboard advertisements along busy highways to lure customers, while a local bank can advertise their grand-opening on promotional key chains and pens. Common broadcasting media include television and radio markets. It is common for many businesses, small or large; to resort to this form of public relations since it provides a fast and efficient method to gain local, regional and national recognition.

Innovation and modern technology advantages

Many new businesses have found fast and effective ways to interact with their customers. For example, online reservation, online shopping, online query submission, online bank account – here banks are trying to provide facilities to their customers by means of internet, now customers need not go to their respective bank's branch. They can do inquiry or transaction online. The businesses are trying to give every possible facility to their customers by using advanced technology and innovative methods. The companies are now providing digital currencies to their customers for easy money transaction. In addition, some company websites can even offer some "virtual" suggestions when a customer decides to purchase items online. These are just some proven ways to gain new business and to keep customers happy.

Present yourself as an expert

Customers are happy and satisfied when they know that their queries are handled by an expert. They believe on experts because they know that they are going to get solution from that expert person. They are hopeful that their problems will be solved more easily and in less time. Therefore it becomes very necessary for you that you should present yourselves as an expert. You must know every minute details of your business if you want to present yourselves as an expert. Once customers will know that you are going to provide solution for their problems then customers will be impressed by you and come to you. As an expert you should know everything about your field. You should not give any indication that you are lagging behind in giving answers or solving the problems. You should look like a confident expert.

Less costs needed to attract new customers

Quality customer service relieves pressure on the organization to attract new customers. Statistics show that it costs more to gain new customers that it is to retain existing ones. The benefit of customer service comes into play here. A thorough customer service program will help maintain an existing customer base rather than lose a percentage of it.

Reputation

A company's reputation depends on not only the products but also the service delivered. It is often stated that when a customer has a bad experience with a company, that customer tells between nine and twelve others. Bad customer service experiences can spread like wildfire. In the age of the Internet and electronic communications, a customer can tell even more people. A company's reputation can be soured, over time, if they continue to provide bad customer service.

Make swift customer e-mail replies

Customers do not want to wait for their queries. They want immediate response to their queries. By doing this you will make your relation with your customers stronger. Do not delay to respond to them. Many customers are usually pleased and impressed by the fast response from a customer service centre, especially if the response is within an hour rather than few hours to days time period. The next day will be your day because you have provided them what they want from you and you will see that your customer base is increasing day by day. Next time they will definitely come to your company.

The customer satisfaction is must

It is a known fact that even though customers, these days, have a wide range of options they prefer to stick to companies with whom they have had a positive experience and build a good rapport. Thus relationship building must be treated as an integral part of developing your business. An excellent customer service is the primary ingredient to ensure that your business thrives. A satisfied buyer will not only buy repeatedly from you, but will also bring in new customers by way of word of mouth or by being a great brand ambassador for your company.

Community involvement

Try to involve more number of people in your business. Give a chance to your customers so that they can rate your product and service. You can interact with your customers for your product or service rating either physically or through internet. Website is the best option to do all this. Give your customers a serious message that their suggestions are important to you and those suggestions will be implemented. By doing this you can get trust of the customers and customers will also have a feeling that you care about them and give importance to them. Through the use of similar online tools, businesses can easily find out the likes and dislikes of their buyers according to customer ratings.

Make returns easy

A liberal return policy is a good thing to have, but having a generous return policy makes it easy for customers to trust you. With that comforting thought in mind, customers will buy more.

Provide new service if customers ask

Customers are the best way to take feedback about your product and service. Customers can tell you exactly what more or less they want from you. Loyal customers can make suggestions on improving a product or service. Customers can ask you for extra services which they need. Companies should be aware of their customer's insights and desires and be willing to offer what the general public is willing to pay for.

So What Could Be the Solution?

17.5 Attracting Customers to Your Trade Show Display

When an individual or group of individuals embarks upon any business venture, one of the most important things they have to cultivate is name recognition.

A trade show is a great place to get your name out there and establish a foothold in your chosen industry. This is an especially important marketing tool if the products you are trying to market are unique and very useful for your customers. With so much competition in this varied arena, your product will become invisible in a sea of business enterprises. You can avoid this however, by taking a few steps towards making your trade show display eye catching and alluring.

Below are guidelines you can utilize to make that happen.

1. Good deal: Good deal will happen only when customers will know about your product/service. You need to first give them a taste of your product/service. To be sure, giving away samples to your customers will be helpful to bring the customers to your booth. Prize drawings and contests are also appealing as they give the consumer a promise of something in return for giving a little of their time to your sales pitch.

2. Make sweeter the pan: Another thing that people cannot resist is something tasty. With this idea in mind, chocolates and ice-cream would be a welcome treat and a reason to stop by your table. Be sure to keep a ready supply of the foodstuffs nearby however, for refills when reserves get low.

3. Interact and get involved: Many trade shows goes sit behind their exhibit and wait for interested parties to come to them which is a mistake. You must be active one and should try to generate interest in customers. Customers like to engage with individuals who are friendly and fun, which is why major companies pay millions to celebrities with charismatic person ality to endorse their products. If being happy go lucky just isn't in your nature, see if you can hire an attractive female model or great reputed personality that has PR experience to address the crowd.

4. A dash of colour: human beings are naturally attracted towards colorful things more easily than the colorless things. Their responses to the visual things are instant. You should make use of this quality of human being while designing banner or poster for your booth. Colorful displays always attract attention. Make sure to do so tastefully, as too much color can end up being confusing and distracting. Decorate the booth with colourful stuffs. Customers at least stop for a while and that the moment you can engage them in your product. A lively, easy to read banner or a nice, brightly colored tablecloth is a great way to add pop without being overbearing.

5. Presentation boards and visuals prompts: power point presentation on large presentation board will be helpful to you to attract interested customers. Visual things can be highlighted more easily than the static one and therefore in a crowd you will be able to catch the attention of the customers. You can make the presentation attractive by making it interactive so that public can have direct access to your presentation and they can see whatever they want to see by their own way. If your presentation is stationary, the rule of colour would definitely apply.

If this is kept up, the business will create the name recognition and appeal that is so essential in helping any new company thrive!

17.6 Marketing Thoughts for Small Businesses

Starting a business is not easy. Double when you do it now when the economy is at a downward trend these days. The present economic climate makes it even more difficult to start one, let alone grow a business that would essentially be a constant in the market.

Starting a business means you not only have to learn and be an expert on the day-to-day essentials of running a business, you also need to be updated on how to attract and get customer to buy whatever it is you are offering on a daily basis. In addition to the regular accounting and bookkeeping responsibilities, as a business owner (you also have to contend with the marketing strategies that would keep customers coming in to your store or shop. This is ultimately how you make money in your business, the more customers that would come in and buy your products and services, the more profits you gain from your business endeavor.

Marketing can help you attract customers so you will make money and marketing is one of the most important elements in business that can determine whether you will succeed or fail in your industry. And depending on what form you will take with your marketing campaigns (catalogs, letterhead printing or print letterheads, sticker printing, brochure printing, flyers, etc.,), your promotional materials can work to make your dreams come true. But you also need to consider that the kind of marketing strategy you apply to your business also depends on what kind of business you are dealing with. Certain kinds of marketing campaigns may work for some, while others may work on different kinds of businesses. It all depends on what your business is and how you implement your ideas to generate the clients you need.

Ultimately, marketing is all about getting your business out there; having your business known by your target clients. And the very first step to a successful marketing is to have a defined brand that would identify you in your market niche. It may be in the form of your logo or your slogan. But definitely, your brand would be the very thing that would represent you and your business in the market. Thus, it is very important that you create for your business a strong brand that would be easily recognized and remembered. You can do this by creating a brand that is professional and uniquely yours. Once you have your brand, it would be easy for you to organize and design promotional materials that you can use to make your target clients know you.

17.7 Interest Your Clients

When deciding to use promotional items, you need think way outside of the box. It should not happen that your item once get into the customers house are thrown out at the corner and making no use. The secret is that you should look different than your competitors. For example- A pen is great for a small gift however, adding a notepad or even a pencil holder along with the pen will give you a promotional item that will stay in front of your potential client as long as you have your company info imprinted on the item and not just the pen.

Here are some guidelines

Find totally unique promotional items because people remember such items. Give your customers those items that are not given by your competitors. Examples for around the office include Rulers, Key chain, Staplers, Pen holder, Letter Openers, Clips, Memo Holders, Magnifiers, Desk Organizers Note Pads and Cubes, Calculators and Paperweights, USB, Flash and Memory Drives, Mouse Pads, Candles and Spa Gifts, Blankets and Throws.

Try to give gifts that will benefit your business. Try to give such gifts which are very close to your business. For example- If you are a medical officer, give away a first aid kit of a stress reliever.

Motivate the customers by all possible means to purchase your products. This small token of appreciation can be something they use every day or something that they can use throughout the week. A small gift always shows appreciation. Most people will purchase another item to get something free.

Plan contest with imprinted promotional items. This way you can afford to give a higher priced item such as bags or even a large gift basket full of goodies.

Using these guidelines should enable you to use imprinted promotional items to your own advantage.

17.8 Using Customer Segmentation as a Marketing Tool

Markets are full of people of different kinds. People are different from each other in terms of age, sex, religion, class, interests, spending and purchasing habits etc. Consumer segmentation is a discipline that classifies these people into several groups that have certain common similarities. Effective consumer segmentation allows the companies to reach out to their target market more effectively and economically.

However, when companies target groups based on their demographics, psychographics or attitudes, it is termed as traditional segmentation. A more evolved segmentation could be when the desired results are achieved by dividing the groups in terms of the revenue that they generate. Now, the market is flooded with companies similar to you. The trick to winning over the consumer is to provide more value to them in return for the money they pay you for your product or service. Value in the sense of better product quality, higher quantity, donation to a cause, a chance to win a raffle, etc., these value additions will in turn help to justify the variations in the price of your product as compared to the competitor's price.

Due to the fact that there are a lot of competitors out there in the market, it is important to perform customer segmentation to gain competitive advantage by identifying your target market and strategically carrying out your marketing plans to benefit each segment individually. This kind of situation can be created by dedicating your resources on strategic planning and research. Let's say for instance that you trade clothes; all types of clothes for every season. However, your target market, which would be pretty much everyone, will include people of different age and social status and as such, the types of clothing that they wear will differ. It is now up to you to set up your marketing campaign in a way that the younger generation is aware that you provide clothing that is considered "hip" to them while ensuring that the parents or the older generation still approves.

Depending on where and when you plan to formulate and run an ad campaign, you will market your products differently to suit the segment of your target market, that will be the most likely to see your ad at that particular point in time. This way you will be maximizing your marketing Rupees and keeping a competitive edge. When you start your own business, you develop a sense of pride that only another entrepreneur can relate to. But maintaining that business and keeping ahead of the competition is not as easy as it seems unless you have a monopoly, which is very unlikely, but even if you do, you will not have it for long. When you start your business, it is wise to get training and have a support team, no matter how much you think that you already know.

17.9 Get New Patrons for Your Business

The key is not just to learn different strategies and techniques to attract more clients in order to increase your income but also to have the ability to attract the type of clients you want and who will pay you the fees you want, whenever you want. A truly amazing skill to have in your range is to be able to attract the right kind of clients.

Figure out what your market really wants.

Steps to help you do this:

- Visibility alone will not give you the momentum you need to secure clients to your liking. Only giving information about your product will not be enough. You must reach to the heart of the customers to know their wants.
- Most customers exactly know about their needs and they also know what to buy. They will not buy articles merely because you think they need them; they buy items that they want to, where they are interested and they think that they will be satisfied by that item.
- No one really needs a 40" flat screen TV but people buy them still. Unless your offerings match up to meet the wants of the market, securing the right kind of clients in good numbers will be difficult. So you've got to keep a close tab on the market and figure out what it is that the market really wants.

Focus on the people who have raised their hands.

You need to be very careful while selling your product or services. You need to have exact information about your customers. Instead of focusing on everyone you need to focus on the customers who really need your product or service. You must then develop a method of converting them into business that pays you well.

See people as people.

Most of the time it will happen that your client being special or different from others will worry you from promoting yourself or your product. The fact is that though they are special or different from the others but still they are people just like you. They have the same thoughts, perceptions, emotions and needs, as you. Keeping this in mind will not only help you increase your knowledge about customers but will also help you to relate to their needs better.

There is nothing personal about rejection.

Don't take anything personal, it is business and you must think in that way only. It is the service or product that you're offering, whatever the reason. Being aware of this will help you approach others openly, honestly and confidently.

Getting new clients is about relationship and not about selling.

Making a strong relationship with your customers are very necessary if you want to successfully sell your product or service. You must make a strong bond with the customers. This can be achieved by being sincere, kind and sympathetic and to have a keen belief in the product or services you provide. Focusing on selling the product to people will not do. Rather, focus on building a relationship with your client; and that will help you achieve great success.

Focusing on different types of customers and their needs

There are various ways to focus on obtaining new customers. Customer-focused marketing can be achieved in several ways. Customer-focused marketing includes information which is compiled about customers. It is a study of the demographics of the types of products which attract certain customers. It goes beyond the existing customer and endeavors toward the acquisition of new customers. The primary purpose is to serve the needs of the customer in order to improve customer relations and provide retention.

Customer lifestyles and trends

The first thing is to target the right audience by focusing on selected groups of customers, but don't worry, appealing to more than one group of customers will attract more buyers interested in your unique product. Customer diversity is the reason to appeal to different groups of customers, because a broader market expands knowledge of the product. This is why it is necessary to know about customer lifestyles. Compiling a list of customers who buy small appliances is one type of buying habit attributed to certain customers. They are usually individuals who work outside the home. Other target audiences are customers who work at home, those with children, singles and retired customers. Whatever their needs may be, they all seek to make improvements in their lifestyle.

Gender is also another consideration in customer-focused marketing. Women are important customers who not only work but take care of families. They make a great many purchases not only for themselves but for others. Singles usually rent and want affordable furnishings; whereas, married customers own their own homes and want new furnishings. This may not be true for every single or married person, but historically, it is a trend. It is important to know that marital status is one consideration, but all customers seek affordable and useful products.

Age groups are important and over the years, studies have shown that succeeding generations spend money differently. According to Let's Talk Business, Issue 73, September 2005, customers born between 1977 and 1994, with an average age of twenty-one, spend most of their money on education and personal appearance. Older adults, or older boomers, whose average age is around fifty, spend money on upgrading their homes and taking vacations. The empty-nesters or seniors, spend more money on insurance, cars and furniture. The chart illustrates other groups and also includes generation X or the thirty something group, who spends money on food for their families.

Advantages of online shopping

Another factor that influences the targeting of customers, is online shopping. The Consumer Behavior Report tracks online shoppers and gives analysis of online shopping trends. Customers will shop on line first, which will allow them to consider the competition, before they make a purchase. Customers get a preview of what to expect before they buy. Prospective on-line shoppers also consider the rating of the product and will often look for discounts. There are some pros and cons to online shopping, but the internet gives a customer an advantage when deciding to buy a product. . It gives them more options and they can compare services and prices.

Customer-focused marketing is about customers and their interest. Combining this knowledge with the use of internet marketing will also help a business attract the greatest customers who want to buy the latest products.

17.10 Innovative Marketing Ideas for Small Businesses

Guerrilla marketing is a term used to describe unconventional marketing tactics, particularly those with low cost or no cost, which rely on time, energy and imagination rather than a big marketing budget, so they are ideal for the cash-strapped small business in the present economic climate. The idea is to target customers in unexpected places, in unexpected ways, to get maximum results from minimum resources and create a unique, engaging and memorable brand experience.

Here are just innovative marketing ideas to get you started:

1. Run a competition to win advertising space on your site. This is a no-cost prize you can use to market your website: free for you but valuable for others.

2. Leave your business card in unexpected places: for instance schools, colleges, government offices or private offices.

3. When you visit the travel agency, saloons, beauty parlors, leave a business card inside each magazine in the waiting room.

4. Add your website's URL to the signature of each email account you use, so it appears on every email you send (personal or business) with an additional comment if appropriate.

5. Give a free product/service to the stylists at your local hairdressers' or barbers' - they will tell their clients all about this crazy person who gives things away. Shopping mall is also one of the best places to interact with the customers.

6. You can run a skit in public - for instance, get a group of students or friends to hold a demo outside your premises with placards reading "This business (your name) is too nice!" or any funny message you choose.

7. Show free demonstrations related to your product or service at local events or venues - maybe your village hall or library or community centre could do with an interesting event to fill up their schedule.

8. Make use of you and your friends and relative wall and project an image of your business/ advertisement on it overnight.

9. Carry a pad of brightly coloured post-it type notes advertising your business wherever you go. (They can be hand-written if you can't afford to get them printed.) Lavatory is a place where people visit frequently; sticking small note about your business will help you. Stick next to the lift buttons in shops or offices; if you write on the back of the notes you can stick them on car windscreens in car-parks, so the driver will see the message when they get in the car.

And if all these have whetted your appetite to start being creative yourself, try brainstorming ideas with your employees, family or friends 'the more off-the wall the better. These are just a few innovative marketing ideas to help you get started.

17.11 Endorse Your Facebook 'Like' Promotional Tool

Facebook is gaining popularity day by day as it gives a chance to the people to interact with their friends and relatives. Millions of people are attached with the facebook. So here you have a great marketing opportunity for your business. Customers will come to your business only when they will know about your business, products and services. Once they will know they will tell to others and therefore customers will help your company to grow. So Facebook provides you that opportunity to expose your business to the world. Now the most important thing is that "How will you use your Facebook for the promotion of your business?" One very effective way is to give your customers gifts.

The promotional items may be unique pen, show piece, photo frame or toys offer a low cost alternative to promoting your Facebook page. These items will definitely motivate the people to purchase your products. These items are affordable and therefore small business owners can do it. Such kind of promotional activities are remembered by the customers for a long time. Choose such promotional items that will be used by the customers and they will always be in touch with that. For example your promotional pen is used by the customers so that pen will always recall them about your company. By visiting your facebook page people will get valuable information about your business but you must also give them information about "what your customers say about your products or services that have actually used it" i.e., customers' comments on products and services. Do not forget to write your company name on our promotional items.

With Facebook you can post your products images and videos. Facebook and other forms of social media are excellent ways of promoting your business or organization. Facebook does not interrupt you with details of a business but rather stays in the background, ready to promote your products and services when people want to look at them. Promotional gifts work in a similar way. Unlike other forms of promotion like TV commercials, phone sales and email spam which interrupt us as we go through are day; promotional gifts keep to themselves until someone chooses to use them. What a perfect low cost incentive to get people to go to your page and click that 'like' button!

17.12 Finding New Customers

If you're a startup, the fastest way to get the cash registers ringing is a little-used method that involves forming "host-beneficiary" relationships with established businesses that cater to a target audience similar to yours. Then you promote yourself to their database with a special offer presented as a gift from the older business.

The beauty of this arrangement is that the startup (the beneficiary) can instantly reach large numbers of highly qualified prospects with the tacit endorsement of the established business (the host). The host is willing to participate because it's a way to reward loyal customers without incurring any costs. The rookie gains new customers, while the veteran gains goodwill.

Women's Clothing and BMWs

One startup that successfully used this technique was a high-end women's clothing boutique. The store arranged to give a free silk kimono to every female customer of a local BMW dealership who brought in a letter sent by the dealership offering the gown as a gift for their past patronage. The kimono had to be picked up at the boutique.

Steps to Success

Host-beneficiary marketing is actually a simple and relatively inexpensive process that will deliver solid results if you follow a few basic rules:

Precisely define your target audience. "Women 35 to 55" might be a start, but it's not enough. Create a detailed profile of your target customer. The more segments you can identify, the more potential hosts you can approach.

The women's clothing boutique that marketed to BMW owners, for example, determined that their likely customers drove certain types of cars, patronized a certain class of hair salon, belonged to a health club and were likely to play bridge. A birdseed store might come up with a list that includes consumers who shop at outdoor equipment outfitters or are affiliated with local conservation groups.

Identify local businesses that serve the same market segments. That's way; you can, not only bring people in the door for your initial offer, but also increase the likelihood that they'll return to give you repeat business.

For a cigar store, logical host partners might include better men's clothiers, upscale shoe stores, luxury car dealerships and country clubs. And don't forget non-commercial organizations like Rotary or Kiwanis.

Develop a clear offer for each prospective partner. Come up with a free or deeply discounted product or service that has a high perceived value for the consumer with a low rupee cost for you.

One new computer support business offered a voucher worth two free hours of computer repair to the small business clients of a local accountant. A framing shop offered free photo framing to a photographic supply store's top 200 customers.

Pitch the plan, highlighting the benefits to the host business. Emphasize that it's a way for the established business to reward their customers at no expense and with virtually no effort. It's also a way to reach out to customers without overtly trying to make a new sale.

Supply a letter for the host's use. Providing a draft "offer" letter that can be sent to the host's customers on the host's letterhead will help put the plan into motion quickly. It will also show the partner how easy it will be for him to participate.

Some businesses will allow the letter to be inserted into their monthly invoices or newsletters at no cost to you. Others will charge or require that you pay for a separate mailing. It's a small price to pay for access to the host business' customer base.

Develop a strategy to convert redeemers to repeat customers. This, after all, is your long-term goal. For the women's boutique that gave away a kimono, the strategy was to encourage browsing and lure shoppers into dressing rooms to try the merchandise. For one new bakery that gave away a chocolate éclair, the approach was to hand out a buy-five-get-one-free VIP card with the free pastry.

Whatever the specific plan, the host-beneficiary method is the single most effective way to quickly attract a critical mass of qualified customers to a new business. Best of all, you're piggybacking on the success of another entrepreneur who has spent years building a solid customer base. For a startup facing so many other challenges, it's just smart business.

17.13 Good Customer Service and Satisfaction

Employees can be taught processes, they can't be taught good customer service. An individual employee's positive personality and attitude is core towards being able to manage customer service situations. Once that foundation is established there are four essential qualities that should be applied to all customer service situations. These qualities are honesty, integrity, reliability and consistency.

Honesty

Always be transparent in customer dealings. Whether the communication is positive or negative, allow for open, clear two way discussion. Don't second guess customers, don't withhold information because it may upset them. Empathies with the customer's situation and be their advocate.

Integrity

Always ensure that promises can be met and see the task through to completion. Ensure statements can be backed up, regardless of whether the information is positive or negative. Provide proof of results.

Reliability

Similar to integrity and honesty, be reliable in customer contact and communication. Keep appointments, set a prompt and efficient expectation. Don't rely on the customer to come to continue to initiate contact. Instead, be responsible for continued follow-up. Show the customer that they can rely on your brand to look after them.

Consistency

Treat all customers with a high priority. When resolving situations ensure there's a process in place, ensure that actions taken are in line with the process. If a process doesn't exist, it's a golden opportunity to create one.

An old saying is "The customer is always right". In the modern world this statement serves to annoy employees more than it does advocate customers. The customer is not always right - however employees don't have to tell them that. Rather than tell any customer they're wrong, provide enough accurate information so that the customer can come to that conclusion themselves. An employee must also be enjoying themselves in order to deliver outstanding customer service. To be successful, an employer must know their staff and constantly ensure employee comfort and satisfaction. After all - shouldn't an employer's staff be considered the employer's customers too!

Positive re-enforcement should be the only tool an employer uses in order to empower employees. Scaring staff into doing whatever it takes to keep customers happy is not the right choice.

17.14 Attracting New Customers

As business owners or sales people looking to attract new sales, you need more tips to attract new customers. You've learned all the tricks and techniques that push customers into making a decision, but when you're pushing your customers, it's easy to feel rejected before you even get started. Chasing customers is tiring - its way more fun when they chase you.

Using the internet is a great way to get your customers to chase you. But you don't have to put all your eggs in one basket. Here are different ways you can attract new customers to your brand.

1. Inviting potential customers to a free workshop is a great way to establish your business, build trust and get your products into the hands of the right people. Prepare a presentation or have guest speakers and be sure to show them your products in action. Make sure that you keep the focus on your visitors and continually remind them of the benefits of your products and what they can do for them. Don't forget to send them home with your contact information, samples, catalogs and coupons for their first order.

2. Having people join your club is a creative way to attract new customers. People want to belong to something, why not your online club. The club should be related to your product or service. You could give away a free e-mail newsletter for club members only. Have a member's only message board, e-mail discussion group or chat room.. Post your advertisements on all the club information.

3. Hold a Draw: It's no secret that people love free stuff, so a draw can make a great promotional tool. As long as the prize is valuable, you'll have no problem getting people to enter your draw. But to ensure that you also reap the benefits of your investment in a prize, you need to ask for something in return.

4. Attend networking events to expand your network, not to sell to the people in the room. Create relationships with people you can brag about. They will brag about you, too.

5. Write down your own article keeping in mind your target customers and submit those articles to news paper, publications or to any famous website so that your target market can read

those articles. Written articles create visibility and credibility for your brand. Establish yourself as the expert and people will be contacting you.

6. Get involved with internet radio. Here is an inexpensive medium that puts your message out for all to listen to and enjoy on their own schedule. Shows can be downloaded, Broadcasted and listened to any time, no matter when it was recorded. If you don't have enough content to start your own show, become a guest on someone else's show who shares the same audience you're after.

7. Invite people to your event that will at least create a small relationship. People love to be included. Once you have succeeded in attracting mass then it is a good time to connect with your customers. Communicate with them and explain the purpose of event. Assure them that you can fulfill their needs by your quality products and services. The secret to a successful invitation is all in the follow up. Do not drop the ball here.

8. Multimedia advertising primarily consists of TV and radio commercials. Similar to print advertising, this tactic is expensive, geographically limited and it must have a specific call to action. As an entrepreneur, there are few situations in which it's beneficial to implement a multimedia advertising campaign, at least at the beginning.

9. **List Your Business on Google and Yahoo.** When we want to find anything, we turn to Google or Yahoo to search — and you can't get any bigger in terms of Web sites than these. Google has a Local Business Directory where you can register your business absolutely free. The search giant even allows restaurants, for example, to post their menus or photos of entrees and enables customers to submit reviews. And here's what's most interesting: You don't even need a site to have a strong Web presence. It's open to all types of small businesses — with hundreds of thousands posted. (Yahoo offers a similar service.)

Stop chasing customers and put your brand in places where they can pull you in on their own schedule. The results are way more fun when your customers chase you.

17.15 Great Customer Service

There are three steps to creating extreme customer service. The steps build upon each other to create a great customer experience that gets your customers bragging about you.

1. Go beyond Satisfaction
2. Manage Customers' Expectations
3. Unconditional Service Guarantee

Step One – Go Beyond Customer Satisfaction

Remember that you're after their business for a lifetime, not only a one-time transaction. Your clients aren't looking for a product. Nor are they looking to be sold on anything. They want solutions. They want help. And you are the expert standing in front of them. Do you really know your product or service inside and out? Can you speak intelligently about the value of your product from the customer's point of view?

Use interactive dialogue – When you follow the same tune as an informal conversation, you can find out why the buyer wants the product. You remove yourself from the role of the seller, to someone trying to help because you care. If you listen, the customer will tell you exactly what they want. You can use this information to exceed their expectations.

Sell the features before the product – If the initial conversation focuses on the added value, the customer will use this information to make comparisons - and you're more likely to get the sale.

Pay attention – Use eye contact, smile, speak clearly and look professional.

Be creative and brainstorm with others – This is where the diversity of your team really wins out. The more ideas you share, the faster new ideas seem to come. Creativity and generosity feed each other.

Your customer will rarely be more excited than you are about your product, so your enthusiasm needs to be contagious. You must be passionate and excited about your brand and let go of any limiting beliefs that may be holding you back.

Step Two – Manage customers' expectations

When follow-up is necessary, telling the customer what to expect can significantly increase his or her satisfaction. When the service investigations department in one Citibank branch instituted this particular procedure, specifying time frames for next steps, customers' satisfaction increased by 40 percent.

Companies should train employees to listen to customers and change fundamental attitudes so that complaints are viewed as opportunities for positive change, not as reasons to be defensive.

British Airway's customer-relations department can now claim to be a true champion of the customer. The retention rate among those who complain to customer relations has more than doubled, while the department's return on investment (the value of business saved plus increased loyalty and new business from referrals relative to the department's total costs) has risen 200 percent.

In training its employees, British Airways tried to help staff understand several things:

- If the company replies to a customer and claims that events did not happen as the customer suggested, then the customer perceives the company to be calling him or her a liar.
- If, after investigating, the company reports back to the customer that events indeed took place as the customer claimed, then the customer can become even more agitated, inferring that the company did not believe him or her at first.
- If the company relays information to the customer that he or she did not know, the customer may think that the company is trying to make excuses for poor service.

To deal with these issues, British Airways' customer-relations department developed a four-step process that it incorporated into all its technical and human systems.

1. Apologize and take up the problem. Customers do not care whose fault the problem was; they want an apology and they want someone to champion their cause.
2. Do it quickly. Aim to reply to the customer the same day and if that is not possible, certainly within 72 hours. British Airways research showed that 40 to 50 percent of customers who contacted it with complaints defected if it took company staff longer than five days to respond. A speedy reply demonstrates a sense of urgency; it shows that the company really cares about the customer's feelings and situation.
3. Assure the customer that the problem is being fixed. Customers can be retained if they are confident that the operational problem they encountered will truly be addressed.
4. Do it by phone. British Airways found that customers with problems were delighted to have a customer-relations person call them.

Step Three – How to Fulfill an Unconditional Service Guarantee?

What is a good service guarantee?

With a good guarantee, you tell your customers where and how to complain and that complaining is worth their time and effort. It also shows that you care. A good guarantee is:

(1) Unconditional

Customers should not need a lawyer to explain the "ifs ands and buts" of a guarantee because ideally there should not be any conditions; a customer is either satisfied or is not. If a company cannot guarantee all elements of its service unconditionally, it should unconditionally guarantee the elements that it can control. Airlines cannot promise on-time arrival, but they can guarantee passengers will be satisfied with airport waiting areas, service on the ground and in the air and food quality.

(2) Easy to Understand and Communicate

A guarantee should be written in simple, concise language that pinpoints the promise. Customers then know precisely what they can expect and employees know precisely what is expected of them. "Five-minute" lunch service, rather than "prompt" service, creates clear expectations.

(3) Meaningful

A good service guarantee is meaningful in two respects. First, it guarantees those aspects of your service that are important to your customers. It may be speedy delivery at lunch time, when many customers are in a hurry to get back to the office, but not at dinner, when fast service is not considered a priority to most patrons. Second, a good guarantee is meaningful financially. It calls for a significant and fair pay out when the promise is not kept. What should it be? A full refund? An offer of free service next time? The answer depends on factors such as the cost of the service, the seriousness of the failure and customers' perception of what is fair.

(4) Easy to Invoke

A customer who is already dissatisfied should not have to jump through hoops to invoke a guarantee; dissatisfaction is only exacerbated when the customer has to talk to different people, fill out forms, make telephone calls, send in written proof of purchase with a full description of the events, wait for a written reply and go somewhere else to see someone to verify all the preceding facts and so on.

(5) Easy to Collect

Customers should not have to work hard to collect a payout. The procedure should be easy and, equally important, quick: on-the-spot, if possible.

17.16 Control Further Costs Unless It Adds Value to Your Customer

As a business professional, you are constantly being enticed by new ways to be successful and create profits. You want a profitable business. You want to offer extreme customer service. You want to improve the quality of your services with fewer mistakes and create more effective use of your time. It's easy to make those decisions, when you know how your business flows.

Ask yourself, does the decision flow with my business model?

There's an acronym to help you filter out your decisions on whether or not a new opportunity is a good investment for you. A helpful quote from Sakichi Toyoda, founder of the Toyota Motor

Company helps bring decisions into a new perspective: "Don't add costs unless it adds value to your customer". To grow your business, your business must FLOW.

F – Friend or Foe. Is this good for my customer or will it alienate them? Can I go back to the drawing board and make this a win-win situation for my business and for my customer? If not, it's a waste and needs to be discarded or re-worked so the customer wins.

L – Leading the Way. Does this decision set me apart from my competition so it's better for my customers? Is it setting a good example for those who follow me? Does it lead the way for bragging customers?

O – Opportunity Costs. Is this a great opportunity for adding value to my customers?

If I spend money on this decision, is it driving me away or leading me closer to my customer relationships? Sometimes, we need to forsake immediate returns in favor of long-term customer relationships. Benjamin Franklin said "A penny saved is a penny earned". The same is true for your customers; A customer saved, is a customer earned.

W – Worthwhile Use of Time. If it takes time and doesn't add value to your customers, it's a waste. Use your prime time for connecting with customers rather than with tasks that don't add value to them. Do you recognize your prime time hours for connecting with your customers?

Toyoda said "Everyone should tackle some great project at least once in their life. You should make an effort to complete something that will benefit society." When you take the time to add value to individual consumers, you are adding value to society. When you help others, you create loyal customers and that helps your business.

17.17 Appreciate Your Customers

When you stop in and tell your customers how much you appreciate their business, you give them something to tell others about. Most of the time it happens that once your transaction is over with your current customer you don't care about that customer and here you do a major mistake. You instantly shift your attention to other customer and don't give value to past customer. Remember that you already have a customer who values your product. Here is somebody who has already bought into your brand. However, once the sale is over, they never hear from you again. That is, unless you're pitching for another sale. You already know that it's less expensive to retain a current customer versus seeking out a new one. So you need to consider the following points.

F – Fuss over your current customers. Discover your customer's key point – and use that. Find out the ways how you can get your customer's attention? A friend of mine felt much fussed over when the service attendant already installed all the necessary softwares in his computer system before his purchase. So he need not have to wait for the installation process or to suggest about different softwares for installation. This didn't cost the company anything, but my friend has told to everyone about the services he got. Use your own gifts and talents to stand out and get your customers to take notice.

R – Reward your customers for referrals. This will motivate them. When they bring new customers to the business then offer them gift that encourages them to do it again. So often, referral bonuses are only paid out if the deal closes – so reward them simply for the introduction. With a few rupees gift cards, you can train that behavior to be repeated and repeated again.

O – Over-deliver, over-exceed, over-do, over-rise, over-reward, over-flow, over-whelm. When your brand shows up in front of your customer, either in person or via email, newsletter or phone call, you give your customers an opportunity to introduce you to someone new. Keeping in contact keeps your brand on the tips of their tongues. Out of sight proves to be disastrous if you are out of mind when it comes to referrals. If your customers don't have you on the tip of their tongue at all times, they won't be referring your business.

G – Give your best. Give your customers a unique thing that they can never get it from anywhere else. Come out with creative ways so that your customers will always remember it. Analyze your customers buying behaviour. Find out what they want? How can you solve their problems? What kind of product or service best suit to your customers? Look at your own business through the eyes of your customers – and if you're too close, ask a real customer to help you out. The very best person to ask about what your customers really want from your business is your customer.

S – Give surprises to your customers. Make your interaction with customers an unforgettable moment. The goal is create moments for your customer to talk about. Create surprises and you will create great customers who turn others onto your brand.

Summary

Customer service support is extremely important for any new business. It involves hiring competent and knowledgeable staff, finding fast, novel ways to respond to consumer inquiries and abiding by the cardinal rule: the customer is always right. In addition, a strong customer service team can be an effective way in which companies can easily establish a solid rapport with existing and prospective consumers in addition to finding out ways to improve products and services.

The reasons behind the new entrepreneurs do not get customers are.

- Entrepreneurs do not find out what customers are for
- Give importance to client's money
- Failure to conduct the primary research
- Failure to follow-up with clients
- Failure by over-marketing
- Unable to focus on the business
- Do not make marketing a priority
- Do not contact professionals
- Do not spend enough time researching the business idea
- Improper determination if the business adds value
- Under-budgeting the marketing costs
- Cannot describe the business in one or two sentences
- Do not consider the demographics.
- Unable to gain an understanding of the business
- Unable to differentiate themselves
- Improper Location
- Non pleasure appearance
- Product has no sizzle
- Improper pricing of products
- Knowledge of the product you are selling
- Unable to create friendly environment with customers
- Advertising

- Underestimating the Competition
- Inability to reach desired sales goals.
- Not cost competitive
- Failure to adapt to changing market conditions
- Wallet is not big enough

Market research involves the systematic gathering, recording and analyzing of data about customers, competitors and the market. This links marketers to consumers by supplying essential information to solve marketing challenges and help with marketing decisions.

Benefits of market research

By conducting thorough market research, entrepreneurs will be able to obtain valuable information about starting their new businesses.

First, market research will enable the business owner to learn of industry trends and which products/services will be in demand.

Second, they will be able to see how the general public responds to their business ideas.

Types of market research

There are two distinct types of market research.

Secondary market research, the business owner gathers already published data, which is easily accessible and nearly free to obtain. Information such as consumer demographics, major competitors and general usage of products is often collected by government agencies and organizations and made available online and in books and publications.

Primary market research is more specific in nature. It contains information regarding a specific product that is brought forth by a company. Focus groups, field studies and simple observations of customer behavior are some ways in which companies obtain primary market research.

Types of customers

There are three main types of customers that every business will encounter.

The "purchaser" is primarily concerned with the cost of a product, not how effective a particular product may be.

The "influencer" is not concerned by the cost of a product but rather if the product being offered will be considered a good purchase.

The end-user will not only be glad to purchase the product but he will actually use the product bought.

Role of public relations campaign

Public Relation is simply accurate, consistent and timely communications that convey the right message to the right audience. This is true across-the-board for businesses of any size. OR "any activity that creates a positive image, fosters goodwill or increase sales.

Public relations campaign includes Define your audience, Define your competition, Website development, Determine your advertising budget and Self vs. hired professionals.

The Importance of Customer Service Support

Surveys suggest that service driven companies are able to charge up to 9 per cent more for the goods and services they offer and grow twice as fast as the average. These are powerful incentives for becoming the best customer-service company in any industry. Equally, poor service has a cost penalty. It costs up to five times as much to go out and get a new customer as to retain those we have.

The factors to be considered are as follows: Good customer care matters, Competitive edge, Association through existing customers, Hire competent staff, Media outlets, Innovation and modern technology advantages, Present yourself as an expert, Automated sales process, Make swift customer e-mail replies, The customer is always right, Community involvement, Get referrals from existing customers and Provide new service if customers ask.

A trade show is a great place to get your name out there and establish a foothold in your chosen industry. This is an especially important marketing tool if the products you are trying to market are unique and very useful for your customers.

The factors to be considered for attracting the new customers to the trade show are Good deal, Make sweeter the pan, Interact and get involved, A dash of color and Presentation boards and visuals prompts.

Interest Your Clients

When deciding to use promotional items, you need think way outside of the box. It should not happen that your item once gets into the customers house are thrown out at the corner and making no use. The secret is that you should look different than your competitors.

The guidelines are as follows:

Find unique imprinted promotional items that will be differentiated from your competitors.

Try to give gifts that enhance your own business.

Use incentives to get customers to purchase from your business.

Plan contest with imprinted promotional items.

For getting new patrons for your business you must do the following:

Figure out what your market really wants.

Focus on the people who have raised their hands.

See people as people.

There is nothing personal about rejection.

Getting new clients is about relationship and not about selling.

Focus on different types of customers and their needs.

Customer lifestyles and trends

Here are just innovative marketing ideas to get you started:

Run a competition to win advertising space on your site

Add your website's URL to the signature of each email account you use

Give a free product/service to the stylists at your local hairdressers' or barbers'

You can run a skit in public

Show free demonstrations related to your product or service at local events or venues

Make use of your wall and your friends and relative wall

Endorse your facebook 'like' promotional tool

With Facebook booming and becoming a great way to gain exposure, it presents businesses with an excellent marketing opportunity. The more people you have following your business, the more people that will learn about your businesses products, services and/or facilities and the more people that will eventually become customers.

Finding new customers

Host-beneficiary marketing is actually a simple and relatively inexpensive process that will deliver solid results if you follow a few basic rules:

Precisely define your target audience.

Identify local businesses that serve the same market segments.

Develop a clear offer for each prospective partner.

Pitch the plan, highlighting the benefits to the host business.

Supply a letter for the host's use.

Develop a strategy to convert redeemers to repeat customers.

Great Customer Service

There are three steps to creating extreme customer service. The steps build upon each other to create a great customer experience that gets your customers bragging about you.

- Go Beyond Satisfaction

  Remember that you're after their business for a lifetime, not only a one-time transaction. Your clients aren't looking for a product. Nor are they looking to be sold on anything. They want solutions. They want help. And you are the expert standing in front of them.
- Manage Customers' Expectations

  When follow-up is necessary, telling the customer what to expect can significantly increase his or her satisfaction. Companies should train employees to listen to customers and change fundamental attitudes so that complaints are viewed as opportunities for positive change, not as reasons to be defensive.
- Unconditional Service Guarantee

  With a good guarantee, you tell your customers where and how to complain and that complaining is worth their time and effort. It also shows that you care. A good guarantee is: Unconditional, Easy to Understand and Communicate, Easy to Collect, Easy to Invoke, and Meaningful.

QUESTIONS

1. Explain what are the problems faced by new small entrepreneurs while interacting with customers and attracting them to their business.
2. What is the importance of market research in business?
3. What is the role of public relation campaign in developing a business?
4. Explain different features of customer service support?
5. Explain innovative ways of attracting customers?

❑ ❑ ❑

CHAPTER – 18

SUPPLIERS RELATED OBSTACLES

LEARNING OBJECTIVES

On completion of this chapter, you should be able to:

☺ *Explain supplier and new small entrepreneur relation.*

☺ *Describe obstacles which are created by suppliers to entrepreneurs.*

☺ *Describe the way of finding good suppliers.*

18.1 Where is Supplier?

The small new entrepreneurs always deal with the problems of the suppliers. First they do not have much information of the suppliers, if they open a business and want to purchase the raw material then they have always the question from where they can get suppliers.

Reliability is the key factor to look for in suppliers. Good suppliers will steer you towards hot-selling items, increasing your sales. If you build a good relationship and your business is profitable for them, suppliers may be willing to bail you out when your customers make difficult demands.

18.2 Don't Pay Bill

Remember, though, that suppliers are in business to make money, If you go to the mat with them on every bill, ask them to shave prices on everything they sell to you or fail to pay your bills promptly, don't be surprised when they stop calling. They are in business to earn money.

BOX 18

Raw Material Assistance (RMA) Scheme

NSIC's Raw Material Assistance (RMA) against the security of Bank Guarantee is of great benefit to MSMEs. Raw Material forms the major chunk of working capital requirement of any industry therefore NSIC has launched the RMA Scheme to cater to the needs of MSMEs. The scheme helps MSMEs to convert their Non-Fund based limits into liquid funds. NSICs RMA requires simple documentation and assistance to the extent of ₹ 2 crores can be provided very quickly. Under this scheme after the sanction of limits we make payment to your Raw Material Suppliers and give you a credit of 90 days. The operations of the scheme are very simple, with no hassles whatsoever. Units who avail this assistance from NSIC also use the opportunity to negotiate for a cash discount with their suppliers and also avail the credit of NSIC. In most cases the cash discount itself is sufficient to offset the Interest payable to NSIC. The maximum amount of assistance under the scheme is ₹ 5 crores. BGs of Nationalized Banks, SBI and its subsidiaries, IDBI Bank and select scheduled and private banks are accepted as security. In those cases where MOU has been signed by NSIC with Raw Material Suppliers, additional discounts like Quantity discounts and MOU discounts are also passed on to small enterprises. The interest rate at present is 10.75 per cent per annum and is calculated as simple interest on daily basis, diminishing balance on actual number of days used. Those units who have been awarded rating under NSIC Performance and Credit Rating Scheme are eligible to avail NSIC RMA at lower interest rates. Those units whose rating is Rating SE 1A have to pay only 9.75 per cent and those with Rating SE2A or SE 1B the interest is 10.25 per cent. Service Charge of @ 1 per cent of the sanctioned limit is charged. Units who want to avai the service have to apply with required documents on prescribed application form and applicable processing Fee as per following slab

(1) Up to ₹ 25 lakhs limit: ₹ 2,500/- + S. tax

(2) Above ₹ 25 lakhs to 50 lakhs: ₹ 5,000/- + S. tax

(3) Above ₹ 50 lakhs to 1 crore: ₹ 10, 000/- + S. tax

(4) Above ₹ 1 Crore: 0.1 per cent of Assistance + tax as applicable

Source: Information received from "NSIC".

As a new business owner, you can't expect to receive the same kind of attention a long-standing customer gets right off the bat. Over time, however, you can develop excellent working relationships that will be profitable for both you and your suppliers.

18.3 Quotes/Proposal

Once you have compiled a list of possible suppliers, ask for quotes or proposals, complete with prices, available discounts, delivery terms and other important factors. Analyze every products price, discounts, terms and conditions. Don't just consider the terms; investigate the potential supplier's financial condition, too. Ask for customer references; call them and find out how well the supplier has performed. By taking feedback from others you can better judge your suppliers. If there have been any problems, ask for details about how they were reconciled. Every supplier relationship hits bumps now and then; the key is to know how the rough spots were handled. Was the supplier prompt and helpful in resolving the problem or defensive and uncooperative?

18.4 Understand Everything

Be open, courteous and firm with your suppliers and they will respond in kind. Tell them what you need and when you need it. Be specific about delivery time. Have a specific understanding about the total cost and expect delivery on schedule. Keep in constant communication with your suppliers about possible delays, potential substitutions for materials or product lines, production quality, product improvements or new product introductions and potential savings. Suppliers often establish a minimum order for merchandise and this minimum may be higher for first orders to cover the cost of setting up a new store account. Some suppliers also demand a minimum number of items per order.

18.5 Who are Quality Suppliers?

The new entrepreneur does not know the quality of the suppliers. The absence of information makes him player at random the person who wants to play but does not have a direction to play. He does not have a proper source from where he can get the information of the reliable suppliers. He is also not the experienced one so that he can apply his experience to get good supplier. So he tries to select those suppliers whom he thinks will be the quality suppliers. Knowing the quality of the supplier is not easy for the new entrepreneurs and without proper guidance they are not able to find quality suppliers for their business.

18.6 Improper Dealing with Supplier

A new entrepreneur does not know how to deal with the suppliers. Some may know but not completely because they are trying their luck for the first time in the business. Most of the questions are not answered to them for e.g., what is the procedure for dealing with the suppliers? What are the business requirements of that? What are the documents that will be required? What price to show etc., that become major obstacles when he does not get the proper answer of his questions. They lack in applying tactics while dealing with suppliers. They are easy hunted by suppliers because of their innocence in the business.

18.7 Suppliers' Retention Problem

If there is much dependency on the suppliers related to the supplies then entrepreneurs try to protect the relationship with the supplier at all level. Even if the entrepreneur is not happy with the suppliers' behaviour still he has to manage the relationship with the suppliers. But sometimes supplier demand increases to such a high level then it becomes difficult for the new entrepreneurs to retain the suppliers. The new entrepreneurs do not have any other options but to follow suppliers. This is the hurdle that really disturbs the new entrepreneurs.

18.8 Supplier Side Delay of Material

Many times the new entrepreneurs suffer from irresponsible nature of the supplier such as supplier's delay in delivering the goods. Here new entrepreneurs face two problems. The first is they already made an agreement with the supplier, so after that they are not in a position to say anything to supplier about delay. They can just say about delay but they cannot make any action about supplier's delay. Prior to agreement they find it difficult to search a supplier. They never think of analysis of supplier and they do not have much money so that they can have a good supplier. Randomly they select supplier and they bear the consequences of selecting bad supplier. Again new entrepreneurs do not have a dominant position in the market so that they can influence the nature of supplier. And for supplier it does not matter whether they follow deadline or not. Because they deal with new business person who does not have at present share in the market, so they do not take their reaction seriously. The second is the new entrepreneurs at least for few months have to bear the nature of the supplier. Their business suffers from the bad performance of the supplier. Entrepreneurs cannot change the suppliers because they have already run out of money. Ultimately for the new entrepreneurs the situation becomes critical.

18.9 Bargaining Power of Suppliers

New entrepreneur as does not have a value or impact in the market in such case he has to be dependent on the suppliers. In such situation the suppliers bargaining power increases and new entrepreneurs cannot do anything either they have to accept all the conditions of the suppliers or quit the suppliers. If the entrepreneur is not capable to handle the supplier then it becomes major obstacles for him.

In those enterprises where the proprietor is directly in charge of the proceedings, vendor management as well as customer handling becomes an all-important priority as they are the ones who have a profound impact on revenue, costs and profitability. And entrepreneurs may not have much problems in keeping businesses – the problem they face, on the other hand, is that of being squeezed by suppliers and customers alike.

A small enterprise invariably would have to deal with heftier organizations for their customers and supply chains and hence, may not be high on bargaining power. And since they are also faced with the might of bigger competitors, they often go out of the way to maintain relationships with suppliers and vendors that would get them businesses. While this may seem alright from a sales point of view, this becomes a problem when the professional relationship morphs into a personal relationship and puts the entrepreneur in a position of disadvantage, where the entrepreneur loses his bargaining power completely and is at the mercy of suppliers and customers who dictate terms. In effect, relationship takes precedence over business and the entrepreneur is unable to negotiate deals in his favour with a supplier with whom he has got too close.

18.10 How to Find and Work with Suppliers

Suppliers are essential to almost every business. Without raw materials to make what you sell or manufacturers to provide what you resell, you will have a tough time growing. There are also many supplies and services your business consumes as part of general overhead, from paper clips to Internet access.

Suppliers and vendors-the terms are used interchangeably here-can do much more than merely supply you with the materials and services you need to do business. They can also be important sources of information, helping you evaluate the potential of new products, track competitors' actions and identify promising opportunities. Vendors can turn into partners, helping you cut costs, improve product designs and even fund new marketing efforts. If you don't make selecting good suppliers and vendors as a part of your growth plan, you're likely to regret it.

Evaluating your suppliers and vendors

Suppliers can be divided into four general categories. They are:

1. **Manufacturers:** Most retailers buy through company salespeople or independent representatives who handle the wares of several different companies. Prices from these sources are usually lowest unless the retailer's location makes shipping freight costly.
2. **Distributors:** Also known as wholesalers, brokers or jobbers, distributors buy in quantity from several manufacturers and warehouse the goods for sale to retailers. Although their prices are higher than a manufacturer's, they can supply retailers with small orders from a variety of manufacturers. (Some manufacturers refuse to fill small orders.) A lower freight bill and quick delivery time from a nearby distributor often compensates for the higher per-item cost.
3. **Independent craftspeople:** Exclusive distribution of unique creations is frequently offered by independent craftspeople who sell through reps or at trade shows.
4. **Import sources:** Many retailers buy foreign goods from a domestic importer, who operates much like a domestic wholesaler. Or, depending on your familiarity with overseas sources, you may want to travel abroad to buy goods.

What makes a good supplier?

A lot of growing companies focus on one trait of their suppliers: price. And price certainly is important when you are selecting suppliers to accompany you as you grow your business. But there's more to a supplier than an invoice-and more to the cost of doing business with a supplier than the amount on a purchase order. Suppliers are the influential factor for the business. Suppliers' business impact has a direct impact on your business. So judging the suppliers with price only could be a great mistake. Number of other factors are there to evaluate. Remember, too, that suppliers are in business to make money. If you go to the mat with them on every bill, ask them to shave prices on everything they sell to you or fail to pay your bills promptly, don't be surprised if they stop calling.

After price, reliability is probably the key factor to look for in suppliers. Good suppliers will ship the right number of items, as promised, on time so that they arrive in good shape. Sometimes you can get the best reliability from a large supplier. These companies have the resources to devote to backup systems and sources so that, if something goes wrong, they can still live up to their responsibilities to you.

Don't neglect small suppliers

New entrepreneurs in the hope to purchase the good quality material always go for the big suppliers but for big suppliers the small new entrepreneurs do not matter because the new small entrepreneurs are not the main source of their income. If you're a big customer of a small company, you'll get more attention and possibly better service and reliability than if you are a small customer of a large supplier. You should also consider splitting your orders among two smaller firms. This can provide you with a backup as well as a high profile.

Do not depend on single supplier only

The new entrepreneurs should protect themselves from depending on the single supplier. This will make you helpless. Try to give order to more number of suppliers. By doing this you will be protected by the exploiting behaviour of the suppliers. You can have proper bargaining position and if you feel that any suppliers is not doing well then you can stop giving order to that supplier.

Stability is another key indicator

Dealing with the good and stable suppliers will benefit your business. You will definitely not need such suppliers who had a history of different businesses. You will need such suppliers who have a history of only one business because that will show their stability in business. A company having good reputation, good customer relationship and long years of experience is always preferred. It shows their stability in the market. Be careful while selecting the suppliers because your suppliers' instability will destroy your business.

Don't forget location

Orders of distant suppliers will cost you and it will also consume your time. If you are not in hurry for your delivery then even distant suppliers are good for you. But if your business consumption rate is very high i.e., your sale is very rapid then you must look for nearby suppliers. If you are doing the business of perishable goods then near suppliers are always preferred. You must know that far located suppliers increase your cost because it is not about months but it is the about the lifetime of the business. For new entrepreneurs where they run their business under limited budget, it will create problem for them. Also, determine supplier price policies before you order. If you order a certain quantity, for instance, you may get free delivery. You may be able to combine two or more orders into one and save on cost. Even you have one option find out the supplier near to your company to prevent extra costs and delivery time.

You need such suppliers who should be in touch with the current market trends and should show you the latest products and services. Your suppliers' company employees should be skilled and well trained so that they can easily explain you. They should be able to offer you a variety of attractive financial terms on purchases. And they should have a realistic attitude towards you, their customer, so that they're willing and eager to work with you to grow both your businesses.

18.11 Changing Your Supplier Relationships

You may not need to find new suppliers to get a new deal. You can usually get discounts, obtain improved service and receive other features you need by making a request of your current suppliers-although it may not be as simple as merely asking. Here are some of the options and negotiating strategies for turning mediocre suppliers into top-shelf ones.

Getting discounts

Business to business commerce is not so easy to do. The businesses that do businesses with the other businesses have wide range of prices, different quality of products, discounts of

50 per cent or more, which depends on the volume of purchase, your terms with the suppliers and your influence on them. So whenever you purchase from your suppliers you must be able to get much as discounts as you want. You must be able to down the prices of products. Remember that apart from you, your suppliers must also earn otherwise they will not do business with you if suppliers will get very less. There are also other ways to get discounts from your suppliers, those are pay early, purchase on bulk, give consistent order, make good relationship etc. For new entrepreneurs it becomes necessary to learn about such practices. When they will have a deal with suppliers, knowledge about it will help them to deal with suppliers.

Improving service

You probably don't and you shouldn't assume your suppliers do, either. If you have a service-related problem with a supplier, bring it to someone's attention. If you don't get satisfaction, move up the chain of command until you get what you want or are as high in management as you can get. Odds are, someone will be concerned and possess enough authority to remedy the situation. Only if you ask for better service and don't get it should you split the relationship.

A better relationship

Having good relation with the suppliers is the part of business. You will definitely get advantages of your better relationship with your supplier. You must assure to your supplier that by doing business with you he will also get profit. Attract him towards your business. Explain them clearly how the performance of supplier is going to give benefit to both i.e., you and supplier. Take him under your trust then you will see that supplier is also taking interest in your business because he also wants to earn profit from your business. Do not treat them outsider, treat them as insider. The new entrepreneurs should remember that your business will do well if you will support and consider your supplier as a part of your business.

18.12 Making a Suppliers' Change

Having fewer suppliers is usually better than having many suppliers. Reducing the number of vendors you deal with, cuts the administrative costs of working with many. Closer relationships with fewer vendors allow you to work together to control costs. Getting rid of troublesome vendors can quickly increase the efficiency of your purchasing and administrative staffs. So how do you decide when to change vendors? Here are key areas to consider:

Unreliability

When your supplier is not fulfilling their responsibilities honestly i.e., late delivery, high price, inconsistent supply and poor quality then you need to change your supplier. Examining the supplier before selection is the good option. Do not hurry in supplier's selection. Supplier has a duty to deliver the goods on time. If suppliers are becoming careless about their responsibilities towards your business then it is better to change them. It may happen that because supplier's company is going through the change phase and therefore he could not be able to deliver the products on time. If this is the reason then you can compromise it. It will ultimately make your relationship with your supplier stronger.

Lack of cost competitiveness

Sometimes suppliers do not change with the changing circumstances. When other suppliers give you quality products in a less price than your suppliers then you need to think on that. First investigate why your suppliers are not providing the same as the others are providing. Find out the problems. Do not change your suppliers without any investigation because you may be wrong. Talk directly with your suppliers and raise the issues. It may happen that your suppliers' explanation will satisfy you. Find out the truth and if you find that everything is ok then continue with your suppliers otherwise change the suppliers. The new entrepreneurs should not be relaxed after dealing with the suppliers. They should continuously do analysis of other suppliers. By this you can know whether your supplier is making you fool or not?

Narrowness

Some suppliers will let you visit their plants, talk to their workers, quiz their managers, obtain and interview references and even examine their financial statements. These are the kinds of suppliers you should seek out. The more you know about your suppliers, the better you can evaluate whether you should continue to do business with them. You will be able to take a decision on the credibility of the suppliers. This will protect you and satisfy you from suppliers' side. If they shut you out, perhaps you should cut them off.

Extra-sale costs

Do not agree on the price suggested by the supplier unless it suits you. Before going to any supplier check their references, their customers, quality of product. Ask supplier's customers are they happy? Make complete evaluation of your supplier and then select your supplier. When you place the order then you have to completely negotiate the terms and conditions. Once you get the delivery then check the products. Are those products up to the mark? Have you got the expected delivery? The new entrepreneurs do not know how to deal with the suppliers and therefore they are fooled by suppliers. Suppliers try to dominate them even if suppliers are not fulfilling the terms and conditions of the agreement. They forcefully deliver their faulty products to the new entrepreneurs. The delivery shows extra costs other than actual agreement costs, their goods are not in good situation and here also suppliers try to fool the entrepreneurs by sending faulty goods. Finally, you may have to train workers to use the newly arrived goods or purchase more equipment and material to make use of them. While some of these costs are inevitable, some are traceable to individual suppliers. If too many costs are being tacked onto the sale prices, check out some other suppliers.

18.13 Dealing Successfully with Suppliers and Advisors

Suppliers and advisors play a critical role in your business. Having a good understanding with them ensures success for your business. If they are aware of the vision of your company and feel satisfied in the association, they will go out of their way to make your business a success.

Dealing with advisors

New entrepreneurs merely give any importance to the advisor. If they want to ask any information they just ask their friends or the one who runs business but these persons also do not have full business knowledge. When entrepreneurs do not take suggestions from the advisor then they face problems in their business. Business advisors can point out the strengths and weaknesses in your business, helping you root out the flaws in your company. In order to get the requisite knowledge and guidance from a business advisor, you need to negotiate with a positive frame of mind and approach the advisor with an open mind.

1. Get a good idea of what you need from an advisor. Then prepare a brief to convey this to the advisor, stating what you want the advisor to do. Give details about your company, employees, targeted profits etc.
2. Decide how frequently you need to meet the advisor.
3. Ask them about the list of suppliers with whom you can meet.

4. Discuss what type of supplier you really want for your business. Share your problem with your advisor. Once your advisor will know everything about your problem then he can more easily solve your problem.
5. Do not hide anything from your advisor. Make a trust on him and then proceed.
6. Make an agreement with your advisor, how frequently you are going to take his help.
7. You need to decide whether the advisor is needed for a one-time project or you need his services more frequently.
8. If your business undergoes restructuring, you need to decide whether to keep the same advisor or hire another one.
9. If you do not like your advisor any more then do not hesitate to replace him by another advisor.

Mutual understanding between you and your suppliers and advisors is essential for a good relation between you.

Striking successful deals with suppliers

When dealing with suppliers, price should not be the only deciding factor. Low price is not very useful if the supplier does not deliver on time, has payment issues and delivers poor quality materials. Here are some ways to negotiate successfully with your suppliers.

(1) When dealing with them, keep in mind price, delivery time, payment mode, maintenance, quality and additional services provided by the supplier. Unless suppliers fulfill all those promises, they are not eligible for your business as a supplier. Their irresponsible nature can destroy your business because you are totally dependent on them.

(2) You need to understand how crucial your businesses' orders are for the supplier. You also need to do a little research into the supplier's history; if other clients were satisfied with its services, or there was a history of delivery default, delayed delivery, poor quality material etc., it becomes necessary for you because they are going to attach with your business their performance will affect your business directly. Do not directly deal with any suppliers. Take time to analyze suppliers and then select the best one.

(3) If you find out that your business is important for the supplier, negotiations will be weighed in your favour. Take advantages of your dominance. Be careful of driving a hard bargain though, as it can make the supplier resentful. While making agreement with the suppliers also keep in mind that there should not be the situation of dispute. Your business cannot run alone so try to make friendly and pleasant environment.

(4) State your needs clearly, from price, quantity, quality to date of delivery, mode of payment etc. Write down agreement of all contracts. Do not do oral contracts. Make document of all meetings. You will have those documents as a proof in case suppliers do fraud with you.

(5) The seniority of the bargaining teams should match, on the supplier as well as purchaser side. As a new entrepreneur do not try to do bargain by yourselves. You do not have any experience. You are not in a position to bargain with suppliers. Always have an experienced person with you otherwise you will be exploited by the unfair practices of the suppliers. This is good strategy to deal with the suppliers when you are new in the business. Having experienced persons with you will increase the probability of your success.

18.14 Finding Suppliers for Successful Business

Strategies for locating new suppliers are as follows:

Attend trade shows

Trade show is the best place to look for suppliers. Here you will be able to find out different suppliers with their products. Here you have a chance to compare the suppliers as all are in one place. You can examine the materials and accordingly can take the decisions. Always attend trade shows. You will know the current trends. Whether you like or do not like it but collect all relevant information about the suppliers. You will get all the suppliers from the world or nation in one place. You will find opportunity to meet with all reputed suppliers.

Seek ideas from current suppliers

Suppliers are also a good source to get valuable information about other suppliers. Ask to your suppliers about other products suppliers. Definitely he will not give you any information about the suppliers who sell the same products. They know much about other suppliers and they can easily give you much information. As in all other cases, be sure to perform thorough due diligence before spending huge amount of money with any new supplier.

Ask competitors for supplier ideas

Well many competitors will not give you any information about the suppliers but even if two to three give you information about suppliers then it is sufficient. Just do not take information only find out more about those suppliers. Find out how much valuable they are for your business. May be you find the supplier of your choice. If in your local area number of business owners are demanding the same products from the same supplier then it will be better to have collective bargaining that will reduce your cost. It takes trust and some extra work, but the savings may be worth the effort.

Become a bargain hunter

One last option is to become a bargain buyer. Many of the larger general store suppliers offer sale pricing on dollar store merchandise. Some conduct monthly sales. Others offer reductions based on quantity purchases. Still others periodically offer closeout pricing on overstocks, package changes and discontinued products. Make sure you receive information about all of the sales and special price offers. Then start purchasing core, in-demand products when they are on sale.

So What Could Be the Solution?

18.15 Make a Good Relationship with Suppliers

They're your hidden growth assets. Follow these guidelines to become a valued customer.

Your approach to suppliers needs to be part of your strategic plan since almost every company, whether product- or service-oriented, is dependent on suppliers. Many business owners seem to get this supplier issue backwards. They think that because they write the order, they're in the dominant position and can exploit it with unreasonable demands, including personal perks.

Let's get this right . . . you need good and reliable suppliers. When you find them, treat them like gold. Work as hard on building a good supplier relationship as you do building a good relationship with your customers. And be loyal to your good suppliers. They are essential to your business's good health and growth.

Let's briefly look at all the ways suppliers can impact your company.

- **Quality:** Supplier components can positively or negatively affect the quality of your product. Higher quality increases customer satisfaction and decreases returns, which adds cash to your bottom line.
- **Test the reputation:** It is vitally necessary to check the reputation of the supplier's service you're contemplating hiring. Ensure the supplier's service you're hiring has a great reputation. You may ask your mates, colleagues or household, if they have ever used supplier's services. They may know a reputed service provider.
- **Timeliness and Reliability:** Reliability is probably the key factor to look for in suppliers. Good suppliers will ship the right number of items, as promised, on time so that they arrive in good shape. Sometimes you can get the best reliability from a large supplier. These companies have the resources to devote to backup systems and sources so that, if something goes wrong, they can still live up to their responsibilities to you.
- **Competitiveness and Stability:** They can give you the one-up on your competition based on their pricing, quality, reliability, technological breakthroughs and knowledge of industry trends. Stability is another key indicator. You'll want to sign up with vendors who have been in business a long time and have done so without changing businesses every few years. A company that has long-tenured senior executives is another good sign and a solid reputation with other customers is a promising indicator that a company is stable.
- **Innovation:** Suppliers can make major contributions to your new product development. If the supplier is innovative then definitely it will help you to promote your business. Innovation makes a product more feasible and helps in decreasing the cost of product. Remember, in this competitive world you cannot live with obsolete technology. You need to be very innovative so that you can attract more number of customers.
- **Finance:** If you've proven to be a considerate, loyal and paying customer, you may be able to tap into your suppliers for additional financing once you hit growth mode—or if you run into a cash crunch. That financing may take the form of postponed debt, extended terms on new purchases, a loan or an investment in your company. All of these improve your cash position.
- **Loyalty:** Another important reason why you ought to make use of good supplier relationship management skills is to promote loyalty with your vendors. This is vital in any business because operations aren't always smooth sailing. When you have established good supplier relations, you can be assured that the suppliers' support goes beyond the top offers with regards to quality and price; but more so, a powerful support in times of a fiscal crisis. They might allow more versatility in terms of payment, for example, should your organization desires it.
- **Operations:** Vendors and suppliers have a big impact in the operations of a business because the goods or services which they offer are an integral part of the worth that you deliver to your customers. To demonstrate clearly, if your supplier provides you with good quality raw materials, that already provides you with the benefit of achieving the level of quality that you intend to provide your clients with.

It is OK to Be a Demanding Customer

Having said how valuable and important a supplier can be to you, I'll now say that you should not be a patsy. You can be a demanding customer—just be fair. State your quality and time needs clearly. Hold your suppliers to their agreements. Make sure they stay competitive. Tell them you never expect to pay higher prices than other purchasers.

There are times you need to replace a supplier because you have outgrown them and they can't perform to your new expectations. Before dropping them, however, you might try to help them change to keep up with you. Also, it's not prudent to rely on one supplier. If that supplier has a strike or a fire, you don't want to be in a position where you'd be shut down too. So keep a backup or multiple suppliers on hand—and don't be embarrassed to tell your key supplier that you're doing so. They will appreciate your honesty.

How to Be a Valued Customer

These ideas assume, of course, that you are a customer that somebody out there wants. In order to be a valued customer to your suppliers, here are a few things you should do:

1. **Always pay on time:** Always pay your bills on time. Remember your supplier is in business because he also wants to earn money like you. Do not let him wait for long time. You can try to convince for favorable pricing but once you have negotiated then do not try to negotiate again and again. Delay in payment can spoil your relationship with the suppliers. So it is better to tell them in advance the reasons for the payment delay. Don't delay the payment. You'll be absolutely amazed at the goodwill and benefits you will earn by observing this simple rule.
2. **Provide adequate lead times:** Try to give suppliers as much lead time as possible on your orders. Unless there's a compelling, competitive reason not to, share with them an honest projection of your needs and keep them abreast of any significant changes in that estimation. When developing your lead times, it helps to be knowledgeable about your suppliers' production methods and needs.
3. **Personalize the relationship:** Visit suppliers' offices. You cannot isolate suppliers from your business. Suppliers are also an important part of your business. So call them in your meetings. Give them clear cut message that in this mutual relationship both the parties will gain. Show trust on your supplier. Invite them to break bread and invite them to your office parties and picnics. Your behaviour will turn your supplier trustworthy for your business.
4. **Share information:** Sharing information with your suppliers will help you in resolving your business issues. Share your business information with them. Supplier is an important part of your business if he is aware of your business then definitely helps your business. Tell them about your changing products, strategies and personnel so that accordingly they can provide you quality material. Many times, you'll find that good suppliers can be to help you find new customers.
5. **Communicate:** ...Good communication with your suppliers will benefit you to get good service. Daily communication with your supplier will make your relation with the supplier strong. Be in contact with your suppliers either by phone or face to face. Show them how important they are for your business and give them an assurance that you will also help their business to grow. Give them respect and show them how important they are for your business?
6. **Clarity:** Always be clear in what your business needs and when you need it. When placing an order always know or agree the cost in advance and ensure it appears on the official order. Disagreement over cost has destroyed some perfect supplier/customer relationships.
7. **Courtesy:** Being courteous to your suppliers pays dividends and costs nothing. Be firm, open and fair but be courteous. Place your orders as far in advance as possible and if it is a rush order say so. Courtesy will always receive a response in kind.

8. **Appreciate:** Show your appreciation of your good suppliers by inviting them to your company functions. This form of socialising can pay very good dividends. It lets your suppliers know you value their contribution to your business.

Developing good relationships with suppliers is not a complicated process. Be communicative, treat them fairly, be demanding (coupled with loyalty) and pay them on time. It's that easy.

18.16 The Characteristics of a Good Supplier

How you deal with your suppliers might impact the results of your enterprise. That is why using good supplier relationship management approaches is a smart investment. You may be thinking that since you are making the orders and payments to suppliers, you are in the dominant position and therefore, might make unreasonable demands. The simple truth is, to make things work in your favour as business owners, whenever you find really good suppliers, you ought to treat them well and you must work towards creating a mutually beneficial relationship with them. Hence the key to running and managing a business successfully means that you have a strong customer base and a stronger supplier base. So how do you decide if a supplier is good and trustworthy?

Before answering that, let us begin with first understanding what defines a good supplier.

"A good supplier is one who can meet all customer expectations, with respect to delivery time, quality of goods and dependability."

Therefore it is logical to infer then that a good supplier is one who meets these qualities. However while the laws of commerce have remained relatively simple, the demands and expectations of the customer keeps evolving. And hence the role of the supplier has changed as well. Keeping in mind the expectations of the customer, the following list contains eight key characteristics of a good supplier:

Timely delivery: Delayed delivery of supplies results in delayed deliveries to the end consumers. This provides an opportunity to supplier's competitors to capture their current customers. So, an ideal supplier takes care of the delivery dates and times and tries to handle the orders promptly and efficiently to keep their customers satisfied and happy.

Constant frequency of delivery (daily basis): If a supplier can keep to supplying goods at constant and smaller frequencies, then the cost advantage is supplemented. Meaning, if a product or part is found to be defective, then the time spent in replacing it is minimal as opposed to having to replace a whole carton or shipment of that item since the delivery is frequent and the supply chain is actively functioning. This is not only cost effective but is also a time and space saver.

Reasonable price: A good supplier always talks in terms of reasonable price. The nature of the supplier is to give benefits to their customers instead of making illegal profit out of their customers. Finding a supplier who offers reasonable price is very necessary because the final price of the product depends on your supplier only.

Minimal paper work: The best way to reduce the paper work is to use technology. Technology has reduced the paper work up to large extent. A good supplier always gives all possible services to their customers. He always tries to reduce the burden of their customers by using technology for e.g., he will be directly taking an order through e-commerce software or other softwares. A good supplier will find ways of reducing the amount of paper work involved.

Quick response/ turnaround time: The world of business is highly unstable and often the gap between demand and supply can be hard to predict. A good supplier will always be prepared to meet such a contingency. Again a frequent and smaller quantity of supplies is the key to eliminating this gap.

Inspection of goods: a good supplier offers warranty and money-back guarantees on products. If a store sells only the highest quality of products, it would not hesitate to put warranty and money-back guarantees. This also speaks of their concern in taking care of their customers.

Take care of you and your business: Good supplier will be more concerned with providing good products and service than making profit out of you. There are other suppliers whose only goal is to make money out of you. It is a good idea to stay away from these kind of people. A good supplier will be more interested with giving you the product that you need whereas a bad supplier will always lure you to buy their most expensive product even though it is not what you need.

Attend to your needs efficiently: A good supplier will have a competent and professional customer service that will always be ready to answer your queries and respond to your concerns immediately. It is a good idea to try out a store's customer service prior to buying from it.

The importance of a good supplier cannot be undermined and it can be said then that a business is as good as its suppliers.

18.17 Find Good Quality Mass Suppliers

Legitimate bulk suppliers include their contact numbers online as well as their office location and address. They will even offer you to view samples of their merchandise so you can gauge whether or not they are up to your standards. Do not fail to do so. The success of your business lies on the quality of the things that your bulk suppliers will sell to you and in turn, to your end customers. Sometimes, it also helps to check out fairs and expos and see if there are any bulk suppliers that are there to invite retailers to a business deal. In fairs and expos, they bring samples of their merchandise as well as the complete list of all products available for bulk orders. It is also a chance to size up a potential competition in case you are currently using a different supplier and experiencing a more askew sales margin.

In choosing a bulk supplier, you should consider pricing as a paramount concern. Aside from items being of high quality, they should also be at the lowest possible price so you can have a larger profit margin. Also, it gives you the flexibility in changing your retail price. Whatever your needs are, the formula is constant. Good reputation plus reliability plus lowest possible price, equals successful retail business. You should really take time to look at all possible bulk suppliers to see which one is the best and the most likely to help you rake in more profits. Do not fail to go the extra mile for your business. It is always wise to exercise prudence when it comes to running a very dynamic type of business. It is also important to minimize risks in order to prevent any loss in profit.

Looking for good bulk suppliers? Finding good suppliers can be difficult. It can be hard to make any decent money on eBay if you can't find good reliable supplies at good prices. If you are serious about finding good wholesalers and suppliers, then you must check out the website link below. If you keep doing things the way you have, then chances are you will get the same results, which I know for a fact are terrible.

18.18 Discover Good Suppliers for Business

How to find suppliers for your business? Locating reliable manufacturers, distributors and service providers is crucial to your small business or home business. Here's where to look for them.

Better, faster, cheaper.

In order for you to give your customers better products, faster service and lower rates, you have to develop a core group of reliable suppliers who cut you good deals on the products and services you buy.

Finding reliable suppliers who will sell to you at low cost is no easy task. In fact, it's not unusual for small businesses to find they can buy certain products cheaper from Wal-Mart than they can from a wholesaler. Nor is it unusual for a wholesaler or distributor to refuse to sell to a very small business. That's because it will take their sales staff the same time to process your 150 order as it would to process a 5,000 order.

Nevertheless, you can develop a core group of suppliers you can trust. Here are tips to help:

Be persistent

You'll need to put considerable effort into finding the best products, prices and suppliers. You can find names of suppliers from trade magazines and newspapers. Internet is the best way to find information on suppliers. You can find detailed information about suppliers online and then it's up to you to contact suppliers and get the best deal. Don't be so focused on getting rock bottom prices that you alienate your suppliers, though. Don't be arrogant otherwise suppliers will not help you when you need it and may ultimately decide they just don't want your business at all.

Shop the ads in trade magazines

Whether you want to buy a pump to use in your laboratory or silver earrings to sell in markets, you're likely to find the products you need advertised in a trade magazine for your business.

If you are just starting out in business and aren't sure what trade publications exist, check the list of free trade publications on Website. You will find one or more trade publications for which you'd get a free subscription. You can also find trade magazines on the Internet. You can take the help of search engine like Google or Yahoo and search for the name of your industry and the term, "trade magazine."

Once you find trade magazines, take all the necessary and important information, browse through all the ads. Ads in magazines and new product listings can help you find new suppliers.

Find suppliers on the web

If you are not able to find any supplier in any magazine, book or in any office then you will definitely find number of suppliers on internet. Go to Google or another major search engine and search for the name of the product you want to purchase followed by a word such as, "manufacturer," "wholesale," or "supplier." If you're looking for readymade dresses for example, type the term "readymade dresses wholesaler" in the search box. Note the search results. If you can't find what you're looking for, try a variation of the original search term, such as "list of wholesalers of readymade dresses." Often you'll see slightly different results just by changing the order of words in your online search.

Find Local Bargains

It is better to find local suppliers for the same goods instead of placing an order from out-of-state vendors. Outside vendor takes much time and money. By local suppliers you will be able to save considerable amount and time on shipping costs and you will get your delivery in less time without paying more on shipping. To narrow your Internet search down to local vendors, use the same search term you did initially and follow that by the name of your country and state or your city and state.

Search for directories of manufacturers on the Internet

Online searching will help you a lot. You will get information about any manufacturer by searching online. You can take the help of governmental sites for getting information e.g., MSME or

EDI etc. The site also has online supplier catalogs with detailed buying and specifying information. District Industries Centre (DIC) contains contact information for companies that supply industrial companies.

Try eBay

Although eBay is probably best known as a place for consumers to buy or auction merchandise, it is also used by businesses selling used and new equipment or supplies. But watch prices. If you find products sold by distributors, depending on what the product is, you may be able to get a better deal through the manufacturer than through eBay.

18.19 Dealing with Suppliers

Establishing good relationships with suppliers puts your business on the road to success.

Making good relationship with suppliers is the key factor in dealing with suppliers. Reliable supplier will guide you to sale your product and to increase your product sales. They can bring a positive change in your business. If you build a good relationship and your business is profitable for them, suppliers may be willing to bail you out when your customers make difficult demands.

Remember, though, that suppliers are in business to make money, If you go to the mat with them on every bill, ask them to shave prices on everything they sell to you, or fail to pay your bills promptly, don't be surprised when they stop calling. As a new business owner, you can't expect to receive the same kind of attention a long-standing customer gets right off the bat. Over time, however, you can develop excellent working relationships that will be profitable for both you and your suppliers.

Once you have compiled a list of possible suppliers, ask for quotes or proposals, complete with prices, available discounts, delivery terms and other important factors. Don't just consider the terms; investigate the potential supplier's financial condition, too. Ask for customer references; call them and find out how well the supplier has performed. If there have been any problems, ask for details about how they were reconciled. Every supplier relationship hits bumps now and then; the key is to know how the rough spots were handled. Was the supplier prompt and helpful in resolving the problem, or defensive and uncooperative?

Be open with your suppliers and they will respond in kind. Tell them what you need and when you need it. Have a specific understanding about the total cost and expect delivery on schedule. Keep in constant communication with your suppliers about possible delays, potential substitutions for materials or product lines, production quality, product improvements or new product introductions and potential savings. Suppliers often establish a minimum order for merchandise and this minimum may be higher for first orders to cover the cost of setting up a new store account. Some suppliers also demand a minimum number of items per order.

Fostering Good Supplier and Sub-contractor Relationships

With ever increasing outsourcing of products and services aimed at increasing profitability, becoming supplier-friendly is as important as being customer friendly.

Businesses are ready for downsizing in order to improve performance, efficiency and to earn more profit. Subcontracting and outsourcing is the best way for the company to achieve the above target. What you have been doing in the past by your own facilities and resources are now outsourced to subcontractors and suppliers. It saves your time and efforts. It is very important that you must treat your suppliers in the same way you treat your staff. You must also care about your suppliers. That's where supplier-friendly measures are increasingly in need.

Essentials that you should know to develop good supplier-friendliness:

Treat Your Suppliers with Dignity

All your interactions with suppliers' personnel should reflect decent interpersonal relationships. Never treat them as a low class people. You actually need them and if you want to have a good relationship with them then you need to respect them and their work. Don't let them wait for you if they need you then you also need them. Don't give them secondary treatment. At the time of price negotiation you must not behave in an arrogant way and try to create a pleasant environment.

Give Appropriate Value to the Quality and Service of Your Suppliers

While dealing with the suppliers you should focus more on "whether you have got desired product" rather than "valuing the supplier". In other words, every supplier's quality, timeliness in delivery, commitment to after-sales service, etc., should have a value in addition to the price.

You will find many suppliers for the same product but each one will have their own quality and advantage. Some may be very good meeting your requirements; some may be above average in product quality; some may be able to develop and offer "specials" out of "ordinary" in times of such need. Each of these unique aspects should be factored into the price.

Look for Long-term Relationships with Your Suppliers

There are several ways by which one can establish long-term supplier-friendly relationships. That include:

- giving a price at which the supplier is comfortable and happy to serve you
- ensuring cash flow by way of payment of advance
- not squeezing too much in credit terms
- ensuring prompt and timely payments without the need for personal follow-up
- providing technical support/collaborative assistance in developing new products, enhancing quality or in solving problems
- offering flexibility in commercial terms and conditions in proportion to the trustworthiness of the supplier and so on.

Encourage Straightforwardness and Corruption-free Dealings with Your Suppliers

You must be careful about the corrupt suppliers. Reject those suppliers who want to make you fool and try to earn profit. Many times the employees in the business favour some suppliers because of the percentage of commission they will get from the suppliers. You need to scan and find out such employees who are not at all honest to the company. When your business grows, your suppliers too should grow. Good supplier-friendly measures should ensure it for the benefit of all stake holders.

Communicate Often

The better you treat suppliers, the better they'll treat you. Be open and straightforward by telling them exactly what you need, when you need it and what you expect to pay. Also keep the lines of communication open, especially with regard to order changes and substitutions you might need or to quality improvements you'd like to see at their end. They'll appreciate the feedback.

Remember that having a few key vendors is better than having too many. This will allow you to establish tight knit relationships that can lead to greater understanding when it comes to cost controls, discounts and payment terms. One good rule of thumb is to maintain a major supplier that receives the bulk of your business and a minor supplier that has the rest. This way you always have a backup should something happen to either one of those relationships.

In today's economy, you need every advantage you can get. Working closely with key suppliers can help your business overcome rough patches and put you on the road to even greater success.

18.20 Where to Find Good Building Material Supplies?

Do you need to find good building material suppliers? Want to add more suppliers to your list? It's a good idea to have a great list. There are many ways to find them. Here are some proven ways to do it. Searching for any building material supplier is relatively easy. Finding a reliable supplier who can provide building material supplies of excellent quality is not very easy. But if you know the techniques, it should not be that hard.

Reliability is important in looking for lumbers supply and other building materials, whether for constructing bridges, power plants, roads, homes, commercial buildings, hospitals, schools and anything else. The word of mouth is a common, but effective strategy of many companies of several types. Hence, you can ask around for a few referrals from contractors, friends, relatives, neighbors and even from the coffee vendor that you happen to buy coffee from. You can then check their reputation by doing some research.

The local chamber of commerce or MSME or Vidarbha Industries Association (VIA) can also be helpful at this point. For sure, they have listing of many building material suppliers. A certain official can provide you all information you may need regarding building supply stores. The chamber of commerce may even give you tips, such as, which stores offer low pricing on materials and have quality products. Understand that there are low quality supplies and high-end building materials. Being able to deliver the right materials, the exact quantity and at the right time is very important. You may request for company profiles of suppliers from the MSME, if it is available. The yellow pages and telephone directory have listings on building suppliers as well. You can scan several telephone directories from different telecommunications in your State. Each building material supplier on it may include company description and profile for everyone's information.

Select the one that has good reputation. Sometimes, they may include on their description of the projects, which they have supplied building materials. Doing an onsite inspection on such projects may give you an idea on the quality of construction materials they have.

Your state government can also help you. The engineering department may have a network of contacts on construction materials providers. They can even give recommendations on which supplier is the best for your project. Engineers and architects have a way of scrutinizing building materials, so anything they say may be valuable. The internet is another place to look for your ideal building material supplier, as the web contains thousands of e-companies. When you search the web, you can narrow down your searches to a few by reading testimonials or reviews of the company's clients. Construction materials suppliers may include on their website information, such as the type of materials they can provide and construction projects that they can have business deals with.

18.21 Relationships with Your Suppliers

It is often a good business practice to maintain a good rapport with your suppliers. Maintaining a healthy relationship with your supplier will, in most cases, benefit both parties financially, but it is what the supplier is willing and able to provide to your business which will ultimately decide how successful the business relationship is!

Having good relationships with your suppliers requires that you:

- settle all accounts on time - if a delay is inevitable, warn your supplier (i.e., before the due date)
- be considerate to sales representatives - never waste their time so they don't waste yours
- avoid submitting orders at the last minute – stock shortages are often a result of poor planning
- all complaints and damage claims should be submitted promptly with evidence - for example, if you receive goods broken, dirty, soiled or water damaged, make sure you return the goods to the supplier – don't discard them.

If you are able to build a good relationship with suppliers, often they will go that extra step for you when you really need help.

Choosing reliable suppliers

An unreliable supplier is a bane to any business. They can close your business. Not only do you risk losing business due to your lack of ability to deliver, it can also be extremely frustrating. If you are having problems with any of your suppliers, then you have to seriously think upon whether to continue relationship with that supplier or not. Often a "threat" of change may also bring your supplier into line.

Poor suppliers are not necessarily the ones that deliver your goods late - they may have a poor sense of timing (always turn up at the most inconvenient time), send the wrong or inferior products, refuse to take returns or offer uncompetitive prices. Your business will lose competitiveness if these problems occur. If you suspect this, you will need to record and report any problems immediately.

Never be afraid of putting a supplier on notice. If you feel that the level of service provided by the supplier is below par, notify them in writing, either by letter, fax or e-mail. Imply that in future you will be claiming for losses arising from their non-compliance or delayed supply (for example, overtime pay when staff has to wait for deliveries) or charging a percentage of the cost of lost sales. Once the supplier's business begins to suffer, often they fall into line rather quickly. You can think on sharing the suppliers of other businessmen.

In the final analysis you may have to decide whether price or service is most important to your business. Paying a little more for reliability, service and perhaps better payment terms may be a better business strategy.

The best thing is to work with a company that provides good quality products and service to you and your customers at fair price.

Over-reliance on one supplier

Never depend on one supplier for your business' goods or services, as this exposes your business to risks if that particular supplier has difficulty producing or delivering or you have problems in dealing with them. Any problems here may mean that your supply also falls short. Remember, a delay in your supply could cripple your business, especially where you may rely on one supplier for most goods or a vital component for your operation.

Losing your supplier can happen and if you are in this vulnerable position, you should take steps to reduce your exposure, including the following:

- Keep a list of alternative suppliers in your file. Take a look at them in comparison to the suppliers you currently have.

- You might discover that changes have occurred that make one of your back-ups more attractive than your regular supplier.
- If nothing else, you may discover new products and/or possible relationships that could be useful in renegotiating supply contracts with your current suppliers.
- Build and maintain good relationships with your current suppliers' sales representatives: that way if a situation arises, such as goods in short supply, you may get serviced quicker.

Warning signs

Look for these warning signs that you may be over reliant on one supplier:

- Your business relies on one large trade creditor. For example, in your creditor ledger, a high proportion is represented by a single supplier.
- The business is trading in a specialized field or a new or developing field and because of the nature of the industry involved, only one supplier is available.
- It may have been easier to deal with one supplier.
- When you first used the supplier your business was not yet established in terms of skills or reputation. Therefore you were unable to negotiate other terms.

What should you do about it?

- Check to see if other suppliers are available who might be willing to give better terms.
- Look to local suppliers to avoid extra transport costs, such as freight, postage, courier or handling costs.
- Now that your business is established, it may be possible to renegotiate your terms of trade with the existing supplier.
- In the longer term you may want to consider producing the materials in-house, especially if you are reliant on a single component. You may even be able to buy the supplier if you have the resources.
- Evaluate the supplier's financial condition. You need to be confident of their ability to perform. Review their operating statement and balance sheet and run a credit check.
- Find out if alternative raw materials can be used or developed. For example, in some circumstances glass may be more appropriate than plastic or vice versa.
- Maintain close ties with your suppliers. This may include taking them to lunch, sending cards for special occasions such as Diwali or Holi or inviting them to business functions and events.

Dealing with poor customer service from your supplier

If your business misses out on the supplies that it needs, this can disrupt the quality of service your business provides to your customers. Similarly, a large number of poor quality items and returns can cost you time and money, even if they are replaced free of charge. Late supplies can also cost you money by having your staff wait around for delayed deliveries.

Invite suggestions from the supplier and then put your own thoughts forward. If possible, this should be a frank, off-the-record discussion with the people who actually work on your account on a day-to-day basis: you're looking for people with titles like project coordinator or account rep. — not vice president or general manager.

Focus on subjects such as these:

- Timing: What are realistic time frames for the various types of work? What can you ask for if you have a real need for faster service?

- Information transfer: What can you do to reduce errors associated with orders and service requests?
- Coordination: What can you do to ensure that your business works effectively with the supplier?

Ask what problems your supplier faces in delivering good service. Perhaps you can't solve those, but understanding your supplier's problems can often help you to plan your work more effectively.

Your paying problems

Sometimes you may find it difficult to meet your suppliers' terms. If so, it is time to address this problem if:

- Your business is incurring considerable penalties as a result of late payment.
- Suppliers are constantly phoning regarding payment progress.
- Your reputation is suffering and your business does not have a good credit rating.

Solutions you should look at include the following:

- Examine your accounting and bill payment process with a view to streamlining it so you have full management and control.
- Examine the timing of your payments to all your suppliers.
- Where the requirements are too burdensome, contact the suppliers and negotiate more reasonable payment terms. As much as possible, use suppliers who offer better, reasonable terms.
- Record all invoices to be paid. Invest in a good accounting software package to help you prepare weekly reports on payments which are due.

Here are few tips of how to maintain a healthy relation with your supplier:

- Always pay on time.
- Discuss vendor's needs and methods of doing business.
- If a vendor or service provider isn't meeting your expectations, discuss it immediately.
- Seek supplier's suggestions.
- When you're the customer, act the way your best customers do.
- Strive to give suppliers enough time to do a great job.
- When you find a good vendor, be loyal.
- Understand vendors' need to make a profit.
- Avoid unreasonable demands.

Summary

The different problems faced by the new small entrepreneurs regarding suppliers are:

- Where is supplier?
- Don't pay bill
- Quotes / proposal
- Understand everything
- Who are quality suppliers?
- Improper dealing with supplier

- Suppliers' retention problem
- Supplier side delay of material
- Bargaining power of suppliers

Suppliers can be divided into four general categories. They are;

- Manufacturers: Most retailers buy through company salespeople or independent representatives who handle the wares of several different companies.
- Distributors: Also known as wholesalers, brokers or jobbers, distributors buy in quantity from several manufacturers and warehouse the goods for sale to retailers.
- Independent craftspeople: Exclusive distribution of unique creations is frequently offered by independent craftspeople who sell through reps or at trade shows.
- Import sources: Many retailers buy foreign goods from a domestic importer, who operates much like a domestic wholesaler. Or, depending on your familiarity with overseas sources, you may want to travel abroad to buy goods.

How do you decide when to change vendors? Here are key areas to consider:

- Unreliability
- Lack of cost competitiveness
- Narrowness
- Extra-sale costs

Dealing with advisors

New entrepreneurs merely give any importance to the advisor. If they want to ask any information they just ask to their friends or the one who runs business but these persons also do not have full business knowledge. When entrepreneurs do not take suggestions from the advisor then they face problems in their business. Business advisors can point out the strengths and weaknesses in your business, helping you root out the flaws in your company. In order to get the requisite knowledge and guidance from a business advisor, you need to negotiate with a positive frame of mind and approach the advisor with an open mind.

Striking successful deals with suppliers

When dealing with suppliers, price should not be the only deciding factor. Low price is not very useful if the supplier does not deliver on time, has payment issues and delivers poor quality materials. Here are some ways to negotiate successfully with your suppliers.

- When dealing with them, keep in mind price, delivery time, payment mode, maintenance, quality and additional services provided by the supplier.
- You need to understand how crucial your businesses' orders are for the supplier.
- If you find out that your business is important for the supplier, negotiations will be weighed in your favor.
- State your needs clearly, from price, quantity, quality to date of delivery, mode of payment etc.
- The seniority of the bargaining teams should match, on the supplier as well as purchaser side.

Strategies for locating new suppliers are as follows: Attend trade shows Seek ideas from current suppliers, Ask competitors for supplier ideas, and become a bargain hunter

The ways suppliers can impact your company are Quality, Test the reputation, Timeliness and Reliability, Competitiveness and Stability, Innovation, Finance, Loyalty, and Operations.

How to Be a Valued Customer

These ideas assume, of course, that you are a customer that somebody out there wants. In order to be a valued customer to your suppliers, here are a few things you should do:

Always pay on time, Provide adequate lead times, Personalize the relationship, Share information, Communicate, Clarity, Courtesy, and Appreciate.

The Characteristics of a good supplier are as follows:

Timely delivery, Constant frequency of delivery (daily basis), Reasonable price, Minimal paper work, Quick response/ turnaround time, Inspection of goods, Take care of you and your business, and Attend to your needs efficiently.

Discover Good Suppliers for Business

How to find suppliers for your business? Locating reliable manufacturers, distributors and service providers is crucial to your small business or home business. Here's where to look for them. Be persistent, Shop the ads in trade magazines, Find suppliers on the web, Find Local Bargains, Search for directories of manufacturers on the Internet and Try eBay.

Essentials that you should know to develop good supplier-friendliness:

Treat Your Suppliers with Dignity; Give Appropriate Value to the Quality and Service of Your Suppliers; Look for Long-term Relationships with Your Suppliers; Encourage Straightforwardness and Corruption-free Dealings with Your Suppliers and Communicate Often

KEYWORDS

Suppliers: A person or company that supplies or sells goods or services.

Manufacturers: A person or organization that produces finished goods from raw materials, especially on a large industrial scale.

Distributors: A company which sells goods for another company which makes those goods.

Vendor: Someone who promotes or exchanges goods or services for money.

Business advisor: *Business advisor means* literally to advise people on their businesses.

Turnaround time: The time taken to complete a job from beginning to end.

Delivery time: The number of days before something will be delivered.

QUESTIONS

1. What are the suppliers related problems of small entrepreneurs?
2. What are the strategies of finding good suppliers?
3. How to maintain good relationship with your suppliers?
4. What are the characteristics of good suppliers?

❑ ❑ ❑

Chapter – 19

Surviving Business Obstacles

LEARNING OBJECTIVES

On completion of this chapter, you should be able to:

- ☺ *Explain the new small entrepreneurs' fear of surviving business.*
- ☺ *Describe reasons of business surviving failure.*
- ☺ *Describe business survival problems of entrepreneurs.*

19.1 Reliability – A Keystone of Entrepreneurship

The recent episode of fraud by the Chairman of Satyam and all the several other frauds perpetrated by other entrepreneurs around the world is a shame on the name of entrepreneurship. These isolated episodes have a tendency to make other entrepreneur's life tougher. People tend to see to other entrepreneurs with less trust. They bring a bad name to the ilk. They are usually followed by tougher regulations, which have a tendency to restrict freedom of business choices for entrepreneurs. Already there are so many rules and regulations that are formed by the government for entrepreneurs. Satyam like situation make the business of the other entrepreneurs very hard at least new entrepreneurs will face tough situation. Now the new entrepreneurs have to pass through more hard legal practices than before. They get less support because now the financers or advisor suddenly do not believe entrepreneurs. They make conduct of business more expensive. Financiers too increase the risk premium and generally make entrepreneurs grovel more to get at their money. The price that genuine entrepreneurs pay for the fault of these incidents is so huge that it is worthy of a self disciplined vigil within the community itself. There is a case for them to become active policemen of themselves and blow the whistle when they see one of their cohorts behaving funny.

When entrepreneurs want funding or raise the funds for the business, there are stages when the entrepreneurs face hardest time for different reasons - at the starting phase when the entrepreneurs start business and once they establish their business successfully.

Starting business phase

When the business is in the starting stage, there is a focused pursuit of a limited objective – may be a small project- driven by a passion to succeed and gambling everything to increase the prospects of success. They become busy in collecting all the necessary stuff for the business. There is not much care given to forms, rules and norms, perhaps not affordable as well, as typically entrepreneurs start poor, are up against established players who are much more powerful. New entrepreneurs focus only on how to get customers for sell and can get profit. They at the low level try to do their best. They have a dream to become successful entrepreneur. Some entrepreneurs mistakenly believe that their only way to succeed is to pursue some short cuts, which seem to work for some time. But that will not always work because legally to become successful entrepreneur, they (new entrepreneurs) must consider every step that is required to grow business. Unfortunately the road that greets entrepreneurs in India is often littered with obstacles and tempting chances for wrongdoing and many fall prey to those temptations and compulsions. Even becoming successful at low level is very hard when you are running the business. Apart from business you have to handle so many other issues. For example any government official can delay in passing your file. This seems it has become the norm rather than the exception. It is unfortunate because, those entrepreneurs of lesser competitiveness and objectivity do fall prey to this and compromise so much of their business future. They never learn the right way of doing business. They always go for such a way which will not provide help to the entrepreneurs for long term. They do not understand competition and believe corruption to be a legitimate part of business. Instead of developing themselves they take the help of others to grow their business, they slowly become dependent for the success of their business. They do not develop strong work culture and leadership within their organization, filling them instead with incompetent staff that will learn to manipulate rather than work smart to ensure business success. Most harmful of all they will earn for themselves an ill reputation, which may be tolerated, but never respected and hence will not ever be the choice partners for financiers and businessmen.

BOX 19

Vencap Success Rate Comparable To US: Study

A third to a fifth of the incubated firms make it to the big league.

The success rate of incubated companies in India is 60-70 per cent, comparable to that in America, says the first such survey conducted by the Department of Science and Technology (DST).

The 'First Status Report on Technology Business Incubation' in India also stated that 20 to 30 per cent of incubated companies make it big. The survey is based on the responses of 28 incubators supported by the DST. Each of these incubators has on an average, 10-15 companies they are fostering. DST supports 55 incubators; there are 120-130 incubators across India.

"For us, a successful entrepreneur or business is one which has managed to survive for five years and above after they graduate from an incubation centre. Those 20-30 per cent who manage to make it big are the ones who have a turnover in excess of ₹ 100 crore," said S K Mittal, the head of DST's National Science and Technology Entrepreneurship Development Board.

DST provides ₹ 2-8 crore funding to each of the incubators, with a target of providing seed fund of at least ₹ 50 lakh per company. Over the past two years, said Mittal, DST and the Technology Development Board have jointly provided funding of ₹ 20 crore.

The study also notes the rise of 'angel funding groups' like Indian Angel Network, Mumbai Angels and TiE Chennai Fund and how this has given an impetus to entrepreneurial ventures in the country.

The next step from DST is to tie-up with other ministries. Some of them have already approached DST, like Ministry of Micro Small and Medium Enterprises, Ministry of Agriculture, Department of Information Technology and banks like the Small Industries Development Bank of India.

DST is also partnering with the Wadhwani Foundation's National Entrepreneurship Network (NEN) for development of mentor programme. A lot of startups die in the early stages, which is healthy. This allows them to come up with a sustainable business model. NEN is also trying to partner with DST to develop some mentors to provide support and guidance to entrepreneurs.

Private venture capital funding backed by US fund houses started to invest in India only from 2000 onwards and clearly win in terms of the investment when compared to government-funded support. The National Science and Technology Entrepreneurship Development Board (NSTEDB) were established in 1982. That, in turn, started the Science and Technology Entrepreneurship Parks (STEP) and Technology Business Incubators (TBIs).

NSTEDB has so far catalyzed 15 STEPs in different parts of India, which have promoted 788 units, generating annual turnover of around Rs 130 crore and employment for 5,000. More than 100 new products and technologies have been developed by STEPs or STEP-promoted entrepreneurs. In addition, over 11,000 have been trained through various skill development programmes conducted by STEPs, say the official figures.

Source: Information received from "Business Standard", 2011.

Entrepreneurs' successful environment phase

The next stage when entrepreneurs work in the successful environment. Entrepreneurs go off track is when the flush of success many times powers them with a sense of invincibility. Entrepreneurs have a taste of success and they try to neglect most of the legal needs of the business because what they think they can manipulate anything. In either case, focus shifts away from managing the business with the edge that ensured its initial success and business falters. Instead of correcting that in the right manner, entrepreneurs resort to short cuts that their newly acquired 'power status' offer them and set down the path of wrongdoings which often brings them to a collapse. What entrepreneurs think that the success they have got is because of their extra efforts that are wrong but they think, that are right and they continue with the wrong practices. They never do the analysis, is there anything wrong with the current procedures? Some of the entrepreneurs went through this process of wrong path; their success was not long lasting but when they redeemed themselves before it was too late and earned a respectful place in society and history by becoming philanthropists!

The initial period of struggle sets the tone for the character and behavior of entrepreneurs through the lifecycle of their ventures. What kind of actions they select becomes the identity of the entrepreneurs because that decides the future behaviour of the entrepreneurs. If at the initial stage they become more used to the illegal process then they continue with that only. Azim Premji in the early 80s, is reputed to have declined to 'take care' of some corrupt officials in his hydrogenated oil plant in Karnataka in the early stages of his entrepreneurial life. As a result, the officials closed the plant on false charges of flouting of excise rules. Azim Premji did not buckle down; let the plant remain shut, while fighting the case legally. It took reportedly three years for him to come out victorious, thanks also to the support of the employees of the plant who were also suffering and reopen the plant. While it was painful, the episode surely sent a clear message. More importantly, it is still remembered and recounted as a legend in principle based entrepreneurial behavior. Mr Premji invested the suffering caused by that incident, including massive financial losses in creating a credibility capital, from which he is still reaping benefits. This early strength in his resume ensured businessmen and financiers around the world respect Mr. Premji as a trusted business partner, aiding him considerably in his ventures to date.

Association of ethics and morality with entrepreneurs' integrity

The new entrepreneurs should not go for the illegal practices while starting the business. There is though a shortcut in the business but that will not help the entrepreneurs for the long time. Somehow in the near future such kinds of entrepreneurs suffer. The entrepreneurs should be the legal one, have honesty and respect in the society. The competitive advantages of integrity as a corner stone of entrepreneurial behavior will lead him to the success. Once an entrepreneur earns the credibility as a person of integrity, doing business becomes that much easier. Partners will seek to do business with such an entrepreneur who they can trust and might be even willing to pay a premium for that feeling of comfort. Your honesty and ethics will help you to attract many supporting hands. Winning the confidence of the partners has a great place in the business. These are people who are required by the entrepreneurs to have success in the life, to grow the business. Financiers will vie with each other to provide funds, as they know their money is relatively safe with such an entrepreneur. Once the entrepreneur sets the limits on acceptable behavior based on principles of integrity, he and his team in the organization know that they cannot resort to short cuts and need to be genuinely competitive to succeed in business. This makes them seek real competitive advantages and conduct business to succeed against not only other routine businesses, but also some that may 'enjoy' advantages due to practicing business without integrity.

Let us take a live example from the field of road contract business. Let us assume, there is one contractor (called Mr X) who behaves with completely integrity and there are others whose integrity quotient let's say varies from awful to 'god-awful'. The challenge that Mr X faces when he bids for a contract are that he needs to take into account the possibility that the bidding process is perverted to favor the others because they may ply bribes or for someone in the bidding organization to let these corrupting bidders know the lowest bid amount, so they can quote a marginally lower prices and win the contract, etc. Can Mr X overcome this challenge while maintaining integrity? Yes. There are many things he can do, including, finding technological solutions to render road building less expensive and hence can quote so low that others without that technology may find it unattractive to bid at those prices. He could resort to the new provisions of Right To Information (RTI) to shed the required extent of transparency in the bidding process. He could build high quality roads on a pro-bono basis to demonstrate the longevity and riding comfort and hence win the support of the users, who could be used to campaign for him. Incidentally these are ideas picked up from several good contractors' real life experiences. Let us not kid ourselves. It is tough to be straight. But who said being an entrepreneur is a cake walk? But setting your behavior right from the beginning, though might make it tougher, straightens a lot of stuff for the lifetime of clean, successful business. Entrepreneurs face very hard time in their life, but they should not therefore adopt the wrong way. You should come up with more competent methods of doing the work. It will take time and efforts also but you will see that you have followed the ethics and people are ready to work with you. Giving into pressures or temptations to cut corners usually sets entrepreneurs on a slippery slide that look so inviting and harmless at the beginning and then keeps getting harmful over time to what Ramalinga Raju calls the 'riding the tiger, without knowing how to get out without being eaten' phenomena.

19.2 Fears of Surviving Business

Lack of commitment

Strategic planning is beneficial in taking a significant decision. So, in companies where the owner and management likes to "hold back" or "hedge bets," work on many things at the same time and "keep all options open," this can be a real problem. This stems from a fear of making a decision and following through with commitment to carry out that decision. Business runs by commitment you must fulfill your commitment. There are two effects of not fulfilling commitment. The first is you lose the trust of others if you have given commitment to others. If you will not support others by fulfilling your responsibilities then others will see you with doubts and they will fear to work with you. The second is you spoil your image as a strong commitment man. You put your business in trouble by not fulfilling your commitment.

Fear of accountability

When in your business you say you are accountable to yourself that means you are not accountable to anyone. Strategic planning brings in accountability to everyone in a system and that causes some real fear and pain to some small business people. Small entrepreneurs do not want to be accountable to any one they do what they think whether it will be a failure or success they are not accountable to anyone.

Fear of failure

Small new entrepreneurs are not the rich persons whatever they will do that directly affects the existence of their business. In small businesses the cost of failure is high and the personal risks are great. Already they do business in uncertainty where they perfectly do not know the future of their business. In large companies, the management is really dealing with someone else's money. In small business and especially with entrepreneurs, one's livelihood is at stake. A great strategic plan can really support the entrepreneur to implement his idea, but a plan can result into a big loss. The small entrepreneurs know that nobody will come to support them if something will go wrong that fear restricts them to go for the strategic planning.

Fear of cost of strategic planning

Small new entrepreneurs always think in terms of cost they do not go for long term results instead they go for the instant results. The fear of cost arises when there is no strategic thinking used to look at the value of strategic planning to the business compared to the cost. Fear also arises when the entrepreneurs wrongly think about the strategic planning as a cost rather than as a tool of investment. They are not ready to invest much in the business but what they want is to get the profit as soon as possible.

Fear of discomfort and confrontation during the strategic planning process

Many small business owners and managers are very fearful and uncomfortable with "confrontations" and they go to great lengths to avoid them. Already the situation of the small business is very critical. They are not ready to involve more issues into their business. They want smoothness in their business and that's why they are ready to sacrifice most of the important things in business instead of having confrontation. They are very uncomfortable in any confrontation and are fearful that they will be confronted with some issue or problem during the strategic planning process that they would rather avoid. Therefore, they decide not to engage in the strategic planning process.

19.3 Small Businesses Failure

New entrepreneurs of small business are not very much serious about strategic planning they think that their business is too small for strategic planning. Or they will offer any number of other excuses why they do not use strategic planning for their business. This is a sad commentary on the thinking of these small business people. They do not realize or comprehend that their business or organization is on the pathway to the business graveyard without a strategic plan. New entrepreneurs do not understand that strategic planning is a tool to grow the business.

Well the real reason they do not do strategic planning is related more to fear than anything else. So the question arises "why are so many of these businesses strategically challenged, strategically averse and/or just plain scared or fearful of strategic planning?" why small entrepreneurs do not go for strategic. Following are the reasons that drive small businesses away from strategic planning.

Success in business is never automatic. It isn't strictly based on luck - although a little never hurts. It requires efforts and a proper planning. It depends primarily on the owner's foresight and organization. What he thinks about the business and how he wants to move forward the business. Even then, of course, there are no guarantees.

Starting a small business is always risky and the chance of success is slim. The new small entrepreneurs have to take many efforts to run a business. According to survey over 50 per cent of small businesses fail in the first year and 95 per cent fail within the first five years.

Following reasons can be considered for small business failure:

- Lack of experience
- Insufficient capital (money)
- Poor location
- Poor inventory management
- Over-investment in fixed assets
- Poor credit arrangements
- Personal use of business funds

- Unexpected growth
- Competition
- Low sales

Choosing a business that isn't very profitable

By unknowingly entrepreneurs select such kind of business where there is not much profit and in or even if there is a profit they are not capable enough to cash that profit. The entrepreneurs must take in deep information of that business after that only they should choose the business. Even though you generate lots of activity, the profits never materialize to the extent necessary to sustain an on-going company.

Fear of strategic planning

Most of the small entrepreneurs even are not aware of the term strategic planning. These things become a major obstacle for the growth of the business of the small entrepreneurs. Fear of being intimidated and overwhelmed by the strategic planning process. Many small business owners and leaders have pre-conceived an idea of what strategic planning is and fear that the process of strategic planning will be too overwhelming for them. Therefore, they feel intimidated by the process and do not want to even start the process.

Inadequate cash reserves

When entrepreneurs start their business, just having the little amount, then the real problem starts. They think that the little amount of money will be sufficient to start the business. They do not properly estimate the real requirement of the business. They have a tendency to solve the problem when that will come but actually they entrap themselves. If you don't have enough cash to carry you through the first six months or so before the business starts making money, your prospects for Success are not good. Consider both business and personal living expenses when determining how much cash you will need.

Fear of past experience

Fear of repeated past bad experiences with strategic planning. Small business leaders may have had some extremely negative and possibly harmful experiences with strategic planning in the past. Most of the small entrepreneurs have thought of that even they have also spent money for that but they did not get proper satisfaction. They may have had a very poor consultant that was brought in and nearly ruined the business. Maybe they spent weeks in meetings without accomplishing one thing because they did not use a professional facilitator. Or maybe they launched a plan without any means of accountability. Here the entrepreneurs are not aware of the good consultants to whom they can contact. So just by bringing the consultant does not solve the problems.

Failure to understand market, customers and customers' buying habits

Entrepreneurs start the business just by looking to the other entrepreneurs' business or thinking that I will earn profit. They do not estimate that who are their customers? You should be able to clearly identify them in one or two sentences. How are you going to reach them? Is your product or service seasonal? What will you do in the off-season? How loyal are your potential customers to their current supplier? Do customers keep coming back or do they just purchase from you one time? Does it take a long time to close a sale or are your customers more driven by impulse buying? Just by copying others, entrepreneurs cannot run business. Entrepreneurs must thoroughly go to the deep knowledge of the implementation of the business.

Failure to price your product or service correctly

Entrepreneurs are not able to perfectly set the price of their services or products. They are the new ones in the business and without taking help of the experienced ones if they will try to do everything then it will have a bad impact on the business. Proper pricing is directly related to the profit of the business. You must clearly define your pricing strategy. You can be the cheapest or you can be the best, but if you try to do both, you'll fail. The new entrepreneurs must know the strategy of the pricing. They should analyze the pricing strategy of the other entrepreneurs who are in the market for long years that will give the idea regarding pricing strategy.

Fear of wastage of time

New entrepreneurs do not want to devote much time to the strategic planning. Fear of the amount of anticipated time and commitment to develop a strategic plan. Small businesses do not have a large corporate staff and are so busy putting out fires and managing day-to-day activities that they believe they will not have time to focus on long-term and strategic thinking. They want to keep working "in the business" but avoid working "on their business. Entrepreneurs think that it will just waste their time and they are not so much confident about the tragic planning. And this translates to a basic fear that if they divert time to strategic planning, the business will fall apart in the meantime.

Failure to adequately anticipate cash flow

The new entrepreneurs' problems are that they do not get credit easily from their supplier and they do not get customers easily there is a time gap. New entrepreneurs are not aware of the proper strategy to play with both the customers and suppliers without loss. When you are just starting out, suppliers require quick payment for inventory. If you sell your products on credit, the time between making the sale and getting paid can be months. The mismanagement of cash flow results in risk of business survival. This two-way tug at your cash can pull you down if you fail to plan for it.

Failure to anticipate or react to competition/ technology/ other changes in the marketplace

Small entrepreneurs are not capable to change instantly. Because change requires something new into your business and it is not possible for the new entrepreneurs. They cannot instantly shift to new technology or process. They cannot suddenly change the taste of the product. It is dangerous to assume that what you have done in the past will always work. Challenge the factors that led to your Success. Do you still do things the same way despite new market demands and changing times? What is your competition doing differently? What new technology is available? Be open to new ideas. Do Experiment. Those who fail to do this end up becoming pawns to those who do.

Fear of benefits of academic theory

Fear of academic or the ivory tower thinking. Small entrepreneurs have their own way of business. They do not go through theory. Even most of them are not aware of those things even if entrepreneurs know they are not much confident about theory and they just want to apply their own experience. They do not show trust on systems, generalizations and formulas. They are fearful about the application of the theory in the real world.

Overgeneralization

Trying to do everything for everyone is a sure road to ruin. Spreading yourself too thin diminishes quality. The market pays excellent rewards for excellent results, average rewards for average results and below average rewards for below average results.

Fear of the facilitation process

The most effective strategic planning meetings use the skills of a professional facilitator. Small business owners and managers may fear that the meetings, no matter how well intended, will end up as gripe sessions or hours of aimless wandering without a clear agenda or purpose.

Overdependence on a single customer

When you start thinking from the point of view of only single customer then here you do a mistake. If you are depending on a single customer for your business then you must stop! Having a large base of small customers is much preferred. Mostly it happens that the small entrepreneurs' customers are already small, in that too they are dependent to some customers only. So if that customer is reluctant to new purchase then it affects the business of the small entrepreneurs. For the new entrepreneurs it becomes difficult to search the new customers. Customers do not suddenly trust on them.

Uncontrolled growth

Slow and steady wins every time. Controlled and predictable growth is always superior to inconsistent one. Growing a business is good but when you are not able to handle your business growth then real problem starts from there. You must have control over your business. You must have manpower to handle the growth. It should not happen that your business is growing but profit is not coming because of mismanagement in handling the business. You may be taking loans to fulfill the growing requirement of your business but don't leverage yourself so far that if the economy stumbles, you'll be unable to pay back your loans. When you go after it all, you usually become less selective about customers and products, both of which drain profits from your company.

Putting up with inadequate management

A common problem faced by Successful companies is growing beyond management resources or skills. As the company grows, you may surpass certain individuals' ability to manage and plan. If a change becomes necessary, don't lower your standards just to fill vacant positions or to accommodate someone within your organization. Decide on the skills necessary for the position and insist the individual has them.

19.4 Troubles Faced For Business Survival

Underestimating the difficulty of starting a business is one of the biggest obstacles entrepreneurs face. However, success can be yours if you are patient, willing to work hard and take all the necessary steps.

One fact reported has been that "8 of 10 small business start-ups are no longer in existence after five years due to lack of management knowledge and skills." While no longer in existence" does not translate into "absolute failure" it appears that the "8 of 10" is extremely high. These are troubling statistics. How can you tell when your business is going to fail and make corrective action? Unable to survive business is the last stage of an organization's life cycle. Business decline, leading to failure is characterized by management who has become reactionary. The result is inadequate or nonexistent planning and inefficient decision-making.

The most common reasons for business to underperform (low productivity, low profits) or fail (bankrupt, cease being) are as follows:

- Poor cash flow management.
- Absence of performance monitoring.

- Lack of understanding or use of performance monitoring information.
- Poor debtor management. A combination of not paying your debtor on time and not coordinating payments with incoming cash flows.
- Over borrowing. The company is overleveraged and debt is not being reduced.
- Over reliance on a few key customers.
- Poor market research leading to an inaccurate understanding of the target customers wants and needs.
- Lack of financial skills and planning.
- Failure to innovate.
- Poor inventory management.
- Poor communications throughout the organization.
- Failure to recognize your own strengths and weaknesses.

Trying to do everything alone

Most of the entrepreneurs try to do all the work of the business by their own. They do not take help of others intentionally or unknowingly. If you do not take external help unknowingly then it means you do not know exactly where you should take the help of others in the business. The new entrepreneurs cannot select the valid or the expert person for their business who can help them in their business. The entrepreneurs who do not take external help intentionally may be because of two reasons the first is that they may be the expert one in their business and do need any help from the outside world. The second is they may have ego. They want to do everything by their own. They think that they are the superior ones and nobody can help them rather they can run their own business in a better way. When the entrepreneurs do not take help from the outside world whatever may be the reasons for that they cannot survive their business. In the competitive world running business alone without any help is very risky. Trying to do everything by yourself and not seeking external help. Whether this external help be as simple as hiring additional staff or going to professional services such as a lawyer, accountant, banker or business coach.

Unwillingness to take responsibility

Any entrepreneur who runs the business must have an honesty to take the responsibility of business failure. If you are trying to run your business and want to earn the profit and in case you do mistakes and because of that your business suffers then you should not blame it to others rather you must try to find out why business is not running? What mistakes you have done? If you will simply blame others for your fault then you will never learn from your mistakes and can never become a successful businessman.

Shortcomings in managerial knowledge

New businesses are more likely to go down because they lack in managerial knowledge, business knowledge and proper financial planning. In contrast, older businesses are more likely to fail because of their resistance to change. These are the conclusions of a new research paper that examines factors underlying corporate bankruptcies and compares the main causes of failure between young and old firms.

Inability to commit

In order for the business to succeed, entrepreneurs must be able to gather information, weigh the facts and then make a prompt decision. The new entrepreneurs are not capable of taking proper decisions. They are not aware about the methods of decision making. They do not know what to do before decision making. What are the factors they should consider while making the decisions? Decision making is not the simple task it requires information, survey and study and many more but the entrepreneurs lack these qualities.

No feasibility analysis

It sounds simple, but the number one reason why businesses succeed or do not survive is because the business owner did not take time to conduct a feasibility analysis, market and business plan. Why? Sometimes an idea is developed that the business owner thinks is good but no one else does. Sometimes an idea is formulated that the business owner believes is so good that the potential customers will find it themselves. And sometimes the business owner thinks that everyone is a potential customer.

Unrealistic expectations

Entrepreneurs set unrealistic expectations from the business. They just want to become a rich person within few years. They do not want to take many efforts. Entrepreneurs forgot that to get something there are steps that they should follow. They should set short term as well as long term goals and then try to achieve that .Many individuals assume not only that most businesses succeed, but that they're lucrative from the get-go. This is definitely not the case. Normally it takes at least a year to develop a profitable business. The first year's goal is usually earning back your investment. Even then, the money has to be reinvested in the business. In other words, in your first year, you should not expect income from the business rather should have other sources of income to live on.

Lack in potential

A clear and consistent finding of prior research is that firms face highest survival risk when they are young and small. But if there are factors other than liabilities of newness and smallness that contribute to firm failure, what are they and how can their influence be mitigated? From the perspective of the resource-based view of the firm, firms will not survive if they are unable to generate self-sustaining levels of organizational rents. For new businesses, the critical challenge then is to establish valuable resources and capabilities before initial asset endowments are depleted. Among older firms, which have survived the liabilities of newness, it is imperative to ensure that resources and capabilities continue to provide value as the competitive landscape changes. Thus, you should observe different causal mechanisms between businesses that fail early and those that fail at a later stage. Young failures should be attributable to inadequate resources and capabilities (relative to initial endowments). Older failures should be attributable to a mismatch between resources and capabilities and strategic industry factors.

Amount of effort exerted

Business demands efforts. If you will put your efforts then the chances of getting success are higher. But when you take efforts for your business there should be consistency in your efforts. It should not happen that some time you take efforts and some time you relax. There should not be any fluctuations in your outcomes. You must always be ready to join any meeting anywhere when that meeting benefits your business. Do not show your laziness here. You must have discipline to work independently. Because it is your business then it should not happen that you are taking decision according to your comfort. You must maintain the same work schedule of the same number of hours virtually every day even if you don't have anything scheduled. When you have your own business then you should not count your working hours. It's your business you cannot work like an employees within specific time. Entrepreneurs should be ready to work at any time for their business. You have to put in long hours and, if necessary, work weekends as well. This is especially true in the start-up stage.

Make your market niche as small as possible

Again, this is counterintuitive—shouldn't you try to appeal to as many people as possible? The paradox is that the more you try to appeal to EVERYONE, the less you will appeal to ANYONE. The entrepreneurs try to target everyone for earning money but they forget that business cannot serve to everyone's need it will create complexity and require more focus. At the initial stage, it is better to focus on the niche because you are not the experienced one nor having enough knowledge or strategy. So better to focus on your niche market otherwise business will suffer.

Lack of Planning

Another fact rarely considered is that the majority of new businesses fail within a few years mostly due simply to poor planning or no planning at all. Successful small businesses don't just happen. They are the result of intentional and well-executed business plans. Many entrepreneurs are so eager to get started that they neglect business planning and jump in headfirst with little more than a dream and an idea. That might cut it in some arenas, but not in small business. If you have already started your business and don't have a business plan, your first priority should be to get one. Fast!

They also fail to allot proper time for administrative tasks. Most new business owners assume the majority of their time will be spent on producing and marketing their product or service. Unfortunately, this isn't the case. An inordinate amount of time is spent on administration - talking on the phone, purchasing supplies and equipment, filling out government forms and taking care of other mundane duties. Internet business-to-business services are helping to cut down the time factor of some of these duties; however, it's still a relevant oversight.

Inexperienced management

The main reason for failure in survival is inexperienced management. Entrepreneurs of bankrupt firms do not have the experience, knowledge or vision to run their businesses. Even as the firm's age and management experience increases, knowledge and vision remain critical deficiencies that contribute to failure. A second key failure happens in financial management. Some of the businesses fail because they are not capable of doing the effective financial planning. Third failure happens in forming a good capital structure. They are not capable in handling the working capital because of their poor planning and most of the time they do not get on time payment from their customers. Both old and young bankrupt businesses suffer this deficiency. Many bankrupt businesses face problems in attaining financing in capital markets; but, it is the internal lack of managerial expertise in many of these businesses that prevents exploration of different financing options.

Inadequate Financing

When the people try to get fund for their business they have wrong perceptions about the funds needed to start a business. They even do not have initial amount for their business. Furthermore, a considerable number have virtually no cash or liquid assets and expect either a bank or the government agencies. In maximum cases the banks or the government are not going to help unless that person invest significant portion of his or her own funds.

Most people mistakenly think that government will provide them with 100 percent financing based solely on their good ideas. But if someone has no cash at all, it usually reflects poorly on his or her ability to manage finances -something the government takes into consideration. Funds may be derived from cash savings, personal credit lines or family loans.

Accept a customer just for the money

When you have started your business and serving the needs of a niche market then accept only those customers who are suited to your business i.e., do not accept the customers who are outside the boundary of your niche. For example if you are serving a particular segment say youths then do not focus on older one unless you establish into the business. Do not be in hurry. Taking on a client outside your niche inevitably results in frustration for you, dissatisfaction on the part of the client and in the end, usually cost you more than you make. Ask any successful business owner and they'll tell you this is true!

Assemble your support team

Look for the people who can help you in the area where you are weak or do not know anything. Some examples: bookkeeper, marketing writer, web designer. Then add the people who give you professional business advice: a lawyer, an accountant, a business coach. Finally, include the people who support you personally: your family, friends and colleagues.

Don't forget to be part of other's support teams, too. Share your expertise at Solo-E, start a networking group where business owners support each other, share a referral with a colleague. Solo Entrepreneurs supporting other Solo Entrepreneurs is what will make us all successful!

19.5 Working Capital Loans – Support to Get Success

Working capital refers to the cash requirements of a business for its day-to-day operations, or more specifically the investment required for the conversion of raw materials to finished products, which the company sells out. In academic terms, working capital is defined as the current assets minus the current liabilities of a business. It is that amount of cash flow the business requires for its daily operations. It is a measure of both a company's efficiency and its short-term financial health.

The lack of working capital and continuous cash flow leads to cash crunches for many new and small business firms. Small businesses often tend to find their current liabilities exceeding their current assets. Lack of proper working capital management often leads to trouble in paying back their creditors in short term and eventually into bankruptcy. Working capital loans are an ideal solution for small businesses, providing them a scope for rapid growth by meeting their short-term financial needs. Working capital loans are not usually for buying fixed assets and investments; instead they are used to clear up accounts payable, wages, short-term credits, advertising and other business obligations.

The lack of working capital and its proper management increases the risk of failure for many small businesses. It prevents them from growing and materializing on many available opportunities. Shortage of necessary working capital is one of the destabilizing factors for a small business. It can substantially jeopardize the regular operations due to the unavailability of essential resources in due course. Working capital loans complement the existing line of credit for the business and provide a continuous cash flow to fuel its growth. It assists the business when it needs to pay its bills and make short-term investments. Working capital loans, unlike the long-term loans, usually reach maturity within a range of one year.

Traditionally collateral was essential to acquire a working capital loan, but innovative companies have come up now with loan programs that do not require any security. There are few basic factors that these lenders look at before they will agree to lend you money for your business. Credit history is one of the primary factors that lenders look into for settling a working capital loan for a business. The business owner's vested interests and ability to repay are other factors taken into consideration by the lenders and clarified on the basis of previous financial statements. These reflect the hard work and personal financial investments along with the cash flow trends of the business.

Broadly speaking, though working capital loans are popular among small business owners unsecured business cash advance is probably a better alternative. Unlike working capital loans, the borrowers are not liable to repay any unsecured cash advance and those payments are settled against the borrower's monthly credit card sales receipts. Business cash advance has also come up big way and is definitely a better finance option for small business.

So What Could Be the Solution?

19.6 Overcoming Obstacles to Starting a Business

If you're thinking of starting a business, you're probably aware of some of the obstacles you face. But, can you overcome them? Here's a look at reasons NOT to start a business - at least if you're not capable of overcoming them with a little work and determination.

1. You Don't Have Initial Money to Start a Business

Starting a business needs at least some initial amount that you must have. You can expect that you'll have some startup expenses and that you'll need to pay estimated taxes, rents etc.

Workarounds for this Obstacle

If you have access to inexpensive credit or investors who are willing to take a chance on your business or if you have friends or significant others who can earn enough to pay your bills while you are getting your business established. You could also consider either starting your business on a part-time basis or taking a part-time job until your business is capable of providing a steady revenue stream.

2. You Dislike Taking Risks

You don't want to take risk because you are not at all ready to confront with the situation that will arise after taking risk. Remember without taking risk you cannot progress and grow your business. An entrepreneur enjoys freedom and independence when he is ready to take risk to grow and earn more profit.

Workarounds for this Obstacle

It is very hard to induce the habit of taking risk in your business. The best thing you can do is to provide some sort of safety net. Having that available should make you feel more confident and will go a long way towards reducing your stress levels. Entrepreneur should be a calculated risk taker. Doing your homework to understand what the real risks are and what their impact could be, will not only help you better prepare for them, but can also help you to better identify which risks you absolutely must avoid in your business.

3. You Lack the Self Discipline Required for a Business

Being your own boss in a business will take a tremendous amount of self-discipline on your part. There will be no one who will tell you about what to do. You will be responsible for your acts. If you will be more focused on your family members than your business and if you will try to misuse your freedom or will show any laziness then chances are very good that you will not be successful in a business.

Workarounds for this Obstacle

Prevent distractions by setting ground rules in the house. Set a schedule for your daily routine and make sure that you should give proper time to your business. Even if your clients aren't setting deadlines for you, set your own and aim to meet them every time. If you're confident you can overcome these obstacles you'll probably want to proceed with your plan. If not, maybe you should think long and hard whether a business is really for you.

4. Unaware about Kind of Business You Want

If you have decided to start a business then only you can decide what type of business you want to open. Your desire and confidence is must for opening the business. If you know you want to start a small business, but don't know what to do - wait until you've figured that out. Otherwise, you'll go from business to business and never realize success.

Workarounds for this Obstacle

You need to do some research work on the availability of the opportunities. Then you must select the one that you like and you are confident enough to handle that business. You need to have a good idea of what your passion in life is all about because if you can follow your passion, your chances for success in your business are much greater because it will drive you to do whatever is necessary to succeed.

5. You Lack the Self Confidence Needed to Run a Business

You must have trust on you if you think that you can run the business successfully. But if your faith on you is not hundred percent or if you are fearing or hesitating from inside then you are basically wasting your efforts, time and money. You should be ready to accept the customers' rejection because every time customers will not be beneficial for your business. You need to have confidence in your abilities or you won't be able to convince others to have confidence in you.

Workarounds for this Obstacle

You can create self confidence by taking the help of mentor. Entrepreneurs' mentor helps the entrepreneurs to establish the business. They show direction to the entrepreneur and helps them where the entrepreneurs are not good or having no knowledge. Sometimes a trusted partner who can help you with your small business can also get you through the rough times.

6. You don't have Enough Time to Run a Business

Starting and running a business is not a fixed time job. It almost takes your all time. You need to do a lot of things before you start a business. You cannot suddenly start the business before starting a business you need to do a research and analysis of market, competitors etc., it requires your lot of time so you should be ready to give your considerable amount of time.

Workarounds for this Obstacle

It's easy to say that we're too busy - for exercise or for operating a business. If you really want your own business you're going to have to find and make the time. See if you can get other family members or friends to help you with some of your obligations. Try to set aside specific times for your business - including the time you'll need for preparation.

19.7 Learn to Delegate Tasks

Delegating tasks and learning to let go could be the key to business growth.

Learning to delegate is an ongoing journey. Half the battle is hiring people who you feel comfortable delegating to. The other half is creating infallible work processes. Some of this simply comes down to good communication. In many small businesses, employees wear many hats. As a result, they are not always sure what their top priority should be. It's your responsibility as the boss to tell them:

- What their tasks and responsibilities are and which of them take priority over others.
- What doing a good job looks like? Don't expect workers to instinctively know; it's up to you to define and describe it. Provide good direction; be specific and give examples.
- The limits of their authority, which might include budgets, time frames and resources at their disposal.
- Reporting criteria. How often do you want to get an update? What should it include? Do you want it in writing or is a verbal report acceptable?
- Where workers stand in terms of their job performance. You can't expect people to make improvements if you don't provide feedback.

Even if you haven't created formal job descriptions and performance reviews—which many small businesses don't — you can still communicate this information to employees. But what if you don't have the right people in place and aren't comfortable delegating certain tasks? You can provide training designed to get employees' skills up to par or shuffle employee positions around. Some employees don't want the responsibility of thinking; they want to work on autopilot. Perhaps there's a place for worker bees in your organization?

If there isn't and nothing is working, you may have to take that difficult step of replacing them with people who will accept responsibility eagerly. That's leadership at its toughest. Once you put the right people, programs and processes into place, your business should practically run itself. It is at that point that you can safely disengage long enough to provide the vision essential to your company's long-term growth.

19.8 Important Learning

Anyone can fail—once. Fail twice and you transcend into a failure. In the face of failure, the only thing that matters is to live to fight another day. The tough-love survival tactics are best extracted from the lessons of failure.

Survival Matters Most

Whatever dream you have seen can never be fulfilled when your business will shut down. So first focus on how you can survive your business. Make an assessment of the current situation. Find out what is wrong about the business. We must be able to find out all the reasons about that. If the situation demands for change then do not hesitate or fear to change. If the market conditions are changed and customers need is also unique then you must be able to change. Change is very essential for the business survival. You cannot remain stick to your concept unless it has demand. We must be willing to change completely, even if the business that survives no longer resembles the business we started. We need to abandon what we hope or believe could happen—especially anything that would absolve us from the need to consider mere survival. Nothing else matters.

The "If . . . Then"

Here's an easy test to determine if you should be taking survival strategy very seriously: Have you made any of these statements for your business? "We can try out new markets for our business"." "We can focus on niche if it is not possible to cover all the customers". "We can make innovative promotional strategies to promote the products". "We can find out easy sources of finance to fulfill financial needs of the business".

If you are thinking in this way that means you are taking survival strategy very seriously.

Money Has a Strong Survival Instinct

Many times the entrepreneurs do one mistake and that is they divert the money of business to other activities and it is totally wrong. If you want to survive your business then you need to form a reserve for your business. This reserve will help your business when your business will be down. Do not use that reserve for any other purpose. Promise to yourselves that you will use that money for your business purpose only. Always remember that even investors will also do not invest in your business unless you put money from your side. So money matters for your business!

Manage Expectations—Your Own and Your Investors'

The giddiness of our expectations made considering radical changes to the business (retrenchments, cost reductions, time delays, even suspending operations in order to withstand any eventuality) a severe disappointment to the investors. But we pressed on. Besides, if we flipped it, whatever problems the business might be having would no longer be our concern.

Be Willing to Fire Yourself

We start business because we think that we have a talent, business knowledge, intelligence and experience that are the key factors for the success of business. After confirming all the success factors we have a strong belief that we can now lead the business. But mostly it does not happen. The entrepreneurs out of so many responsibilities have two main responsibilities that business management and financial management. The entrepreneurs have two roles one is of manager and second is of investor. As a manager we must be able to manage the whole human resources and non human resources. We must be able to run the business even in troubles. As an investor we must be able to fulfill the financial needs of the business. We must find out the easy and cheap sources of finance. But if you are not able to fulfill the responsibilities of these two roles then it is better to fire yourself instead of blaming others for your failure.

19.9 Role of Finance in Small Business Success

Accounting, bookkeeping, financial management, call it what you will, is more than a necessary but boring task. Money is a resource that you are using to help create your future — your many futures: next week, next month, next year, ten years from now. To the degree that you do not have control over your money, you are not controlling those futures. The future starts now, today. So the correct approach is, "Here is how much money I have. How do I use it to get where I want to be in a year?"

See? Two necessary conditions: knowing how much money you have and knowing where you want to get to. These conditions lead to the following necessary, basic rules of business finances.

(1) Keep business money separate from personal money. If you put personal money into the business, it becomes business money.

(2) Keeping the record of money coming in a business and money going out of the business is very essential. This will give a clear picture of spending and earning of the business. For one thing, it will save you a lot on taxes to have accurate records. But even more important, you will be able to accurately evaluate your progress towards the goals you have set and adjust your current actions accordingly.

(3) The first place you should look for the money to start your business is in the mirror. Most new small businesses are started using funds, at least partially, from the new owner himself. Even

if you are looking for outside investors, they will want to see that you are sharing some of the financial risk.

(4) Keeping aside money out of the profit always helps the business. You must develop the habit of doing this no matter how hard things are or how much you owe, keep a steadily growing fund and never use it for any personal purpose. This fund is not a reserve, to be used for emergencies. This fund is never used, except maybe, someday, as a down payment on a building. At that time this fund will help you.

(5) Where almost all small business owners fall down. They don't have the complete idea of using the money they have to get where they want to be. So get this straight, right now. Part of where any small business owner wants to be is solvent and you don't become solvent by spending everything you make. Always set some aside.

(6) Spend only what is absolutely needed, even if you have more cash than usual. It is very easy to splurge on new equipment or extra advertising or whatever, when the money is there. Don't do it. Spend what you need to and set the rest aside. This fund is a reserve, a temporary surplus, completely separate from your other don't-touch fund.

(7) Make tax savings your top priority in business planning. Some do only worry during tax season. However, making tax savings your priority in business planning proves to be an excellent way to save money on taxes. Better yet, plan your tax for a full year of business operation. This way, you can manage your business expenses, purchases and investments with tax savings in mind.

(8) Invest in marketing to attract clientele. Sometimes the most creative marketing ideas evolve from no budget. Effective delivery of customers is what's important — much more than any old school, often boring, marketing process. Skip the norm; go for wow.

(9) **Commit to excellence.** Whether you're cleaning houses, baking cupcakes or consulting for companies, decide you will always deliver excellent products and services with a positive attitude. This will distinguish you from most competitors.

If borrowing is necessary for some major equipment, fine, so long as the payments can be covered by the income like any other regular expense. These rules will keep any small business on the path to becoming a big one. No one can reasonably be expected to follow them all perfectly, all the time, but come as close as you can. You will find that by focusing on future income and future expenses, you will have much more control over that future, so you can make it better.

SUMMARY

When entrepreneurs want funding or raise the funds for the business, there are stages when the entrepreneurs face hardest time for different reasons - at the starting phase when the entrepreneurs start business and once they establish their business successfully.

Starting business phase

When the business is in the starting stage, there is a focused pursuit of a limited objective – may be a small project- driven by a passion to succeed and gambling everything to increase the prospects of success. They at the low level try to do their best. They have a dream to become successful entrepreneur. Some entrepreneurs mistakenly believe that their only way to succeed is to pursue some short cuts, which seem to work for some time.

Entrepreneurs' successful environment phase

The next stage when entrepreneurs work in the successful environment. Entrepreneurs go off track is when the flush of success many times powers them with a sense of invincibility.

Entrepreneurs have a taste of success and they try to neglect most of the legal needs of the business because what they think they can manipulate anything.

Association of ethics and morality with entrepreneurs' integrity

The new entrepreneurs should not go for the illegal practices while starting the business. There is though a shortcut in the business but that will not help the entrepreneurs for the long time. Somehow in the near future such kinds of entrepreneurs suffer. The entrepreneurs should be the legal one, have honesty and respect in the society.

Fears of surviving business includes Lack of commitment, Fear of accountability, Fear of failure, Fear of cost of strategic planning and Fear of discomfort and confrontation during the strategic planning process.

Following reasons can be considered for small business failure:

Choosing a business that isn't very profitable

Fear of strategic planning

Inadequate cash reserves

Fear of past experience

Failure to understand market, customers and customers' buying habits

Failure to price your product or service correctly

Fear of wastage of time

Failure to adequately anticipate cash flow

Failure to anticipate or react to competition/ technology/ other changes in the marketplace

Fear of benefits of academic theory

Overgeneralization

Fear of the facilitation process.

Overdependence on a single customer

Uncontrolled growth

Putting up with inadequate management

Troubles faced for business survival

Underestimating the difficulty of starting a business is one of the biggest obstacles entrepreneurs face. However, success can be yours if you are patient, willing to work hard and take all the necessary steps.

The most common reasons for business to underperform (low productivity, low profits) or fail (bankrupt, cease being) are as follows:

Trying to do everything alone, Unwillingness to take responsibility, Shortcomings in managerial knowledge, Inability to commit, No feasibility analysis, Unrealistic expectations, Lack in potential, Amount of effort exerted, Make your market niche as small as possible, Lack of Planning, Inexperienced management, Inadequate Financing, Accept a customer just for the money, and Assemble your support team.

Overcoming Obstacles to Starting a Business

If you're thinking of starting a business, you're probably aware of some of the obstacles you face. But, can you overcome them? Here's a look at reasons NOT to start a business - at least if you're not capable of overcoming them with a little work and determination.

You Don't Have Initial Money to Start a Business

If you have access to inexpensive credit or investors who are willing to take a chance on your business or if you have friends or significant others who can earn enough to pay your bills while you are getting your business established.

You Dislike Taking Risks

It is very hard to induce the habit of taking risk in your business. The best thing you can do is to provide some sort of safety net.

You Lack the Self Discipline Required for a Business

Prevent distractions by setting ground rules in the house. Set a schedule for your daily routine and make sure that you should give proper time to your business.

You don't have Enough Time to Run a Business

It's easy to say that we're too busy - for exercise or for operating a business. If you really want your own business you're going to have to find and make the time.

You Lack the Self Confidence Needed to Run a Business

You can create self confidence by taking the help of mentor. Entrepreneurs' mentor helps the entrepreneurs to establish the business.

Unaware about Kind of Business You Want

You need to do some research work on the availability of the opportunities. Then you must select the one that you like and you are confident enough to handle that business.

Delegating tasks and learning to let go could be the key to business growth.

Learning to delegate is an ongoing journey. Half the battle is hiring people who you feel comfortable delegating to. The other half is creating infallible work processes. Some of this simply comes down to good communication. In many small businesses, employees wear many hats. As a result, they are not always sure what their top priority should be.

Important Learning

Anyone can fail—once. Fail twice and you transcend into a failure. In the face of failure, the only thing that matters is to live to fight another day. The tough-love survival tactics are best extracted from the lessons of failure. Those tactics are Survival Matters Most; The "If . . . Then"; Money Has a Strong Survival Instinct; Manage Expectations—Your Own and Your Investors' and Be Willing to Fire Yourself.

KEYWORDS

Business ethics: Business ethics is the behavior that a business adheres to in its daily dealings with the world.

Strategic plan: A broadly-defined plan aimed at creating a desired future.

Cash reserves: A company's reserves in cash deposits or bills kept in case of urgent need.

Cash flow: Cash which comes into a company from sales (cash inflow) or the money which goes out in purchases or overhead expenditure (cash outflow).

Feasibility analysis: The process of determining whether or not a project is feasible.

Niche marketing: It is where you are marketing to a certain sector of people.

Delegation: Delegation means assigning your responsibilities.

Business *growth*: Expansion of a firm's operations from its own (internally generated) resources, without resorting to borrowing or acquisition.

QUESTIONS

1. Why do small entrepreneurs not capable of sustaining their business? Explain.
2. Why do small businesses fail? Give reasons.
3. What is the role of finance in small business success?
4. What is working capital? How it can be utilized for running business successfully?

❑ ❑ ❑

CHAPTER – 20

MARKETING OBSTACLES

LEARNING OBJECTIVES

On completion of this chapter, you should be able to:

- ☺ *Explain marketing obstacles that are faced by new small entrepreneurs.*
- ☺ *Describe barriers to entrepreneurs' entry.*
- ☺ *Describe marketing issues and challenges.*

The new small entrepreneurs open the business; collect all necessary stuff for the business. But opening business is not sufficient unless you have marketing strategies about your products and services and knowledge about marketing it in the market in such a way so that number of customers know about your products or services and try to purchase it. The new entrepreneurs lack marketing knowledge, they have very limited marketing information and in absence of any proper guidance the new entrepreneurs face the following obstacles.

20.1 Marketing Problems

Customers demand discounts

Entrepreneurs deal with the problems of where they should give discount or not. Whether this strategy will work or not? Even if they want to give discount how much discount they should give so that they can earn profit and can attract the customers the new entrepreneurs are always in confusion unless they have the supporting hands. Some entrepreneurs think that by giving the heavy discounts they will definitely attract the customers. It is true also because during financial crisis customers prefer such discounts. But there is a big problem with discounting once you drop your prices, it is nearly impossible to raise them again. Entrepreneurs must find other ways to persuade customers to buy, mainly through offering improved service. Offer customers better terms of trade (by giving them longer to pay), offer priority delivery or think about giving them a little gift with every purchase.

Understanding the customer

The entrepreneurs who open a business need not necessarily have a degree of MBA or they are from the business family. They do not know anything about the customers. They do not know strategies for the customers. They simply open the business and wait for the customers. What they think is that opening business is enough they do not know that there are still so many tasks that they have to perform for their business. But there is no one who can tell them about such things.

Poor sales executives' performances

Entrepreneurs deal with the problems of employees' performance. They are not the expert or not the HR. They try to solve problems by their own. The small entrepreneurs never keep HR person because the business is not so big. They may appoint the leader but when leader will be competent then it's okay otherwise they face the problem of employees performance. Sales environment can be very competitive and sales people can be very aggressive and clever to sell their products. But good entrepreneurs never give up and find out a way to go beyond the barriers. Entrepreneurs should go for a brainstorming session with all employees to create a sales process that everyone can do. Naturally, this should be led by your sales stars, which will hopefully pass on tips and advice to help other members of their group start climbing towards their level.

Unaware about sales process

New entrepreneurs are not aware of the sales process. They do not know different model which they can take for their own business. They just try to copy the others and want results. They do not know perfectly when the sales will increase, if increase what preparation they must do? Sales cycle (from lead generation through to client management) generally stretches out when the economy slows as customers guard their cash and it is during these times that a robust sales process becomes crucial. A sales process really needs to have three phases - a sales process for creating an opportunity; a sales process for managing opportunities; and a sales process for retaining and growing accounts won.

BOX 20

Marketing Intelligence Cell

Objective: *To collect and disseminate both domestic as well as international marketing intelligence for the benefit of MSMEs. This cell, in addition to spreading awareness about various programmes / schemes for MSMEs, will specifically maintain database and disseminate information on the following:*

- *Database of Bulk Buyers (Product wise) Buyers in Government / Public Sector Undertakings.*
- *Database of Rate Contracts of various Government Department and PSUs.*
- *Information on Tenders Floated by Government Department and PSUs.*
- *Database of Indian Exporters to various Countries with Products.*
- *Database of International Buyers with Products.*
- *Database of Technology Suppliers and Projects for MSMEs*
- *List of Micro and Small Enterprises registered with NSIC for Government Purchases, Raw Material Assistance, Performance and Credit Rating Schemes, List of MSMEs Industrial Association.*

National Small Industries Corporation (NSIC), ISO: 9001:2008 certified company and a Government of India Enterprise has been working to fulfill its mission of promoting, aiding and fostering the growth of Micro, Small and Medium Enterprises in the country. Over a period of five decades of transition, growth and development, NSIC has proved its strength within the country and abroad by promoting modernization, up gradation of technology, quality consciousness, strengthening linkages with large and medium enterprises and enhancing exports-projects and products from small industries. NSIC operates through country wide network of 123 offices and Technical Centres in the country. In addition, NSIC has 48 Training-cum-Incubation Centres with a large professional manpower; NSIC provides a package of services as per the need of MSME sector. To manage operations in African countries, NSIC operates from its office in Johannesburg, South Africa.

In stepping up its efforts to market the products of MSMEs, NSIC has set up a Specialized Marketing Intelligence Cell to collect and disseminate both domestic and international marketing intelligence in coordination with other relevant department/ agencies. This Cell provides a single point contact to collect database relating to bulk buyers in Government, Public and Private sectors, the detail of exporters, international buyers and technology suppliers. Besides, the information on trade leads and product wise buyers and sellers as well as database relating to DGS & D suppliers with prices of their products, shall also be provided by this NSIC Marketing Intelligence Cell to help MSMEs in getting appropriate information at one place and at the right time which will enable MSMEs in enhancing their ability to gauge and be at par with the global demand.

In the current era of globalization, MSMEs need marketing information about the changing pattern of fashions / tastes in the domestic and international market besides information about the trends in exports and potential for exports. These are the vital inputs for making MSMEs aware about their marketing strategy. MSMEs need to be provided with market related information, new avenues for their products, new business practices, both domestically as well as overseas. MSMEs are handicapped because of the non availability of information pertaining to Central Government / State Government policies and programmes.

Source: Information received from "NSIC".

Lack of total knowledge about business

Entrepreneurs also had a big problem - no-one in the organisation actually knew how to sell. They could work on tenders, they could manage projects, but the business just hadn't needed to be sales focused in the past. Now they needed help. Technical people do not have information about the sales marketing and in such situation they cannot move forward.

In such situation the entrepreneurs should concentrate on getting the firm's top management to understand the importance of putting sales at the centre of the firm's strategy and to demonstrate that everyone in the firm had a role in selling, from the admin staff to the accountants to the project managers. It's about getting everybody and the same page and getting everyone to understand how they engage customers.

Customers don't seem to "get"

The entrepreneurs face the problems of their identity. They do not know that in market they must first have to create their identity for what they think that customers should know them in the market. The entrepreneurs' messages about company to the customers are not clear. The customers remain confused. The message of the entrepreneurs should clearly indicate their business strengths and problem solving nature. It becomes very hard for them to create identity in the market because number of companies exists in the market. Businesses must give a clear, concise message of what exactly their business does before they can even think of making a sale.

Basic solution is that you need to have a clear marketing message of intent. What do you do? How do people understand what you do? You need to sell the right way and to do that you need to ask what it is exactly that you do for people." Being pro-active and talking to people is great, but if you're not clear about what you do then they're not going to understand.

Unclear about sales and marketing planning

Entrepreneurs are confused about from where they should start their sales marketing. They find it difficult to search for such a good place from where they can start. They open the business but about sales marketing they remain blank. They do not know what areas are profitable for them. If they do not get answer they start at random with any area. Companies cannot afford to be complacent in a downturn and must figure out a plan to survive and part of that strategy involves setting clear sales targets.

First you need to decide the numbers that you want. If you want to generate X amount of revenue then do reverse engineering decide on average sales and out of that how many sales you should generate each year, how many customers will be required by you to reach that number and how many employees you will need to accomplish the work.

Just relying on the internet is not good because number of customers in India at least do not go for internet surfing. So you must also contact the people. You need to look at details. Know what markets you need to be targeting. Who do you need to be in front of and how often do you need to do that?

Unable to take leads

Entrepreneurs do not have a proper database of their customers, suppliers or the people who interact with their business. They just maintain the data with simple word or excel files. They do not know where there is any software they can use. What is the use of database for analysis? Analysis is also major part of the business, it benefits to the business. They even do not think about that. The database helps the entrepreneurs to have a record of the customers and once they will have a database they can better serve their customers.

"Remind them that you exist. Fill them in on any new products or services you're offering. A bit of database pruning doesn't go off track, too. Get rid of the dead wood and work hard on satisfying the needs of your top 20 per cent of customers (most likely they're giving you 80 per cent of your business). Too many times you run around chasing new business and you forget about the 'gold' sitting in our databases. You assume our top customers will always be loyal and you forget to reward them for having got us where we are. They've brought us to the party; the least we can do is dance with them."

No money for sales staff incentives

Incentives motivate the people to work more. If you can give incentives to your employees for their great work then definitely their performance will improve and they will help in progress of business. But at the initial stage of the business the small entrepreneurs do not have money for incentives. Structuring the incentives for the sales executives is not easy task particularly when the market economy is not strong enough. If for small entrepreneurs it is not possible to give financial rewards then they can focus on non-financial rewards in the short term, such as flexible working arrangements or time off for a special occasion. Then, depending on whether sales targets have been made, sales staff should get financial bonuses at the end of the year.

Can't afford to carry inventory

New entrepreneurs face the problems of inventory. It becomes hard for them to bear the cost of inventory. Businesses that run with low inventories in a boom period face problems - to free up working capital, there has been a need to run down inventory levels. Of course, this creates another problem - selling stuff that you don't have is a good way to annoy customers.

To solve the problem entrepreneurs must follow the rule of 80/20. That mean you must focus on 20 per cent of products. These are the products that are valuable from the customers' point of view. You need to have these products in stock. These products will help you to generate 80 per cent of revenue. You should be able to run down inventory levels across the rest of your range.

No idea about marketing campaign

The entrepreneurs remain blank when the question comes about marketing campaign. They do not know the exact place or customers from where they can start their campaign. Brian Walker, principal and founder of retail consultancy The Retail Doctor, says the days of the mass marketing campaign are fast diminishing. For example, sending a catalogue or flyer to every home in your area just won't work - instead, you need to target your marketing to the people who you know are actually interested in your product.

He suggests any such campaign will need to be multi-disciplined; online, direct email marketing and advertisements in appropriate media. A campaign based around a loyalty or rewards type program can be particularly effective, as you can be certain you are targeting those customers who want your goods.

"It's about protecting the margin as best you can," Walker says. "Think of ways of giving them a reason to come to you."

Unsure about marketing

New entrepreneurs' first problem is that they do not know the exact marketing plan or strategy. The second problem is that they do not know the area or place of their marketing campaign. Even if they are following the marketing campaign they are not sure whether it will work or not, whether customers will come or not. They remain confused about their business and strategies. The entrepreneurs need to focus on marketing that will deliver them a solid return on investment.

In this critical time you should invest your money carefully. It's easy to not get a return on your investment and effectively waste your money, which is what you don't want to do right now when you're trying to stockpile cash. Your strategy should be such that you must get return on investment for marketing. You must give your customers a specific reason to buy. Not necessarily a discount, but points of differentiation like a special flavour for the month or a new product. Simply from a marketing perspective, it's just about being pro-active and getting out there."

Cannot afford expensive media space for marketing

For the new entrepreneurs it is very hard to get the space in the news paper as it is very costly for them. Already they lack finance for their own business in such situation they always try to save their money for some other purpose of the business. But they also want to do advertise about their business it becomes big problem for them. During a downturn, many businesses are making decisions based on fear that the economy will continue to deteriorate. But that businesses should do all they can to communicate with ad agencies to pick up good deals while the time is right?

With the decrease in advertising spend across the country, media buying costs are coming down and there are some great deals to be had. During tough times consumers are more conscious of value and tend to spend more time at home and TV spend can become increasingly effective.

You must have a good relationship with your media partners and advertising agencies; work with them for mutual benefit. If their business doesn't survive, you will be forced to find new partners, which could take significant time to get them up to speed.

Measurement of marketing campaign

The new entrepreneurs do not properly evaluate the marketing campaign. Even they do not have any effective method to judge the effectiveness of the marketing campaign. Researching is very lengthy process but it is the way to get clear idea about your marketing campaign. If your ad can attract many customers that means your marketing strategies have worked. It is different thing whether they purchase or not. It is not necessary that customers will purchase the product but what is necessary that they should at least come to your company. If customers are coming to your company it means your marketing campaign is effective. "You don't have a marketing problem, you have a selling problem. Before you run the ad again, you'd better get up to speed with sales techniques, otherwise you're going to get the same results again and again.

Not enough customers for store

The new small entrepreneurs are not capable of attracting the huge customers to their business. They open the business, hire the employees and now they think that customers will come automatically. Definitely it is right but the percentage of such customers is very less. Opening the business is not enough unless you promote your business by advertising or by promotional activities. But the fact is that small entrepreneurs cannot spend such a huge amount of money on the promotional activities. The other thing is that they do not train their employees properly to sell the products to the customers. They totally depend upon the skills of the employees to sell their products instead of giving the proper training to that employee to for selling the products. On an average just 20 per cent to 25 per cent of people who walk into a store actually buy anything and 60 per cent of transactions have no add-on component. Think on it, how can you improve it? Entrepreneurs should focus on training their staff in marketing and sales promotions. By doing this entrepreneurs will definitely get success in collecting the crowd.

Sales field just isn't working

Many entrepreneurs spend too much trying to sell a product while ignoring how a customer thinks before they buy it. Many businesses do not have knowledge of customer's need and their decision-making process - that's the most important aspect of selling. Entrepreneurs do not ask the customers what really they want. Are you satisfying the needs of the customers? What's important for the customers when they buy? They just crap on about functions and features and price, but don't really ask what is important.

Remember that a customer doesn't always know what they want. More important is the process by which they make a decision. Your fundamental need may be a phone - that's not rocket science - but the process by which they decide which phone is the key to your sales strategy."

Only attracting poor, not big customers

The new entrepreneurs are not able to distinguish between the different types of customers. Some customers are profit provider, some customers are of medium importance and some customers are not at all profitable those customers come one or two times. The entrepreneurs provide their equal time to every customer to attract them but the fact is that they waste their time by not distinguishing the customers from the poor customers. What they need to do is look at their existing customer base. So don't spend too much time on customers that aren't profitable. Just identify the customers who can generate profits for you. Remember all customers are not equal.

Customers aren't coming back

Most of the time customers do not come back. The reason is that the new entrepreneurs do not know how to handle them. When the customers they have high expectations and if at that time entrepreneurs are not able to fulfil their expectations then customers do not have any reason to come back. The entrepreneurs mostly do not satisfy the customers query properly, they lack convincing power and they do not have a skilled labour. You need to give them a reason.

Confusion about selling in a new area

When the entrepreneurs try to do a business in the new area without knowing anything about the area then they take the high risk. Without proper analysis they try to open their business in a new area. The new entrepreneurs should protect themselves from opening the business in the new area without much information.

20.2 Making A Way into New Markets

Strategies for small entrepreneurs to penetrate new markets

Small-scaled businesses may find it difficult to enter new markets where established players already exist. Here are some suggestions to overcome these barriers of entry.

A barrier of entry is defined as an obstruction that makes it difficult for a company to enter into an industry. There are several forms of entry barriers that are commonly seen in established markets. The following will provide you insights of different obstructions and solutions for small business owners to penetrate the market.

Economies of scale (high cost problem)

Without a doubt, this is a problem for small business. Larger, more established businesses enjoy economies of scale as they are able to lower their production costs just by their sheer size. Small businesses always begin operating with high costs and usually incur losses during the initial years of their operations, which may inevitably lead to their demise. The small businesses are not able to increase the size of the plant or increase the number of the products.

The new entrepreneurs suffer from this reality. The small entrepreneurs can give tough competition to the others on the bases of their quality. They are producing fewer products but if they are more focusing on the quality of the products then definitely they can compete with the big players. Small-scaled businesses can start, however, by being realistic. A prudent forecast of sales and profits will indicate a reasonable level of costs in the first few years. Purchasing only the minimum capital (physical and human) will help curb high costs. Small business owners are required to work harder during the first few years and to make more sacrifices financially to pave for success in the long-run.

High capital requirements

High capital requirements are inherent in start-up businesses. Financial resources can be a massive barrier especially if a company is reliant on expensive raw material. The new small entrepreneurs cannot purchase expensive raw material. Again, financial planning is of the essence here. Small companies have to learn to work within their means. Financing for small-scaled businesses is, however, available, but is incumbent on a strong business plan with reasonable but promising financial forecasts. Applying for a loan from a bank / corporation / consortium is possible but small companies have to ensure that they factor in the costs in repayment into their financial forecasts.

High switching costs and product differentiation

To increase customer sales, small-businesses have to win over consumers from existing providers. The small entrepreneurs face many problems like first, they have to attract the customers from existing players to their business, second they have to put all their efforts to become more competent than the existing entrepreneurs. This can be expensive for customers as they may already be comfortable with their current facilities and fees. Similarly, high-scaled branding and advertising that translates into product differentiation will entice consumers to remain with their larger providers.

Customers show less trust on the new entrepreneurs as a result of that it is not the easy job for the new entrepreneurs to attract the customers and to sustain them. So instead of focusing on the big one they should focus on the niche. A niche target market is a specific group of consumers who have a specific requirement. Small businesses by doing market analysis and R&D should come up with the products or services for the particular segment of the market and should cater their needs. For small companies it is not possible to reach to the large number of customers. Contrary to this for reputed companies it is easy to reach to the large customers and they more focus on establishing relationship with the customers. So here small businesses have a chance to concentrate on building rapport with their own niche target markets to boost their presence in the market. This allows smaller companies to demonstrate their own expertise and product branding.

Lack of access to distribution channels

Small businesses have low bargaining power and usually begin with shaky business networks. Because of this, it is easy to lose out on business opportunities to the big corporations in the market. The small new entrepreneurs are not in position to have bargain with the distributors. The cost is very high. Even if they think that few distribution channels are good for them they cannot just use it.

The new entrepreneurs can do one thing they should concentrate on few segments of the customers instead of serving all the segments of the customers. For example, for selling the chocolate they should concentrate only on kids but not youths or more. They should have a market niche. This would help eliminate the main competition with the big players in the market. The big players are serving different segments and you are serving the different segments. Alternatively, small companies can find ways to "complement" the networking channels (with their niche products and services) to increase bargaining presence in the industry.

Internet marketing is the good option. Internet marketing is the best way for the small new entrepreneurs to get to the customers. The Internet is a less costly and very effective tool in today's business world, especially where distribution channels are involved. Marketing your products or services through internet is less costly; involves user friendly technology and small business reach to billions. If the Internet marketing strategy lives with the business model, small-firm owners may quickly work their way up to larger distribution channels.

Lack of marketing new business

Many entrepreneurs have great ideas for products and services, but often they don't know how to market them. The entrepreneurs always deal with the problem of how customers will be aware of my business. The entrepreneurs have every good thing with them, they have idea and they have product or service but they lag in marketing the product or service. The most common question is: How do I create awareness, buzz and drive traffic to my business products or services? There are number of ways that can be done. There's traditional advertising promotion through newspapers, the Yellow Pages and other things of that nature.

You must surf the internet to get quality and valuable information. Consumers do not want to wait they want instant action from the company that may be related to solutions or answers. When people have high expectations from the company at that time your responsibilities are also increased. Customers need to get answers to their questions quickly. They need to know what products or services you offer, how to find them and what differentiates you from your competition.

Lack of strategies in attracting the customers

The new entrepreneurs when make the strategies they do not consider the help of their friends, relatives or neighbors for their business. They forget to consider them; the entrepreneurs should know that their business is small so they should take the help of every person who will ultimately do mouth advertising of their business. This will be the cheapest and effective source of the advertising. The first customers typically come in via word-of-mouth. It could be a referral from a friend, neighbor, colleague or other businesses owner who let people know in conversation that your business is opening. When you will actually open your business then it will be better if you will communicate the date of opening to your prospective customers. It's also a good time to consider the value of membership with your local chamber of commerce, because the chambers often promote new-business openings within their community.

Biggest challenges in landing that first customer

As a new business owner, you need to constantly promote your business or service in every available venue. The entrepreneurs think that only some places will be effective for them for advertising about the business but by doing this they reduce the probability of attracting the customers. The new entrepreneurs think that opening business in a crowded place will do everything but it is not the fact. You have limited time and often have limited funds. It would be wise to get assistance from a mentor or coach and to reach out to others who have expertise or who have been successful in opening a business previously.

If you're launching an independent consulting business, you want to target organizations of a size that would need your expertise. Make a list and start calling each one at a time. Ask for referrals from colleagues and follow up on every one. Once you get your first client, ask that person for referrals and a letter of recommendation.

Common marketing mistakes that new business owners make

No marketing plan: A marketing plan isn't just for big business, it is just as important for small businesses. In fact, it's probably more critical. So take time to write down your marketing plan for the next 12 months at least and stick to it! Not knowing target audience: Do you know who your target audience is for the products/services that you offer? Defining your target audience will give you a good idea on where to advertise/market your business. Who is responsible for marketing? Who in your business is responsible for marketing? For most small businesses it is the owner themselves. If this is the case, are you holding yourself accountable for your marketing efforts? No tracking of marketing performance: If you don't currently measure the results of your marketing campaigns then how will you know whether they were effective? Inconsistent branding: It really does add to your credibility if your branding is consistent across all areas of your business. This includes your business cards, invoices, letterhead, website, blog pages and all forms of advertising.

New business owners unclear about their customers

New entrepreneurs do not try to understand their customers but they just try to sell their products. They want customers for their products and they search for those customers but instead they can mold their product according to the need of the customers that will really help the entrepreneurs. You want to completely understand who your customers are and the need that you are fulfilling. This will allow you to provide concise and accurate information that drives the potential customer to your business. Test your marketing message on a mentor, adviser, coach or someone who you believe represents your customer base. Ask them specific questions about whether or not the message gets across.

New business and marketing

Often small-business owners are active and visible within their communities. They create positive relationships with local media. They are civically active, so that their commitment to the community shows beyond just their business. What they also do well and that's important, is developing and executing a marketing plan and monitoring their results and adjusting as necessary.

You want to play to your strengths. If that doesn't achieve the desired result, then it's certainly time to look at other opportunities and work on developing other tools, techniques and capabilities to promote your business.

Mr. Ramesh Reddy, owner of Bear shop originally attempted to market his custom-made teddy bears through local stores. When that didn't work as well as he intended, he began selling them from a push-cart in downtown. His bears then became popular and he began wholesaling them to specialty stores. He also changed his marketing materials so that they talked about the quality of the bears — how they have 14 stitches per inch. By promoting their unique traits, he differentiated his bears from all others on the market.

Marketing challenges of first-time business owners and expectation

For new business owners to be prepared, they need to include a detailed marketing plan as part of their overall business plan and strategy. The plan would consider different marketing or promotional alternatives, costs and budgets and the resulting plan would be appropriate for a business that has taken all factors into account.

A marketing plan should include a market analysis, which is an analysis of the potential customers and the area you're targeting. You want to find out who are going to be your customers, their income level and all the demographics of the surrounding area. Say you're planning to open a fine-dining establishment in a neighborhood where the average income is relatively low. Then you're opening a business that could possibly be challenged from the start. Your marketing plan also should include a good analysis of your competition. You need to research the strengths and weaknesses of your competitors and their products or services.

Then you can start developing your marketing messages. You want to base them on your analysis of your target customer and competition and consider the various delivery mechanisms, such as paid advertising, public relations and the Web.

Best way to market a new business without spending a lot

Word-of-mouth remains a good way to drive traffic, but it doesn't work by itself. You can't rely on that as your sole way of getting business. Distributing press releases about new products or services often provides quality exposure in local newspapers or other publications at low or no cost. You could write educational articles for trade journals or newspapers and make yourself available to speak at local functions, service clubs or other gatherings.

20.3 Marketing Issues for Young Progressing Business

Initial marketing focus

The new entrepreneurs do not have an experienced one who can tell them the marketing strategy. They start their marketing without any proper focus. A venture's first strategic marketing issue involves potential founders rather than customers. Without support, no company can succeed. They should start the business with the experienced person who will guide them in every area of the business.

Marketing the company vs. promoting products

The young entrepreneurs do not exactly know where to promote the company or the product. After establishing the business they suddenly go for marketing the products or services. A young unknown company has to be accepted within its marketplace before it can effectively market to targeted end-user customers. Young companies must be what they are. Not every prospect will value innovation and agility. But the right ones will.

Marketing had better feed selling

Once a young company is positioned, if its marketing program isn't specifically designed to fulfill its current sales objectives, its marketing effort should be re-evaluated. But the new entrepreneurs do not know whether they are going in the right direction or not. They lack complete skills or sometimes they do not bother to reevaluate their marketing strategies. New entrepreneurs do anything (task) for their business. They do not pay much attention to reevaluation because of lack of time. New entrepreneurs' current results can only create future possibilities.

Focus on getting marketing fund

Your business' first strategic marketing focus should not be the end user customers or attractive location rather the business focus should be to market the business to appropriate sources of funding. Your initial funding sources should be employees, relatives, family and friends, third-party angel investors, a venture capital fund, a corporate partner, a licensee or some combination of these. It is a fact that getting money is not easy for the entrepreneurs. But entrepreneurs do mistake of expecting money from the wrong sources. For example, new and small entrepreneurs cannot go to any nationalized bank for loans. The banks will not entertain them because banks do not provide loans to very small businesses. So for a young business, its first challenge is to find the sources of fund from where they can get money. The sources those are readily available to give required fund for business. They should not waste their time to get the funding from the place where they cannot get the fund.

If entrepreneurs try to compete with inadequate resources or with·resources that do not match its situation, then they will make their problems more complex. The entrepreneurs should think on that, they should first collect all the relevant resources that will form the base of their business depending on that only they can move forward.

Less importance to company promotion

In the commercial marketplace, before promoting the products or services you must promote your company name. You must tell the customers about your company. What is the purpose of your company? What is the background of your company? How do you value the customers and try to help them by your services and products? The new entrepreneurs forget that they should first promote their company. They should first earn the reputation for the company. Young ventures, especially brand-new companies, often overlook the fact that the marketplace has never heard of the company and that this can truly make a difference. For winning the trust of the customers you should assure the customers about your company. Create the image of the company. Many young entrepreneurs offer innovative product with different features, functionalities, outlooks and that to in low prices. It is good for the customers. But they suffer from only one limitation and that is their business is new and small.

To provide comfort for targeted prospects, you market company at the outset of the marketing message. Newness, innovation and the pioneering spirit are positive marketing messages. It is well-accepted that these values are more likely to be found in smaller, younger, less traditionally structured companies.

Fulfillment of the objectives of your current sales program

If you have positioned your business in the market then you must be very seriously and carefully implement your marketing strategies. Otherwise you cannot fulfill the objectives of your current sales program. Young and innovative entrepreneurs are overconfident about their products or services offerings. Such entrepreneurs think that the features and functionality of their products or services will be recognized and accepted by the customers. The fact is that though their products or services are superior but unless these provide the real benefits to the customers it is of no use. You should not be in an illusion that making the superior product will lead the sales. You have to market it in such a way that it will generate customers' needs. This should be a lesson to entrepreneurs who are now in the pre-launch or early growth stage.

When the entrepreneurs offer attractive products with many features and functionality and that too competitively priced but even after that their marketing program fail to generate actual sales? The answer is customers are not interested much in the features or the functionality of the product but they are more interested in what are the benefits they will get from it? Is that product going to satisfy their needs? If the answer is yes then only customers will purchase the products. So while marketing products you need to promote the benefits of products to the customers. Explain them how this product cares about them? How it will help them to solve their problems? And you will see your sales are increasing day by day. If you were to make modifications to improve the effectiveness of your program, what would you change? Why? Look at companies that are clearly succeeding. What do they appear to be doing right? How could you apply some of their techniques to your own company?

The peculiar marketing issue

Some enthusiastic entrepreneurs commence their business without talking to their prospective customers. They have an idea. They think that it is very attractive and demanding. They see huge profits in it and without any second thought they convert their idea into the business. They are so overconfident that they even do not care to ask customers in the market about the viability of their business idea. A niche market is not necessarily a marketing opportunity. The issue is validation.

Looking over its portfolio, one early-stage venture fund analyzed the characteristics of companies that had become successful. In all but one case, the CEO of every successful company had previously "carried a bag" (i.e., had experience in actually *calling on prospects and customers*). And in all but one case, the CEO of every successful company had actually called on deal targeted companies as a basis for creating the company's business plan and its marketing program. The information and candid feedback that can be provided by prospective customers is invaluable. Access may be easier than you might imagine. Yes, sometimes even *before* you have either a product to sell or even have formed the company.

20.4 Marketing Rules for the Encouraged Entrepreneur

The following laws will provide guidance on how to act, think and work in a slant way. You can apply these laws to all areas of your life, work and business to get bigger results from the time you invest.

Multiple rewards

Utilize your time in such a way so that you can be rewarded multiple times for your efforts and the hours invested by you. Focus on productive work and time. Package your time, efforts and knowledge into the quality product. Utilize your time properly because once time will pass it will never come again?

Mistakes are gifts

Don't disappoint with your mistakes. Mistakes are the way to learn the things. Mistakes teach us but only when you will do a deep analysis of your mistakes. Try to find out what went wrong and next time what precautions you will take. It gives you clue about your tasks, work or strategies where you have done mistakes and how to improve it. The mistakes will aware you for the future mistakes. It gives you the correct information that you should apply for the best results and next time you will see that your decision is the best one.

Know when to stop

If you are doing something wrong unknowingly or not comfortable with the present tasks then, be prepared to stop what you're doing. You should have a deadline for your every task. Try to complete those tasks on time. But if you are not capable to do it then take stop and try to do something different. Don't continue with the business otherwise you and your business will suffer. Do not involve yourselves in a single project for a long time. Make a list of all mistakes and good things that you have learned for the project. Analyze those factors and better do in near future.

Use your force

Think logically; try to get maximum from the small one. Do such an innovative work that will have a big impact. Try to use business tactics and knowledge. Try to learn from the others' success stories and take all the relevant ideas. Focus will help but there are other forms of leverage too. Here are just two. Make a communication with everyone who can help you in the business. You don't have to do it all yourself. Use your network. Ask and you shall receive. Give and you shall get.

Don't be busy - be effective

Don't waste your hours simply being "busy". Being busy does not cause you to be wealthy. So don't be busy – be effective. Involve in more productive work instead of the unproductive work. Protect yourselves from wasting the time. Remember the 80:20 rule. Typically 20 per cent of the things you do will be responsible for 80 per cent of the results you get. So focus on the 20 per cent that gets the result.

Always look for the easy route

A single task can be done in a different way. Do not immediately start your work on the task. First analyze it think on different alternatives to accomplish the tasks and then select the best one most suited for your task. You must select a best technique to run your business. Think logically while running business. Think broadly, one task can be done in different way, look that task which suits best to your business.

Measure progress by what you reap

Your success will tell you about your progress. How much efforts you will take will not matter until it will lead you towards the success. Analyze your outcomes and compare it with the inputs the output should be more than input. Measurement of the progress gives true picture of your business. Ask questions to yourselves, have I increased my customers' base? Have I increased profit? Have I grown my business? And so many questions you can ask. It tells you where you are lagging and where you are gaining strength so that accordingly you can make improvement into your business.

So What Could Be the Solution?

20.5 Top Marketing

What is marketing?

Mark Stevens: Marketing is the most misunderstood work in business; ask 100 people what marketing is and you'll get 100 different answers. You get back: advertising, websites, good service, etc. It's all of those things, but the essence of marketing is that it's the movement of the business from one level of profitable revenue to the next. Marketing has to be a driver of business growth, so if you're doing a million in revenue one year, the next year you need to be doing a million and a half and then you take it to 2 million and so on. You can't stay where you are. You need a catalyst for growth. Accounting can't drive growth, HR can't drive growth, organizational structure can't drive growth—these are all important structures, but marketing is the engine for growth. The only valid definition of marketing is the ability to take a company from one level of profitable revenue and continue to do that.

Most common misperception people have about marketing

A common misperception about marketing is that there is a single, sure-fire selling technique that will work (or is most likely to work) in every situation; this is not at all the case. Since marketing and selling are, at the most basic level, about understanding people and treating them the way they wish to be treated, the most successful salespeople will be those who adjust their technique to match the personality of the prospect. Failure to adjust your sales technique to your prospect's personality type is likely to sour your relationship and lower your chances of successfully closing.

Learning to alter your approach to sales in this manner is difficult and may initially seem counter-intuitive. Most of us have a clear idea of how we like to be treated and when we attempt to sell something to a prospect, we naturally treat them in a way that would appeal to us if we were a prospect. This works well when our communication style, personality and motivation are similar to those of the prospect; it does not work when there are fundamental differences between us.

Guidelines for creating a successful business plan

Most small-business owners really start off with the desire that they will grow something of substance; they just don't know how. It is the self-reliant kind of person who starts a business, so sometimes he takes that self reliance to extremes and doesn't delegate anything to anyone. Then he is held hostage by his own limited situation.

Very few, maybe 1 percent, really truly want to stay a small business: "I don't want any employees, I don't want any hassles and I don't want anybody to manage." That's not a small-business owner though, that's a self-employed person. If you want a business, then you do have to learn how to manage and know how to manage five, 10 or more employees. And then you should want to grow it. Because if you believe in the value of growing and you believe that your products are really superb and are better than anybody else's, you should want to grow your business and have people enjoy them far away. It's not really difficult to manage people—you have to understand leadership. It's not a popularity contest and you're going to sometimes make decisions that people will be unhappy with. If you are open to ideas from employees and listen to them and then make a decision, that's all you have to do.

A useful equation that applies to every business is "C" plus "A" plus "M" equals PG.

C=Capture Attrition happens, so you must continuously capture clients or customers.

Solution: Capture through your website, internet marketing, events, etc.

A=Amplify Once you have a relationship with a customer or client, you need to grow it. You need to cross-sell them, up-sell them enhance the relationship and get referrals. Oftentimes businesses, once they turn a prospect into a customer or client, lose the sort of lust they had when they pursued that person as a client.

Solution: Give them the same level of wonderful support you did in the beginning. Ensure that your customers know the full range of products or services offered.

M=Maintain: You maintain customers not by giving them loyalty points but by providing exceptional products and level of service.

Solution: Do things they don't expect. For example, I was at home improving when a salesperson at my favorite store drove out and brought me a royal blue sweater (my favorite color) from a designer I liked. You can't leave a business that does those kind of things for you.

PG=Perpetual Growth If you do all three things, you will have perpetual growth. The problem is businesses tend to stop doing one, two or even three of those things. How many businesses actually do these type of things? Not very many, which is good news for your business.

Grow a business using marketing

You need to contact your existing client base. It's almost free—you just send e-mails making them aware of the fact that "By the way, we have these 10 products you may not know about and because you're a good customer, if you purchase one of your regular items, we'll give you a sample of one of the other products for free." Instead of doing those things, many businesses simply advertise. The biggest argument for doing your marketing yourself is the cost. Small entrepreneurs are also finding that doing their own advertising and promotions is not only less expensive, but also much more effective. As a business owner, you know your product and your market well.

Word-of-Mouth marketing has an important role in growing business. Building trust and credibility for your product may not be addressed by advertising, even if you have the funds for it. To foster faith, your products or services must be vouched as superior, beneficial or useful by someone close to your customer or someone your customer trusts. It can come in the form of a glowing recommendation from a friend, an endorsement from a credible member of the industry or a storeowner or perhaps from family members.

Specialty marketing: Television ads can get lost in the clutter. Print ads may be forgotten after you close the magazine or publication. But your company name or ad will always be with the consumer if you emblazon or print it in a key chain, mouse pad, notepad, calculator, pens, mugs and other giveaways. Specialty advertising or promotional products represent one of the most powerful and most affordable form of marketing that every small business owner should explore.

Event marketing: Sponsoring events can turn your products into public spectacles and, as a result, transform your marketing into news events. Events help launch products, gain wider distribution, build awareness and just plain sell.

Determine the right media

In order to determine the right media to purchase there are a few questions you need to ask yourself:

What is your true message? - What exactly do you want customers to know about your business and what will be the impact of your advertising on them? Is your advertising designed to promote your business name, products or services or is it designed to bring customers to your place of business?

Who and where is your target market? - If you are selling computer equipment are your customers in city or in the village? If in the city then, TV and internet will be the best media for advertising and if customers are in village then you need to rely on news paper or radio for advertising.

Cost per thousand? - Advertising must always be an investment never an expense. Media sales people are going to talk to you in terms of cost per thousand. What you should be concerned with is *cost per customer*. How much does advertising cost to bring a target market customer into your place of business? Cost per thousand is immaterial if most of the audience is not your target market. The cost per customer would probably make this advertising too costly for a satisfactory return on your advertising investment.

How much time should a new business owner spend on marketing?

He or she should never stop thinking about marketing. The person who owns the business should always think of himself or herself as the marketer-in-chief. It should be the most important thing he or she does because it's the growth of the business; the business owner shouldn't just hand it off to other people or another firm. Someone else can do it, but the person who owns the business should always be involved.

Many new business owners are experts in their services or products but aren't well versed in marketing strategies. What to do?

They have to recognize that while they're the expert in the operations of the business—how the factory works or the retail store works—those aspects don't grow the business. You have to become a marketer. The reason small businesses fail is because they stop thinking about marketing. It's also why big businesses fail. It's why General Motors is failing now, because the senior management of General Motors stopped thinking about hybrids and creating cutting-edge cars. They just stopped doing it, whereas Toyota never stopped thinking about marketing and making products more and more appealing. A lot of small-business owners start businesses in areas of their expertise—they're IT specialists, computer fixers or chefs, for example. It's important to maintain skills as a chef, but you have got to think, how am I going to market my restaurant? Otherwise you'll be cooking for yourself.

20.6 Coupons for Attracting Buyers

Starting a business of your own is not easy but with the use of good promotion you can surely reach your goals. Promoting it using coupons will be a great start because it can easily be recognize by the buyers especially if they can save more with the discount that you offer. However, you need to study first how every procedure is being done because once you started it wrong you might lose everything. Do some research first and choose guidelines that you can use. Pick a design for your coupon that is informative and of course attractive.

Online Coupons Spur Immediate Action

Whether consumers buy in stores or online, they're researching and shopping on the internet before making a purchase. So it's no surprise that the convenience of online coupons make them popular with customers. In fact, as many as 62 percent of adults look for coupons for online stores before making a purchase, according to a Benchmark Survey on Consumer Coupon Behavior by Harris Interactive for RetailMeNot, a coupon website.

- **Send coupons by e-mail:** The advantage of internet is that no need to have physical interaction with the customers. You can directly send the coupons to the registered customers. For whatever purpose you are distributing the coupons, reward your customers with coupons immediately and increase your sales. Do not delay in rewarding the coupons. Follow the example of major retailers, such as the popular clothing chain Westside, which headlined a recent e-mail promotion, Enjoy a special 25 per cent offer from Westside to share with friends and family; four days only, Shop Now.
- **Convenient Access:** Online coupons can be easily accessed through the convenient use of internet. Coupons are being offered online through the use of company websites or coupon publishing sites. With just a click on a computer mouse, a consumer will be able to purchase items from high end sites and stores at discounted prices. For example, UPrinting discount postcards and posters can be offered through online coupons published on the company website. Online coupons for the said prints can be easily accessed through the internet.
- **Offer savings on your main web page:** when you are offering coupons online then highlight it on the main page of your website. Your offer should be strong enough to attract the customers. As customers are searching for the coupons online they should get it without any difficulty. Integrate your coupon promotion with your overall campaign by using your other marketing tactics to drive shoppers to your website in order to take advantage of your offer. You can use TV commercials featuring actress to send cost-conscious consumers to its website.
- **Post on coupon sites:** Thirty-five percent of all online adults visit coupon websites at least occasionally, according to the Harris Interactive survey. These sites are growing in popularity and while some charge for posting coupons, others are free. Most allow customers to search for savings by product category and a few, including retailmenot.com and couponcodesindia.com, help shoppers find locally available coupons. If you want to reach dedicated coupon users, evaluate the top coupon sites and test market your offers at several.

And keep in mind; it's not too late to use off-line tactics to stimulate sales. Newspaper ads—the tried and true holiday standby for many retailers—continue to perform when they carry the right coupon offer and the paper's readership closely matches the advertiser's target audience. And a coupon distributed to customers in your retail store can bring even last-minute shoppers back if the coupon remains valid until festivals. No matter how you distribute them, you can be sure customers will respond to the savings and convenience of coupons.

20.7 Creating a Marketing Plan

Firms that are successful in marketing invariably start with a marketing plan. Large companies have plans with hundreds of pages; small companies can get by with a half-dozen sheets. Put your marketing plan in a three-ring binder. Refer to it at least quarterly, but better yet monthly. Leave a tab for putting in monthly reports on sales/manufacturing; this will allow you to track performance as you follow the plan. The plan should cover one year. For small companies, this is often the best way to think about marketing. Things change, people leave, markets evolve and customers come and go. Later on create a section of your plan that addresses the medium-term future—two to four years down the road. But the bulk of your plan should focus on the coming year.

Keep your marketing plan simple**.** Many small business owners get so involved in details that they lose sight of their goals. By keeping your plan simple, you will create a clear roadmap that focuses on what you need to accomplish. Write your marketing plan down (as opposed to thinking about it and keeping it in your head). It is important to have a document that will remind you what you are trying to accomplish. A marketing plan template is an excellent place to start. Be direct and be clear. If you're not sure, ask a friend, relative, colleague or employee to read your plan. They should immediately grasp your goals. Don't build in too much flexibility**.** You may be tempted to plan for various market contingencies. If your market changes that quickly, then you should incorporate that into your plan. But create a strategy you can keep to - that's the purpose of having a plan in the first place. Review your marketing plan often - quarterly or even monthly**.** That doesn't mean you have to revise it every month. But take some time to evaluate it and make sure you're on track. Finally....never stop marketing! Once you have your plan in place, you need to take action. Commit yourself to your marketing program. Don't let yourself stagnate. Keep at it and you'll be giving your business the opportunity to flourish.

Who should see your plan? All the players in the company. Firms typically keep their marketing plans very, very private for one of two very different reasons: Either they're too skimpy and management would be embarrassed to have them see the light of day, or they're solid and packed with information . . . which would make them extremely valuable to the competition. You can't do a marketing plan without getting many people involved. No matter what your size, get feedback from all parts of your company. This is especially important because it will take all aspects of your company to make your marketing plan work.

A marketing plan, as a stand-alone plan outside of the business plan, is normally developed and implemented by managers or teams that have marketing-only responsibility. It doesn't deal with the overall financial health of the business or other important elements like production, administration, product development and cash flow. The business plan is about the whole business, while the marketing plan is just about the marketing and sales. So which comes first depends a lot on context. A lot of people develop the marketing plan first but only as the key driver for the complete business plan, not as a separate plan. A marketing person will develop the marketing portion first, while a finance specialist might not. A separate stand-alone marketing plan is usually something that emerges as a need after a company is already started and has a team in place. And if it isn't very carefully synchronized with the business plan, there will be problems.

Effective marketing, planning and promotion begin with current information about the marketplace. Do your research: Look on the Internet, talk to customers, study the advertising of other businesses in your community and consult with any relevant industry associations. Once you have all the necessary information, take these steps for writing your plan.

1. Introduction

The plan is designed to provide the reader with the necessary information to fully understand the following:

- Purpose of the Marketing Plan
- Organization Mission Statement
- Organizational background information

2. Define Your Business

- What is your product or service? Describe attributes, pricing, distribution and promotion.
- What is the target market? Are you targeting one town, a region or a national audience?
- Who are your distributors? Describe channels, purchase process and demographics.
- Who are your competitors? Describe direct competitor, strength and weakness and competitive trends.
- How do you differentiate from the other competitors?
- What price will you be asking for your service or products?
- How does the competition promote itself?
- What is your financial condition? Describe current sales analysis and profitability analysis.
- How will you promote your business?
- What is the impact of external forces? Describe social-cultural, economic, political and technical forces.
- Where will you set up your business?
- How will you distribute products?

3. Marketing Strategies and Objectives

- What is your marketing strategy? Describe market growth, market stability, cost control and market exit.
- What are your financial objectives? Describe customers' sales, channel sales, margins and profitability.
- What are your marketing objectives? Describe market share, customers, promotional objectives, channel objectives, market research and R & D objectives.

4. Define Your Customers

- What is your current customer base? Think about it in terms of age, sex, income and geographic location.
- How will your customers get information about your product or service? Will it be by print, TV, radio, Internet? Word-of-mouth? Event marketing?
- What is the buying behaviour of your customers? Where they shop, what they like, watch, listen to?
- What are the qualities, your customers want to see in your product or service? Selection, handiness, service, reliability, availability, durability?
- What features about your product or service do you need to improve to better serve the customers?
- What are your prospective customers? How will you reach them?

5. Tactical Marketing Programs

Details and timetables are presented for six key decision areas:

- Who are your target markets? Describe target market tactics.
- What is your product? Consider all aspects of product decisions (branding, labeling and packaging) and not just the product itself.
- What is your promotion strategy? Promotion consists of four major areas – advertising, sales promotion, public relations and personal selling – though not all may be used.
- What is product pricing? Describe discounting and payment terms.
- What is your distribution channel? Describe tactical decisions regarding Types of channels used, Level of market coverage, Outlets handling product, Perceived product positioning, Distribution costs and Identify planned changes.

6. Define Your Plan and Budget

- What are the previous marketing techniques you have used to communicate to your customers?
- What methods have been most effective?
- What are your costs compared to sales?
- What is your cost per customer?
- What marketing methods will you use to attract new customers?
- What percentage of profits can you allocate to your marketing campaign?
- What marketing tools can you implement within your budget? Newspapers, magazines, Internet, direct mail, telemarketing, community outreach, sponsorships?
- What methods are you using to test your marketing ideas?
- What methods are you using to measure results of your marketing campaign?

20.8 Exposing Products to a Trade Show

Trade shows offer inventors and entrepreneurs the opportunity to reach a large number of potential buyers and retailers. You'll meet buyers seeking products like yours and even if you don't make a sale on the spot, your presence creates awareness about your product. So, you've taken the plunge and decided to exhibit your invention or new product idea at a tradeshow. What's next? How do you prepare? How can you optimize your time at the show? Here are guidelines to help you maximize your experience.

Here are some strategies for maximizing your trade show experience:

Decoration of Booth

While the decoration and styling of the booth is important, make sure that you do not overdo it. The booth should be designed in such a manner that while it manages to attract footfalls, it does not take away the focus away from your products. So, instead of pasting posters and pictures on the walls, just go for smartly coordinated solid colors that look stylish and attractive.

Find Shows That Fit

The most important thing you can do before attending a trade show is to make sure you choose the right one. You need to make the most of your time and money and a poor choice can be a waste of both. Be sure to make your choice based on the potential returns. To choose appropriate trade shows, consider the following:

- **Ask your best customers (or target customers) which trade shows they attend:** For example, if your best customer is a locally owned house wares store, ask the owner which trade show she attends to choose her products. Chances are, there'll be other buyers like her there from around the region or country interested in your product, too.
- **Consider cost:** Smaller, regional shows are often less expensive than larger, national ones. Your booth rental can cost anywhere from hundreds to thousands of rupees, depending on the show. When you consider the time and preparation involved, a bigger, more costly show may be a better investment.
- **Examine the nature of the attendees:** Some shows, for instance, may be dominated by buyers who represent regional or independent stores, while others may be mainly attended by mass retailers. Still others will target niche buyers like grocery or drug-stores. Be sure your product is a potential match for the buyers who'll be attending.

Find Ways to Maintain Contact

Don't throw those business cards away. Find reasons to periodically stay in touch with contacts you feel may be relevant. Let contacts know you're exhibiting at a trade show. Let them know when you've made changes/improvements to your invention. But don't inundate them with letters and phone calls. The idea is to keep your new product idea in their minds, not to pester anyone to the point of alienating them. During the tradeshow, network with other exhibitors, listen to feedback and remember what you liked or didn't like about other booth displays. Don't be so involved in putting your idea out there that you forget to do some information gathering and learning.

The location of your booth can also be critical to your success. When registering to exhibit, get a map of the show layout to choose your preferred locations. Here are a few things to remember when scouting your site:

- Locations near the main entry are typically highly desired.
- People tend to veer right after entering rooms.
- A corner location can benefit from traffic coming from multiple directions.
- You can request placement near specific vendors at some shows. Avoid being placed near a huge booth that will dwarf yours, near direct competitors or at dead-end points in the traffic pattern.

Working the Show

A few weeks before a trade show, you can start creating some pre-show buzz. Send a letter or postcard to key prospective customers to let them know you'll be at the show. Include your booth number and information on what you'll be exhibiting. Also, consider including a promotional element to entice them to come visit your booth—a drawing for a prize or a small giveaway to all visitors.

Once you're at the trade show, make the most of your time. Engage with potential buyers as they pass by. Another way of attracting visitors is by hiring models and professionals to advertise your product through live presentations and talks at your booth. If the person you hire is good enough at his or her job, then large number of footfalls at your stall is almost guaranteed.

Tools of the Trade

Remember to bring these key items to the show:

- Receipt book
- Order forms
- Stapler
- Organizer or folder for orders

- Product sell sheets
- Business cards
- Product samples
- A bowl of candy to entice people to stop
- A promotional giveaway, usually a small, inexpensive item with your logo
- Supplies including packing tape, scissors, pens, a dolly and a small broom

Here are some good trade show tips anyone can use to get the most out a trade show:

(1) Don't sit.
(2) Avoid chatting with your other staff or co-workers.
(3) Live by the 80/20 rule.
(4) Train your trade show team.
(5) Call them while they're hot.
(6) Offer some booth love.
(7) Always be on.

Can't-Miss Guidelines

We've also learned a few additional lessons along the way about dos and don'ts for exhibiting at a trade show.

- Wear comfortable shoes. The high-heeled may look fantastic, but your look of anguish at the end of the day will surely undermine your sales efforts.
- Bring someone along so your booth is never unattended. Take occasional breaks to walk around the show and regain your energy.
- Don't eat in your booth.
- Try not to chat too much with your booth neighbors, especially when they're speaking to potential buyers.
- Identifying new products helps stop prospects. The word "new" stops the viewer's eye and creates a double-take. The prospect is challenged by the word new and wants to investigate.
- Consider doing a prize drawing giveaway. Think of what's hot and what people would want to win and consider your audience. Giveaways to bring home to the kids are always popular.
- Look into travel deals negotiated by the trade show for hotels, car rentals and airlines. Then search on your own for potentially better deals through discount travel sites.
- Round tables are better than square counters. Square and rectangular shapes create the impression that the visitor should stand on one side and the seller on the opposite. They serve as a barrier and reduce the quality of interaction. Round shapes eliminate the perception of positioning and create a more friendly side-by-side conversation with the visitor.

Keep it in Perspective

While trade shows can be a great way to make sales, be sure to set realistic expectations. A trade show should be one component of your overall sales plan. In other words, don't expect to make your entire investment back at your first show. In addition to potential sales, remember to value what else you can gain by exhibiting at a trade show — new contacts, industry knowledge, feedback about your product and product and brand awareness.

20.9 Small Business Promotion

Don't Advertise Like a Big Business

Copying a big business will be a mistake. Big businesses advertise to create name recognition, earn reputation and future sales. A small business can't afford to do that as it needs huge money. You must design your own advertising for selling products and making your customers aware about your products. One way to accomplish this is to always include an offer in your advertising - and an easy way for prospective customers to respond to it.

Offer a Cheaper Version

It is not always possible that the prospective customers will be able to pay your product or service price. Some customers are ready to pay low price for low quality product. If you will not sell products to those customers that means you are losing your customers and that is not beneficial for your business. You can avoid losing sales to many of these customers by offering a smaller or stripped down version of your product or service at a lower price.

Offer a Premium Version

Contrary to the above point not all customers are looking for a cheap price or low quality product. Most of the customers are ready to pay any price of the product if they get quality product. You can boost your average size sale and your total revenue by offering a more comprehensive product or service ...or by combining several products or services in a special premium package offer for a higher price.

Try Some Unusual Marketing Methods

Look for some unconventional marketing methods your competitors are overlooking. You may discover some highly profitable ways to generate sales and avoid competition. For example, print your best small ad on a postcard and mail it to prospects in your targeted market. A small ad on a postcard can drive a high volume of traffic to your website or generate a flood of sales leads for a very small cost.

Trim Your Ads

Reduce the size of your ads so you can run more ads for the same cost. You may even be surprised to find that some of your short ads generate a better response than their longer versions.

Focus your marketing efforts. Sending a postcard to 10,000 people in your city (I get plenty of these, believe me!) is not a useful strategy unless you know that those individuals may clearly have a need for what you do. Most small businesses have a focused niche and they need to create mechanisms to reach their target customers efficiently, not spend money on broad-based advertising or mailings.

Set up Joint Promotions with Other Small Businesses

Joint promotion for small business is a good idea. If you are not capable of promoting your product alone then joint promotion will help you to promote your product. The advantage here is that the probability of product sales increases. Customers get something extra apart from your single product or service. Contact some non-competing small businesses serving customers in your market. You can offer to publicize each other products or services to your customers. This usually produces a large number of sales for a very low cost.

Offer an Assessment

An assessment is an excellent way to engage prospective customers in a way that doesn't feel like selling and is value-added. It could be as simple as a questionnaire that you score and interpret, to an on-site, half-day working session to assess their needs and come up with the outline of a solution. You can charge for the assessment (people value what they pay for more than something that is free!), offer it for nothing, or refund the price if the customer goes ahead with a purchase.

Show Customers Why They Should Keep Doing Business with You

Just because someone has bought from you in the past does not mean they will continue to do so in the future. In today's business climate you need to constantly prove to your existing customers why it makes sense to continue buying your product/service. What can you do to reinforce this to your customers?

Take Advantage of Your Customers

Your customers already know and trust you. It's easier to get more business from them than to get any business from somebody who never bought from you. Take advantage of this by creating some special deals just for your existing customers ...and announce new products and services to them before you announce them to the general market.

Also, convert your customers into publicity agents for your business. Develop an incentive for them to tell associates and friends about the value of your products or services. An endorsement from them is more effective than any amount of advertising - and it is much cheaper.

Offer extended support and service

This is important. People are sometimes impulsive and need to be reassured about their purchase. Most big-box sales are final with limited exception for refunds. You could instill more trust in your prospects by having a favorable guarantee policy. Perhaps your product requires support – offer extended or premium support. The name of the game is to bundle it with your service, not bend them over a barrel when they purchase.

Summary

The new small entrepreneurs open the business; collect all necessary stuff for the business. But opening business is not sufficient unless you have marketing strategies about your products and services and knowledge about marketing it in the market in such a way so that number of customers know about your products or services and try to purchase it.

Marketing problems faced by the new entrepreneurs are as follows:

Customers demand discounts

Understanding the customer

Poor sales executives' performances

Unaware about sales process

Lack of total knowledge about business

Customers don't seem to "get"

Unclear about sales and marketing planning

Unable to take leads

No money for sales staff incentives

Can't afford to carry inventory

No idea about marketing campaign

Unsure about marketing

Cannot afford expensive media space for marketing

Measurement of marketing campaign

Not enough customers for store

Sales field just isn't working

Only attracting poor, not big customers

Customers aren't coming back

Confusion about selling in a new area

Making a way into new markets for entrepreneurs' involves the following:

Strategies for small entrepreneurs to penetrate new markets

Economies of scale (high cost problem)

High capital requirements

High switching costs and product differentiation

Lack of access to distribution channels

Lack of marketing new business

Lack of strategies in attracting the customers

Biggest challenges in landing that first customer

Common marketing mistakes that new business owners make

New business owners unclear about their customers

New business and marketing

Marketing challenges of first-time business owners and expectation

Best way to market a new business without spending a lot

Marketing issues for young progressing business are:

Initial marketing focus

Marketing the company vs. promoting products

Marketing had better feed selling

Focus on getting marketing fund

Less importance to company promotion

Fulfillment of the objectives of your current sales program

The peculiar marketing issue

Marketing rules for the encouraged entrepreneur are Multiple rewards, Mistakes are gifts, Know when to stop, Use your force, Don't be busy - be effective, Always look for the easy route and Measure progress by what you reap.

A useful equation that applies to every business is "C" plus "A" plus "M" equals PG.

PG=Perpetual Growth, If you do all three things, you will have perpetual growth.

M=Maintain, You maintain customers not by giving them loyalty points but by providing exceptional products and level of service.

C=Capture, Attrition happens, so you must continuously capture clients or customers.

A=Amplify, Once you have a relationship with a customer or client, you need to grow it. You need to cross-sell them, up-sell them enhance the relationship and get referrals.

Online Coupons Spur Immediate Action

Whether consumers buy in stores or online, they're researching and shopping on the internet before making a purchase. So it's no surprise that the convenience of online coupons make them popular with customers.

Send coupons by e-mail: Customers who've registered to receive your e-mails are your best prospects. Reward them—and win immediate sales—by e-mailing coupons for online and off-line savings.

Offer savings on your main web page: With consumers scrutinizing every purchase, they're visiting more websites and spending less time per page than ever before. That means your main page has to grab and hold them with a strong coupon offer.

Post on coupon sites: Thirty-five percent of all online adults visit coupon websites at least occasionally, according to the Harris Interactive survey. These sites are growing in popularity and while some charge for posting coupons, others are free.

Marketing Plan

Firms that are successful in marketing invariably start with a marketing plan. Large companies have plans with hundreds of pages; small companies can get by with a half-dozen sheets. Put your marketing plan in a three-ring binder. Refer to it at least quarterly, but better yet monthly. Leave a tab for putting in monthly reports on sales/manufacturing; this will allow you to track performance as you follow the plan. The plan should cover one year.

Marketing Plan provides you with several major benefits.

Steps for writting marketing plan arel introduction, Define your business, mkting startegies subjectives, define your customers, bactical mkting programs and Define your plan and budget.

Here are some strategies for maximizing your trade show experience:

Decoration of Booth, Find Shows That Fit, Ask your best customers, Consider cost, **Examine** the nature of the attendees, **Find Ways to Maintain Contact,** Working the Show, Collect tools of the Trade, Can't-Miss Guidelines, and Keep it in Perspective.

Small business promotion guidelines:

Don't Advertise Like a Big Business

Offer a Cheaper Version

Offer a Premium Version

Try Some Unusual Marketing Methods

Trim Your Ads

Focus your marketing efforts

Set up Joint Promotions with Other Small Businesses

Offer an Assessment

Show Customers Why They Should Keep Doing Business with You

Take Advantage of Your Customers

Offer extended support and service

Keywords

Market: A market is a place which allows the purchaser and the seller to invent and gather information and let them carry out exchange of various products and services.

Marketing: *Marketing* is finding out what people want, why they want it and how much.

Marketing plan: A marketing plan outlines the specific actions you intend to carry out to interest potential customers.

***Sales process*:** *Sales process* refers to a systematic process of repetitive and measurable milestones.

Marketing campaign: A document or presentation that outlines your targeted demographic, how you plan to reach them and how much it will cost.

***Economies of scale*:** The decrease in unit cost of a product or service resulting from large-scale operations, as in mass.

***Switching costs*:** *Switching costs* are costs that occur when switching suppliers, brands, products or into a new marketplace.

Sales promotions: Sales promotions are designed to increase consumer demand, stimulate market demand or improve product availability for a limited time.

Public relations: The practice of managing the flow of information between an organization and its audiences.

***Coupon*:** A *coupon* is a ticket or document that can be exchanged for a financial discount or rebate when purchasing a *product*.

Questions

1. What are the marketing problems of small entrepreneurs?
2. What are the marketing issues for young progressing business?
3. What do you mean by marketing plan? What are its contents?
4. How do entrepreneurs utilize trade show for promoting their products?
5. What are the strategies of small business promotion?

❑ ❑ ❑

CHAPTER – 21

PROFIT EARNING OBSTACLES

LEARNING OBJECTIVES

On completion of this chapter, you should be able to:

☺ *Explain what are the different obstacles faced by new small entrepreneurs in earning profit.*

☺ *Describe obstacles to success in business*

21.1 Critical Situation to Profitability

If you take time to make some profitability predictions – you have to know where "there" is before you can get there - about when you'll break even and become profitable, you can let go of some of that cash-strapped anxiety and focus on actually starting a business.

Most of the entrepreneurs in India go to business because they want to earn the profit. But profit making is not so easy to the small new entrepreneurs. Many requirements are there that the entrepreneurs have to fulfill and for that they must have money.

Improper cash to start business

The new entrepreneurs' problems are always the cash. If they want to earn the profit then they have to invest money in the business. They have an idea they have plan but they do not have money to implement the plan in reality and to earn money. The new entrepreneurs always struggle for the money. The money restricts them to take a risk where they think they can earn profit but because of less money they are not ready to take any risks. Sometimes they do wrong projection of money with respect to the business. They invest whole money before fulfilling the requirements of the business. But, seriously, before you can put together your cash flow projection, you'll need to know how much money you have to start and operate your business.

Making money in business

The new entrepreneurs just start the business but they lag in doing proper planning regarding how to earn the profit. They lag in interaction with the different people who are really important for the progress of the business and to earn profit. Sometimes others do not entertain them properly and do not show trust also. They are new so they cannot take advantage by reducing the cost of their services or product. They cannot take the advantage of suppliers or customers. If you want to make money then you must do some market research and competitive analysis to understand the growth potential of your business. By analyzing the pricing of others' products or services in the market you should set such a price of your products/services so that you can grab the opportunities in the market.

Lack in business tactics

Entrepreneurs must know the business tactics to earn the profit. They should come up with the creative ideas it is not necessary that every creative idea will need money. Some ideas even require less money and are more profitable. For example instead of customers coming to you, you can go to the customers. Have you thought about the timing of your revenue opportunity? You must use every possible tools of marketing to grow business. For example you can use discounts, coupons, demo, contest, free samples many more and then you would be in a position to estimate the month-by-month revenue of your business.

Way of spending money on business

Running the business requires at least initial amount, too, so your next step is to take a look at your expenses. The new entrepreneurs are not able to calculate the exact expenses on business. They spend money whenever they need to spend. They do not have any plan to spend money. Even most of the entrepreneurs record expenses in mind only. They do not write down all the expenses and therefore they do not have a proper understanding of their expenditure. Spending money on the business requires logic and strategies. You must have clear picture in mind how you are going to spend money on the bushiness. Invest where it is necessary. Do not invest at once; try to take credit so that you can use rest of the money with you for some other work. Think about

BOX 21

Development through Clustering

Across the globe in at least fifty developed and transition economies, the Micro, Small and Medium Enterprises (MSMEs) producing same or similar range of products have often been found to naturally co-exist in typical geographical locations – "clusters".

While clusters have benefited from natural external economies; only those have excelled, where firms have gone for promotion of selective "active cooperation" or "targeted joint action" and also taken the benefits of linking to winner value chain within and outside the cluster. As a result, clusters worldwide are being acknowledged as a strategic mechanism through which the regions and nations can attain higher level of industrial development.

International experience has proven that clustering and networking of enterprises helps enhance economic growth and encourage technical progress among MSMEs. Research studies on clusters suggest that the competitiveness advantages of MSMEs grouped in clusters, are based on the three aspects: specialization, cooperation and flexibility. Many of the cluster stories indicate a strong networking between large firms and small firms and the proximity to raw materials and business clients.

As per the current estimates there are about 6500 clusters in India and about 80 per cent of the goods / services are being produced by these clusters. Development of these clusters will have an impact on both employment as well as poverty alleviation. The Ministry of Micro, Small and Medium Enterprises (MSME), Government of India (GoI) has adopted the cluster approach as a key strategy for enhancing the productivity and competitiveness as well as capacity building of micro and small enterprises and their collectives. In this context, a scheme "Upgradation of Technology and Management Programme (UPTECH)" was launched in 1998.

What is Cluster

Clusters can be defined as sectoral and geographical concentration of enterprises of clusters in particular Micro, Small and Medium Enterprises (MSME) facing common opportunities and threats.

Hence a cluster can be defined as a group of companies who partner together for the purpose of improving their performance through mutual learning and sharing.

Source: Information received from "MSME".

exactly when payment is due for each expense - you're not doing yourself any favours by paying bills before they're due, since that money could be sitting in your bank account working for you by accruing interest.

Cash shortages during months with negative cash flow

You must have a plan for backup for those months when you know you're going to come up short. New entrepreneurs are not ready to face such situation. They do not have any plan what they will do after six months when there will be no season of business. They live in current environment only, current market and with current competitors only. They do not have any alternate plan; if business passes through 'X' direction then is there any 'Y' direction as an alternate plan. Measuring profitability is all about planning and you may have already lined up a wealthy friend or family member to provide a short-term loan or have credit cards or home equity for financing on an as-needed basis. Or maybe you still have savings that you've set aside as operating capital. No matter what the source, make sure you can spell out where you'll be getting that extra cash from and how much is available to you. The main thing is that you must continue your business.

Put it all together for profitability measurement and use it wisely!

Entrepreneurs must know about cash management. If entrepreneurs will not go through cash management thoroughly then they will not have proper information about how to utilize cash, when to take a loan. Cash Management Report might look scary to your non-financial types, but it's built around a relatively simple process - you enter the numbers you collected through your research, the formulas and linkages in the Excel workbook work their magic. You see a final report that has incorporated all of your hard work into a two–year cash flow forecast for your new business.

Accurate cost calculation of the required items in your business is very necessary otherwise proper estimation could not have been possible. Just do not rely only on cash management report you should put an accounting system in place in addition to this document. If you feel uncomfortable then you can take the help of any accountant.

Cash management is strategic report, utilize it simultaneously with your business plan. It should be a star by which you steer your financial ship, but it's highly likely that you'll see some differences between it and your actual revenues and expenses. To make sure you get the most value out of it, compare your actual expenses and revenues to it on a monthly basis. Look for differences between the two reports and figure out how to correct or "balance" them, just as you would with your cheque book. That's how you'll figure out how to apply your cash reserves to cover any shortages.

Knowing what makes a business profitable

The main thing for entrepreneurs is when their business will begin to earn profit? Every entrepreneur will have different answer for it but profitability measurement is as clear as knowing when your business has more cash coming in than going out in a given month.

The new entrepreneurs know only that their customers will give them profit. They will sell the products or services and earn the profit. But they do not know, there are few factors that are responsible to earn the profit. For example planning, promotion, best services etc., they do not know, if they want to earn the profit then they themselves have to get to the customers ask them about their needs and accordingly serve them. They never do prediction about what will happen in the future from where profit will come. Who will be responsible for earning the profit?

Some businesses are more seasonal and might therefore experience profitability at certain times of year (such as a landscaping or pool-cleaning business in the summer) and experience a negative or break-even cash flow at other times of the year. Before entering into the business you must know whether your business is the all time business or the seasonal one and what is your planning about the months when there will be no business?

But if you know what could happen in tough months then you can manage the tough months from the wealth of good months for e.g., increasing the hotel room rate located in hill stations in summer seasons. Your focus should be to earn more in seasons to compensate off-seasons. Even by taking more efforts you can turn your tough months into the good months by generating interest of the customers during non seasonal period. To generate need about cold drinks in winter, try to give your customers additional value apart from normal cold drinks. You can give them cold drink having medicinal qualities or enrich it with nutrition or try to give them flavours that are available in winter only.

Finally even if you are not sure what to do then it is better to make contact with the established and experienced business owners in your field. Ask them what they have done in the same situation? Gain their knowledge of handling the business in non season. What are the different strategies they have used for surviving the business? For example the hotels in cold places lower their room fare to attract customers and they get success also. That will help the business to know the hidden things and prepare according to the challenges you will face. It's very dangerous to guess about these things, so don't be shy when it comes to profitability measurement - do your homework and planning.

Delay in payment by customers

New entrepreneurs have fewer customers as compared to the old one. They earn their profit from those customers only. At the initial stage the entrepreneurs try to give better services to those customers because they want to win the trust of their customers but here they have problems. They already have fewer customers and in such cases, they become dependent to their customers and if customers do not pay money instantly or after some days then it affects their business. They cannot move forward without getting the required money to run the business.

Dependency on customers

The new entrepreneurs have complete dependency on customers for their profit. For example the new entrepreneurs are selling their products to other business. It is very difficult for the new entrepreneurs to get customers and once they get customers they cannot easily leave them. They want to have a strong relationship with the customers and therefore they are ready to bear any difficulties. As soon as they sell their products to other business, the other business is always in dominant position. So they start utilizing the new entrepreneurs business for their own purpose. For example dominant business does not make payment on time to new entrepreneurs, gives less payment and does not treat them well also. New entrepreneurs are not in a position to have an argument with dominant business. Otherwise their relationship with dominant business will break and therefore they do not want to take any risk. But the fact is that the new entrepreneurs suffer a lot; they suffer from low income and delay in payment. As a result of that, their business progress becomes slow.

21.2 Obstacles to Success in the Business

When the entrepreneurs got land in the commercial area then they start their business from there only. They do not go for the separate business land. A number of home-based entrepreneurs earn as much as 10,000 - 30,000 per month in their business. They're living their dreams — traveling the globe, spending time with family and friends and contributing to worthwhile causes. You can too.

The journey from start-up to achievement in business, however, is not always smooth playing. Like a seasoned mariner, you must identify the obstructions along the way and know how to navigate your business around them — otherwise you risk sinking your hopes for financial freedom. What are some of the obstacles that could threaten your success in business?

Unclear vision

What is your dream about your business? Where do you want to take your business? If you don't know your final destination— the ultimate objective of your business – how can you judge yourselves about your progress? You should at least have an approximate estimation of your business. You could stay busy in managing the resources and still take your business nowhere.

The new entrepreneurs lack vision. They do not have any destination where they want to reach. They have only one vision to sell products or services and earn money. For example, they do not think about becoming number one in local area or city. Unless they promise themselves where they want to reach, they will run business but they cannot expand their business.

Define and visualize "success" in terms of your business. What does your destination look like? Instead of saying, "I want to earn more than I am right now and travel more often," say, "I will earn 40,000 a month within one year and buy a land in three years." The more apparent and perfect your goal, the more likely you'll achieve it. Therefore set targets to achieve your goals. Start planning from single day. At the end of everyday figure out, are you following your plan and reaching to your target?

No plan

Without proper planning profit is not possible. The new entrepreneurs' problem is that they never do any planning for the business in terms of profit. If you will wake up in the morning then you should know what your today's tasks are. A business revolves around customers. For attracting the customers requires strategy. The strategy should be planned and applied in a logical way. Without plan you do not know what to do next. You cannot measure your business, your performance. Once you will have the plan you will have the accountability. You will know the tasks and responsibilities to perform. Without a plan, you could not set clear and challenging goals. Outline the practical steps necessary to achieve your objective. What can you do today to move your business forward? Remember, a dream without a plan will remain unfulfilled.

Discouraging influences

When the people in your surrounding don't have knowledge what you do may ask, "When will you get a job? Don't disappoint from such discouraging remarks. Be focused on your work. They are enough to break your enthusiasm. Interact with the people who have knowledge, interest and ready to help you in your business. Make a friendship with positive attitude people. You will be benefited by their attitude, perception and thinking power. You will get more insight about your business. The lone person suffers from limited knowledge. You should share knowledge with the people you think will help you in your business. You can get idea from others also that will be beneficial for you and ultimately it will help to earn more profit in your business.

Lack of knowledge

Many entrepreneurs don't take their businesses seriously. As a result they give up; failing to achieve the wealth they had been seeking. As Leonard W. Clements, in his book *Inside Network Marketing* writes, "So many distributors work the business wrong, then claim the business is wrong when it doesn't work."

The entrepreneurs must have full knowledge of the business. They should gain every minute to big information about the business they are doing. The cannot earn the profit when they know very less about their business. For example if the entrepreneurs want to open a restaurant they should know from where they can get grains, wheat or rice in less price after that only they can manipulate their profit. They cannot be dependent on the single one for their business. The problem of the new entrepreneurs is, they start their business with little knowledge and then they suffer.

Fear of rejection

This is the most difficult obstacle to overcome. It keeps you from making business-building phone calls, going to networking meetings or sharing your products and services with someone who needs them. If you stop with the fear that people will reject you then you cannot progress. You should not fear to do any experiment with your business. If you think you can get your customers from bank, offices or colleges then do not hesitate or fear what they will say because they will provide you profit. With fear of rejection you will lose the opportunity to earn profit. Just go and talk about your business. Assure them how you are going to satisfy the requirements of their organization. Explain them about your skills and expertise. Rejection should not be the question but instead you should continue with your mission.

Inadequate training and support

Mostly the new entrepreneurs are not trained in the business nor are they from the business family background. They do not get the logic of business easily. Some entrepreneurs give up because they feel isolated and lack consistence, accountability and training. These individuals, after few months of minimal profit in the business, figure that business is not for them and quit. They are confident enough that business is not for them. They feel very nervous. The entrepreneurs must take proper training or at least suggestions from the experienced one to get in deep knowledge. After that they will learn to earn the profit. This creates a win-win relationship for everyone.

Short-term mentality

Narrow thinking of the entrepreneurs hampers their business profit. When they become satisfied with the current customers or with the current earnings then they cannot go beyond certain limits. When entrepreneurs do not try to think in a long way then they put a boundary on the growth and expansion of their business. By doing this they become a salaried employee who works, only for a limited time with Sunday holiday. Without vision, entrepreneurs cannot imagine about their business. If your business is doing very well then you should try to expand it. Number of competitors are there in the market. If you will be lazy or satisfied with the current situation then others will take the benefits of opportunities, earn good profit and will grow their business.

Business-focus

The entrepreneurs do business but they do not have a special focus on the customers. They just take the customers as it is. They treat every customer same. If they will behave like this then they are doing the mistakes. They should have a focus on the customers' value, what kind of customers they really want? They should give more value to the customers who come again and again than customers who come only once. Entrepreneurs do not focus on these things. Customers are the source of revenue; if they will not come then profit will go down. People can tell if you are genuinely concerned about them or if you are acting out of self-interest. Absorb yourself in meeting your prospect's needs.

Lack of interest

When entrepreneurs go in such a business where they do not have much interest then they do not take the business responsibility from their heart. The business becomes just formality for them. Business requires hardworking, interaction with every person who is attached with the business after that only the entrepreneurs can think that they will earn the profit. Some entrepreneurs believe that success in business means you get others to sell for you. While they want the benefits of marketing, their unwilling to do whatever it takes to achieve them.

At the moment of apathy, focus on why you chose your business. What are your goals? Why did you decide to become a home-based entrepreneur? When you renew your mind with thoughts of how your business can empower you to live out your dreams, you'll cheer yourself on to further achievement.

Lack of self-discipline

Many people choose business to be their own boss. With freedom comes responsibility, however. Many first-time home entrepreneurs don't know how to handle it. When they become their own boss and they are the first time entrepreneurs they do not take business affairs very seriously, they become lazy. They do not have any higher authority. But the true entrepreneurs are the disciplined ones. They do not need any supervision; they know their work and responsibilities. But the new small entrepreneurs misuse freedom and therefore they mismanage the business events. Sometimes they ignore most of the issues because they do not really have any desire to work on those issues. They do work for their business but not so much instantly. They give less time to business and more time to freedom, keep the things as it is and so forth. Your business will remain a hobby until you commit to performing those tasks necessary to build your organization.

21.3 Think More than Attracting New Customers!

When you're just starting out in business, it's a safe bet that you need more clients. But what if you have been up and running for a while and you're still not making as much money as you would like? You may be in the habit of thinking that attracting new clients is the answer, but this isn't always the case. There are many reasons why a business might not be earning enough.

Start by looking at your gross revenue — the total amount your customers pay you over the course of a year. How does it compare to others in the same line of business? Ask some trusted colleagues or check with your professional association for any statistics they may have. What percentage of your gross revenue remains after you cover cost of sales? This is your gross profit. As a service business, you may have no cost of sales. If, however, you are selling books, tapes or software or accepting credit cards, your inventory cost and credit card fees need to be deducted from your earnings before making other calculations.

Now deduct your business expenses from your gross profit. What percentage of gross profit remains? Is this a typical percentage for your business? If you can't gather comparable data from colleagues, your professional association or a published source compare your profit margin (net income divided by gross profit) to a desired goal of 70 per cent.

Low revenue

The new entrepreneurs mostly face the problem of low revenue. They do every possible work for their business but still they are not able to increase business revenue. You can earn more revenue by increasing the rate which may mean finding a market that is willing to pay more. For example, rich people are ready to pay higher prices, because mostly they are not price sensitive to small price change. Always search for the customers who are ready to give you big orders. For example, instead of organizing one day picnic try to organize two to three weeks travel tour. As you will think big so you will also need more people to work. Do not fear if you are handling a big tour, hire more employees so that you can maintain your quality of work. You should also work to increase your passive income by selling products created by you or others, reselling some of your existing work or licensing a process you have developed.

Low profits

Look for ways to cut expenses by reducing your overhead or focusing on your most profitable line of business. Most of the time entrepreneurs in a hope to improve the process invest more than the real requirement. It will affect the income of the business as you are diverting your money to the less important area. You must be very clear about the business areas where you want to invest money. Don't waste your money on unproductive work. For example, your restaurant requires three servants but you have kept four servants in a hope to give better services to your customers. But it has actually increased your cost and lowered your profit. Consider cutting back on advertising or mailings and using more referral-based marketing strategies. Seek out customers who will give you repeat business or long-term contracts.

Too few customers

Too few customers definitely affect the business. In business customers are the kings. All the strategies are formulated just to attract the customers. Low revenue combined with not enough billable work to keep you busy means you really don't have enough customers. The best strategy to attract the customers is to go to customers' door instead of customers coming to your door. If you don't have a marketing plan, it's time to create one. Focus your plan on the most attractive service you have to offer and the most lucrative market, rather than diffusing your energy by marketing several different service lines to more than one type of customer.

If your marketing plan is not working then you need to look for a new market and new customers where you can generate appeal for your product or services. Many times to go into the new market is not easy, so at that time, you can make a partnership with someone who can benefit your business. Entrepreneurs must generate the new market if they see that there is no market for their business.

Poor pricing strategy

The most common method for setting prices is to start at the unit cost and then mark up the price to achieve a profit, so-called "cost-plus" pricing. Unfortunately, cost has little to do with how a product or service is valued by customers, which can lead to systematic under pricing. For example, if a widget costs ₹ 1000 to manufacture and you sell it to a customer for ₹ 1250 when that customer would gladly have paid ₹ 1750; you have left ₹ 500 worth of value on the table.

Even worse, cost-based pricing can lead to prices that are greater than what the market will bear. Because unit cost is related to sales volume, high prices lead to fewer sales, which in turn increase unit cost, leading to a further round of price increases.

As Thomas Nagle and John Hogan point out in The Strategy and Tactics of Pricing, failing to account for the effect of price on sales volume — and hence costs — have led to numerous business failures over the years once they enter a "death spiral" of price increases to allocate fixed costs across a smaller volume of sales. You should instead let anticipated prices, based on the product's perceived value to customers; determine the *cost structure*, not the other way round. Consequently, pricing strategy and customer value should be addressed in the earlier stages of planning a new business.

Too little time

Most of the time it happens that you want to earn more money but because you do not have enough time, that's why you are not capable to earn more money. When you are serving your customers all hours per week, with more potential customers in the pipeline than allowing customers to wait for your service is not the good option and here you need to hire an employee. When entrepreneurs see that there is huge customers but employees are less then they should hire the employees to serve the customers. If you are not able to hire more employees then think about subcontracting work to a trusted associate and keeping a percentage of their billings.

Look customers should not feel uncomfortable. If more customers are coming to the business then you cannot let them wait because of less number of employees. So it is better to tie up with some others to get the help in business in return pay some money. There are six statistics every service business owner should know: revenue, expenses, profit margin, number of customers, average sales amount and billable time. If you don't have the answers, start tracking these measurements today.

So What Could Be the Solution?

21.4 Maximize Profit for Your Online Business

Who would not want to earn? People take on a job because they want to earn. Others put in a business so that they could produce more profit. And what is good to know is even if people are already earning, they still want some more, more and even more. Does that desire for more profits ever end? No, because once you earn some bucks and dreamt of growing big, you would maximize everything to earn. This is true even with online business. You need to use all your resources so that you can maximize your profits.

Here are some guidelines on how to do that.

1. Since you have already established trust with your existing customers, offer them new products. If you have built a good reputation with the first transaction with your customers, they are more likely to make another business transaction with you.
2. Cross promote or upsell your other products. You can maximize the profits you get from each client by offering them products that are relevant to their first purchase. For instance, if they have bought mobile phone from you, offer them downloadable ringing tones, wall papers or mobile games.
3. Establish affiliate programs for your business. In this way, you would be able to minimize on the cost of advertising and yet maximize the potential sales since you would have more channels of reaching different clients.
4. If you are providing services, you can outsource your other tasks. For instance, if you are running a copywriting business, you can hire writers to do work for you. More writers mean more jobs done that can result to more profits for you.
5. You can also add a low cost bonus for your products. For example, you can provide an eBook half its price if customers will buy a certain product from you.
6. Freebies can also do the trick. You can encourage more sales once people know that you are giving out stuffs for no cost at all.

21.5 Approach to Maximize Business Revenue

Starting a franchise is not enough. You have to have a plan to keep your business running properly. Yes, your franchisor will be there to guide you, but you need to take initiative in this area, too. Here are following ways to increase your business profit:

1. Choose the right location: It is an important decision in business. Most of the business fails because of bad location selection. Before choosing a location, there are many factors you should look into. Make sure the customers can come easily to your location and whether they can park their car if needed. Checking customers' feasibility is very important because if customers find more feasible place than yours, then they will stop coming to your shop. Also, checking out the competition is necessary as is the proximity of an anchor store if you are a restaurant or retail location going into a shopping center.

2. Advertise effectively: Each business has its own way of doing this. Your franchisor will have an effective marketing and advertisement plan, but you are always free to advertise on your own. While doing advertisement don't rely on single media. You can use multiple media for advertisement for e.g., radio, TV, magazines or news paper. If your franchise opportunity is new in the place, it will help to increase the business, if you advertise locally in your area.

3. Develop a Great Business Plan: The process of developing a business plan forces you to think through every critical element that will determine your business success. You must have a plan for selecting your products and services, developing your marketing, selecting the right people, getting the money you need, designing your sales process, arranging for distribution, service and collection of payments and many other factors.

Especially, you must be absolutely clear about the critical numbers in your business. There is always one number that is more indicative and predictive of your success than any other and you must decide what it is. It may be number of sales, size of sales, profitability of sales, number of repeat purchases per customer or rate of growth. There are thirty-five different measures that may be applicable to your business and you must be absolutely clear about which measure is most important to you.

4. Don't let seasonal slumps hit you: There are some businesses, which are highly seasonal such as putting up decorative Christmas lights or lawn care. If you are starting a franchise of such a concept, keep the off-periods in mind. You can either use that period in networking among your peers or planning for the coming season. Whatever you do, don't forget to send regular customers seasonal greetings. That way, they will come back to you time and again whenever they will need your services.

5. Use a home office in the beginning if possible: Using home as an office will save your money of rent if you would have hired an office. There are many franchise opportunities that can be operated from home in the beginning. If you are running such a franchise, make use of it during the initial stages. The saved amount can be used for other purposes of business. At the initial stage of your business your every rupee will help you. Even if you are planning to open an office then do not suddenly go for buying costly furnitures. Today the cost of furniture and decoration is very high. Think on it. If the franchisor is not strict about the office decoration then you can use used furnitures. Buying used furnitures are less costly. There are many stores that specialize in selling these kinds of equipments.

6. Develop and operate a Customer Strategy programme of how you and your staff are going to treat, look after and communicate with your customers. This will be the most beneficial programme in your business that will increase your customer satisfaction, loyalty and referrals.

7. Network: There is nothing that beats the power of networking in building a successful business whether big or small. Invest your time in discovering and building relationships with likeminded people including advisors and mentors. This network comes in handy when you need any counsel or support of any kind.

A big part of networking will be attending the annual seminars and meetings of your franchisor. Never miss any of them, if you want to learn ways to increase your profit margin.

8. Surround Yourself with Great People: Your ability to interview, select, hire and deploy excellent people is the control valve on your success in business. Fortunately, you can become excellent at the process of finding and keeping good people with a little instruction, guidance and practice.

The best companies have the best people. The second best companies have the second best people. The third best companies are on their way out of business. Sometimes, the selection or de-selection of a single person can have a major difference on your business results.

9. You can buy used equipments: You don't need to have the latest or finest equipment to start your business, but as far as it is still valuable you can go for it. Purchasing used equipment, furniture, tools and other business related items can help keep your start-up costs in check. Before equipping your office and buying furniture, decide what your real needs are in terms of being able to work professionally, what you need to make a professional impression and to maintain a healthy cash flow. You can buy brand new equipment and buy fancier furniture if your business is generating enough income. Reward yourself with a modular desk only after your business as started generating profit. Remember, when buying used products know the actual cost of the products if brand new and be sure it is still in a good working condition.

21.6 Maximizing Earnings

All businesses work on one central goal and that is maximizing profits. There could be different approaches to achieving this target. One could either enhance revenues through expanding the business and introducing new products. Another way to tackle the problem is by focusing on minimizing fixed and variable costs, such as production costs and marketing costs. One could also combine these two approaches to maximize the benefits. Some effective steps that an organization can take to achieve its profit targets are:

Action Steps

Retain the existing customer base

It is widely acknowledged that the cost of retaining existing customers is less than that of gaining new ones. Formulate strategies to win customer loyalty by enhancing your customer service and being open to accepting and implementing customer feedback. You could also strengthen the bond by rewarding your regular customers with discounts and freebies and introducing loyalty programs.

Use offline and online marketing strategies

Marketing your products and services effectively on both the offline and online advertising spaces can help you maximize business visibility and attract more customers. Strengthening your market position and improving brand image through effective marketing strategies could go a long way in boosting revenues. This would eventually help you enhance business profits.

Expand beyond brick and mortar stores

While brick and mortar stores are essential, offering your customers the facility to order your products and services online could drastically increase sales. Meanwhile, online stores require limited infrastructure, helping you save immensely on your fixed costs. Alternatively, you could join e-commerce sites, such as Amazon and eBay.

Expanding into high-margin products and services

Another way of drastically improving your profits is by introducing high-margin products and services. While launching these products and services in a specific market, do not forget to check for their demand. You could take the services of mailing list brokers to gauge demand. You must also focus on providing the products and services that give you an edge over your competitors.

Taking measures to reduce taxes

Implement measures, such as giving to charities and making donations, induct family members into the business and keep proper records. These will help you obtain tax benefits. Alternatively, you can significantly reduce your tax burdens by forming an offshore company. Offshore companies are becoming increasingly popular as investment vehicles. The formation of a business outside your registration jurisdiction can also help you increase confidentiality. This could go a long way in helping you enhance your profits further.

Your profit is your income minus your expenses. At a very simple level, you can increase your profit by generating more income and cutting back on costs. Of course, there is a balance to be struck; for example, you may be able to make more sales by spending more on marketing.

Setting a Price

Whether you are selling a product or a service, you need to decide on a price. Basic economics dictates that the higher your price, the fewer sales you will make (but the more profit you will make from each sale).

In practice, things are a little more complicated.

If you set your price low, you will have to sell lots of units to cover your costs and make a profit. If you set your price too high, you may find that you have no customers at all! To some extent, your price will depend on what your competitors are charging for equivalent things and how much demand there is for them. Ultimately, one way or another, the market will dictate the price it wants to pay. One way to set a price is to ask up front what people are willing to pay.

You could use focus groups for this, but a better strategy could be to test the market directly: make sales at different prices and see how price-sensitive your customers really are. For example, suppose you have written a book, but you aren't sure what to charge for it. If you have a mailing list of 300 potential customers, you could send three batches of 100 marketing letters, with the price set at ₹ 8, ₹ 10 and ₹ 12 in each respective batch. Then see what response you get and use that to set the price for everyone else. Money talks!

Controlling Your Costs

There are two types of costs: fixed and variable.

Fixed costs are things that are independent of the amount of trade you do and the growth of your business. Things such as rent, utilities and, to some extent, your wage bill are the same regardless of whether you make one sale or a thousand. The more sales you make, the less impact your fixed costs have on your profit per item.

Variable costs increase as you do more work or manufacture more products. The cost of raw materials is a major factor towards the variable costs of a manufacturing business.

Your sale price should take variable costs into account, so covering your fixed costs is normally more of a concern. Because your costs have a direct impact on the profit you make, you need to control them carefully and cut back on costs whenever you can do so without suffering a reduction of quality in the service you provide.

The Role of Marketing

Marketing is an expense. But it is a necessary outlay – if nobody knows about your business, you will find it difficult to make sales and to see growth. You need to judge how much to invest in marketing so that this investment is more than covered by the increased income it generates.

Good Relationship with Suppliers

(a) Suppliers experiencing low capacity offer better discounts.

(b) Suppliers can suggest different methods, processes, materials or manufacturing tolerances to help you save money.

(c) Pay your bills early or on time to receive Supplier incentive discounts. Late payments will result in higher costs being levied in the future.

(d) Have excellent communication lines established with your Suppliers which can be very helpful when you hit a downturn in sales and find meeting obligations difficult.

(e) Develop a Supplier Business Plan

A Balancing Act

Maximizing your profit is a balancing act. Nobody said it was going to be easy! You need to set prices that make you competitive while charging as much as the market will comfortably bear. You need to spend a certain amount of money on marketing to build awareness of your brand, but at a level that is maintainable from the increased income it generates. And you need to cut costs ruthlessly wherever you can do so without compromising the quality of your service.

21.7 Profitable e-commerce Solutions for Maximizing Business

The unbeaten promotion of products and services along with efficient and safe business transactions boosts up the company's revenue. Uphold your professional and valuable retail presence on the internet and strategically reach the niche in the market attracting large number of clients and consumers at your end.

Entrepreneurs can judiciously invest up front with minimal capital with online retail business option. Suitable for small businesses as well, it has turned out to be popular these days and renders ample opportunities for giving vent to your creative ideas or talent. Ideal to be run as a solo, parent, home-based or part-time entrepreneur, this business revolves round the importance of comprehending the target consumers and their preferences. An extensive market research complimented with focused financial resource including dynamic website designing, creating finest product and implementation of a strategic marketing program during the initial start up phase serves as a milestone in online retail business. Moreover, the rapid pace of market competition and the changing market trends has enhanced the demand of e-commerce shopping cart software. Booming e-commerce solutions these days, carry attractive and accessible features for the success in the industry and helps focus on your budget and business requirements. An affordable range of e-commerce solution not only facilitates in attaining desired profitability but also motivates customer service thereby increasing revenue and strengthening image or brand of the company.

Define your e-business statement today with effective and feature-rich e-commerce solution and help your customers to complete their transactions in a quick and reliable fashion. This will not only help in building excellent communication with your new visitors but also facilitate in maintaining strong relation with the regular customers.

21.8 Lucrative Financial Plan

If you don't keep track of how much money you're making, you have no idea whether your business is successful or not. You can't tell how well your marketing is working. You need to know what your net profit is. If you don't, there's no way you can know how to increase it. To be successful in business, you need to make a financial plan and check it against the facts on a monthly basis, then take immediate action to correct any problems. Here are steps you should take:

Create a Financial Plan: Preparing a financial plan will always help you as it shows a clear cut roadmap of your business. It shows how much clear you are for your business. You must estimate the revenue you are expecting from your business every month and project what will be the expenses of your business. If you need it, get help from business planning books, software or an accountant.

Review the Plan at Least Quarterly

While a mature business in a static industry might be able to get away with reviewing its financial plan annually, it's better to review it at least quarterly. One small business owner looks over certain numbers every other month. Everything in business starts with gross profit, so project and review every cost area in company bimonthly.

Evaluating operations

Each time you prepare an income statement, actual sales and costs are compared with those you projected in your original profit plan. This permits detection of areas of unsatisfactory performance so that corrective action can be taken.

Make Adjustments Right Away: If revenues are lower than expected, increase efforts in sales promotion and marketing or look for ways to increase your rates. Analyze your business systematically and try to find out is there any wastages of resources or money, find ways to cut back. Take the help of experts if required to solve the problem. There are other businesses like yours around. Analyze others business and get information on what other businesses are doing in the same situation. What is their secret for operating profitably?

Planning purchasing requirements

The volume of expected sales may be more than the business' usual suppliers can handle or expected sales may be sufficient to permit taking advantage of quantity discounts. In either case, advance knowledge of purchasing requirements will permit taking advantage of cost savings and ensure that purchased goods are readily available when needed.

Thinking about the future

Too often, small businesses neglect to plan ahead: thinking about where they are today, where they will be next year or the year after. As a result, opportunities are overlooked and crises occur that could have been avoided. Development of the profit plan requires thinking about the future so that many problems can be avoided before they arise.

Pay Yourself a Salary: If you are incorporated, you may already be doing this. If not, allocate an amount to owner's compensation on a monthly basis. Each month that your business meets its profitability goal, pay yourself the full amount. When you miss your target, dock your "pay" and when you exceed it, pay yourself a "bonus." Writing yourself a monthly paycheque will give you a strong incentive to keep your business profitable.

It's About Profit, Not Revenue: It doesn't matter how many thousands of rupees you are bringing in each month if your expenses are almost as high or higher. If profit is increasing and simultaneously cost is also increasing then there is no use of it. Always try to increase profit and decrease cost. Many high-revenue businesses have gone under for this very reason — don't be one of them.

21.9 Elegant Money-Saving Tactics

Buying Brainpower

Sometimes it's not what you buy, but how you buy that will save you money. Check out these smart shopping tips:

- **Stretch your budget with barter.** Swapping one product or service for another is a good way to avoid cash outlays-and unload slow-moving inventory. If you'd rather not bargain with other businesses directly, hire a commissioned barter broker (listed in the Yellow Pages under "Barter"), or join a commercial barter club or exchange.
- **Time your payments.** Ask suppliers if they give discounts for early payment. If not, it's to your advantage to pay your bills-including utilities, taxes and suppliers-as late as possible without incurring a fee. The longer money is in your account, the longer it's earning interest for you.
- **Join an association.** Many trade and business associations have reasonable membership fees and offer discounts on everything from insurance, travel and car rental to long-distance phone service, prescriptions and even golf course fees.
- **Seek at least three bids on everything.** Even mundane purchases merit shopping around. If you quote a competitor's lower price, a supplier or vendor will often match that price to win your business.

Employee Economics

Hiring a full time employee could be costly for you. If you are not ready to hire a full time employee because of your low economy then you can choose an option of employee leasing. Employee leasing is an option in which you turn over your work force to a professional employer organization that leases your employees back to you-can save your substantial cash on employee benefits.

The other option to you is to hire temporary employees when your business is low to handle surges in business. Another way to get free or low-cost help-and give college students a chance to learn the ropes-is by hiring interns. Check with your local university for more information.

Insurance Intelligence

Buying insurance is one of those necessary evils all smart entrepreneurs put up with. But that doesn't mean you have to break the bank. Here are some cost-cutting ideas:

- **Save by association.** When looking for insurance, check with your trade association. Many associations offer competitive group insurance.
- **Raise your deductible.** Raising the deductible on your insurance usually lowers your premiums. Even if you end up having to pay the deductible, it's likely to be less than the amount you save.
- **Make a foul-weather friend.** By arranging for an alternative place to run your business in case of a major disaster, you may be able to save on business interruption insurance, advises the Insurance Information Institute. For instance, you could arrange with a firm in the same industry to use their facilities in case of damage and *vice-versa.*

Office Overhead

Small office essentials can nickel-and-dime you to death, unless you buy smart. Purchase recycled printer cartridges. Check Google or your Yellow Pages for a local recycled printer cartridge supplier. You can also find free forms online that you can download customize and print. Another way to save money is buying used equipment. You can save up to 60 percent with used computer equipment, copiers and office furniture.

Penny-Pinching Promotions

Want to market your business on a budget? The people you know can help. Here are three ways the people in your network can assist your marketing efforts: 1. Split advertising and promotion costs with neighboring businesses. Jointly promote a sidewalk sale or take your marketing alliance further by sharing mailing lists, distribution channels and suppliers with businesses that sell complementary goods or services. 2. Ask the people you know for help. The kind of support you'd most like to get from your contacts is referrals-the names of specific individuals who need your products and services. So go ahead and ask! Your contacts can also give prospects your name and number. As the number of referrals you receive increases, so does your potential for increasing the percentage of your business generated through referrals. 3. Got a happy customer? By telling others what they've gained from using your products or services in presentations or informal conversations, your sources can encourage others to use your products or services.

Up-to-Date

Here are some of the most effective and least expensive items you may want to buy to bring your older computers back up to speed:

- **Hard Drives:** One of the most important features of any computer is its ability to store large amount of data. Whether you need desktop drives to back up your primary hard drives or store your digital video files or a portable large-capacity drive to carry a hefty business presentation, there are several solutions that may help to meet your needs.
- **CD-ROM/R/RW and DVD-ROM/R/RW Drives:** Upgrading to a speedier CD-ROM drive may be just what you need to give your system a valuable boost in performance.
- **Processor Upgrades and Accelerators:** Processor upgrades and accelerators allow you to increase the overall performance of a computer by allowing it to process information faster. Accelerators do this by shifting operational functionality and providing additional cache memory, thereby freeing up the computer's main processor so it can do its real job-running software applications.
- **Memory:** While everything that has already been mentioned can help increase the usability of your current computers, one of the most tried and true ways to improve performance is to simply install more random access memory, otherwise known as RAM.

Shopping List

If your company is going to expend the time and resources on new technology purchases, they need to be worthwhile. Keep in these tips next time your company is ready to do some serious tech buying:

1. **Renegotiate existing contracts for services such as network support and consulting.** Telecom is especially ripe for bargains. Start by setting benchmarks for rates and auditing bills to ensure you're not overpaying. Then instead of buying all long-distance, local phone and other telecom services from one vendor, dual-source it. Vendors will treat you better and charge you less.
2. **Make sure you need whatever new technology you do buy.** Inventory all PCs, printers and software. Look for opportunities to consolidate purchases, standardize configurations and root out duplication.
3. **Set up a system to keep doing it.** Pick a team of people from IT and other departments and meet with them regularly to discuss what they need and how to save on it.

Buy Smarter

You must be very careful while investing money in technology. You must be able to get return on technology that you have chosen for your business. You can't afford to have a key business hardware component go down without protection. A warranty will give you peace of mind. It's as important to know when not to skimp as it is to know when to go for the extra discount.

Discount stores have decent-size technology sections and can net you good value on everything from laptops to printer cartridges. What you won't get is a lot of one-on-one service. If you're sure of what you want, go ahead and look out for good deals. If you need to ask questions, go somewhere else.

You can also save money by working closely with a value-added reseller (VAR). This is a good route to explore for large purchases where you want the reseller to also be the installer. The reseller will be up on the latest special offers and promotions that fit your needs. Selecting the right VAR is also important. See how long they have been in business and whether they have experience serving your particular market.

Leave No (Paper) Trail

Drowning in paper? Technology can help you reduce or even eliminate your need for paper. Try the following options to free your office from stacks and stacks of paper that threaten to overwhelm:

- **Computers:** PCs, laptops and handhelds can be combined for document creation mobility and flexibility, stamping out rampant paper use.
- **Scanners:** Scanners create digital images so that documents can be exchanged electronically and preserved easily. When scanning, remember to employ image compression to maintain network performance and make sure to choose a single, standardized electronic document format so that images can be indexed and searched easily.
- **e-mail:** e-mail is a great substitute for paper memos. Effective e-mail systems should allow users to filter content and file messages electronically by topic. They also should let workers combine e-mail with fax and voice-mail retrieval in a unified messaging system.
- **Storage systems:** Affordable, robust storage technology is essential for high-speed, centralized electronic information management. Check out low-cost systems built upon RAID (Redundant Array of Independent Disks) technology or ISCSI-based storage-area networks.
- **Fax over IP (Internet protocol):** The boring old fax goes high-tech with a Web-or e-mail-based fax capability that eliminates the need to send hard copies.
- **Wireless local area networks:** Wi-Fi LANs are spreading like wildfire, making electronic information mobile, portable and easily accessible to workers anywhere.
- **Secure remote access:** Virtual private networks (VPNs) ensure that home workers and road warriors get secure, confidential access to the company intranet, abolishing the need to lug around a briefcase full of documents.
- **E-learning systems:** Workers in training can say good-bye to books and binders when they use online or Web-based training systems.
- **Advanced printers:** Printers that print on both sides of a sheet can significantly reduce paper use.

Back It Up!

At any time, you could lose your computer equipment, whether it's a laptop that gets stolen or a desktop that's lost in a house fire. So be prepared: Back up your data weekly-or even daily. Some backup options include portable hard drives, DVD-writers and online data.

There are also several networked data storage options, including:

- **Direct Attached Storage:** Known as DAS, this technology attaches storage media (like disk arrays and tape backup) directly to servers.

- **Network Attached Storage:** Called NAS, this standalone, self-contained solution connects directly to a LAN, rather than to a server. The separation of data from servers tends to improve performance.
- **Storage Area Network:** SANs create a separate, dedicated high-performance network that is highly secure and scalable.
- **ISCSI SAN:** This type of SAN offers most of the strengths of the Fibre Channel SAN, but it's easier to install, has lower-cost connections, is much easier to manage and grows with your business.
- **Managed Storage Network:** Managed storage services are offered by specialized service providers. Businesses can contract with these providers, who implement and maintain the storage network on an outsourced basis.

Regardless of which backup method you choose, remember it's better to be safe than sorry when it comes to your data.

SUMMARY

Critical situation to profitability:

Improper cash to start business

The new entrepreneurs' problems are always the cash. If they want to earn the profit then they have to invest money in the business. They have an idea they have plan but they do not have money to implement the plan in reality and to earn money.

Making money in business

The new entrepreneurs just start the business but they lag in doing proper planning regarding how to earn the profit. They lag in interaction with the different people who are really important for the progress of the business and to earn profit.

Lack in business tactics

Entrepreneurs must know the business tactics to earn the profit. They should come up with the creative ideas it is not necessary that every creative idea will need money. Some ideas even require less money and are more profitable.

Way of spending money on business

Running your business is going to cost you some money, too, so your next step is to take a look at your expenses. The new entrepreneurs are not able to calculate the exact expenses on business. They do not write down all the expenses and therefore they do not have a proper understanding of their expenditure.

Cash shortages during months with negative cash flow

New entrepreneurs are not ready to face such situation. They do not have any plan what they will do after six months when there will be no season of business.

Put it all together for profitability measurement and use it wisely!

Entrepreneurs must know about cash management. If entrepreneurs will not go through cash management thoroughly then they will not have proper information about how to utilize cash, when to take a loan.

Knowing what makes a business profitable

The important question for the entrepreneurs is when profitability is going to happen for business? The answer is different for everyone, but profitability measurement is as clear as knowing when your business has more cash coming in than going out in a given month.

Delay in payment by customers

New entrepreneurs already have fewer customers and in such cases they become dependent to their customers and if customers do not pay money instantly or after some days then it affects their business.

Dependency on customers

New entrepreneurs are not in a position to have an argument with dominant business. Otherwise their relationship with dominant business will break and therefore they do not want to take any risk. The fact is that the new entrepreneurs suffer a lot; they suffer from low income and delay in payment.

Obstacles to success in the business are Unclear vision, No plan, Discouraging influences, Lack of knowledge, Fear of rejection, Inadequate training and support, Short-term mentality, Business-focus, Lack of interest and Lack of self-discipline.

Think More than Attracting New Customers!

When you're just starting out in business, it's a safe bet that you need more clients. But what if you have been up and running for a while and you're still not making as much money as you would like? You may be in the habit of thinking that attracting new clients is the answer, but this isn't always the case. There are many reasons why a business might not be earning enough.

Low revenue

The new entrepreneurs mostly face the problem of low revenue. They do every possible work for their business but still they are not able to increase business revenue. You can earn more revenue by increasing the rate which may mean finding a market that is willing to pay more.

Low profits

Look for ways to cut expenses by reducing your overhead or focusing on your most profitable line of business. Most of the times the entrepreneurs in a hope to make the process better invest more than the actual requirement.

Too few customers

The best strategy to attract the customers is to go to customers' door instead of customers coming to your door.

Poor pricing strategy

The most common method for setting prices is to start at the unit cost and then mark up the price to achieve a profit, so-called "cost-plus" pricing. Unfortunately, cost has little to do with how a product or service is valued by customers, which can lead to systematic under pricing.

Too little time

It's possible that you simply don't have enough time to earn more money. When you are consistently spending over all hours per week serving clients, with more potential customers in the pipeline than you can realistically serve, it's time to hire an employee or bring in a junior partner.

Approach to maximize business revenue

Starting a franchise is not enough. You have to have a plan to keep your business running properly. Yes, your franchisor will be there to guide you, but you need to take initiative in this area, too. Here are following ways to increase your business profit:

Choose the right location

Advertise effectively

Develop a Great Business Plan

Don't let seasonal slumps hit you

Use a home office in the beginning if possible

Develop and operate a Customer Strategy programme

Network

Surround Yourself with Great People

You can buy used equipments

Some effective steps that an organization can take to achieve its profit targets are:

Retain the existing customer base

It is widely acknowledged that the cost of retaining existing customers is less than that of gaining new ones.

Use offline and online marketing strategies

Marketing your products and services effectively on both the offline and online advertising spaces can help you maximize business visibility and attract more customers.

Expand beyond brick and mortar stores

While brick and mortar stores are essential, offering your customers the facility to order your products and services online could drastically increase sales.

Expanding into high-margin products and services

Another way of drastically improving your profits is by introducing high-margin products and services.

Taking measures to reduce taxes

Implement measures, such as giving to charities and making donations, induct family members into the business and keep proper records. These will help you obtain tax benefits.

Setting a price

Whether you are selling a product or a service, you need to decide on a price. Basic economics dictates that the higher your price, the fewer sales you will make (but the more profit you will make from each sale).

Controlling your costs

There are two types of cost: fixed and variable.

The role of marketing

You need to judge how much to invest in marketing so that this investment is more than covered by the increased income it generates.

Maintain Good Relationship with Suppliers:

A balancing act

Maximizing your profit is a balancing act. Nobody said it was going to be easy! You need to set prices that make you competitive while charging as much as the market will comfortably bear.

Lucrative Financial Plan

If you don't keep track of how much money you're making, you have no idea whether your business is successful or not. You can't tell how well your marketing is working. You need to know what your net profit is!

Create a Financial Plan, Review the Plan at Least Quarterly, Evaluating operations, Make Adjustments Right Away, Planning purchasing requirements, Thinking about the future,

Pay Yourself a Salary and It's About Profit, Not Revenue.

Elegant Money-Saving Tactics:

Buying Brainpower

Sometimes it's not what you buy, but how you buy that will save you money. The smart shopping tips are Stretch your budget with barter, Time your payments, Join an association and seek at least three bids on everything.

Employee Economics

Employee leasing -in which you turn over your work force to a professional employer organization that leases your employees back to you-can save your substantial cash on employee benefits.

Insurance Intelligence

Buying insurance is one of those necessary evils all smart entrepreneurs put up with. But that doesn't mean you have to break the bank. The cost-cutting ideas are make a foul-weather friend, Save by association and Raise your deductible.

Office Overhead

Small office essentials can nickel-and-dime you to death, unless you buy smart. Purchase recycled printer cartridges. Check Google or your Yellow Pages for a local recycled printer cartridge supplier.

Penny-Pinching Promotions

Want to market your business on a budget? The people you know can help. Here are three ways the people in your network can assist your marketing efforts:

1. Split advertising and promotion costs with neighboring businesses.
2. Ask the people you know for help.
3. Got a happy customer? By telling others what they've gained from using your products or services in presentations or informal conversations, your sources can encourage others to use your products or services.

Shopping List

If your company is going to expend the time and resources on new technology purchases, they need to be worthwhile. Keep in these tips next time your company is ready to do some serious tech buying:

Set up a system to keep doing it.

Make sure you need whatever new technology you do buy.

Renegotiate existing contracts for services such as network support and consulting.

Buy Smarter

Investing in technology for your business doesn't have to send you to the poor house, as long as you know how to get the most out of what you can spend. You can't afford to have a key business hardware component go down without protection. A warranty will give you peace of mind. It's as important to know when not to skimp as it is to know when to go for the extra discount.

KEYWORDS

Profit: A financial benefit that is realized when the amount of revenue gained from a business activity exceeds the expenses, costs and taxes needed to sustain the activity.

Pricing: Pricing is a method adopted by a firm to set its selling price.

Pricing Strategy: It takes into view factors such as a firm's overall marketing objectives, consumer demand, product attributes, competitors' pricing and market and economic trends.

Business plan: A business plan is a document that summarizes the operational and financial objectives of a business and contains the detailed plans and budgets showing how the objectives are to be realized.

Marketing Strategy: Marketing Strategy is a set of specific ideas and actions that outline and guide decisions on the best.

Financial plan: Financial plan section is the section that determines whether or not your business idea is viable and is a key component in determining whether or not your business plan is going to be able to attract any investment in your business idea.

QUESTIONS

1. Why do small entrepreneurs lag in earning a huge profit?
2. What are the different approaches to maximize business revenue?
3. How can you maximize your profit in online business?
4. How does e-commerce help your business in generating the revenue?
5. What are the different money saving strategies? Explain.

❑ ❑ ❑

Chapter – 22

Government Policies/Grants Obstacles

LEARNING OBJECTIVES

On completion of this chapter, you should be able to:

- ☺ *Explain the obstacles faced by the new small entrepreneurs when deal with government.*
- ☺ *Describe **governmental measures** to help first generation entrepreneurs*
- ☺ *Describe the problems of entrepreneurs of high official costs of starting a business.*

For any new business, government approval is must without it, it is impossible to run the business. When the new entrepreneurs open the business they face many difficulties as far as getting government approval is concerned. The first difficulty is about documents requirements. They do not know what are the documents required for registration of the business. The new entrepreneurs anyhow have to arrange for the registration of the business because they cannot move forward. This procedure is very complex, time consuming and can take many months. Following are the obstacles that are faced by the new entrepreneurs when deal with government for registration of the business.

22.1 Complex Document Procedures

A new entrepreneur does not have much knowledge about the document procedure for setting up a new business. Even if he wants to start his own business he may not be able to start the business because of documents requirement. And when he starts to collect the required documents that are needed for the business he faces many problems; as he may have partial knowledge of the documents and he continuously faces different problems when dealing with such kind of things. In this stage the complexity of the process is enough to break the enthusiasm of the entrepreneur. He thinks just by having the business idea he can run the business but when the legal requirements come and that requirements are not fulfilled as soon as possible it delays his business which may even affect his business. For new entrepreneurs these things are not as easy as the experienced entrepreneur.

22.2 Instantaneous Change in Policies

Government creates rules and frameworks where businesses are able to compete against each other. From time to time the government changes these rules and frameworks forcing businesses to change the way they operate. Business is thus keenly affected by government policy. Key areas of government policy that affects business are:

- **Economic policy**

A key area of government economic policy is the role that the government gives to the state in the economy. Between 1945 and 1979 the government increasingly interfered in the economy by creating state run industries which usually took the form of public corporations. However, from 1979 onwards we saw an era of privatization in which industries were sold off to private shareholders to create a more competitive business environment.

- **Taxation policy**

It affects business costs. For example, a rise in corporation tax (on business profits) has the same effect as an increase in costs. Businesses can pass some of this tax on to consumers in higher prices, but it will also affect the bottom line. Other business taxes are environmental taxes (e.g., landfill tax) and VAT (value added tax). VAT is actually passed down the line to the final consumer but the administration of the VAT system is a cost for business.

- **Interest rates**

Another area of economic policy relates to Interest rates. In this country the level of interest rates is determined by a government appointed group - the Monetary Policy Committee which meets every month. A rise in interest rates raises the costs to business of borrowing money and also causes consumers to reduce expenditure (leading to a fall in business sales).

Government spending policy also affects business. For example, if the government spends more on schools, this will increase the income of businesses that supply schools with books,

BOX 22

Single Window Clearance

The Single Window Clearance Committee under the Chairmanship of District Collector has been functioning efficiently in Tiruppur with a view to quicken the process of providing all the required Industrial clearances / licenses for SSI units / MSMEs from various statutory authorities under one roof.

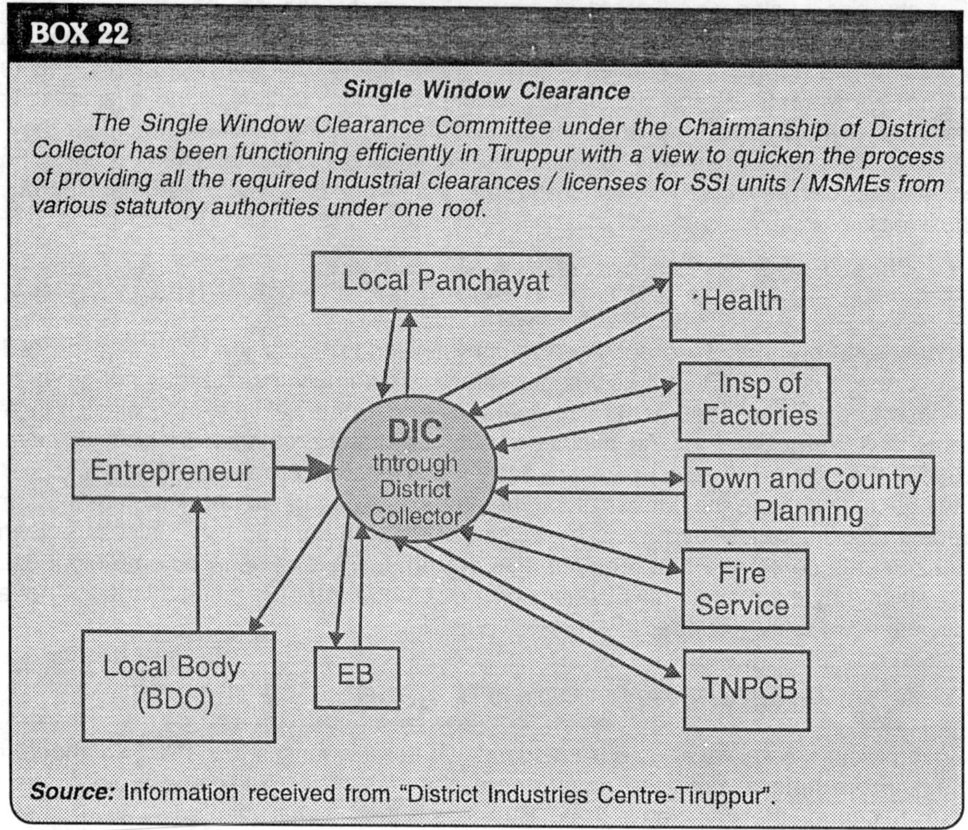

Source: Information received from "District Industries Centre-Tiruppur".

equipment etc. Government also provides subsidies for some business activity - e.g., an employment subsidy to take on the long-term unemployed.

- **Legal changes**

The government of the day regularly changes laws in line with its political policies. As a result businesses continually have to respond to changes in the legal framework.

Examples of legal changes include:

- The creation of a National 'Minimum Wage'.
- The requirement for businesses to cater for disabled people, by building ramps into offices, shops etc.
- Providing increasingly tighter protection for consumers to protect them against unscrupulous business practice. For example: consumer forum for the welfare of consumers.
- Creating tighter rules on what constitutes fair competition between businesses.
- Introduction of new legal practices.

22.3 Document Process Delay

The new entrepreneurs already have a very less knowledge about the documents required for opening the business. When they want to open the business they are not given correct information by the government agencies. Every time they miss some documents therefore it wastes their time and delays in opening the business. The speed of document clearance is very slow. It takes much time. Ultimately the new entrepreneurs frustrated because of the slow nature of the government offices.

22.4 No Information about Government Policies

Most of the time it happens the new entrepreneurs are not aware about government policies. They open business by their own without knowing the assistance available for them by government side. They do everything by their own. They do not have any idea about any assistance they can get from government side. Though government is trying to provide many facilities to the young entrepreneurs for opening their business but the fact is that most of the entrepreneurs are not able to take advantages of the government schemes and most of the entrepreneurs do not have any information about such schemes. If they would have known about it then definitely it would help them a lot. New entrepreneurs must always go through various sources of information. They can get information about government policies, rules and regulations from News channels, official government websites, news papers, government agencies, entrepreneurship development institutes etc.

22.5 Cumbersome Government Attitude

The government attitude is not serious about the new entrepreneurs business. They do not care about them. The new entrepreneurs are not given full information. The lack of entrepreneurial initiatives, the large debt burden and the bureaucratic red tapism can be accorded as obstacles to the growth and development of India. We understand reforms, we all understand liberalization –but what we need here is discipline, considering the licensing and regulatory nightmares faced by potential Indian Entrepreneurs. The challenges faced by an entrepreneur in the 21st century emphasize the need for a spirit of risk taking and Initiative.

22.6 Corruption/ Bribe

Entrepreneurs interviewed said they faced corruption at some time during their entrepreneurial journey while dealing with government procedure and officials.

Most of the new entrepreneurs any how face the hurdle of corruption. If he wants to open the business then he has to follow them at any cost. Here we can categorise the situation the First one where an entrepreneur knows that he has to face this problem and he prepares himself, he collects money and ready to pass the documents or to get the approval or to open the business without any hurdles or to save his time wastage, useless efforts. And in the other situation the entrepreneur doesn't know anything about such happenings and even if he knows about it or as soon as he knows about it then he is not ready to pay bribe that is actually demanded. Here he has two options either he can collect money that really lowers down his desire of entrepreneurship and if he wants to go through the legal one then he suffers a lot and that really create hurdles for the desired person who wants to become an entrepreneur.

In recent years, the detrimental effects of bureaucratic corruption gained attention from development economists as well as international financial institutions and policymakers. Corruption, which was previously ignored and mentioned only with caution, has taken a center stage. Nonetheless, corruption is not a new phenomenon. It is as old as government itself. The current literature on corruption highlights its harmful effects on growth (see Klitgaard 1988, Shleifer and Vishny 1993, Mauro 1995, Cheung 1996 and Bardhan 1997). However, until recently the growth literature did not adequately explain why corruption is low in some countries and endemic in others. (1) The relevant analytical problem is not to assess the harmfulness of corruption but why different political systems foster different levels of corruption. We cannot discern any useful prognosis from the literature on corruption so long as the causes of corruption are not clearly identified. Moreover, the empirical studies on the effects of corruption on economic growth are besieged by endogenous problems. Few of these empirical studies take into account the possibility that economic growth or the lack of it can increase or decrease the level of corruption.

The prevailing view is that corruption is harmful to economic growth. Mauro (1995) finds that corruption lowers investment and consequently, economic growth. Using data from a large sample of countries, he finds that corruption, red tape and bureaucratic inefficiency are negatively correlated with economic growth. Klitgaard (1988) suggests that when political power translates corruptly into economic gains, corruption redistributes resources from the poor to the rich and encourages malfeasance and rent seeking. In corrupt societies, government bureaucrats compete for positions of economic power and spend their time and energy in the pursuit of rents. This rent-seeking activity, in turn, affects the capacity of public institutions to provide services. (2) Corruption adversely distorts incentives and creates uncertainties about the expected benefits of productive activities, forcing entrepreneurs to undertake costly and inefficient loss-avoiding behaviors. Shleifer and Vishny (1993) suggest that corruption is a tax on economic activity that is more costly than legal taxes. Unlike taxation, corruption is illegal and real resources are wasted to avoid detection. The need to keep the transactions secret directs resources to hard-to-detect activities with no regard for economic consequences.

Contrary to this prevailing view that corruption is harmful to economic development, some studies suggest that it might be beneficial and enhance efficiency. (3) Left (1964) long ago proffered that corruption circumvents inefficient and cumbersome government regulations. He argues that corruption mitigates the distortionary effects of government policies and allows entrepreneurs to avoid bureaucratic delays. A direct payment to corrupt officials reduces the transactions cost of business and energizes corrupt civil servants who would have otherwise engaged in delaying tactics. (4) Left also claims that corruption generates a social benefit and serves as a mechanism for political participation and influence for minorities and foreign corporations. Left (1979: 328) remarks: "In most underdeveloped countries, interest groups are weak and political parties rarely permit the participation of elements outside the contending cliques. Consequently, graft may be the only institution allowing other interests to achieve articulation and representation in the political process."

Scott (1972) also argued that what is considered corruption in the West is in fact a continuation of traditional gift giving in less developed countries (LDCs). The imposition of Western values and attitudes has transformed this traditional gift exchange in LDCs into corruption. Tullock (1996) also claims that illicit payments are a substitute for higher wages. Corruption therefore saves money for the government that it would have otherwise paid in higher salaries. Lui (1996) makes the case that what some people call corruption is nothing but a fee for under priced services. He suggests that corruption restores the price mechanism and improves the allocation of resources in distorted and heavily regulated markets.

Reassessing the Relationship between Corruption and Economic Growth

22.7 Red Tapism

Red tapism is a derogatory term which refers to a hard-and-fast obligation to official procedures and formalities. It stands in sharp contrast to speeding up processes without compromising with quality or other attributes. The telltale signs of red tapism can be traced from unnecessary delays in decision making and implementation of plans. Red tape usually comprises of unneeded paper works, issuing of licenses getting held up for ages, having too many officials for a relatively insignificant job that can easily be handled without much fuss and so on.

By making deliberate delays unprofitable and rewarding promptness. Most delays occur in the garb of bureaucratic requirements for the sake of forcing people to cough up money just out of exasperation. When detected, such cases should invite exemplary punishment instead of warnings or just an order to do in any case.

22.8 Poor Infrastructure

With regard to infrastructure, India projects a poor show. The facilities like roads, highways, railways, ports, airports, power and telecom are in bad state causing high transport and supply-chain costs, it said.

Entrepreneurship is currently constrained by multiple factors and challenges; it is the young start-ups within the industry that face the toughest hurdles. For these companies, developing new revenue streams are the biggest roadblocks. Funding and access to capital is the other constraint these young entrepreneurs face, reflecting the fragile nature of their cash flows and nascent stage of venture capital. Being small in size and not so well known, these companies also had problems in attracting key personnel.

Organizations operating also challenged by the lack of industry-institution linkages, the absence of a consortium approach to R&D and the paucity of global-class talent.

Some of the other challenges facing by the entrepreneurs include the following:

- Access to capital and key technologies
- Lack of a domestic market to experiment and development capabilities.
- An acute shortage of equity (risk) capital, to support the development of the industry (both large and small) and infrastructure outside of the government.
- High entry barriers, including relatively larger investment and resources, a gestation period, technological complexity and end market and marketing knowledge
- Lack of resources for brand building

22.9 Providing the Growth Drivers

Clearly, the industry and the government have to work closely to provide a fillip. A host of initiatives can be jointly undertaken to catalyze the growth of this emerging industry. These include the following:

- Improve the level of funding and encourage networking between the seekers and givers.
- Increase the talent pool of target areas.
- Increase the access to test and development facilities at national scientific organizations.
- Introduce policies that foster a balance between innovations and facilitate technology diffusion.

- Ø Improve business training facilities.
- Ø Encourage innovation to ensure global competitiveness.

22.10 Registration of Company

Entrepreneurs face difficulty and delays in meeting various government requirements such as:

Obtaining Licenses

Entrepreneurs said they faced problems while obtaining various clearances and licences. Obtaining the necessary licenses to construct a warehouse/infrastructure remains extremely costly in India. It is also complex and time consuming, requiring 20 procedures and 270 days. India fares poorly when compared with the South Asia average of 16 procedures and 226 days. India ranks 155th in the world on the ease of licensing. Requirements vary considerably across states. It takes 159 days to fulfill all regulatory requirements to build a warehouse in Bhubaneshwar—the shortest within India. At the other end of the spectrum it takes 522 days in Ranchi. The number of procedures is lowest in Bhubaneshwar (16) and highest in Patna and Ranchi (25).

- **Current scene:** Industrial Licensing is governed by the Industries (Development and Regulation) Act, 1951. The Industrial Policy Resolution of 1956 identified the following three categories of industries: those that would be reserved for development in public sector, those that would be permitted for development through private enterprise with or without State participation and those in which investment initiatives would ordinarily emanate from private entrepreneurs. Over the years, keeping in view the changing industrial scene in the country, the policy has undergone modifications. Industrial licensing policy and procedures have also been liberalized from time to time. A full realization of the industrial potential of the country calls for a continuation of this process of change.

- **Obstacles:** The winds of change have been with us for some time. The industrial licensing system has been gradually moving away from the concept of capacity licensing. The system of reservations for public sector undertakings has been evolving towards an ethos of greater flexibility and private sector enterprise has been gradually allowed to enter into many of these areas on a case by case basis. Further impetus must be provided to these changes which alone can push this country towards the attainment of its entrepreneurial and industrial potential. This calls for bold and imaginative decisions designed to remove restraints on capacity creation, while at the sametime, ensuring that over-riding national interests are not jeopardized.

- **Overcome:** In the above context, industrial licensing will henceforth be abolished for all industries, except those specified, irrespective of levels of investment. These specified industries, will continue to be subject to compulsory licensing for reasons related to security and strategic concerns, social reasons, problems related to safety and over-riding environmental issues, manufacture of products of hazardous nature and articles of elitist consumption. The exemption from licensing will be particularly helpful to the many dynamic small and medium entrepreneurs who have been unnecessarily hampered by the licensing system. As a whole the Indian economy will benefit by becoming more competitive, more efficient and modern and will take its rightful place in the world of industrial progress.

22.11 Registering the Property

India ranks 110th on the ease of registering property. The process takes six procedures and 62 days, placing India among the upper half of South Asia countries. By contrast it takes only 1 day in Norway, 32 in China and 47 in Brazil. Costs are also high. Entrepreneurs must pay 8 per cent of the property value to register a transfer of ownership. On average in South Asia property registration costs 5 per cent of the property value. It is only 3 per cent in China and there is no cost in Saudi Arabia. Within India, it takes the least time to register property in Bengaluru and Hyderabad (35 days) and the most time in New Delhi (138 days) and in Kolkata (155 days). It costs the least in Ranchi (6 per cent of property value) and the most in Bhubaneshwar (14 per cent). The difference in time across cities is due to the different amount of time needed in each city to mutate a property title and to register the transfer at the sub-registrar. The different rates of stamp duty and transfer charges account for the differences in costs.

22.12 The Official Costs of Starting a Business Are High

A recent report of the International Finance Corporation ranked 17 different states on the ease of doing business by surveying the major cities in these states. The findings were not very surprising as Ludhiana in Punjab, home to some efficient small and medium industries, emerged on top, while Kochi and Kolkata in the Left-ruled Kerala and West Bengal languished at the bottom, probably an indication of the insufficient enthusiasm of the official machinery for encouraging entrepreneurship.

What accounts for these substantial differences in doing business across the major cities in India? The study has investigated this issue in detail by looking at the number of procedures for starting a business, the problems with dealing in construction permits, the time for registering property and other similar aspects like trading across borders, paying taxes, enforcing contracts and the steps for closing down a business.

The problems of doing business in India start right at the beginning when the entrepreneur registers his business. The process takes at least one month in Mumbai, which ironically has the fastest procedure. It goes up to 40-41 days in Bengaluru or Kochi, at the higher end. The substantial difference in the days taken for setting up a business in the best and the worst cities is difficult to understand as the number of procedures required for the process do not vary significantly. The count showed that it ranged from a minimum of 11 in Jaipur to 13 in Ahmedabad. In fact a large number of cities have more procedures for setting up business than the two ranked at the bottom.

Smart working of the state machinery is evident in cities like Ahmedabad and New Delhi, which have set up a mechanism for electronic payment of stamp duty by companies. These cities and Mumbai, also encourage on line application of VAT registration. The cities in states like Andhra Pradesh and Orissa have consolidated the registration for VAT and profession tax under the same authority. The aim should be to create a one-stop-shop for all pre- and post-registration requirements, says the report.

So, one can say that rather than the number of procedures it is the efficiency of the administration and accountability that accounts for substantial disparities in the speed of setting up a business. And procedures for starting a business in India have to be substantially overhauled if they are to attain the global benchmarks achieved in a country like New Zealand, where it takes just one day to get things started. Till then, Indian businesses would be forced to remain officially unacknowledged and unregulated in the informal sector, with their activities remaining largely unreported in the official statistics that play an important role in dictating policy.

Surprisingly, the efficiency of the cities alters substantially when we look at the second indicator of doing business, namely the ease of dealing with construction permits. Mumbai, which ranked in the forefront in the ease of starting a business, falls sharply to the bottom end with the time requirement position touching 200 days.

Only Kochi and Kolkata, which were at the bottom of the earlier list, did worse than Mumbai with the time taken extending to 224 and 258 days respectively. The most efficient state in dealing with construction permits was Hyderabad where it took only 80 days. However, Bengaluru, which lagged at the bottom end in the ease of doing business, made it way up to the second rank when it came to dealing with construction permits, by ensuring that it took only 97 days to deal with construction permits. But the achievement of Hyderabad and Bengaluru in cutting down the days for approving construction projects to 80 and 97 respectively has to be lauded as it took an average of 158 days even in the OECD countries.

Mumbai's slack performance in approving construction projects is explained by the excessive number of procedures prescribed. A businessman had to plod through 37 procedures to make his case for proceeding with construction. In sharp contrast, the procedures have been whittled down to just 15 in cities like Bengaluru, Chennai and Ahmedabad. The bulk of delays for the tardy progress of construction project approvals are attributed to problems created by utilities and inspectors. Their delays increased the time for clearance by around 160 days in Kochi, 100 days in Mumbai and 80 days in Kolkota.

The scope for improvement on the construction permits front is considerable as some cities like Hyderabad and Bengaluru have been able to cut down the required time for clearance by utilities and inspectors to around 30-35 days. These cities have emerged at the forefront by using cutting edge technologies like digitalised zoning plans, computerised building permit process and improved handling of applications, all of which seem to have been completed neglected in Kochi and Mumbai. The report advocated that the cities should go ahead with the computerisation of construction-related permits and approvals, rationalize and consolidate pre-approval clearances and increase administrative efficiency to ensure faster gains.

But the inefficiencies in starting a business and getting construction permit approvals pale in comparison with the more important aspect of securing property rights. This is reflected in the considerable disparity in time taken to register property which varied from just 24 days in Jaipur to 126 days in Bhubaneshwar. Kolkata, as usual, was ranked second from the bottom with the time being 155 days. Surprisingly, Kochi did comparatively better by ensuring property registration in 27 days. But there is substantial scope for improving the situation in other major metros like Delhi, Mumbai and Chennai where the time taken was 55, 44 and 48 days, respectively.

22.13 List of Industries in Respect of which Industrial Licensing will be Compulsory

1. Coal and Lignite.
2. Petroleum (other than crude) and its distillation products.
3. Distillation and brewing of alcoholic drinks.
4. Sugar.
5. Animal fats and oils.
6. Cigars and cigarettes of tobacco and manufactured tobacco substitutes.
7. Asbestos and asbestos-based products.

8. Plywood, decorative veneer and other wood based products such as particle board, medium density fibre board, block board.
9. Raw hides and skins, leather, chamois leather and patent leather.
10. Tanned or dressed fur skins.
11. Motor cars.
12. Paper and Newsprint except bagasse-based units.
13. Electronic aerospace and defense equipment; All types.
14. Industrial explosives, including detonating fuse safety fuse, gun powder, nitrocellulose and matches.
15. Hazardous chemicals.
16. Drugs and Pharmaceuticals (according to Drug Policy).
17. Entertainment electronics (VCRs, colour TVs, C.D. Players, Tape Recorders).
18. White Goods (Domestic Refrigerators, Domestic Dishwashing machines, Programmable Domestic Washing Machines, Microwave ovens, Air conditioners).

Note: The compulsory licensing provisions would not apply in respect of the small-scale units taking up the manufacture of any of the above items reserved for exclusive manufacture in small scale sector.

22.14 Governmental Measures to Help First Generation Entrepreneurs

Recognizing the importance of small and medium enterprises in the growth of Indian economy in terms of their contribution to country's industrial production, exports, employment and creation of entrepreneurial base, the Central and State Governments are undertaking several policy measures and incentives as well as implementing schemes and programmes for promotion and development of these enterprises. For this, entrepreneurship development and training is one of the key steps, particularly, for the first generation entrepreneurs. Entrepreneurship Development Programmes (EDPs) of various durations are being organized on regular basis by a number of organizations, such as, National and State level **Entrepreneurship Development Institutes (EDIs); Micro, Small and Medium Enterprises Development Institutes (MSMEDIs)** – formerly called Small Industries Service Institutes (SISIs); National and State level Industrial Development Corporations, Banks and other training institutions/agencies in private and public sector; etc. These EDPs aim to create new entrepreneurs by cultivating their latent qualities of entrepreneurship and enlightening them on various aspects necessary for setting up micro and small enterprises. Besides, Skill Development Programmes (SDPs) and Entrepreneurship-Cum-Skill Development Programmes (ESDPs) are also being organized by various public as well as private training institutions.

However, there are still wide spread variations in the success rate, in terms of actual setting up and successful running of enterprises, by the EDP/SDP/ESDP trained entrepreneurs.

Also, new entrepreneurs generally face difficulties in availing full benefits under available schemes of the Governments / financial institutions, completing and complying with various formalities and legal requirements under various laws/regulations, in selection of appropriate technology, etc. In order to bridge the gap between the aspirations of the potential entrepreneurs and the realities, there is a need to support and nurture the potential first generation entrepreneurs by giving them handholding support during the initial stages of setting up and managing their enterprises. Accordingly, the scheme called '**Rajiv Gandhi Udyami Mitra Yojana (RGUMY)**' has been launched to provide handholding support and assistance to the potential first generation entrepreneurs, who have already successfully completed EDP/SDP/ESDP or vocational training from ITIs, through the selected lead agencies, like 'Udyami Mitras'. This helps such entrepreneurs in the establishment and management of the new enterprise, in dealing with various procedural and legal hurdles as well as in completion of various formalities required for setting up and running of the enterprise, etc. The work profile of Udyami Mitras include networking, coordinating and follow up with various Government departments/ agencies/ organizations and regulatory agencies for channelizing the benefits available under various schemes to the first generation entrepreneurs and help them in setting up their enterprise.

22.15 Some of the other governmental measures for small and medium enterprises include:

- The Ministry of Micro, Small and Medium Enterprises has been implementing the **'Scheme of Surveys, Studies and Policy Research'** with a view to regularly/periodically collect, from primary, secondary and other sources, relevant and reliable data on various aspects and features of micro, small and medium enterprises (MSMEs) engaged in manufacturing and services (whether in the category of tiny/small scale industries, khadi, village industries or coir) as a composite group or specific segments thereof. It aims to study and analyse, on the basis of empirical data or otherwise, the constraints and challenges faced by the MSMEs as well as the opportunities available to them, in the context of liberalisation and globalisation of the economy. It further aims to use the results of these surveys and analytical studies for policy research and designing appropriate strategies and measures of intervention by the Government, by itself or in public private partnership mode, to assist and enable these enterprises in facing the challenges and availing of the opportunities with a view to enhancing their efficiency and competitiveness as well as expanding generation of sustainable employment by them.
- **Micro, Small and Medium Enterprises Development Act, 2006** has been enacted to facilitate the promotion and development as well as enhance the competitiveness of micro, small and medium enterprises and for matters connected therewith or incidental thereto. For this, it included the establishment of specific funds, notification of particular schemes/programmes, progressive credit policies and practices, preference in Government procurements to products and services of these enterprises, following more effective mechanisms for mitigating their problems, etc. It provides the first-ever legal framework for recognition of the concept of 'enterprise' which comprises both manufacturing (those engaged in the manufacture/production of goods pertaining to any industry) and service ((those engaged in providing/rendering of services) entities. Under the Act, three tiers of enterprises, namely 'micro, small and medium' have been defined for the first time. The Act also provides statutory consultative mechanism at the national level with balanced representation of all sections of stakeholders, particularly, these enterprises and with a wide range of advisory functions.
- The progressive de-reservation of products in the MSMEs aimed at providing opportunities for technological up gradation, promotion of exports and economies of scale, with a view to encourage modernization and enhance competitiveness in the sector. As on 13 March 2007, 125 items were dereserved. As on 8th February, 2008, 79 items more were dereserved. At present, the total number of items reserved for exclusive manufacture in the micro and small scale sector is 35.

- The National Manufacturing Competitiveness Programme (NMCP) has been launched to provide support to the manufacturing sector, particularly small and medium enterprises sector, in their endeavour to become competitive. It consists of **ten components and programmes** as the initiatives for development and promotion of MSMEs.
- Credit is one of the critical inputs for the promotion of small and medium enterprises. It is a part of the priority sector lending policy of the banks. Accordingly, several schemes and policies have been undertaken to provide adequate credit to such enterprises. One of such scheme is the **Credit Linked Capital Subsidy Scheme (CLCSS)** which was launched to facilitate technology up gradation by upfront capital subsidy to small, micro and medium enterprises, including tiny, khadi, village and coir industrial units, on institutional finance (credit) availed by them for modernization of their production equipment (plant and machinery) and techniques in specified sub-sectors/ products approved under the Scheme.
- Besides, the State and Union Territories (UTs) Governments are executing several promotional and developmental projects/schemes as well as providing a number of supporting incentives for development and promotion of MSME sector in their respective States/UTs. These schemes/ projects are executed through State Directorate of Industries, who have District Industries Centers (DICs) under them to implement Central/State level schemes. Around 30 MSME-DIs and 28 Branch MSME-DIs have been set up in State capitals and other industrial cities all over the country, with a view to provide assistance/ consultancy to prospective entrepreneurs as well as to existing units; conduct EDPs, Management Development Programmes, Skill Development Programmes, etc. Also, the State Industrial Development and Financial Institutions and State Financial Corporations look after the needs of the MSME sector.

SUMMARY

For any new business government approval is must without it, it is impossible to run the business. When the new entrepreneurs open the business they face many difficulties as far as getting government approval is concerned.

The problems faced by the new entrepreneurs in getting legal documents are:

Complex Document Procedures

Instantaneous Change in Policies

- Economic policy
- Taxation policy
- Interest rates
- Legal changes

Document Process Delay

No Information about Government Policies

Cumbersome Government Attitude

Corruption/ Bribe

Red-Tapism

Poor Infrastructure

Registration of Company

Entrepreneurs face difficulty and delays in meeting various government requirements such as:

Obtaining Licenses

Entrepreneurs said they faced problems while obtaining various clearances and licences. Obtaining the necessary licenses to construct a warehouse/infrastructure remains extremely costly in India. It is also complex and time consuming, requiring 20 procedures and 270 days.

Registering the Property

India ranks 110th on the ease of registering property. The process takes six procedures and 62 days, placing India among the upper half of South Asian countries. By contrast it takes only one day in Norway, 32 in China and 47 in Brazil.

The Official Costs of Starting a Business Are High

The problems of doing business in India start right at the beginning when the entrepreneur registers his business. The process takes at least one month in Mumbai, which ironically has the fastest procedure. It goes up to 40-41 days in Bengaluru or Kochi, at the higher end.

So, one can say that rather than the number of procedures it is the efficiency of the administration and accountability that accounts for substantial disparities in the speed of setting up a business. And procedures for starting a business in India have to be substantially overhauled if they are to attain the global benchmarks achieved in a country like New Zealand, where it takes just one day to get things started.

Governmental Measures to Help First Generation Entrepreneurs

Recognizing the importance of small and medium enterprises in the growth of Indian economy in terms of their contribution to country's industrial production, exports, employment and creation of entrepreneurial base, the Central and State Governments are undertaking several policy measures and incentives as well as implementing schemes and programmes for promotion and development of these enterprises.

Entrepreneurship Development Programmes (EDPs) of various durations are being organized on regular basis by a number of organizations, such as, National and State level **Entrepreneurship Development Institutes (EDIs); Micro, Small and Medium Enterprises Development Institutes (MSMEDIs)** to create new entrepreneurs by cultivating their latent qualities of entrepreneurship and enlightening them on various aspects necessary for setting up micro and small enterprises. **'Rajiv Gandhi Udyami Mitra Yojana (RGUMY)'** has been launched to provide handholding support and assistance to the potential first generation entrepreneurs.

KEYWORDS

Economic policy: The actions taken by a government to influence its economy.

Taxation: The act of levying a tax, or of imposing taxes, as on the subjects of a state, by government or on the members of a corporation or company, by the proper authority.

Red-Tapism: Excessive formality and routine required before official action can be taken.

First Generation Entrepreneurs: Who first time start their own business and do not have any business background.

Interest rate: An *interest rate* is the rate at which interest is paid by a borrower for the use of money that he borrows from a lender.

Registration of Company: A government official whose duty is to ensure that companies are properly registered and that, when registered, they file accounts and other information correctly.

QUESTIONS

1. What are the different problems faced by the new small entrepreneurs while getting government approval for opening the business?
2. What do you mean by Red Tapism? How it impacts the growth of new entrepreneurs?
3. What are the different measures taken by the Indian Government to help First Generation Entrepreneurs?
4. How does government make the process of assisting the new small entrepreneurs more effective? Give suggestions.

❑ ❑ ❑

Chapter – 23

Family Responsibility Obstacles

LEARNING OBJECTIVES

On completion of this chapter, you should be able to:

- ☺ *Explain obstacles created by family to the new small entrepreneurs.*
- ☺ *Describe the importance of family for the new entrepreneurs.*
- ☺ *Describe family support to entrepreneurs.*

It's difficult enough to give up the comforts of the corporate world to start a business. Without support of family and friends the journey can be challenging. To win the support of family takes time to explain the business and build a solid business plan. If others can see how entrepreneurs have taken the time to think it through and minimize the risks, they will be more supportive.

23.1 Importance of Family Responsibility

The support which family provides in terms of tolerance for failure and the help to stand up again is best. It is short lead time required to bounce back and the moral and material support, in case of failure, that puts family-based entrepreneurial activity in an advantageous position.

Family business success is down to "having a clear vision, mobilizing oneself with full conviction, the energy to work, not fearing change but pursuing it, having a dedicated team and a bit of luck!"

23.2 Family Pressure for Earning

The new entrepreneur faces many problems as far as family is concerned. Most of the entrepreneurs from India belong to middle class family where the thinking of family members about business is not good. The expectations of the middle class members are more towards doing a good job instead of opening a business. They do not want to take a risk which involves risk taking, financial support and even after that assurance cannot be given that, business will run and money will come back. These are the things that motivate the family not to go for business but rather to go for a job. This becomes hurdles for the entrepreneur when he has his own dream of becoming the entrepreneur and wants to open his own business. Unless and until he gets his family member's support he cannot open the business because up to that time also he is not fully dependent. Though he has entrepreneurial qualities but because of the family pressure he gives up his dream and goes for the job.

23.3 No Money/Little Assistance

Many entrepreneurs do not get complete financial assistance from the family. The belief of the family does not coincide with the business plan. The family members do not trust on the business. They think that the business is not for them and therefore they do not want their family members to go for the business. Opening the business requires huge money and the family members are not ready to give such a huge amount for the business. They just give or sometimes do not give money for opening the business. So the young entrepreneurs cannot do anything for such situation and they try to collect money from other sources i.e., from friends, relatives, banks and government schemes. The problem of the entrepreneurs from the family is that even if they have all the possible qualities of the entrepreneurs but without family support their speed of opening the business becomes slow.

23.4 No Supporting Hand

The entrepreneurs who do not get support from family have to do lot of tasks by themselves only. Either they can handle the business or they hire the employees to have a support in the business. But the fact is that for the entrepreneurs the probability of getting such an employee who can handle the business is very less. An employee never takes the business seriously, their

BOX 23

FICCI Ladies Organisation (FLO)

Established in 1983, FLO is the women Wing of FICCI, the Federation of Indian Chambers of Commerce and Industry which is the apex body of industry and chambers of commerce in India.

As an all India forum for women, FLO has members comprising of entrepreneurs, professionals, executives and others, who may not be working full time or are homemakers wanting to contribute to developmental initiatives.

FLO believes that the resources and strengths of women need to be channelised, to help develop their full potential. The primary objective of FLO is to promote entrepreneurship and professional excellence in women. It does this through its educational and vocational training programmes, talks, seminars, panel discussions and workshops on a vast range of subjects especially concerning women and business.

FLO works closely with the Ministry of MSME or Microcredit, Small and Medium Enterprises as well as with the Hans Seidel Foundation from Germany.

The training programmes are organised all over India especially in the smaller towns and semi-urban areas at three levels: ***At the grass root level****, emphasis is given on entrepreneurship development programmes for crafts-persons and others especially in the remote areas of different states of India.*

At the middle level*, women who wish to set up their own industry are given similar entrepreneurial development training to help them in developing skills for product identification, preparation of project reports, identify sources for funding, etc. Some training programmes are related to general business while others are specific to an industry.*

At the senior level *women who are already in business or profession are provided with skill enhancement programmes like sophisticated management techniques, international marketing, human resource development, financial accountancy, Information technology etc.*

Besides these, FLO receives and takes delegations abroad to promote bilateral trade, internationalism and networking among women.

The widespread network of FICCI has helped FLO reach out to more women around the globe. One of FLO's strength is its enormously powerful parent - FICCI, with its nationwide membership of:

- *1000 Chambers of Commerce*
- *450 Trade Associations*
- *1500 corporates*
- *It represents 2,50,000 business organisations.*

This translates into a vast network of organizations, government bodies and individuals who can be leveraged to contribute.

Source: Information received from "FICCI Ladies Organisation (FLO)".

performance is not good and therefore the entrepreneurs suffer from such things. Entrepreneurs cannot be on the entire place at all times, the entrepreneurs who have family support get one supervisor, the trusted one from the family so those entrepreneurs are relaxed about their business when they go out of their business for some business purpose. The entrepreneurs who run business without family support take many efforts to run the business, to handle the tasks and to grow the business.

23.5 No Time for Family

The entrepreneurs are so busy in their business that they cannot give proper time to their family. If the entrepreneurs are married and have children then they do not give proper time to their children and wife/husband. They bear two responsibilities the first one is of their family and the second is of their business. Many times they do not fulfill the requirements of their family, in such situation if the wife/ husband of the entrepreneurs support them in such critical situation then those entrepreneurs are able to give full time to their business without any stress but the same is not possible with the entrepreneurs who by any reason do not get support. For the entrepreneurs the family support is a must. It is also one of the important factors for the success of the entrepreneurs.

23.6 No Encouragement for the Business

The entrepreneurs who do not get family support for the business become lonely. They do not get encouragement for their business. They do not have any person with whom they can share their thoughts, or solve the business problems. They are under stress because they have to face the problems alone; they do not have at least moral support. They find it difficult to be mentally strong. These things lower the confidence of the entrepreneurs.

23.7 Less Prone to take Risk

The entrepreneurs who have family and are from poor and financially weak background are not able to take the risk so easily, even if they are very much sure that they will get success. They are not able to take risk because they have their limitations they have the responsibilities of their family also, with this fear if something will go wrong they do not take any risk in the business. If they are financially strong then definitely they take risk but the fact is that most of the small entrepreneurs are not the rich ones.

23.8 Force to take Family Business Only

The new entrepreneurs who have family business are always forced to take family business. They are not supported by the family members for their new business. For the entrepreneurs from the business family background it is not easy for them to divert to other business, even if they have all the business ideas and plans, they are not motivated for the other business. The family believes in the traditional business that will be moving forward by their next generation, it becomes hurdle for them to open the new business.

23.9 Family Support to Entrepreneur

The biggest strength in a family-run business is "the support and the availability of committed resources within the family to manage different aspects of businesses." Family support is must to new small entrepreneurs so that they can have more focus on their business and feel relaxed from family side. Otherwise most of the time with the stress of family and business both, the entrepreneurs cannot work properly and therefore their business suffers.

23.10 Tradition of Single Family

In today's world the tradition of living in joint family is decreasing. The couple who lives in joint family enjoys the benefits of family support for their children and for their personal work. They can share their problems with the family members and can ease their stress. If they do a major mistake in their life then joint family can absorb the shock of that mistake. The couple will not suffer much from their mistakes. The probability of diverting from the good path is very less in joint family because the old one from the family by their experience educate the others about what is good and what is bad. But as the tradition of joint family is decreasing day by day so the benefits are also decreasing. A person who does not live in a joint family cannot dare to take such a decision that can have a bad impact on their family. He is not able to take a risk. So a person who is very much enthusiastic to open a business cannot open a business easily because he does not have that support system in the form of joint family that is required by him in case he takes wrong decision.

23.11 Traditional Attitude of Family

The family members may be parent, uncle-aunty or grandparents they always dream about their children as a manager, officer or supervisor in any reputed company and accordingly they give education to their children. They invest money to educate them and to make them more competent. They take all efforts to fulfill their dreams and if their children get government job then they become very happy. They never want to see their children as businessman because it involves many risks and secondly they don't know anything about business and therefore trying to open a business is not a good idea for them. According to them opening a business is very risky and it will spoil the career of their children. With that fear in mind they are not at all ready to allow their children to open the business. So lastly the desire of their children does not matter for them as they are very much sensitive to the future of their children.

23.12 Women Entrepreneurs Family Problems

Women entrepreneurs face number of problems right from the commencement till running the business. The women entrepreneurs' family responsibilities towards family and society restrict them to fully devote their time for the business.

The basic family problems faced by women entrepreneurs are as follows:

Family ties

Women in India are very sensitively attached to their families. For them their family comes first. They are supposed to attend to all the household work, to look after the children and other members of the family. They are over burdened with family responsibilities like extra attention to husband, because they are not at all in a position to bear the anger of their husband or family members. In such a situation, it becomes difficult for them to fully concentrate and run the business successfully.

Look after children

The children in a family are very much attached to their mother. So as a mother it becomes very difficult for them to neglect their children. If women entrepreneurs live in a joint family then somewhat their problem gets solved but it totally depends on the nature of the family members. If they are helpful then it's ok otherwise their business focus gets divided into children and business and they are not able to run their business properly.

Male dominated society

In our society females are not treated equal to males. Women's self decisions are not taken in a good way in Indian society. Women are not allowed to take decisions by their own. Their entry to business requires the approval of the head of the family. Women are totally dependent to others in a family. It is not easy for women to start a business as they are the only person in family who look after the children, home and family members. Husband does not allow his wife to open a business because of his fear of who will look after the family and home work? If he allows her then family work will get shattered and children will lag in their study. Most of the women in India they themselves do not want to become an entrepreneur because of the above problems.

Family support

In India, women are bogged down by family ties and relationships and have to walk a tightrope between business and home. A woman's business success depends a great deal on the support she gets from her family members. In the male dominant world it is very hard for the women to come out with an idea of opening and running a business. Women want to open the business but it is not easy for them to come out of their family responsibilities because they do not have any support system in their absence.

Not able to neglect any family events

Most of the social events in Indian family cannot be completed without women. Most of the festivals demand women presence and if they are not present at that time then it is not tolerated by the family heads and members. The act is considered against the discipline of their respective religion. As far as men are considered the men can escape from their responsibilities but for women it is not at all easy to escape. Running the business requires your presence but because of family obligation it is not possible for the women to remain present in the business continuously.

So What Could Be the Solution?

23.13 Working with Family Members

The reality of small businesses is that family members are often called upon — or given the opportunity — to be a part of the business. Sometimes, as in my case, they're used in a pinch. But many other times, entrepreneurs turn to family members as employees, lenders or investors. Working with members of your family has the potential to be a very trying, sticky and challenging situation. It can bring out the best in you and your relatives—and also the worst in your working relationships. It can cause you to minimize or overlook errors or omissions that your relative commits or it can make you excessively hypercritical and condescending.

Just why does this happen? Working with family members is difficult for any number of reasons:

- You know so much about the other person—you've been privy to intimate information about them.
- You've most likely had arguments or negative conflicts with them.
- You have years of experiences with them, both positive and negative.
- You know the other person's "hot and cold buttons," the thoughts, feelings and behaviors that reward, cajole and pacify or punish, threaten and dismiss the other person.

- Maybe you don't like your relative or conversely, you're very close with that person, which means you could either be overly critical or overly protective of them.
- You may provide too much supervision or teamwork—or you may provide too little.

So how do you begin to correct the situation?

First, you need to approach the other person and acknowledge that the current relationship isn't working optimally, that something is either "too right" or "too wrong," too positive or too negative.

Second, R-E-S-P-E-C-T! The way you speak to each other as family business partners can be very different than how you speak to your other colleagues, but should it be? Make it a priority to promote a work atmosphere that is more professional and less personal.

Third, you need to agree to meet together or with an experienced, neutral, fearless and objective HR manager or external consultant.

Fourth, **Differentiate Business Discussions.** Once a family member or friend starts to work with you, there may be times when you will have to have discussions about business or work performance. Such conversations should have an entirely different tone than personal conversations would. Come up with ways to differentiate these discussions by designating certain settings for discussing business. For example, you may have business discussions in a conference room or set up specific times to address work matters. At all other times, the discussion of business would be off limits, allowing your personal relationship to continue to flourish.

Fifth, Define Business Roles. Before you agree to work with family, the related parties should draft a detailed description of each family member's role and responsibilities to the business. A detailed job description helps prevent one family member from feeling as if he is carrying other family member's weight or prevent one family member from encroaching into another family member's job. When working with others who are not family, those situations are annoying but not serious. When working with family, those situations are often taken personally and create big problems for the business and the family relationship.

Sixth, you need to clarify the specific goals each of you agrees to meet so that behaviors and attitudes are directed towards meeting the company's goals and mission. Ensure that any statement of goals you create is specific, can be measured and assessed and can be successfully achieved.

Seventh, Consider Using A Mediator. Instead of being the person to deal directly with your family member or friend, have another trusted employee serve as a direct manager or work closely with that person. Not only will it be easier to convey information that your family member or friend may not want to hear, but you'll be able to keep at arm's length distance between the two of you and there's less likely to be perceptions of favoritism.

Eighth, Succession Planning: Family businesses that plan ahead for change are more likely to have a smooth transition when the founder or founders are ready to retire. If you wait until the time comes, advises management expert Peter Drucker, it will be too late. He advises hiring an outsider to manage and plan succession. The family should agree ahead of time that this person will objectively evaluate and choose the most qualified candidate to take the wheel when the current chief officer is ready to hand it off.

The **ninth,** Don't Blur the Lines: As family and business partners you can often mix 'love and praise', versus 'respect and feedback'. There can be too much emphasis on personal feelings and too little on metrics and goals; you need to keep personal feelings from dominating the office place for the sake of the business.

The **tenth** and final step involves showing the positive quality of interpersonal relationships. Just because you're related to someone doesn't mean you need to love them or worship them, especially on the job. Nor does it mean that the company is a playground for working out family problems. What *is* required is that you demonstrate respect for other people, especially your relatives. You needn't be fawning or ostentatious with your praise or criticism of them, but you do need to be professional and appropriate, whatever the true nature of your feelings and attitudes toward others, especially family.

23.14 Prepare Yourself for Business

This means that we have to be willing to ask ourselves the really tough questions — questions you should be asking yourself too.

1. **Do you love your business as much as your family?**

   Let's be clear: You always have to love and provide for your family. However, there are times—especially in today's environment of hand-to-hand combat — when many of your normal family experiences have to be put on hold in order to tend to your business. You have to maximize profits in your business so your family life can continue on a reasonable basis.

2. **Do you take responsibility for every aspect of your business?**

   It is your business. It is your creation. You are liable for your faults. If employees do not work properly then it is your fault. You have selected them; you have taken interview; you have evaluated them. So you are responsible for their wrong act. You must be ready to take responsibility. Stop blaming the employees and ask yourself what you have done to improve their mistakes? If you train your employees, teach them, make them skillful and after that if some employees do not follow your directions and instructions and continue to make the same mistakes then replace them. Conventional wisdom places too much emphasis on limiting employee turnover. Turnover can be good because it allows you to get rid of the dead wood.

3. **Do you work on weekends?**

   The entrepreneurs never have a fixed time for work as the service men have. You can never say that today is Sunday or holiday so I don't want to work. Start working on weekends also if you do not work who knows you will lose any good opportunity on that day only. You can give this time to those works that you did not do and that were also not so much important because of your busy schedule. Weekends are a good time to meet prospective employees to know their problems and demands, to find out any small problems if exist in business.

4. **Are you aware of all of your customers and their needs?**

   You must know who are your customers? Who will buy it? It is important to know who is buying the product or the service. More important thing to ask yourselves is - do I have enough customers? What customers like? And what customers don't like? If you sell to a small market - consider it again before you start your venture, because you could end up having higher expenses than incomes.

5. **Does your ego get the best of you?**

   Never rest on your success (sales and profits). In business everyday is not the same day. You need to prepare plan and think on how can you earn more money? You need to make money every day. Don't rest on your laurels. Exorcise the ego.

6. **Are you clear in your directions?**

   You must be very much clear about your desires from the business and employees. You must have your expectations in written form so that there should not be any ambiguity. When you say something, say it with conviction and stand by it.

7. **Do you pay for performance?**

   You must know the mentality of your employees. You must know how can you make them happy and get the work done. Money is the best way to motivate the employees for their work. Employees work better when they know they'll be rewarded financially. If someone does a good job, reward them with bonuses, tell the other employees about his/her performance. By doing this employee will feel good and will put more efforts. If not, be sure they make less. Weed out the ones who are not serious about making your business as successful as it can be.

8. **Do you pay yourself well?**

   Always pay yourself first. If you're not happy with your salary, you know there's more work to be done. Vendors like to pretend they have your interests at heart, but they really care more about themselves than about you. You are not in business to make them rich, so they can always wait a few days for their money.

9. **Are you a defeatist?**

   One of the qualities of entrepreneur is he never gives up. Even if the economy is not good but you cannot just say that my business is not working because the economy is down. These excuses will make you weak. This is the time when you need to work hard for your business. You'll be surprised at the energy that comes when your hard work starts paying off.

10. **Are you satisfied?**

    You shouldn't be. You must always try to think well than the present. There is always a room for making the things better. It's that little extra those differentiate you from the other business and make you unique in the market. This differentiation will lead you to a success. Failure isn't an option. Commit to doing whatever it takes. You must be very much clear about how much profit you want from your business. Focus on it. Don't wish for it or imagine what it would be like. Force it into reality. Fight for every sale. Learn to love winning.

23.15 Engaging Family in Your Startup Business

If you are starting a business be sure to involve your family right from the start. Don't wait until problems and resentment arise over your long work hours or until you hear "all you ever talk about is your business - you don't care about us anymore."

Treat your business as a family grass-roots effort and get loved ones excited about it right from the start. Remember: If they are not cheering you on or working by your side, your family may someday rally against you in protest if they feel less important to you than the business.

If you don't involve your spouse/partner or children they are likely to resent the time you will need to spend developing and running your business. *You* might not mind working weekends or long into the night because you are excited about your business, but your *family* will. When people who are used to getting your time and attention see your energies is being diverted to a business, they are likely to see the business as competition and complain.

Involve Your Family in Your Business

More will be the people more will be the chances of getting good ideas. If you want an excellent idea for your business then it will be a good option to involve your family members in your business. Explain them what kind of idea you want then ask them about their ideas. You must listen to them very carefully. Do not take them lightly. It is not necessary that ideas come after investing huge money or contacting to the experienced and intelligent experts but it can come from any one. If you will not take the ideas of your family members seriously then they will not show interest and will stop thinking. You must give importance to their thoughts. Who knows that the excellent idea will come out from your child? By involving your family members you will be benefited because now you are not thinking alone but many brains are working for your business. As you have a support of your family members so you can focus on other work. For small entrepreneurs it is a good deal if someone is helping them for solving their problems and there is no need of any paid assistant.

23.16 Taking Loan from Friends and Family

Tap into this popular source of startup financing

Most businesses have started with money from four or five different sources. After self-financing, the second most popular source for business start-up money is comprised of friends, relatives and business associates. "Family and friends are great sources of financing."These people know you have integrity and will grant you a loan based on the strength of your character." It makes sense. People with whom you have close relationships know you're reliable and competent, so there should be no problem in asking for a loan, right? So how can eager entrepreneurs keep their personal relationships from going belly-up when borrowing start-up capital? Here are a few guidelines to consider:

Tell your friend exactly why you need to borrow money

Tell your friends exactly why you need to borrow money. You can draft a letter explaining how the money will be used and what you intend to get out of the temporary loan. This may help ease your friends' concerns about lending money to you.

Setting up a loan or investment with friends or family

If you decide to accept a loan or investment from friends or family it is best practice to approach it as if it were a formal finance deal.

This will involve:

- Presenting your business plan
- Preparing a business case
- Taking professional advice
- Having a formal, written agreement

Before approaching a friend or family member you should create or revise your business plan so that you can show them the new plan for your business and their investment in it. Make your proposal with the same considerations as you would for approaching a bank manager. The friend or relative will need to know how their money will be put to use and what the bigger picture for your business is. Make them aware of all risks and worst-case scenarios. You need to make a business case to a prospective lender or investor that will persuade them to finance your business instead of their own personal plans.

Choose lenders carefully

Some friends and family members may not be capable of offering "no strings attached" loans and may consider someone's indebtedness to them as a free license to meddle with their business and their life. Any friends or family members who may have ulterior motives for helping an investor out should be left off the list, according to Entrepreneur.com. Additionally, it can be worthwhile to "think outside the box" when considering potential sources of capital, according to *Expert Business Source,* an online publication dedicated to small business issues. Parents, aunts and childhood friends are only a small portion of the potential lender pool. Consider extended relations and family acquaintances as well.

Borrowers should be realistic

Borrowers should be realistic about what a practical repayment plan would be and not try to borrow more than they can repay. You have to treat it the same as any kind of loan and be realistic. If you're considering borrowing money from someone close to you, first draw up a contract. Put it in writing and make it as businesslike as possible. Even get it notarized by a notary public. This will help protect the borrower as well as the lender. In case of a lawsuit, both parties will be held to the terms of the agreement. To further sweeten the deal, borrowers should put something of their own on the table — and be ready to kiss it goodbye should they default.

Pay Back the Loan

Pay back the loan, starting as soon as possible immediately, if you can. Don't let the loan sit out their unpaid. Start making payments, even if they are small. Determine an amount of interest on the loan, even if the lender says it's not necessary. You are paying back the loan and including interest is a great good-faith gesture and it may save the relationship.

Consider a Limited Partner Arrangement

If the person really wants to participate in the business, consider bringing the person in as a partner, but as a limited partner rather than a full (general) partner. A limited partner has less say in the day-to-day operations, which might be easier for you in running the business. The person might also be more comfortable with having limited personal liability. Having an agreement in writing, setting out all the terms and conditions and agreeing on the "What if" situations will help you keep your family and friends in the fold instead of making enemies.

Be realistic

Don't make false promises because they're your friends and family, you may feel the urge to dazzle them with suggestions that they're all going to become rich, fast. But starting a business can be extremely challenging and this is a tough economy. When you're borrowing from friends and family and if you can, under-promise and over-deliver, but above all, when structuring your repayments, pad in some extra time for unexpected problems — like having your own clients or vendors dragging their feet in paying *you* back.

23.17 Young Entrepreneurs' Family Balance

Overcoming to Overachieving: Business Lessons for a Young Entrepreneur, by a Young Entrepreneur

Before you begin your new and exciting venture into the business world, take time out to enjoy what you have already accomplished. Realize that what you are doing may not become a total success in the end and what you are more importantly gaining is business experience. Take a good look at the other young people you come in contact with everyday and understand the strides you have taken to set yourself apart from those around you and the benefits these efforts will earn you. Just by trying you have become an "overachiever" in your peer group.

As a young entrepreneur, there are certain business related and personal related obstacles you will have to endure in order to become successful. Some factors are real, such as where you will get your initial funding and where you will find time to manage your business, family and school responsibilities all at once. Your age or experience levels are nothing more than mental games you will play with yourself that will hinder your performance and success. As a young entrepreneur, you must overcome in order to (over)achieve.

In your first attempt at building a successful business you will undoubtedly come across times of trouble. To preempt feelings of failure during these inevitable situations, begin by taking a walk around the local mall. There you will find many of your peers working in jobs that they do not enjoy. These jobs will never serve a purpose in their lives other than paying for their current expenses. At the mall you will also find others, much older than you, working in dead-end jobs in which they have no control over their future or their success. They wake up, go to work, come home, go to sleep and start over again in the morning. You, however, are involved in a dynamic business experience that will help you throughout your life. Your age should never concern you. It should be used to your advantage rather than becoming a detriment to your success.

Understand that your youth enables you to do many things in business and take risks that older people in the same position could not. You are young, without a wife and three kids, unlike your competition. You can take chances and not have to worry about feeding your children every day. Your youth grants you energy and a sharp mind. Use these factors to separate yourself from older competitors. You should view yourself as a "young gun" of business and take things head on, because if your business flops, so what? You can always go back to McDonald's, but you can never regain your youth. If you need steady income while your business is still developing, use your part time job to your advantage. It could be the only source of capital you have at first. Once again, if either your job or your new business doesn't work out, so be it, you can always make up for it in the future and you'll be wiser as well.

It is prudent to take a step back and evaluate your position before embarking on a business venture. It may be difficult to gain funds for your business and a part time job may be the only way you will be able to achieve your business goals. Some persons are fortunate when starting out because they (and their parents) had planned ahead and began saving money from the time they were a small child. If you have not already done so, go to the bank and open a savings account. Not a checking account, but a savings account that you will not withdraw from unless needed to advance your business. Begin to grow your funds in the bank while your business is still young. As you grow and expand the money can be used and replaced. Save as much of your paycheque as you can while being able to pay your everyday expenses. As your business grows and you are able to support yourself, you should then focus your attention fully on developing your business.

College and college work are other obstacles that are unique to younger entrepreneurs. It is important to set your priorities straight. No matter how successful your business is becoming or how much your business needs to be worked on; you must keep your college work as your top priority. It is easy to ignore assignments and lose focus in college because of the million rupees ideas floating around in your head. Be sure to understand that college is what will help you later in life as you continue your business career. Set homework time aside every day and keep your grades in order. No one wants to deal with a businessperson who has failed out of college.

Summary

It's difficult enough to give up the comforts of the corporate world to start a business. Without support of family and friends the journey can be challenging. To win the support of family takes time to explain the business and build a solid business plan. If others can see how entrepreneurs have taken the time to think it through and minimize the risks, they will be more supportive.

The family problems faced by the entrepreneurs while running a business are as follows:

- Importance of family responsibility
- Family pressure for earning
- No money/ little assistance
- No supporting hand
- No time for family
- No encouragement for the business
- Less prone to take risk
- Force to take family business only
- Family support to entrepreneur

Women Entrepreneurs Family Problems

Women entrepreneurs face number of problems right from the commencement till running the business. The women entrepreneurs' family responsibilities towards family and society restrict them to fully devote their time for the business.

The basic family problems faced by women entrepreneurs are as follows:

Family Ties,

Look after Children,

Male Dominated Society,

Family Support,

Not Able To Neglect Any Family Events.

Working with family members: The required tasks are as follows:

- First, you need to approach the other person and acknowledge.
- Second, R-E-S-P-E-C-T.
- Third, you need to agree to meet together.
- Fourth, Differentiate Business Discussions.
- Fifth, Define Business Roles.
- Sixth, you need to clarify the specific goals each of you agrees to meet.
- Seventh, Consider Using A Mediator.
- Eighth, Succession Planning.
- Ninth, don't blur the Lines.
- Tenth and final step involves showing the positive quality of interpersonal relationships.

Prepare yourself for business

This means that we have to be willing to ask ourselves the really tough questions—questions you should be asking yourself too.

- Do you love your business as much as your family?
- Do you take responsibility for every aspect of your business?
- Do you work on weekends?
- Are you aware of all of your customers and their needs?
- Does your ego get the best of you?
- Are you clear in your directions?
- Do you pay for performance?
- Do you pay yourself well?
- Are you a defeatist?
- Are you satisfied?

How to Involve Your Family in Your Business

Being a good listener is an important skill all business owners need to develop; it validates people and when you open your mind to new ideas and concepts it will help you grow your business faster.

Start by practicing with your own family.

Ask your family (including children) for ideas and strategies and listen carefully.

Get young children to color "idea" pictures (and hang them on your wall.)

Tap into this popular source of startup financing.

Loans from friends and family offer some substantial benefits. Rates are typically lower, terms tend to be more flexible and the approval process is significantly simpler than with traditional loans.

So how can eager entrepreneurs keep their personal relationships from going belly-up when borrowing start-up capital? Here are a few guidelines to consider:

Tell your friend exactly why you need to borrow money.

Setup a loan or investment with friends or family.

Choose lenders carefully.

Borrowers should be realistic.

Pay Back the Loan.

Consider a Limited Partner Arrangement.

Be realistic.

Young Entrepreneurs' Family Balance

Overcoming to Overachieving: Business Lessons for a Young Entrepreneur, by a Young Entrepreneur

As a young entrepreneur, there are certain business related and personal related obstacles you will have to endure in order to become successful. Some factors are real, such as where you will get your initial funding and where you will find time to manage your business, family and school responsibilities all at once. Your age or experience levels are nothing more than mental games you will play with yourself that will hinder your performance and success. As a young entrepreneur, you must overcome in order to (over)achieve.

KEYWORDS

Business Role: A prescribed or expected behavior associated with a particular position or status in a group or organization.

Interpersonal relationship: An interpersonal relationship is the nature of interaction that occurs between two or more people.

Business Goals: Goals simply take the organization's vision and looks at where it is going and maps out the steps to get there.

Strategic planning: A strategic planning process delivers a set of defined initiatives (projects) that achieve a desired set of business goals.

QUESTIONS

1. Explain in detail the family related problems faced by the new small entrepreneurs?
2. What are the problems faced by women entrepreneurs in India. Explain.
3. What do the entrepreneurs need to know while running a family business? Explain.
4. How can you turn your family members, friends and relatives into a good source of finance?

❑ ❑ ❑

CHAPTER – 24

CULTURAL OBSTACLES

LEARNING OBJECTIVES

On completion of this chapter, you should be able to:

☺ *Explain what are the cultural obstacles faced by new small entrepreneurs while opening business.*

☺ *Discuss the responsibilities of entrepreneurs towards their culture.*

☺ *Describe cultural attitude towards new business.*

☺ *Describe the barriers to entrepreneurs and discrimination with entrepreneurs.*

Motives impel men to action. Entrepreneurial growth requires proper motives like profit-making, acquisition of prestige and attainment of social status. Ambitious and talented men would take risks and innovate if these motives are strong. The strength of these motives depends upon the culture of the society. The new entrepreneurs if get proper cultural support then definitely it helps them to get success in their business. The following are the cultural obstacles faced by the new entrepreneurs.

24.1 Cultural Attitude

Entrepreneurs take most of the values from their culture only. Their attitude, behaviour, interaction, thinking most of the human behaviours are decided by their culture only. For entrepreneurs it becomes difficult to overcome that. For the entrepreneurs from particular background that background creates the attitude of the entrepreneurs. They think everything from the mindset that they have developed from their family, relatives or the surroundings. Entrepreneurship can develop in a society in which cultural norms permit variability in the choice of paths of life. Unfortunately, the Indian culture consists of a network of benefits that in many ways run counter to entrepreneurship. For example, Indians believe that being passive and content with the *status quo* is healthier for the inner soul than striving to improve one's situation. They believe that peace of mind can be achieved from spiritual calm rather than from materialism. They keep this thing in mind and when they do business these things reflect in their business behaviour also.

24.2 Sensitive to Emotional Resemblance

People in India are more sensitive to emotional resemblance in the workplace than to work and productivity. They think by their heart. They cannot become so rude. Their culture restricts them to something against their culture. But sometimes doing this they also break the law of the business i.e., they should behave professionally and should be the disciplined one. Moreover the entrepreneurs should think the business in term of business only. They should be ready to fulfill the requirements of their business without any restriction generated by their culture.

24.3 Caste System

Caste system is very critical in India like country. In India caste system has very much influence on the human being. Caste decides the business of the person. The person who wants to do business other than their traditional business is not so easy for that person. Even sometimes family does not support them to go for the other business. The person who wants to start their other business then at that time the different caste people of that business creates barriers to them. This becomes really difficult for that person to open business. The caste system has impeded class mobility for centuries. The caste system and its series of obligations reinforce the practice of following a family occupation rather than launching a new venture. An entrepreneur needs to work around the clock and this has kept some people away from their own start-ups. After all, compared with other countries, family life in India is more important. People, even today, think that taking up a job is much better than taking a risk and starting a venture. If a job is taken up after college, the person will soon have a comfortable existence. The other scenario could be starting a venture after working for four to five years. This requires a lot of commitment and courage to leave the present job. As time passes by, the risk-taking capacity goes down.

BOX 24

Accelerating Women Entrepreneurs (AWE)

AWE is an alliance-based marketing campaign for the global women entrepreneurs movement – created to tell the story of women entrepreneurs and of how, by Accelerating Women Entrepreneurs, AWE can mitigate poverty, increase prosperity and advance peace.

The campaign is designed to attract attention, energy and resources to support women entrepreneurs worldwide to exponentially accelerate the number, scale and positive impact of women entrepreneurs around the world, particularly in developing countries.

By engaging global audiences, including academia, governments, multi-national corporations, NGOs, community groups, entrepreneurs, executives and professionals AWE wants to:

- *Foster widespread recognition of the social and economic value and high leverage, of investing in women entrepreneurs world-wide and of the role women entrepreneurs play in advancing broadly distributed prosperity and promoting peace;*
- *Effect legal reforms that facilitate enterprise creation for women around the world, especially for women living in poverty; and*
- *Attract capital, technical expertise, mentoring and other resources to support women entrepreneurs to flourish.*

The AWE Alliance – catalyzed by FLOW to facilitate multi-sector collaboration, draw on the assets, resources and capabilities of various Alliance Partners and advance the shared objectives of the program while also addressing specific partner organizational needs and objectives.

- *Media partners will provide programming and advertising time and content.*
- *Retail partners will provide point-of-sale exposure and opportunities for action.*
- *Other corporate partners will provide product and promotional tie-ins, distribution channels and access to stakeholders.*
- *Non-profit partners will provide content, credibility, access to stakeholders and relationships.*
- *Ongoing grass-roots marketing and public relations will provide sustained, extensive exposure for the program and program partners.*

Who is FLOW?

A corporation founded by John Mackey, co-founder and CEO of Whole Foods Market and innovative educator Michael Strong and a broad coalition of partners. FLOW is founded on a belief that the creativity, innovation and generative power of entrepreneurs and entrepreneurship are a key to addressing the challenges and opportunities facing humanity and that the process of entrepreneurship in itself fosters nourishing.

FLOW ideas and FLOW action are based on commitments to:

- *Cultivate human nourishing*
- *Practice non-violence, non-coercion and radical tolerance*
- *Promote freely-chosen, mutually beneficial solutions*
- *Criticize by creating!*

FLOW is also committed to rigorous, intellectual integrity and to the principles of transparency, dialog and collaboration. The word "FLOW" refers to an optimal state of human experience in which individuals are fully engaged in creative endeavours, experiencing fulfillment, happiness and well-being; and the means by which increases in the free global flow of goods, services, capital, people and information will accelerate human progress and well-being.

Source: Information received from "FLOW".

24.4 Not Taking into Account the Religion, Region or Background of your Counterpart

As an entrepreneur it becomes necessary for the entrepreneurs that they should understand the culture of others with whom they want to do business. The entrepreneurs never try to learn the culture of their partners with whom they are doing business. Sometimes the entrepreneurs behave in their own manner when they interact with others. But the fact is that as a new entrepreneur you should understand that you require other persons for your business. You should know him thoroughly. You should have all the cultural information of other person with whom you are doing business. These are the things that the entrepreneurs should know and it really affects the business. The Indian entrepreneurs though are very rich but they are very attached with their culture; they cannot tolerate any indiscipline with their culture. If you know the others' culture and you are very respectful about the others' culture then definitely it will help you for the business. India has 23 languages and half a dozen major religions, including Hinduism, Christianity, Buddhism, Jainism and Sikhism.

You must customize your approach. "A Punjabi-speaking Sikh machine shop owner in Delhi may behave very differently from a Gujarati-speaking vegetarian Jain in Mumbai. In that sense, India is like Europe. You wouldn't do business in Sweden the same way as you would in Croatia, would you?"

The entrepreneurs face many problems when they deal with different religion, region business persons. They behave same with all kind of persons. They forgot that it will not work. Their ideas may be interesting for one religion person so the other religion person may not take any interest in that. It is because of their mindset. Their thinking has the influence of their region, background and religion.

24.5 Missing the Social Nuances

The Indian entrepreneurs have a tendency that they suddenly do not say 'No' to anything unless that is the illegal one. Business people in India, as a general rule, don't like to say no. even if they think that they dislike some points in the business deal they will never say no. They think that they will hurt the sentiments of the others or the other person will get angry and become unhappy.

Most of the time the other person after knowing the tendency or the nature of entrepreneurs, try to exploit that new entrepreneur. The culture of India is such that we do not want to hurt anyone and the entrepreneurs apply the same thing in business also. But the entrepreneurs must make difference with their business partners and non business partners. When it comes to business they should behave more logically, focused and aggressively. They should know that they are in the business to earn the profit and to progress the business.

24.6 Cultural Values

Value systems and cultural norms affect the acceptability and perceived utility of entrepreneurial activity. Thus, whereas Western culture tends to encourage the drive to achieve that McClelland (1961) found to be a key aspect of the entrepreneurial personality, the Indian culture consists of a network of beliefs that in many ways run counter to entrepreneurship. An entrepreneur if does business he will do the business with their cultural values. For example, Indians believe that be the satisfied one. Do not go for wealth. Peace is the secret of life. They believe that peace of mind can be achieved from spiritual calm rather than from materialism. Work, in and of itself, is not valued in India and is done with involvement only when done for a nurturing superior; otherwise, it gets perfunctory attention.

The Indian entrepreneurs when start their business they always keep these things in mind that they should not do something against their cultural values. They do business with their beliefs and discipline. But sometimes these become problems when the others do not do the same thing. The other entrepreneurs will do anything to achieve profit or progress in the business and that person achieves that progress too. The new entrepreneur finds himself in dilemma whether he is correct or not.

Western theorists-in societies where people value control-interpret passivity withdrawal and submissiveness as inward behaviors, which in Western culture are signs of relinquished control. In India, much energy and creativity (which may have been manifested in entrepreneurial behavior in the context of a different culture) is redirected towards aligning oneself with the environment status quo (accepting destiny).

When a culture is such that people are conditioned to believe in an external locus of control (emphasis on destiny, for instance), self-efficacy may be low, resulting in low levels of entrepreneurial effort. Many researchers have found correlations between self-efficacy and subsequent task performance (Bandura 1982; Bandura and Adams 1977; Bandura, Adams and Beyer 1977; Bandura, Adams, Hardy and Howells 1980; Chambliss and Murray 1979; Feltz 1982; and Locke et al. 1984). In India, an external locus of control has been reinforced by the caste system, which has impeded class mobility for centuries. Gadgil (1959), Medhora (1965) and Weber (1958), among others, observed that the caste system and its series of obligations reinforces the practice of following a family occupation rather than launching a new venture. two Furthermore, as noted by Nafziger (1971), it used to be that leading entrepreneurs tended to belong to communities in which caste divisions were not rigidly observed! . As summarized by Hoselitz, “entrepreneurship can develop only in a society in which cultural norms permit variability in the choice of paths of life” (1960, p.155).

24.7 Culture Diffusion

When a cultural item diffuses, it typically does not keep spreading and spreading forever. Instead it tends to diffuse outward from its place of origin, encounter one or more barrier effects—things that inhibit cultural diffusion—and stop spreading.

Culture diffusion has created problems for the new entrepreneurs. They are new in the market they do not know the business strategies. When they start business they do not keep in mind the cultural diffusion effects. They do the business keeping in mind about the particular culture. For example a restaurant may serve the food according to the need of Indian culture only but as the other cultures are diffusing into the society and people are trying the other culture i.e., they eat Chinese or burger then in such situation it is not good for the entrepreneurs to serve the food according to the Indian culture. They should study the different culture and accordingly try to serve the food. This will be possible only when they start giving importance to the other culture also.

Social barrier effects consist of characteristics that differentiate human groups and potentially limit interaction between them; thus inhibiting the spread of culture. Examples include language, religion, race and ethnicity and a history of conflict between specific cultural communities. Islam, for instance, nowadays acts as a social barrier in many Middle Eastern countries by discouraging adoption of certain styles of western dress and music. For much of human history, therefore, barrier effects tended to isolate cultural communities from each other, inhibiting their ability to share cultural characteristics. Today, however, traditional barrier effects are being overwhelmed by modern means of communication. Isolation is on the decline. Cultural characteristics are diffusing as never before.

Adoption of a new culture item is often accompanied by disuse of an old one. Hence, global decline in cultural diversity is a significant modern trend. Virtually hundreds of languages spoken by formerly isolated peoples will disappear during the next 50 years because, due to diffusion of "modern global languages" (such as English, Spanish and French), they are not being passed on to the next generation.

24.8 Barriers to Entrepreneurs

Physical barriers in the workplace

Physical barriers in the workplace include:

- Marked out territories and empires into which strangers are not allowed. They are not accepted by the other people. The new entrepreneurs are not welcome by the old people. They create barriers to them. The old one fears of the competition or lose of the business to the strangers. They instead of taking the competition from the new one, they try to restrict them to come into the business.
- Closed office doors, barrier screens and separate areas for people of different status. The Low class people are treated in a different way than high class people. The low class entrepreneurs are not treated well as others are treated. The high status entrepreneurs have more attitudes they never behave normally with the low status entrepreneurs. If the low status entrepreneurs are in the same business then the high status entrepreneurs try to restrict them in the business even by some illegal means. New entrepreneurs become helpless in such situation.
- Large working areas or working in one unit that is physically separate from others.

  Research shows that one of the most important factors in building cohesive teams is proximity. As long as people still have a personal space that they can call their own, nearness to others aids communication because it helps us get to know one another. The new entrepreneurs are not given the chance to prove themselves. The government authority or any other institutes suffer from proximity. They try to take the people to whom they are familiar. They do not go for the qualities of the entrepreneur but they will support those people who are from their caste, religion or their friends, relatives. Such kind of things can never provide a good platform to the new entrepreneurs. They suffer from the biasness of the respective authority.

Perceptual Barriers

The entrepreneurs have more impact of their family, friends, relatives and religion. These relationships decide the perception of the entrepreneur. How does he think? How does he behave? How does he solve the problem? These things are right whenever there is no competition or the competition is between the same kinds of people. But the situation changes when the entrepreneurs have a competition with the totally different people. In this situation the culture may become barrier or boost the life of the entrepreneur. An entrepreneur from the traditional and religious background will not give a tough competition to the entrepreneur from the modern and open minded background

Emotional barriers

Entrepreneurs' emotional barriers have a major impact on the entrepreneurs. They fear to show trust on others. They cannot risk suddenly. They think so much on the issue or plan. The thinking itself destroies their business. They do not become free to others but in business interacting with others is the requirement of the business. The entrepreneurs should interact with every person who is attached with the business. One of the chief barriers to open and free communications is the emotional barrier. It is comprised mainly of fear, mistrust and suspicion. The roots of our emotional mistrust of others lie in our childhood and infancy when we were taught to be careful what we said to others. Entrepreneurs' problem is that they do not face the risk but try to protect from the risks.

Behavioural barriers

The entrepreneurs do not mix themselves to any group. They always search the reason to belong to the group. The reason may be caste, religion or anything. Because of this behaviour they normally keep themselves away from the group where they are not getting the things that they want. An entrepreneur should mix in any group where they see the business opportunities without thinking any other cultural reason. When we join a group and wish to remain in it, sooner or later we need to adopt the behaviour patterns of the group. These are the behaviours the group accepts as signs of belonging. The group rewards such behaviour through acts of recognition, approval and inclusion. The groups which are happy to accept you and where you are happy to conform, there is a mutuality of interest and a high level of win-win contact. Where, however, there are barriers to your membership of a group, a high level of game-playing replaces good communication.

Language barriers

Language that describes what we want to say in our terms may present barriers to others who are not familiar with our expressions, buzz-words and jargon. When we express our communication in such language, it is a way of excluding others. In a global market place the greatest compliment we can pay another person is to talk in their language. In India itself many languages are there. Those languages have their own way of expressing the thoughts and this differs from language to language. So entrepreneurs must have knowledge about the different culture in a country. The different caste or religion people have their own way of business language. Entrepreneurs if will have a knowledge then they can convey them or negotiate with them in those people's way. A Marwari may behave in a different style than a Guajarati people behave. The entrepreneurs if will have a knowledge then they will understand the different people that will benefit them in their business.

Gender barriers

Women entrepreneurs are not treated the way the male entrepreneurs are treated they are not given the full freedom, they are less trusted. It is not expected by the traditional thinking family that women will work in the business. These things create obstacles for becoming entrepreneur even if female has all the required qualities to become an entrepreneur. There are distinct differences between the speech patterns in a man and those in a woman. A woman speaks between 22,000 and 25,000 words a day whereas a man speaks between 7,000 and 10,000. In childhood, girls speak earlier than boys and at the age of three, have a vocabulary twice that of boys.

The reason for this lies in the wiring of a man's and woman's brains. When a man talks, his speech is located in the left side of the brain but in no specific area. When a woman talks, the speech is located in both hemispheres and in two specific locations. This means that a man talks in a linear, logical and compartmentalized way, features of left-brain thinking; whereas a woman talks more freely mixing logic and emotion, features of both sides of the brain. It also explains why women talk for much longer than men each day.

24.9 Some Tips for Entrepreneurs

Since many Indians are proficient in English, you need not worry about the language barrier. But here are additional things to consider when doing business in India:

- India's culture is very family-centric, so be a human being and pull out the photos of your kids. Give equal importance to your business also.
- There are still differences among the genders in India. Women are also the best problem solver, best entrepreneur. Try to involve them in your business they are hard workers. Give them the equal chance to help you in your business. Exploit their complete potential into your business.
- Gift-giving is customary in India and a nice way to cement a business friendship, but it's often not expected during the first meeting. If you go that route, stay away from white and black wrapping paper. Those colors are considered bad luck. If your colleague is a Hindu, avoid giving anything that's made out of leather. Many Hindus are vegetarian and may not appreciate it. And remember—it's a global economy. Chances are, if you bring something American, they can buy it at their local shopping mall. So try to find a gift that's unique to your state or town.

So What Could Be the Solution?

24.10 Promoting Entrepreneurship Culture

The formation of an entrepreneurship culture is the prerequisite of a successful Entrepreneurship Environment (**EE**) in India's higher education system. Students and faculty members will involve in EE more vigorously only if the whole society supports entrepreneurship and entrepreneurs are respected for their skills, work and talent risk-taking capability.

The formation of an entrepreneurship culture can be done through opening institutes that promote entrepreneurship, providing opportunities to the one who has talent to become entrepreneur so that more and more people will try to become entrepreneur. Documentation of cases on real entrepreneurs, success stories and video films will present the true picture of the entrepreneurs and that will motivate the people to become entrepreneur. India is doing well in this direction. Since the formation of an entrepreneurship culture acts in accordance with the development of the national economy, it will be a long and hard process in India.

Creating an Entrepreneurship Environment

In India, although many business regulations were removed during the 1990s, many of the old bureaucrats remain. The development and improvement of infrastructure in India will be slow process because of its less developed economy. But states have a major role to play. States can come up with the good policies either by their own or with the help of central government that can promote entrepreneurship and can solve the problems of entrepreneurs. There is a need of creating friendly environment for entrepreneurs. For example, the "single window scheme" needs to be implemented. With the deepening of reform, a favorable Entrepreneurship Environment will be formed and this in turn will benefit EE in the higher education system.

Refining Techniques of Entrepreneurship Education

Entrepreneurship education is not like the other typical business education. Opening a business is a different activity from running a business. EE must address the unclear nature of business entry and should give enough information on that. For overcoming the problems of business EE must include training programmes, skill development programmes, management development programmes, personality development, new product development, workshop on creative thinking and practical knowledge on existing and emerging technologies. Other areas identified as important for EE include an awareness of entrepreneur career options; sources of venture capital; business plan preparation; idea protection; ambiguity tolerance. Developing these qualities will help the people to develop their entrepreneurial personality and thus will help them to face the challenges confidently associated with each stage of business development and find out the solutions logically. The following learning tools are useful in EE: business plans; student business start-ups; consultation with practicing entrepreneurs; computer simulations; behavioral simulations; interviews with entrepreneurs, environmental scans; "live" cases; field trips and the use of video and films.

Students' selection for entrepreneurship should not be done in random. Those students must be selected who have a potential to become entrepreneur and in the next phase those students need to be motivated. After the motivation phase, they should be given special entrepreneurship training.

And finally, students have to be provided with proper and adequate support. At present, besides the special entrepreneurship training, EE in Indian educational institutions also needs to instill certain basic ideas in doing business. For instance, in doing business, being punctual is very important. University students need to be reminded of the importance of this basic trait.

Cultural and structural barriers to women's entrepreneurship include:

- women's belief that making large amounts of money is dirty and is associated with immoral behaviour, such as prostitution
- qualities associated with making money – such as assertiveness and ambition – are associated with men
- qualities associated with women – such as altruism and self-sacrifice – can keep women from seeing themselves as entrepreneurs
- women are permitted to have money but not in large sums and if they have it they have to hide the fact, claiming that it belongs to a male relative, because money makes women independent and Zimbabwean men do not like independent women
- Structural barriers include women's lack of marketable skills, lack of time or ability to travel, the lack of land, capital and other assets, limited education and their position as family providers.

Recommendations for changes in approaches to women's entrepreneurship include:

- Training in vocational skills, business skills and marketing is necessary but is not sufficient to promote women's entrepreneurship.
- Training needs should be identified through participatory approaches and should focus on education, solving problems and providing information.
- Conventional training does not recognize cultural barriers: training needs to challenge beliefs about women, men, money and power.
- Existing approaches fail to discuss and transfer the behavioural skills that make an individual an entrepreneur. Women need to develop personal empowerment skills, such as assertiveness, skills in negotiating, time-management skills and self awareness.
- Macro-economic policies need to create a climate favourable to women's entrepreneurship. This means recognizing that women's work is equal to men's.

24.11 Decisive Success Factors for Entrepreneurship

Factor 1: Overcoming distrust: One critical success factor for the entrepreneurial settlers is to win the trust of local population and economic. Succeeding with innovations seems to create trust and make future innovations easier. This may partly be explained by the notion of trust developed in a much-quoted article by Mayer et al. (1995) in which trust is defined as '*The willingness of a party to be vulnerable to the actions of another party based on the expectations that the other will perform a particular action important to the trustor, irrespective of the ability to monitor and control that other party*' (p. 712). They argue that trust depends on four dimensions: the trustor's propensity to trust and the trustee's demonstration of ability, integrity and benevolence. The entrepreneur must be reliable and he must demonstrate that he wants the best not just for him- or herself but also for the local community. The four entrepreneurial settlers have all developed a capacity to care for the local community, a local patriotism. The geographical point of view may be a way of 'showing good intentions' which makes trust building and networking easier. It is also a moral driving engine of open innovation.

Factor 2: Educating people to appreciate a service: This is the major task of an entrepreneur. Here the entrepreneur has a great role to play. He has to educate the people about the importance of the service. How it will benefit the people? What are the advantages of it? And how it will solve their problems? There is seldom a clear want for a service. People cannot initially see the use of it. They are unknown about the importance of it. Therefore an entrepreneur must educate or develop people's taste for a given service. He should teach people to appreciate and understand a service and see it in the right proportions.

Factor 3: Linking innovation to a strategic arena. This leads to the next incident, which consists in linking innovation activities to a strategic arena where people with different preconditions, interests, powers and morals are interacting. It is in this context that people learn to appreciate the new services.

Linking innovations to a strategic arena, including networking, serves different purposes like *(a)* providing a context for learning about a service, *(b)* weaving together different ideas and interests so that the different groups that should be involved in the service are prepared to do so, *(c)* achieving resources for coordination and *(d)* increasing the ability to mutually benefit from innovation. The importance of these networks is further evident as most of the service innovations discussed would simply not have been possible in the absence of these networks.

Factor 4: Sustaining moral entrepreneurship and entrepreneurship with care: It follows from the above incidents that the entrepreneurial settlers analyzed are not, strictly speaking, entrepreneurial individuals in the Schumpeterian sense. Individual economic benefits are not the only driving engine. They are much more composite entrepreneurs who possess different drives and capabilities that make them fall under concepts such as social, moral, lifestyle, political and, as a central aspect, network entrepreneurs. They are furthermore characterized by a willingness to fight against distrust and they are local patriots. Last, but not least, they possess the drive and the capabilities to educate the population. Without these non-economic entrepreneurial characteristics none of these entrepreneurs would probably have become successful entrepreneurs.

SUMMARY

Motives impel men to action. Entrepreneurial growth requires proper motives like profit-making, acquisition of prestige and attainment of social status. Ambitious and talented men would take risks and innovate if these motives are strong. The strength of these motives depends upon the culture of the society.

The following are the cultural obstacles faced by the new entrepreneurs.

- Cultural attitude
- Sensitive to emotional resemblance

- Caste system
- Not taking into account the religion, region or background of your counterpart
- Missing the social nuances
- Cultural values
- Culture diffusion

Physical barriers in the workplace include:

Marked out territories and empires into which strangers are not allowed.

Large working areas or working in one unit that is physically separate from others.

The office doors are closed, barrier screens and separate areas for the people of different status.

Perceptual Barriers

The entrepreneurs have more impact of their family, friends, relatives, religion. These relationships decide the perception of the entrepreneur. How does he think? How does he behave? How does he solve the problem?

Emotional barriers

Entrepreneurs' emotional barriers have a major impact on the entrepreneurs. They fear to show trust on others. They cannot risk suddenly. They think so much on the issue or plan. The thinking itself destroy their business.

Behavioural barriers

The entrepreneurs do not mix themselves to any group. They always search the reason to belong to the group. The reason may be caste, religion or anything.

Language barriers

Language that describes what we want to say in our terms may present barriers to others who are not familiar with our expressions, buzz-words and jargon. When we express our communication in such language, it is a way of excluding others.

Gender barriers

Women entrepreneurs are not treated the way the male entrepreneurs are treated they are not given the full freedom, they are less trusted. It is not expected by the traditional thinking family that women will work in the business.

Promoting entrepreneurship culture

The formation of an entrepreneurship culture can be done through a host of interventions like the use of media, the creation of literature for inculcating entrepreneurial values, documentation of cases, success stories, video films and behavioral exercises, etc.

Creating an Entrepreneurship Environment

The "single window scheme" needs to be implemented. With the deepening of reform, a favorable Entrepreneurship Environment will be formed and this in turn will benefit EE in the higher education system.

Refining Techniques of Entrepreneurship Education

Entrepreneurship education is different from a typical business education. Business entry is a fundamentally different activity from managing a business. EE must address the equivocal nature of business entry. To this end, the EE must include skill-building courses in negotiation, leadership, new product development, creative thinking and exposure to technology innovation. Other areas identified as important for EE include an awareness of entrepreneur career options; sources of venture capital; idea protection; ambiguity tolerance. These are characteristics that define the entrepreneurial personality from which one draws when faced with the challenges associated with each stage of venture development.

Decisive success factors for entrepreneurship are as follows:

Factor 1: Overcoming distrust:

Factor 2: Educating people to appreciate a service

Factor 3: Linking innovation to a strategic arena

Factor 4: Sustaining moral entrepreneurship and entrepreneurship with care

Keywords

***Attitude*:** An *attitude* is made up of what you think, what you do and what you feel.

Culture: Culture is the way of life of a particular society or group of people, including pattern of thoughts, beliefs, behaviour, customs, traditions, rituals, dress and language, as well as art, music and literature.

Caste system: A *caste system* is a social system where people are ranked.

Cultural Values: The values that most people agree are fundamental to society.

Cultural diffusion: The ideas and things in one culture "borrowed" by another culture.

Entrepreneurship: Entrepreneurship is a process undertaken by an entrepreneur to establish and to develop a new enterprise.

Physical barriers: Marked out territories and empires into which strangers are not allowed.

Emotional barriers: They fear to show trust on others.

Behavioural barriers: The entrepreneurs do not mix themselves to any group.

Entrepreneurial Culture: Entrepreneurial Culture is a business culture which is typically informal, with a focus on creativity and the pursuit of new opportunities.

Entrepreneurship education: Entrepreneurship education is the process of providing individuals with the concepts and skills necessary to recognize new business opportunities.

Questions

1. What are the cultural obstacles faced by new small entrepreneurs while opening business? Explain.
2. Write down in detail about different barriers to entrepreneurs?
3. How can you create an entrepreneurial environment in India?
4. What are the cultural barriers to women entrepreneurs?

❑ ❑ ❑

Chapter – 25

Personal Competence Obstacles

LEARNING OBJECTIVES

On completion of this chapter, you should be able to:

☺ *Explain the personal competence impact on new small entrepreneurs and their business.*

☺ *Describe weaknesses of entrepreneurs.*

☺ *Describe the role of entrepreneurial development in business.*

25.1 Need of Entrepreneurial Competences for Successful Business

Becoming an entrepreneur for any person is not an easy task. If you've determined that you do not want to work in corporate and be your own boss. As you start preparation how to start your own business, you start listing down what you want to do and what you can do. You want to do a little bit of everything - for your business. You do market research, product and service planning, Web design, write, with a five years experience in legal and administrative support. But then, you think, "What skills are required to succeed as an entrepreneur?"

If you want to start a business, you will need a large array of entrepreneurial skills to succeed in today's competitive market. You must have multi skills to be an entrepreneur. You must possess basic skills necessary to enable you to start, build up, finance and market your own business. There are number of qualities and skills you need to have, including marketing skills, management skills and personal competence.

Entrepreneurship skill is a primary need for the establishment of any kind of business activities. If a person has developed such skill he can become an Entrepreneur. Every entrepreneur likes to

BOX 25

Two thirds of all small business operators worldwide started their new company in the last two years in an increasingly difficult environment. They feel increasingly ignored by politicians. The three most important demands to their governments: Put more pressure on banks to give loans, make more programs to support start-ups and introduce harsher penalties for customers who fail to pay their bills on time.

A recent global survey shows that three quarters of small businesses feel ignored by their governments. The worst responses came from entrepreneurs in Spain, Mexico and the United States. Only entrepreneurs in India, France and China reported positive public initiatives.

The problems of small business founders differ in each country. While those in India, Mexico, South Africa and Western Europe are finding it difficult to access credit from banks, in the U.S. and Canada funds are still flowing sufficiently. But in those locations there are fears about falling income and rising taxes.

Late payments are a particular problem in China, Spain, South Africa and India. The European Union is currently considering a law to resolve this issue, yet it will only penalize those who do not pay their bills after 60 days. Greater start-up funds are particularly sought by respondents in South Africa, Japan, France and China.

In comparing the political initiatives in individual countries, it appears that the best support comes from the Scandinavian countries, South America (except Argentina), India and France. However, it seems that entrepreneurs from the unsupportive countries are the ones who need the most help to expand - the greater the expansion plans, the greater the unmet need for government support.

The results were published as part of a Regus Global Study, undertaken by the business center operators twice a year. More than 5,500 entrepreneurs from 78 countries participated in this survey in August and September 2010.

Source: Information received from "Deskmag-The Co working Magazine".

see himself as a successful businessman. But it is up to him how much he is capable of taking the risk. Whether he is ready to face all efforts and challenges that come in his way?

Entrepreneurs must have all the required qualities that define them as a successful businessman. If the entrepreneurs will lag in those traits then they have to suffer in any area of their business where they lag the required trait. Definitely it is not possible for any person to have all the entrepreneurial qualities, no entrepreneurs are complete. There is difference between two entrepreneurs that is why one entrepreneur touches the heights of the business than others just run the normal business. The required skills of the entrepreneurs are always in connection with the personality traits. The personality traits have a greater influence on the entrepreneurship.

Entrepreneurial competence is required for performing the task efficiently and effectively. It is the determination and passion of the person. It demonstrates the keenness of the entrepreneurs how they interact with the business situation? How they overcome the problem? Whether they are energetic or not? Competence gives the entrepreneurs all the required qualities to drive the business. If the entrepreneurs do not have competency then they will never overcome the problems, face the challenge and ultimately the whole business will come down. Competence is responsible for the business growth. It may be skill, knowledge, motivation, quality of personality and interest. As per the research study of entrepreneurship, some major entrepreneurial competences are very much required for the successful entrepreneurship.

For example he must have intelligence by this only he will come up with new techniques or new ideas to run the business. He must have knowledge of the business without which he cannot progress the business. Their lack of knowledge will make him dumb.

Successful entrepreneur is always capable using his strengths to grab the opportunities. He should have that much smartness also. They use all their intelligence to catch the opportunities. These opportunities may be related to personal growth, new product or business. A successful entrepreneur is always active and all his actions should be faster than the requirements. They quickly react to their ideas. It may be job order or demand by the situation or expansion of business to the new location or launching the new products, adopting new technology or introduction of new brand of existing product or introducing a new product.

A real entrepreneur is ready to face all challenges. He never gives-up. He thinks logically with his mind. He thinks from profit perspective. He is not lazy one, not discourage himself by the failure. He is ready to repeat the same action 'n' number of times to achieve the goal. Collecting required information is also a skill entrepreneur is ready to visit any place or meet specialists or he has the courage to conduct personal research related to his business and demand. Individual businessmen should be concerned with quality of actions. It may be quality of production or quality of service or quality of performance of job quality which is one of the major requirements for the successfulness of the business.

Committed entrepreneur is concerned with the completion of job. Entrepreneur is an owner of the business. They know how to complete the task within deadline. They are very hard workers. They take all the efforts to complete the work within the deadline. They have a great respect to time. To sustain the orders or demand, they should do hard work to finish the task within time frame. The entrepreneurs are full of motivation. They are motivated for many things. They should be able to motivate his employees regarding progress of business. Entrepreneurship is always opposite to the bureaucratic type behavior. Utilizing all available resources for the completion of job within time and required quality and also it depends on the efficiency of the system. They know the proper utilization of the resources to make a product. They never waste their resources. They take complete benefits of their resources.

Planning is first most important requirement. Without planning it is not possible to run the business also. There should be a systemic plan with sub goals in order to reach the goal. Goal setting is important task of the business. The entrepreneurs are very clear about their goals. They continuously hard work, take risks and accept challenges to achieve the goals. They are focused on their goals. Plan guides entrepreneur to move in right path. It also helps to anticipate future threats and entrepreneur can develop alternatives to face the difficult situation. Problems in business may arise any moment. But it is a challenge to the skill and experience of the entrepreneur. He should identify new ideas which are potential to face the situation for achieving the goal and should discover innovative ideas for solving common problems.

Person without self confidence cannot do anything in this world. When a person wishes to recognize as entrepreneur he must have confidence on himself, his ability and skill. We can measure one's self confidence how much he is ready to take the risk.

Entrepreneur should always be assertive. While dealing with customers, suppliers or people connected with his business. He should be assertive to his employees. While delegating the responsibilities and show the courage to confront to bring discipline in world environment.

Entrepreneur's convincing power has important role in the growth of the business. Convincing skill is connected to marketing strategy. Entrepreneur should be able to convince customers to buy the product and able to convince finance provider to easy obtain financial assistance and suppliers for supplying the product in reasonable rate.

Outside influencers are having their own role in the development of the business. These influencers may be agents, friends, competitive firms, government authorities. Entrepreneur should develop good business contacts and should be able to use agents and friends for the accomplishment of business goals. Instead of depending on employees, for entrepreneur it is better to personally supervise the business. His presence in workplace is important which helps to avoid fraud other problems due to the ignorance of employees.

Committed honesty and hard working employees are really assets of the organization. If the business is in good profitable position entrepreneur should not hesitate to take the actions to introduce various welfare schemes for the welfare of his employees. It will increase employee morale and loyalty.

25.2 Weaknesses of Entrepreneurs

Do Not Have Skills for Entrepreneurs

There are some basic skills you need to adopt as an entrepreneur to run any kind of business.

Lack of sales and marketing skills

When the Entrepreneurs are new to business then they do not know the tactics of the marketing. They are not aware about the skills that are required for the sales and marketing. Sales and marketing are the two most important skills you must have when you plan to start your own business. A business is nothing if it has no customers. The new small entrepreneurs try to sell without any plan and strategy. You may have the fanciest computer with the latest graphics software, but if no one is knocking at your door to hire you as a graphic designer, then you better rethink why you are in business in the first place. To have revenues and profits, you first need to have customers. To get the customers you should know the different marketing skills to increase the sales.

Planning a business and executing the plan is a difficult process. Entrepreneurs plan their business; but when they actually implement it they find difficulty in reaching the target customers.

Reaching to the target customers involve many different methods. You need to understand the marketing concepts, customers' behavior, their perception, their needs and their taste. You must have the knowledge of different marketing tools, their budget and effectiveness. Once you will have such knowledge you will be able to select the tools that your budget permits. Direct interaction with the customers will give you many ideas.

Entrepreneurs forget that they also need money for their marketing purpose. When they lack budget they do not do any planning instead they do business according to their convenience. It would be extremely helpful if you possess excellent written and oral communication skills to help you sell your products and services (more so if you are a solo entrepreneur who will be doing everything by yourself). You can also hire sales executives who are good in communication skills, body language, negotiations, convincing and personality. You need to interact with the people to tell them about your business and your specialty. You need to write ads, press releases and story ideas about your business. Starting a business is a time to get out of your timid self and begin to aggressively market your venture. That's the only way you can succeed.

Mistrust

The desire for control leads them to show strong distrust in people who work for them. They do not trust anyone in the business. They do not have any trust on the employees nor on the business partners etc. They think that the others may take undue advantages of their trust. They are afraid and remain doubtful. If they are too paranoid, they become easy praise for investors, partners and clients who adapt it to manipulate them to gain control. Yet, this trait is a double edged sword. It can make them more alert to the people in the surrounding who might attempt to con them. Don't you see it all around you: why bosses in small companies tend to be misers compared to those in big companies? They are afraid that when they spend on their employees, they will be taken advantage of. So, being trapped in the state of distrust, their first defence is to ensure that they exploit a lot more from employees.

Financial know-how

You are in business to make money. Therefore, the most important skill you must have is the ability to handle money well. This includes knowing the sources of money, proper utilization of money, spend when it is needed, take decision on new vs. old purchase and buy vs. lease. You should know the proper manipulation of the money. The entrepreneurs may not know where to use credit and where to use debit. They do not know how much they have to invest? When do they have to purchase the equipments? When do they have to take equipments on rent? How much to carry on hand. Entrepreneurs need to think about it. You also need to identify the best pricing structure for your business in order to get the best kind of return for your products or services.

Only having money is not enough for the success of business. Look at the failed dot-coms with funding of as much as 100 million rupees. Even if they are awash with cash, they still end up as a failure because they were not able to manage their money well. The entrepreneurs must know the better combination of the credit and debit. If you have learned the tactics of managing the money then you know better how to run the business in fluctuating market. The important thing is to always focus on the bottom-line. You should have a record of every spending. Always ask yourself: "How much will this contribute to my bottom line?" If it will not give your business anything in return financially, better think twice before opening your wallet.

Ego

Every entrepreneur has an ego and usually it is a strong one. If you don't have an ego, it's hard to believe that you are an entrepreneur. Ego is good but it should not hurt others in the business. That's the unfortunate reality because of the many characteristics which an entrepreneur possesses. They should not be the egoistic person; they are in business where they will need the help of number of persons to run the business. They cannot run business without anyone's help. However, there are varying degrees of ego in every entrepreneur. Sometimes, personal ego can be detrimental to the growth of the company. Every person wants respect from others, if you will not respect others or treat them in a wrong way then you may not get proper support that you want from them. It is always important for the entrepreneur to think about how his or her startup as an organization is greater than them. They should give value to each person who is helping them to grow the business. The other is that the entrepreneur has to learn humility through the hard way.

Decline in self-motivation skills

Entrepreneurs are always in the illusion that now they are the boss and they do not have to do much; they just hire the people and they will do everything in the business. They forget that in the small business they cannot sit relaxed. Market is full of competition in such case the relaxation will be costly for the entrepreneurs. As an entrepreneur, you do not have the luxury of bosses and bureaucracy to tell you what needs to be done. Everything rests on your shoulder - from thinking where to get money to fund the business, to develop the product, to determine how to reach the customer and so on. You need to be smart enough to know when you need to go ahead and when to stop. The self motivation is must in the business. Entrepreneurs start their business with zeal but after sometime they become lazy. They also become lazy when business does well in the market. They become the satisfied ones.

If you want to grow your business then you must be an initiator with clear business objectives. You must have a belief on yourself. You must be confident enough to implement your ideas. If you will hesitate or fear then you can never sell your ideas to the customers even if your ideas are best. More importantly, you must be willing to focus your energy and work hard towards each and every step that will make your enterprise a success. The business is yours if you will not take the efforts then how you will expect that others will work hard for your business. You should not be the lazy one but the active one. You must have extra drive and commitment to make sure that you are taking the necessary steps to make your dream of a successful business a reality.

Control freak

Most entrepreneurs desire control. Entrepreneurs are people who want to make a difference in other people's lives. The motivation to create something new and innovative or redefine how people conceive the traditional markets bring them not only creativity but also the unfortunate trait of possibly being a control freak. Their obsession with control affects their ability to move or delegate demonstrates how badly at times they get along with other people. They do not treat the others in a good manner. If the entrepreneur is a nonconformist in the first place, they will have serious difficulty in dealing with issues on dominance and submission and worst, they are suspicious of authority. They should definitely have a control over the business but their behavior should not be the worst one. Most entrepreneurs want to create their own environment. They do not want to be at the mercy of others, which makes them very intolerant of incompetency.

Time management skills

Time has an important role in business. If properly managed then it can give you success and if improperly managed then your business will not survive. You must have a time table for your business activities. When you wake up in the morning, you must have a clear idea what tasks you are going to do today. You should have perfect planning of the day and the record of how much you have completed the work. The new entrepreneurs cannot give their much time because they have to do everything in their business. They have a little budget so they take care of all the work but here they face the problem of not giving the time to the whole business. Some issues in the business need quick settlement. If those issues are not given proper time then business suffers. Especially if you are running a one-person operation, you must design the whole day in such a manner so that from morning to evening you should be able to do multi-tasks in sequence. In the morning type document or send e-mails, in afternoon handle all marketing activities and in evening do bookkeeping. In between you may have to go to the banks for depositing and withdrawing money. So plan it and select those banks that are on your way. Planning your time is the best way to perform the tasks sequentially and on time. You simply have to know how to manage time and prioritize your tasks.

Administration skills

Most of the new entrepreneurs do not have good administration skills. They face many problems without any solutions. They properly do not know the exact solutions; sometimes they even don't know that there are problems in the business. They are not capable of handling each and every task. They need a proper training to get the skills of the administration. They should develop themselves in terms of billing, printing invoices, collecting payments and managing receivables. If you can take the assistance of paid assistant then it will help you a lot. Even if you lack knowledge in administration work then select such an assistant who are the experienced ones and can handle the burden of administrative work. However, for new small entrepreneurs it is not easy to hire paid assistant. They already run out of money so it becomes their distant dream. Starting a business is never easy, even if you have the perfect background and possess all the above skills. Having all the needed skills and qualities will not even ensure your success. But having these basic skills will, at least, lessen the pain of the start-up process, giving you greater chance in seeing your business grow and prosper.

Get conned easily

Most young entrepreneurs will begin with idealism and fervor and work on passion to keep their startup going. Being young and brash, they usually let both successes and failures overwhelm them. Their lack of experience with the real world makes them naive about dealing with people. There are many examples in how human error could occur. The first example is that they may not be sharp enough to see that the supplier makes more money out of them by delivering lesser goods. Another example involves their business partners are not delivering what they promised. Sometimes, these awkward situations can land young entrepreneurs into trouble.

25.3 Entrepreneurial Development Role

Entrepreneur as a self-employed

The emotional driving force behind the self-employed person is not security but a desire for greater control over his or her life, career and destiny. They do not want to work under any one. Relinquishing that control to a boss every day from nine to five is not their idea of happiness and they believe that they could do their job just as well without an employer – and perhaps without the need for other employees. They want more autonomy. They want their own control on work. They want to do things in their own way. And they usually begin by creating a situation where they do the same type of work they did while an employee, but they figure out how to do it by themselves and for themselves.

They believe that "if we can do better then why should we work under someone else". They do not want any intermediaries between them and customers. They want to directly interact with customers. They make the mistake of not envisioning a business that will run by itself without their constant supervision and handholding and they don't picture creating an enterprise that thrives on involving others in a teamwork effort.

Entrepreneur as a manager

Those with a managerial outlook are often in a great position to succeed as entrepreneurs, expect for two big misconceptions that leads to massive problems. Many managers believe that if a business is not working properly, then cost cut is the best strategy. They start cost cutting plus they start throwing out employees but this only aggravates the situation because it fails to address the underlying root cause of the difficulty or lack of profitability. Another mistaken belief that is common to this mindset is that success cannot be achieved without growing the business. They believe in expansion of the business. Though expansion of the business signifies that your business is growing, but it is also not necessary that if you have a big infrastructure then only you will grow. The important thing is that you must have a gut to run the business depending upon all the laws and strategies of the business. You must have solutions for all issues generated in your business. Many managerial entrepreneurs go into bankruptcy thanks to vigorous growth, but they never figure out why. Managers always believe in giving the orders, they always try to take someone in the business that is less in knowledge than them because they do not want anyone who can surpass them in talent and knowledge. To give orders and be in charge requires no great skill or aptitude, but to be a leader – one who knows how to inspire and train others to rise to greater heights – is a rare quality.

Entrepreneur as a leader

The entrepreneur as a leader knows exactly how to lead the people inside the business? How to motivate them? How to give direction to the business? He knows the proper ways to utilize the resources and to get the benefits of the teamwork so that business can earn profits. He takes decision collectively and participates all the employees for their suggestions. He believes in collective success rather than individual success therefore he uses the word 'We' rather than 'I'. For example he says "we are running a successful business" rather than "I am running a successful business". This kind of entrepreneur has created an organization that is more self-sufficient and self-sustaining and by doing so has created more wealth, personal freedom and free time.

He is ready to give responsibilities and authority to others as he believes that others should also have a feeling of achievement. He has confidence on others. He believes in distributing the responsibilities to the desired person. The leader can therefore focus not so much on sales and revenues, but on net profits. While the business continues to run smoothly – and generate more transactions – the owner/leader concentrates on fine tuning it for increased profitability while letting others handle the day-to-day operational details.

Entrepreneur as an investor

Entrepreneurs always try to generate more profits. They manage the resources properly and utilize it in such a way so that more returns should come. But apart from that they also have a challenge of managing the money so that more money can be generated. Investing for maximum returns involves smart leverage of assets and the entrepreneurial investor will often leverage the success of the first business to create a second or third company based on the same model or system. Many investors buy the others businesses then develop it and sell it to others. So apart from their own business of selling products/services they also do the business of selling entire business. Such entrepreneurs do not want to earn profits just by involving in their business but they also search other ways to earn profits. So instead of permanently remaining in one business the investors buy them, ensure that they have valuable equity or attractive allure and potential and then sell them to other entrepreneurs or would-be entrepreneurs. They collect necessary resources, employees, build infrastructure, expose the business to customers, invest money and legally build a running business. The quality of these entrepreneurs is that they are good in starting and opening the business but they cannot run the business themselves for a long time. They do not want to be the manger of the business who handles all types of issues while running the business. They start business appoint necessary authority and either they sell it to someone else or run the business in partnership with others. By doing this they are free to open other business and likewise they earn profit. They do not want to bind themselves into the responsibilities of running business. They are the investors. They invest money and earn profit. Working smart replaces working hard and the rewards – both financial and personal – are abundant.

The real true entrepreneur

The real entrepreneurs are the entrepreneurs who give birth to a new idea, take every effort to convert this idea into the business, run that business successfully, face challenges and issues, take calculated risks, form business plan, identify customers and competitors, make strategies, design effective public relations campaign and anyhow survive the business. So an entrepreneur is a one man army who fulfills so many responsibilities in their life time to run business and to get profit out of that. They learn from their mistakes, get knowledge from others' experience and always think to grow the business and because of this it is possible for them to reach the ultimate goal and realize their dreams in a really life-changing way.

25.4 The Not to Have Qualities for Entrepreneurs

Everybody can become an entrepreneur but those must have at least the essential qualities of the entrepreneur. Entrepreneurs can be differentiating by judging their qualities. Two entrepreneurs may be same or different. If they are different that means one has all the necessary qualities of the entrepreneur and other lacks all those qualities. And some traits are common to all successful entrepreneurs. While – quite naturally – individual entrepreneurs have many unique traits that are not common to other entrepreneurs, all entrepreneurs do share a kind of strength, a certain type of foundation and attitude and a special drive and willingness.

Lack of confidence

Entrepreneurs must have confidence but all entrepreneurs do not have this quality. Some new entrepreneurs lack confidence. Confidence is a property of the entrepreneur. Not all of us are born with confidence, but that does not mean we are not capable of it. And because of lack of confidence the entrepreneurs cannot do any work properly. Those entrepreneurs lack in self esteem and they are unable to accept challenges because of the fear of not completing those challenging tasks. They lack in their strength. They are not confident about their own strengths. They have fewer beliefs in themselves and therefore do not progress after some level. They remain stagnant or become failure in tough competition.

Lack of feeling a sense of ownership

The lack of self esteem is not a good symbol for the entrepreneurs. Taking responsibility for getting things done – and doing them with care and attention – means to act like an owner. But lack of responsibility in the entrepreneurs suffers the whole business. They do not give proper direction to the business. They become dependent on others for progress of the business. They do not find solution so easily or unable to take the decisions. They leave the things in bad shape they are unable to estimate the problems and solving them. They always fear of getting failure that brings restriction to their business. Sometimes they do not solve the problems and let the problems as it is. The entrepreneurs must have a sense of ownership and responsibility. While a sense of ownership makes for a stellar employee, the entrepreneur knows that the goal is not to be owned by the enslavement of too much responsibility. Rather than controlling situations in an attempt to possess them, the entrepreneur teaches other people how to take charge. In that way the clever entrepreneur uses individual accountability in the ultimate pursuit of profitability, teamwork and overall success.

Unable to communicate

Entrepreneurs know the importance of human resource in business. One business interact with their employees, customers, suppliers, business partners etc., all are the form of human being if you could not have been able to have a good relation with them then these relations will either make or break your business. Here the role of communication is very important. The entrepreneurs should work on their communication skills it may be in the form of verbal, non verbal, body language, written or oral. When entrepreneurs do not posses these qualities they become unable to maintain the relationship with the other people who are valuable for the growth of the company. They do not properly interact with the people of foreign language or national language. They are unable to put their thought, clearly and as a result of that they do not win the trust of others. The entrepreneurs must sharpen themselves with communication skills. And to support communication, they should take advantage of all available tools and resources. Those might include foreign language or public speaking classes, computer and telecom technology or search engine optimization as it relates to sales and marketing or specialized writing such as that needed for grants, business proposals, mission statements or policy manuals. At last the entrepreneurs should also be a good listener what others are communicating to them. Improper listening could cost you in business dealings.

Lack of passionate about learning

Entrepreneurs when do not have passion about their business then they take the business as a formality. They do not learn the things easily; they do not search the important information that will be useful for the business. Every time they need help to get the knowledge. They themselves do not ask the question why the business is not growing. What can we do to grow the business? Where we can get the useful information? They do not do any research for their business. They also do not quickly learn from their own mistakes, which means they are more prone to keep repeating them due to overconfidence, ego or blindness to one's own faults, shortcomings or errors in judgment. They do not try to get more knowledge from the experience of others and to become more educated. They are the laze ones. Because of the lack of passion for education, entrepreneurs miss the opportunity to learn from the people who either know more than they do or know things that are different from what they know. They never enrich themselves with knowledge while also making a concerted effort to grow that knowledge by sharing it with others.

Lack of team player

Business is an integrate activity. You cannot run your business alone. Business is a good example of team work. If you do not have a quality of team work then you cannot accomplish any task. If you do not have a habit of working with others then your business can never survive. There is no need to do everything alone in business. You must be able to utilize the benefits of team work. You must be very effective in developing and maintaining relationships with your employees, suppliers or partners. But the problem is that they never take the advantage of the good relationship. They become failure to maintain the relationship. One man cannot possess every possible trait and if entrepreneurs will try to do everything by their own then they will be good in something but become failure in most of the things. The entrepreneurs must learn to work in a team. They should know how to utilize the characteristics of different members in a team. The successful entrepreneurs leverage teamwork to get the heavy lifting done without breaking stride.

System-orientations

The good system has one property here you can make predictions about the outcome with less and less exertion of energy or resources. Entrepreneurs have more love for their systems than their people, they believe in system based solutions than people based solutions. If the person gets the job done but falls sick or leaves, the job is threatened. But if a system is created to get the job done, anyone can step in and follow the blueprint to get the desired result. Similarly, when troubleshooting and problem solving, the entrepreneur will first examine and study the system – because a flaw in the system will produce a flawed outcome each and every time. Designing, implementing and perfecting systems is one of the most useful and rewarding skills of an entrepreneur.

Lack of dedication

Entrepreneurs should have dedication to fulfill number of requirements of the business. Though they see many dreams but they lack their desire to fulfill the requirements. They just fulfill some requirements of the business but they do not care about the remaining requirements. For example they will fulfill the requirement of taking employees but what about their training they do not care about it. Some entrepreneurs lack dedication to their work. They run business according to their mood but they do not fold themselves according to the business. They lack in fulfillment of their plans, visions and dreams and that tenacity of purpose generates electricity throughout the whole organization. Companies fail because they try to achieve many things at once and because of that they lose their business main focus. You must clearly specify the goals, write down your objectives and narrow the margin of error. The real entrepreneurs do not follow multiple objectives at a single time rather they follow one by one different objectives with their full dedication. They show their willingness and commitment to their work. No matter what that might mean in terms of rising to meet a challenge or acting above and beyond the call of duty, the entrepreneur shows steadfast dedication.

Grateful

Entrepreneurs learn to take nothing for granted in this world. That gives them the agility and flexibility to adapt to changes and demands, while it also invests in them a thankfulness that reminds them that riches and wealth are not about "stuff", but are about fulfillment, satisfaction and the pleasure that comes from one's accomplishments and contributions.

Lack of being optimistic

If the entrepreneurs are not optimistic then they cannot earn the profit and cannot run the business. You must have a positive attitude for your business. Don't lose your enthusiasm after one failure. Instead of getting nervous collect your energy and try again. Your positive attitude will give you success. The entrepreneurs who are not optimistic they cannot enjoy the business. Do not think on failure only. It will waste your time. Now plan about what you will do next? You must be ready to face the challenges. Your negative feelings will make you fearful and unsure. The growth requires patience, hope if these are absent in the entrepreneurs then business cannot grow. Such kind of entrepreneurs cannot give impetus to their business for greater accomplishments.

Gregarious

Some entrepreneurs are always serious in their business. They think that seriousness is the secret of the success. If it could be then just by becoming serious most of the entrepreneurs can have success in their business. it is true that seriousness is necessary for the success of the business but more important is responsibility. They should be responsible to their business it does not matter whether they are serious or smiling. Because business is all about people, entrepreneurs tend to be socially outgoing. New entrepreneurs just want the authority and therefore they neglect the part of some funny time with their employees. They do not share ideas, products and services and that excitement is contagious to their employees, clients, friends and other contacts both within and beyond the business sphere. They do not discuss their business issue with their employees but try to hide all the things. But the fact is that they should enjoy their business, people and should show trust on them. Human resource experts, career counselors and business psychologists all agree that those who do jobs they enjoy and are good at have higher rates of success and broader measures of satisfaction. Entrepreneurs know that firsthand, from their own experience and they tend to be a fun-loving group of people both on and off the job.

A leader by example (lack leadership)

Entrepreneurs not only lead themselves through self-motivation as self-starters who jump into tasks with enthusiasm, but they also have skills in leading others. But few new small entrepreneurs lack leadership. They do not know the importance of teamwork and they do not understand the need to appreciate others, support them and reward them accordingly. They just think that whatever success their business is getting because of themselves only. In contrary to above they blame others for their failure. True leaders do not fear. They take the responsibility of their failure. They never blame to others for their failure. This is the quality which makes them more prosper. Leaders who share their power and their time can accomplish extraordinary things. The best leaders understand that leadership is the liberation of talent; hence they gain power not only by constantly giving it away, but also by not grabbing it back."

Afraid of risk or success

New entrepreneurs are afraid of the success and risk. That make them handicap to do something new in the business. That restricts them for doing the experiment with their business. Many people could be successful if they only took chances. And many people who take chances and become somewhat successful find the realization of their dreams an overwhelming possibility, so they sabotage their continued success by retreating back into a comfort zone of smallness. The entrepreneurs who do not want to take risk have lazy, scared and uncompetitive kind of personality they want protection and that's why they fear to bring any innovative idea. Entrepreneurs are not immune to fear. But they prioritize their approach to life so that the fear of failure, frustration, boredom, drudgery and dissatisfaction far outweighs the lingering fear of success.

25.5 Recognizing the Entrepreneur Within

The attitude, mindset, passion and character that define the successful entrepreneur are sometimes hard to pinpoint, specify or sum up in a profile. It is possible to imitate major qualities of the true entrepreneur, nurture and develop them or to acknowledge whether or not we are actually suited to an entrepreneurial career. Everyone cannot become an entrepreneur and everybody needs to understand it. Otherwise it will be wastage of time, money and efforts if someone later realizes that he is not made for entrepreneurship. To become entrepreneur you must have at least maximum qualities of that.

For others who are ideally fitted for an entrepreneurial career – getting knowledge of entrepreneur's qualities, attitude and their lifestyle will help them in fulfilling their entrepreneurial dream and achieving their aspirations. Checklist of the desirable qualities of entrepreneurs can be referred as a guideline to better clarify our sense of purpose. It can help us reach objectives and route to greater attainment of higher goals and bigger benchmarks.

Being an entrepreneur requires that you are intelligent, focused and passionate. As such, most business fail in the first year because the entrepreneur either doesn't have those qualities or makes one of the following mistakes.

Lack in business plan

The new entrepreneurs lack in making the business plan. They are not thorough with their business plan. If you lag in preparing the business plan then how can you expect to accomplish anything if you haven't actually sat down and made a map of your goals? A complete and attractive business plan that clearly shows your intention about business is must if you intend to succeed. The biggest reason behind this is that it requires you to do some research into your industry, better understand your market and have a cohesive grasp of what you intend to do. Most of the entrepreneurs do not have such a talent to write down detail business plan. They have rough idea but they lag in proper R&D for the business plan. Even more importantly if you want investment, you are going to need something other than an elevator pitch.

Lack in rapid expansion

Some entrepreneurs do not have a potential to handle many businesses but still they try to handle the businesses because they want to expand their business. They want to earn more profit but they lag in handling the business affairs. They become incapable to handle so many businesses. Don't expand your business until you become capable to handle it otherwise it will be costly for you. The proper way is to get the proper training to get the full knowledge and then try to handle the things. One of the other more common mistakes a new and growing company makes is trying to appear bigger than they are by hiring too many employees and getting a plush office.

Running out of money

Some entrepreneurs are not able to handle money properly. They mismanage money. They lack the knowledge and they run out of money. If you don't have a business plan, you most likely didn't make sales projections, expense budgets, etc. Therefore, you will most likely run out of money. Taking the help of accountant will solve your finance related issues. When entrepreneurs try to do everything by their own then they entrap themselves in a net where they cannot come out easily. If you can't obtain angel funding or other investment, consider a small business loan.

Not having a solid marketing plan

Some entrepreneurs are not competent enough to make marketing plan for their product. They suffer from their poor planning. The entrepreneurs must know how are you going to reach your customers? Did you assume that you were just great and they would come flocking to you? Be sure to have a firm grasp on your competitors' strategies and a large enough budgets to experiment with different marketing tactics. They are incapable of analyzing the marketing trend and converting that trend into the best marketing plan.

Not creating a distinct brand

Normally it has been seen that the entrepreneurs do not take the branding of their business seriously. They are interested in just selling the products or services. They do not have any idea to boost the name of the company. They are not capable of distinguishing their business from the others. You must think about yourselves. What makes you unique? Your brand must reflect your qualities and your thinking. For example if you think that the products or the services must be of great quality then definitely you will try to give quality services and products to your customers. Create such a great impression of your products / services so that customers could never forget your company.

Not being passionate

Some new entrepreneurs do business because they think that just by having the business they will become rich. But they do not take their business from their heart. They do not take efforts to grow their business. Sometimes they become satisfied with their current earning and remain constant and do not do anything. If you are not passionate about what you are doing. Just quit.

Being a quitter

Entrepreneurs most of the times do not get success. They do not have entrepreneurial qualities but they continue with their business and suffer from losses. Such kind of entrepreneurs should either quit the business or must take proper training of entrepreneurship from the reputed or good institutes. Many successful businesses have started out as failures. If your strategy is not working then be ready to change, rethink on your work, improve it then implement it. If that doesn't work, rinse and repeat. Just keep going. The moment you stop trying, you've failed and so has your business.

So What Could Be the Solution?

25.6 Thinking like an Entrepreneur

On a trip down south, at Nagpur you marvel at the size of the oranges and the price at which they are available. You buy in dozens and consume these merrily en route. This is consumer's mindset.

On the contrary, an entrepreneurially thinking individual, he may buy and enjoy the oranges as well, would also start thinking what if I arrange for their transportation and sale at my place... if volume-weight factor and perishability is the constraint how about packaged orange juice... where would the technology come from, Italy? Would Indians like to consume packaged juices when by the roadside they can get fresh juice? Exports? Which are the countries that could serve as the potential market? What would be their quality expectations?

25.7 Entrepreneurial Competencies Entrepreneurs Must Have

A competence is an underlying characteristic of persons, which results in effective and or superior performance in a job. A job competence is an underlying characteristics of a person, in that it may be motive ,traits, skills ,aspect of one's self-image a body of knowledge ,set of skills and cluster of appropriate motives/ traits that an individual possess to perform a given task. The knowledge of entrepreneurial competence has been sharpened over the last three decades. The following is a list of major competencies that contribute towards top performance.

(a) **Initiative:** acting out of choice rather than compulsion, taking the lead rather than waiting for others to start.

(b) **Sees and Acts on Opportunities:** A mindset where one is trained to look for business opportunities from everyday experiences. Recall 'oranges' example.

(c) **Persistence:** A 'never say die' attitude, not giving up easily, striving Information seeking continuously until success is achieved.

(d) **Knowing:** Knowing who knows, consulting experts, reading relevant material and an overall openness to ideas and information.

(e) **Concern for High Quality of Work:** Attention to details and observance of established standards and norms.

(f) **Commitment to Work Contract:** Taking personal pains to complete a task as scheduled.

(g) **Efficiency Orientation:** Concern for conservation of time, money and effort.

(h) **Systematic Planning:** Breaking up the complex whole into parts, close examination of the parts and inferring about the whole; e.g., simultaneously attending to production, marketing and financial aspects (parts) of the overall business strategy (the whole).

(i) **Problem solving:** Observing the symptoms, diagnosing and curing.

(j) **Self-confidence:** Not being afraid of the risks associated with business and relying on one's capabilities to successfully manage these.

(k) **Assertiveness:** Conveying emphatically one's vision and convincing others of its value.

(l) **Persuasion:** Eliciting support of others in the venture.

(m) **Use of Influence Strategies:** Providing leadership.

(n) **Monitoring:** Ensuring the progress of the venture as planned.

(o) **Concern for Employee Welfare:** Believing in employee well being as the key to competitiveness and success and initiating programmes of employee welfare.

(p) **Information Seeker:** A successful entrepreneur always keeps his eyes and ears open and is receptive to new ideas which can help him in realizing his goals. He is ready to consult expert for getting their expert advice.

25.8 The Role of Prior Work Experience

Project work, summer training as well as prior work experience hone the entrepreneurial competencies. Whichever area you might decide upon to start a venture be it a school, restaurant, garments, courier service, interior decoration etc., along with the educational qualifications, if any, you need to acquire practical experience in that field. For it is while you get on the job training/ experience that you familiarize yourself with all aspects of the venture. You can learn as to how to handle customers, suppliers and government officials, financiers. You will also be able to acquaint yourself with the nitty-gritty's of the production process, bottlenecks like power disruptions, delay or non-availability of raw materials and a host of other things. Day-to-day dealings of the various facets of business will equip you to handle your own venture deftly, with confidence and with minimal of costly mistakes.

25.9 Developing Entrepreneurial Capability

Competency finds expression in human behavior. Development of entrepreneurial competency is seen in the following method or procedure.

The procedure involves four steps.

1. Competency Recognition
2. Self-Assessment
3. Competency Application
4. Feed back

Competency Recognition:

The first step involved in developing a particular competency is first to understand and recognize a particular competence.

Self Assessment:

In this step we have to see whether one possesses the particular competence or not. If yes, then to see how friendly one exhibits the same in his particular portion of one's competence. It can be ascertained by posing and answering relevant question to a competence

Competency Applications:

After assessing one's position regarding a particular competency, one need to practice the same on continuous basis in various activities. In order to make a new behavior a part of one's personality, the particular behavior/competency needs to be applied frequently even in the simplest activities 'that one performs in one's day-to-day life. This is because "practice makes a man perfect'.

Feed Back:

In this stage one needs to make an introspection of the same in order to sharpen and strengthen one's competency. This is called feedback. Thus feedback means to know the strengths and weaknesses of one's new behaviour. This helps one know how the new behaviour has been rewarding. This enables one to sustain or give up the exhibition of a particular behaviour also competence in his life.

25.10 Astonishing Businessman

There are different common factors to those who build net fortunes of one million dollars or more.

The factors compiled here are summarized from the research done by Thomas Stanley Ph.D. on over 1100 actual millionaires (many are multi-millionaires) in the U.S. today.

(1) Live Well Below Your Means

Don't be fooled. The 'average' millionaire doesn't look like a millionaire! The key word here is frugal, frugal and frugal. The typical person in America is a consumptionist. It's in their blood. They work hard, make money and spend it well. Not the typical millionaire! They play great defence (saving and investing) as well as offense (making money). Millionaires on average claimed their spouses were as frugal or more than they were. It's a family affair: Sacrifice high consumption today, for financial freedom tomorrow.

(2) Spend Your Time, Energy and Money in Ways that Build Wealth

Do investment planning. Go to seminars. Hire good attorneys, tax accountants, mentors and coaches. Learn to identify and invest in assets that produce income. The wealthy spend money when the investment will protect and grow their assets. Millionaires also know the details: How much is spent each month and on food, clothing and shelter. The non-wealthy say they don't have time to plan, while the wealthy make time to plan. But here's the shocker: The average millionaire spends 8.5 hours per month planning, while the non-affluent spend 4.5 hours or less planning. How can 4 more hours per week impact your future? Make it happen and the odds are in your favor of joining the truly wealthy!

(3) Choose Financial Independence over Displaying High Social Status

The wealthy run highly efficient operations both in business and at home. Most live in average neighborhoods and drive average cars. They're not interested in keeping up with the Jones' – because the Jones' aren't financially free. It takes lots of energy to consume big mortgages, change homes every few years, buy the most recent model cars and wear the latest fashions. The wealthy drive typically American made cars! Japanese cars come in 2nd place; half of these are Toyota Camrys. Yes, significant value per dollar is the key here. The Millionaire's Motto: You aren't what you drive. The status cars – Lexus, BMW's, Mercedes? At 6.4 per cent or less per each brand.

(4) Don't Accept Economic Support from Your Parents once Outside the Home

Sounds painful doesn't it? It's a fact that has taught the wealthy how to earn, keep and invest money. Parents of the wealthy do not or cannot, provide "economic outpatient care". The results are clear: The more dollars the adult children receive, the fewer they accumulate. Those who are given less are motivated to accumulate more on their own merits. An amazing fact: 80 per cent of millionaires are first generation millionaires; they have made their money on their own, in their lifetime. Many of these folks have been immigrants to the U.S., starting out with minimal cash on hand. Work hard to learn and generate wealth — it CAN be done and happens in America every day.

(5) Teach your children to be economically self-sufficient to foster a "Wealth Mind-Set"

Provide your children fish and they will eat for a day. Teach them to fish and they will eat for a lifetime. As you might guess, children who grew up to be affluent, who had affluent parents, were taught to be disciplined and intentional with their money. Robert Kyosaki, author of Rich Dad Poor Dad, didn't cave in when his son asked for a car at 16 years old, even when the neighbor kids were being given cars by their parents. He gave his son ₹ 40000 and a subscription to the Wall Street Journal and a few books on investing in the stock market. Now Rich Dad's son watches more CNN than MTV. He has the motivation and is getting an education that will provide him for a lifetime, well beyond his first car purchase.

(6) Become Proficient in Targeting Market Opportunities

Find your niche, like the wealthy do. Follow where the money flows and look for specialized opportunities. Why not target the wealthy themselves? Yes, they are frugal, especially first generation self-made wealthy. BUT...they spend openly on investing in themselves and their families. Investment advice and services, business training, software, tax advice, legal, medical, dental, health, real estate and education are top priorities. They pay well for products and services that protect and grow their assets. Remember the majority of the wealthy are self-employed entrepreneurs followed by medical professionals and business executives.

(7) Choose the Right Occupation

You now have a good idea of what the affluent do. 20 per cent are retirees. Of the remaining 80 per cent, most of these are self-made businessmen and women. Keep in mind that entrepreneurs are four times more likely to become millionaires than those who work for others. There is no one business or group of business more likely to breed millionaire-hood. Some are lecturers, others medical professionals, farmers, small manufacturers and corner mom and pop stores. The most important predictor is the characteristics of the owner, than the type of business. It's the winning combination of skills and attitude that hit's the wealth target.

25.11 Entrepreneurial Proficiencies in Business

Entrepreneurial Competencies

There are different entrepreneurial competencies that a would-be entrepreneur should possess:

Organizing ability

An entrepreneur should be wise enough in choosing the people with whom he will work. He must choose people who possess skills that are needed for the improvement and success of the business.

Problem-solving ability

An entrepreneur should be rational rather than emotional in handling obstacles. He is also firm enough when making decisions without hurting others.

Ability to absorb setbacks and recovery

Analysis in absorbing setbacks and recovery of the business are important competencies of the entrepreneur. Accepting and analyzing the difficulties encountered help in the improvement and success of the business.

Human relations ability

Personality factors such as emotional stability, personal relations, sociability, consideration and tactfulness are important contributors to the entrepreneur manager's success in small business. One of the most important facets of human relations is one's ability to put himself in someone else's place and know how the other person feels. This is the ability to practice empathy.

When running a business, he is expected to give a fair price to his customers. He should never cheat on his customers because his business solely depends on them. He must always take good care of these people. If he gives them a fair price for his products and services, he can be sure that they'll keep coming back to patronize what he has for them. Through this, his relationship with them will become stronger and they'll have a feeling that his business can be trusted. This is very important if he wants to stay for more years in the business world. Business is about people, it's about building lasting relationships with people. Everyday entrepreneurs interact and deal with people - from customers, to suppliers, investors, employees, creditors and other third party entities. Potential entrepreneurs must develop competency in human relations. They should maintain good relations with others and must have the ability to inspire and drive other people especially employees and subordinates.

Communications ability

Entrepreneurs should have an ability to communicate effectively both orally and in writing. Communication also means that both the sender and the receiver understand and are understood. Entrepreneurs should be able to explain, discuss, sell and market their goods or service. It is important to be able to interact effectively with your business team. Additionally, entrepreneurs need to be able to express themselves clearly both verbally and in writing. They also should have strong reading comprehension skills to understand contracts and other forms of written business communication.

Effective written communication is much more difficult to achieve than effective oral communication. For example, the teacher might walk into his class and in a pleasant voice, with a smile, say, "This class can go jump in the lake." Very few students would be offended, although they might be puzzled. On the other hand, if the instructor wrote the same message on the blackboard and left it for the class to read, he would probably receive a wide range of reactions, from anger to amusement.

The small business manager who can effectively communicate with customers, employees, suppliers and creditors will be more likely to succeed than the manager who cannot. Communication is considered a social skill and inventors and engineers, for example, aren't known to be social butterflies. Founders have to communicate their ideas and products to investors, business partners and the rest of the team. Then, hopefully, come customers, distribution channels and going public or merging with an attractive buy-out candidate. Communication is not just talking, but also writing, body language and "actions speak louder than words."

Ability to make sound decisions and to take full responsibility for decisions made

An entrepreneur is the leader, the boss. All those under him are dependent on the decisions he makes. Thus, he should have a sound judgment which will be fair to all.

Persistence and patience to wait until the business really becomes successful

Failure in running a business is not an obstacle for entrepreneurs. It will instead be a challenge to their abilities to handle it. Searching for the best way to succeed is a necessary skill for them.

Technical knowledge on how to operate the business

A basic knowledge in handling a business is necessary for entrepreneurs in order to be able to organize and manage a business.

Sense of independence and self-confidence

An entrepreneur should have trust in himself and in his work. His sound judgment, self-confidence and independence in his job will enable him to succeed.

Good health and enthusiasm

An entrepreneur who is physically as well as mentally fit would have a good chance of success. He will be able to grapple with the problems in the business.

25.12 Entrepreneurial Leadership Personality

"Always bear in mind that your own resolution to succeed is more important than any other." – Abraham Lincoln, US-President, 1861-1865

In order to become a fully functioning, successful individual in whichever endeavor you choose to undertake, you must first cultivate the right attitude and behavioral traits. Nowhere else is this fact more true as than when we consider the dominant characteristics needed for entrepreneurial leadership?

There are effective executives and directors in many fields but most leadership development programs neither focus on increasing entrepreneurship nor do they employ innovative training methods. However, you can acquire, develop and robustly practice the requisite entrepreneurial leadership skills.

According to the late great management expert, **Peter F. Drucker**, *"The entrepreneur always searches for change, responds to it and exploits it as an opportunity. Innovation is the specific instrument of entrepreneurship. (It's the entrepreneurial) act that endows resources with a new capacity to create wealth."*

Entrepreneur extraordinaire, **Sir Richard Branson**, explains why he changed his mind and became one because he originally *"wanted to be an editor or a journalist (and) I wasn't really interested in being an entrepreneur, but I soon found I had to become (one) in order to keep my magazine going."*

So in a very real sense, Sir Richard, Bill Gates, Steve Jobs and others like them already had attributes of the leadership mind-set and they were behaving in similar ways as leaders do too. If you hope to successfully initiate any commercial, governmental or public service undertaking, you will have to learn, exhibit and embrace the characteristics of entrepreneurial leadership.

What types of character traits do entrepreneurs have? Are those behaviors really important? In a word, these characteristics are important because if you don't possess them, you will have lower chances in terms of business success. The characteristics are as follows:

Risk Assessor – This is a very important characteristic of an entrepreneur. If you're not willing to take any risk, then you will not succeed as a businessperson. Many organizational executives are willing to take any risk which presents itself as a breakthrough or never-before-tried opportunity. But without taking the time and effort to thoroughly evaluate or explore the potential pitfalls of new idea, you are not very likely to succeed in your venture. In the everyday course of the business, you will encounter a lot of problems and challenges which you need to decide the soonest. Some risks are worth taking after careful evaluation especially if it's for the good of the business. If you're not a risk taker, then you're not an effective entrepreneur and you're bound to fail in your business undertaking.

Wise, Smart and Accepting of New Ideas – Most people think that only smartness is needed for becoming a good and successful executive but apart from that knowledge, your desire to know new things and to do new things, positive attitude, leadership are also necessary traits for winning in your entrepreneurial enterprise.

You cannot become a successful and influencing entrepreneur just by having one or two qualities. You need to be interactive, communicative and supportive that will help you to serve your business in better way. Today's complex and competitive environment compel you to show your intelligence, knowledge of changing circumstances and emerging trends. Those attributes will help you earn the respect and trust of your clients and all your associates or partners.

Executive Leadership Development – Leadership is the basic quality of entrepreneurs. An entrepreneur leads and this keeps him forward in any field. A quality of a person's leadership is clear from how he handles a problem and generating resources. An enterprise with a good leadership is always prominent in the market.

Today's innovative training programs have a capability to sharpen the ordinary man with the necessary business skills and entrepreneurial qualities. The training programs can change the attitude of the common person from negative to positive. Your executive leadership skills will help you to run your business and your personal qualities and behaviors help you direct, organize and motivate people. These abilities will enable you to handle your business affairs with greater ease and positive emotions.

An Inner Passion for Your Enterprise – One essential characteristic of successful entrepreneurs is the amount and scope of their enthusiastic, dynamic, passionate zeal they have for their business. A dynamic and enthusiastic entrepreneur is always pragmatic and approach problems to solve them rather than run away from them. He finds solution to the problems systematically and solves them in the interest of his enterprise. A dynamic and enthusiastic entrepreneur always believes in a win-win situation.

It is not possible for any executive leadership development or innovative training programs to create extensive interest and desire for your business. It is your responsibility to generate interest and passion for your business. It is your determination, eagerness and feeling of achievement that will support you to successfully grow your business.

Honesty, Integrity and Trustworthy – Optimistic relationships is the foundation of every organization. Normally it has been seen that entrepreneurial leadership dedicate and invest 80 per cent of their time into developing, constructing and making strong relations with customers, suppliers and other stakeholders.

Your honesty, integrity and trustworthy nature will help you to earn the reputation and customers', creditors, investor's and other stakeholders' loyalty in the market. Your goodwill will increase. Apart from the above traits there are also other behavioral traits needed to ensure success in your entrepreneurial activities. The five attributes listed above will help you handle most of your organizational responsibilities, duties and obligations.

These traits also form the basis for successful careers in any industry or profession. If, however, you can equip yourself with the means to improve your performance, some additional time spent in innovative training courses will put you over the top. If you plan on using an executive leadership development program to sharpen your competence in these characteristics, all you'll need to do is study market trends carefully, think of a few strategic options for your venture, provide the capital and you'll be ready to take entrepreneurial leadership action.

"The real issue is not talent as an independent element, but talent in relationship to will, desire and persistence. Talent without these things vanishes and even modest talent with those characteristics grows." – **Milton Glaser**

SUMMARY

Becoming an entrepreneur is not an easy task. If you've decided that you want to get out of the corporate rat-race and be your own boss. As you begin planning how to start your own business from home, you begin listing down what you want to do and what you can do, what are the basic things that you require. You tell yourself that you love to do a little bit of everything - you can do research, Web design, write, with a five years experience in legal and administrative support. But then, you ask yourself, "What skills do I really need to succeed as an entrepreneur?"

Weaknesses of entrepreneurs are as follows:

- Do Not Have Skills for Entrepreneurs
- Lack of sales and marketing skills
- Mistrust
- Financial know-how
- Ego
- Decline in self-motivation skills
- Control freak
- Time management skills
- Administration skills
- Get conned easily

Entrepreneur as a self-employed

The emotional driving force behind the self-employed person is not security but a desire for greater control over his or her life, career and destiny. They do not want to work under any one. Relinquishing that control to a boss every day from nine to five is not their idea of happiness and they believe that they could do their job just as well without an employer – and perhaps without the need for other employees.

Entrepreneur as a manager

Those with a managerial outlook are often in a great position to succeed as entrepreneurs, expect for two big misconceptions that lead to massive problems. Many managers believe that if a business is not working properly, then cost cut is the best strategy. They start cost cutting plus they start throwing out employees but this only aggravates the situation because it fails to address the underlying root cause of the difficulty or lack of profitability.

Entrepreneur as a leader

The entrepreneur as a leader enjoys remarkable benefits by knowing how to step aside and let the business – and those employees working in it – operate as a profit center not reliant upon the owner's constant hands-on participation. He as a leader gives direction to the business.

Entrepreneur as an investor

With a business that generates profits, the entrepreneur who has succeeded this far can begin to accept another exciting challenge, that of managing money so that it works to produce more money. Investing for maximum returns involves smart leverage of assets and the entrepreneurial investor will often leverage the success of the first business to create a second or third company based on the same model or system.

The real true entrepreneur

The real entrepreneurs are the entrepreneurs who are responsible for having a great idea, turning that idea into real one i.e., into business, then running business with that idea successfully, handling issues and challenges of doing business, forming strategies, taking risks and giving tough competition to the competitors and surviving the business.

The not to have qualities for entrepreneurs are:

- Lack of confidence
- Lack of feeling a sense of ownership
- Unable to communicate
- Lack of passionate about learning
- Lack of team player
- System-orientations
- Lack of dedication
- Grateful
- Lack of being optimistic
- Gregarious
- A leader by example (lack leadership)
- Afraid of risk or success

As such, most business fails in the first year because the entrepreneur either doesn't have those qualities or makes one of the following mistakes.

- Lack in business plan
- Lack in rapid expansion
- Running out of money
- Not having a solid marketing plan
- Not creating a distinct brand
- Not being passionate
- Being a quitter

Entrepreneurial competencies entrepreneurs must have:

A competence is an underlying characteristic of persons, which results in effective and or superior performance in a job. The following is a list of major competencies that contribute towards top performance.

Initiative, Sees and Acts on Opportunities, Persistence, Knowing, Concern for High Quality of Work, Commitment to Work Contract, Efficiency Orientation, Systematic Planning, Problem solving, Self-confidence, Assertiveness, Persuasion, **Information Seeker,** Monitoring, Concern for Employee Welfare, and Use of Influence Strategies

Developing Entrepreneurial Capability:

Competency finds expression in human behavior. Development of entrepreneurial competency is seen in the following method or procedure.

The procedure involves four steps.

- Competency Recognition
- Self-Assessment
- Competency Application
- Feed back

Entrepreneurial proficiencies in business involve:

- Entrepreneurial Competencies
- Organizing ability
- Problem-solving ability
- Ability to absorb setbacks and recovery
- Human relations ability
- Communications ability
- Ability to make sound decisions and to take full responsibility for decisions made
- Persistence and patience to wait until the business really becomes successful
- Technical knowledge on how to operate the business
- Sense of independence and self-confidence
- Good health and enthusiasm

Entrepreneurial Leadership Personality

In order to become a fully functioning, successful individual in whichever endeavor you choose to undertake, you must first cultivate the right attitude and behavioral traits. Nowhere else is this fact more true as than when we consider the dominant characteristics needed for entrepreneurial leadership.

The characteristics are:

Risk assessor, wise, smart and accepting of new ideas, executive leadership development, an inner passion for your enterprise and honesty, integrity and trustworthy.

KEYWORDS

Competency: A core *competency* is fundamental knowledge, ability or expertise in a specific subject area or skill set.

Self-motivation: The ability to keep yourself going and being productive and using initiative.

Time management: analysis and control of the amount of time spent on different work activities.

Self-employed: If you work for yourself either part time or full time – without being on a salary or commission from an employer.

Manager: An individual who is in charge of a certain group of tasks or a certain subset of a company.

Leadership: *It* involves motivating and directing followers primarily through appealing to their own self-interest.

Team Player: A person who can function effectively as part of a group of individuals, sharing information and striving towards a common goal.

Marketing plan: A marketing plan outlines the specific actions you intend to carry out to interest potential customers.

Self- Assessment: An evaluation of one's own abilities and failings.

Optimistic: A tendency to expect the best possible outcome or dwell on the most hopeful aspects of a situation.

QUESTIONS

1. What is the need of entrepreneurial competences for the success of business?
2. What are the reasons due to which an entrepreneur becomes a weak entrepreneur?
3. Write down in detail about the different roles of entrepreneurs in an organization.
4. Write down in detail about the negative factors that hamper the entrepreneurial development?
5. Entrepreneurs' qualification or experience what matters more? Explain.

❑ ❑ ❑

BIBLIOGRAPHY

- Schiffman Leon G., Consumer Behaviour, Pearson Educational Asia, New Delhi, First Edition, 2002.
- Srivastava K.K., Consumer Behaviour, Galgotiya Publishing Co., New Delhi, First Edition, 2002.
- Saxena Rajan, Consumer Behaviour, Tata Mcgraw Hill Pub. Co. Ltd., New Delhi, First Edition, 2002.
- Chunawala S.A., Marketing Management Vol.-II, Tata Mcgraw Hill Pub. Co. Ltd., New Delhi, First Edition, 1998.
- Luck David J., Marketing Research, Prentice Hall of India, New Delhi, First Edition, 2001.
- Kumar Dileep M.C., Luck David J., Marketing Research, Kalyani Publishers, New Delhi, First Edition, 2010.
- Rathor B.S., Advertising Management, Himalaya Pub. House, New Delhi, First Edition, 2001.
- Mishra M.N., Modern Marketing Research, Himalaya Pub. House, Mumbai, First Edition, 1999.
- Advertising Theory and Practice, Himalaya Pub. House, Mumbai, First Edition, 2002.
- Sontakki C.N., Marketing Management, Kalyani Publishers, New Delhi, First Edition, 2004.
- Giram Shivkumar, Consumer Protection and Redress, Himalaya Pub. House, New Delhi, First Edition, 2002.
- Mishra M.N., Sales Promotion and Advertising, Himalaya Pub. House, New Delhi, First Edition, 2002.
- Jha S.M., Social Marketing, Himalaya Pub. House, Mumbai, First Edition, 2002.
- Jha S.M., Services Marketing, Himalaya Pub. House, Mumbai, First Edition, 2003.
- Chunawala S.A., Foundations of Advertising, Himalaya Pub. House, Mumbai, First Edition, 2002.
- Gopalakrishnan P, Purchasing and Materials Management, Tata Mcgraw Hill Pub. Co. Ltd., New Delhi, First Edition, 2001.
- Kincaid Judith W., Customer Relationship Management, Dorling Kindersley (I) Pvt. Ltd., New Delhi, First Edition, 2001.
- Chopra Sunil, Supply Chain Management, Dorling Kindersley (I) Pvt. Ltd., New Delhi, Third Edition, 2006.
- Jefkins Frank, Advertising, Macmillan India Ltd., New Delhi, Third Edition, 2002.
- Woodruffe Helen, Service Marketing, Macmillan India Ltd., New Delhi, 2001.
- Palmer Adrian, Services, Oxford and IBH Pub. Co., New Delhi, Second Edition, 2009.
- Rangaraj N., Logistics And Supply Chain Management, Macmillan India Ltd., New Delhi, Second Edition, 2001.
- Pezzullo Mary Ann, Marketing Financial Services, Macmillan India Ltd., New Delhi, First Edition,1998.
- Nag A., Marketing Strategy, Macmillan India Ltd., New Delhi, First Edition,2002.
- Sahay B.S., Supply Chain Management, Macmillan India Ltd., New Delhi, First Edition,2002.
- Seth Rajeev K., Marketing of Banking Services, Macmillan India Ltd., New Delhi, First Edition,1997.
- Ramkishan Y., Rural Marketing, Jaico Publishing House, Mumbai, First Edition,2002.
- Belding Shaun, Dealing With The Customer, Macmillan India Ltd., New Delhi, First Edition,2001.
- Grover S.K., Marketing A Strategic Orientation, S. Chand And Co. Ltd., New Delhi, First Edition,2003.
- Walker C. Orville, Marketing Strategy, Tata Mcgraw Hill Pub.co. Ltd., New Delhi, First Edition,2000.
- Assael Henry, Consumer Behaviour, Asian Books Private Limited., New Delhi, First Edition,2001.
- Balagopal T.A.S., Export Marketing, Himalaya Pub. House, Mumbai, First Edition,1994.
- Gosney John W., Customer Relationship, Prentice Hall of India, New Delhi, First Edition,2001.
- Still Richard R., Sales Management, Prentice Hall of India, New Delhi, First Edition,1983.
- Gopalakrishnan P, Electronic Marketing In 21st Century, Himalaya Pub. House, Mumbai, First Edition, 2001.
- Cherunilam Francis, Business Marketing, Himalaya Pub. House, Mumbai, First Edition, 2000.
- Patankar Sanjay V., Services Management, Himalaya Pub. House, Mumbai, First Edition, 2001.

- Venugopal Vasanti, Services Marketing, Himalaya Pub. House, Mumbai, First Edition, 2002. -
- Rugimbana Robert, Cross Cultural Marketing, Thomson South Western, Singapore, First Edition, 2003.
- Parameswaran M.G., Understanding Consumers, Tata Mcgraw Hill Pub. Co. Ltd., New Delhi, First Edition, 2003.
- E- Marketing, Prentice Hall of India, New Delhi, First Edition, 2003.
- Bhattacharjee C., Brand Building, Himalaya Pub. House, Mumbai, First Edition,2009.
- Singh P.P., Web Advertising And Online Marketing, Deep and Deep Publications, New Delhi, First Edition,2004.
- Berman Barry, Retail Management, Pearson Educational Asia, New Delhi, Eighth Edition,2002.
- Pradhan Swapna, Retailing Management, Tata Mcgraw Hill Pub. Co. Ltd., New Delhi, First Edition,2004.
- Srivastava R.K., Product Management and New Product, Excel Books, New Delhi, First Edition,2009.
- Brue Greg, Six Sigma for Managers, Tata Mcgraw Hill Pub. Co. Ltd., New Delhi, First Edition,2005.
- Mantravadi Pramod, E-marketing The Emerging Trend, ICFAI Center For Management Research, Hyderabad, First Edition, 2002.
- Fillis Ian, Creative Marketing For Smes, ICFAI Center for Management Research, Hyderabad, First Edition, 2005.
- Suresh K., Effective Sales Promotions, ICFAI Center for Management Research, Hyderabad, First Edition, 2005.
- Kaushesh Anshu, Innovations In Marketing, ICFAI Center for Management Research, Hyderabad, First Edition, 2003.
- Suresh K., ST-enabled Retailing, ICFAI Center for Management Research, Hyderabad, First Edition,2005.
- Thakur L.K., Internet Marketing, Author Press, New Delhi, First Edition, 2005.
- Rao T. Srinivasa, Changing Life Style and Consumers, Deep and Deep Publications, New Delhi, First Edition,2006.
- Web Marketing in A Week, Hodder and Stoughton Education, London, Gabay J. Jonathan, First Edition, 2007.
- Mohanty Malay Kumar, Fundamentals of Entrepreneurship, Kalyani Publishers, New Delhi, First Edition, 2010.
- Saibaba Rudra, Fundamentals of Entrepreneurship, Kalyani Publishers, New Delhi, First Edition, 2010.
- Ray Rajeev, Entrepreneurship, Oxford and IBH Pub. Co., New Delhi, First Edition, 2008.
- Basotia G.R., Handbook of Entrepreneurship Development, Mangal Deep Publications, New Delhi, First Edition, 1999.
- Khanka S.S., Entrepreneurial Developement, S. Chand and Co. Ltd., New Delhi, First Edition, 2000.
- Batra G.S., Entrepreneurship and Small-Scale Industries, S. Chand and Co. Ltd., New Delhi, First Edition, 1999.
- Peters Hisrich, Entrepreneurship, Tata Mcgraw Hill Pub. Co. Ltd, New Delhi, First Edition, 2000.
- Khanka S.S., Entrepreneural Development, S. Chand and Co. Ltd., New Delhi, First Edition, 2002.
- Desai Vasant, Dynamics of Entrepreneurial Development, Himalaya Pub. House, Mumbai, First Edition, 1998.
- Chandak N.N., Entrepreneurial Development, Professional Publishers, Nagpur, First Edition, 1998.
- Colombo Plan Staff College, Entreprenurship Development, Tata Mcgraw Hill Pub. Co. Ltd, New Delhi, First Edition, 1999.
- Wadhawa Raj K., Entrepreneur And Enterprise Management, Kanishka Publishers, New Delhi, First Edition, 1998.
- Saini J.S, Entrepreneurship, S. Chand and Co. Ltd., New Delhi, First Edition, 2001.
- Sudha G.S., Principles of Business Management, Ramesh Book Depot, New Delhi, First Edition, 2004.
- Reddy Venugopal, Wealth Creation Through Entrepreneurship, Himalaya Pub. House, Mumbai, First Edition, 2009.

- Nagarajan R. Project Management, New Age International Publication, New Delhi, Second Edition, 2004.
- Zimmerer Thomas W., Essentials Of Entrepreneurship, Prentice Hall of India, New Delhi, Fourth Edition, 2005.
- Janakiram B., Management Entrepreneurship, Excel Books, New Delhi, First Edition, 2010.
- Prasad Laxhman, Entrepreneurial Climate, Excel Books, New Delhi, First Edition, 2008.
- Prasad R., Enterpreneurship, ICFAI Center for Management Research, Hyderabad, First Edition, 2003.
- Kaplan Jack M., Patterns of Entrepreneurship, John Wiley and Sons Inc., New York, First Edition, 2003.
- Sarwate Dilip M., Entrepreneurial Development, Everest Publishing House, Pune, Eighth Edition, 2003.
- Ceo Speak, The Art of Entrepreneurship, Vision Book Pvt. Ltd., New Delhi, First Edition, 2006.
- Desai Vasant, Small Scale Industries And Entrepreneurship, S. Chand and Co. Ltd., Mumbai, Eighth Edition, 1995.
- James Richard, Project Management Survival, Kogan Page India Private Ltd., New Delhi, First Edition, 2008.
- Paul Roberts, Guide to Project Management, Viva Books Private Ltd., New Delhi, First Edition, 2008.
- Sontakki V.C., Project Management, Himalaya Pub. House, Mumbai, First Edition, 2006.
- Developing New Entrepreneurs, Entrepreneurship Development Institute, Ahmedabad, First Edition, 1987.
- Kanitkar Ajit, In Search of Identity, Entrepreneurship Development Institute, Ahmedabad, First Edition, 1992.
- Sebastian Jose, Not Born-the Created Entrepreneurs, Entrepreneurship Development Institute, New Delhi, First Edition, 1994.
- Budgeting, Entrepreneurship Development Institute, Ahmedabad.

❑ ❑ ❑

INDEX

A

B

C